W9-DDJ-990

Method Chaining (373): Make modifier methods return the host object, so that multiple modifiers can be invoked in a single expression.

Model Ignorant Generation (567): Hardcode all logic into the generated code so that there's no explicit representation of the Semantic Model.

Model-Aware Generation (555): Generate code with an explicit simulacrum of the semantic model of the DSL, so that the generated code has generic-specific separation.

Nested Closure (403): Express statement subelements of a function call by putting them into a closure in an argument.

Nested Function (357): Compose functions by nesting function calls as arguments of other calls.

Nested Operator Expression (327): An operator expression that can recursively contain the same form of expression (for example, arithmetic and Boolean expressions).

Newline Separators (333): Use newlines as statement separators.

Notification (193): Collects errors and other messages to report back to the caller.

Object Scoping (385): Place the DSL script so that bare references will resolve to a single object.

Parse Tree Manipulation (455): Capture the parse tree of a code fragment to manipulate it with DSL processing code.

Parser Combinator (255): Create a top-down parser by a composition of parser objects.

Parser Generator (269): Build a parser driven by a grammar file as a DSL.

Production Rule System (513): Organize logic through a set of production rules, each having a condition and an action.

Recursive Descent Parser (245): Create a top-down parser using control flow for grammar operators and recursive functions for nonterminal recognizers.

Regex Table Lexer (239): Implement a lexical analyzer using a list of regular expressions.

Semantic Model (159): The model that's populated by a DSL.

State Machine (527): Model a system as a set of explicit states with transitions between them.

Symbol Table (165): A location to store all identifiable objects during a parse to resolve references.

Syntax-Directed Translation (219): Translate source text by defining a grammar and using that grammar to structure translation.

Templated Generation (539): Generate output by handwriting an output file and placing template callouts to generate variable portions.

Textual Polishing (477): Perform simple textual substitutions before more serious processing.

Transformer Generation (533): Generate code by writing a transformer that navigates the input model and produces output.

Tree Construction (281): The parser creates and returns a syntax tree representation of the source text that is manipulated later by tree-walking code.

Domain-Specific Languages

The Addison-Wesley
Signature Series

Kent Beck, Mike Cohn, and Martin Fowler, Consulting Editors

LEADING LEAN SOFTWARE DEVELOPMENT
Mary Poppendieck
Tom Poppendieck

SUCCEEDING WITH AGILE
Software Development Using Scrum
Mike Cohn

AGILE TESTING
A Practical Guide for Testers and Agile Teams
Lisa Crispin
Janet Gregory

GROWING OBJECT-ORIENTED SOFTWARE, GUIDED BY TESTS
Steve Freeman
Nat Pryce

PATTERNS OF ENTERPRISE APPLICATION ARCHITECTURE
Martin Fowler

✦ Addison-Wesley

Visit **informit.com/awss** for a complete list of available products.

T he **Addison-Wesley Signature Series** provides readers with practical and authoritative information on the latest trends in modern technology for computer professionals. The series is based on one simple premise: Great books come from great authors. Books in the series are personally chosen by expert advisors, world-class authors in their own right. These experts are proud to put their signatures on the covers, and their signatures ensure that these thought leaders have worked closely with authors to define topic coverage, book scope, critical content, and overall uniqueness. The expert signatures also symbolize a promise to our readers: You are reading a future classic.

PEARSON

✦ Addison-Wesley   **Cisco Press**   EXAM/**CRAM**   **IBM** Press.   **QUE**   ⠶ PRENTICE HALL   **SAMS** | Safari" Books Online

Domain-Specific Languages

Martin Fowler

With Rebecca Parsons

✦✦Addison-Wesley

Upper Saddle River, NJ • Boston • Indianapolis • San Francisco
New York • Toronto • Montreal • London • Munich • Paris • Madrid
Sydney • Tokyo • Singapore • Mexico City

Many of the designations used by manufacturers and sellers to distinguish their products are claimed as trademarks. Where those designations appear in this book, and the publisher was aware of a trademark claim, the designations have been printed with initial capital letters or in all capitals.

The authors and publisher have taken care in the preparation of this book, but make no expressed or implied warranty of any kind and assume no responsibility for errors or omissions. No liability is assumed for incidental or consequential damages in connection with or arising out of the use of the information or programs contained herein.

The publisher offers excellent discounts on this book when ordered in quantity for bulk purchases or special sales, which may include electronic versions and/or custom covers and content particular to your business, training goals, marketing focus, and branding interests. For more information, please contact:

U.S. Corporate and Government Sales
(800) 382–3419
corpsales@pearsontechgroup.com

For sales outside the United States please contact:

International Sales
international@pearson.com

Visit us on the Web: informit.com/aw

Library of Congress Cataloging-in-Publication Data:

Fowler, Martin, 1963-
  Domain-specific languages / Martin Fowler.
      p. cm.
  Includes index.
  ISBN 0-321-71294-3 (hardcover : alk. paper) 1. Programming languages (Electronic computers)
2. Domain-specific programming languages. I. Title.
  QA76.7.F687 2010
  005.13--dc22

                                                                        2010026229

Copyright © 2011 Martin Fowler

All rights reserved. Printed in the United States of America. This publication is protected by copyright, and permission must be obtained from the publisher prior to any prohibited reproduction, storage in a retrieval system, or transmission in any form or by any means, electronic, mechanical, photocopying, recording, or likewise. For information regarding permissions, write to:

Pearson Education, Inc
Rights and Contracts Department
501 Boylston Street, Suite 900
Boston, MA 02116
Fax (617) 671 3447

ISBN-13: 978–0–321–71294–3
ISBN-10:   0–321–71294–3
Text printed in the United States on recycled paper at Courier in Westford, Massachusetts.
First printing, September 2010

For Cindy
— Martin

Contents

Preface

Domain-specific languages have been a part of the computing landscape since before I got into programming. Ask an old Unix-hand or Lisp-hand and they'll happily bore you to tears on how DSLs have been a useful part of their bag of tricks. Despite this, they've never become a very visible part of the computing landscape. Most people learn about DSLs from someone else, and they often learn only a limited set of available techniques.

I've written this book to try to change this situation. My intention is to introduce you to a wide range of DSL techniques, so that you can make an informed choice about whether to use a DSL in your work and what kinds of DSL techniques to employ.

DSLs are popular for several reasons, but I will highlight the two main ones: improving productivity for developers and improving communication with domain experts. A well-chosen DSL can make it easier to understand a complicated block of code, thus improving the productivity of those working with it. It can also make it easier to communicate with domain experts, by providing a common text that acts as both executable software and a description that domain experts can read to understand how their ideas are represented in a system. This communication with domain experts is a benefit more difficult to achieve, but the resulting gain is much broader because it helps unclog one of the worst bottlenecks in software development—the communication between programmers and their customers.

I should also not overstate the value of DSLs. I frequently say that whenever you're discussing the benefits, or indeed the problems, of DSLs, you should consider substituting "DSL" with "library." Much of what you gain with a DSL you can also gain by building a framework. Indeed, most DSLs are merely a thin facade over a library or framework. As a result, the costs and benefits of a DSL are less than people think, but these costs and benefits are not understood as well as they should be. Knowing good techniques reduces the cost of building a DSL considerably—and my hope in this book is to enable that. The facade may be thin, but it is often useful and worth building.

Why Now?

DSLs have been around for ages, yet in recent years they've generated a significant uptick in interest. At the same time, I decided to spend a couple years writing this book. Why? While I don't know if I can provide a definitive explanation for the general uptick, I can share a personal perspective.

At the turn of the millennium, there was a sense of an overwhelming standardization in programming languages—at least in my world of enterprise software. For a couple of years, Java was The One Future Language, and even when Microsoft challenged that statement with C#, it was still very much a similar language. New development was dominated by compiled, static, OO languages with a C-like syntax. (Even Visual Basic got made to look as close to this as it could.)

But it soon became clear that not everything sat well with this Java/C# hegemony. There were bits of important logic that didn't fit well with those languages—which led to the rise of XML configuration files. Programmers were soon joking that they were writing more lines of XML than of Java/C#. Partly, this was due to a desire to modify behavior at runtime, but it was also a desire to express aspects of behavior in a more custom way. XML, despite its very noisy syntax, allows you to define your own vocabulary and provides a strong hierarchic structure.

But the noise of XML ended up being too much. People complained of angle brackets hurting their eyes. There was a desire to get the benefits of XML config files without the cost of XML.

Now our narrative reaches the mid-noughties and the explosive appearance of Ruby on Rails. Whatever Rails' place is as a practical platform (and I think it's a good one), it's had a huge impact on how people think about library and framework design. A big part of the modus operandi of the Ruby community is a more fluent approach—trying to make interacting with a library feel like programming in a specialized language. This is a strand of thinking that goes back to one of oldest programming languages, Lisp. This approach also saw flowerings in what you would think as the stony ground of Java/C#: Both languages have seen fluent interfaces become more popular, probably due to the lasting influence of the original creators of JMock and Hamcrest.

As I looked at all of this, I felt a sense of a knowledge gap. I saw people using XML where a custom syntax would be more readable and not harder to do. I saw people bending Ruby into complicated contortions when a custom syntax would be easier. I saw people playing around with parsers when a fluent interface in their regular language would be a lot less work.

My hypothesis is that these things are happening because of a knowledge gap. Skilled programmers don't know enough about DSL techniques to make an informed decision about which ones to use. That's the kind of gap I enjoy trying to fill.

Why Are DSLs Important?

I'll talk about this in more detail in "Why Use a DSL?," p. 33 but I see two primary reasons why you should be interested in DSLs (and thus the techniques in this book).

The first reason is to improve programmer's productivity. Consider this fragment of code:

```
input =~ /\d{3}-\d{3}-\d{4}/
```

You may recognize it as a regular expression match, and probably you know what it's matching. Regular expressions are often criticized for being cryptic, but think of how you would write this pattern match if all you could use were regular control code. How easy would it be to understand and modify that code, compared to a regular expression?

DSLs are very good at taking certain narrow parts of programming and making them easier to understand and therefore quicker to write, quicker to modify, and less likely to breed bugs.

The second reason for valuing DSLs goes beyond programmers. Since DSLs are smaller and easier to understand, they allow nonprogrammers to see the code that drives important parts of their business. By exposing the real code to the people who understand the domain, you enable a much richer communication channel between programmers and their customers.

When people talk about this kind of thing, they often say that DSLs will allow you to get rid of programmers. I'm extremely skeptical of that argument; after all, it was said of COBOL. Although there certainly are languages, such as CSS, written by people who don't call themselves programmers, it's the reading that matters more than the writing. If a domain expert can read, and mostly understand, the code that drives a key part of her business, then she can communicate in a much more detailed fashion with the programmer who actually types in the code.

This second reason for using DSLs isn't easy to achieve. But the rewards are worth the effort. Communication between programmers and their customers is the biggest bottleneck in software development, so any technique that can address it is worth its weight in single malts.

Don't Be Frightened by the Size of This Book

The thickness of this book may be a bit intimidating to you; it certainly makes me gulp to see how much there is here. I'm wary of big books, because I know we all only have so much time to read—so a big book is a big investment of time (which is much more valuable than the cover price). Therefore, I've used a format that I prefer in cases like this: a duplex book.

A **duplex book** is really two books under one cover. The first book is a narrative book, designed to be read cover to cover. My aim with the narrative book is to provide a brief overview of the topic, enough to get a broad understanding but not to do any detailed work. My target for a narrative section is no more than 150 pages, so it is a manageable amount to read.

The second, and larger, book is reference material, which is designed not to be read cover to cover (although some people do) but instead to be dipped into when needed. Some people like to read the narrative first to get a broad overview of the subject and then dive into those bits of the reference section that interest them. Others like to dive into the interesting parts of the reference section as they work through the narrative. The purpose of the split is for me to give you an idea of what's skippable and what isn't—then you can choose when you wish to skip and when you want to delve deeper.

I've also tried to make the reference bits reasonably self-standing, so if you want someone to use *Tree Construction (281)* you can tell them to read just that pattern and get a good idea of what to do, even if their memory of the narrative is a little hazy. This way, once you've absorbed the narrative overview, it becomes a reference book that's handy to grab when you need to look up some details.

The main reason the book is so large is that I haven't figured out how to make it shorter. One of my primary aims in this book is to provide a resource that explores the breadth of different techniques available for DSLs. There are books out there that talk about code generation, or Ruby metaprogramming, or using *Parser Generator (269)* tools. With this book, I want to sweep across all these techniques so that you can better understand their similarities and differences. They all play a role in a broader landscape, and my aim here is to provide a tour of that landscape while giving you enough detail to get started with the techniques I'm talking about.

What You'll Learn

I've designed this book as a wide-ranging guide on different kinds of DSLs and the approaches to building them. Often, when people start experimenting with DSLs, they pick up only one technique. The point of this book is to show you a broad variety of techniques, so that you can evaluate which one is the best for your circumstances. I've provided details and examples on how to implement many of these techniques. Naturally, I cannot show you everything you can do, but there is enough to get you started and help you through the early decisions.

The early chapters should give you a good idea of what a DSL is, when DSLs come in useful, and what is their role compared to a framework or library. The implementation chapters will give you a broad start in how to build external and internal DSLs. The external DSL material will show you the role of a parser, the usefulness of a *Parser Generator (269)*, and different ways of using a parser to parse an external DSL. The internal DSL section will show you how to think about the various language constructs you can use in a DSL style. While this won't tell you how to best use your particular language, it will help you understand how techniques in one language correspond to those in others.

The code generation section will outline different strategies for code generation, should you need to use it. The language workbench chapter is a very brief overview of a new generation of tools. For most of this book I concentrate on techniques that have been used for decades; language workbenches are more of a future technique that is promising but unproven.

Who Should Read This Book?

My primary target audience for this book is professional software developers who are considering building a DSL. I imagine such a reader as someone with at least a couple of years of programming experience and thus comfortable with the basic ideas of software design.

If you're deeply involved in language design, you probably won't find much new in this book in terms of material. What I hope you will find useful is the approach I've used to organizing and communicating this information. Although there is a huge amount of work done in language design, particularly in academia, very little of this makes its way into the professional programming world.

The first couple of chapters of the narrative section should also be useful to anyone wondering what a DSL is and why it may be worth using. Reading the full narrative section will provide an overview on the various implementation techniques to use.

Is This a Java Book or a C# Book?

As with most books I write, the ideas here are pretty much independent of programming language. One of my top priorities is to uncover general principles and patterns that can be used with whatever programming language you happen to be using. As such, the ideas in the book should be valuable to you if you are using any kind of modern OO language.

One potential language gap here is functional languages. While I think much of this book will still be relevant, I don't have enough experience in functional languages to really know to what extent their programming paradigm would alter the advice here. The book is also somewhat limited for procedural languages (i.e., non-OO languages like C) because several of the techniques I describe rely on object orientation.

Although I am writing about general principles here, in order to describe them properly I believe I need to show examples—which require a particular programming language to be written in. In choosing a language for examples, my primary criteria is how widely read the language is. As a result, almost all examples in this book are in Java or C#. Both are widely used in the industry; both have a familiar C-like syntax, memory management, and libraries that remove many awkward contortions. I am not claiming that these are the best languages to write DSLs in (in particular, because I don't think they are), but they are the best languages to help communicate the general concepts I'm describing. I've tried to use both languages pretty much equally, tipping the balance only when one of them made things a bit easier. I've also tried to avoid elements of the language that require too much knowledge of the syntax, although that's a difficult tradeoff since a good use of internal DSLs often involves exploiting syntactic quirks.

There are a few ideas which absolutely require a dynamic language and thus cannot be illustrated in Java or C#. In those cases I've turned to Ruby since it's the dynamic language I'm most familiar with. It also helps that it's well-suited to writing DSLs with. Again, despite my personal familiarity and considerable liking of the language, you should not infer that these techniques are not applicable elsewhere. I enjoy Ruby a lot, but the only way you can get my language bigotry to become evident is by dissing Smalltalk.

I should mention that there are many other languages for which DSLs are appropriate, including many that are specially designed to make it easier to write internal DSLs. I don't mention them here because I haven't done enough work with them to feel confident about pontificating on them. You should not interpret that as any negative opinion on them.

In particular, one of the difficult things about trying to write a language-independent book on DSLs is that the usefulness of many techniques depends very directly on the features of a particular language. You should always be aware of the fact that your language environment can severely change the tradeoffs compared to the broad generalizations I have to make.

What's Missing

One of the most frustrating parts of writing a book like this is the moment when I realize that I have to stop. I've put a couple of years of work into writing this, and I believe I have a lot of useful material for you to read. But I'm also conscious of the many gaps that remain. They are all gaps I'd like to fill, but doing so would take a significant amount of time. My belief is that it's better to have an incomplete published book than wait years for a complete book—if a complete book is even possible. So here I mention the main gaps that I could see but didn't have time to cover.

I've already alluded to one of these—the role of functional languages. There is a strong history of DSL construction in modern functional languages based on ML and/or Haskell—and I've pretty much ignored this work in my book. It's an interesting question how much a familiarity with functional languages and their DSL usage would affect the structure of the material in this book.

Perhaps the most frustrating gap for me is the lack of a decent discussion of diagnostics and error handling. I remember being taught at university how the truly hard part of compiler writing is diagnostics—and thus I realize I'm glossing over a considerable topic by not covering it properly here.

My favorite section of this book is the section on alternative computational models. There is so much more I could write about here—but again, time was my enemy. In the end I decided I'd have to do with less alternative computational models than I would like—hopefully there's still enough to inspire you to explore some more.

The Reference Book

While the narrative book is a pretty normal structure, I feel I need to talk a bit more about the structure of the reference section. I've divided the reference section into a series of topics grouped into chapters to keep similar topics together. My aim was that each topic should generally be self-standing—once you've read the narrative, you should be able to dive into a particular topic for more detail without looking into other topics. Where there are exceptions, I mention that at the start of the corresponding topic.

The majority of the topics are written as patterns. The focus of a pattern is a common solution to a recurring problem. So if a common problem is "How do I structure my parser?", two possible patterns for the solution are *Delimiter-Directed Translation (201)* and *Syntax-Directed Translation (219)*.

There's been a lot written about patterns in software development in the last twenty years or so, and different authors have different views on them. For me, patterns are useful because they provide a good way of structuring a reference section like this. The narrative will tell you that if you want to parse text, these two patterns are likely candidates; the patterns themselves will give you more information on selecting one and enough to get you started on implementing it.

Although I've written most of the reference section using a pattern structure, I haven't used it for every case. Not all of the reference topics felt like solutions to me. With some topics, such as *Nested Operator Expression (327)*, a solution didn't really seem to be the focus of the topic, and the topic didn't fit the structure I'm using for patterns; so in these cases, I didn't use a pattern-style description. There are other cases that are hard to call patterns, such as *Macro (183)* or *BNF*

(229), but using the pattern structure seemed like a good way to describe them. On the whole, I've been guided by whether the pattern structure, in particular the separation of "how it works" and "when to use," seems to work for the concept I'm describing.

Pattern Structure

Most authors use some kind of standard template when writing about patterns. I'm no exception, both in using a standard template and in having one that's different from everyone else's. My template, or pattern form, is the one I first used in P of EAA [Fowler PoEAA]. It has the following form.

Perhaps the most important element is the **name**. One of the biggest reasons I like using patterns as my reference topics is that it helps create a strong vocabulary to discuss the subject. There's no guarantee that this vocabulary will be widely used, but at least it encourages me to be consistent in my own writing, while giving others a starting point should they wish to use it.

The next two elements are the **intent** and **sketch**. They are there to briefly summarize the pattern. They are a reminder of the pattern, so if you already "have the pattern" but don't know the name, they can jog your memory. The intent is a sentence or two of text, while the sketch is something more visual. Sometimes I use a diagram for sketch, sometimes a brief code example—whatever I think will quickly convey the essence of the pattern. When I use a diagram, I sometimes use UML, but am quite happy to use something else if I think it will convey the meaning more easily.

Next comes a slightly longer **summary**, usually around a motivating example. This is a couple of paragraphs, and again is there to help people get an overview before diving into the details.

The two main body sections of the pattern are *How it works* and *When to use it*. The ordering of the two is somewhat arbitrary; if you're trying to decide whether to use a pattern, you may only want to read the "when" section. Often, however, the "when" section doesn't make much sense without knowing how it works.

The last sections are examples. Although I do my best to explain how a pattern works in the "how" section, often you need an example, with code, to really get the point. Code examples are dangerous, however, because they show only one application of the pattern, and some people may think it's that application that is the pattern, rather than the general concept. You can use the same pattern a hundred times, making it a little different every time, but I only have limited space and energy for examples. So, always remember that the pattern is much more than the particular example shows.

All of the examples are deliberately very simple, focused only on the pattern in question. I use simple, independent examples because they match my goal of making each reference chapter independent of others. Naturally, there'll be a host of other issues to deal with when you apply the pattern to your circumstances, but with a simple example I feel you at least have a chance of understanding the core point. Richer examples can be more realistic, but they would force you to deal with a bunch of issues extraneous to the pattern you are studying. So my aim is to show you the pieces, but leave to you the challenge of assembling them together for your particular needs.

This also means that my primary aim in the code is understandability. I've not taken into account performance issues, error handling, or other things that distract from the pattern's essence.

I try to avoid code that I think is hard to follow, even if it's more idiomatic for the language I'm using. This is a particularly awkward balance for internal DSLs that often rely on obscure language tricks in order to enhance the flow of the language.

Many patterns will miss out a section or two if I feel there isn't anything compelling to put into that section. Some patterns don't have examples because the best examples are in other patterns—when that happens, I do try to point them out.

Acknowledgments

As usual when I write a book, there's a lot of other people who have done a great deal to help making the book happen. While my name may be on it, there are many other people who greatly improved its quality.

My first thanks go to my colleague **Rebecca Parsons**. One of my concerns about writing a book on this topic has been delving into an area with a great deal of academic background that I'm seriously under-aware of. Rebecca has been a huge help here, since she has a strong background in language theory. On top of that, she's one of our leading technical troubleshooters and strategists, so she combines the academic background with a lot of practical experience. She would have liked, and is certainly qualified, to play a bigger role in this book, but ThoughtWorks find her far too useful. I'm glad for the many hours of talks she's been able to give me.

When it comes to reviewers, an author always hopes for (and, kind of, dreads) the reviewer who goes through everything and finds tons of problems, both small and large. I've been lucky to find **Michael Hunger** who has played this role remarkably well. From the earliest days this book appeared on my website, he's been pummeling me with my errors and how to fix them—and believe me, that's a pummeling I need. Just as importantly, Michael has played a big role in pushing me to describe techniques utilizing static typing, particularly with respect to statically typed *Symbol Tables (165)*. He has made tons of further suggestions, which would take another two books to do justice to; I hope to see these ideas explored in the future.

Over the last couple of years, I've given tutorials on this material in conjunction with my colleagues **Rebecca Parsons, Neal Ford,** and **Ola Bini.** Besides giving these tutorials, they've done much to shape the ideas in them and in this book, leading me to steal quite a few thoughts.

ThoughtWorks have generously given me a great deal of time to write this book. After spending so much of my life determined to never work for a company, I'm glad to have found a company that makes me want to stay and actively play a role in building it.

I've had a strong group of official reviewers who have gone through this book, found errors, and suggested improvements:

David Bock	David Ing
Gilad Bracha	Jeremy Miller
Aino Corry	Ravi Mohan
Sven Efftinge	Terance Parr
Eric Evans	Nat Pryce
Jay Fields	Chris Sells
Steve Freeman	Nathaniel Schutta
Brian Goetz	Craig Taverner
Steve Hayes	Dave Thomas
Clifford Heath	Glenn Vanderburg
Michael Hunger	

A small but important thank you is due to **David Ing** who suggested the title for a Zoo of DSLs.

One of the nice things about being a series editor is that I've acquired a really good team of authors who are an outstanding sounding board for questions and ideas. Of these, I particularly want to thank **Elliotte Rusty Harold** for his wonderfully detailed comments and review.

Many of my colleagues at ThoughtWorks have acted as sources for ideas. I want to thank everyone who has let me poke around in projects over the last few years. I see far more ideas than I can write about, and I really enjoy having such a rich seam to mine from.

Several people made useful comments on the Safari Books Online roughcut, which I managed to make use of before we went to print: **Pavel Bernhauser, Mocky, Roman Yakovenko, tdyer.**

My thanks to those at Pearson who published this book. **Greg Doench** was the acquisition editor who looked after the overall process of publishing the book. **John Fuller** was the managing editor who oversaw the production.

Dmitry Kirsanov turned my sloppy English into something worthy of a book. **Alina Kirsanova** composed the book into the layout you now see and produced the Index.

Part I

Narratives

Chapter 1

An Introductory Example

When I start to write, I need to swiftly explain what it is I'm writing about; in this case, to explain what a domain-specific language (DSL) is. I like to do this by showing a concrete example and following up with a more abstract definition. So, here I'm going to start with an example to demonstrate the different forms a DSL can take. In the next chapter I'll try to generalize the definition into something more widely applicable.

1.1 Gothic Security

I have vague but persistent childhood memories of watching cheesy adventure films on TV. Often, these films would be set in some old castle and feature secret compartments or passages. In order to find them, heroes would need to pull the candle holder at the top of stairs and tap the wall twice.

Let's imagine a company that decides to build security systems based on this idea. They come in, set up some kind of wireless network, and install little devices that send four-character messages when interesting things happen. For example, a sensor attached to a drawer would send the message D2OP when the drawer is opened. We also have little control devices that respond to four-character command messages—so a device can unlock a door when it hears the message D1UL.

At the center of all this is some controller software that listens to event messages, figures out what to do, and sends command messages. The company bought a job lot of Java-enabled toasters during the dot-com crash and is using them as the controllers. So whenever a customer buys a gothic security system, they come in and fit the building with lots of devices and a toaster with a control program written in Java.

For this example, I'll focus on this control program. Each customer has individual needs, but once you look at a good sampling, you will soon see common patterns. Miss Grant closes her bedroom door, opens a drawer, and turns on a light to access a secret compartment. Miss Shaw turns on a tap, then opens either

3

of her two compartments by turning on the correct light. Miss Smith has a secret compartment inside a locked closet inside her office. She has to close a door, take a picture off the wall, turn her desk light on three times, open the top drawer of her filing cabinet — and then the closet is unlocked. If she forgets to turn the desk light off before she opens the inner compartment, an alarm will sound.

Although this example is deliberately whimsical, the underlying point isn't that unusual. What we have is a family of systems that share most components and behaviors, but have some important differences. In this case, the way the controller sends and receives messages is the same across all the customers, but the sequence of events and commands differs. We want to arrange things so that the company can install a new system with the minimum of effort, so it must be easy for them to program the sequence of actions into the controller.

Looking at all these cases, it emerges that a good way to think about the controller is as a state machine. Each sensor sends an event that can change the state of the controller. As the controller enters a state, it can send a command message out to the network.

At this point, I should confess that originally in my writing it was the other way around. A state machine makes a good example for a DSL, so I picked that first. I chose a gothic castle because I get bored of all the other state machine examples.

1.1.1 Miss Grant's Controller

Although my mythical company has thousands of satisfied customers, we'll focus on just one: Miss Grant, my favorite. She has a secret compartment in her bedroom that is normally locked and concealed. To open it, she has to close the door, then open the second drawer in her chest and turn her bedside light on — in either order. Once these are done, the secret panel is unlocked for her to open.

I can represent this sequence as a state diagram (Figure 1.1).

If you haven't come across state machines yet, they are a common way of describing behavior — not universally useful but well suited to situations like this. The basic idea is that the controller can be in different states. When you're in a particular state, certain events will transition you to another state that will have different transitions on it; thus a sequence of events leads you from state to state. In this model, actions (sending of commands) occur when you enter a state. (Other kinds of state machines perform actions in different places.)

This controller is, mostly, a simple and conventional state machine, but there is a twist. The customers' controllers have a distinct idle state that the system spends most of its time in. Certain events can jump the system back into this idle state even if it is in the middle of the more interesting state transitions, effectively resetting the model. In Miss Grant's case, opening the door is such a reset event.

Introducing reset events means that the state machine described here doesn't quite fit one of the classical state machine models. There are several variations

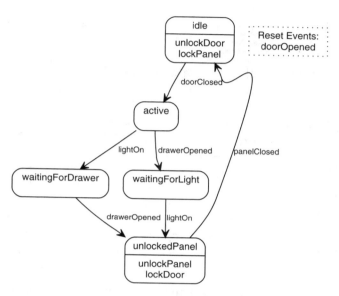

Figure 1.1 *State diagram for Miss Grant's secret compartment*

of state machines that are pretty well known; this model starts with one of these but the reset events add a twist that is unique to this context.

In particular, you should note that reset events aren't strictly necessary to express Miss Grant's controller. As an alternative, I could just add a transition to every state, triggered by doorOpened, leading to the idle state. The notion of a reset event is useful because it simplifies the diagram.

1.2 The State Machine Model

Once the team has decided that a state machine is a good abstraction for specifying how the controllers work, the next step is to ensure that abstraction is put into the software itself. If people want to think about controller behavior with events, states, and transitions, then we want that vocabulary to be present in the software code too. This is essentially the Domain-Driven Design principle of *Ubiquitous Language* [Evans DDD]—that is, we construct a shared language between the domain people (who describe how the building security should work) and programmers.

When working in Java, the natural way to do this is through a *Domain Model* [Fowler PoEAA] of a state machine.

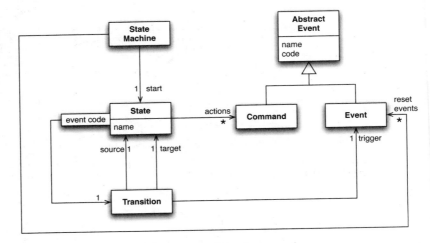

Figure 1.2 *Class diagram of the state machine framework*

The controller communicates with the devices by receiving event messages and sending command messages. These are both four-letter codes sent through the communication channels. I want to refer to these in the controller code with symbolic names, so I create event and command classes with a code and a name. I keep them as separate classes (with a superclass) as they play different roles in the controller code.

```
class AbstractEvent...
  private String name, code;

  public AbstractEvent(String name, String code) {
    this.name = name;
    this.code = code;
  }
  public String getCode() { return code;}
  public String getName() { return name;}
```

```
public class Command extends AbstractEvent
```

```
public class Event extends AbstractEvent
```

The state class keeps track of the commands that it will send and its outbound transitions.

```
class State...
  private String name;
  private List<Command> actions = new ArrayList<Command>();
  private Map<String, Transition> transitions = new HashMap<String, Transition>();
```

```
class State...
  public void addTransition(Event event, State targetState) {
    assert null != targetState;
    transitions.put(event.getCode(), new Transition(this, event, targetState));
  }
```

```
class Transition...
  private final State source, target;
  private final Event trigger;

  public Transition(State source, Event trigger, State target) {
    this.source = source;
    this.target = target;
    this.trigger = trigger;
  }
  public State getSource() {return source;}
  public State getTarget() {return target;}
  public Event getTrigger() {return trigger;}
  public String getEventCode() {return trigger.getCode();}
```

The state machine holds on to its start state.

```
class StateMachine...
  private State start;

  public StateMachine(State start) {
    this.start = start;
  }
```

Then, any other states in the machine are those reachable from this state.

```
class StateMachine...
  public Collection<State> getStates() {
    List<State> result = new ArrayList<State>();
    collectStates(result, start);
    return result;
  }

  private void collectStates(Collection<State> result, State s) {
    if (result.contains(s)) return;
    result.add(s);
    for (State next : s.getAllTargets())
      collectStates(result, next);
  }
```

```
class State...
  Collection<State> getAllTargets() {
    List<State> result = new ArrayList<State>();
    for (Transition t : transitions.values()) result.add(t.getTarget());
    return result;
  }
```

To handle reset events, I keep a list of them on the state machine.

```
class StateMachine...
  private List<Event> resetEvents = new ArrayList<Event>();

  public void addResetEvents(Event... events) {
    for (Event e : events) resetEvents.add(e);
  }
```

I don't need to have a separate structure for reset events like this. I could handle this by simply declaring extra transitions on the state machine like this:

```
class StateMachine...
  private void addResetEvent_byAddingTransitions(Event e) {
    for (State s : getStates())
      if (!s.hasTransition(e.getCode())) s.addTransition(e, start);
  }
```

I prefer explicit reset events on the machine because that better expresses my intent. While it does complicate the machine a bit, it makes it clear how a general machine is supposed to work, as well as the intention of defining a particular machine.

With the structure out of the way, let's move on to the behavior. As it turns out, it's really quite simple. The controller has a handle method that takes the event code it receives from the device.

```
class Controller...
  private State currentState;
  private StateMachine machine;

  public CommandChannel getCommandChannel() {
    return commandsChannel;
  }

  private CommandChannel commandsChannel;

  public void handle(String eventCode) {
    if (currentState.hasTransition(eventCode))
      transitionTo(currentState.targetState(eventCode));
    else if (machine.isResetEvent(eventCode))
      transitionTo(machine.getStart());
      // ignore unknown events
  }

  private void transitionTo(State target) {
    currentState = target;
    currentState.executeActions(commandsChannel);
  }
```

```
class State...
  public boolean hasTransition(String eventCode) {
    return transitions.containsKey(eventCode);
  }
  public State targetState(String eventCode) {
    return transitions.get(eventCode).getTarget();
  }
  public void executeActions(CommandChannel commandsChannel) {
    for (Command c : actions) commandsChannel.send(c.getCode());
  }

class StateMachine...
  public boolean isResetEvent(String eventCode) {
    return resetEventCodes().contains(eventCode);
  }

  private List<String> resetEventCodes() {
    List<String> result = new ArrayList<String>();
    for (Event e : resetEvents) result.add(e.getCode());
    return result;
  }
```

It ignores any events that are not registered on the state. For any events that
are recognized, it transitions to the target state and executes any commands
defined on that target state.

1.3 Programming Miss Grant's Controller

Now that I've implemented the state machine model, I can program Miss Grant's
controller like this:

```
Event doorClosed = new Event("doorClosed", "D1CL");
Event drawerOpened = new Event("drawerOpened", "D2OP");
Event lightOn = new Event("lightOn", "L1ON");
Event doorOpened = new Event("doorOpened", "D1OP");
Event panelClosed = new Event("panelClosed", "PNCL");

Command unlockPanelCmd = new Command("unlockPanel", "PNUL");
Command lockPanelCmd = new Command("lockPanel", "PNLK");
Command lockDoorCmd = new Command("lockDoor", "D1LK");
Command unlockDoorCmd = new Command("unlockDoor", "D1UL");

State idle = new State("idle");
State activeState = new State("active");
State waitingForLightState = new State("waitingForLight");
State waitingForDrawerState = new State("waitingForDrawer");
State unlockedPanelState = new State("unlockedPanel");

StateMachine machine = new StateMachine(idle);
```

```
idle.addTransition(doorClosed, activeState);
idle.addAction(unlockDoorCmd);
idle.addAction(lockPanelCmd);

activeState.addTransition(drawerOpened, waitingForLightState);
activeState.addTransition(lightOn, waitingForDrawerState);

waitingForLightState.addTransition(lightOn, unlockedPanelState);

waitingForDrawerState.addTransition(drawerOpened, unlockedPanelState);

unlockedPanelState.addAction(unlockPanelCmd);
unlockedPanelState.addAction(lockDoorCmd);
unlockedPanelState.addTransition(panelClosed, idle);

machine.addResetEvents(doorOpened);
```

I look at this last bit of code as quite different in nature from the previous pieces. The earlier code described how to build the state machine model; this last bit of code is about configuring that model for one particular controller. You often see divisions like this. On the one hand is the library, framework, or component implementation code; on the other is configuration or component assembly code. Essentially, it is the separation of common code from variable code. We structure the common code in a set of components that we then configure for different purposes.

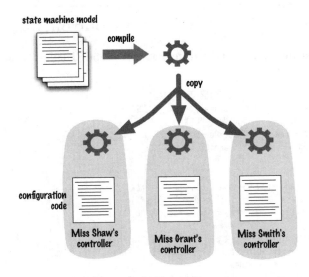

Figure 1.3 *A single library used with multiple configurations*

Here is another way of representing that configuration code:

```xml
<stateMachine start = "idle">
  <event name="doorClosed" code="D1CL"/>
  <event name="drawerOpened" code="D2OP"/>
  <event name="lightOn" code="L1ON"/>
  <event name="doorOpened" code="D1OP"/>
  <event name="panelClosed" code="PNCL"/>

  <command name="unlockPanel" code="PNUL"/>
  <command name="lockPanel" code="PNLK"/>
  <command name="lockDoor" code="D1LK"/>
  <command name="unlockDoor" code="D1UL"/>

  <state name="idle">
    <transition event="doorClosed" target="active"/>
    <action command="unlockDoor"/>
    <action command="lockPanel"/>
  </state>

  <state name="active">
    <transition event="drawerOpened" target="waitingForLight"/>
    <transition event="lightOn" target="waitingForDrawer"/>
  </state>

  <state name="waitingForLight">
    <transition event="lightOn" target="unlockedPanel"/>
  </state>

  <state name="waitingForDrawer">
    <transition event="drawerOpened" target="unlockedPanel"/>
  </state>

  <state name="unlockedPanel">
    <action command="unlockPanel"/>
    <action command="lockDoor"/>
    <transition event="panelClosed" target="idle"/>
  </state>

  <resetEvent name = "doorOpened"/>
</stateMachine>
```

This style of representation should look familiar to most readers; I've expressed it as an XML file. There are several advantages to doing it this way. One obvious advantage is that now we don't have to compile a separate Java program for each controller we put into the field—instead, we can just compile the state machine components plus an appropriate parser into a common JAR, and ship the XML file to be read when the machine starts up. Any changes to the behavior of the controller can be done without having to distribute a new JAR. We do, of course, pay for this in that many mistakes in the syntax of the configuration can only be detected at runtime, although various XML schema systems can help with this a bit. I'm also a big fan of extensive testing, which catches most of the errors with compile-time checking, together with other faults that type checking can't spot. With this kind of testing in place, I worry much less about moving error detection to runtime.

A second advantage is in the expressiveness of the file itself. We no longer need to worry about the details of making connections through variables. Instead, we have a declarative approach that in many ways reads much more clearly. We're also limited in that we can only express configuration in this file—limitations like this are often helpful because they can reduce the chances of people making mistakes in the component assembly code.

You often hear people talk about this kind of thing as declarative programming. Our usual model is the imperative model, where we command the computer by a sequence of steps. "Declarative" is a very cloudy term, but it generally applies to approaches that move away from the imperative model. Here we take a step in that direction: We move away from variable shuffling and represent the actions and transitions within a state by subelements in XML.

These advantages are why so many frameworks in Java and C# are configured with XML configuration files. These days, it sometimes feels like you're doing more programming with XML than with your main programming language.

Here's another version of the configuration code:

```
events
    doorClosed   D1CL
    drawerOpened D2OP
    lightOn      L1ON
    doorOpened   D1OP
    panelClosed  PNCL
end

resetEvents
    doorOpened
end

commands
    unlockPanel PNUL
    lockPanel   PNLK
    lockDoor    D1LK
    unlockDoor  D1UL
end

state idle
    actions {unlockDoor lockPanel}
    doorClosed => active
end

state active
    drawerOpened => waitingForLight
    lightOn      => waitingForDrawer
end
```

```
state waitingForLight
  lightOn => unlockedPanel
end

state waitingForDrawer
  drawerOpened => unlockedPanel
end

state unlockedPanel
  actions {unlockPanel lockDoor}
  panelClosed => idle
end
```

This is code, although not in a syntax that's familiar to you. In fact, it's a custom syntax that I made up for this example. I think it's a syntax that's easier to write and, above all, easier to read than the XML syntax. It's terser and avoids a lot of the quoting and noise characters that the XML suffers from. You probably wouldn't have done it exactly the same way, but the point is that you can construct whatever syntax you and your team prefer. You can still load it in at runtime (like the XML) but you don't have to (as you don't with the XML) if you want it at compile time.

This language is a domain-specific language that shares many of the characteristics of DSLs. First, it's suitable only for a very narrow purpose—it can't do anything other than configure this particular kind of state machine. As a result, the DSL is very simple—there's no facility for control structures or anything else. It's not even Turing-complete. You couldn't write a whole application in this language; all you can do is describe one small aspect of an application. As a result, the DSL has to be combined with other languages to get anything done. But the simplicity of the DSL means it's easy to edit and process.

This simplicity makes it easier for those who write the controller software to understand it—but also may make the behavior visible beyond the developers themselves. The people who set up the system may be able to look at this code and understand how it's supposed to work, even though they don't understand the core Java code in the controller itself. Even if they only read the DSL, that may be enough to spot errors or to communicate effectively with the Java developers. While there are many practical difficulties in building a DSL that acts as a communication medium with domain experts and business analysts like this, the benefit of bridging the most difficult communication gap in software development is usually worth the attempt.

Now look again at the XML representation. Is this a DSL? I would argue that it is. It's wrapped in an XML carrier syntax—but it's still a DSL. This example thus raises a design issue: Is it better to have a custom syntax for a DSL or an XML syntax? The XML syntax can be easier to parse since people are so familiar with parsing XML. (However, it took me about the same amount of time to write the parser for the custom syntax as it did for the XML.) I'd contend that the custom syntax is much easier to read, at least in this case. But however you view this choice, the core tradeoffs of DSLs are the same. Indeed, you can argue that most XML configuration files are essentially DSLs.

Now look at this code. Does this look like a DSL for this problem?

```
event :doorClosed, "D1CL"
event :drawerOpened,  "D2OP"
event :lightOn, "L1ON"
event :doorOpened,  "D1OP"
event :panelClosed, "PNCL"

command  :unlockPanel, "PNUL"
command  :lockPanel,   "PNLK"
command  :lockDoor,    "D1LK"
command  :unlockDoor,  "D1UL"

resetEvents :doorOpened

state :idle do
  actions :unlockDoor, :lockPanel
  transitions :doorClosed => :active
end

state :active do
  transitions :drawerOpened => :waitingForLight,
              :lightOn => :waitingForDrawer
end

state :waitingForLight do
  transitions :lightOn => :unlockedPanel
end

state :waitingForDrawer do
  transitions :drawerOpened => :unlockedPanel
end

state :unlockedPanel do
  actions :unlockPanel, :lockDoor
  transitions :panelClosed => :idle
end
```

It's a bit noisier than the custom language earlier, but still pretty clear. Readers whose language likings are similar to mine will probably recognize it as Ruby. Ruby gives me a lot of syntactic options that make for more readable code, so I can make it look very similar to the custom language.

Ruby developers would consider this code to be a DSL. I use a subset of the capabilities of Ruby and capture the same ideas as with our XML and custom syntax. Essentially I'm embedding the DSL into Ruby, using a subset of Ruby as my syntax. To an extent, this is more a matter of attitude than of anything else. I'm choosing to look at the Ruby code through DSL glasses. But it's a point of view with a long tradition—Lisp programmers often think of creating DSLs inside Lisp.

This brings me to pointing out that there are two kinds of textual DSLs which I call external and internal DSLs. An **external DSL** is a domain-specific language represented in a separate language to the main programming language it's working with. This language may use a custom syntax, or it may follow the syntax of another representation such as XML. An **internal DSL** is a DSL represented within the syntax of a general-purpose language. It's a stylized use of that language for a domain-specific purpose.

You may also hear the term **embedded DSL** as a synonym for internal DSL. Although it is fairly widely used, I avoid this term because "embedded language" may also apply to scripting languages embedded within applications, such as VBA in Excel or Scheme in the Gimp.

Now think again about the original Java configuration code. Is this a DSL? I would argue that it isn't. That code feels like stitching together with an API, while the Ruby code above has more of the feel of a declarative language. Does this mean you can't do an internal DSL in Java? How about this:

```
public class BasicStateMachine extends StateMachineBuilder {

  Events doorClosed, drawerOpened, lightOn, panelClosed;
  Commands unlockPanel, lockPanel, lockDoor, unlockDoor;
  States idle, active, waitingForLight, waitingForDrawer, unlockedPanel;
  ResetEvents doorOpened;

  protected void defineStateMachine() {
    doorClosed. code("D1CL");
    drawerOpened. code("D2OP");
    lightOn.    code("L1ON");
    panelClosed.code("PNCL");

    doorOpened. code("D1OP");

    unlockPanel.code("PNUL");
    lockPanel.  code("PNLK");
    lockDoor.   code("D1LK");
    unlockDoor. code("D1UL");

    idle
      .actions(unlockDoor, lockPanel)
      .transition(doorClosed).to(active)
      ;

    active
      .transition(drawerOpened).to(waitingForLight)
      .transition(lightOn).    to(waitingForDrawer)
      ;

    waitingForLight
      .transition(lightOn).to(unlockedPanel)
      ;
```

```
waitingForDrawer
  .transition(drawerOpened).to(unlockedPanel)
  ;

unlockedPanel
  .actions(unlockPanel, lockDoor)
  .transition(panelClosed).to(idle)
  ;
  }
}
```

It's formatted oddly, and uses some unusual programming conventions, but it is valid Java. This I would call a DSL; although it's more messy than the Ruby DSL, it still has that declarative flow that a DSL needs.

What makes an internal DSL different from a normal API? This is a tough question that I'll spend more time on later ("Fluent and Command-Query APIs," p. 68), but it comes down to the rather fuzzy notion of a language-like flow.

Another term you may come across for an internal DSL is a **fluent interface**. This term emphasizes the fact that an internal DSL is really just a particular kind of API, designed with this elusive quality of fluency. Given this distinction, it's useful to have a name for a nonfluent API—I'll use the term **command-query API**.

1.4 Languages and Semantic Model

At the beginning of this example, I talked about building a model for a state machine. The presence of such a model, and its relationship with a DSL, are vitally important concerns. In this example, the role of the DSL is to populate the state machine model. So, when I'm parsing the custom syntax version and come across:

```
events
  doorClosed D1CL
```

I would create a new event object (new Event("doorClosed", "D1CL")) and keep it to one side (in a *Symbol Table (165)*) so that when I see doorClosed => active I could include it in the transition (using addTransition). The model is the engine that provides the behavior of the state machine. Indeed you can say that most of the power of this design comes from having this model. All the DSL does is provide a readable way of populating that model—that is the difference from the command-query API I started with.

From the DSL's point of view, I refer to this model as the *Semantic Model (159)*. When people discuss a programming language, you often hear them talk about syntax and semantics. The syntax captures the legal expressions of the program—everything that in the custom-syntax DSL is captured by the grammar. The semantics of a program is what it means—that is, what it does when it executes. In this case, it is the model that defines the semantics. If you're used to using *Domain Models* [Fowler PoEAA], for the moment you can think of a Semantic Model as very close to the same thing.

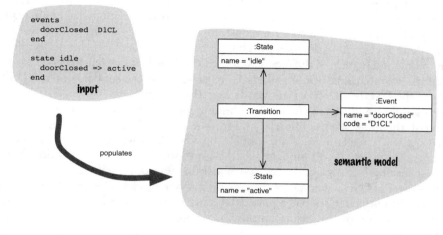

Figure 1.4 *Parsing a DSL populates a Semantic Model (159).*

(Take a look at *Semantic Model (159)* for the differences between Semantic Model and Domain Model, as well as the differences between a Semantic Model and an abstract syntax tree.)

One opinion I've formed is that the Semantic Model is a vital part of a well-designed DSL. In the wild you'll find some DSLs use a Semantic Model and some do not, but I'm very much of the opinion that you should almost always use a Semantic Model. (I find it almost impossible to say some words, such as "always," without a qualifying "almost." I can almost never find a rule that's universally applicable.)

I advocate a Semantic Model because it provides a clear separation of concerns between parsing a language and the resulting semantics. I can reason about how the state machine works, and carry out enhancement and debugging of the state machine without worrying about the language issues. I can run tests on the state machine model by populating it with a command-query interface. I can evolve the state machine model and the DSL independently, building new features into the model before figuring out how to expose them through the language. Perhaps the most important point is that I can test the model independently of futzing around with the language. Indeed, all the examples of a DSL shown above were built on top of the same Semantic Model and created exactly the same configuration of objects in that model.

In this example, the Semantic Model is an object model. A Semantic Model can also take other forms. It can be a pure data structure with all behavior in separate functions. I would still refer to it as a Semantic Model, because the data structure captures the particular meaning of the DSL script in the context of those functions.

Looking at it from this point of view, the DSL merely acts as a mechanism for expressing how the model is configured. Much of the benefits of using this approach comes from the model rather than the DSLs. The fact that I can easily configure a new state machine for a customer is a property of the model, not the DSL. The fact that I can make a change to a controller at runtime, without compiling, is a feature of the model, not the DSL. The fact I'm reusing code across multiple installations of controllers is a property of the model, not the DSL. Hence the DSL is merely a thin facade over the model.

A model provides many benefits without any DSLs present. As a result, we use them all the time. We use libraries and frameworks to wisely avoid work. In our own software, we construct our models, building up abstractions that allow us to program faster. Good models, whether published as libraries or frameworks or just serving our own code, can work just fine without any DSL in sight.

However, a DSL can enhance the capabilities of a model. The right DSL makes it easier to understand what a particular state machine does. Some DSLs allow you to configure the model at runtime. DSLs are thus a useful adjunct to some models.

The benefits of a DSL are particularly relevant for a state machine, which is particular kind of model whose population effectively acts as the program for the system. If we want to change the behavior of a state machine, we do it by altering the objects in its model and their interrelationships. This style of model is often referred to as an *Adaptive Model (487)*. The result is a system that blurs the distinction between code and data, because in order to understand the behavior of the state machine you can't just look at the code; you also have to look at the way object instances are wired together. Of course this is always true to some extent, as any program gives different results with different data, but there is a greater difference here because the presence of the state objects alters the behavior of the system to a significantly greater degree.

Adaptive Models can be very powerful, but they are also often difficult to use because people can't see any code that defines the particular behavior. A DSL is valuable because it provides an explicit way to represent that code in a form that gives people the sensation of programming the state machine.

The aspect of a state machine that makes it such a good fit for an Adaptive Model is that it is an alternative computational model. Our regular programming languages provide a standard way of thinking about programming a machine, and it works well in many situations. But sometimes we need a different approach, such as *State Machine (527)*, *Production Rule System (513)*, or *Dependency Network (505)*. Using an Adaptive Model is a good way to provide an alternative computational model, and a DSL is good way to make it easier to program that model. Later in the book, I describe a few alternative computational models ("Alternative Computational Models," p. 113) to give you a feel of what they

are like and how you might implement them. You may often hear people refer
to DSLs used in this way as declarative programming.

In discussing this example I used a process where the model was built first,
and then a DSL was layered over it to help manipulate it. I described it that way
because I think that's an easy way to understand how DSLs fit into software development. Although the model-first case is common, it isn't the only one. In a
different scenario, you would talk with the domain experts and posit that the
state machine approach is something they understand. You then work with them
to create a DSL that they can understand. In this case, you build the DSL and
model simultaneously.

1.5 Using Code Generation

In my discussion so far, I process the DSL to populate the *Semantic Model (159)*
and then execute the Semantic Model to provide the behavior that I want from
the controller. This approach is what's known in language circles as **interpretation**.
When we interpret some text, we parse it and immediately produce the result
that we want from the program. (Interpret is a tricky word in software circles,
since it carries all sorts of connotations; however, I'll use it strictly to mean this
form of immediate execution.)

In the language world, the alternative to interpretation is compilation.
With **compilation**, we parse some program text and produce an intermediate
output, which is then separately processed to provide the behavior we desire.
In the context of DSLs, the compilation approach is usually referred to as
code generation.

It's a bit hard to express this distinction using the state machine example, so
let's use another little example. Imagine I have some kind of eligibility rules for
people, perhaps to qualify for insurance. One rule might be age between 21 and 40.
This rule can be a DSL which we can process in order to test the eligibility of
some candidate like me.

With interpretation, the eligibility processor parses the rules and loads up the
semantic model while it executes, perhaps at startup. When it tests a candidate,
it runs the semantic model against the candidate to get a result.

In the case of compilation, the parser would load the semantic model as part
of the build process for the eligibility processor. During the build, the DSL processor would produce some code that would be compiled, packaged up, and incorporated into the eligibility processor, perhaps as some kind of shared library.
This intermediate code would then be run to evaluate a candidate.

Our example state machine used interpretation: We parsed the configuration
code at runtime and populated the semantic model. But we could generate
some code instead, which would avoid having the parser and model code in the
toaster.

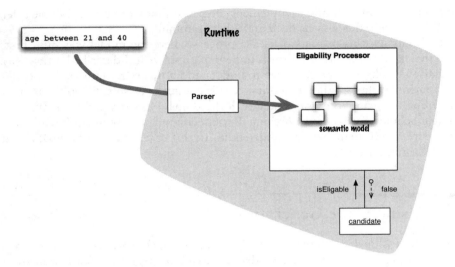

Figure 1.5   *An interpreter parses the text and produces its result in a single process.*

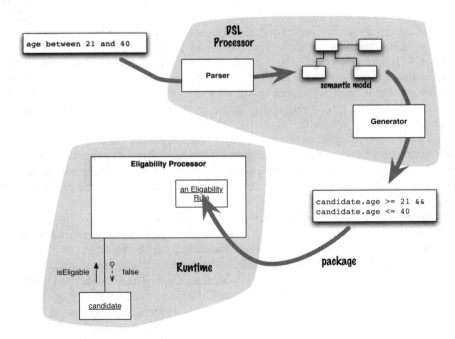

Figure 1.6   *A compiler parses the text and produces some intermediate code which is then packaged into another process for execution.*

Code generation is often awkward in that it often pushes you to do an extra compilation step. To build your program, you have to first compile the state framework and the parser, then run the parser to generate the source code for Miss Grant's controller, then compile that generated code. This makes your build process much more complicated.

However, an advantage of code generation is that there's no particular reason to generate code in the same programming language that you used for the parser. In this case, you can avoid the second compilation step by generating code for a dynamic language such as Javascript or JRuby.

Code generation is also useful when you want to use DSLs with a language platform that doesn't have the tools for DSL support. If we had to run our security system on some older toasters that only understood compiled C, we could do this by having a code generator that uses a populated Semantic Model as input and produces C code that can then be compiled to run on the older toaster. I've come across recent projects that generate code for MathCAD, SQL, and COBOL.

Many writings on DSLs focus on code generation, even to the point of making code generation the primary aim of the exercise. As a result, you can find articles and books extolling the virtues of code generation. In my view, however, code generation is merely an implementation mechanism, one that isn't actually needed in most cases. Certainly there are plenty of times when you must use code generation, but there are even plenty of times where you don't need it.

Using code generation is one case where many people don't use a Semantic Model, but parse the input text and directly produce the generated code. Although this is a common way of working with code-generating DSLs, it isn't one I recommend for any but the very simplest cases. Using a Semantic Model allows you to separate the parsing, the execution semantics, and the code generation. This separation makes the whole exercise much simpler. It also allows you to change your mind; for example, you can change your DSL from an internal to an external DSL without altering the code generation routines. Similarly, you can easily generate multiple outputs without complicating the parser. You can also use both an interpreted model and code generation off the same Semantic Model.

As a result, for most of my book, I'm going to assume that a Semantic Model is present and is the center of the DSL effort.

I usually see two styles of using code generation. One is to generate "first-pass" code, which is expected to be used as a template but is then modified by hand. The second is to ensure that generated code is never touched by hand, perhaps except for some tracing during debugging. I almost always prefer the latter because this allows code to be regenerated freely. This is particularly true with DSLs, since we want the DSL to be the primary representation of the logic that the DSL defines. This means we must be able to change the DSL easily whenever we want to change behavior. Consequently, we must ensure that any generated code isn't hand-edited, although it can call, and be called by, handwritten code.

1.6 Using Language Workbenches

The two styles of DSL I've shown so far—internal and external—are the traditional ways of thinking about DSLs. They may not be as widely understood and used as they should be, but they have a long history and moderately wide usage. As a result, the rest of this book concentrates on getting you started with these approaches using tools that are mature and easy to obtain.

But there is a whole new category of tools on the horizon that could change the game of DSLs significantly—the tools I call **language workbenches**. A language workbench is an environment designed to help people create new DSLs, together with high-quality tooling required to use those DSLs effectively.

One of the big disadvantages of using an external DSL is that you're stuck with relatively limited tooling. Setting up syntax highlighting in a text editor is about as far as most people go. While you can argue that the simplicity of a DSL and the small size of the scripts means that may be enough, there's also an argument for the kind of sophisticated tooling that modern IDEs support. Language workbenches make it easy to define not just a parser, but also a custom editing environment for that language.

All of this is valuable, but the truly interesting aspect of language workbenches is that they allow a DSL designer to go beyond the traditional text-based source editing to different forms of language. The most obvious example of this is support for diagrammatic languages, which would allow me to specify the secret panel state machine directly with a state transition diagram.

A tool like this not only allows you to define diagrammatic languages; it also allows you to look at a DSL script from different perspectives. In Figure 1.7 we see a diagram, but it also displays lists of states and events and a table to enter the event codes (which could be omitted from the diagram if there's too much clutter there).

This kind of multipane visual editing environment has been available for a while in lots of tools, but it's been a lot of effort to build something like this for yourself. One promise of language workbenches is that they make it quite easy to do this; indeed I was able to put together an example similar to Figure 1.7 quite quickly on my first play with the MetaEdit tool. The tool allows me to define the *Semantic Model (159)* for state machines, define the graphical and tabular editors in Figure 1.7, and write a code generator from the Semantic Model.

However, while such tools certainly look good, many developers are naturally suspicious of such doodleware tools. There are some very pragmatic reasons why a textual source representation makes sense. As a result, other tools head in that direction, providing post-IntelliJ-style capabilities—such as syntax-directed editing, autocompletion, and the like—for textual languages.

My suspicion is that, if language workbenches really take off, the languages they'll produce won't be anything like what we consider a programming

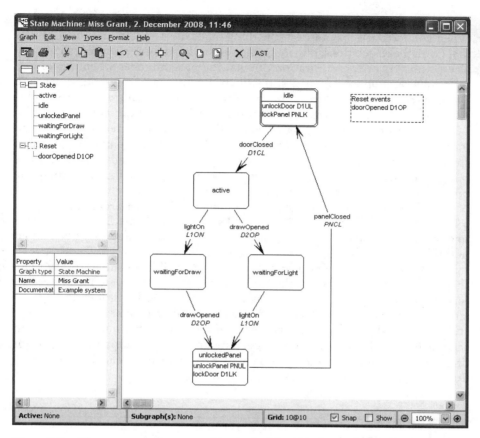

Figure 1.7 *The secret panel state machine in the MetaEdit language workbench (source: MetaCase)*

language. One of the common benefits of such tools is that they allow non-programmers to program. I often sniff at that notion by pointing out that this was the original intent of COBOL. Yet I must also acknowledge a programming environment that has been extremely successful in providing programming tools to nonprogrammers who program without thinking of themselves as programmers—spreadsheets.

Many people don't think about spreadsheets as a programming environment, yet it can be argued that they are the most successful programming environment we currently know. As a programming environment, spreadsheets have some interesting characteristics. One of these is the close integration of tooling into the programming environment. There's no notion of a tool-independent text representation that's processed by a parser. The tools and the language are closely intertwined and designed together.

A second interesting element is something I call **illustrative programming.** When you look at a spreadsheet, the thing that's most visible isn't the formulae that do all the calculations; rather, it's the numbers that form a sample calculation. These numbers are an illustration of what the program does when it executes. In most programming languages, it's the program that's front-and-center, and we only see its output when we make a test run. In a spreadsheet, the output is front-and-center and we only see the program when we click in one of the cells.

Illustrative programming isn't a concept that's got much attention; I even had to make up a word to talk about it. It could be an important part of what makes spreadsheets so accessible to lay programmers. It also has disadvantages; for one thing, the lack of focus on program structure leads to lots of copy-paste programming and poorly structured programs.

Language workbenches support developing new kinds of programming platforms like this. As a result, I think the DSLs they produce are likely to be closer to a spreadsheet than to the DSLs that we usually think of (and that I talk about in this book).

I think that language workbenches have a remarkable potential. If they fulfill this they could entirely change the face of software development. Yet this potential, however profound, is still somewhat in the future. It's still early days for language workbenches, with new approaches appearing regularly and older tools still subject to deep evolution. That is why I don't have that much to say about them here, as I think they will change quite dramatically during the hoped-for lifetime of this book. But I do have a chapter on them at the end, as I think they are well worth keeping an eye on.

1.7 Visualization

One of the great advantages of a language workbench is that it enables you to use a wider range of representations of the DSL, in particular graphical representations. However, even with a textual DSL you can obtain a diagrammatic representation. Indeed, we saw this very early on in this chapter. When looking at Figure 1.1, you might have noticed that the diagram is not as neatly drawn as I usually do. The reason for this is that I didn't draw the diagram; I generated it automatically from the *Semantic Model (159)* of Miss Grant's controller. Not only do my state machine classes execute; they are also able to render themselves using the DOT language.

The DOT language is part of the Graphviz package, which is an open source tool that allows you to describe mathematical graph structures (nodes and edges) and then automatically plot them. You just tell it what the nodes and edges are, what shapes to use, and some other hints, and it figures out how to lay out the graph.

Using a tool like Graphviz is extremely helpful for many kinds of DSLs because it gives you another representation. This **visualization** representation is similar to the DSL itself in that it allows a human to understand the model. The visualization differs from the source in that it isn't editable—but on the other hand, it can do something an editable form cannot, such as a render diagram like this.

Visualizations don't have to be graphical. I often use a simple textual visualization to help me debug when I'm writing a parser. I've seen people generate visualizations in Excel to help them communicate with domain experts. The point is that, once you have done the hard work of creating a Semantic Model, adding visualizations is really easy. Note that the visualizations are produced from the model, not the DSL, so you can do this even if you aren't using a DSL to populate the model.

Chapter 2

Using Domain-Specific Languages

After going through the examples in the last chapter, you should now have a good feel for what a DSL is, even though I haven't given any general definition yet. (You can find some more examples in "A Zoo of DSLs," p. 147.) Now I'll move on to that definition and discuss the benefits and problems of DSLs. I want to do this early on to provide some context before I start talking about implementing them in the next chapter.

2.1 Defining Domain-Specific Languages

"Domain-specific language" is a useful term and concept, but one that has very blurred boundaries. Some things are clearly DSLs, but others can be argued one way or the other. The term has also been around for a while and, like most things in software, has never had a very firm definition. For this book, however, I think a definition is valuable.

Domain-specific language (noun): a computer programming language of limited expressiveness focused on a particular domain.

There are four key elements to this definition:

- **Computer programming language:** A DSL is used by humans to instruct a computer to do something. As with any modern programming language, its structure is designed to make it easy for humans to understand, but it should still be something executable by a computer.

- **Language nature:** A DSL is a programming language, and as such should have a sense of fluency where the expressiveness comes not just from individual expressions but also from the way they can by composed together.

- **Limited expressiveness:** A general-purpose programming language provides lots of capabilities: supporting varied data, control, and abstraction structures. All of this is useful but makes it harder to learn and use. A DSL

27

supports a bare minimum of features needed to support its domain. You can't build an entire software system in a DSL; rather, you use a DSL for one particular aspect of a system.

- **Domain focus:** A limited language is only useful if it has a clear focus on a small domain. The domain focus is what makes a limited language worthwhile.

Notice that the domain focus comes last in that list, and is merely a consequence of the limited expressiveness. Many people use a literal definition of DSL as a language for a specific domain. But literal definitions are often incorrect: We don't call coins "compact disks" even though they are disks that rather more compact than those disks that we do apply the term to.

I divide the DSLs into three main categories: external DSLs, internal DSLs, and language workbenches.

- An **external DSL** is a language separate from the main language of the application it works with. Usually, an external DSL has a custom syntax, but using another language's syntax is also common (XML is a frequent choice). A script in an external DSL will usually be parsed by a code in the host application using text parsing techniques. The Unix tradition of little languages fits this style. Examples of external DSLs that you probably have come across include regular expressions, SQL, Awk, and XML configuration files for systems like Struts and Hibernate.

- An **internal DSL** is a particular way of using a general-purpose language. A script in an internal DSL is valid code in its general-purpose language, but only uses a subset of the language's features in a particular style to handle one small aspect of the overall system. The result should have the feel of a custom language, rather than its host language. The classic example of this style is Lisp; Lisp programmers often talk about Lisp programming as creating and using DSLs. Ruby has also developed a strong DSL culture: Many Ruby libraries come in the style of DSLs. In particular, Ruby's most famous framework, Rails, is often seen as a collection of DSLs.

- A **language workbench** is a specialized IDE for defining and building DSLs. In particular, a language workbench is used not just to determine the structure of a DSL but also as a custom editing environment for people to write DSL scripts. The resulting scripts intimately combine the editing environment and the language.

Over the years, these three styles have developed their own communities. You'll find people who are very experienced in internal DSLs but have no idea how to build an external DSL. I find this problematic because, as a result, people may not choose the best tool for the job. I remember talking to a team who had used very clever internal DSL processing techniques to support a custom syntax that,

I'm convinced, would have been much easier as an external DSL. But, since they didn't know how to build external DSLs, they didn't have that option open to them. Hence it's important to me in this book to present both internal and external DSLs clearly so you'll have that information. (I'm rather more sketchy on language workbenches as they are so new and still evolving.)

Another way of looking at a DSL is as a way of manipulating an abstraction. In software development, we build abstractions and then manipulate them, often on multiple levels. The most common way to build in abstraction is by implementing a library or framework; the most common way to manipulate this framework is through command-query API calls. In this view a DSL is a front-end to a library providing a different style of manipulation to the command-query API. In this context, the library is the *Semantic Model (159)* of the DSL. A consequence of this is that DSLs tend to follow libraries, and indeed I consider a Semantic Model to be a necessary adjunct to a well-built DSL.

When people talk about DSLs, it's easy to think that building the DSL is the hard work. In fact, usually the hard work is building the model; the DSL then just layers on top of it. It still takes effort to get a DSL that works well, but that effort is usually much smaller than for building the underlying model.

2.1.1 Boundaries of DSLs

As I said, DSLs are a concept with blurry boundaries. While I don't think anyone would disagree that regular expressions are a DSL, there's plenty of cases that are open to reasonable argument. As a result I think it's worth talking about some of these cases here as they help provide a better idea of how to think about DSLs.

Each style of DSL has different boundary conditions, so I'll discuss them separately. As we go through these, it's worth remembering that the distinguishing characteristics of DSLs are their language nature, domain focus, and limited expressiveness. As it turns out, the domain focus isn't a good boundary condition—the boundaries more commonly revolve around limited expressiveness and the language nature.

I'll start with internal DSLs. Here, the boundary question is the difference between an internal DSL and the normal command-query API. In many ways, an internal DSL is nothing more than a quirky API (as the old Bell labs saying goes, "Library design is language design"). In my view, the heart of the difference is the language nature. Mike Roberts suggested to me that a command-query API defines the vocabulary of the abstraction, whereas an internal DSL adds a grammar.

A common way of documenting a class with a command-query API is to list all the methods it has. When you do this, each method should make sense on its own. You have a list of "words," each with a somewhat self-sufficient meaning. The methods of an internal DSL often only make sense in the context of a larger expression in the DSL. In the Java internal DSL example earlier, I had a method called to that specified the target state of a transition. Such a method would be a bad name in a command-query API, but fits inside a phrase like `.transition(lightOn).to(unlockedPanel)`.

As a result, an internal DSL should have the feel of putting together whole sentences, rather than a sequence of disconnected commands. This is the basis for calling these kinds of APIs fluent interfaces.

Limited expressiveness, for an internal DSL, is obviously not a core property of the language, since the language of an internal DSL is a general-purpose language. In this case, limited expressiveness comes from the way you use it. When forming a DSL expression, you limit yourself to a small subset of the general language features. It's common to avoid conditions, looping constructs, and variables. Piers Cawley called this a pidgin use of the host language.

With external DSLs, the boundary is with general-purpose programming languages. Languages can have a domain focus but still be general-purpose languages. A good example of this is R, a language and platform for statistics; it is very much targeted at statistics work, but has all the expressiveness of a general-purpose programming language. Thus, despite its domain focus, I would not call it a DSL.

A more obvious DSL is regular expressions. Here, the domain focus (matching text) is coupled with limited features—just enough to make text matching easy. One common indicator of a DSL is that it isn't Turing-complete. DSLs usually avoid the regular imperative control structures (conditions and loops), don't have variables, and can't define subroutines.

It's at this point where many people will disagree with me, using the literal definition of a DSL to argue that languages like R should be counted as a DSL. The reason I put a strong emphasis on limited expressiveness is that it is what makes the distinction between DSLs and general-purpose languages useful. The limited expressiveness gives DSLs different characteristics, both in using them and in implementing them. This leads to a different way of thinking about DSLs compared to general-purpose languages.

If this boundary isn't fuzzy enough, let's consider XSLT. XSLT's domain focus is that of transforming XML documents, but it has all the features one might expect in a regular programming language. In this case, I think the way it is used matters more than the language itself. If XSLT is being used to transform XML, then I would call it a DSL. However, if it's being used to solve the eight queens problem, I would call it a general-purpose language. A particular usage of a language can put it on either side of the DSL line.

Another boundary with external DSLs is with serialized data structures. Is a list of property assignments (`color = blue`) in a configuration file a DSL? I think that here, the boundary condition is the language nature. A series of assignments lacks fluency, so it doesn't fit the criteria.

A similar argument applies to many configuration files. Many environ-ments these days provide a lot of their programmability through some kind of configuration files, often using XML syntax. In many cases, these XML configurations are effectively DSLs. However, this may not always be the case. Sometimes, the XML files are intended to be created by other tools, so XML is only used for serialization and not intended to be used by humans. In that case, since humans aren't expected to use it, I wouldn't classify it as a DSL. Of course it's still valuable to have a storage format that is human-readable, as it can be useful in debugging. The question isn't whether it's human-readable or not, but whether the representation is a human's main way of interacting with that aspect of the system.

One of the biggest issues with these kinds of configuration files is that, even though they aren't intended to be human-edited, they end up being the primary editing mechanism in practice. In this case the XML becomes a DSL by accident.

With language workbenches, the boundary is between a language workbench and any application that allows a user to design their own data structure and forms—something like Microsoft Access. After all, it's possible to take a state model and represent it in a relational database structure (I've seen far worse ideas). You can then produce forms to manipulate the model. There are two questions here: Is Access a language workbench, and is the thing you define a DSL?

I'll start with the second question. Since we are building a particular application for the state machine, we have both domain focus and limited expressiveness. The critical issue is that of the language nature. If we are putting data in forms and saving them in a table, there usually isn't a real language-like feel to it. A table can be an expression of a language nature—FIT ("FIT," p. 155) and Excel both use a tabular representation and both have a language feel to them (I would consider FIT to be domain-specific and Excel general-purpose). But most appli-cations do not try to achieve that kind of fluency; they just create forms and windows that don't stress the interconnections. For example, the textual interface of the Meta-Programming System Language Workbench has a feel very different from most form-based UIs. Similarly, few applications allow you to lay out a diagram to define how things are put together in the manner of MetaEdit.

As to whether Access is a language workbench, I'd go back to the design intent. Access wasn't designed to be a language workbench, although you can use it that way if you really want. Look at how many people use Excel as a database—even though it wasn't designed to be one.

In a broader sense, is a purely human jargon a DSL? A common example that's bandied around is the language used to order a coffee at Starbucks: "Venti, half-caf, nonfat, no-foam, no-whip latte." The language is nice because it has limited expressiveness, a domain focus, a sense of grammar as well as vocabulary. It falls outside my definition, however, because I use "domain-specific language" to refer to computer languages only. If we implemented a computer language to understand Starbucks expressions, then that would truly be a DSL, but the words we spout when getting our caffeine fix are a human language. I use **domain language** to mean a domain-specific human language and reserve "DSL" for computer languages.

So, what has this discussion of the boundaries of DSLs taught us? Hopefully, one thing that is clear is that there are few sharp boundaries. Reasonable people can disagree on what is a DSL. Tests like language nature and limited expressiveness are themselves very blurry, so we should expect the result to exhibit the same blur. And not everyone will use the boundary conditions that I do.

In this discussion, I've excluded many things from being a DSL, but this doesn't mean that I don't consider them valuable. The purpose of a definition is to help in communication so different people can have the same idea of what we're talking about. For this book, it helps make clear whether the techniques I describe are relevant. I find that this definition of DSLs helps target the techniques I describe more effectively.

2.1.2 Fragmentary and Stand-alone DSLs

The secret panel state machine example I used in "Using Domain-Specific Languages," p. 27 is a stand-alone DSL. By this I mean that you can look at a block of DSL script, typically a single file, and it is all DSL. If you are familiar with the DSL but not with the host language of the application, you should be able to understand what the DSL does because the host language either isn't there (in the external case) or is subdued by the internal DSL.

Another way DSLs appear is in a fragmentary form. In this form, little bits of DSL are used inside the host language code. You can think of them as enhancing the host language with additional features. In this case, you can't really follow what the DSL is doing without understanding the host language.

For an external DSL, a good example of a fragmentary DSL is regular expressions. You don't have a whole file of regular expressions in a program, but you have little snippets interspersed with regular host code. Another example of this is SQL, often used in the form of SQL statements within the context of a larger program.

Similar fragmentary approaches are used with internal DSLs. A particularly fruitful area of internal DSL development has been in the unit testing world. In particular, expectation grammars in mock object libraries are short bursts of DSLs within a larger host code context. A popular language feature for internal fragmentary DSLs is *Annotations (445)* which allow you to add metadata to the host code programming elements. This makes annotations suitable for fragmentary DSLs but useless for stand-alone ones.

The same DSL can be used in both stand-alone and fragmentary contexts; SQL is a good example of this. Some DSLs are designed to be used in a fragmentary form, others in a stand-alone form, and still others can swing both ways.

2.2 Why Use a DSL?

Now, I hope, we're pretty much on board with what a DSL is. The next question is why should we consider using one.

DSLs are a tool with limited focus. They aren't like object orientation or agile processes which introduce a fundamental shift into the way we think about software development. Instead, DSLs are a very specific tool for very particular conditions. A typical project might use half a dozen or so DSLs in various places—indeed, many already do.

In "Languages and Semantic Model," p. 16, I kept saying that a DSL is a thin veneer over a model, where the model might be a library or framework. This phrase should remind us that whenever you think about the benefits (or disadvantages) of a DSL, it's important to separate the benefits provided by the model from the benefits of the DSL. It's a common mistake to confuse the two.

DSLs have the potential to realize certain benefits. When you are considering using a DSL, you should weigh these benefits and decide which of them are applicable to your circumstances.

2.2.1 Improving Development Productivity

The heart of the appeal of a DSL is that it provides a means to more clearly communicate the intent of a part of a system. If you read Miss Grant's controller definition in a DSL form, it's easier for you to understand what it's doing than through the command-query API of the model.

This clarity isn't just an aesthetic desire. The easier it is to read a lump of code, the easier it is to find mistakes, and the easier it is to modify the system. So, for the same reason that we encourage meaningful variable names, documentation, clear coding constructs—we should encourage DSL usage.

People often underestimate the productivity impact of defects. Not only do defects detract from the external quality of software, they also slow developers down by sucking up time in investigations and fixes, sowing confusion about the behavior of the system. The limited expressiveness of DSLs makes it harder to say wrong things and easier to see when you've made an error.

The model alone provides a considerable improvement in productivity. It avoids duplication by gathering together common code; above all, it provides an abstraction to think about the problem that makes it easier to specify what's going on in an understandable way. A DSL enhances this by providing a more expressive form to read and manipulate that abstraction. A DSL can help people learn how to use an API since it shifts focus to how different API methods should be combined together.

An interesting example of this I've come across is using a DSL to wrap an awkward third-party library. The DSL's usual advantages of a more fluent interface are magnified when the command-query interface is poor. In addition, the

DSL only has to support the actual client usage, which can significantly reduce the surface area that the client developers need to learn.

2.2.2 Communication with Domain Experts

I believe that the hardest part of software projects, the most common source of project failure, is communication with the customers and users of that software. By providing a clear yet precise language to deal with domains, a DSL can help improve this communication.

This benefit is more nuanced than the simple productivity argument. For a start, many DSLs aren't suitable for domain communication—the DSLs for regular expressions or build dependencies don't really fit in here. Only a subset of stand-alone DSLs really apply to this communication channel.

When people talk about DSLs in this context, it's often along the lines of "Now we can get rid of programmers and have business people specify the rules themselves." I call this argument the COBOL fallacy—since that was the expectation with COBOL. It's a common argument, but I don't think it improves with repetition.

Despite the COBOL fallacy, I do think DSLs can improve communication. It's not that domain experts will write the DSLs themselves; but they can read them and thus understand what the system thinks it's doing. By being able to read DSL code, domain experts can spot mistakes. They can also talk more effectively to the programmers who do write the rules, perhaps by writing some rough drafts that can be refined into proper DSL rules.

I'm not saying that domain experts should never write DSLs themselves. I have run into too many cases where a team had succeeded in getting domain experts to write significant bits of behavior using a DSL. However, I still think the biggest gain from using a DSL in this way comes when domain experts start reading it. Focusing on reading can be the first step towards writing the DSL, with the advantage that you lose nothing if you don't take that further step.

My focus on DSLs as something for domain experts to read does introduce an argument against using DSLs. If you want domain experts to understand the content of a *Semantic Model (159)*, you can do this just by providing a visualization of the model. It's worth considering whether a visualization alone is a more efficient route than supporting a DSL. And it's useful to have visualizations in addition to a DSL.

Involving domain experts in a DSL is very similar to involving domain experts in building a model. I've often found great benefit by building a model together with domain experts; constructing a *Ubiquitous Language* [Evans DDD] deepens the communication between software developers and domain experts. A DSL provides another technique to engage that communication. Depending on the circumstances, you might find domain experts participating in the model and the DSL, or the DSL only.

Indeed some people find that trying to describe a domain using a DSL is useful even if the DSL is never implemented. It can be beneficial just as a platform for communication.

So, all in all, involving domain experts in a DSL is difficult to achieve but has a high payoff. And even if you can't get the domain experts' involved, you may still get enough of a gain in developer productivity to make the DSL worth the effort.

2.2.3 Change in Execution Context

When talking about why we might want to express our state machine in XML, one strong reason was that the definition could be evaluated at runtime rather than compile time. This kind of reasoning, where we want code to run in a different environment, is a common driver for using a DSL. For XML configuration files, shifting logic from compile time to runtime is a common reason.

There are other useful shifts in execution context. One project I looked at needed to trawl though databases to find contracts that matched certain conditions and tag them. They wrote a DSL to support specifying these conditions and used it to populate a *Semantic Model (159)* in Ruby. It would be slow to read all of the contracts into memory to run the query logic in Ruby, but the team could use the Semantic Model representation to generate SQL to do the processing in the database. Writing the rules in SQL directly was too difficult for the developers, let alone the business people. However, the business people could read (and in this case, write) the appropriate expressions in the DSL.

Using a DSL like this can often make up for limitations in a host language, allowing us to express things in a comfortable DSL and then generate code for the actual execution environment to use.

A model can facilitate this kind of shift. Once you have a model, it's easy to either execute it directly or generate code from it. Models can be also be populated from a forms-style interface as well as a DSL. A DSL has a couple of advantages over using forms. DSLs are often better than forms at representing complicated logic. Furthermore, we can use the same code management tools, such as version control systems, to manage these rules. When rules are entered via a form and stored in a database, version control is often neglected.

This relates to a spurious benefit of a DSL. I've heard people argue that the good thing about a DSL is that it allows the same behavior to be executed in different language environments. One could write business rules that generate code in C# and Java, or describe validations that can run in C# on the server and Javascript on the client. This is a spurious benefit because you can gain this just by using a model; you don't need a DSL at all. A DSL can make it easier to understand these rules, but that's a separate issue.

2.2.4 Alternative Computational Model

Mainstream programming is pretty much all done using an imperative model of computation. This means that we tell the computer what things to do in what sequence, control flow is handled using conditionals and loops, we have variables—indeed lots of things that we take for granted. Imperative computation has become popular because it's relatively easy to understand and easy to apply to lots of problems. However, it isn't always the best choice.

The state machine is a good example of this. We can write imperative code and conditionals to handle this kind of behavior—it can be pretty nicely structured too. But thinking of it as a state machine is often more helpful. Another common example is defining how to build software. You can do it with imperative logic, but after a while most people recognize that it's easier to do with a *Dependency Network (505)* (e.g., to run tests, your compilations must be up-to-date). As a result, languages designed for describing builds (such as Make and Ant) use dependencies between tasks as their primary structuring mechanism.

You often hear such nonimperative approaches referred to as declarative programming. The notion is that these styles allow you to declare *what* should happen, rather than work through the imperative statements that describe *how* the behavior works.

You don't need a DSL to use an alternative computational model. The core behavior of an alternative computational model comes from a *Semantic Model (159)*, as the state machine example illustrates. However, a DSL can make a big difference as it makes it much easier for people to manipulate declarative programs that populate the Semantic Model.

2.3 Problems with DSLs

Having talked about when to use a DSL, it makes sense that I talk a bit about when not to use them, or at least about the problems involved in using them.

Fundamentally, the only reason to not use a DSL is if you don't see any of the benefits of a DSL apply to your situation—or at least, you don't see the benefits being worth the cost of building the DSL.

Even when DSLs are applicable, they do come with problems. On the whole, I think these problems are currently overstated, usually because people aren't familiar enough with how to build DSLs and how they fit the broader software development picture. Also, many commonly stated problems with DSLs stem from the same confusion between DSL and model that plague many stated DSL benefits.

Many problems with DSLs are specific to one of the particular styles of DSL, and to understand these issues you need to have a deeper understanding of how these DSLs are implemented. As a result, I'll leave the discussion of these problems till later; for now, I'll just look at the broad problems in line with what we've currently discussed.

2.3.1 Language Cacophony

The most common objection I hear to DSLs is what I call the **language cacophony problem**: the concern that languages are hard to learn, so using many languages will be much more complicated than using a single one. Having to know multiple languages makes it harder to work on the system and to introduce new people to the project.

When people talk about this concern, there's a couple of misconceptions that they commonly have. The first is that they often mistake the effort of learning a DSL with the effort of learning a general-purpose language. DSLs are far simpler than a general-purpose language, and thus far easier to learn.

Many critics understand this, but still object to DSLs because, even if they are relatively easy to learn, having many DSLs makes it harder to understand what's going on in a project. The misconception here is forgetting that a project will always have complicated areas that are hard to learn. Even if you don't have DSLs, you will typically have many abstractions in your codebase that you need to understand. Usually, these abstractions are captured by libraries in order to make them tractable. Even if you don't have to learn several DSLs, you still have to learn several libraries.

So the true learning cost question is how much harder it is to learn a DSL than to learn the underlying model on its own. I'd argue that the incremental cost of learning the DSL is quite small compared to the cost of understanding the model. Indeed, since the whole point of a DSL is to make it easier to understand and manipulate the model, having a DSL should reduce the learning cost.

2.3.2 Cost of Building

A DSL may be a small incremental cost over its underlying library, but it's still a cost. There's still code to write, and above all to maintain. Thus, like any code, it has to pull its weight. Not every library benefits from having a DSL wrapper over it. If a command-query API does the job just fine, then there's no value in adding another API on top of it. Even if a DSL might help, sometimes it would just be too much effort to build and maintain for the marginal benefit.

The maintenance of the DSL is an important factor. Even a simple internal DSL may cause problems if most of the development team finds it difficult to understand. External DSLs in particular add a lot of moving parts to the process, with parsers that are often intimidating for developers.

One of the things that inflates the cost of adding a DSL is the fact that people aren't used to building them. There are new techniques to learn. Although you shouldn't ignore these costs, you should remember that learning curve costs can be amortized across multiple times that you might use a DSL in the future.

Also, remember that the cost of a DSL is the cost over the cost of building the model. Any complicated area needs some mechanism to manage the complexity, and if it's complicated enough to consider a DSL, it's almost certainly complicated enough to benefit from a model. A DSL may help you think about the model and reduce the cost of building it.

This leads to the related issue—that encouraging DSLs will lead to many bad DSLs being built. Indeed I expect many bad DSLs to be built, just as there are plenty of libraries with bad command-query APIs. The question is whether a DSL will make things worse. A good DSL can wrap a bad library and make it easier to deal with (although I'd rather fix the library if I can). A bad DSL is a waste of resources to build and maintain, but that can be said of any bad code.

2.3.3 Ghetto Language

The ghetto language problem is a contrast to the language cacophony problem. Here, we have a company that's built a lot of its systems on an in-house language which is not used anywhere else. This makes it difficult for them to find new staff and to keep up with technological changes.

In analyzing this argument, I begin by noting that if you're writing whole systems in a language, that means it isn't a DSL (at least by my definition) but a general-purpose language. Although you can use many of the DSL techniques for building general-purpose languages, I would very strongly urge you not to do so. Building and maintaining a general-purpose language is a big undertaking that condemns you to a lot of work and a life in a ghetto. Don't do that.

I think there are a couple of real issues implied by the ghetto language problem. The first of these is that there's always a danger for a DSL to accidentally evolve into a general-purpose language. You take your DSL and gradually add new features; today you add conditional expressions, another day you add loops, and whoops—you're Turing-complete.

The only defense against this is to guard firmly against it. Make sure you have a clear sense of what narrow problem the DSL is focused on. Question any new features that seem to fall outside that mission. If you need to do more, consider using more than one language and combining them, instead of letting one DSL grow too big.

The same problem can plague frameworks. A good library has a clear sense of purpose. If your product pricing library includes an implementation of the HTTP protocol, you're suffering from essentially the same failure to separate concerns.

The second issue is that of building yourself what you should be taking from outside. This applies to libraries as much as DSLs. For example, there's little reason now to build your own object-relational mapping system. My general rule with software is that if it's not your business, don't write it yourself—always look to take it from somewhere else. In particular, with the rise of open source tools it often makes sense to work on extending an existing open source effort than writing your own from scratch.

2.3.4 Blinkered Abstraction

The usefulness of a DSL is that it provides an abstraction that you can use to think about a subject area. Such an abstraction is really valuable; it allows you to express the behavior of a domain much more easily than if you think in terms of lower-level constructs.

However, any abstraction, be it a DSL or a model, always carries with it a danger—that of putting blinkers on your thinking. With a blinkered abstraction, you spend more effort on fitting the world into your abstraction than the other way around. You see this when you come across something that doesn't fit in with the abstraction—and you burn time trying to make it fit, instead of changing the abstraction to easily absorb the new behavior. Blinkering tends to occur once you've got comfortable with an abstraction and you feel it's bedded down—at this point it's natural to be worried by the prospect of uprooting it.

Blinkered abstractions are a problem with any abstraction, not just a DSL, but there is a concern that a DSL can make it worse. Since a DSL provides a more comfortable way of manipulating an abstraction, it can make you more reluctant to change it. This problem can be exacerbated when using the DSL with domain experts, who often are even more reluctant to change an abstraction once they get used to it.

As with any abstraction, you should always look at a DSL as something that's evolving, not finished.

2.4 Wider Language Processing

This book is about domain-specific languages, but it's also about techniques for language processing. The two overlap, because 90% of the use of language processing techniques in an average development team is for DSLs. But these techniques can be used for some other things as well and I would be remiss not to discuss some of these.

I ran into an excellent example of this when visiting a ThoughtWorks project team. They had the task of communicating to a third-party system by sending messages whose payload was defined by COBOL copybooks. COBOL copybooks are a data structure format for records. There were a lot of them, so my colleague Brian Egge decided to build a parser for the subset of COBOL copybook syntax in use and generate Java classes to interface to these records. Once he'd built the parser, he could happily interface to as many copybooks as he needed; none of the rest of the code needed to know about COBOL data structures, and any changes could be handled with a simple regeneration. It would be an appalling

stretch to call COBOL copybooks a DSL—but the same basic techniques that
we use for external DSLs did the trick.

So, just because I talk about these techniques in the context of DSLs shouldn't
stop you from applying them to other problems. Once you've got the hang of
language processing ideas, there are many ways you can use them.

2.5 DSL Lifecycle

In this opening, I introduced a DSL by first describing a framework and its
command-query API, and then layering a DSL on top of the API to make it easier
to manipulate. I used this approach because I think it's easier to understand DSLs
that way, but it's not the only way that people use DSLs in practice.

A common alternative is to define the DSL first. In this mode, you begin with
some scenarios and write those scenarios down in the way you'd like the DSL to
look. If the language is part of the domain functionality, it's good to do this with
a domain expert—this is a good first step to using the DSL as a communication
medium.

Some people like to start with statements that they expect to be syntactically
correct. This means that for an internal DSL, they'll stick to the syntax of the
host language. For an external DSL they'll write statements they are confident
they can parse. Others are more informal at the beginning and then take a second
pass through the DSL to get it close to a reasonable syntax.

So, doing the state machine in this case, you'd sit down with some people who
understand the customers' needs. You'd come up with a set of example controller
behaviors, either based on what people wanted in the past, or on something you
think they'll desire. For each of these, you would try to write them in some DSL
form. As you work through various cases, you'll modify the DSL to support new
capabilities. By the end of the exercise, you'll have worked through a reasonable
sample of cases and will have a pseudo-DSL description of each of them.

If you're using a language workbench, you'll need to do this stage outside the
workbench using a plain text editor, or regular drawing software, or pen and
paper.

Once you have a representative set of pseudo-DSLs, you can start implementing
them. Implementing here involves designing the state machine model in the host
language, the command-query API for the model, the concrete syntax of the DSL,
and the translation between the DSL and the command-query API. People do
this in different ways. Some might like to do little bits at a time across all these
elements: building a little bit of the model, adding the DSL to drive it, and
hooking that thread all up with tests. Others might prefer to build and test
the framework first and then layer the DSL over it. Yet others might like to

get the DSL in place, then build the library, and fit them together. As I'm an incrementalist, I prefer thin slices of end-to-end functionality, so I go with the first of the three.

So I might start with a simplest of the cases that I see. I'd program a library that can support that case, using test-driven development. I'd then take the DSL and implement that, tying it to the framework I'd built. I'd be happy to make some changes to the DSL to make it easier to build, although I would run those changes past the domain expert to ensure we still share a common communication medium. Once I have one controller working, I'd pick the next one. I would evolve the framework and tests first, then evolve the DSL.

This doesn't mean that the model-first route is a bad one; indeed its often an excellent choice. Usually it is used when you don't think about using a DSL at first, or you're not sure you'll need one. You thus build the framework, work with it for a while, and then decide that a DSL would be a useful addition. In this case, you might have a state machine model up and running and used by many customers. You then realize that it's harder than you'd like to add new customers, so you decide to try a DSL.

Here are a couple approaches you can use to grow a DSL on top of the model. A language-seeded approach slowly builds the DSL on top of the model, treating the model as a mostly black box. We would start by looking at all the controllers we currently have and sketching out pseudo-DSL for each one. Then we'd implement the DSL scenario by scenario, much as in the earlier case. We usually wouldn't make any deep changes to the model, although I would be happy to add methods to the model to help support the DSL.

With a model-seeded approach, we'd add fluent methods to the model first, to make it easier to configure the model, and then gradually draw them away into a DSL. This approach is more oriented towards internal DSLs; you can think of it as a heavy refactoring of the model to derive the internal DSL. An appealing aspect to the model-seeded approach is that it's very gradual, so it doesn't inflict a notable cost to build the DSL.

There are many cases, of course, where you don't even know you have a framework. You might build several controllers and only then realize that there is a lot of common functionality. I'd then refactor the system to create separation between the model and the configuration code. This separation is the vital step. While I might have a DSL in mind while doing it, I'd be more inclined to get the separation done first, before putting the DSL on top.

While I'm here, I should stress something that I wish I didn't need to. Do make sure all your DSL scripts are kept under some form of version control system. A DSL script becomes part of your code and thus should be under version control just like everything else. The great thing about textual DSLs is that they play well with version control systems, allowing you to keep a clear track of the changes to the behavior of your system.

2.6 What Makes a Good DSL Design?

When people reviewed this book, they often asked for tips on creating a good design for the language. After all, language design is tricky and we want to avoid a proliferation of bad languages. I'd love to have a good advice to share, but I confess I don't have a clear idea in my mind.

The overall goal for a DSL, as with any writing, is clarity for the reader. You want your typical reader, which may be a programmer or a domain expert, to be able to understand what the sentences in the DSL mean, as quickly and clearly as possible. While I don't feel I can say much about how to do that, I do think it's valuable to keep that goal in mind as you work.

I'm generally a fan of iterative design, and this is no exception. Try out ideas on your target audience. Be prepared to provide multiple alternatives and see how people react. Getting a good language will involve trying and rejecting lots of missteps. Don't worry about wrong turns; the more of those you make and correct, the more likely you are to find a good path.

Don't be afraid to use the jargon of the domain in the DSL and in its *Semantic Model (159)*. If the users of the DSL are familiar with the jargon, then they should see it in the DSL. Jargon is there to enhance communication within a domain even if it sounds gibberish to those outside.

Do take advantage of the common conventions in your regular life. If everyone uses Java or C#, then use "//" for your comments and "{" and "}" for any hierarchic structures.

One area where I do think you need a specific caution is this: Don't try to make the DSL read like natural language. There have been various attempts to do that with general-purpose languages, with Applescript as the most obvious example. The trouble is that such attempts lead to a lot of syntactic sugar which complicates understanding of the semantics. Remember that a DSL is a programming language, so using it should feel like programming, with the greater terseness and precision that programming has compared to a natural language. Trying to make a programming language look like natural language puts your head into the wrong context; when you're manipulating a program, you must always remember you're in a programming language environment.

Chapter 3

Implementing DSLs

At this point you should have a good sense of what a DSL is and why you might
be interested in using one. It's time now to delve into the techniques that you'll
need to start building a DSL. Although many of these techniques vary between
internal and external DSLs, there is also much that they have in common. In
this chapter, I'll concentrate on the common issues for internal and external
DSLs, moving onto specific issues in the next chapter. I'll also ignore language
workbenches for the moment; I'll get back to them much later on.

3.1 Architecture of DSL Processing

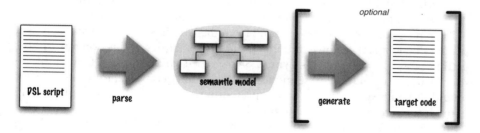

Figure 3.1 *The overall architecture of DSL processing that I usually prefer*

Perhaps one of the most important things to talk about is the broad structure of
how DSL implementations work—what I might call the architecture of a DSL
system.

By now you should be getting tired of me saying that a DSL is a thin layer over
a model. When I refer to a model in this context I call it the *Semantic Model
(159)* pattern. The basic idea behind this pattern is that all the important semantic

43

behavior is captured in a model, and the DSL's role is to populate that model via a parsing step. This means that the Semantic Model plays a central role in how I think about DSLs—indeed almost all of this book assumes you are using one. (I'll talk about alternatives to a Semantic Model at the end of this section, when I have enough context to discuss them.)

Since I'm an OO bigot, I naturally assume that a Semantic Model is an object model. I like rich object models that combine data and processing. But a Semantic Model doesn't need to be like that; it can also be just a data structure. While I'd always rather have proper objects if I can, using a data model form of Semantic Model is better than not using a Semantic Model at all. So, although I'll be assuming proper behavioral objects in the discussion in this book, remember that data structures are an option you may also see.

Many systems use a *Domain Model* [Fowler PoEAA] to capture the core behavior of a software system. Often a DSL populates a significant portion of a Domain Model. I do like to keep the notions of Domain Model and Semantic Model different. The Semantic Model of a DSL is usually a subset of the application's Domain Model, as not all parts of the Domain Model are best handled by the DSL. In addition, DSLs may be used for tasks other than populating a Domain Model, even when one is present.

The Semantic Model is a completely normal object model, which can be manipulated in the same way as any object model you might have. In the state example, we can populate the state machine by using the command-query API of the state model, and then run it to get our state behavior. In a sense, it's thus independent of the DSL, although in practice the two are close siblings.

(If you come from a compiler background you may be wondering whether the Semantic Model is the same as an abstract syntax tree. The short answer is that it's a different notion; I'll explore that in "The Workings of a Parser," p. 47.)

Keeping a Semantic Model separate from the DSL has several advantages. The primary benefit is that you can think about the semantics of this domain without getting tangled up in the DSL syntax or parser. If you're using a DSL at all, it's usually because you're representing something pretty complex, for otherwise you wouldn't be using it. Since you're representing something quite complex, that's enough for it to deserve its own model.

In particular, this allows you to test the Semantic Model by creating objects in the model and manipulating them directly. I can create a bunch of states and transitions and test to see if the events and commands run, without having to deal with parsing at all. If there are problems in how the state machine executes, I can isolate the problem in the model without having to understand how the parsing works.

An explicit Semantic Model allows you to support multiple DSLs to populate it. You might start with a simple internal DSL, and later add an external DSL as a alternative version that's easier to read. Since you have existing scripts and existing users, you might want to keep the existing internal DSL and support both. Since both DSLs can parse into the same Semantic Model, this isn't difficult. It also helps to avoid any duplication between the languages.

More to the point, having a separate Semantic Model allows you to evolve the model and language separately. If I want to change the model, I can explore that without changing the DSL, adding the necessary constructs to the DSL once I get the model working. Or I can experiment with new syntaxes for the DSL and just verify that they create the same objects in the model. I can compare two syntaxes by comparing how they populate the Semantic Model.

In many ways, this separation of the Semantic Model and DSL syntax mirrors the separation of domain model and presentation that we see in designing enterprise software. Indeed on a hot day I think of a DSL as another form of user interface.

The comparison between DSLs and presentations also suggests limitations. The DSL and the Semantic Model are still connected. If I add new constructs to the DSL, I need to ensure they are supported in the Semantic Model, which often means modifying the two at the same time. However, the separation does mean I can think about semantic issues separately from parsing issues, which simplifies the task.

The difference between internal and external DSLs lies in the parsing step—both in what is parsed and in how the parsing is done. Both styles of DSL will produce the same kind of Semantic Model, and as I implied earlier there's no reason to not have a single Semantic Model populated by both internal and external DSLs. Indeed, this is exactly what I did when programming the state machine example where I have several DSLs all populating a single Semantic Model.

With an external DSL, there is a very clear separation between the DSL scripts, the parser, and the Semantic Model. The DSL scripts are written in a clearly separate language; the parser reads these scripts and populates the Semantic Model. With an internal DSL, it's much easier for things to get mixed up. I advocate having an explicit layer of objects (*Expression Builders (343)*) whose job is to provide the necessary fluent interfaces to act as the language. DSL scripts then run by invoking methods on an Expression Builder which then populates the Semantic Model. Thus in an internal DSL, parsing the DSL scripts is done by a combination of the host language parser and the Expression Builders.

This raises an interesting point—it may strike you as a little odd to use the word "parsing" in the context of an internal DSL. I'll confess it's not something I'm entirely comfortable with either. I have found, however, that thinking of the parallels between internal and external DSL processing is a useful point of view. With traditional parsing, you take a stream of text, arrange that text into a parse tree, and then process that parse tree to produce a useful output. With parsing an internal DSL, your input is a series of function calls. You still arrange them into a hierarchy (usually implicitly on the stack) in order to produce useful output.

Another factor in the use of the word "parsing" here is that several cases don't involve handling the text directly. In an internal DSL, the host language parser handles the text, and the DSL processor handles further language constructs. But the same occurs with XML DSLs: The XML parser translates the text into XML elements, and the DSL processor works on these.

At this point it's worth revisiting the distinction between internal and external DSLs. The one I used earlier—whether or not it's written in the base language of your application—is usually right, but not 100% so. An example edge case is if your main application is written in Java but you write your DSL in JRuby. In this case I'd still classify the DSL as internal, in that you'd use the techniques from the internal DSL section of this book.

The true distinction between the two is that internal DSLs are written in an executable language and parsed by executing the DSL within that language. In both JRuby and XML, a DSL is embedded into a carrier syntax, but we execute the JRuby code and just read the XML data structures. Most of the time, an internal DSL is done in the main language of the application, so that definition is generally more useful.

Once we have a Semantic Model, we then need to make the model do what we want. In the state machine example, this task is to control the security system. There are two broad ways we can do this. The simplest, and usually the best, is just to execute the Semantic Model itself. The Semantic Model is code and as such can run and do all it needs to.

Another option is to use code generation. Code generation means that we generate code which is separately compiled and run. In some circles, code generation is seen as an essential part of DSLs. I've seen talks about code generation assuming that to do any DSL work, you have to generate code. In the rare event that I see someone talking or writing about *Parser Generators (269)*, they inevitably talk about generating code. Yet DSLs have no inherent need for code generation. A lot of the time the best thing to do is just to execute the Semantic Model.

The strongest case for code generation is when there is a difference between where you want to run the model and where you want to parse the DSL. A good example of this is executing code in an environment that has limited language choices, such as on limited hardware or inside a relational database. You don't want to run a parser in your toaster or in SQL, so you implement the parser and Semantic Model in a more suitable language and generate C or SQL. A related case is where you have library dependencies in your parser that you don't want in the production environment. This situation is particularly common if you are using a complex tool for your DSL, which is why language workbenches tend to do code generation.

In these situations, it's still useful to have a Semantic Model in your parsing environment that can run without generating code. Running the Semantic Model allows you to experiment with the execution of the DSL without having to simultaneously understand how the code generation works. You can test parsing and semantics without generating code, which will often help you run tests more quickly and on isolating problems. You can do validations on the Semantic Model that can catch errors before generating code.

Another argument for code generation, even in an environment where you could happily interpret the Semantic Model directly, is that many developers find the kind of logic in a rich Semantic Model difficult to understand. Generating code from the Semantic Model makes everything much more explicit and less like magic. This could be a crucial point in a team with less capable developers.

But the most important thing to remember about code generation is that it's an *optional* part of the DSL landscape. It's one of those things that are absolutely essential if you need them, yet most of the time you don't. I think of code generators as snowshoes: If I'm hiking in winter over deep snow I really have to have them, but I'd never carry them on a summer day.

With code generation, we see another benefit to using a Semantic Model: It decouples the code generators from the parser. I can write a code generator without having to understand anything about the parsing process, and test it independently too. That alone is enough to make the Semantic Model worthwhile. In addition, it makes it easier to support multiple code-generation targets should I need them.

3.2 The Workings of a Parser

So the differences between internal and external DSLs lie entirely in parsing, and indeed there are many differences in detail between the two. But there are a lot of similarities, too.

One of the most important similarities is that parsing is a strongly hierarchical operation. When we parse text, we arrange the chunks into a tree structure. Consider the simple structure of a list of events from the state machine. In the external syntax, it looked something like this:

```
events
  doorClosed D1CL
  drawerOpened D2OP
end
```

We can look at this composite structure as an event list containing a list of events, with each event having a name and a code.

We can take a similar view in the Ruby internal DSL.

```
event :doorClosed "D1CL"
event :drawerOpened "D2OP"
```

Here there's no explicit notion of an overall list, but each event is still a hierarchy: an event containing a name symbol and a code string.

Whenever you look at a script like this, you can imagine that script as a hierarchy; such a hierarchy is called a **syntax tree** (or parse tree). Any script can be turned into many potential syntax trees—it just depends on how you decide to break it down. A syntax tree is a much more useful representation of the script than the words, for we can manipulate it in many ways by walking the tree.

If we are using a *Semantic Model (159)*, we take the syntax tree and translate it into the Semantic Model. If you read material in the language community, you'll often see more emphasis placed on the syntax tree—people execute the syntax tree directly or generate code off the syntax tree. Effectively, people can use the syntax tree as a semantic model. Most of the time I would not do that, because the syntax tree is very tied to the syntax of the DSL script and thus couples the processing of the DSL to its syntax.

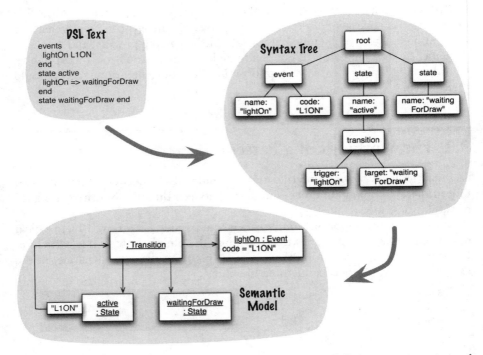

Figure 3.2 *A syntax tree and a semantic model are usually different representations of a DSL script.*

I've been talking about the syntax tree as if it's a tangible data structure in your system, like the XML DOM. Sometimes it is, but often it isn't. A lot of the time the syntax tree is formed on the call stack and processed as we walk it. As a result, you never see the whole tree, just the branch that you are currently processing (which is similar to the way XML SAX works). Despite this, it's usually helpful to think about a ghostly syntax tree hiding in the shadows of the call stack. For an internal DSL, this tree is formed by arguments in a function call (*Nested Function (357)*) and by nested objects (*Method Chaining (373)*).

Sometimes, you don't see a strong hierarchy and you have to simulate it (*Function Sequence (351)* with the hierarchy simulated with *Context Variables (175)*). The syntax tree may be ghostly, but it's still a useful mental tool. Using an external DSL leads to a more explicit syntax tree; indeed, sometimes you actually do create a full-blown syntax tree data structure (*Tree Construction (281)*). But even external DSLs are commonly processed with the syntax tree forming and pruning continuously on the call stack. (I've referenced a few patterns above that I haven't described yet. You can safely ignore them on your first read, but the references will be helpful on a later pass.)

3.3 Grammars, Syntax, and Semantics

When you work with a language's syntax, an important tool is a grammar. A **grammar** is a set of rules which describe how a stream of text is turned into a syntax tree. Most programmers have come across grammars at some point in their lives, as they are often used to describe the programming languages we all work with. A grammar consists of a list of production rules, where each rule has a term and a statement of how it gets broken down. So, a grammar for an addition statement might look like `additionStatement := number '+' number`. This would tell us that if we see the language sentence 5 + 3, the parser can recognize it as an addition statement. Rules mention each other, so we would also have a rule for a number telling us how to recognize a legal number. We can compose a grammar for a language with these rules.

It's important to realize that a language can have multiple grammars that define it. There is no such thing as *the* grammar for a language. A grammar defines the structure of the syntax tree that's generated for the language, and we can recognize many different tree structures for a particular piece of language text. A grammar just defines one form of a syntax tree; the actual grammar and syntax tree you'll choose will depend on many factors, including the features of the grammar language you're working with and how you want to process the syntax tree.

The grammar also only defines the syntax of a language—how it gets represented in the syntax tree. It doesn't tell us anything about its semantics, that is, what an expression means. Depending on the context, 5 + 3 could mean 8 or 53; the syntax is the same but the semantics may differ. With a *Semantic Model (159)*, the definition of the semantics boils down to how we populate the Semantic Model from the syntax tree and what we do with the Semantic Model. In particular, we can say that if two expressions produce the same structure in the Semantic Model, they have the same semantics, even if their syntax is different.

If you're using an external DSL, particularly if you use *Syntax-Directed Translation (219)*, you're likely to make explicit use of a grammar in building a parser. With internal DSLs, there won't be an explicit grammar, but it's still useful to think in terms of a grammar for your DSL. This grammar helps you choose which of the various internal DSL patterns you might use.

One of the things that makes talking about a grammar tricky for internal DSLs is that there are two parsing passes and thus two grammars involved. The first is the parsing of the host language itself, which obviously depends on the host grammar. This parsing creates the executable instructions for the host language. As the DSL part of that host language executes, it will create the ghostly syntax tree of the DSL on the call stack. It's only in this second parse that the notional DSL grammar comes into play.

3.4 Parsing Data

As the parser executes, it needs to store various bits of data about the parse. This data could be a complete syntax tree, but a lot of the time that isn't the case—and even when it is, there's other data that usually needs to be stored to make the parse work well.

The parse is inherently a tree walk, and whenever you are processing a part of a DSL script, you'll have some information about the context within the branch of the syntax tree that you're processing. However, often you need information that's outside that branch. Again, let's take a fragment of a state machine example:

```
commands
  unlockDoor D1UL
end

state idle
  actions {unlockDoor}
end
```

Here we see a common situation: A command is defined in one part of the language and referred to somewhere else. When the command is referred to as part of the state's actions, we're on a different branch of the syntax tree from where the command was defined. If the only representation of the syntax tree is on the call stack, then the command definition has disappeared by now. As a result, we need to store the command object for later use so we can resolve the reference in the action clause.

In order to do this, we use a *Symbol Table (165)*, which is essentially a dictionary whose key is the identifier unlockDoor and whose value is an object that represents the command in our parse. When we process the text unlockDoor D1UL, we create an object to hold that data and stash it in the Symbol Table under the key unlockDoor. The object we stash may be the semantic model object for a command, or it could be an intermediate object that's local to the syntax tree. Later, when we process actions {unlockDoor}, we look up that object using the Symbol Table to capture the relationship between the state and its actions. A Symbol Table is thus

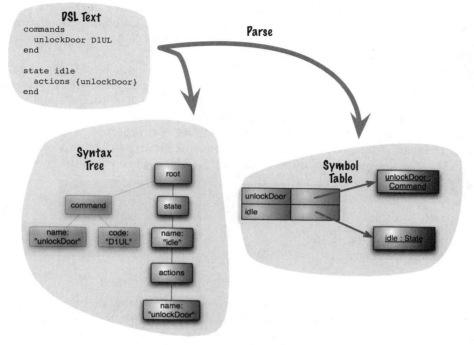

Figure 3.3 *Parsing creates both a parse tree and a symbol table.*

a crucial tool for making the cross-references. If you actually do create a full syntax tree during the parse, you can theoretically dispense with a Symbol Table, although usually it's still a useful construct that makes it easier to stitch things together.

At this point I'm going to finish this section by lurching into a couple of more detailed patterns. I'm mentioning them here because they are used in both internal and external DSLs, so this is a good spot even though most of this chapter is at a higher level.

As the parse continues, you'll need to keep its results. Sometimes all the results can be weaved into a Symbol Table, sometimes a lot of information can be kept on the call stack, sometimes you'll need additional data structures in the parser. In all of these cases the most obvious thing to do is to create *Semantic Model (159)* objects as your results; often, however, you'll need to create intermediate objects because you can't create Semantic Model objects till later in the parse. A common example of such an intermediate object is a *Construction Builder (179)* which is an object that captures all the data for a Semantic Model object. This is useful when your Semantic Model object has read-only data after construction, but you gradually gather the data for it during parsing. A Construction Builder has the same fields as the Semantic Model object, but makes them read-write, which gives you somewhere to stash the data. Once you have all the data, you can create the Semantic Model object. Using a Construction Builder complicates the parser but I'd rather do that than alter the Semantic Model to forgo the benefits of read-only properties.

Indeed sometimes you might defer all creation of Semantic Model objects till you've processed all the DSL script. In this case the parse has distinct phases: first, reading through the DSL script and creating intermediate parsing data, and second, running through that intermediate data and populating the Semantic Model. The choice of how much to do during the text processing and what to do afterwards usually depends on how the Semantic Model needs to be populated.

The way you parse an expression often depends on the context that you are working in. Consider this text:

```
state idle
  actions {unlockDoor}
end

state unlockedPanel
  actions {lockDoor}
end
```

When we process actions {lockDoor}, it's important to know that this is in the context of the unlockedPanel state and not the idle state. Often, this context is supplied by the way the parser builds and walks the parse tree, but there are many cases where it's difficult to do that. If we can't find the context by examining the parse tree, then a good way to deal with it is by holding the context, in this case the current state, in a variable. I call this kind of variable a *Context Variable (175)*. This Context Variable, like a Symbol Table, can hold a Semantic Model object or some intermediate object.

Although a Context Variable is often a straightforward tool to use, in general I prefer to avoid them as much as possible. The parsing code is easier to follow if you can read it without having to mentally juggle Context Variables, just as lots of mutable variables make procedural code more complicated to follow. Certainly there are times when you can't avoid using a Context Variable, but I tend to see them as a smell to be avoided.

3.5 Macros

Macros (183) are a tool that can be used with both internal and external DSLs. They used to be used pretty widely, but are less common now. In most contexts I'd suggest avoiding them, but they are occasionally useful, so I need to talk a little about how they work and when you might use them.

Macros come in two flavors: textual and syntactic. Textual macros are the simplest to understand; they allow you to substitute some text for some other text. A good example of where they can be handy is specifying colors in a CSS file. For all but a few fixed cases, CSS forces you to specify colors with color codes, such as #FFB595. Such a code is not very meaningful; what's worse, if you use the same color in multiple places, you have to repeat the code. This, like any form of code duplication, is a Bad Thing. It would be better to give it a name that's meaningful in your context, like MEDIUM_SHADE, and define in one place that MEDIUM_SHADE is #FFB595.

Although CSS (at least currently) doesn't let you do that, you can use a macro processor to handle such situations. Just create a file which is your CSS file but with MEDIUM_SHADE where you need your color. The macro processor then does a simple text substitution to replace MEDIUM_SHADE with #FFB595.

That's a very simple form of macro processing; more involved ones can use parameters. A classic example of this is the C preprocessor that can define a macro to replace sqr(x) with x * x.

Macros provide a lot of opportunities to create DSLs, either within a host language (as the C preprocessor does) or as a stand-alone file transformed into a host language. The downside is that macros have a number of awkward problems that make them difficult to use in practice. As a result, textual macros have pretty much fallen out of favor, and most mavens like me advise against them.

Syntactic macros also do substitution, but they work on syntactically valid elements of the host language, transforming from one kind of expression to another. The language that's most famous for its heavy use of syntactic macros is Lisp, although C++ templates may be a better-known example. Using syntactic macros for DSLs is a core technique for writing internal DSLs in Lisp, but you can only use syntactic macros in a language that supports them; I therefore don't talk about them much in this book, since relatively few languages do.

3.6 Testing DSLs

Over the last couple of decades I've become quite a bore on the subject of testing. I'm a big fan of test-driven development [Beck TDD] and similar techniques that put testing into the forefront of programming. As a result, I can't think about DSLs without thinking about testing them.

With DSLs, I can break testing down into three separate areas: testing the *Semantic Model (159)*, testing the parser, and testing the scripts.

3.6.1 Testing the Semantic Model

The first area I think about is testing the *Semantic Model (159)*. These tests are about ensuring that the Semantic Model behaves the way I expect it to—that, as I execute it, the right outputs happen depending on what I place in the model. This is standard testing practice, the same as you would use with any framework

of objects. For this testing, I don't really need the DSL at all—I can populate the
model using the basic interface of the model itself. This is good, as it allows me
to test the model independently of the DSL and the parser.

Let me illustrate this with the secret panel controller. Here, my Semantic
Model is the state machine. I can test the Semantic Model by populating it with
the command-query API code I used at the beginning of the Introduction (p. 9),
which doesn't require any DSL.

```
@Test
public void event_causes_transition() {
  State idle = new State("idle");
  StateMachine machine = new StateMachine(idle);
  Event cause = new Event("cause", "EV01");
  State target = new State("target");
  idle.addTransition(cause, target);
  Controller controller = new Controller(machine, new CommandChannel());
  controller.handle("EV01");
  assertEquals(target, controller.getCurrentState());
}
```

The above code demonstrates that I can simply test the Semantic Model in
isolation. However, I should point out that the real test code for this case will
be more involved and should be better factored.

Here are a couple of ways to better factor this kind of code. First off, we can
make a bunch of small state machines which provide minimal fixtures for testing
various features of the Semantic Model. To test that an event triggers a transition,
all we need is a simple state machine with an idle state and two outbound
transitions to separate states.

```
class TransitionTester...
  State idle, a, b;
  Event trigger_a, trigger_b, unknown;

  protected StateMachine createMachine() {
    idle = new State("idle");
    StateMachine result = new StateMachine(idle);
    trigger_a = new Event("trigger_a", "TRGA");
    trigger_b = new Event("trigger_b", "TRGB");
    unknown = new Event("Unknown", "UNKN");
    a = new State("a");
    b = new State("b");
    idle.addTransition(trigger_a, a);
    idle.addTransition(trigger_b, b);
    return result;
  }
```

When we want to test commands, however, we might just want a smaller
machine with just a single state off our idle state.

```
class CommandTester...
  Command commenceEarthquake = new Command("Commence Earthquake", "EQST");
  State idle = new State("idle");
  State second = new State("second");
  Event trigger = new Event("trigger", "TGGR");

  protected StateMachine createMachine() {
    second.addAction(commenceEarthquake);
    idle.addTransition(trigger, second);
    return new StateMachine(idle);
  }
```

These different test fixtures can be run, and tests probed, in similar ways. I can make this easier by giving them a common superclass. The first thing this class provides is the ability to set up a common fixture—in this initializing, a controller and a command channel with the supplied state machine.

```
class AbstractStateTesterLib...
  protected CommandChannel commandChannel = new CommandChannel();
  protected StateMachine machine;
  protected Controller controller;

  @Before
  public void setup() {
    machine = createMachine();
    controller = new Controller(machine, commandChannel);
  }

  abstract protected StateMachine createMachine();
```

I can now write tests by firing events at the controller and checking the state.

```
class TransitionTester...
  @Test
  public void event_causes_transition() {
    fire(trigger_a);
    assertCurrentState(a);
  }
  @Test
  public void event_without_transition_is_ignored() {
    fire(unknown);
    assertCurrentState(idle);
  }
```

```
class AbstractStateTesterLib...
  //-------- Utility methods ------------------------
  protected void fire(Event e) {
    controller.handle(e.getCode());
  }
  //------- Custom asserts ------------------------
  protected void assertCurrentState(State s) {
    assertEquals(s, controller.getCurrentState());
  }
```

The superclass provides *Test Utility Methods* [Meszaros] and *Custom Assertions* [Meszaros] to make the tests easier to read.

An alternative approach for testing the Semantic Model is to populate a larger model that demonstrates many features of the model, and run multiple tests on that. In this case, I can use Miss Grant's controller as a test fixture.

```
class ModelTest...
  private Event doorClosed, drawerOpened, lightOn, doorOpened, panelClosed;
  private State activeState, waitingForLightState, unlockedPanelState,
                idle, waitingForDrawerState;
  private Command unlockPanelCmd, lockDoorCmd, lockPanelCmd, unlockDoorCmd;
  private CommandChannel channel = new CommandChannel();
  private Controller con;
  private StateMachine machine;

@Before
public void setup() {
  doorClosed = new Event("doorClosed", "D1CL");
  drawerOpened = new Event("drawerOpened", "D2OP");
  lightOn = new Event("lightOn", "L1ON");
  doorOpened = new Event("doorOpened", "D1OP");
  panelClosed = new Event("panelClosed", "PNCL");
  unlockPanelCmd = new Command("unlockPanel", "PNUL");
  lockPanelCmd = new Command("lockPanel", "PNLK");
  lockDoorCmd = new Command("lockDoor", "D1LK");
  unlockDoorCmd = new Command("unlockDoor", "D1UL");

  idle = new State("idle");
  activeState = new State("active");
  waitingForLightState = new State("waitingForLight");
  waitingForDrawerState = new State("waitingForDrawer");
  unlockedPanelState = new State("unlockedPanel");

  machine = new StateMachine(idle);

  idle.addTransition(doorClosed, activeState);
  idle.addAction(unlockDoorCmd);
  idle.addAction(lockPanelCmd);

  activeState.addTransition(drawerOpened, waitingForLightState);
  activeState.addTransition(lightOn, waitingForDrawerState);

  waitingForLightState.addTransition(lightOn, unlockedPanelState);
  waitingForDrawerState.addTransition(drawerOpened, unlockedPanelState);

  unlockedPanelState.addAction(unlockPanelCmd);
  unlockedPanelState.addAction(lockDoorCmd);
  unlockedPanelState.addTransition(panelClosed, idle);

  machine.addResetEvents(doorOpened);
  con = new Controller(machine, channel);
  channel.clearHistory();
}
```

```
@Test
public void event_causes_state_change() {
  fire(doorClosed);
  assertCurrentState(activeState);
}

@Test
public void ignore_event_if_no_transition() {
  fire(drawerOpened);
  assertCurrentState(idle);
}
```

In this case, I again populated the Semantic Model using its own command-query interface. As the test fixtures get more complex, however, I can simplify the test code by using the DSL to create fixtures. I can do this if I have tests for the parser.

3.6.2 Testing the Parser

When we're using a *Semantic Model (159)*, the job of the parser is to populate the Semantic Model. So our testing of the parser is about writing small fragments of DSL and ensuring that they create the right structures in the Semantic Model.

```
@Test
public void loads_states_with_transition() {
  String code =
    "events trigger TGGR end " +
    "state idle " +
    "trigger => target " +
    "end " +
    "state target end ";
  StateMachine actual = StateMachineLoader.loadString(code);

  State idle = actual.getState("idle");
  State target = actual.getState("target");
  assertTrue(idle.hasTransition("TGGR"));
  assertEquals(idle.targetState("TGGR"), target);
}
```

Poking around in the Semantic Model like this is rather awkward, and may result in breaking encapsulation on the objects in the Semantic Model. Therefore another way to test the output of the parser is to define methods to compare Semantic Models and use those.

```
@Test
public void loads_states_with_transition_using_compare() {
  String code =
    "events trigger TGGR end " +
    "state idle " +
    "trigger => target " +
    "end " +
    "state target end ";
  StateMachine actual = StateMachineLoader.loadString(code);

  State idle = new State("idle");
  State target = new State("target");
  Event trigger = new Event("trigger", "TGGR");
  idle.addTransition(trigger, target);
  StateMachine expected = new StateMachine(idle);

  assertEquivalentMachines(expected, actual);
}
```

Checking complex structures for equivalence is more involved than the regular notions of equality would suggest. We also need more information than just a Boolean answer, since we want to know what's different between the objects. As a result, I have a comparison that uses a *Notification (193)*.

```
class StateMachine...
  public Notification probeEquivalence(StateMachine other) {
    Notification result = new Notification();
    probeEquivalence(other, result);
    return result;
  }

  private void probeEquivalence(StateMachine other, Notification note) {
    for (State s : getStates()) {
      State otherState = other.getState(s.getName());
      if (null == otherState) note.error("missing state: %s", s.getName()) ;
      else s.probeEquivalence(otherState, note);
    }
    for (State s : other.getStates())
      if (null == getState(s.getName())) note.error("extra state: %s", s.getName());
    for (Event e : getResetEvents()) {
      if (!other.getResetEvents().contains(e))
        note.error("missing reset event: %s", e.getName());
    }
    for (Event e : other.getResetEvents()) {
      if (!getResetEvents().contains(e))
        note.error("extra reset event: %s", e.getName());
    }
  }
}
```

```
class State...
  void probeEquivalence(State other, Notification note) {
    assert name.equals(other.name);
    probeEquivalentTransitions(other, note);
    probeEquivalentActions(other, note);
  }

  private void probeEquivalentActions(State other, Notification note) {
    if (!actions.equals(other.actions))
      note.error("%s has different actions %s vs %s", name, actions, other.actions);
  }

  private void probeEquivalentTransitions(State other, Notification note) {
    for (Transition t : transitions.values())
      t.probeEquivalent(other.transitions.get(t.getEventCode()), note);
    for (Transition t : other.transitions.values())
      if (!this.transitions.containsKey(t.getEventCode()))
        note.error("%s has extra transition with %s", name, t.getTrigger());
  }
```

The approach of this probe is to walk through the objects in the Semantic Model and record any differences in a Notification. This way I find all differences instead of stopping at the first one. My assertion then just checks to see if the Notification has any errors.

```
class AntlrLoaderTest...
  private void assertEquivalentMachines(StateMachine left, StateMachine right) {
    assertNotificationOk(left.probeEquivalence(right));
    assertNotificationOk(right.probeEquivalence(left));
  }

  private void assertNotificationOk(Notification n) {
    assertTrue(n.report(), n.isOk());
  }

class Notification...
  public boolean isOk() {return errors.isEmpty();}
```

You may think I'm being paranoid by doing the equivalence assertion in both directions, but usually the code *is* out to get me.

Invalid Input Tests

The tests I've just discussed are positive tests, in that they ensure that a valid DSL input creates the correct structures in the *Semantic Model (159)*. Another category of tests are negative tests, which probe what happens if I submit invalid DSL input. This goes into the whole area of error handling and diagnostics, which is out of scope for this book, but I won't let that stop me briefly mentioning invalid input tests here.

The idea with invalid input tests is to throw various kinds of invalid input at the parser. The first time you run such a test, it's interesting to see what happens. Often you'll get an obscure but violent error. Depending on the amount of diagnostic support you want to provide with the DSL, that may be enough. It's worse if you supply an invalid DSL, parse it, and get no error at all. This would violate the principle of "fail fast"—that is, that errors should show up as early and loudly as possible. If you populate a model in an invalid state and have no checks for that, you won't find out there's a problem till later. At that point, there is a distance between the original fault (loading an invalid input) and the later failure, and that distance makes it harder to find the fault.

My state machine example has very minimal error handling—a common feature of book examples. I probed one of my parser examples with this test, just to see what would happen.

```
@Test public void targetStateNotDeclaredNoAssert () {
  String code =
    "events trigger TGGR end " +
    "state idle " +
    "trigger => target " +
    "end ";
  StateMachine actual = StateMachineLoader.loadString(code);
}
```

The test passed just fine, which is a bad thing. Then, when I tried to do anything with the model, even just print it, I got a null pointer exception. I'm fine with this example being somewhat crude—after all, its only purpose is pedagogical—but a typo in an input DSL could lead to much lost time debugging. Since this is my time, and I like to pretend to myself that it's valuable, I'd rather it failed fast.

Since the problem is that I'm creating an invalid structure in the Semantic Model, the responsibility to check for this problem is that of the Semantic Model—in this case, the method that adds a transition to a state. I added an assertion to detect the problem.

```
class State...
  public void addTransition(Event event, State targetState) {
    assert null != targetState;
    transitions.put(event.getCode(), new Transition(this, event, targetState));
  }
```

Now I can alter the test to catch the exception. This will tell me if I ever change the behavior of this output, as well as document what kind of error this invalid input causes.

```
@Test public void targetStateNotDeclared () {
  String code =
    "events trigger TGGR end " +
    "state idle " +
    "trigger => target " +
    "end ";
  try {
    StateMachine actual = StateMachineLoader.loadString(code);
    fail();
  } catch (AssertionError expected) {}
```

You'll notice that I only put in an assertion for the target state and not for the trigger event, which also could be null. My reason for this is that a null event will cause an immediate null pointer exception due to the event.getCode() call. This fulfills the fast-fail need. I can check this with another test.

```
@Test public void triggerNotDeclared () {
  String code =
    "events trigger TGGR end " +
    "state idle " +
    "wrongTrigger => target " +
    "end " +
    "state target end ";
  try {
    StateMachine actual = StateMachineLoader.loadString(code);
    fail();
  } catch (NullPointerException expected) {}
```

A null pointer exception does fail fast, but isn't as clear as the assertion. In general, I don't do not-null assertions on my method arguments, as I feel the benefit isn't worth the extra code to read. The exception is when this leads to a null that doesn't cause an immediate failure, such the null target state.

3.6.3 Testing the Scripts

Testing the *Semantic Model (159)* and the parser does unit testing for the generic code. However, the DSL scripts are also code, and we should consider testing them. I do hear arguments along the lines of "DSL scripts are too simple and obvious to be worth testing," but I'm naturally suspicious of that. I see testing as a double-check mechanism. When we write code and tests, we are specifying the same behavior using too different mechanisms, one involving abstractions (the code) and the other using examples (the tests). For anything of lasting value, we should always double-check.

The details of script tests very much depend on what it is you're testing. The general approach is to provide a test environment that allows you to create text fixtures, run DSL scripts, and compare results. It's usually some effort to prepare such an environment, but just because a DSL is easy to read doesn't mean people won't make mistakes. If you don't provide a test environment and thus don't have a double-check mechanism, you greatly increase the risk of errors in the DSL scripts.

Script tests also act as integration tests, since any errors in the parser or Semantic Model should cause them to fail. As a result, it's worth sampling the DSL scripts to use a few for this purpose.

Often, alternative visualizations of the script are a useful aid in testing and debugging DSL scripts. Once you have a script captured in the Semantic Model, it's relatively easy to produce different textual and graphical visualizations of the script's logic. Presenting information in multiple ways often helps people find errors—indeed, this notion of a double check is the heart of why writing self-testing code is such a valuable approach.

For the state machine example, I begin by thinking about the examples that would make sense for this kind of machine. To my mind, the logical approach would be to run scenarios, each scenario being a sequence of events sent to the machine. I then check the end state of the machine and the commands it has sent out. Building up something like this in a readable way naturally leads me to another DSL. That's not uncommon; testing scripts is a common use of DSLs as they fit well with the need for a limited, declarative language.

```
events("doorClosed", "drawerOpened", "lightOn")
      .endsAt("unlockedPanel")
      .sends("unlockPanel", "lockDoor");
```

3.7 Handling Errors

Whenever I write a book, I reach a point where I recognize that, as with writing software, I have to cut the scope in order to get the book published. While this means that an important topic isn't covered properly, I reason that it's better to have a useful but incomplete book than a complete book that never gets finished. There are many topics I'd like to have explored further in this book, but the top of that list is error handling.

During a compiler class at university, I remember being told that parsing and output generation are the easy part of compiler writing—the hard part was giving good error messages. Appropriately, error diagnostics was as beyond the scope for that class as it has become for this book.

The out-of-scopeness of decent error messages goes further than that. Good diagnostics are a rarity even in successful DSLs. More than one highly useful DSL package does little in the way of helpful information. Graphviz, one of my favorite DSL tools, will simply tell me syntax error near line 4, and I feel somewhat lucky even to get a line number. I've certainly come across tools that just fall over, leaving me to do a binary search with commenting out lines in order to find just where the problem is.

One can rightly criticize such systems for their poor error diagnostics, but diagnostics are yet another thing to be traded off. Any time spent on improving error handling is time not spent adding other features. The evidence from many DSLs in the wild is that people do tolerate poor error diagnostics. After all, DSL scripts are small, so crude error finding techniques are more reasonable with them than with general-purpose languages.

I'm not saying this to persuade you to not work on error diagnostics. In a heavily used library, good diagnostics can save a lot of time. Every tradeoff is unique, and you have to decide based on your own circumstances. It does, however, make me feel a little bit better about not devoting a section of this book to the subject.

Despite the fact that I can't give the topic the in-depth coverage I'd like to, I can say something that will hopefully get you started in thinking more about error diagnostics, should you decide to provide greater support.

(One thing that I should mention is the crudest error-finding technique of all—commenting out. If you use an external DSL, make sure that you support comments. Not just for the obvious reasons, but also to help people find problems. Such comments are easiest to work with when they are terminated by line endings. Depending on the audience, I'd use either "#" (script style) or "//" (C style). These can be done with a simple lexer rule.)

If you follow my general recommendation to use a *Semantic Model (159)*, then there are two places where error handling can live: the model or the parser. For syntactic errors, the obvious place to put the handling is in the parser. Some syntactic errors will be handled for you: host language syntax errors in an internal DSL or grammar errors when using a *Parser Generator (269)* in an external DSL.

The situation where you have a choice between parser and model is handling semantic errors. For semantics, both places have their strengths. The model is really the right place to check the rules of semantically well-formed structures. You have all the information structured the way you need to think about it, so you can write the clearest error checking code here. Additionally, you'll need the checking here if you want to populate the model from more than one place, such as multiple DSLs or using a command-query interface.

Putting error handling purely in the Semantic Model does have one serious disadvantage: There's no link back to the source of the problem in the DSL script, not even an approximate line number. This makes it harder for people to figure out what went wrong, but this may not be an intractable problem. There is some experience that suggests that a purely model-based error message is enough to find the problem in many situations.

If you do want the DSL script context, then there are a few ways to get it. The most obvious one is to put the error detection rules in the parser. However, the problem with this strategy is that it makes it much harder to write the rules, as you are working on the level of the syntax tree rather than the semantic model. You also have a much greater risk of duplicating the rules, with all the problems that code duplication entails.

An alternative is to push syntactic information into the Semantic Model. You might add a line number field to a semantic transition object, so that when the Semantic Model detects an error in that transition, it can print the line number from the script. The problem is that this can make the Semantic Model much more complicated as it has to track the information. Additionally, the script may not map that cleanly to the model, which could result in error messages that are more confusing than helpful.

The third strategy, and the one that sounds best to me, is to use the Semantic Model for error detection, but trigger error detection in the parser. This way, the parser will parse a hunk of DSL script, populate the Semantic Model, and then tell the model to look for errors (if populating the model doesn't do that directly). Should the model find any, the parser can then take those errors and supply the DSL script context it knows. This separates the concerns of syntactic knowledge (in the parser) and semantic knowledge (in the model).

A useful approach is to divide error handling into initiation, detection, and reporting. This last strategy puts initiation in the parser, detection in the model, and reporting in both, with the model supplying the semantics of the error and the parser adding syntactic context.

3.8 Migrating DSLs

One danger that DSL advocates need to guard against is the notion that first you design a DSL, then people use it. Like any other piece of software, a successful DSL will evolve. This means that scripts written in an earlier version of a DSL may fail when run with a later version.

Like many properties of DSL, good and bad, this is very much the same as what happens with a library. If you take a library from someone, write some code against it, and they upgrade the library, you may end up stuck. DSLs don't really do anything to change that; the DSL definition is essentially a published interface, and you have to deal with the consequences just the same.

I started using the term **published interface** in my Refactoring book [Fowler Refactoring]. The difference between published and the more common "public" interface is that a published interface is used by code written by a separate team. Therefore, if the team that defines the interface wants to change it, they can't easily rewrite the calling code. Changing a published DSL is an issue with both internal and external DSLs. With nonpublished DSLs, it may be easier to change an internal DSL if the language concerned has automated refactoring tools.

One way to tackle the problem of changes to DSLs is to provide tools that automatically migrate a DSL from one version to another. These can be run either during an upgrade, or automatically should you try to run an old-version script.

There are two broad ways to handle migration. The first is an **incremental migration** strategy. This is essentially the same notion that's used by people doing evolutionary database design [Fowler and Sadalage]. For every change you do to your DSL definition, create a migration program that automatically migrates DSL scripts from the old version to the new version. That way, when you release a new version of the DSL, you also provide scripts to migrate any code bases that use the DSL.

An important part of incremental migration is that you keep the changes as small as you can. Imagine you are upgrading from version 1 to 2, and have ten changes that you want to make to your DSL definition. In this case, don't create just one migration script to migrate from version 1 to 2; instead, create at least ten scripts. Change the DSL definition one feature at a time, and write a migration script for each change. You may find it useful to break it down even more and add some features with more than one step (and thus more than one migration). This may sound like more work than a single script, but the point is that migrations are much easier to write if they are small, and it's easy to chain multiple migrations together. As a result, you'll be able to write ten scripts much faster than one.

The other approach is model-based migration. This is a tactic you can use with a *Semantic Model (159)*. With **model-based migration** you support multiple parsers for your language, one for each released version. (So you only do this for versions 1 and 2, not for the intermediate steps.) Each parser populates the semantic model. When you use a semantic model, the parser's behavior is pretty simple, so it's not too much trouble to have several of them around. You then run the appropriate parser for the version of script you are working with. This handles multiple versions, but doesn't migrate the scripts. To do the migration, you write a generator from the semantic model that generates a DSL script representation. This way, you can run the parser for a version 1 script, populate the semantic model, and then emit a version 2 script from the generator.

One problem with the model-based approach is that it's easy to lose stuff that doesn't matter for the semantics but is something that the script writers want to keep. Comments are the obvious example. This is exacerbated if there's too much smarts in the parser, although then the need to migrate this way may encourage the parsers to stay dumb—which is a Good Thing.

If the change to the DSL is big enough, you may not be able to transform a version 1 script into a version 2 semantic model. In this case, you may need to keep a version 1 model (or an intermediate model) around and give it the ability to emit a version 2 script.

I don't have a strong preference among these two alternatives.

Migration scripts can be run by script programmers themselves when needed, or automatically by the DSL system. If it's to be run automatically, it's very useful to have the script record which version of the DSL it is so the parser can detect it easily and trigger the resulting migrations. Indeed, some DSL authors argue that all DSLs should have a mandatory version statement in a script so it's easy to detect out-of-date scripts and support the migration of scripts. While a version statement may add a bit of noise to the script, it's something that's very hard to retrofit.

Of course another migration option is not to migrate—that is, to keep the version 1 parser and just let it populate the version 2 model. You should help people migrate, and they will need to if they want to use more features. But supporting the old scripts directly, if you can, is useful since it allows them to migrate at their own pace.

Although techniques like this are quite appealing, there is the question of whether they are worth it in practice. As I said earlier, the problem is exactly the same as with widely used libraries, and automated migration schemes have not been used much there.

Chapter 4

Implementing an Internal DSL

Now that I've gone through some general issues in implementing DSLs, it's time to go into the specifics of implementing particular flavors of DSLs. I've decided to start with internal DSLs as they are often the most approachable form of DSLs to write. Unlike external DSLs, you don't need to learn about grammars and language parsing, and unlike language workbenches, you don't need any special tools. With internal DSLs you work in your regular language environment. As a result, it's no surprise that there's been a lot of interest in internal DSLs in the last couple of years.

When you use internal DSLs, you are very much constrained by your host language. Since any expression you use must be a legal expression in your host language, a lot of thought in internal DSL usage is bound up in language features. A good bit of the recent impetus behind internal DSLs comes from the Ruby community, whose language has many features which encourage DSLs. However, many Ruby techniques can be used in other languages too, if usually not as elegantly. And the doyen on internal DSL thinking is Lisp, one of the world's oldest computer languages with a limited but very appropriate set of features for the job.

Another term you might hear for an internal DSL is **fluent interface**. This was a term coined by Eric Evans and myself to describe more language-like APIs. It's a synonym for an internal DSL looked at from the API direction. It gets to the heart of the difference between an API and a DSL—the language nature. As I've already indicated, there is a gray area between the two. You can have reasonable but ill-defined arguments about whether a particular language construction is language-like or not. The advantage of such arguments is that they encourage reflection on the techniques you are using and on how readable your DSL is; the disadvantage is that they can turn into continual rehashes of personal preferences.

4.1 Fluent and Command-Query APIs

For many people, the central pattern of a fluent interface is that of *Method Chaining (373)*. A normal API might have code like this:

```
Processor p = new Processor(2, 2500, Processor.Type.i386);
Disk d1 = new Disk(150, Disk.UNKNOWN_SPEED, null);
Disk d2 = new Disk(75, 7200, Disk.Interface.SATA);
return new Computer(p, d1, d2);
```

With Method Chaining, we can express the same thing with:

```
computer()
  .processor()
    .cores(2)
    .speed(2500)
    .i386()
  .disk()
    .size(150)
  .disk()
    .size(75)
    .speed(7200)
    .sata()
  .end();
```

Method Chaining uses a sequence of method calls where each call acts on the result of the previous calls. The methods are composed by calling one on top of the other. In regular OO code, these are usually derided as "train wrecks": The methods separated by dots look like train cars, and they are wrecks because they often are a sign of code that is brittle to changes in the interfaces of the classes in the middle of the chain. Thinking fluently, however, Method Chaining allows you to easily compose multiple method calls without relying on a lot of variables, which gives you code that seems to flow, feeling more like its own language.

But Method Chaining isn't the only way to get this sense of flow. Here is the same thing using a sequence of method call statements, which I call a *Function Sequence (351)*:

```
computer();
  processor();
    cores(2);
    speed(2500);
    i386();
  disk();
    size(150);
  disk();
    size(75);
    speed(7200);
    sata();
```

As you can see, if you try to lay out and organize a Function Sequence in an appropriate way, it can read as clearly as Method Chaining. (I use "function" rather than "method" in the name, as you can use this in a non-OO context with function calls while Method Chaining needs object-oriented methods.) The point here is that fluency isn't as much about the style of syntax you use as it is about the way you name and factor the methods themselves.

In the early days of objects, one of the biggest influences on me and many others was Bertrand Meyer's book *Object-Oriented Software Construction*. One of the analogies he used to talk about objects was to treat them as machines. In this view, an object was a black box, its interface being a series of displays to view the observable state of the object and buttons that you could press to change the object. This effectively offers a menu of different things you can do with the object. This style of interface is the dominant way we think about interacting with software components; it is so dominant that we don't even think of giving it a name, hence my coining of the term "command-query interface" to describe it.

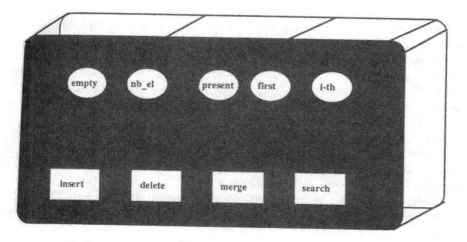

Figure 4.1   *The original figure from OOSC that Bertrand Meyer used to illustrate the machine metaphor. The ovals represent query buttons that have indicator lights to reveal the state of the machine when you press them, but do not alter the machine's state. The rectangles are command buttons that do alter state, causing the machine to start "screeching and clicking," but lacking any indicator lights to tell you what the noise is all about.*

The essence of fluent interfaces is that they approach thinking about using components differently. Instead of a box of objects, each sporting lots of buttons, we think linguistically of composing sentences using clauses that weave these objects together. It's this mental shift that is the core difference between an internal DSL and just calling an API.

As I've mentioned earlier, it's a very fuzzy difference. Treating APIs as languages is also an old and well-regarded analogy that goes back before objects were the norm. There's plenty of cases that could be argued as command-query or fluent. But I do think that, despite its fuzziness, it's a helpful distinction.

One of the consequences of the differences between the two styles of interface is that the rules about what makes a good interface are different. Meyer's original machine metaphor is very apt here. The figure appeared in a section of OOSC that introduced the principle of command-query separation.

Command-query separation says that the various methods on an object should be divided into commands and queries. A query is a method that returns a value, but does not change the observable state of the system. A command may change the observable state, but should not return a value. This principle is valuable because it helps us identify query methods. Since queries don't have side effects, you can call them multiple times and change the order of using them—without changing the results of calling them. You have to be much more careful with commands because they do have side effects.

Command-query separation is an extremely valuable principle in programming, and I strongly encourage teams to use it. One of the consequences of using Method Chaining in internal DSLs is that it usually breaks this principle—each method alters state but returns an object to continue the chain. I have used many decibels disparaging people who don't follow command-query separation, and will do so again. But fluent interfaces follow a different set of rules, so I'm happy to allow it there.

Another important difference between a command-query and fluent interface is in the naming of the methods. When you're coming up with names for a command-query interface, you want the names to make sense in a stand-alone context. Often, if people are looking for a method to do something, they'll run their eyes down the list of methods on a web document page or in an IDE menu. As a result, the names need to convey clearly what they do in that kind of context—they are the labels on the buttons.

With fluent interfaces, naming is quite different. Here, you concentrate less on each individual element in the language, but more on the overall sentences that you can form. As a result, you can often have methods whose names make no sense in an open context, but read properly in the context of a DSL sentence. With DSL naming, it's the sentence that comes first; the elements are named to fit in with that context. DSL names are written with the context of the specific DSL in mind, while command-query names are written to work without any context (or in any context, which is the same thing).

4.2 The Need for a Parsing Layer

The fact that a fluent interface is a different kind of interface to a command-query one can lead to complications. If you mix both styles of interface on the same class, it's confusing. I therefore advocate keeping the language-handling elements of a DSL separate from regular command-query objects by building a layer of *Expression Builders (343)* over regular objects. Expression Builders are objects whose sole task is to build up a model of normal objects using a fluent interface—effectively translating fluent sentences into a sequence of command-query API calls.

The different nature of the interfaces is one reason for Expression Builders, but the primary reason is a classic "separation of concerns" argument. As soon as you introduce some kind of language, even an internal one, you have to write code that understands that language. This code will often need to keep track of data that is only relevant while the language is being processed—parsing data. Understanding the way in which the internal DSL works is a reasonable amount of work, and it's not needed once you've populated the underlying model. You don't need to understand the DSL or how it works to understand how the underlying model operates, so it's worth keeping the language-processing code in a separate layer.

This structure follows the general layout of DSL processing. The underlying model of command-query interface objects is the *Semantic Model (159)*. The layer of Expression Builders is (part of the) parser.

I've puzzled a bit over using the term "parser" for this layer of Expression Builders. Usually we use "parser" in the context of parsing text. In this case, the host language parser manipulates the text. But there are many parallels between what we do with Expression Builders and what a parser does. The key difference is that while a traditional parser arranges a stream of tokens into a syntax tree, the input for the Expression Builders is a stream of function calls. The parallels to other parsers are that we still find it useful to think of arranging these function-call parse nodes into a tree, we use similar parsing data structures (such as *Symbol Table (165)*), and we still populate a Semantic Model.

Separating the Semantic Model from Expression Builders introduces the usual advantages of a Semantic Model. You can test the Expression Builders and the Semantic Model independently. You can have multiple parsers, mixing internal and external DSLs or supporting multiple internal DSLs with multiple Expression Builders. You can evolve the Expression Builders and the Semantic Model independently. This is important since DSLs, like any other software, are hardly ever fixed. You need to be able to evolve the software, and often it's useful to change the underlying framework without changing the DSL scripts or vice versa.

There is an argument for not using Expression Builders, but only when the Semantic Model objects use fluent interfaces themselves, rather than a command-query interface. There are some cases where it makes sense for a model to use a fluent interface, if that's the main way people will interact with it. In most situations, however, I prefer a command-query interface on a model. The command-query interface is more flexible in how it can be used in different contexts. A fluent interface often needs temporary parsing data. In particular, I object to mixing a fluent and a command-query interface on the same objects—that's just too confusing.

As a result, I'll be assuming Expression Builders for the rest of this book. Although I acknowledge that you may not have to use Expression Builders all the time, I do think you should use them most of the time, so I'll write with that majority case in mind.

4.3 Using Functions

Since the beginning of computing, programmers sought to package up common code into reusable chunks. The most successful packaging construct we've come up with is the function (also called subroutine, procedure, and method in OO-land). Command-query APIs are usually expressed in functions, but DSL structures are also often built primarily on functions. The difference between a command-query interface and a DSL centers around how functions are combined.

There are a number of patterns for combining functions to make a DSL. At the beginning of this chapter I showed two. Let's recap, as I've forgotten what I wrote back there. First, *Method Chaining (373)*:

```
computer()
  .processor()
    .cores(2)
    .speed(2500)
    .i386()
  .disk()
    .size(150)
  .disk()
    .size(75)
    .speed(7200)
    .sata()
  .end();
```

Then, *Function Sequence (351)*:

```
computer();
  processor();
    cores(2);
    speed(2500);
    i386();
  disk();
    size(150);
  disk();
    size(75);
    speed(7200);
    sata();
```

These are different patterns for combining functions, which naturally leads to the question of which one you should use. The answer involves various factors. The first factor is the scope of the functions. If you use Method Chaining, the functions in the DSL are methods that need to only be defined on the objects that take part in the chain, usually on an *Expression Builder (343)*. On the other hand, if you use bare functions in a sequence, you have to ensure the functions resolve properly. The most obvious way to do this is to use global functions, but using globals introduces two problems: complicating the global namespace and introducing global variables for parsing data.

Good programmers these days are nervous about any global stuff, as it makes it harder to localize changes. Global functions will be visible in every part of a program, but ideally you want the functions to only be available within the DSL processing bit. There are various language features that can remove the need to make everything global. A namespace capability allows you to make functions look global only when you import a particular namespace (Java has static imports).

The global parsing data is the more serious problem. Whichever way you do a Function Sequence, you'll need to manipulate *Context Variables (175)* in order to know where you are in parsing the expression. Consider the calls to diskSize. The builder needs to know which disk's size is being specified, so it does that by keeping track of the current disk in a variable—which it updates during the call to disk. Since all the functions are global, this state will end up being global too. There are things you can do to contain the globality—such as keeping all the data in a singleton—but you can't get away from global data if you use global functions.

Method Chaining avoids much of this because, although you still need some kind of bare function to begin the chain, once you've started, all parsing data can be held on the Expression Builder object that the chaining methods are defined on.

You can avoid all this globalness with Function Sequence by using *Object Scoping (385)*. In most cases this involves placing the DSL script in a subclass of an Expression Builder so that bare function calls are resolved against methods in the Expression Builder superclass. This handles both globalness problems. All the functions in the DSL are defined only in the builder class, and thus localized.

Furthermore, since these are instance methods, they connect directly to data on the builder instance to store the parsing data. That's a compelling set of advantages for the cost of placing the DSL script in a builder subclass, so that's my default option.

A further advantage of using Object Scoping is that it may support extensibility. If the DSL framework makes it easy to use a subclass of the scoping class, the user of DSL can add their own DSL methods to the language.

Both Function Sequence and Method Chaining require you to use Context Variables in order to keep track of the parse. *Nested Function (357)* is a third function combination technique that can often avoid Context Variables. Using Nested Function, the computer configuration example looks like this:

```
computer(
  processor(
    cores(2),
    speed(2500),
    i386
  ),
  disk(
    size(150)
  ),
  disk(
    size(75),
    speed(7200),
    SATA
  )
);
```

Nested Function combines functions by making function calls arguments in higher-level function calls. The result is a nesting of function invocations. Nested Functions have some powerful advantages with any kind of hierarchic structure, which is very common in parsing. One immediate advantage is that, in our example, the hierarchic structure of the configuration is echoed by the language constructs themselves—the disk function is nested inside the computer function just as the resulting framework objects are nested. The nesting of the functions thus reflects the logical syntax tree of the DSL. With Function Sequence and Method Chaining, I can only hint at that syntax tree through strange indentation conventions; Nested Function allows me to reflect that tree within the language (although I still format the code rather differently to how I'd format regular code).

Another consequence is the change in evaluation order. With a Nested Function, the arguments to a function are evaluated before the function itself. This often allows you to build up framework objects without using a Context Variable. In this case, the processor function is evaluated and can return a complete processor object before the computer function is evaluated. The computer function can then directly create a computer object with fully formed parameters.

A Nested Function thus works very well when building higher-level structures. However, it isn't perfect. The punctuation of parentheses and commas is more explicit, but it can also feel like noise compared to the indentation conventions alone. (This is where Lisp scores highly, its syntax works extremely well with Nested Functions.) A Nested Function also implies using bare functions, so it runs into the same problems of globalness as Function Sequence—albeit with the same Object Scoping cure.

The evaluation order can also lead to confusion if you are thinking in terms of a sequence of commands rather than building up a hierarchic structure. A simple sequence of Nested Functions ends up being evaluated backwards to the order they are written, as in third(second(first)). My colleague Neal Ford likes to point out that if you want to write the song "Old MacDonald Had a Farm" with Nested Functions, you'd have to write the memorable chorus phrase as o(i(e(i(e())))). Both Function Sequence and Method Chaining allow you to write the calls in the order they'll be evaluated.

Nested Function also usually loses out in that the arguments are identified by position rather than name. Consider the case of specifying a disk's size and speed. If all I need for these are two integers, then all I really need is disk(75, 7200), but that doesn't remind me which is which. I can solve that by having Nested Functions that just return the integer value and write disk(size(75), speed(7200)). That's more readable, but doesn't prevent me from writing disk(speed(7200), size(75)) and getting a disk that would probably surprise me. To avoid this problem, you end up returning some richer intermediate data—replacing the simple integer with a token object—but that's an annoying complication. Languages with keyword arguments avoid this problem but, sadly, this useful syntactic feature is very rare. In many ways, Method Chaining is a mechanism that helps you supply keyword arguments to a language that lacks them. (Soon I'll discuss *Literal Map (419)* which is another way to overcome the lack of named parameters.)

Most programmers see the heavy use of Nested Function as unusual, but this really reflects how we use these function combination patterns in normal (non-DSL) programming. Most of the time, programmers use Function Sequence with small dashes of Nested Function and (in an OO language) Method Chaining. However, if you're a Lisp programmer, Nested Function is something you use often in regular programming. Although I'm describing these patterns in the context of DSL writing, they are actually general patterns we use to combine expressions. It's just that what makes a good combination differs when we think of an internal DSL.

I've written about these patterns so far as if they were mutually exclusive, but in fact you'll usually use a combination of these (and further patterns that I'll describe later) in any particular DSL. Each pattern has its strengths and weaknesses, and different points in a DSL have different needs. Here's one possible hybrid:

```
computer(
  processor()
    .cores(2)
    .speed(2500)
    .type(i386),
  disk()
    .size(150),
  disk()
    .size(75)
    .speed(7200)
    .iface(SATA)
);
computer(
  processor()
    .cores(4)
);
```

This DSL script uses all three patterns that I've talked about so far. It uses Function Sequence to define each computer in turn, each computer function uses Nested Function for its arguments, each processor and disk is built up using Method Chaining.

The advantage of this hybrid is that each section of the example plays to the strengths of each pattern. A Function Sequence works well for defining each element of a list. It keeps each computer definition well separated into statements. It's also easy to implement, as each statement can just add a fully formed computer object to a result list.

The Nested Function for each computer eliminates the need for a Context Variable for the current computer, as the arguments are all evaluated before the computer function is called. If we assume that a computer consists of a processor and a variable number of disks, then the arguments lists of the function can capture that very well with its types. In general, Nested Function makes it safer to use global functions, as it's easier to arrange things so the global function just returns an object and doesn't alter any parsing state.

If each processor and disk have multiple optional arguments, then that works well with Method Chaining. I can call whatever values I wish to set to build up the element.

However, using a mix also introduces problems. In particular, it results in punctuational confusion: Some elements are separated with commas, others with periods, others with semicolons. As a programmer, I can figure it out—but it can also be difficult to remember which is which. A nonprogrammer, even one who is only reading the expression, is more likely to be confused. The punctuational differences are an artifact of the implementation, not the meaning of the DSL itself, so I'm exposing implementation issues to the user—always a suspicious idea.

So, in this case I wouldn't use exactly this kind of hybrid. I'd be inclined instead to use Method Chaining instead of Nested Function for the computer function. But I'd still use Function Sequence for the multiple computers, as I think that's a clearer separation for the user.

This tradeoff discussion is a microcosm of the decisions you'll need to make when building your own DSL. I can provide some indication here of the pros and cons of different patterns—but you'll have to decide on the blend that works for you.

4.4 Literal Collections

Writing a program, whether in a general-purpose language or a DSL, is about composing elements together. Programs usually compose statements into sequences, and compose by applying functions. Another way to compose elements is to use *Literal List (417)* and *Literal Map (419)*.

A Literal List captures a list of elements, either of different types or of the same type, with no fixed size. In fact, I've already slipped an example of Literal List past you. Look again at the *Nested Function (357)* version of the computer configuration code:

```
computer(
  processor(
    cores(2),
    speed(2500),
    i386
  ),
  disk(
    size(150)
  ),
  disk(
    size(75),
    speed(7200),
    SATA
  )
);
```

If I collapse the lower-level function calls here, I get code that looks like this:

```
computer(
  processor (...),
  disk(...),
  disk(...)
);
```

The contents of the call to computer is a list of elements. Indeed in a curly-brace language like Java or C#, a varargs function call like this is a common way to introduce a Literal List.

Other languages, however, give you different options. In Ruby, for example, I could represent this list using Ruby's built-in syntax for literal lists.

```
computer [
  processor(...),
  disk(...),
  disk(...)
]
```

There's little difference here, except that I have square brackets instead of parentheses, but I can use this kind of list in more contexts than just within a function call.

C-like languages do have a literal array syntax {1,2,3} that could be used as a more flexible Literal List, but you're usually quite limited as to where you can use it and what you can put in it. Other languages, like Ruby, allow you to use literal lists much more widely. You can use varargs functions to handle most of these cases, but not all of them.

Scripting languages also allow a second kind of literal collection: a Literal Map, also called hash or dictionary. With it, I can represent the computer configuration like this (again in Ruby):

```
computer(processor(:cores => 2, :type => :i386),
        disk(:size => 150),
        disk(:size => 75, :speed => 7200, :interface => :sata))
```

The Literal Map is very handy for cases like setting the processor and disk properties here. In these cases, the disk has multiple subelements all of which are optional but may only be set once each. *Method Chaining (373)* is good for naming the subelements, but you have to add your own code to ensure each disk mentions its speed only once. This is baked into the Literal Map and is familiar to people using the language.

A still better construct for this would be a function with named parameters. Smalltalk, for example, would handle this with something like diskWithSize: 75 speed: 7200 interface: #sata. However, even fewer language have named parameters than have a Literal Map syntax. But if you're using such a language, then using named parameters is a good way of implementing a Literal Map.

This example also introduces another syntactic item that's not present in curly languages: the symbol data type. A **symbol** is a data type that, on first sight, is just like a string, but is there primarily for lookups in maps, particularly *Symbol Tables (165)*. Symbols are immutable and are usually implemented so the same value of the symbol is the same object, to help with performance. Their literal form doesn't support spaces and they don't support most string operations, as their role is symbol lookup rather than holding text. Elements above, like :cores, are symbols—Ruby indicates symbols with a leading colon. In languages without symbols, you can use strings instead, but in languages with a symbol data type you should use it for this kind of purpose.

This is a good point to talk a little about why Lisp makes such an appealing language for internal DSLs. Lisp has a very convenient Literal List syntax: (one two three). It also uses the same syntax for function calls: (max 5 14 2). As a result, a Lisp program is all nested lists. Bare words (one two three) are symbols, so the syntax is all about representing nested lists of symbols, which is an excellent basis for an internal DSL—provided you're happy with your DSL having the same fundamental syntax. This simple syntax is both a great strength and a weakness of Lisp. It's a strength because it is very logical, making perfect sense if you follow it. Its weakness is that you have to follow what is an unusual syntactic form—and if you don't make that jump, it all seems like lots of irritating, silly parentheses.

4.5 Using Grammars to Choose Internal Elements

As you can see, there are many different choices for the elements of an internal DSL. One technique that you can use to choose which one to use is to consider the logical grammar of your DSL. The kinds of grammar rules that you create when using *Syntax-Directed Translation (219)* can also make sense in thinking about an internal DSL. Certain kinds of expressions, with their *BNF (229)* rules, suggest certain kinds of internal DSL structures.

Structure	BNF	Consider...
Mandatory list	`parent ::= first second third`	*Nested Function (357)*
Optional list	`parent ::= first maybeSecond? maybeThird?`	*Method Chaining (373), Literal Map (419)*
Homogenous bag	`parent ::= child*`	*Literal List (417), Function Sequence (351)*
Hetrogenous bag	`parent ::= (this | that | theOther)*`	Method Chaining
Set	n/a	Literal Map

If you have a clause of mandatory elements (parent ::= first second), then Nested Function works well. The arguments of a Nested Function can match the rule elements directly. If you have strong typing, then type-aware autocompletion can suggest the correct items for each spot.

A list with optional elements (parent ::= first maybeSecond? maybeThird?) is more awkward for Nested Function, as you can easily end up with a combinatorial explosion of possibilities. In this case, Method Chaining usually works better as the method call indicates which element you are using. The tricky element with Method Chaining is that you have to do some work to ensure you only have one use of each item in the rule.

A clause with multiple items of the same subelement (parent ::= child*) works well with a Literal List. If the expression defines statements at the top level of your language, then this is one of the few places I'd consider Function Sequence.

With multiple elements of different subelements (parent ::= (this | that | theOther)*), I'd move back to Method Chaining since, again, the method name is a good signal of which element you are looking at.

A set of subelements is a common case that doesn't fit well with BNF. This is where you have multiple children, but each child can only appear at most once. You can also think of this as a mandatory list where the children can appear in any order. A Literal Map is a logical choice here; the issue you'll normally run into is the inability to communicate and enforce the correct key names.

Grammar rules of the at-least-once form (parent ::= child+) don't lend themselves well to the internal DSL constructs. The best bet is to use the general multiple element forms and check for at least one call during the parse.

4.6 Closures

Closures are a programming language capability that's been around for a long time in some programming language circles (such as Lisp and Smalltalk) but that has only recently begun to raise its head in more mainstream languages. They go under various names (lambdas, blocks, anonymous functions). A short description of what they do is this: They allow you to take some inline code and package it up into an object that can be passed around and evaluated whenever it suits you. (If you've not come across them yet, you should read *Closure (397)*.)

In internal DSLs, we use closures as *Nested Closures (403)* within DSL scripts. A Nested Closure has three properties that make it handy for use in DSLs: inline nesting, deferred evaluation, and limited-scope variables.

When I talked earlier about *Nested Function (357)*, I said that one of its great features is that it allows you to capture the hierarchic nature of the DSL in a way that is meaningful to the host programming language, instead of suggesting the hierarchy with indentation, as you have to do with *Function Sequence (351)* and *Method Chaining (373)*. A Nested Closure also has this property, with the additional advantage that you can put any inline code into the nesting—hence the term **inline nesting**. Most languages have restrictions on what you can put into function arguments, which limits what you can write in a Nested Function, but a Nested Closure allows you to break those limitations. This way you can nest more complicated structures, such as allowing a Function Sequence inside the Nested Closure in a way that wouldn't be possible inside a Nested Function. There's also an advantage in that many languages make it easier to syntactically nest multiple lines inside a Nested Closure than inside a Nested Function.

Deferred evaluation is perhaps the most important capability that Nested Closure adds. With Nested Function, the arguments to the function are evaluated before the enclosing function is called. Sometimes this is helpful, but sometimes (as in the Old MacDonald example) it's confusing. With a Nested Closure, you have complete control about when the closures are evaluated. You can alter the order of evaluation, not evaluate some at all, or store all the closures for later evaluation. This becomes particularly handy when the *Semantic Model (159)* is one that takes strong control of the way a program executes—a form of model that I call an *Adaptive Model (487)* and will describe in much more detail in "Alternative Computational Models," p. 113. In these cases, a DSL can include sections of host code within the DSL and put these code blocks into the Semantic Model. This allows you to intermix DSL and host code more freely.

The final property is that a Nested Closure allows you to introduce new variables whose scope is limited to that closure. By using **limited-scope variables** it can be easier to see what the methods in the language are acting on.

Now is a good time for an example to illustrate some of this. I'll start by another example for the computer builder.

```ruby
#ruby...
  ComputerBuilder.build do |c|
    c.processor do |p|
      p.cores 2
      p.i386
      p.speed 2.2
    end
    c.disk do |d|
      d.size 150
    end
    c.disk do |d|
      d.size 75
      d.speed 7200
      d.sata
    end
  end
```

(I use Ruby here, as Java doesn't have closures whereas C#'s closure syntax is a bit too noisy and thus doesn't really show the value of a Nested Closure.)

Here we see a good example of inline nesting. The calls to processor and disk both contain code which is several statements of Ruby. This also illustrates limited-scope variables for the computer, processor, and disks. These variables add a bit of noise, but can make it easier for people to see what objects are being manipulated where. It also means that this code doesn't need global functions or *Object Scoping (385)*, for functions such as speed are defined on the limited-scope variables (which in this case are *Expression Builders (343)*).

With a DSL like the computer configuration, there isn't really much need for deferred evaluation. This property of closures kicks in more when you want to embed bits of host code in the structure of a model.

Consider an example of where you want to use a set of validation rules. Commonly, in an object-oriented environment we think of an object being valid or not, and have some code somewhere to check its validity. Validation may be more involved in that it's often contextual—you validate an object in order to do something to it. If I'm looking at data about a person, I might have different validation rules to check if that person is eligible for one insurance policy rather than another. I might specify the rules in a DSL form like this:

```
// C#...
  class ExampleValidation : ValidationEngineBuilder {
    protected override void build() {
      Validate("Annual Income is present")
        .With(p => p.AnnualIncome != null);
      Validate("positive Annual Income")
        .With(p => p.AnnualIncome >= 0);
```

In this example, the contents of the function call With is a closure that takes a person as an argument and contains some arbitrary C# code. This code can be stored in the Semantic Model and executed as the model runs—which provides a lot of flexibility in choosing your validations.

Nested Closure is a very useful DSL pattern, but it's often frustratingly awkward to use. Many languages (such as Java) don't support closures. You can get around a lack of closures with other techniques, such as function pointers in C or command objects in an OO language. Such techniques are valuable to support Adaptive Models in such languages. However, these mechanisms require a lot of unwieldy syntax that can add a debilitating amount of noise to a DSL.

Even languages that do support closures often do so with an awkward syntax. C#'s has got steadily better with ongoing versions, but is still not as clean as I'd like. I was used to Smalltalk's very clean closure syntax. Ruby's closure syntax is almost as clean as Smalltalk's, which is why Nested Closures are so common in Ruby. Oddly enough, Lisp, despite it's first-class support for closures, also has an awkward syntax for them—which it deals with by using macros.

4.7 Parse Tree Manipulation

Since I've invoked the name of Lisp and its macros, there's a natural segue into *Parse Tree Manipulation (455)*. The segue is there because of Lisp's macros, which are widely used to make closures more syntactically palatable, but perhaps find their greatest power in being able to do some clever code writing tricks.

The basic idea behind Parse Tree Manipulation is to take an expression in the host programming language and, instead of evaluating it, get its result—to consider the parse tree as data. Consider this expression in C#: aPerson.Age > 18. If I take this expression with a binding for the variable aPerson and evaluate it, I'll get a Boolean result. An alternative, available in some languages, is to process this expression to yield the parse tree for the expression (Figure 4.2).

When I have the parse tree like this, I can manipulate it at runtime to do all sorts of interesting things. One example is to walk the parse tree and generate a

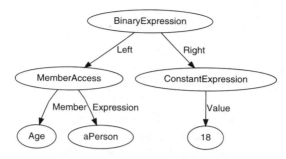

Figure 4.2   *A parse tree representation of* `aPerson.Age > 18`

query in another query language, such as SQL. This is essentially what .NET's Linq language does. Linq allows you to express many SQL queries in C#, which many programmers prefer.

The strength of Parse Tree Manipulation is in allowing you to write expressions in the host language that can then be converted into different expressions that populate the *Semantic Model (159)* in ways that are beyond just storing the closure itself.

In C#'s case above, this manipulation is done with an object model representation of the parse tree. In Lisp's case, this manipulation is done by macro transformations on Lisp source code. Lisp is well suited to this because the structure of its source code is very close to that of a syntax tree. Parse Tree Manipulation is more widely used in Lisp for DSL work—so much so that Lispers often wail at the lack of macros in other languages. My view is that manipulating an object model of the parse tree in C# style is a more effective way of doing Parse Tree Manipulation than Lisp macros—although this may be due to my lack of practice with Lisp's macro processing.

Whatever mechanism you use, the next question is how important Parse Tree Manipulation is as a technique for DSLs. One very prominent use is in Linq—a Microsoft technology that allows you to express query conditions in C# and turn them into different query languages for various target data structures. In this way, one C# query can be turned into SQL for relational databases and XPath for XML structures, or kept in C# for in-memory C# structures. It's essentially a mechanism that allows application code to do runtime code translation, generating arbitrary code from C# expressions.

Parse Tree Manipulation is a powerful, but somewhat complex, technique that hasn't been supported much by languages in the past, but these days has been getting a lot more attention due to its support in C# 3 and Ruby. Since it's relatively new (at least outside the Lisp world), it's hard to evaluate how truly useful it is. My current perception is that it's a marginal technique—something that is rarely needed but very handy on the occasions when that need arises. Translating queries to multiple data targets the way Linq does is a perfect example of its usefulness; time will tell what other applications may emerge.

4.8 Annotation

When the C# language was launched, many programmers sneered that it was really just a warmed-over Java. They had a point, although there's no need to sneer at a well-executed implementation of proven ideas. However, one example of a feature that wasn't a copy of mainstream ideas was **attributes**, a language feature later copied by Java under the name of *Annotations (445)*. (I will use the Java name since "attribute" is such an overloaded term in programming.)

An Annotation allows a programmer to attach metadata to programming constructs, such as classes and methods. These annotations can be read during compilation or at runtime.

For an example, let's assume we wish to declare that certain fields can only have a limited valid range. We can do this with an annotation like this:

```
class PatientVisit...
  @ValidRange(lower = 1, upper = 1000, units = Units.LB)
  private Quantity weight;
  @ValidRange(lower = 1, upper = 120, units = Units.IN)
  private Quantity height;
```

The obvious alternative to this would be to put range-checking code into the setter of the field. However, the annotation has a number of advantages. It reads more clearly as a bound for the field, it makes it easy to check the range either when setting the attribute or in a later object validation step, and it specifies the validation rule in such a way that could be read to configure a GUI widget.

Some languages provide a specific language feature for such number ranges (I remember Pascal did). You can think of Annotations as a way of extending the language to support new keywords and capabilities. Indeed, even existing keywords might have been done better with Annotations—from a green field I'd argue that access modifiers (private, public, etc.) would be better that way.

Since Annotations are so closely bound to the host language, they are suited for fragmentary DSLs and not stand-alone DSLs. In particular, they are good at providing a very integrated feel of adding domain-specific enhancements to the host language.

The similarities between Java's annotations and .NET's attributes are pretty clear, but there are other language constructs that look different while doing essentially the same thing. Here's Ruby on Rails' way of specifying an upper limit for the size of a string:

```
class Person
  validates_length_of :last_name, :maximum => 30
```

The syntax is different in that you indicate which field the validation applies to by providing the name of the field (:last_name) rather than placing the Annotations next to the field. The implementation is also different in that this is actually a class method that's executed when the class is loaded into the running system, rather than a particular language feature. Despite these differences, it's still about adding metadata to program elements, and it's used in a way similar to Annotations. So I think it's reasonable to consider it essentially the same concept.

4.9 Literal Extension

One of the things that have caused the recent spike in interest in DSLs is the use of DSL expressions in Ruby on Rails. A common example of its DSL expressions is a fragment like 5.days.ago. Most of that expression is *Method Chaining (373)*, such as we've already seen. The new part is the fact that the chain begins on a literal integer. The tricky bit here is that integers are provided by the language or by standard libraries. In order to start a chain like this, you need to use *Literal Extension (481)*. To do this, you need to be able to add methods to external library classes—which may or may not be a capability of the host language. Java, for example, does not support this. C# (through extension methods) and Ruby do.

One of the dangers of Literal Extension is that it adds methods globally, while they should only be used within the often limited context of DSL usage. This is a problem with Ruby, compounded by the fact that there's no easy mechanism in the language to find where the extension was added. C# handles this by putting extension methods in a namespace that you need to explicitly import before you can use them.

Literal Extension is one of those things that you don't need to use terribly often, but can be very handy when you do—it really gives the sense of customizing the language for your domain.

4.10 Reducing the Syntactic Noise

The point of internal DSLs is that they are just expressions in the host language, written in a form that makes them read well as a language. One of the consequences of this form is that they bring with them the syntactic structure of the host language. In some ways this is good, as it provides a syntax familiar to many programmers, but others find some of the syntax annoying.

One way to reduce the burden of this syntax is write chunks of DSL in a syntax that is very close the host language, but not exactly the same, and then use simple text substitution to convert it to the host language. This *Textual Polishing (477)* can convert a phrase like 3 hours ago to 3.hours.ago or, more ambitiously, 3% if value at least $30000 to percent(3).when.minimum(30000).

While it's a technique I've seen described a few times, I have to say I'm not a big fan of it. The substitutions get convoluted pretty quickly, and when they do it's much easier to use a full external DSL.

Another approach is to use syntax coloring. Most text editors provide customizable text coloring schemes. When communicating with domain experts, you can use a special scheme that de-emphasizes any noisy syntax, for example by coloring it a light grey on white background. You can even go so far as to make it disappear by coloring it the same as the background.

4.11 Dynamic Reception

One of the properties of dynamic languages, such as Smalltalk or Ruby, is that they process method invocations at runtime. As a result, if you write aPerson.name and no name method is defined on the person, the code will compile happily and only raise an error at runtime (unlike C# or Java, where you will get a compilation error). While many people see this as a problem, dynamic language advocates can take advantage of this.

The usual mechanism used by these languages is to handle such an unexpected call by routing it to a special method. The default action of this special method (method_missing in Ruby, doesNotUnderstand in Smalltalk) is to raise an error, but programmers can override the method to do other things. I call this overriding *Dynamic Reception (427)* since you are making a dynamic (runtime) choice on what is a legal method to receive. Dynamic Reception can lead to a number of useful idioms in programming, particularly when using proxies where you often want to wrap an object and do something with its method invocations without needing to know exactly which methods are being called.

In DSL work, a common use of Dynamic Reception is to move information from method arguments into the method name itself. A good example of this is Rails Active Record's dynamic finders. If you have a person class with a firstname field, you may want to find people by their first names. Instead of defining a find method for every field, you could have a generic find method that takes the field name as argument: people.find_by("firstname", "martin"). This works, but feels a bit odd since you would expect "firstname" to be part of the method name rather than a parameter. Dynamic Reception allows you to write people.find_by_firstname("martin") without having to define the method in advance. You override the missing method handler to see if the invoked method begins with find_by, process the name to extract the field name, and turn it into an invocation of the fully parametrized method. You can do this all in one method, or in separate methods, such as people.find.by.firstname("martin").

The crux of Dynamic Reception is that it gives you the option to move information from parameters to method names, which in some cases can make expressions easier to read and understand. The danger is that it can only take so much—you don't want to find yourself doing complicated structures in a sequence of method names. If you need anything more complicated than a single list of things, consider using something with more structure (such as *Nested Function (357)* or *Nested Closure (403)*) instead. Dynamic Reception also works best when you are doing the same basic processing with each call, such as building up a query based on property names. If you are handling dynamically received calls differently (i.e., you have different code to process firstname and lastname), then you should be writing explicit methods without relying on Dynamic Reception.

4.12 Providing Some Type Checking

Having looked at something that requires a dynamic language, it's now time to flip over into the world of static languages and look at some ways to benefit from static type checking.

There is a long-running, and potentially endless, debate about whether it's better to have static type checking in a language or not. I don't really want to revisit that here. Many people consider type checking at compile time to be very valuable, while others claim that you don't find many errors from such type checking that aren't caught by good tests—which are always needed.

There's a second argument in favor of using static typing. One of the great benefits of modern IDEs is that they provide some excellent support based on static typing. I can type the name of a variable, hit a control key combination, and get a list of methods that I can invoke on that variable based on the variable's type. The IDE can do this because it knows the types of the symbols in the code.

Most similar symbols in a DSL, however, don't have this support, because we need to represent them as strings or symbol data types and hold them in our own symbol table. Consider this fragment of Ruby from the gothic security example (p. 14):

```
state :waitingForLight do
  transitions :lightOn => :unlockedPanel
end
```

Here :waitingForLight is a symbol data type. If we were to translate this code into Java, we'd see something like this:

```
state("waitingForLight")
      .transition("lightOn").to("unlockedPanel");
```

Again, our symbols are just primitive strings. I have to wrap waitingForLight in a method so I can chain methods onto it. When I'm entering the target state, I have to type `unlockedPanel` rather than select from a list of states with the IDE's autocompletion mechanism.

What I'd rather have is this:

```
waitingForLight
      .transition(lightOn).to(unlockedPanel)
      ;
```

This not only reads better, avoiding the state method and noisy quotes; I also get proper type-aware autocompletion for my triggering events and target states. I can make full use of the IDE's capabilities.

To do this, I need a way to declare symbol types (such as `state`, `command`, `event`) in my DSL processing mechanism, and then declare the symbols I use in a particular DSL script (such as `lightOn` or `waitingForLight`). One way of doing this is a *Class Symbol Table (467)*. In this approach, the DSL processor defines each symbol type as a class. When I write a script, I put it in a class and declare fields for my symbols. So, to define a list of states, I begin by creating a `States` class for the symbol type. I define the states used in a script by a field declaration.

```
Class BasicStateMachine...
   States idle, active, waitingForLight, waitingForDrawer, unlockedPanel;
```

The result, like many DSL constructs, looks rather strange. I would never normally advocate a plural name for a class such as used here for `States`. But it does result in an editing experience that meshes much more closely with the general experience of Java programming.

Chapter 5

Implementing an External DSL

With internal DSLs, you can do a great deal to define a language that has that elusive flow, but in the end you are always limited by conforming to the syntactic structure of the host language. External DSLs provide a greater syntactic freedom—the ability to use any syntax you like.

Implementing an external DSL differs from internal DSLs in that the parsing process operates on pure text input which is not constrained by any particular language. The techniques we can use to parse text are essentially those that have been in use for decades in parsing programming languages. There is also a long-running language community developing these tools and techniques.

But there is a catch. The tools and writings of the programming language community almost always assume you are working with a general-purpose language. DSLs are lucky to get a mention in passing. While many of the principles apply equally to general-purpose and domain-specific languages, there are differences. In addition, you don't need to understand as much to work with DSLs, which essentially means you don't need to go all the way up the learning curve that you'd need to go for a general-purpose language.

5.1 Syntactic Analysis Strategy

When we're parsing an external DSL, we need to take the stream of text and break it up into some kind of structure that we can use to figure out what that text says. This initial structuring is referred to as syntactic analysis. Let's consider the following code which might be a variation on programming my introductory state machine ("Gothic Security," p. 3).

```
event doorClosed  D1CL
event drawerOpened D2OP
command unlockPanel PNUL
command lockPanel PNLK
```

Syntactic analysis is about recognizing that the line `event doorClosed D1CL` is an event definition and telling it apart from a command definition.

The simplest way to do it is one that, I'm sure, you've done yourself, even if you've never dabbled with serious parsing. Divide the input text into lines, then process each line. If it starts with `event`, you know it's an event; if it starts with `command` you know it's a command. You can then break up the line accordingly to find the key bits of information. This style I refer to as *Delimiter-Directed Translation (201)*. The general idea is to pick some delimiter characters that break the input into statements (usually line endings), chop the input into separate statements using that delimiter, and then feed each chunk into a separate processing step to figure out what's on the line. Usually, there's some clear marker in the line that tells you what kind of statement you are dealing with.

Delimiter-Directed Translation is very simple to use and uses tools that most programmers are familiar with—string splitting and regular expressions. Its limitation is that it doesn't give you any inherent way to handle the hierarchic context of your input.

Let's assume that I formulated my definitions thus:

```
events
  doorClosed  D1CL
  drawerOpened  D2OP
end

commands
  unlockPanel PNUL
  lockPanel   PNLK
end
```

Now splitting it up into lines isn't quite enough. There isn't enough information on the line `doorClosed D1CL` to tell if this is an event or a command I'm defining. There are ways to do this (and I explore one in an example for Delimiter-Directed Translation) but you'll have to do it yourself. The more hierarchic context you get, the more effort you have to spend on managing it yourself.

In order to handle DSLs with this kind of structure, the next step is to use *Syntax-Directed Translation (219)*. In this technique, we first define a formal grammar for the input language, for example:

```
list : eventList commandList;
eventList : 'events' eventDec* 'end';
eventDec  : identifier identifier;
commandList : 'commands' commandDec* 'end';
commandDec : identifier identifier;
```

If you've read any book on programming languages, you've encountered the notion of a grammar. A grammar is a way of defining the legal syntax of a programming language. Grammars are almost always written in some form of *BNF (229)*. Each line is a production rule; it states a name followed by the legal elements of that rule. So, in the above example, the line `list : eventList commandList;`

says that the element list consists of an eventList followed by a commandList. Items in quotes are literals and a "*" indicates that the preceding element may appear many times. So eventList : 'events' eventDec* 'end'; says that an event list consists of the word events followed by some number of eventDecs, followed by the word end.

A grammar is a good way of thinking about the syntax of a language, whether you are using Syntax-Directed Translation or not. Indeed it's helpful for thinking about internal DSLs as well, as illustrated by my table for internal DSL elements ("Using Grammars to Choose Internal Elements," p. 79). It works particularly well for Syntax-Directed Translation because you can translate it fairly mechanically into a parser.

The kind of parser that's generated from Syntax-Directed Translation is very capable of handling hierarchic structures like these; after all, this kind of thing is essential for general-purpose languages. As a result, you can handle many things that are awkward with Delimiter-Directed Translation much more easily.

How do you go from a grammar to a parser? As mentioned earlier, it's a pretty mechanical process, and there are various ways to turn a BNF into some kind of parsing algorithm. There are many years of research into doing this, and that research spawned lots of techniques. In this book, I've selected three broad approaches.

Recursive Descent Parser (245) is a classic way to perform this conversion. The recursive descent algorithm is an easy to understand approach to parsing that takes each grammar rule and turns it into a control flow representation inside a function. Each rule in the grammar turns into a function in the parser, and there are clear patterns you follow to turn each BNF operator into control flow.

A more hip and modern way is the *Parser Combinator (255)*. Here, each rule is turned into an object, and we compose the objects into a structure that mirrors the grammar. You still need the elements of the Recursive Descent Parser, but these are packaged up into combinator objects that you can just compose together. This allows you to implement a grammar without knowing the details of the Recursive Descent Parser algorithms.

The third option does much of what this book is all about. A *Parser Generator (269)* takes a flavor of BNF and uses it as a DSL. You write your grammar in this DSL, and Parser Generator then generates a parser for you.

The Parser Generator is the most sophisticated approach; such tools are very mature and can handle complex languages very efficiently. Using BNF as a DSL makes it easy to understand and maintain the language, since its syntax is clearly defined and automatically tied to the parser. On the downside, they do take a bit of time to learn and, since they mostly use code generation, they complicate the build process. You may also not have a good Parser Generator available for your language platform, and it's not trivial to write one yourself.

A Recursive Descent Parser may be less powerful and efficient, but it is powerful and efficient enough for a DSL. It thus makes a reasonable option if the Parser Generator isn't available or feels too heavyweight to introduce. The biggest problem with Recursive Descent Parser is that the grammar gets lost in the control flow, which makes the code far less explicit than I'd like.

As a result, I prefer the Parser Combinator for cases where you can't or don't want to use a Parser Generator. A Parser Combinator follows basically the same algorithm as a Recursive Descent Parser but allows you to represent the grammar explicitly in the code that composes the combinators together. While this code may not be quite as clear as a true BNF, it can be pretty close — particularly if you introduce internal DSL techniques.

With either of these three techniques, Syntax-Directed Translation makes it much easier than Delimiter-Directed Translation to handle languages that have any kind of structure to them. The biggest downside of Syntax-Directed Translation is that it's a technique that isn't as widely known as it should be. Many people are under the impression that using it is quite hard. I think that this fear often comes from the fact that Syntax-Directed Translation is usually described in the context of parsing a general-purpose language—which introduces a lot of complexities that you don't face with a DSL. I hope this book will encourage you to try and work with Syntax-Directed Translation for yourself, and you'll discover that it's really not that tough to do.

For most of this book, I'm going to use Parser Generator. I find that the maturity of the tooling and the explicitness of the grammar make it easier to talk about the various concepts that I want to explain. In particular, I use the ANTLR Parser Generator—a mature, widely available, open source tool. One of its advantages is that it is a sophisticated form of a Recursive Descent Parser, which means it fits in well with the understanding you may get by using Recursive Descent Parser or Parser Combinator. Particularly if you are new to Syntax-Directed Translation, I think ANTLR is a good place to start.

5.2 Output Production Strategy

When we want to parse some input, we have to know what we want to do with the result—what is our output going to be? I've already argued that most of the time, the output we should build is a *Semantic Model (159)*, which we can then either interpret directly or use as an input for code generation. I won't rehash that argument again now, other than to point out that this is immediately a significant difference to the underlying assumptions you may find in the established language community.

Within that community, there is a strong emphasis on code generation, and parsers are usually constructed to directly produce the output code with no Semantic Model in sight. This is a reasonable approach for general-purpose languages, but it isn't the approach I suggest for DSLs. This difference is important to bear in mind when you read material produced by the language community—which includes most documentation for tools such as *Parser Generators (269)*.

Given that our output is a Semantic Model, our options boil down to using one or two steps. The single-step way is *Embedded Translation (299)*, where you place calls directly in the parser to create the Semantic Model during the parsing process. In this approach, you gradually build up the Semantic Model while you are going through the parse. As soon as you understand enough of the input to recognize a part of the Semantic Model, you go ahead and create it. Often you'll need some intermediate parsing data before you can actually create the objects in the Semantic Model—this usually involves storing some information in *Symbol Tables (165)*

The alternative route is the two-step route—*Tree Construction (281)*. In this approach, you parse the input text and produce a syntax tree that captures the essential structure of that text. You also populate a Symbol Table to handle cross-references between different parts of the tree. You then run a second phase that walks the syntax tree and populates the Semantic Model.

The great advantage of using Tree Construction is that this splits up the task of parsing into two simpler tasks. While recognizing the input text, you can focus only on how to build up the syntax tree. Indeed, many Parser Generators provide a DSL for tree construction that further simplifies this part of the process. Walking the tree to populate the Semantic Model is then a more regular programming exercise, and you have the whole tree to examine in order to determine what to do. If you've written code to process XML, you can liken Embedded Translation to using SAX and Tree Construction to using a DOM.

There is also a third option—*Embedded Interpretation (305)*. Embedded Interpretation runs an interpretation process during the parse itself, and its output is the final result. A classic example of Embedded Interpretation is a calculator that takes in arithmetic expressions and produces the answer as a result. Therefore, Embedded Interpretation doesn't produce a Semantic Model. Although Embedded Interpretation does come up from time to time, it's a rare case.

You can also use Embedded Translation and Tree Construction without a Semantic Model; indeed, this is quite common when using code generation. Most examples you see of Parser Generators will do one of these. Although it may make sense, particularly for simpler cases, it's an approach I recommend only rarely. Usually I find the Semantic Model overwhelmingly helpful.

So, most of the time the choice is between Embedded Translation and Tree Construction. This decision depends on the costs and benefits of that intermediate syntax tree. The great benefit of Tree Construction is that it splits the parsing problem into two. Usually it's easier to combine two simple tasks than to write one more complicated task. This becomes increasingly true as the complexity of the overall translation increases. The more involved the DSL and the greater the distance between the DSL and the Semantic Model, the more useful it is to have an intermediate syntax tree, particularly if you have tooling support to create an abstract syntax tree.

I seem to be making a convincing argument here for Tree Construction. Certainly, a common argument against it—the memory that the syntax tree takes up—withers away when processing small DSLs on modern hardware. But despite the many reasons that favor Tree Construction, I'm not entirely convinced—sometimes it feels that building up and walking the tree is more trouble than it's worth. I have to write the code to create the tree and code to walk it—often, it's easier to just build the Semantic Model right there and then.

So, I'm conflicted on the choice. Other than the vague notion that increasing complexity of translation favors Tree Construction, I have mixed feelings. My best advice is to try a little of both and see which you prefer.

5.3 Parsing Concepts

If you start reading about parsing and using *Parser Generators (269)*, you'll soon run into a whole bunch of fundamental concepts of that world. In order to make sense of *Syntax-Directed Translation (219)*, you'll need to understand many of these, albeit not to the extent that traditional compiler books assume, since we're dealing with DSLs rather than general-purpose languages here.

5.3.1 Separated Lexing

Usually *Syntax-Directed Translation (219)* is divided into two stages, lexing (also scanning or tokenizing) and syntactic analysis (also referred to, confusingly, as parsing). The lexing stage takes the input text and transforms it into a stream of tokens. Tokens are a data type with two primary attributes: type and content. In our state machine language, the text state idle would turn into two tokens.

```
[content: "state", type: state-keyword]
[content: "idle", type: identifier]
```

It's pretty easy to write a lexer using a *Regex Table Lexer (239)*. This is simply a list of rules that match regular expressions to token types. You read the input stream, find the first regexp that matches, create a token of the corresponding type, and repeat all that with the next part of the stream.

The syntactic analyzer then takes this stream of tokens and arranges it into a syntax tree, based on the grammar rules. However, the fact that the lexer does its work first has some significant consequences. Firstly, it means that I have to be careful about how I use my text. I might have a state declared like this: state initial state, intending to name my state initial state. This is tricky because, by default, the lexer will classify the second "state" as a state keyword, not an identifier. To avoid this, I have to use some scheme of *Alternative Tokenization (319)*. There are various ways to do Alternative Tokenization, depending a great deal on my parser tool.

The second consequence of this is that whitespace is generally discarded before the parser gets to see anything. This makes syntactic whitespace more difficult to deal with. **Syntactic whitespace** is whitespace that is part of the syntax of the language—such as using newlines as statement separators (*Newline Separators (333)*) or using indentation to indicate structure in the manner of Python.

Syntactic whitespace is inherently a knotty area because it intermixes the syntactic structure of the language with formatting. In many ways, it makes sense for these to match—our eye uses formatting to infer structure, so it's advantageous for the language to use it the same way. However, there's just enough edge cases where the two needs don't quite line up, which introduces a lot of complications. This is why many language people really hate syntactic whitespace. I've included some information on Newline Separators here, as they are a common form of syntactic whitespace, but I ran out of time to dig into syntactic indentation in any depth, leaving only enough time for a few notes in "Syntactic Indentation," p. 337.

The reason for the lexer to be separated like this is that it makes it much easier to write each of the two elements. It's another case of decomposing a complicated task into two simpler tasks. It also improves performance, particularly on the more limited hardware that many of these tools were originally designed for.

5.3.2 Grammars and Languages

If you were exceptionally sharp-eyed earlier on, you might have noticed that I talked about writing *a* grammar for a language. Many people have the misconception that one can have *the* grammar for a language. While it's true that a grammar formally defines the syntax of a language, it's quite easy for more than one grammar to recognize the same language.

Let's take the following input, from the gothic security system:

```
events
   doorClosed  D1CL
   drawOpened  D2OP
end
```

I can write a grammar for this input that looks like this:

```
eventBlock    : Event-keyword eventDec* End-keyword;
eventDec      : Identifier Identifier;
```

But I can also write a grammar that looks like this:

```
eventBlock    : Event-keyword eventList End-keyword;
eventList     : eventDec*
eventDec      : Identifier Identifier;
```

Both of these are valid grammars for this language. They will both recognize the input—meaning they will turn the input text into a parse tree. The resulting parse trees will be different, and thus the way I write my output generation code will differ.

There are many reasons for why you can get different grammars. The primary reason is that different *Parser Generators (269)* use different grammars, in terms of both syntax and semantics. Even with a single Parser Generator, you can have different grammars depending on how you factor your rules, which is the variation I've shown above. Just like with any code, you refactor your grammars to make them easier to understand. Another aspect that alters how you factor your grammar is the output production code; I often end up altering my grammar to make it easier to organize the code that translates source into the semantic model.

5.3.3 Regular, Context-Free, and Context-Sensitive Grammars

This is a good moment to dip our toes in some language theory, in particular the way in which the programming language community classifies grammars. This scheme, called the **Chomsky hierarchy**, was developed by the linguist Noam Chomsky in the 1950's. It was based on looking at natural languages, rather than computer languages, but it derives its classification from the mathematical properties of a grammar used to define their syntactic structure.

Regular, context-free, and context-sensitive are the three categories that concern us. They form a hierarchy, in that all grammars that are regular are context-free, and all grammars that are context-free are context-sensitive. The Chomsky hierarchy strictly applies to grammars, but people use it for languages too. To say that a language is regular means that you can write a regular grammar for it.

The difference between the classes depends on certain mathematical characteristics of the grammar. I'll leave that to proper language books to explain; for our purposes, the key distinction is what kind of fundamental algorithm you need for the parser.

A **regular grammar** is important to us because it can be processed using a **finite-state machine**. This is important because regular expressions are finite-state machines, hence a regular language can be parsed using regular expressions.

In terms of computer languages, regular grammars have one big problem: They can't deal with nested elements. A regular language can parse an expression like 1 + 2 * 3 + 4 but can't parse 1 + (2 * (3 + 4)). You may hear people saying that regular grammars "can't count." In parsing terms this means that you can't use a finite-state machine to parse a language that has nested blocks. Obviously, this is bit of a bummer when it comes to computer languages, as any general-purpose language has be able to do arithmetic. It also affects block structure—programs like this:

```
for (int i in numbers) {
  if (isInteresting(i)) {
    doSomething(i);
  }
}
```

need nested blocks, so are not regular.

To handle nested blocks, you need to step up to a context-free grammar. I find this name rather confusing, because the way I look at things, a context-free grammar does add hierarchic context to your grammar, allowing it to "count." A **context-free grammar** can be implemented using a **push-down machine**, which is a finite-state machine with a stack. Most language parsers use context-free grammars, most *Parser Generators (269)* use them, and both *Recursive Descent Parser (245)* and *Parser Combinator (255)* produce a push-down machine. As a result, most modern programming languages are parsed using context-free grammars.

Although context-free grammars are so widely used, they can't handle all the syntactic rules that we might like. The common exception case to context-free grammars is the rule that you must declare a variable before you use it. The problem here is that the declaration of a variable often occurs outside the particular branch of the hierarchy you are in when you use the variable. While a context-free grammar can hold hierarchic context, that's not enough context to handle this case—hence the need for *Symbol Tables (165)*.

The next step up in the Chomsky hierarchy is context-sensitive grammars. A context-sensitive grammar could handle this case, but we don't know how to write general context-sensitive parsers. In particular, we don't know how to generate a parser from a context-sensitive grammar.

I made this dip into language classification theory primarily because it gives you some insight into which tool to use for processing a DSL. In particular, it tells you that if you use nested blocks, you'll need something that can handle a context-free language. It also argues that if you need nested blocks, you're likely to be better off with *Syntax-Directed Translation (219)* rather than *Delimiter-Directed Translation (201)*.

It also suggests that if you only have a regular language, you don't need a push-down machine to process it. As it turns out, you may find that it's easier to use a push-down machine in any case. Once you've got used to using them, they are sufficiently straightforward, so it usually isn't overkill to use one even for a regular language.

This division is also part of why we see separated lexing. Lexing is usually done with a finite-state machine, while syntactic analysis uses a push-down machine. This limits what you can do in the lexer, but allows the lexer to be faster. There are exceptions to this; in particular, I use ANTLR for most examples in this book, and ANTLR uses a push-down machine for both lexing and syntactic analysis.

There are some parser tools out there that only handle regular grammars. Ragel is one better-known example. Also, you can use lexers on their own to recognize a regular grammar. However, if you're getting into Syntax-Directed Translation, I'd suggest starting with a context-free tool.

While the notions of regular and context-free grammars are the most common ones you're likely to run into, there is a relative newcomer that is also interesting.

This is a form of grammar called a **Parsing Expression Grammar (PEG)**. PEGs use a different form of grammar which can handle most context-free situations and some context-sensitive ones. PEG parsers don't tend to separate lexing, and it seems that a PEG is more usable than a context-free grammar in many situations. However, as I write this, PEGs are still relatively new, and tools are both rare and immature. This may change, of course, by the time you read this, but that's the reason I don't talk much about PEGs in this book. The best known PEG parsers are Packrat parsers.

(The line between the PEGs and more traditional parsers is not solid, however. ANTLR, for example, has incorporated many ideas from PEGs.)

5.3.4 Top-Down and Bottom-Up Parsing

There are many ways you can write a parser, and as a result, there are many kinds of *Parser Generators (269)* out there, many with interesting differences. One of the biggest distinguishing features, however, is whether a parser is top-down or bottom-up. This affects not just the way it works, but also the kinds of grammars it can work with.

A top-down parser begins with the highest level rule in the grammar, and uses it to decide what to try and match. So, in an event list grammar like this:

```
eventBlock     : Event-keyword eventDec* End-keyword;
eventDec       : Identifier Identifier;
```

with input like this:

```
events
   doorClosed  D1CL
   drawOpened  D2OP
end
```

the parser would work by first trying to match an eventBlock and therefore looking for an event keyword. Once it sees the event keyword, it then knows it wants to match an eventDec and looks inside that rule to know if it needs to match an identifier. In short, a top-down parser uses the rules as goals to direct it what to look for.

It won't shock you if I say that a bottom-up parser does the opposite. It starts by reading the event keyword, then checks if the input so far is enough to match a rule. As it isn't (yet), it puts it aside (this is called *shifting*) and takes the next token (an identifier). This is still not enough to match anything, so it shifts again. But with the second identifier, it can now match the eventDec rule, so it can now *reduce* the two identifiers to an eventDec. It similarly recognizes the second line of input; then, when it reaches the end keyword, it can reduce the whole expression to an event block.

You will often hear top-down parsers referred to as LL parsers and bottom-up parsers as LR parsers. The first letter refers to the direction in which the input is scanned, and the second to how the rules are recognized (L is left-to-right, i.e. top-down, R is right-to-left, hence bottom-up). You will also hear bottom-up parsing referred to as shift-reduce parsing, as the shift-reduce approach is the most likely approach to bottom-up parsing that you'll run into. There are a number of variants of LR parsers, such as LALR, GLR, and SLR. I'm not going to go into the details of these variations here.

Bottom-up parsers are usually considered harder to write and understand than top-down ones. This is because most people find it harder to visualize the order in which the rules are processed with a bottom-up approach. While you don't have to worry about writing a parser if you use a Parser Generator, you often have to understand, roughly, how it works in order to debug problems. Probably the best-known family of Parser Generators is the Yacc family, which is a bottom-up (LALR) parser.

The recursive descent algorithm is a top-down parsing algorithm. As a result, *Recursive Descent Parser (245)* is a top-down parser, as is *Parser Combinator (255)*. If that's not enough, the ANTLR Parser Generator is also based on recursive descent, and is thus top-down.

The big disadvantage for top-down parsers is that they cannot deal with **left recursion**, which is a rule of the form:

```
expr: expr '+' expr;
```

Rules like this push the parser into an endless recursion trying to match expr. People disagree about how big a problem this limitation is in practice. There is a simple, mechanical technique called left-factoring that you can use to get rid of left recursion, but the result is a grammar that isn't as easy to follow. The good news for top-down parsers, however, is that you only really run into this problem when dealing with *Nested Operator Expressions (327)*, and once you understand the idioms for Nested Operator Expressions, you can churn them out relatively mechanically. The resulting grammar will still be not as clear as for a bottom-up parser, but knowing the idiom will get you there much quicker.

In general, different Parser Generators have various restrictions on the kind of grammars they can handle. These restrictions are driven by the parsing algorithms they use. There are also plenty of other differences, such as how you write actions, how you can move data up or down the parse tree, and what the grammar syntax is like (BNF vs. EBNF). All of these affect how you write your grammar. Perhaps the most important point is to realize that you shouldn't treat the grammar as a fixed definition of the DSL. Often, you'll need to alter the grammar to make the output production work better. Like any other code, the grammar will change depending on what you want to do with it.

If you are pretty comfortable with these concepts, they probably play an important role in deciding which parser tool to use. For more casual users, they probably don't make a difference as to which tool to use, but are useful to bear in mind as they alter how you work with the chosen tool.

5.4 Mixing-in Another Language

One of the biggest dangers that you face with an external DSL is that it may accidentally evolve to become a general-purpose language. Even if things don't deteriorate that far, a DSL can easily become overly complex, particularly if you have a lot of special cases that need particular treatment but are only used rarely.

Imagine we have a DSL that allocates sales leads to salesmen based on the kind of product that's being asked for and the state in which the customer is based. We might have rules like:

```
scott handles floor_wax in WA;
helen handles floor_wax desert_topping in AZ NM;
brian handles desert_topping in WA OR ID MT;
otherwise scott
```

Now, what happens if Scott starts regularly playing golf with a big shot of Baker Industries, which gives him links into all sorts of companies called Baker This and Baker That? We decide to handle this problem by assigning to him all floor wax leads with companies whose names start with "baker" in the New England states.

There may be a dozen of special cases like this, all of which need extending the DSL in a particular direction. But including special tweaks for individual cases may add a lot of complication to the DSL. For those rare cases, it's often worthwhile to handle them using a general-purpose language by using *Foreign Code (309)*. Foreign Code embeds a small bit of a general-purpose language into the DSL. This code isn't parsed by the DSL's parser; rather, it is just slurped as a string and put into the *Semantic Model (159)* for later processing. Here, this may lead to a rule like this (using Javascript as the foreigner):

```
scott handles floor_wax in MA RI CT when {/^Baker/.test(lead.name)};
```

This isn't as clear as extending the DSL would be, but this mechanism can handle a wide range of cases. Should regex matching become a common condition, we can always extend the language later.

In this case, the general-purpose language I've used is Javascript. Using a dynamic language is useful for Foreign Code because it allows you to read and interpret the DSL script. You can also do Foreign Code with a static language, but then you have to use code generation and weave the host code into the generated code. This technique is familiar to people who use *Parser Generators (269)* since this is how most Parser Generators work.

This example uses general-purpose code, but you can also use the same technique with another DSL. This approach would allow you to use different DSLs for different aspects of your problem—which very much fits the philosophy of using several small DSLs rather than one larger DSL.

Sadly, using multiple external DSLs together in this way isn't very easy to do with current technology. Current parser technologies aren't well suited to mixing different languages together with modular grammars ("Modular Grammars," p. 339).

One of the problems with using Foreign Code is that you need to tokenize the Foreign Code differently to how you scan the code in your main language, so you need to use some approach of *Alternative Tokenization (319)*.

The simplest approach for Alternative Tokenization is to quote the embedded code inside some clear delimiters that can be spotted by the tokenizer and thus slurped as a single string, as I did above by putting the Javascript between curly brackets. Such an approach allows you to grab the different text easily, but may add some noise to the language.

Alternative Tokenization isn't just for handling Foreign Code. There are cases where, depending on the parsing context, you may want to interpret what should usually be a keyword as part of a name, such as state `initial` state. Quoting can do the trick (state `"initial state"`), but the other implementations of Alternative Tokenization which I discuss in that pattern may involve less syntactic noise.

5.5 XML DSLs

Right at the beginning of this book, I argued that many of the XML configuration files that we deal with are effectively DSLs. Other than an occasional snark, I haven't talked any more about XML DSLs yet, holding my fire till I've had a chance to talk more about external DSLs.

I'm not saying that all configuration files are DSLs. In particular, I like to draw a distinction between property lists and DSLs. A property list is a simple list of key/value pairs, perhaps organized into categories. There's not much syntactic structure here—none of that mysterious language nature that's key to something being a DSL. (Although I will say that XML is too noisy for property lists—I much prefer the INI file approach for things like that.)

Many configuration files do have a language nature to them, and are thus DSLs. If done in XML, I do see them as external DSLs. XML isn't a programming language; it's a syntactic structure with no semantics. Therefore, we process it by reading the code into tokens rather than interpreting it for execution. DOM processing is essentially *Tree Construction (281)*, SAX processing leads to *Embedded Translation (299)*. I think of XML as a carrier syntax for the DSL, in much the same way that an internal DSL's host language provides a carrier syntax. (An internal DSL also provides carrier semantics.)

My problem with XML as a carrier syntax is that it introduces far too much syntactic noise—lots of angle brackets, quotes, and slashes. Any nesting element needs both opening and closing tags. The result is too many characters expended on syntactic structure as opposed to real content. This makes it much harder to understand what the code is trying to say—which spoils the whole purpose of DSLs.

Despite this, there are a couple of arguments for XML. The first one is that humans shouldn't have to write XML in the first place—special UIs should capture the information and just use XML as a human-readable serialization mechanism. This is a reasonable argument, although it takes us away from the DSL territory, with XML becoming a serialization mechanism rather than a language. A particular task may handled with a forms-and-fields UI as an alternative to using a DSL. What I have seen is much talk of having a UI over XML, but not so much action. If you spend a significant amount of time looking at XML (or diffs of XML), then the fact that you have a UI is incidental.

I often hear the point that XML parsers exist off-the-shelf, and as a result you don't need to write your own. I think this argument is rather flawed, stemming from a confusion about what parsing is. In this book, I look at parsing as the whole route from input text to the *Semantic Model (159)*. The XML parser only takes us part of the way—typically to a DOM. We still have to write code to traverse the DOM and do something useful. This is what *Parser Generators (269)* can also do; ANTLR can easily take some input text and produce a syntax tree—which is the equivalent of the DOM. My experience is that, once you get moderately familiar with a Parser Generator, it takes no longer to use it than XML parser tools. Another point is that programmers are typically more familiar with XML parsing libraries than Parser Generators, but my view is that the time cost of learning to use a Parser Generator is a price worth paying.

One irritation with dealing with custom external DSLs is the inconsistency that they breed when dealing with things like quoting and escaping. Anyone who's spent time working with Unix configuration files appreciates this annoyance, and XML does provide a single scheme that works very solidly.

I've generally skimmed over error handling and diagnostics in this book, but that shouldn't be a reason to ignore the fact that XML processors usually do a good job here. You'll have to work harder to get good diagnostics with a typical custom language; how hard depends on how good a parser toolkit you're working with.

XML comes with technologies that allow you to easily check if the XML is reasonable without executing it, by comparing it to a schema. Various schema formats exist for XML: DTDs, XML Schema, Relax NG, all of which can check various things about the XML and also support more intelligent editing tools. (I write this book in XML and welcome the support that a Relax NG schema provides to my Emacs.)

Apart from parser tools that generate trees or events, you can also get binding interfaces that can easily translate XML data to fields in objects. These are less useful for DSLs, as the structure of the Semantic Model will rarely match that of the DSL to allow you to bind XML elements to the Semantic Model. You may be able to use binding with a translation layer, but it's doubtful that this will buy you much over walking an XML tree.

If you use a Parser Generator, then the grammar DSL can define many of the checks that an XML schema provides. But few tools can take advantage of a grammar. We can write something ourselves, of course, but the plus of XML is that such tools already exist for it. Often, an inferior but prevalent approach ends up being more useful than superior technologies.

I concede the point, but still believe that the syntactic noise of XML is too much for a DSL. The key to a DSL is readability; tooling helps with writing, but it's the reading that really counts. XML has its virtues—it's really good at text markup like this book—but as a DSL carrier syntax it just imposes too much noise for my taste.

This raises a connected point of other carrier syntaxes. Some of these syntaxes have got traction recently as ways to textually encode structured data; good examples are JSON (www.json.org) and YAML (www.yaml.org). Many people, including myself, like these syntaxes because they carry much less syntactic noise than XML. However, these languages are very much oriented towards structuring data, and as a result lack the flexibility you need to have a truly fluent language. A DSL is different from a data serialization, just like a fluent API is different from a command-query API. Fluency is important for a DSL to be easily readable, and a data serialization format makes too many compromises to work well in that context.

Chapter 6

Choosing between Internal and External DSLs

Now that we've gone through the details of implementing internal and external DSLs, we're now at a point where we can better understand their strengths and weaknesses. This gives us enough information to decide which of the two techniques to use, and indeed to decide if a DSL is appropriate at all.

One of the great difficulties is the lack of information to base your choice on. Only a few people do much with DSLs, and those that do tend to only use one or two techniques, and so can't really compare the different styles. This issue is further complicated by the fact that many of the techniques in this book aren't widely known. My hope is that this book will help people build DSLs more easily, but until it's been out in the wild for a while, we can't tell what effect it has on decisions on using a DSL or choosing one kind of DSL. So, my thoughts on this topic are more speculative than I would like.

6.1 Learning Curve

At first glance, the learning curve costs seem to favor using an internal DSL. After all, an internal DSL is really just a funky kind of API, and you are using facilities of a language you already know. With an external DSL, you have to learn about parsers, grammars, and *Parser Generators (269)*.

There's some truth to this, but the picture is rather more nuanced. There is certainly a bunch of new concepts to learn with *Syntax-Directed Translation (219)*, and the way you drive parsers with grammars can sometimes seem like magic. It's not as bad as many people fear it is, but if you've not worked with these kinds of tools before, I would recommend that you work with some trial examples first to become familiar with the tools before you make any estimates on doing the real work.

105

Sadly, the learning curve for Syntax-Directed Translation is made worse by the poor documentation for most Parser Generator tools. Even the documentation that is there tends to be written for people working on general-purpose languages rather than DSLs. For many tools, the only documentation is a Ph.D. thesis. There's a crying need to do more to make Parser Generator tools accessible to those who want to use them for DSL work but don't have a background in the language community.

There is the point that you can use *Delimiter-Directed Translation (201)* instead. The tools here are much more familiar—breaking up strings, regular expressions, no need for grammars. There are limits to where you can go with Delimiter-Directed Translation, and most of the time I think it's better to face the learning curve of Syntax-Directed Translation, but Delimiter-Directed Translation is an option to keep in mind, particularly for a regular language.

Using an XML carrier syntax is another way to avoid the cost of learning Syntax-Directed Translation. In this case, I certainly think that learning Syntax-Directed Translation is worth the cost, as the resulting language is so much clearer to read.

On the other hand, internal DSLs aren't necessarily as easy as you might think. Although you are using a familiar language, you are doing it in a very odd way. Internal DSLs often rely on obscure tricks in the host language to produce something that's fluent. So, even if you know the language well, you may need to spend some time finding out about the tricks available to you in your particular language. The patterns in this book should help you get started by suggesting what to look for, but you'll find particular language tricks that aren't here. Finding these and sorting out how to use them presents a learning curve of its own. The bright side is that you can mount this learning curve slowly, learning new techniques as you develop the DSL. This contrasts with Syntax-Directed Translation where you have to learn much more just to get going.

So, despite the fact that the difference is smaller than you might initially think, I'd still say that internal DSLs are easier to learn.

When considering the learning curve, remember that it applies not just to you but to anyone who wants to touch your code. Using an external DSL is likely to be less approachable for others who don't want to put much effort into learning how to use it.

6.2 Cost of Building

If you're using a DSL technique for the first time, the major cost is the cost of ascending the learning curve. Once you're familiar with the technique, that cost will go away, but there's still some cost involved in providing a DSL.

When we're thinking about the cost of building a DSL, it's important to separate the cost of building the model from the cost of building the DSL that layers over it. In this discussion, I'm going to take the presence of the model as a given. It's true that in many cases the model will be built in conjunction with the DSL, but the model has its own justification.

With an internal DSL, the extra effort involved is creating a layer of *Expression Builders (343)* over the model. The Expression Builders are relatively straightforward to write, but most of the effort isn't in getting them to work but in fiddling with the language so that you have something that works well. This Expression Builder cost won't appear if you are putting the fluent methods directly in the model, but that may lead to other costs if people find these methods confusing compared to a command-query API.

With an external DSL, the equivalent cost is building the parser. Once you are up to speed with *Syntax-Directed Translation (219)*, it's actually quite quick to write a grammar and the translation code. My current sense is that the cost of developing a parser is similar to that of building an Expression Builder layer.

Once you are familiar with Syntax-Directed Translation, I don't think it is any harder than using an XML carrier syntax, and is easier than using *Delimiter-Directed Translation (201)* unless the language is quite simple.

So, my sense at the moment is that, once you are familiar with the techniques, there's no big difference in cost for building an internal or external DSL.

6: Choosing between Internal and External DSLs

6.3 Programmer Familiarity

Many people argue that with an internal DSL, programmers who use it are using the language that they are familiar with, which makes it easier to work with than a new, external DSL. To some extent this is true, but I don't think the difference is as marked as most people think. The odd fluent interface style takes at least a little to get used to, although rather less than it does to learn how to build it. An external DSL is also not hard to learn as it is, by definition, rather simple. Echoing the syntactic conventions of your usual programming language can help make it more approachable.

Other than the syntactic element, the biggest difference is often that of the tools. If your host language is one with a sophisticated IDE, then you get to keep that familiar tooling with an internal DSL. You may need to use a more complicated technique like *Class Symbol Table (467)* to preserve the tool's support, but this way you can keep enjoying the IDE's strengths. With external DSLs, however, you're unlikely to be offered anything but the most basic level of editing support. You'll usually have to fall back to a regular text editor. It's not too difficult to support syntax highlighting, and most text editors are very configurable in that regard, but things like type-aware autocompletion are almost certainly beyond you.

6.4 Communication with Domain Experts

Internal DSLs are always tied to the syntax of the host language. The result will almost always be some constraints on how you can express things, together with some amount of syntactic noise. While this is unlikely to be a big factor for programmer users (who are used to these elements), domain experts are a different matter. The degree of constraints and syntactic noise also depends on the language; some languages are better suited for DSLs than others.

Even the best internal DSLs, however, don't offer the same syntactic flexibility as an external DSL. The size of the comfort gap will depend on particular domain experts, but such is the value of the communication channel that I'd be inclined to push that bit harder and use an external DSL if it looks like it could make the difference.

If you're not comfortable with building an external DSL, but not sure how well an internal DSL will fly with domain experts, you can try using an internal DSL first, then switch later if you think it's worthwhile. Since you can use the same *Semantic Model (159)* for both, the incremental cost of building two DSLs isn't really that great.

6.5 Mixing In the Host Language

An internal DSL is really nothing more than a convention to use certain fluent methods to do things. There's nothing to stop you from arbitrarily mixing DSLish code with regular imperative code. This wafer-thin boundary between the DSL and the host language has properties that may be beneficial or problematic—depending on what you are trying to do.

A benefit of this thin boundary is that it allows you to use the host language freely when you don't have the constructs of the internal DSL available to you. So, if you need to express arithmetic in your DSL, there's no point in making DSL constructs for this; just use the features of the host language. If you need to build abstractions on top of the DSL, you can use the abstraction facilities of the host language.

This strength is particularly nice when you need to put chunks of imperative code inside your DSL. A good example of this is using a DSL to describe how to build software. Build languages that use a *Dependency Network (505)*, such as Make and Ant, have been around for a long time. Both Make and Ant are external DSLs, and both are very good at expressing the Dependency Network that you need for builds. However, the content of many build tasks requires more complex logic, and often the dependencies themselves need abstractions layered on top of them. Ant has thus suffered from sliding into generality, acquiring all manner of imperative constructs that don't suit its nature or syntax.

Here, the contrast is with an internal DSL, such as the Rake language which is a Ruby internal DSL for building software. Being able to freely mix the Dependency Network with imperative code in *Nested Closures (403)* makes it much easier to describe complicated build actions. Using Ruby's objects and methods to build abstractions on top of the Dependency Network helps describe the higher-level structure of the build.

It's not impossible to mix external DSLs with host code. You can embed host code into DSL scripts as *Foreign Code (309)*. Similarly, you can embed DSLs into general-purpose code as strings—which is how we typically embed things like regular expressions and SQL today. But the mixing is awkward. Tools usually don't know what you are doing and thus are clunky in how they work. It's hard to integrate symbols between the two environments, so things like referring to a host code variable within a DSL fragment become difficult. If you want to intermix host and DSL code, then an internal DSL is almost always the way to go.

6: Choosing
between Internal
and External DSLs

6.6 Strong Expressiveness Boundary

The ability to freely mix host and DSL code isn't always a positive. It only really works if the users of the DSL are comfortable with the host language. It thus doesn't usually apply to the case where you have domain experts reading your DSL. Throwing lumps of a host language into the DSL will usually only raise a communication barrier that the DSL was supposed to avoid.

Intermixing is also unhelpful in cases where you want DSLs to be written by a different group of programmers. Indeed, often the benefit of a DSL is that it produces a restricted range of what can be done. This restriction can make it easier to understand what to do, and serves as a barrier to bugs. If you have a DSL with strong boundaries, that limits the kinds of things you need to test for. Pricing rules in a DSL aren't going to send arbitrary messages to your integration server or alter your order processing workflow. With a general-purpose language, anything is possible, so you have to watch the boundaries through convention and review. An external DSL's limitations reduce what you have to watch for. Most of the time, this is good as it protects you from mistakes, but it may also help with security as well.

6.7 Runtime Configuration

One of the main reasons that XML DSLs have become so popular is that they allow you to alter the execution context of the code from compile time to runtime. For situations where you are using a compiled language and want to alter the behavior of the system without recompiling, this is an important factor. External DSLs allow you to do this since you can easily parse them at runtime, translate into a *Semantic Model (159)*, and then execute that model. (Of course if you are programming in an interpreted language, then everything is at runtime anyway, so this isn't an issue.)

One approach is to use interpreted languages in conjunction with a compiled language. You can then write an internal DSL in the interpreted language. In this scenario, many of the common benefits of an internal DSL may be attenuated. Unless most of the team is familiar with the dynamic language, you won't get the language familiarly benefit of internal DSLs. Tooling for the dynamic language is often poorer. You won't be able to easily mix the dynamic language and static language constructs, but a full dynamic language also means you can't put firm boundaries around the DSL. That's not to say you shouldn't use an internal DSL in this way—there are plenty of cases where these potential issues aren't applicable. But this attenuation does lead to more situations where an external DSL meshes better with a static host language.

6.8 Sliding into Generality

One of the most successful DSLs of modern times is Ant. Ant is a language for specifying builds for Java; it's an external DSL in XML syntax. In a discussion about DSLs, James Duncan Davidson, Ant's creator, asked: "How do we prevent disasters like Ant occurring?"

Ant is both a roaring success and a nightmare. It filled a huge gap in Java development at the time, but since then, its success has forced many teams to face its flaws. There are many problems with Ant, its XML syntax (which I also thought was a good idea at the time) is perhaps the most noticeable. But the real issue behind Ant is that over time, it steadily grew in capability so that it no longer has the limited expressiveness that a DSL needs.

This is a common road to heck. People with a Unix background will often use the example of Sendmail. It happens because the demands placed on the DSL get steadily greater, leading to more features and greater complexity—and, drop by drop, all the clarity that a good DSL has leaks out.

This danger always exists with external DSLs—and, like most issues in design, has no simple answer. It needs a constant attention and determination to not let things get too complex. There are alternatives. One is to let other languages develop for more complicated cases. Instead of extending one language, you can introduce other languages for particular and difficult cases. You can layer another language over the base DSL whose output is that base DSL. This can be a useful technique to allow abstractions to be built in a language that lacks abstraction-building features. Internal DSLs are often a good choice when this kind of complexity grows, because they allow you to mix DSL and general-purpose elements.

Since internal DSLs are melded in with a general-purpose host language, they don't suffer from this problem. An analogous problem may arise when mixing with the host language gets so intertwined that you lose any sense of DSLness.

6: Choosing between Internal and External DSLs

6.9 Composing DSLs

I've been saying ad nauseam that you want small DSLs that are very limited in their capabilities. So, to get real work done, you have to integrate your DSLs with one or more general-purpose languages. You can also compose DSLs together.

With internal DSLs, composing is as easy as mixing them with the host language. You can also use the host language's abstraction features to help make the composition work.

With external DSLs, such composition is more difficult. To do this composition with *Syntax-Directed Translation (219)*, you need to be able to write independent grammars for different languages, and yet be able to compose the grammars together. Most *Parser Generators (269)*, however, don't have facilities to handle this case—another consequence of their focus on supporting general-purpose programming languages. As a result, you need to use *Foreign Code (309)* if you want to compose DSLs, which is more clunky that it need be. (There is some work going on to provide tools that support more composition, but they are currently rather immature.)

6.10 Summing Up

My conclusion is that there is no conclusion. I don't see a clear, general advantage for internal or external DSLs. I'm not even sure I see some general guidelines to pontificate. I hope I've given you enough information thus far to help you judge what would best suit your particular situation.

One thing I do want to stress, however, is that experimenting in both directions need not be as expensive as you think. If you use a *Semantic Model (159)*, it's relatively easy to layer on multiple DSLs, both internal and external. This gives you lots of opportunity for experimentation to find an approach that works well for you.

An approach that Glenn Vanderburg finds useful is to use an internal DSL early on, when you're still trying to understand what you want to do with it. That way you have easy access to facilities from the host language and a more seamless environment to evolve in. Once things settle down, and there's a need for some of the advantages of an external DSL, you can then build one. Again, a Semantic Model makes this process much easier.

There is another option that I haven't mentioned yet—using a language workbench. I'll come to that in "Language Workbenches," p. 129.

Chapter 7

Alternative Computational Models

When people talk about the benefits of using DSLs, you often hear them say that they support a more declarative approach to programming. I confess to having a problem with the word "declarative"; it often seems to be used as a very broad brush. In general, however, declarative means "something other than imperative."

Mainstream programming languages follow the imperative computational model. The imperative model defines computation through a sequence of steps: do this, do that, if (red) do the other. Conditionals and loops vary the steps, and steps can be grouped together into functions. Object-oriented languages add bundling together of data and process, as well as polymorphism—but are still grounded in an the imperative model.

The imperative model gets quite a bit of flak thrown at it, particularly from academics, but it has continued to be our fundamental computational model since the early days of computing. I think this is because it's easy to understand: Sequences of actions are something that is straightforward to follow.

When we talk about ease of understanding, there are really two different kinds of understanding in play. The first is understanding the intent of the program—what are we trying to achieve with it. The second form of understanding is of the implementation—how the program works to satisfy the intent. The imperative programming model is particularly good with the latter: You can read the code and see what it's doing. To get more details, you can step through with a debugger—the sequence of the statements in the source code corresponds exactly to what happens in the debugger.

Where the imperative approach doesn't always work so well is in the understanding of intent. If the intent is a sequence of actions, fine; but often, our intentions aren't best expressed that way. In these cases, it is often worth considering a different computational model.

I'll start with a simple example. Often, you run into situations where you need to state the consequences for different combinations of conditions. A small example of this might be scoring points to assess car insurance, where you might see something like Figure 7.1.

Figure 7.1   *A simple decision table for car insurance*

This kind of table is a common way for people to think about this kind of problem. If we turn this table into imperative C# code, we'd see something like this:

```
public static int CalcPoints(Application a) {
  if ( a.HasCellPhone &&  a.HasRedCar) return 7;
  if ( a.HasCellPhone && !a.HasRedCar) return 3;
  if (!a.HasCellPhone &&  a.HasRedCar) return 2;
  if (!a.HasCellPhone && !a.HasRedCar) return 0;
  throw new ArgumentException("unreachable");
}
```

My normal style of writing Boolean conditions is rather more terse, something like this:

```
public static int CalcPoints2(Application a) {
  if (a.HasCellPhone)
    return (a.HasRedCar) ? 7 : 3;
  else return (a.HasRedCar) ? 2 : 0;
}
```

But in this case I prefer the first, longer way of writing it because the code corresponds more closely to the intent of the domain expert. The tabular nature of how she thinks about it is similar to the way the code is laid out.

There's similarity between the table and the code, but they're not quite the same. The imperative model forces the various if statements to be executed in a particular order, which isn't implied by the decision table. This means that I'm adding an irrelevant implementation artifact to my representation of the table. For decision tables this isn't a big deal, but it can matter for other alternative computational models.

A potentially more serious shortcoming of an imperative representation is that it removes some useful opportunities. One of the nice things about a decision table is that you can check it to ensure you don't miss a permutation, or that you don't accidentally repeat a permutation.

An alternative to using imperative code is to create a decision table abstraction and then configure it for this particular case. If I do that, I could represent this table with something like this:

```
var table = new DecisionTable<Application, int>();
table.AddCondition((application) => application.HasCellPhone);
table.AddCondition((application) => application.HasRedCar);
table.AddColumn( true,  true, 7);
table.AddColumn( true, false, 3);
table.AddColumn(false,  true, 2);
table.AddColumn(false, false, 0);
```

I now have a more faithful representation of the original decision table. I no longer specify the order of evaluating the conditions in the imperative code; that's left to the insides of the decision table (this lack of ordering may be handy to exploit concurrency). More importantly, the decision table can check for a properly formed set of conditions and tell me if I've missed anything in my configuration. As a bonus, I shift my execution context from compile time to runtime and can thus change the rules without a recompile.

I call this style of representation an *Adaptive Model (487)*. The term "adaptive object model" has been around for a while to describe how this is done as an OO model; take a look at writings by Joe Yoder and Ralph Johnson [Yoder and Johnson]. But you don't need to use objects to do something like this—storing data structures that capture behavioral rules is common in databases too. Most decent OO models have objects contain behavior as well as data, but the defining thing about an Adaptive Model is that the behavior is largely defined by the instances of the model and how they are wired together. You cannot understand what behavior to expect without looking at the configuration of instances.

You don't need a DSL to use an Adaptive Model. Indeed, DSLs and Adaptive Models are separate notions that can be used independently of each other. Even so, I suspect it should be obvious to you that Adaptive Models and DSLs go together like wine and cheese. Throughout this book, I've harped on and on about making the DSL parse build a *Semantic Model (159)*. Often, this Semantic Model is an Adaptive Model that provides an alternative computational model for a part of a software system.

The big negative of using an Adaptive Model is that the behavior it defines is implicit; you can't just look at the code to see what happens. On top of this, while the intention is usually easier to understand, the implementation is not. This becomes important when things go wrong and you need to debug. It's often much harder to find faults with an Adaptive Model. I often hear people complain that they can't find the program and can't understand how it works. As a result, Adaptive Models have a reputation for being hard to maintain. Often, I hear about people taking months to figure out how it works. If they finally figure it out, the Adaptive Model can make them very productive, but before they do (and many people never do) it's a nightmare.

This implementation comprehension problem with Adaptive Models is a real issue, and one that rightly deters many people from using them, despite the very real benefits you can get once you become comfortable with how they work. One of the benefits I see with DSLs is that they make it easier to understand how an

Adaptive Model fits together and thus easier to program it. With a DSL, you can at least see the program. It doesn't take away all the issues of understanding how the general Adaptive Model works, but being able to more clearly see the specific configuration can give you a significant leg up.

Alternative computational models are also one of the compelling reasons for using a DSL, which is why I've spent a big chunk of time on them in this book. If your problem can be easily expressed using imperative code, then a regular programming language works just fine. The key benefits of a DSL—greater productivity and communication with domain experts—really kick in when you are using an alternative computational model. Domain experts often think about their problems in a nonimperative way, such as via a decision table. An Adaptive Model allows you to capture their way of thinking more directly in a program, and the DSL allows you to communicate that representation more clearly to them (and yourself).

7.1 A Few Alternative Models

There are many possible computational models out there, and I'm not going to provide a comprehensive picture of them in this book. What I can do is provide a small sample of common ones. These will help you in the common cases, but I also hope they may spark you imagination to come up with specific computational models for your domain.

7.1.1 Decision Table

Since I've already mentioned *Decision Tables (495)*, I might as well start with them. It's a pretty simple form of an alternative computational model, but well suited to a DSL. Figure 7.2 is a relatively simple example.

Premium Customer	X	X	Y	Y	N	N	
Priority Order	Y	N	Y	N	Y	N	conditions
International Order	Y	Y	N	N	N	N	
Fee	150	100	70	50	80	60	consequences
Alert Rep	Y	Y	Y	N	N	N	

Figure 7.2 *A decision table for handling orders*

The table consists of a number of rows of conditions, followed by a number of rows of consequences. The semantics are straightforward; in this case, you take an order and check it against the conditions. One column of conditions should match, and then the consequences on that column apply. So, if we have a premium customer with a domestic, priority order, there's a fee of $70 and we alert a representative to handle the order.

In this case, each condition is a Boolean condition, but more complicated decision tables can have other forms of conditions, such as numeric ranges.

Decision tables are particularly easy to follow for nonprogrammers, so they work well in communicating with domain experts. Their tabular nature makes them natural for editing in a spreadsheet, so this is one case of a DSL where direct editing by a domain expert is more likely than not.

7.1.2 Production Rule System

The general notion of modeling logic by dividing it up into rules, each of which has a condition and a consequent action, is a *Production Rule System (513)*. Each rule can be specified individually in a style similar to a bunch of if-then statements in imperative code.

```
if
  passenger.frequentFlier
then
  passenger.priorityHandling = true;

if
  mileage > 25000
then
  passenger.frequentFlier = true;
```

With a Production Rule System, we specify these rules in terms of their conditions and actions, but we leave it to the underlying system to execute them and tie them together. In the example I just showed, there is a link between the rules in that if the second rule is true (and thus "fired," as it's said in the local lingo), that may affect whether the first rule should be fired.

This characteristic, where firing some rules changes whether other rules should be fired, is called **chaining**, and is an important characteristic of a Production Rule System. Chaining allows you to write rules individually, without thinking of their broader consequences, and then let the system figure out those consequences.

This benefit is also a danger. A Production Rule System relies a lot on implicit logic, which can often do things that weren't anticipated. Sometimes this unanticipated behavior can be beneficial, but sometimes it can be harmful, leading to an incorrect result. These errors are often precisely due to the fact that the writers of the rules haven't taken into account how rules interact.

Problems due to implicit behavior are a common issue with alternative computational models. We are relatively used to the imperative model, but still make lots of mistakes with it. With alternative models, we are even more prone to problems because we often cannot reason easily about what will happen just by looking at the code. A bunch of rules embedded in a rule base will often produce surprising results, for good or ill. One consequence of this, which applies to most cases where you implement an alternative computational model, is that it's important to produce a tracing mechanism so you can see what exactly happened on an execution of the model. With Production Rule System, this means the ability to record which rules fired and provide that record easily when required, so that a puzzled user or programmer can see the chain of rules that led to an unexpected conclusion.

Production Rule Systems have been around for a long time, and there are many products that implement them and provide sophisticated tools for capturing and executing the rules. Despite this, it can still be useful to write a small Production Rule System within your own code. Like any case where you roll your own alternative computational model, you can usually get away with something relatively simple when you do it at a small scale with a particular domain in mind.

Although chaining is certainly an important part of a Production Rule System, it actually isn't mandatory. Sometimes it's useful to write a Production Rule System without chaining, a good example for which is a set of validation rules. With validation, you are often just capturing a bunch of conditions where the action is raising an error. Although you don't need chaining, thinking of the behavior as a set of independent rules is still useful.

You can argue that a *Decision Table (495)* is a form of Production Rule System where each column in the Decision Table corresponds to a single rule. While this is true, I think it misses the point. With a Production Rule System, you focus on the behavior one rule at a time; with a Decision Table, you focus on the entire table. That shift in thinking is an essential part of the two models, making them different mental tools.

7.1.3 State Machine

I opened this book with another popular alternative computational model—the *State Machine (527)*. A State Machine models the behavior of an object by dividing it into a set of states and triggering behavior with events so that, depending on the state the object is in, each event leads to a transition to a different state.

Figure 7.3 indicates that we can cancel an order in the collecting and paid states, either of which will transition the order to the cancelled state.

The State Machine has the core elements of states, events, and transitions, but there are a lot of variations that build on that basic structure. Variations particularly appear in how the State Machine initiates actions. A State Machine is a common choice because many systems can be thought of as reacting to events by going through a series of states.

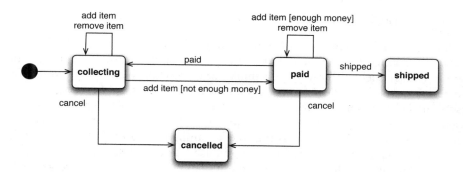

Figure 7.3 *A UML state machine diagram for an order*

7.1.4 Dependency Network

One of the most familiar alternative models in the daily work of software developers is the *Dependency Network (505)*. It's familiar because this model underpins build tools such as Make, Ant, and their derivatives. In this model, we look at the tasks that need to be done and capture the prerequisites for each task. For example, the task to run tests may have the compile and load data tasks as prerequisites, both of which have the generate code task as a prerequisite. With these dependencies stated, we can then invoke the test task, and the system figures out which other tasks need to be done and in what order. Furthermore, even though the generate code task appears twice in the list (because it's listed twice as a prerequisite) the system knows it only needs to run it once.

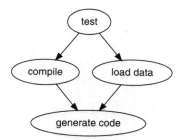

Figure 7.4 *A possible dependency network for building software*

A Dependency Network is thus a good choice when you have computationally expensive tasks with dependencies between them.

7.1.5 Choosing a Model

7: Alternative
Computational
Models

I find it hard to come up with particular guidelines as to when to choose a particular computational model. It really all boils down to a sense that the computational model fits the way you think about your problem. The best way to determine whether it does fit is to try it out. Initially, just try it on paper by describing behaviors using simple text and diagrams. If a model seems to pass that simple desk check, then it's worth building it, perhaps as a prototype, to see how it works in action. My feeling is that the key thing is to get the *Semantic Model (159)* working properly, but it may help to use a simple DSL to help in this process. I'd put more effort into tuning the model first, however, before getting a very readable DSL. Once you have a reasonable Semantic Model in place, it's relatively easy to experiment with different DSLs to drive it.

There are many more alternative computational models than these. If I had more time to spend on this book, I'd like to spend it on writing up more of them. It strikes me that a book of computational models would be a good book for somebody to write.

Chapter 8

Code Generation

So far in my discussion of implementing DSLs, I've talked about parsing some DSL text, usually with the aim of populating a *Semantic Model (159)*, and putting interesting behavior in that model. In many cases, once we can populate the Semantic Model our work is done—we can just execute the Semantic Model to get the behavior we're looking for.

While executing the Semantic Model directly is usually the easiest thing to do, there are plenty of times when you can't do that. You may need your DSL-specified logic to execute in a very different environment, one where it's difficult or impossible to build a Semantic Model or a parser. It's in these situations that you can reach for code generation. By using code generation, you can take the behavior specified in the DSL and run it in almost any environment.

When you use code generation, you have two different environments to think about: what I shall call the DSL processor and the target environment. The DSL processor is where the parser, Semantic Model, and the code generator live. This needs to be a comfortable environment to develop these things. The target environment is your generated code and its surroundings. The point of using code generation is to separate the target environment from your DSL processor because you can't reasonably build the DSL processor in the target environment.

Target environments come in various guises. One case is an embedded system where you don't have the resources to run a DSL processor. Another is where the target environment needs to be a language that isn't suitable for DSL processing. Ironically, the target environment may itself be a DSL. Since DSLs have limited expressiveness, they usually don't provide abstraction facilities that you need for a more complex system. Even if you could extend the DSL to give you abstraction facilities, that would come at the price of complicating the DSL—perhaps enough to turn it into a general-purpose language. So, it can be better to do that abstraction in a different environment and generate code in your target DSL. A good example of this is specifying query conditions in a DSL and then generating SQL. We might do this to allow our queries to run efficiently in the database, but SQL isn't the best way for us to represent our queries.

Limitations of the target environment aren't the only reason to generate code. Another reason may be the lack of familiarity with the target environment. It may be easier to specify behavior in a more familiar language and then generate the less familiar one. Another reason for code generation is to better enforce static checking. We might characterize the interface of some system with a DSL, but the rest of the system wishes to talk to that interface using C#. In this case, you might generate a C# API so that you get compile-time checking and IDE support. When the interface definition changes, you can regenerate the C# and have the compiler help you identify some of the damage.

8.1 Choosing What to Generate

One of the first things to decide when generating code is, what kind of code are you going to generate? The way I look at things, there are two styles of code generation you can use: *Model-Aware Generation (555)* and *Model Ignorant Generation (567)*. The difference between the two lies in whether or not you have an explicit representation of the *Semantic Model (159)* in the target environment.

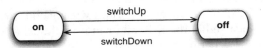

Figure 8.1   *A very simple state machine*

As an example, let's consider a *State Machine (527)*. Two classic alternatives for implementing a state machine are nested conditionals and state tables. If we take a very simple state model, such as Figure 8.1, a nested conditional approach would look like this:

```
public void handle(Event event) {
  switch (currentState) {
    case ON:  switch (event) {
            case DOWN:
               currentState = OFF;
          }
    case OFF: switch (event) {
               case UP : currentState = ON;
          }
  }
}
```

We have two conditional tests nested one inside the other. The outer conditional looks at the current state of the machine and the inner conditional switches on the event that's just been received. This is Model Ignorant Generation because the logic of the state machine is embedded into the control flow of the language—there's no explicit representation of the Semantic Model.

With Model-Aware Generation we put some representation of the semantic model into the generated code. This needn't be exactly the same as that used in the DSL processor, but it will be some form of data representation. For this case, our state machine is a touch more complicated.

```
class ModelMachine...
  private State currentState;
  private Map<State, Map<Event, State>> states = new HashMap<State, Map<Event, State>>();

  public ModelMachine(State currentState) {
    this.currentState = currentState;
  }
  void defineTransition(State source, Event trigger, State target) {
    if (! states.containsKey(source)) states.put(source, new HashMap<Event, State>());
    states.get(source).put(trigger, target);
  }
  public void handle(Event event) {
    Map<Event, State> currentTransitions = states.get(currentState);
    if (null == currentTransitions) return;
    State target = currentTransitions.get(event);
    if (null != target) currentState = target;
  }
```

Here I'm storing the transitions as nested maps. The outer map is a map of states, whose key is the state name, and value is a second map. This inner map has the event name as the key and the target state as the value. This is a crude state model—I may not have explicit state, transition, and event classes—but the data structure captures the behavior of the state machine. As a result of being data-driven, this code is entirely generic and needs to be configured by some specific code to make it work.

```
modelMachine = new ModelMachine(OFF);
modelMachine.defineTransition(OFF, UP, ON);
modelMachine.defineTransition(ON, DOWN, OFF);
```

By putting a representation of the Semantic Model into the generated code, the generated code takes on the same split between generic framework code and specific configuration code that I talked about in the introduction. Model-Aware Generation preserves the generic/specific separation while the Model Ignorant Generation folds the two together by representing the Semantic Model in control flow.

The upshot of this is that if I use Model-Aware Generation, the only code I need to generate is the specific configuration code. I can build the basic state machine entirely in the target environment and test it there. With Model Ignorant Generation, I have to generate much more code. I can pull out some code into library functions which don't need to be generated, but most of the critical behavior has to be generated.

As a result, it's much easier to generate code using Model-Aware Generation. The generated code is usually very simple. You do have to build the generic section, but since you can run and test it independently of the code generation system, this usually makes it much easier to do.

My inclination, therefore, is to use Model-Aware Generation as much as possible. However, often it isn't possible. Often, the whole reason for using code generation is that the target language can't represent a model easily as data. Even if it can, there may be processing limitations. Embedded systems often use Model Ignorant Generation because the processing overhead of code generated with Model-Aware Generation would be too great.

There's another factor to bear in mind if it's possible to use Model-Aware Generation. If you need to change the specific behavior of the system, you can replace only the artifact corresponding to the configuration code. Imagine we're generating C code; we can put the configuration code into a different library than the generic code—this would allow us to alter the specific behavior without replacing the whole system (although we'd need some runtime binding mechanism to pull this off).

We can go even further here and generate a representation that can be read entirely at runtime. We could generate a simple text table, for example:

```
off switchUp   on
on  switchDown off
```

This would allow us to change the specific behavior of the system at runtime, at the cost of the generic system having the code to load the data file at startup.

At this point, you're probably thinking that I've just generated another DSL which I'm parsing in the target environment. You could think of it this way, but I don't. To my mind, the little table above isn't really a DSL because it isn't designed to be for human manipulation. The textual format does make it human-readable, but that's more of a useful feature for debugging. It's primarily designed to make it really easy to parse, so we can quickly load it into the target system. When designing such a format, human readability comes a distant second to simplicity of parsing. With a DSL, human readability is a high priority.

8.2 How to Generate

Once you've thought about what kind of code to generate, the next decision is how to go about the generation process. When generating a textual output, there are two main styles you can follow: *Transformer Generation (533)* and *Templated Generation (539)*. With Transformer Generation, you write code that reads the *Semantic Model (159)* and generates statements in the target source code. So for the states example, you might get hold of the events and generate the output code to declare each event, likewise with the commands, and again for each state. Since the states contain transitions, your generation for each state would involve navigating to the transitions and generating code for each of these too.

With Templated Generation, you begin by writing a sample output file. In this output file, wherever there is something specific to a particular state machine, you place special template markers that allow you to call out to the Semantic Model to generate the appropriate code. If you've done templated web pages with tools like ASP, JSP, and the like, you should be familiar with this mechanism. When you process the templates, it replaces the template references with generated code.

8: Code
Generation

With Templated Generation, you are driven by the structure of your output. With Transformer Generation, you may be driven by either input, output, or both.

Both approaches to code generation work well, and to choose between them, you're usually best off to experiment with each and see which one seems to work best for you. I find that Templated Generation works best when there's a lot of static code in the output and only a few dynamic bits—particularly since I can look at the template file and get a good sense of what gets generated. As a consequence of this, I think you're more likely to use Templated Generation if you are using *Model Ignorant Generation (567)*. Otherwise—actually, most of the time—I like Transformer Generation.

I've discussed these as opposite approaches, but that doesn't mean you can't mix them. Indeed, usually you do. If you're using Transformer Generation, you'll probably use string format statements to write out a little chunk of code—and these are miniature cases of Templated Generation. Despite this, I think it's useful to have a clear idea of what your overall strategy is and be conscious about switching over. As with most things involving programming, the moment you stop being thoughtful about what you are doing is the moment when you start making an unmaintainable mess.

One of the biggest problems in using Templated Generation is that the host code used to generate variable output may start to overwhelm the static template code. If you're generating Java to generate C, you want the template to be mostly C and minimize any Java in the template. I find *Embedment Helper (547)* a vital pattern here. All the complexity of figuring out how to generate the variable elements of the template should be hidden in a class that's called by simple method calls in the template. That way you only have the bare minimum of Java in your C.

Not only does this keep your template clear, it usually also makes it easier to work with your generation code. The Embedment Helper can be a regular class, edited with tools that are aware they are editing Java. With sophisticated IDEs, this makes a big difference. If you embed a lot of Java in a C file, the IDEs usually can't help you. You may not even get syntax highlighting. Each callout in a template should be a single method call; anything else should be inside the Embedment Helper.

A good example of where this is important is the grammar files for *Syntax-Directed Translation (219)*. I've often come across grammar files that are full of long code actions, essentially blocks of *Foreign Code (309)*. These blocks are woven into the generated parser, but their size buries the structure of the grammar; an Embedment Helper helps a great deal by keeping the code actions small.

8.3 Mixing Generated and Handwritten Code

Sometimes you can generate all the code that needs to execute in the target environment, but more often than not, you will mix generated and handwritten code.

The general rules to follow here are:

- Don't modify generated code.

- Keep generated code clearly separate from handwritten code.

The point of using code generation from a DSL is that the DSL becomes the authoritative source for that behavior. Any generated code is just an artifact. If you go in and manually edit the result of the code generation, you'll lose those changes when you regenerate. This causes extra work on generation, which is not just bad in its own right but also introduces a reluctance to change the DSL and generate when necessary, undermining the whole point of having a DSL. (It is sometimes useful to generate a scaffold to get you started on handwritten code, but that's not the usual situation with DSLs.)

As a result, any generated code should never be touched by hand. (One exception is inserting trace statements for debugging.) Since we want them to never be touched, it makes sense to keep them apart from the handwritten code. My preference is to have files clearly separated into all-generated or all-handwritten. I don't check generated code into a source code repository, since it can be regenerated at will during the build process. I prefer to keep generated code in a separate branch of the source code tree.

In a procedural system, where the code is organized into files of functions, this is pretty easy to achieve. However, object-oriented code, with classes that mix data structure and behavior, often complicates this separation. There are plenty of times where you have one logical class, but some parts of the class need to be generated and some handwritten.

Often, the easiest way to handle this is to have multiple files for your class; you can then split the generated and handwritten code up as you wish. However, not all programming environments allow this. Java does not, recent versions of C# do—under the name of "partial classes." If you're working with Java, you can't simply split the files in a class.

One popular option was to mark separate areas of the class as generated or handwritten. I always found this a clunky mechanism, one that often leads to mistakes as people edit the generated code. It also usually means that it's impossible to avoid checking in generated code—which confuses the version control history.

A good solution to this is *Generation Gap (571)* where you split generated and handwritten code using inheritance. In the basic form, you generate a superclass and handwrite a subclass which can augment and override generated behaviors. This keeps the file separation between generated and handwritten code while allowing a lot of flexibility in combining both styles in a single class. The disadvantage is that you need to relax visibility rules. Methods that might otherwise be private have to be relaxed to protected to allow overriding and calling from a subclass. I find such relaxation a small price to pay for keeping the generated and handwritten code separate.

The difficulty of keeping the generated and handwritten code separate seems to be proportional to the pattern of calls between generated and handwritten code. A simple flow of control, such as *Model Ignorant Generation (567)* where the generated code calls handwritten code in a one-way flow, makes it much easier to separate the two artifacts. So, if you have difficulty keeping handwritten and generated code separate, it may be worth thinking about ways to simplify the control flow.

8.4 Generating Readable Code

A tension that comes out from time to time when talking about code generation is how readable and well-structured you need to make the generated code. The two schools of thought are those that think that generated code should be as clear and readable as handwritten code, and those that feel that such concerns are irrelevant for generated code, since it should never be modified by hand.

In this debate, I lean towards the group that says that generated code should be well-structured and clear. Although you shouldn't ever have to hand-edit generated code, there will be occasions where people will want to understand how it works. Things will go wrong and require debugging, and then it's much easier to debug clear, well-structured code.

Therefore, I prefer to generate code almost as good as that I would write by hand—with clear variable names, good structure, and most of the habits I use normally.

There are exceptions. Perhaps the primary exception is that I'm less concerned if it's going to take extra time to get the right structure. I'm less inclined to spend the time to figure out or create the best structure with generated code. I worry less about duplication; I don't want the obvious and easy-to-avoid duplication, but I don't stress about it to the degree I do with handwritten code. After all, I don't have to worry about the modifiability, only the readability. If I think some duplication is clearer, I'll certainly leave it in. I'm also happier to use comments, since I can ensure that generated comments are kept up-to-date with generated code. Comments can refer back to structures in the *Semantic Model (159)*. I'll also compromise clear structure to meet performance goals—but that's true for handwritten code too.

8.5 Preparse Code Generation

Through most of this section, I've concentrated on code generation as the output of the DSL script, but there is another place where code generation can play a role. In some cases, you need to integrate with some external information when writing your DSL script. If you are writing a DSL about linking territories for salespeople, then you might want to coordinate with a corporate database used by salespeople. You may want to ensure that the symbols you use in your DSL scripts match those in the corporate database. One way of doing this is to use code generation to generate information you need while writing your scripts. Often, this kind of checking can be done when populating the *Semantic Model (159)*, but there are times when it's useful to have the information in source code too, particularly for code navigation and static typing.

An example of this would be where you are writing an internal DSL in Java/C# and you want your symbols that refer to salespeople to be statically typed. You can do this by code-generating enums to list your salespeople and importing those enums into your script files [Kabanov et al.].

8.6 Further Reading

The most extensive book available on code generation techniques is [Herrington]. You may also fine Marcus Voelter's set of patterns in [Voelter] useful.

Chapter 9

Language Workbenches

The techniques I've written about so far have been around, in some form or another, for a long time. The tools that exist to support them, such as *Parser Generators (269)* for external DSLs, are similarly well seasoned. In this chapter, I'm going to spend some time looking at a set of tools that are rather more shiny and new—tools that I call language workbenches.

Language workbenches are, in essence, tools that help you build your own DSLs and provide tool support for them in the style of modern IDEs. The idea is that these tools don't just provide an IDE to help create DSLs; they support building IDEs for editing these DSLs. This way, someone writing a DSL script has the same degree of support that a programmer who uses a post-IntelliJ IDE.

As I write this, the language workbench field is still very young. Most tools have barely left beta stage. Even those that have been out for a while haven't garnered enough experiences to draw many conclusions. Yet there's immense potential here—these are tools that could change the face of programming as we know it. I don't know whether they will succeed in their endeavors, but I am sure that they are worth keeping an eye on.

This immaturity means that this topic is especially difficult to write about. I've wondered long and hard about what to say about language workbenches in this book. In the end, I decided that the fact that these tools are so new and volatile means I cannot write much in a book like this. Much of what I write now will be out-of-date by the time you read it. As ever in my work, I'm looking for core principles that don't change much, but they are hard to identify in such a rapidly moving field. So I decided to just write this one chapter and not provide any more details in the reference section of the book. I also decided to only cover a few aspects of language workbenches here—those that I felt were relatively stable. Even so, you should take this chapter with caution and keep an eye on the Web to find out about more recent developments.

9.1 Elements of Language Workbenches

Although language workbenches differ greatly in what they look like, there are common elements that they share. In particular, language workbenches allow you to define three aspects of a DSL environment:

- *Semantic Model (159)* **schema** defines the data structure of the Semantic Model, together with static semantics, usually by using a meta-model.

- **DSL editing environment** defines a rich editing experience for people writing DSL scripts, through either source editing or projectional editing.

- **Semantic Model behavior** defines what the DSL script does by building off the Semantic Model, most commonly with code generation.

Language workbenches use a Semantic Model as the core part of the system. As a result, they provide tools to help you define that model. Instead of defining the Semantic Model with a programming language, as I've assumed for this book, they define it within a special meta-modeling structure that allows them to use runtime tools to work on the model. This meta-modeling structure helps them provide their high degree of tooling.

As a result of this, there is a separation between schema and behavior. The Semantic Model schema is essentially a data model without much behavior. The behavioral aspects of the Semantic Model come from outside the data structure—mostly in the form of code generation. Some tools expose the Semantic Model allowing you to build an interpreter, but thus far code generation is the most popular way to make the Semantic Model run.

One of the most interesting and important aspect of language workbenches is their editing environments. This is perhaps the key aspect that they bring to software development, providing a much richer range of tools for populating and manipulating a Semantic Model. These vary from something close to assisted textual editing, to graphical editors that allow you to write a DSL script as a diagram, to environments that use what I call "illustrative programming" to provide an experience closer to working with a spreadsheet than that of a regular programming language.

Going much deeper than this would raise the problems of the tools' newness and volatility, but there are a couple of general principles that I feel will have some lasting relevance: schema definition and projectional editing.

9.2 Schema Definition Languages and Meta-Models

Throughout this book, I've been stressing the usefulness of using a *Semantic Model (159)*. Every language workbench I've looked at uses a Semantic Model and provides tools to define it.

There is a notable difference between language workbenches' models and the Semantic Models I've used so far in this book. As an OO bigot, I naturally build an object-oriented Semantic Model that combines both data structure and behavior. However, language workbenches don't work that way. They provide an environment for defining the schema of the model, that is, its data structure, typically using a particular DSL for the purpose—the schema definition language. They then leave the behavioral semantics as a separate exercise, usually through code generation.

9: Language
Workbenches

At this point, the word "meta" begins to enter the picture, and things start looking like an Escher drawing. This is because the schema definition language has a semantic model, which is itself a model. The schema definition language's Semantic Model is the meta-model for a DSL's Semantic Model. But the schema definition language itself needs a schema, which is defined using a Semantic Model whose meta-model is the schema definition language whose meta-model is the . . . (swallows self).

If the above paragraph didn't make perfect sense to you (and it only makes sense to me on Tuesdays) then I'll take things more slowly.

I'll begin with a fragment of the secret panel example, specifically the movement from the active state to the waiting-for-light state. I can show this fragment with the state diagram in Figure 9.1.

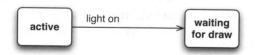

Figure 9.1 *A simple state diagram of a light switch*

This fragment shows two states and a transition connecting them. With the Semantic Model I showed in the Introduction ("The State Machine Model," p. 5), I interpret this model as two instances of the state class and one instance of the transition class, using the Java classes and fields I defined for the Semantic Model. In this case, the schema for the Semantic Model is Java class definitions. In particular, I need four classes: state, event, string, and transition. Here's a simplified form of that schema:

```
class State {
...
}

class Event {
  ...
}

class Transition {
  State source, target;
  Event trigger;
  ...
}
```

The Java code is one way to represent that schema; another way is to use a class diagram (Figure 9.2).

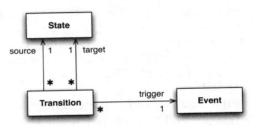

Figure 9.2 *A class diagram for a simple state machine schema*

The schema of a model defines what you can have in the contents of the model. I can't add guards to my transitions on my state diagram unless I add them in the schema. This is the same as any data structure definition: classes and instances, tables and rows, record types and records. The schema defines what goes into the instances.

The schema in this case is the Java class definitions, but I can have the schema as a bunch of Java *objects* rather than classes. This would allow me to manipulate the schema at runtime. I can do a crude version of this approach with three Java classes for classes, fields, and objects.

```
class MClass...
  private String name;
  private Map<String, MField> fields;

class MField...
  private String name;
  private MClass target;
```

```
class MObject...
  private String name;
  private MClass mclass;
  private Map<String, MObject> fields;
```

I can use this environment to create a schema of states and transitions.

```
private MClass state, event, transition;
private void buildTwoStateSchema() {
  state = new MClass("State");
  event = new MClass("Event");

  transition = new MClass("Transition");
  transition.addField(new MField("source", state));
  transition.addField(new MField("target", state));
  transition.addField(new MField("trigger", event));
}
```

9: Language
Workbenches

Then, I can use this schema to define the simple state model of Figure 9.1.

```
private MObject active, waitingForDrawer, transitionInstance, lightOn;
private void buildTwoStateModel() {
  active = new MObject(state, "active");
  waitingForDrawer = new MObject(state, "waiting for drawer");
  lightOn = new MObject(event, "light on");
  transitionInstance = new MObject(transition);
  transitionInstance.set("source", active);
  transitionInstance.set("trigger", lightOn);
  transitionInstance.set("target", waitingForDrawer);
}
```

It can be useful to think of this structure as two models, as illustrated in Figure 9.3. The base model is the fragment of Miss Grant's secret panel; it contains the MObjects. The second model contains the MClasses and MFields and is usually referred to as a meta-model. A **meta-model** is a model whose instances define the schema for another model.

Since a meta-model is just another Semantic Model, I can easily define a DSL to populate it just like I do for its base model—I call such a DSL a **schema definition language**. A schema definition language is really just a form of data model, with some way of defining entities and relationships between them. There are lots of different schema definition languages and meta-models out there.

When rolling a DSL by hand, there usually isn't much point in creating a meta-model. In most situations, using the structural definition capability of your host language is the best bet. A language you have is much easier to follow, as you are using familiar language constructs both for the schema and for the instances. In my crude example, if I want to find the source state of my transition, I have to say something like aTransition.get("source") rather than aTransition.getSource(); this makes it much harder to find what fields are available, forces me to do my own type checking, and so on. I'm working despite my language rather than with it.

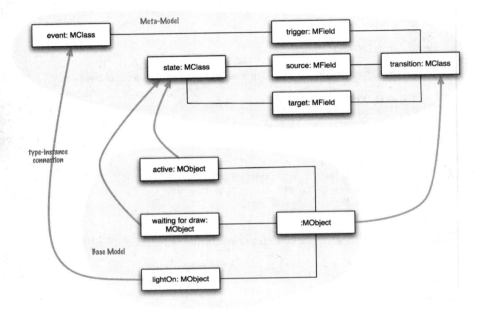

Figure 9.3 *Meta-model and base model for a state machine*

Perhaps the biggest argument for not using a meta-model in this situation is that I lose the ability to make my Semantic Model a proper OO domain model. While the meta-model does a tolerable, if kludgy, job of defining the structure of my Semantic Model, it's really hard to define its behavior. If I want proper objects that combine both data and behavior, I'm much better off with using the language's own mechanism for schema definition.

These tradeoffs work differently for language workbenches. In order to provide good tooling, a workbench needs to examine and manipulate the schema of any model I define. This manipulation is usually much easier when using a meta-model. In addition, the tooling of language workbenches overcomes many of the common disadvantages of using a meta-model. As a result, most language workbenches use meta-models. The workbench uses the model to drive the definition of editors and to help with adding in the behavior that can't exist in the model.

The meta-model, of course, is just a model. As with any other model, it has a schema to define its structure. In my crude example, that schema is one that describes MClass, MField, and MObject. But there's logically no reason why this schema can't be defined using a meta-model. This then allows you to use the workbench's own modeling tools to work on the schema definition system itself, allowing you to create meta-models using the same tools that are used to write DSL scripts. In effect, the schema definition language is itself just another DSL in the language workbench.

Many language workbenches take this approach, which I refer to as a boot-strapped workbench. In general, a bootstrapped workbench gives you more confidence that the modeling tools will be sufficient for your own work, since the tool can define itself.

But this is also the point where you start to think of yourself as inside an Escher drawing. If models are defined using meta-models, which are just models defined using meta-models—where does it all end? In practice, the schema definition tools are special in some way, and there's some stuff that's hard-coded into the workbench to make it work. Essentially, the special thing about a schema definition model is that it's capable of defining itself. So although you can imagine yourself popping up an infinite ladder of meta-models, at some point you reach a model that can define itself. That's quite weird in its own way, of course. On the whole I find it easiest not to think about it too hard, even on a Tuesday.

A common question is what is the difference between a schema definition language and a grammar. The short answer is that a grammar defines the concrete syntax of a (textual) language, while the schema definition language defines the structure of the schema of a Semantic Model. A grammar will thus include lots of things that describe the input language, while a schema definition language will be independent of any DSL used to populate the Semantic Model. A grammar also implies the structure of the parse tree; together with tree construction rules, it can define the structure of a syntax tree. But a syntax tree is usually different from a Semantic Model (as I've discussed in "The Workings of a Parser," p. 47).

When defining a schema, we can think of it in terms of data structures: classes and fields. Indeed, a lot of schema definition is about thinking of the logical data structure in which we can store the elements of a Semantic Model. But there's a further element that can appear in a schema—structural constraints. These are constraints on what makes valid instances of the Semantic Model, equivalent to invariants in Design by Contract [Meyer].

Structural constraints usually are validation rules that go beyond what can be expressed within the data structure definition. Data structure definition itself implies constraints—we can't say anything in the Semantic Model that its schema can't store. Our state model above says there's only one target state for a transition; we can't add more because there's nowhere to put it in. That's a constraint that is defined and enforced by the data structure.

When we talk about structural constraints, we usually mean those that aren't due to the data structure—we can store it, but it's illegal. This might be a limitation imposed on a data structure, such as saying that a person's number of legs must be 0, 1, or 2 even if we are storing that attribute in an integer field. Constraints can be arbitrarily complicated, involving a number of fields and objects—for example, saying that a person cannot be her own ancestor.

Schema definition languages often come with some way of expressing structural constraints. This may be as limited as allowing you to attach ranges to attributes, or it may be a general-purpose language to allow you to express any constraint. One usual limitation is that structural constraints cannot change the Semantic

9: Language Workbenches

Model, they can only query it. In this way, these constraints are a *Production Rule System (513)* without any chaining.

9.3 Source and Projectional Editing

One of the most notable features of many language workbenches is their use of a projectional editing system, not the source editing system that most programmers are used to. A **source-based** editing system defines the program using a representation that's editable independently of the tools used to process that representation into a running system. In practice that representation is textual, which means the program can be read and edited with any text-editing tool. This text is the source code of the program. We turn it into an executable form by feeding the source code into a compiler or interpreter, but the source is the key representation that we programmers edit and store.

With a **projectional editing** system, the core representation of the program is held in a format specific to the tool that uses it. This format is a persistent representation of the *Semantic Model (159)* used by the tool. When we want to edit the program, we start up the tool's editing environment, and the tool can then project editable representations of its Semantic Model for us to read and update. These representations may be text, or they may be diagrams, tables, or forms.

Desktop database tools, such as Microsoft Access, are good examples of projectional editing systems. You don't ever see, let alone edit, the textual source code for an entire Access program. Instead, you start up Access and use various tools to examine the database schema, reports, queries, etc.

Projectional editing gives you a number of advantages over a source-based approach. The most obvious one is that it allows editing through different representations. A state machine is often best thought of in a diagrammatic form, and with a projectional editor you can render a state machine as a diagram and edit it directly in that form. With source, you can only edit it in text, and although you can run that text through a visualizer to see the diagram, you can't edit that diagram directly.

A projection like this allows you to control the editing experience to make it easier to enter the correct information and disallow incorrect information. A textual projection can, given a method call on an object, only show you the legal methods for that class and only allow you to enter a valid method name. This gives you a much tighter feedback cycle between the editor and the program and allows the editor to give more assistance to the programmer.

You can also have multiple projections, either at the same time or as alternatives. A common demonstration of the Intentional Software's language workbench shows a conditional expression in a C-like syntax. With a menu command, you can switch that same expression to a Lisp-like syntax, or to a tabular form. This allows you to use whichever projection best fits the way you want to look at the information for the particular task at hand, or to follow an individual programmer's preference. Often, you want multiple projections of the same information—such as showing a class' superclass as a field in a form and also in a class hierarchy in another pane of the editing environment. Editing either of these updates the core model which, in turn, updates all projections.

These representations are projections of an underlying model, and thus encourage semantic transformations of that model. If we want to rename a method, this can be captured in terms of the model rather than in terms of text representations. This allows many changes to be made in semantic terms as operations on a semantic model, rather than in textual terms. This is particularly helpful for doing refactorings in a safe and efficient manner.

9: Language
Workbenches

Projectional editing is hardly new; it's been around for at least as long as I've been programming. It has many advantages, yet most serious programming we do is still source-based. Projectional systems lock you into a specific tool, which not only makes people nervous about vendor lock-in, but also makes it hard to create an ecosystem where multiple tools collaborate over a common representation. Text, despite its many faults, is a common format; so tools that manipulate text can be used widely.

A particularly good example of where this has made a big difference is source code management. There's been a great deal of interesting developments in source code management over the last few years, introducing concurrent editing, representation of diffs, automated merging, transactional repository updates, and distributed version control. All of these tools work on a wide range of programming environments because they operate only on text files. As a result, we see a sad situation where many tools that could really use intelligent repositories, diffs, and merges are unable to do so. This problem is a big deal for larger software projects, which is one reason why larger software systems still tend to use source-based editing.

Source has other pragmatic advantages. If you're sending someone an email to explain how to do something, it's easy to throw in a text snippet, whereas explaining through projections and screenshots can be much more trouble. Some transformations can be automated very well with text processing tools, which is very useful if a projectional system doesn't provide a transformation you need. And while a projectional system's ability to only allow valid input can be helpful, it's often useful to type in something that doesn't work immediately, as a temporary step, while thinking through a solution. The difference between helpful restriction and constraints on thinking is often a subtle one.

One of the triumphs of modern IDEs is that they provide a way to have your cake and eat it. You work fundamentally in a source-based way, with all the advantages that implies; however, when you load your source into an IDE, it creates a semantic model that allows it to use all the projectional techniques to make editing easier—an approach I call **model-assisted source editing**. Doing this requires a lot of resources; the tool has to parse all the sources and requires a lot of memory to keep the semantic model, but the result comes close to the best

9: Language
Workbenches

of both worlds. To be able to do this, and to keep the model updated as the programmer edits, is a difficult task.

9.3.1 Multiple Representations

One concept I find handy when thinking about the flow of source and projectional editing is the notion of representational roles. Source code plays two roles: It is the editing representation (the representation of the program that we edit) and the storage representation (the representation that we store in persistent form). A compiler changes this representation into one that is executable—that is, one that we can run on our machine. With an interpreted language, the source is an executable representation as well.

At some point, such as during compilation, an abstract representation is generated. This is a purely computer-oriented construct that makes it easier to process the program. A modern IDE generates an abstract representation in order to assist editing. There may be multiple abstract representations; the one the IDE uses for editing may not be the same as the syntax tree used by the compiler. Modern compilers often create multiple abstract representations for different purposes, such as a syntax tree for some things and a call graph for others.

With projectional editing, these representations are arranged differently. The core representation is the *Semantic Model (159)* used by the tool. This representation is projected into multiple editing representations. The model is stored using a separate storage representation. The storage representation may be human-readable at some level—for example, serialized in XML—but it isn't a representation any sane person would use for editing.

9.4 Illustrative Programming

Perhaps the most intriguing consequence of projectional editing is its support for what I call **illustrative programming**. In regular programming, we pay most attention to the program, which is a general statement of what should work. It's general because it's a text that describes the general case, yielding different results with different inputs.

But the most popular programming environment in the world doesn't work like that. The most popular environment, in my unscientific observation, is a spreadsheet. Its popularity is particularly interesting because most spreadsheet programmers are **lay programmers**: people who don't consider themselves to be programmers.

With a spreadsheet, the most visible thing is an illustrative calculation with a set of numbers. The program is hidden away in the formula bar, visible just one cell at a time. The spreadsheet fuses the execution of the program with its definition, and makes you concentrate on the former. Providing a concrete illustration of the program output helps people understand what the program definition does, so they can more easily reason about behavior. This is, of course, a property shared with the heavy use of testing, but with the difference that in a spreadsheet, the test output has more visibility than the program.

I chose the term "illustrative programming" to describe this, partly because "example" is so heavily used (and "illustration" isn't) but also because the term "illustration" reinforces the explanatory nature of the example execution. Illustrations are meant to help explain a concept by giving you a different way of looking at it—similarly, an illustrative execution is there to help you see what your program does as you change it.

When trying to make a concept explicit like this, it's useful to think about the boundary cases. One boundary is the notion of using projections of program information during editing, such as in an IDE that shows you the class hierarchy while you are working on the code. In some ways this is similar, as the hierarchy display is continuously updated as you modify the program, but the crucial difference is that the hierarchy can be derived from static information about the program. Illustrative programming requires information from the actual running of the program.

I also see illustrative programming as a wider concept than the ability to easily run code snippets in an interpreter that's a much beloved feature of dynamic languages. Interpreting snippets allows you to explore execution, but it doesn't put the examples front and center, the way that a spreadsheet does with its values. Illustrative programming techniques push the illustration to the foreground of your editing experience. The program retreats to the background, peeping out only when we want to explore a part of the illustration.

I don't think that illustrative programming is all goodness. One problem I've seen with spreadsheets and with GUI designers is that, while they do a good job of revealing what a program does, they de-emphasize program structure. As a result, complicated spreadsheets and UI panels are often difficult to understand and modify. They are often rife with uncontrolled copy-and-paste programming.

This strikes me as a consequence of the fact that the program is de-emphasized in favor of the illustrations, and the programmers often don't think to take care of it. We suffer enough from a lack of care of programs even in regular programming, so it's hardly shocking that this occurs with illustrative programs written by lay programmers. But this problem leads to programs that quickly become unmaintainable as they grow. The challenge for future illustrative programming environments is to help develop a well-structured program behind the illustrations—although the illustrations may also force us to rethink what a well-structured program is.

The hard part of this may well be the ability to easily create new abstractions. One of my observations on rich client UI software is that they get tangled because the UI builders think only in terms of screens and controls. My experiments here suggest that you need to find the right abstractions for your program, which will take a different form. But these abstractions won't be supported by the screen builder, for it can only illustrate the abstractions it knows about.

Despite this problem, illustrative programming is a technique we should take more seriously. We can't ignore the fact that spreadsheets have become so popular with lay programmers. Many language workbenches focus their attention on enabling lay programmers, and projectional editing leads to illustrative programming which could be a vital part of their eventual success.

9.5 Tools Tour

Thus far, I've been reluctant to mention any actual language workbenches in this section. With such a volatile field, anything I say about tools is likely to be out of date by the time this book is published, let alone by the time you read it. But I decided to do it anyway in order to provide a feel for the variety of tools in this world. Remember, however, that the actual details of the tools are almost certainly not going to be true when you read this.

Perhaps the most influential, and certainly the most sophisticated is the Intentional Workbench by Intentional Software (http://intentsoft.com). This project is led by Charles Simonyi, who is well known for his pioneering work at PARC on early word processors and leading the development of Microsoft Office. His vision is of a highly collaborative environment that includes programmers and nonprogrammers working in a single integrated tool. As a result, the Intentional Workbench has very rich projectional editing capabilities and a sophisticated meta-modeling repository to tie it all together.

The biggest criticisms of Intentional's work are how long they've been beavering away at it and how secretive they are. They have also been rather active on the patent front, which alarms many in this field. They did start doing some meaningful public presentations in early 2009 and have demonstrated what looks like a highly capable tool. It supports all sorts of projections: text, tables, diagrams, illustrations, and all combinations.

Although Intentional is the oldest language workbench in terms of its development, I believe the oldest released tool is MetaEdit from from MetaCase (www.metacase.com). This tool is particularly focused on graphical projections, although it also supports tabular projections (but not text). Unusually, it isn't a bootstrapped environment; you use a special environment for schema and projection definition. Microsoft has a DSL tools group with a similar style of tool.

Meta-Programming System (MPS) by JetBrains (www.jetbrains.com) takes another route at projectional editing, preferring a structured text representation. It also targets much more at programmer productivity rather than close involvement of domain experts in the DSLs. JetBrains has made a significant advancement of IDE capabilities with their sophisticated code editing and navigation tools and thus has built a strong reputation for developer tooling. They see MPS as the foundation for many future tools. A particularly important point is that most MPS code is open source. This might be a vital factor in getting developers to move into a very different kind of programming environment.

Another open source effort is Xtext (www.eclipse.org/Xtext), built on top of Eclipse. Xtext is notably different in that it uses source editing rather than projectional editing. It uses ANTLR as a parser back-end and integrates with Eclipse to provide model-assisted source editing for DSL scripts in a style similar to editing Java in Eclipse.

9: Language Workbenches

Microsoft's SQL Server Modeling project (formerly known as "Oslo") uses a mix of textual source and projections. It has a modeling language, currently called M, which allows you to define a *Semantic Model (159)* schema and a grammar for a textual DSL. The tool then creates a plugin for an intelligent editor that gives you model-assisted source editing. The resulting models go into a relational database repository, and a diagrammatic projectional editor (Quadrant) can manipulate these models. The models can be queried at runtime, so the whole system could work entirely without code generation.

I'm sure this little tour isn't comprehensive, but it gives you a flavor of the variety of tools in this space. Lots of new ideas are popping up, and it is still far too early to predict what combination of technical and business ideas will lead to a success. Purely in terms of technical sophistication, Intentional would surely take the prize, but as we know it's often a lesser technology hitting the most important targets that wins in the end.

9.6 Language Workbenches and CASE tools

Some people look at language workbenches and see many parallels with CASE tools that were supposed to revolutionize software development a couple of decades ago.

For those who missed that saga, CASE (short for Computer-Aided Software Engineering) tools would allow you to express the design of your software using various diagrammatic notations and then generate your software for you. They were the future of software development in the 90s, but have since faded away.

On the surface, there are a few similarities. The central role of a model, the use of meta-models to define it, and projectional editing with diagrams were all characteristics of CASE tools.

The key technological difference is that CASE tools did not give you the ability to define your own language. MetaEdit is a language workbench probably closest to a CASE tool—but its facilities to define your own language and control code generation from your model are very different from what CASE tools provided.

There is a strand of thought that OMG (Object Management Group) MDA (Model-Driven Architecture) could play a large role in the DSL and language workbench landscape. I'm skeptical of this, as I see the OMG MDA standards as too unwieldy for a DSL environment.

Perhaps the most important difference, however, is cultural. Many people in the CASE world looked down on programming and saw their role as automating something that would then die out. More people in the language workbench community come from a programming background and are looking to create environments that make programmers more productive (as well as increase collaboration with customers and users). A result of this is that language workbenches tend to have strong support for code generation tools—as this is central to producing a useful output from the tool. This aspect tends to get missed during demonstrations, as it's less exciting than the projectional editing side, but it's a sign of how seriously we should take the resulting tool.

9.7 Should You Use a Language Workbench?

I don't know if you're as tired of reading this disclaimer as I am of writing it, but I'll say it again. This is a new and volatile area, so what I say now could easily be invalid by the time you read it. Even so, here goes.

I've been keeping an eye on these tools for the past few years because I think they have extraordinary potential. If language workbenches pull off their vision, they could completely change the face of programming, altering our idea of a programming language. I should stress that it is a potential, and could end up like nuclear fusion's potential to solve all of our energy needs. But the fact that the potential is there means it's worth keeping an eye on developments in this space.

However, the newness and volatility of the field means that it's important to be cautious at the moment (early 2010). A further reason for caution is that the tools inherently involve a significant lock-in. Any code you write in one language workbench is impossible to export into another one. Some kind of interoperability standard may come some day, but it will be very hard. As a result, any effort you commit to working in a language workbench could be lost if you run into a wall or there are vendor problems.

One way to mitigate this is to treat the language workbench as a parser rather than a full DSL environment. With a full DSL environment, you design the *Semantic Model (159)* in the language workbench's schema definition environment and generate pretty full-featured code. When you treat the language workbench as a parser, you still build the Semantic Model the usual way. You then use the language workbench to define the editing environment with a model that's geared to *Model-Aware Generation (555)* against your Semantic Model. That way, should you run into issues with your language workbench, it's only the parser that's affected. The most valuable stuff is in the Semantic Model which isn't locked in. You will also find it easier to come up with an alternative parser mechanism.

My thought above, like much of using language workbenches, is somewhat speculative. But I do think the potential of these tools means they are worth experimenting experimenting with. Although it's a risky investment, the potential returns are considerable.

9: Language
Workbenches

Part II

Common Topics

Chapter 10

A Zoo of DSLs

As I've said at the beginning of this book, the software world is full of DSLs. Here I want to show a brief summary of a few of them. I haven't picked them out of any desire to show the best; it's just a selection of those I've come across and considered suitable to show the variety of different kinds of DSL that exist. It's a tiny fraction of DSLs that exist out there, but I hope even a small sample can give you a taste of the full population.

10.1 Graphviz

Graphviz is both a good example of a DSL and a useful package for anyone working with DSLs. It is a library for producing graphical renderings of node-and-arc graphs. Figure 10.1 shows an example stolen from Graphviz's website.

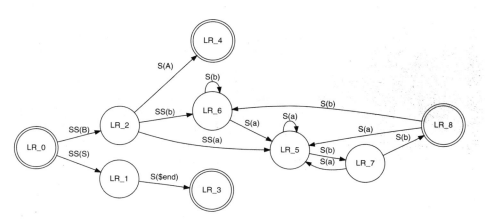

Figure 10.1 *An example use of Graphviz*

147

To produce this diagram, you provide the following code in the DOT language, which is an external DSL:

```
digraph finite_state_machine {
  rankdir=LR;
  size="8,5"
  node [shape = doublecircle]; LR_0 LR_3 LR_4 LR_8;
  node [shape = circle];
  LR_0 -> LR_2 [ label = "SS(B)" ];
  LR_0 -> LR_1 [ label = "SS(S)" ];
  LR_1 -> LR_3 [ label = "S($end)" ];
  LR_2 -> LR_6 [ label = "SS(b)" ];
  LR_2 -> LR_5 [ label = "SS(a)" ];
  LR_2 -> LR_4 [ label = "S(A)" ];
  LR_5 -> LR_7 [ label = "S(b)" ];
  LR_5 -> LR_5 [ label = "S(a)" ];
  LR_6 -> LR_6 [ label = "S(b)" ];
  LR_6 -> LR_5 [ label = "S(a)" ];
  LR_7 -> LR_8 [ label = "S(b)" ];
  LR_7 -> LR_5 [ label = "S(a)" ];
  LR_8 -> LR_6 [ label = "S(b)" ];
  LR_8 -> LR_5 [ label = "S(a)" ];
}
```

This example shows two kinds of things on the graph: nodes and arcs. Nodes are declared with the node keyword, but don't have to be declared. Arcs are declared using the -> operator. Both nodes and arcs can be given attributes listed between square brackets.

Graphviz uses a *Semantic Model (159)* in the form of a C data structure. The Semantic Model is populated by a parser using *Syntax-Directed Translation (219)* and *Embedded Translation (299)* written in Yacc and C. The parser makes good use of *Embedment Helper (547)*. As it's C, it doesn't have a helper object, but a set of helper functions which are called in the grammar actions. As a result, the grammar itself is quite readable with short code actions that don't obstruct the grammar. The lexer is handwritten, which is fairly common with Yacc parsers despite the presence of the Lex lexer generator.

The real business of Graphviz occurs once the Semantic Model of nodes and arcs is populated. The package figures out how to lay the graph out onto a diagram and has rendering code that can render the graph in various graphics formats. All of this is independent of the parser code; once the script is turned into the Semantic Model, everything else is based on those C data structures.

The example I show uses semicolons as statement separators, but these are entirely optional.

10.2 JMock

JMock is a Java library for *Mock Objects* [Meszaros]. Its authors have written several mock object libraries, which have evolved their ideas of a good internal DSL for defining expectations on the mocks ([Freeman and Pryce] is an excellent paper that talks about this evolution).

Mock objects are used in testing. You begin the test by declaring **expectations,** which are methods that an object expects will be called on it during the test. You then plug in the mock object to the actual object you are testing and stimulate that actual object. The mock object then reports if it received the correct method calls, thus supporting *Behavior Verification* [Meszaros].

10: A Zoo of DSLs

To illustrate JMock's DSL, I'll go through a couple of eras of its evolution, beginning with the first library named JMock (JMock 1) that its authors dub the Cenozoic era [Freeman and Pryce]. Here are some example expectations:

```
mainframe.expects(once())
  .method("buy").with(eq(QUANTITY))
  .will(returnValue(TICKET));
```

This says that, as part of a test, the mainframe object (which is a mock mainframe) expects the buy method to be called once on it. The parameter to the call should be equal to the QUANTITY constant. When called, it will return the value in the TICKET constant.

Mock expectations need to be written in with test code as a fragmentary DSL, so an internal DSL is a natural choice for them. JMock 1 uses a mix of *Method Chaining (373)* on the mock object itself (expects) and *Nested Function (357)* (once). *Object Scoping (385)* is used to allow the Nested Function methods to be bare. JMock 1 does the Object Scoping by forcing all tests using mocks to be written in a subclass of their library class.

In order to make the Method Chaining work better with IDEs, JMock uses progressive interfaces. This way, with is only available after method, which allows the autocompletion in IDEs to guide you through writing the expectations in the right way.

JMock uses *Expression Builder (343)* to handle the DSL calls and translate them onto a *Semantic Model (159)* of mocks and expectations. [Freeman and Pryce] refers to the Expression Builders as a *syntax layer* and the Semantic Model as the *interpreter layer*.

An interesting lesson in extensibility came from the interplay of Method Chaining and Nested Function. The Method Chaining defined on the Expression Builder is tricky for users to extend, since all the methods you can use are defined on the Expression Builder. However, it's easy to add new methods in the Nested Function since you define them on the test class itself, or use your own subclass of the library superclass used for Object Scoping.

This approach works well, but still has some problems. In particular, there is the constraint that all tests using mocks must be defined in a subclass of the JMock library class so that Object Scoping can work. JMock 2 used a new style of DSL that avoided this problem; in this version, the same expectation reads like this:

```
context.checking(new Expectations() {{
    oneOf(mainframe).buy(QUANTITY);
    will(returnValue(TICKET));
}}
```

With this version, JMock now uses Java's instance initialization to do the Object Scoping. Although this does add some noise at the beginning of the expression, we can now define expectations without being in a subclass. The instance initializer effectively forms a *Closure (397)*, making this a use of *Nested Closure (403)*. It's also worth noting that instead of using Method Chaining everywhere, the expectations now use *Function Sequence (351)* to separate the method call part of the expectation from specifying the return value.

10.3 CSS

When I talk about DSLs, I often use the example of CSS.

```
h1, h2 {
  color: #926C41;
  font-family: sans-serif;
}
b {
  color: #926C41;
}

*.sidebar {
  color: #928841;
  font-size: 80%;
  font-family: sans-serif;
}
```

CSS is an excellent example of a DSL for many reasons. Primarily, it's a good example because most CSS programmers don't call themselves programmers, but web designers. CSS is thus a good example of a DSL that's not just read by domain experts, but also written by them.

CSS is also a good example because of its declarative computational model, which is very different from imperative models. There's no sense of "do this, then do that" that you get with traditional programming languages. Instead, you simply declare matching rules for HTML elements.

This declarative nature introduces a good bit of complexity into figuring out what's going on. In my example, an h2 element inside a sidebar div matches two different color rules. CSS has a somewhat complicated specificity scheme to figure out which color will win in such situations. However, many people find it hard to figure out how these rules work—which is the dark side of a declarative model.

CSS plays a well-focused role in the web ecosystem. While it's pretty much essential these days, the thought of using only it to build an entire web application is ludicrous. It does its job pretty well, and works with a mix of other DSLs and general-purpose languages inside a complete solution.

CSS is also quite large. There's a lot to it, both in the basic language semantics and in the semantics of the various attributes. DSLs can be limited in what they can express, but still have a lot to learn.

CSS fits in with the general DSL habit of limited error handling. Browsers are designed to ignore erroneous input, which usually means that a CSS file with a syntax error misbehaves silently, often making for some annoying debugging.

Like most DSLs, CSS lacks any way to create new abstractions—a common consequence of the limited expressiveness of DSLs. While this is mostly fine, there are some features that are annoyingly missing. The sample CSS shows one of these—I can't name colors in my color schemes, so I have to use meaningless hex strings. People commonly complain about the lack of arithmetic functions that would be useful when manipulating sizes and margins. The solutions to this are the same as with other DSLs. Many simple problems, such as named colors, can be solved with *Macros (183)*.

Another solution is to write another DSL that is similar to CSS and generates CSS as output. SASS (http://sass-lang.com) is an example of this, providing arithmetic operations and variables. It also uses a very different syntax, preferring syntactic newlines and indentation to CSS's block structure. This is a common solution: use one DSL as a layer on top of another to provide abstractions the underlying DSL misses. The overlayed DSL needs to be similar (SASS uses the same attribute names), and the user of the overlayed DSL usually also understands the underlying DSL.

10.4 Hibernate Query Language (HQL)

Hibernate is a widely used object-relational mapping system which allows you to map Java classes onto the tables of a relational database. HQL provides the ability to write queries in a SQLish form in terms of Java classes that can be mapped to SQL queries against a real database. Such a query might look like this:

```
select person from Person person, Calendar calendar
where calendar.holidays['national day'] = person.birthDay
    and person.nationality.calendar = calendar
```

This allows people to think in terms of Java classes rather than database tables, and also avoid dealing with the various annoying differences between different databases' SQL dialects.

The essence of HQL processing is to translate from an HQL query to a SQL query. Hibernate does this in three steps:

- HQL input text is transformed using *Syntax-Directed Translation (219)* and *Tree Construction (281)* into an HQL abstract syntax tree (AST).

- The HQL AST is transformed into a SQL AST.

- A code generator generates SQL code from the SQL AST.

In all these cases, ANTLR is used. In addition to using a token stream as an input to ANTLR's syntactic analyzer, you can use ANTLR with an AST as input (this is what ANTLR calls a "tree grammar"). ANTLR's tree construction syntax is used to build both the HQL and SQL ASTs.

This path of transformations, input text ▶ input AST ▶ output AST ▶ output text, is a common one with source-to-source transformation. Like in many transformation scenarios, it's good to break down a complex transformation into several small transformations that can be easily plugged together.

You can think of the SQL AST as the *Semantic Model (159)* for this case. The meaning of the HQL queries is defined by the SQL rendering of the query, and the SQL AST is a model of SQL. More often than not, ASTs are not the right structure for a Semantic Model, as the constraints of a syntax tree usually help more than they hinder. But for source-to-source translation, using an AST of the output language makes a great deal of sense.

10.5 XAML

Ever since the beginning of full-screen user interfaces, people have experimented with how to define the screen layout. The fact that this is a graphic medium has always led people to use some kind of graphic layout tool. Often, however, greater flexibility can be achieved by performing the layout in code. The trouble is that code may be an awkward mechanism. A screen layout is primarily a hierarchic structure, and stitching together a hierarchy in code is often more fiddly than it ought to be. So, with the appearance of Windows Presentation Framework, Microsoft introduced XAML as a DSL to lay out UIs.

(I confess I find Microsoft's product naming to be remarkably banal these days. Good code names like "Avalon" and "Indigo" get turned into boring acronyms like WPF and WCF. Although it does invite a fantasy of seeing "Windows" turned one day into "Windows Technology Foundation.")

XAML files are XML files that can be used to lay out an object structure; with WPF, they can lay out a screen, as in this example I stole from [Anderson]:

```
<Window x:Class="xamlExample.Hello"
  xmlns="http://schemas.microsoft.com/winfx/2006/xaml/presentation"
  xmlns:x="http://schemas.microsoft.com/winfx/2006/xaml"
  Title="Hello World">
  <WrapPanel>
    <Button Click='HowdyClicked'>Howdy!</Button>
    <Button>A second button</Button>
    <TextBox x:Name='_text1'>An editable text box</TextBox>
    <CheckBox>A check box</CheckBox>
    <Slider Width='75' Minimum='0' Maximum='100' Value='50' />
  </WrapPanel>
</Window>
```

Microsoft is a fan of graphical design surface, so when working with XAML you can use a design surface, a text representation, or both. As a textual representation, XAML does suffer from XML's syntactic noise, but XML does work fairly well on hierarchic structures like this. The fact that it bears a strong resemblance to HTML for laying out screens is also a plus.

XAML is a good example of what my old colleague Brad Cross refers to as a compositional (rather than computational) DSL. Unlike my initial state machine example, XAML is about how to organize relatively passive objects into a structure. Program behavior usually doesn't depend strongly on the details of how a screen is laid out. Indeed, one of XAML's strengths is that it encourages separating the screen layout from the code that drives the behavior of the screen.

A XAML document logically defines a C# class, and indeed there is some code generation. The code is generated as a partial class, in this case xamlExample.Hello. I can add behavior to the screen by writing code in another partial class definition.

```
public partial class Hello : Window {
  public Hello() {
    InitializeComponent();
  }
  private void HowdyClicked(object sender, RoutedEventArgs e) {
    _text1.Text = "Hello from C#";
  }
}
```

This code allows me to wire behavior together. For any control defined in the XAML file, I can tie an event on that control to a handler method in the code (HowdyClicked). The code can also refer to controls by name in order to manipulate them (_text1). By using names like this, I can keep the references free of the structure of the UI layout, which allows me to change it without having to update the behavior code.

XAML is usually thought of in the context of UI design, as it's almost always described together with WPF. However, XAML can be used to wire up instances of any CLR classes, so it could be used in many more situations.

The structure that XAML defines is a hierarchy. DSLs can define hierarchy, but they can also define other structures by mentioning names. Indeed this is what Graphviz does using references to names to define a graph structure.

DSLs to lay out graphical structures like this are quite common. Swiby (http://swiby.codehaus.org) uses a Ruby internal DSL to define screen layout. It uses *Nested Closure (403)* which provides a natural way of defining a hierarchic structure.

While I'm talking about DSLs for graphical layout, I can't help but mention PIC—an old, and rather fascinating, DSL. PIC was created in the very early days of Unix, when graphical screens were still unusual. It allows you to describe a diagram in a textual format and then process it to produce the image. As an example, the following code produces Figure 10.2:

```
.PS
A: box "this"
move 0.75
B: ellipse "that"
move to A.s; down; move;
C: ellipse "the other"
arrow from A.s to C.n
arrow dashed from B.s to C.e
.PE
```

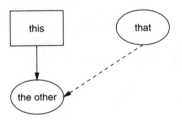

Figure 10.2 *A simple PIC diagram*

The written form is mostly obvious; the only hint is that you refer to connection points on shapes by compass points, so A.s means the "south" point on shape A. Textual descriptions like PIC aren't so popular in the days of WYSIWYG environments, but the approach can be rather handy.

10.6 FIT

FIT (http://fit.c2.com) is a testing framework developed by Ward Cunningham in the early noughties (FIT stands for Framework for Integrated Test). Its aim is to describe testing scenarios in the form that a domain expert can understand. The basic idea has been extended by various tools since, in particular Fitnesse (http://fitnesse.org).

Looking at FIT as a DSL, there are a couple of things that make it interesting. The first is its form; at the heart of FIT is the notion that nonprogrammers are very comfortable with specifying examples in a tabular form. So a FIT program is a collection of tables, typically embedded in HTML pages. In between the tables, you can put any other HTML elements, which are treated as comments. This allows a domain expert to use prose narrative to describe what they want, with tables providing something that's processable.

FIT tables can take different forms. The most program-like form is the action fixture, which is essentially a simple imperative language. It's simple in that there are no conditionals or loops, just a sequence of verbs:

eg.music.Realtime			
enter	select	2	pick an album
press	same album		find more like it
check	status	searching	
await	search complete		
check	status	ready	
check	selected songs	2	

Each table is connected to a fixture that can translate the verbs into actions against the system. The *check* verb is special, in that it carries out a comparison. When the table is run, an output HTML is created which is the same as the input page except that all the check rows are colored either green or red, depending on whether the comparison matches or not.

Apart from this limited imperative form, FIT works with a number of other table styles. Here's one that defines tabular output data from a list of objects (in this case, the search above):

eg.music.Display					
title	artist	album	year	time()	track()
Scarlet Woman	Weather Report	Mysterious Traveller	1974	5.72	6 of 7
American Tango	Weather Report	Mysterious Traveller	1974	3.70	2 of 7

The header line defines various methods to be invoked against the collection of objects in the list. Each row compares against an object, defining the expected value from the object for its columns attribute. When the table is run, FIT compares the expected values against actual values, again using green/red coloring. This table follows the imperative table earlier, so you get an imperative table (called an *action fixture* in FIT) to navigate the applications, followed by a declarative table of expected results (called a *row fixture*) to compare to what the application displays.

This use of tables as source code is unusual, but it's an approach that could be used more often. People like specifying things in tabular form, whether it's examples for test data or more general processing rules such as a *Decision Table (495)*. Many domain experts are very comfortable with editing tables in spreadsheets, which can then be processed into source code.

The second interesting thing about FIT is that it's a testing-oriented DSL. In recent years, there's been quite a growth in interest for automated testing tools, with several DSLs created for organizing tests. Many of these have been influenced by FIT.

Testing is a natural choice for a DSL. Compared to general-purpose programming languages, testing languages often require different kinds of structures and abstractions, such as the simple linear imperative model of FIT's action tables. Tests often need to be read by domain experts, so a DSL makes a good choice, usually with a DSL purpose-written for the application at hand.

10.7 Make et al.

A trivial program is trivial to build and run, but it isn't long before you realize that building code requires several steps. So, in the early days of Unix, the Make tool (www.gnu.org/software/make) provided a platform for structuring builds. The issue with builds is that many steps are expensive and don't need to be done every time, so a *Dependency Network (505)* is a natural choice of programming model. A Make program consists of several targets linked through dependencies.

10: A Zoo of DSLs

```
edit : main.o kbd.o command.o display.o
            cc -o edit main.o kbd.o command.o
main.o : main.c defs.h
            cc -c main.c
kbd.o : kbd.c defs.h command.h
            cc -c kbd.c
command.o : command.c defs.h command.h
            cc -c command.c
```

The first line of this program says that edit depends on the other targets in the program; so, if any of them is not up-to-date, then, after building them, we must also build the edit target. A Dependency Network allows me to minimize build times to a bare minimum while ensuring that everything that needs to be built is actually built. Make is a familiar external DSL.

To me, the most interesting thing about build languages like Make isn't so much their computational model as the fact that they need to intermix their DSL with a more regular programming language. Apart from specifying the targets and the dependencies between them (a classic DSL scenario), you also need to say how each target gets built—which suggests a more imperative approach. In Make, this means using shell script commands, in this example the calls to cc (the C compiler).

In addition to language intermixing in the target definitions, a simple Dependency Network suffers when the build gets more complex, requiring further abstractions on top of the Dependency Network. In the Unix world, this has led to the Automake toolchain, where Makefiles are generated by the Automake system.

A similar progression is visible in the Java world. The standard Java build language is Ant, which is also an external DSL using an XML carrier syntax. (Which, despite my dislike of XML carrier syntax, did avoid Make's horrendous problems caused by allowing tabs and spaces in syntactic indentation.) Ant started simple, but ended up with embedded general-purpose scripts and other systems, like Maven, generating Ant scripts.

For my personal projects, the build system I prefer these days is Rake (http://rake.rubyforge.org). Like Make and Ant, it uses a Dependency Network as its core computational model. The big difference is that it is an internal DSL in Ruby. This allows you to write the contents of the targets in a more seamless manner, but also to build larger abstractions more easily.

Here is an example culled from the Rakefile that builds this book:

```
docbook_out_dir = build_dir + "docbook/"
docbook_book = docbook_out_dir + "book.docbook"

desc "Generate Docbook"
task :docbook => [:docbook_files, docbook_book]

file docbook_book => [:load] do
  require 'docbookTr'
  create_docbook
end
```

```
def create_docbook
  puts "creating docbook"
  mkdir_p docbook_out_dir
  File.open(docbook_book, 'w') do |output|
    File.open('book.xml') do |input|
      root = REXML::Document.new(input).root
      dt = SingleDocbookBookTransformer.new(output,
                       root, ServiceLocator.instance)
      dt.run
    end
  end
end
```

The line task :docbook => [:docbook_files, docbook_book] is the Dependency Network, saying that the :docbook depends on the other two targets. Targets in Rake can be either tasks or files (supporting both task-oriented and product-oriented styles of Dependency Network). The imperative code for building a target is contained in a *Nested Closure (403)* after the target declaration. (See [Fowler rake] for more on the nice things you can do with Rake.)

Chapter 11

Semantic Model

The model that's populated by a DSL.

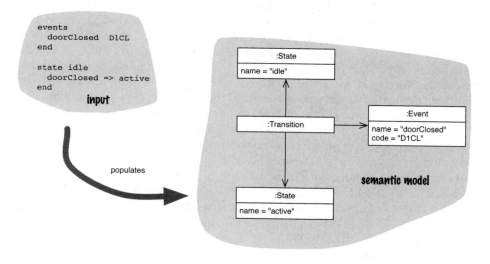

11.1 How It Works

In the context of a DSL, a semantic model is a representation, such as an in-memory object model, of the same subject that the DSL describes. If my DSL describes a state machine, then my Semantic Model might be an object model with classes for state, event, etc. A DSL script defining particular states and events would correspond to a particular population of that schema, with an event instance for each event declared in the DSL script. The Semantic Model is thus the library or framework that the DSL populates.

In this book, my Semantic Models are in-memory object models, but there are other ways of representing them. You could have a data structure, with the behavior of a state machine coming from functions that act upon that data. The model need not be in-memory; the DSL could populate a model held in a relational database.

The Semantic Model should be designed around the purpose of the DSL. For a state machine, the purpose is to control behavior using a *State Machine (527)* computational model. Indeed, the Semantic Model should be usable without a DSL present. You should be able to populate a Semantic Model through a command-query interface. This ensures that the Semantic Model fully captures the semantics of the subject area, and allows independent testing of itself and the parser.

A Semantic Model is a notion very similar to that of a *Domain Model* [Fowler PoEAA]. I use a separate term because although Semantic Models are often subsets of Domain Models, they don't have to be. I use Domain Model to refer to a behaviorally rich object model, while a Semantic Model may be data alone. A Domain Model captures the core behavior of an application, while a Semantic Model may play a supporting role. A good example of this is an object-relational mapper that coordinates data between an object model and a relational database. You could use a DSL to describe object-relational mappings, and the resulting Semantic Model would consist of the *Data Mappers* [Fowler PoEAA], not the Domain Model that is the subject of the mapping.

A Semantic Model is usually different from a syntax tree because they serve separate purposes. A syntax tree corresponds to the structure of the DSL scripts. Although an abstract syntax tree may simplify and somewhat reorganize the input data, it still takes fundamentally the same form. The Semantic Model, however, is based on what will be done with the information from a DSL script. It often will be a substantially different structure, and usually not a tree structure. There are occasions when an AST is an effective Semantic Model for a DSL, but these are the exception rather than the rule.

Traditional discussions of languages and parsing don't use a Semantic Model. This is part of the difference between working with DSLs and with general-purpose languages. A syntax tree usually makes a suitable structure to base code generation for a general-purpose language, so there's less desire to have a different Semantic Model. From time to time, a Semantic Model is used; for instance, a call graph representation is very useful for optimization. Such models are referred to as intermediate representations—they are usually intermediate steps before code generation.

The Semantic Model can often precede the DSL. This happens when you decide that a portion of a Domain Model might be better populated from a DSL than from the regular command-query interface. Alternatively, you can build a DSL and Semantic Model together using the discussions with domain experts both to refine the expressions of the DSL and the structure of the Domain Model.

The Semantic Model can either hold the code to execute itself (interpreter style), or be the basis for code generation (compiler style). Even if you are using code generation, it's useful to provide interpretation to help with testing and debugging.

The Semantic Model is usually the best place for validation behavior, since you have all the information and structures in place to express and run the validations. In particular, it's useful to run validations before either running the interpreter or generating code.

11: Semantic Model

Brad Cross introduced the distinction of computational and compositional DSLs [Cross]. This distinction has much to do with the kind of Semantic Models they produce. A compositional DSL is about describing some kind of composite structure in textual form. Using XAML to describe a UI layout is a good example of this—the primary form of the Semantic Model is how the various elements are composed together. The state machine example is more a case of a computational DSL, in that the Semantic Model it produces feels more like code than data.

Computational DSLs lead to a Semantic Model that drives computation, usually with an alternative computational model instead of the usual imperative one. The Semantic Model for this is usually an *Adaptive Model (487)*. You can do a lot more with a computational DSL, but people often find them more difficult to work with.

It's usually helpful to think of the Semantic Model as having two distinct interfaces. One interface is the **operational interface**—the one that allows clients to use a populated model in the course of their work. The second is the **population interface** which is used by the DSL to create instances of the classes in the model.

The operational interface should assume the Semantic Model has already been created and make it easy for other parts of the system to take advantage of it. I've often found that a good mental trick for API design is to assume that the model is, magically, already there, and then ask myself how I would use it. This can be counterintuitive, but I find it better to define the operational interface before I think about the population interface, even though a running system will have to execute the population interface first. This is a general rule of thumb for me with any objects, not just DSLish ones.

The population interface is only used to create instances of the model and may only be used by the parser (and test code for the Semantic Model). Although we seek to decouple the Semantic Model and the parser(s) as much as possible, there is always a dependency in that the parser obviously needs to see the Semantic Model in order to populate it. Despite this, by building a clear interface we can reduce the chances of an implementation change in the Semantic Model forcing us to change the parser.

11.2 When to Use It

My default advice is to always use a Semantic Model. I'm always rather uncomfortable when I say "always" because usually I find such absolute advice a strong sign of closed-minded thinking. In this case, it may be my limited imagination but I only see very few cases when you might not want to use a Semantic Model, and these are all in very simple situations.

I find that a Semantic Model brings many compelling advantages. A clear Semantic Model allows you to test the semantics and the parsing of the DSL separately. You can test the semantics by populating the Semantic Model directly and executing tests against the model; you can test the parser by seeing if it populates the Semantic Model with the correct objects. If you have more than one parser, you can test if they produce semantically equivalent output by comparing the population of the Semantic Model. This makes it easy to support multiple DSLs and, more commonly, to evolve the DSL separately from the Semantic Model.

The Semantic Model increases the flexibility in parsing as well as in execution. You can execute the Semantic Model directly, or you can use code generation. If you're using code generation, you can base it off the Semantic Model which completely decouples it from parsing. You can also execute both the Semantic Model and the generated code—which allows you to use the Semantic Model as a simulator for the generated code. A Semantic Model also makes it easier to have multiple code generators because the independence from the parser avoids any need to duplicate parser code.

But the most important part of using a Semantic Model is that it separates thinking about semantics from thinking about parsing. Even a simple DSL contains enough complexity to justify dividing it up into two simpler problems.

So what are the few exceptions I envisage? One case is simple imperative interpretation where you just want to execute each statement as you parse it. A classic calculator program where you evaluate simple arithmetic expressions is a good example of this. With arithmetic expressions, even if you don't interpret them immediately, their abstract syntax tree (AST) is pretty much what you would have in a Semantic Model anyway, so there's no value in having a separate syntax tree and Semantic Model for that case. That's an example of a more general rule: If you can't think of a more useful model than the AST, then there's little point creating a separate Semantic Model.

The most common case where people don't use a Semantic Model is when they're generating code. In this approach, the parser can generate an AST and the code generator can work directly off the AST. This is a reasonable approach, provided the AST is a good model of the underlying semantics and you don't mind coupling the code generation logic to the AST. If that isn't the case, you may well find it simpler to transform the AST to a Semantic Model and do a simpler code generation from that.

Such is my bias, however, that I'd always start by assuming I need a Semantic Model. Even if thinking through convinces me that one isn't necessary, I'd stay alert to increasing complexity and put one in as soon as I start seeing any complication coming into my parsing logic.

Despite my high regard for Semantic Model, it's only fair to point out that using a Semantic Model isn't part of the DSL culture in the functional programming world. The functional programming community has a long history of DSL thinking, and my experience with modern functional languages is no more than occasional experimentation. So, although my inclinations tell me that a Semantic Model would be useful even in that world, I have to confess that I don't have enough knowledge of functional programming to have any confidence in those inclinations.

11: Semantic Model

11.3 The Introductory Example (Java)

There's lots of examples of Semantic Models in this book, precisely because I favor using Semantic Model so much. A useful one to illustrate the point is the one I use in the initial example—the secret panel controller state machine. Here, the Semantic Model is the state machine model. I didn't use the term Semantic Model in the discussion initially, since my purpose in the introduction was to introduce the notion of a DSL. As a result, I found it easier to assume that the model was built first and the DSL layered on top of it. This still makes the model a Semantic Model but, since we are thinking inside out, it's not such a good way to approach the discussion.

However, the classic strengths of a Semantic Model are all there. I can (and did) test the state machine model independently of writing the DSLs. I did some refactoring of the implementation of the model without having to touch the parsing code, because my implementation changes didn't alter the population interface. Even if I did have to alter these methods, most of the time the changes would be easy to follow from the parser code because that interface marks a clear boundary.

While it's not terribly common to support multiple DSLs for the same Semantic Model, this was a requirement for my example. A Semantic Model made this relatively easy. I had multiple parsers with both internal and external DSLs. I could test them by ensuring they create equivalent populations of the Semantic Model. I could easily add a new DSL and parser without duplicating any code in other parsers or altering the Semantic Model. This advantage also worked for output. In addition to having the Semantic Model execute directly as a state machine, I could use it to generate multiple code generation examples, as well as visualizations.

Apart from being used as the basis for execution and other outputs, the Semantic Model also provided a good place for validation checks. I can check that I don't have any unreachable states or states that you can't get out of. I can also check that all the events and commands are used in the definitions of states and transitions.

Chapter 12

Symbol Table

A location to store all identifiable objects during a parse to resolve references.

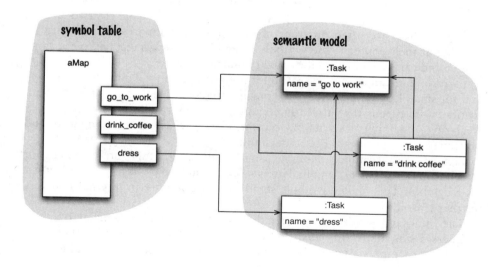

Many languages need to refer to objects at multiple points within the code. If we have a language that defines a configuration of tasks and their dependencies, we need a way for one task to refer to its dependent tasks in its definition.

In order to do this, we come up with some form of symbol for each task; while processing the DSL script, we put these symbols in a Symbol Table that stores the link between the symbol and an underlying object that holds the full information.

12.1 How It Works

The essential purpose of a Symbol Table is to map between a symbol used to refer to an object in a DSL script and the object that symbol refers to. A mapping like this naturally fits with the notion of a map data structure, so it's no surprise that the most common implementation of a Symbol Table is a map with the symbol as a key and the *Semantic Model (159)* object as a value.

One question to consider is the kind of object that should be used as the key in the Symbol Table. For many languages, the most obvious choice is a string, since the text of the DSL is a string.

The main case to use something other than a string is with languages that support a symbol data type. Symbols are like strings in a structural sense—a symbol is fundamentally a sequence of characters—but they usually differ in behavior. Many string operations (concatenation, substrings, etc.) do not make sense for symbols. The principal task of symbols is to be used for lookup, and symbol types are usually designed with that in mind. So, while the two strings, "foo" and "foo", are often different objects and are compared for equality by looking at their contents, the symbols :foo and :foo always resolve to the same object and can be compared for equality much faster.

Performance can be a good reason for preferring symbol data types to strings, but for small DSLs it may not make much difference. The big reason to prefer a symbol data type is that it clearly communicates your intention in using it. By declaring something as a symbol, you state clearly what you are using it for and thus make your code easier to understand.

Languages that support symbols usually have a particular literal syntax for them. Ruby uses :aSymbol, Smalltalk uses #aSymbol, and Lisp treats any bare identifier as a symbol. This makes symbols stand out all the more in internal DSLs—a further reason to use them.

The values in a symbol table can either be final model objects or intermediate builders. Using model objects makes the Symbol Table act as result data, which is good for simple situations—but putting a builder object as the value often provides more flexibility, at the cost of a bit more work.

Many languages have different kinds of objects that need to be referred to. The introductory state model needs to identify states, commands, and events. Having multiple kinds of things to refer to means you have to choose between a single map, multiple maps, or a special class.

Using a single map for your Symbol Table means that all lookups for any symbol use the same map. An immediate consequence of this is that you can't use the same symbol name for different kinds of things—you can't have an event with the same name as a state. This may be a useful constraint to reduce confusion in the DSL. However, using a single map makes it harder to read the processing code as it's less clear what kind of thing is being manipulated when you refer to the symbol. I therefore don't recommend this option.

With multiple maps, you have a separate map for each kind of objects you are referring to. For example, a state model may have three maps for events, commands, and states. You may think of this as one logical Symbol Table or three Symbol Tables. Either way, I prefer this option to a single map, as it's now clear in the code which kind of object you are referring to in the processing steps.

Using a special class means having a single object for the Symbol Table with different methods to refer to the different kinds of objects stored in there: getEvent(String code), getState(String code), registerEvent(String code, Event object), etc. This can sometimes be useful, and it does give a natural place to add any specific symbol-processing behavior. Most of the time, however, I don't find a compelling need to do this.

In some cases, objects are referred to before they are properly defined—these are called forward references. DSLs don't usually have strict rules about declaring identifiers before you use them, so forward references often make sense. If you allow forward references, you need to ensure that any reference to a symbol will populate the entry in the symbol table if it isn't already there. This will often push you to use builders as the values in the symbol table, unless the model objects are very flexible.

If there's no explicit declaration of symbols, you also need to be wary of misspelled symbols, which can be a frustrating source of errors. There may be some way you can detect misspelled symbols, and putting that kind of checking in will prevent a lot of hair-pulling. This problem is one reason to require that all symbols are declared in some way. If you choose to require an explicit declaration, remember that symbols don't need to be declared before usage.

More complicated languages often have nested scopes, where symbols are only defined in a subset of the overall program. This is very common in general-purpose languages, but much rarer in simpler DSLs. If you do need to do this, you can support this by using a *Symbol Table for Nested Scopes* [parr-LIP].

12.1.1 Statically Typed Symbols

If you are doing an internal DSL in a statically typed language, such as C# or Java, you can easily use a hashmap as your Symbol Table with strings as keys. A line of such a DSL might look something like this:

```
task("drinkCoffee").dependsOn("make_coffee", "wash");
```

Using strings like this certainly will work, but it comes with some disadvantages.

- Strings introduce syntactic noise, since you have to quote them.

- The compiler can't do any type checking. If you misspell your task names, you only discover that at runtime. Furthermore, if you have different kinds of objects that you identify, the compiler can't tell if you refer to the wrong type—again, you only discover this at runtime.

- If you use a modern IDE, it can't do autocompletion on strings. This means you lose a powerful element of programming assistance.

- Automated refactorings may not work well with strings.

You can avoid these problems by using some kind of statically typed symbol. Enums make a good simple choice, as does a *Class Symbol Table (467)*.

12.2 When to Use It

Symbol Tables are common to any language-processing exercise, and I expect you'll almost always need to use them.

There are times when they aren't strictly necessary. With *Tree Construction (281)*, you can always delve around in the syntax tree to find things. Often, a search on the *Semantic Model (159)* that you're building up could do the job. But sometimes, you need some intermediate store, and even when you don't, it often makes life easier.

12.3 Further Reading

[parr-LIP] provides a lot of detail on using various kinds of Symbol Table for external DSLs. Since Symbol Table is also a valuable technique for internal DSLs, many of these approaches are likely to be appropriate for internal DSLs as well.

[Kabanov et al.] provides some useful ideas for using statically typed symbols in Java. As usual, these ideas are often usable in other languages too.

12.4 Dependency Network in an External DSL (Java and ANTLR)

Here's a simple dependency network:

```
go_to_work -> drink_coffee dress
drink_coffee  -> make_coffee wash
dress -> wash
```

The task on the left-hand side of "->" is dependent on the tasks named on the right-hand side. I'm parsing this using *Embedded Translation (299)*. I want to be able to write the dependencies in any order and return a list of the heads—that is, those tasks that aren't a prerequisite of any other task. This is a good example of where it's worthwhile to keep track of the tasks in a Symbol Table.

As is my habit, I write a loader class to wrap the ANTLR parser; this will take input from a reader:

```
class TaskLoader...
  private Reader input;
  public TaskLoader(Reader input) {
    this.input = input;
  }

  public void run() {
    try {
      TasksLexer lexer = new TasksLexer(new ANTLRReaderStream(input));
      TasksParser parser = new TasksParser(new CommonTokenStream(lexer));
      parser.helper = this;
      parser.network();
    } catch (IOException e) {
      throw new RuntimeException(e);
    } catch (RecognitionException e) {
      throw new RuntimeException(e);
    }
  }
}
```

12: Symbol Table

The loader inserts itself as the *Embedment Helper (547)* to the generated parser. One of the helpful things it provides is the symbol table, which is a simple map of task names to tasks.

```
class TaskLoader...
  private Map<String, Task> tasks = new HashMap<String, Task>();
```

The grammar for this DSL is extremely simple.

```
grammar file...
  network : SEP? dependency (SEP dependency)* SEP?;
  dependency
    : lhs=ID '->' rhs+=ID+
      {helper.recognizedDependency($lhs, $rhs);}
    ;
```

The helper contains the code that handles the recognized dependency. To link together the tasks, it both populates and uses the Symbol Table.

```
class TaskLoader...
  public void recognizedDependency(Token consequent, List dependencies) {
    registerTask(consequent.getText());
    Task consequentTask = tasks.get(consequent.getText());
    for(Object o : dependencies) {
      String taskName = ((Token)o).getText();
      registerTask(taskName);
      consequentTask.addPrerequisite(tasks.get(taskName));
    }
  }
}
```

```
private void registerTask(String name) {
  if (!tasks.containsKey(name)) {
    tasks.put(name, new Task(name));
  }
}
```

Once the loader has run, it can be asked for the heads of the graph.

```
class TaskLoader...
  public List<Task> getResult() {
    List<Task> result = new ArrayList<Task>();
    for(Task t : tasks.values())
      if (!tasksUsedAsPrerequisites().contains(t))
        result.add(t);
    return result;
  }

  public Set<Task> tasksUsedAsPrerequisites() {
    Set<Task> result = new HashSet<Task>();
    for(Task t : tasks.values())
      for (Task preReq : t.getPrerequisites())
        result.add(preReq);
    return result;
  }
```

12.5 Using Symbolic Keys in an Internal DSL (Ruby)

Symbol Tables come from the world of parsing, but they are just as useful with internal DSLs. For this example, I use Ruby to show the use of a symbol data type, which is the type to use if you have it in your language. Here's the simple DSL script with breakfast tasks and prerequisites:

```
task :go_to_work => [:drink_coffee, :dress]
task :drink_coffee => [:make_coffee, :wash]
task :dress => [:wash]
```

Each task is referred to in the DSL by Ruby's symbol data type. I use *Function Sequence (351)* to declare the list of tasks, with the details of each task shown using a *Literal Map (419)*.

The *Semantic Model (159)* is simple to describe, just a single task class.

```ruby
class Task
  attr_reader :name
  attr_accessor :prerequisites

  def initialize name, *prereqs
    @name = name
    @prerequisites = prereqs
  end

  def to_s
    name
  end
end
```

The DSL script is read by an *Expression Builder (343)* that uses *Object Scoping (385)* with instance_eval.

```ruby
class TaskBuilder...
  def load aStream
    instance_eval aStream
    return self
  end
```

The Symbol Table is a simple dictionary.

```ruby
class TaskBuilder...
  def initialize
    @tasks = {}
  end
```

The task clause takes the single hash association argument and uses it to populate the task information.

```ruby
class TaskBuilder...
  def task argMap
    raise "syntax error" if argMap.keys.size != 1
    key = argMap.keys[0]
    newTask = obtain_task(key)
    prereqs = argMap[key].map{|s| obtain_task(s)}
    newTask.prerequisites = prereqs
  end
  def obtain_task aSymbol
    @tasks[aSymbol] = Task.new(aSymbol.to_s) unless @tasks[aSymbol]
    return @tasks[aSymbol]
  end
```

The implementation of a Symbol Table using symbols is the same as with strings for identifiers. However, you should use symbols if they are available.

12.6 Using Enums for Statically Typed Symbols (Java)

Michael Hunger has been a very diligent reviewer of this book; he has steadily urged me to describe using enums as statically typed symbols, as it is a technique he's had much success with. Many people like static typing for its ability to find errors, which isn't something I'm as enthused about since I feel that static typing catches few errors that won't be caught by decent testing—which you need with or without static typing. But one great advantage of static typing is that it works well with modern IDEs. It's nice to just be able to type Control-Space and get a list of all the symbols that are valid for this point in a program.

I'll use the task example again, with exactly the same *Semantic Model (159)* as earlier. The Semantic Model has strings for task names, but in the DSL I'll use enums. That will not only give me autocompletion, but it will also guard against typos. The enum is simple.

```
public enum TaskName {
  wash, dress, make_coffee, drink_coffee, go_to_work
}
```

I can use this to define my task dependencies like this:

```
builder = new TaskBuilder(){{
  task(wash);
  task(dress).needs(wash);
  task(make_coffee);
  task(drink_coffee).needs(make_coffee, wash);
  task(go_to_work).needs(drink_coffee, dress);
}};
```

I'm using Java's instance initializer here for *Object Scoping (385)*. I also use a static import for the task name enum, which allows me to use the bare task names in the script. With these two techniques, I'm able to write the script in any class without needing to use inheritance that would force me to write it in a subclass of the *Expression Builder (343)*.

The task builder builds up a map of tasks; each call to task registers a task in the map.

```
class TaskBuilder...
  PrerequisiteClause task(TaskName name) {
    registerTask(name);
    return new PrerequisiteClause(this, tasks.get(name));
  }
  private void registerTask(TaskName name) {
    if (!tasks.containsKey(name)) {
      tasks.put(name, new Task(name.name()));
    }
  }
  private Map<TaskName, Task> tasks = new EnumMap<TaskName, Task>(TaskName.class);
```

The prerequisite clause is a child builder class.

```
class PrerequisiteClause...
  private final TaskBuilder parent;
  private final Task consequent;

  PrerequisiteClause(TaskBuilder parent, Task consequent) {
    this.parent = parent;
    this.consequent = consequent;
  }
  void needs(TaskName... prereqEnums) {
    for (TaskName n : prereqEnums) {
      parent.registerTask(n);
      consequent.addPrerequisite(parent.tasks.get(n));
    }
  }
}
```

I made the child builder a static inner class of the task builder so it could access private members of the task builder. I could have gone further and made it an instance inner class; then I wouldn't have needed the reference to the parent. I didn't do this as it may be hard to follow for readers less familiar with Java.

Using enums like this is quite easy, and it's nice that it doesn't force inheritance or constraints on where you can write DSL script code—an advantage compared to a *Class Symbol Table (467)*.

With an approach like this, bear in mind that if the set of symbols needs to correspond to some external data source, you can write a step that reads the external data source and code-generates the enum declarations, so that everything is kept in sync [Kabanov et al.].

A consequence of this implementation is that I have a single namespace of symbols. This is fine when you have multiple little scripts that share the same set of symbols, but sometimes you want different scripts to have different sets of symbols.

Suppose I have two sets of tasks, one devoted to morning tasks (such as those above) and the other dedicated to snow shoveling. (Yes, I'm thinking of that as I look at my driveway today.) When I'm working on morning tasks, I only want to see them offered to me by my IDE, and similarly for snow-shoveling tasks.

I can support this by defining my task builder in terms of an interface and having my enums implement that interface.

```
public interface TaskName {}

class TaskBuilder...
  PrerequisiteClause task(TaskName name) {
    registerTask(name);
    return new PrerequisiteClause(this, tasks.get(name));
  }
  private void registerTask(TaskName name) {
    if (!tasks.containsKey(name)) {
      tasks.put(name, new Task(name.toString()));
    }
  }
  private Map<TaskName, Task> tasks = new HashMap<TaskName, Task>();
```

I can then define some enums and use them for a specific group of tasks by selectively importing the ones I need.

```
import static path.to.ShovelTasks.*;

enum ShovelTasks implements TaskName {
  shovel_path, shovel_drive, shovel_sidewalk, make_hot_chocolate
}

builder = new TaskBuilder(){{
  task(shovel_path);
  task(shovel_drive).needs(shovel_path);
  task(shovel_sidewalk);
  task(make_hot_chocolate).needs(shovel_drive, shovel_sidewalk);
}};
```

If I want even more static type control, I could make a generic version of the task builder that would check that it's using the correct subtype of TaskName. But if you're primarily interested in good IDE usability, then selectively importing the right set of enums is good enough.

Chapter 13

Context Variable

Use a variable to hold context required during a parse.

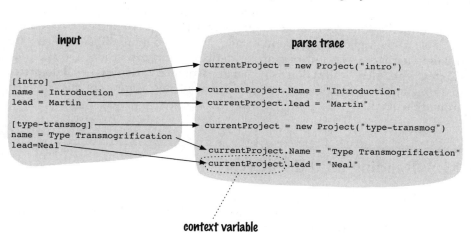

context variable

Imagine you are parsing a list of items, capturing data about each one. Each bit of information about an item can be captured independently, but you also need to know which particular item you are capturing information for.

A Context Variable does this by keeping the current item in a variable and reassigning it as you move to a new one.

13.1 How It Works

You have a Context Variable whenever you have a variable named something like currentItem which you update periodically during the parse as you move from one item to another in the input script.

175

A Context Variable can be a *Semantic Model (159)* object or a builder. A Semantic Model is superficially more straightforward, but this is only true if all its properties are mutable when the parse needs them to be changed. If this is not the case, it's usually best to use some kind of builder to gather the information and create the Semantic Model object when done—something like a *Construction Builder (179)*.

13.2 When to Use It

There are lots of places where you have to keep context during a parse, and a Context Variable is an obvious choice. It's easy to create and get going.

Context Variables are problematic, however, particularly as you get more of them. By their nature, they are mutable state that has to be kept track of, and bugs adore this kind of mutable state. It's easy to forget to update the Context Variable at the right moment, and debugging can get quite difficult. There are usually alternative ways of organizing the parse that can reduce the need for Context Variables. While I don't say that any Context Variable is evil, I do prefer to use techniques that don't need them—and you'll see mentions of this scattered around the book.

13.3 Reading an INI File (C#)

I wanted a very simple example to illustrate what a Context Variable looks like, and the old INI file format is a good illustration. Although it can seem somewhat old-fashioned—it was "improved" by the Registry in Windows—it still remains a lightweight and readable way to handle a simple list of items with properties. Alternative formats like XML and YAML can handle more complex structures, but at a cost of readability and parsing difficulty. If your needs are simple enough for an INI file, it remains a reasonable choice.

For my example, here is a list of project codes and some property data for each one:

```
[intro]
name = Introduction
lead = Martin

[type-transmog]
name = Type Transmogrification
lead=Neal


#line comment
```

```
[lang] #group comment
name = Language Background Advice
lead = Rebecca # item comment
```

Although there's no standard form for an INI file format, the basic elements are property assignments, separated into sections. In this case, each section is a project code.

The *Semantic Model (159)* is trivial.

```
class Project...
  public string Code { get; set; }
  public string Name { get; set; }
  public string Lead { get; set; }
```

The INI file format is easy to read using *Delimiter-Directed Translation (201)*. The basic structure of the parser implements the usual approach of breaking the script into lines and parsing each one.

```
class ProjectParser...
  private TextReader input;
  private List<Project> result = new List<Project>();

  public ProjectParser(TextReader input) {
    this.input = input;
  }
  public List<Project> Run() {
    string line;
    while ((line = input.ReadLine()) != null) {
      parseLine(line);
    }
    return result;
  }
}
```

The first statements in the line parser just handle blanks and comments.

```
class ProjectParser...
  private void parseLine(string s) {
    var line = removeComments(s);
    if (isBlank(line)) return ;
    else if (isSection(line)) parseSection(line);
    else if (isProperty(line)) parseProperty(line);
    else throw new ArgumentException("Unable to parse: " + line);
  }
  private string removeComments(string s) {
    return s.Split('#')[0];
  }
  private bool isBlank(string line) {
    return Regex.IsMatch(line, @"^\s*$");
  }
}
```

The Context Variable—currentProject—appears for parsing sections; at this point I assign to it.

```
class ProjectParser...
  private bool isSection(string line) {
    return Regex.IsMatch(line, @"^\s*\[");
  }
  private void parseSection(string line) {
    var code = new Regex(@"\[(.*)\]").Match(line).Groups[1].Value;
    currentProject = new Project {Code = code};
    result.Add(currentProject);
  }
  private Project currentProject;
```

I then use the Context Variable when parsing a property.

```
class ProjectParser...
  private bool isProperty(string line) {
    return Regex.IsMatch(line, @"=");
  }
  private void parseProperty(string line) {
    var tokens = extractPropertyTokens(line);
    setProjectProperty(tokens[0], tokens[1]);
  }
  private string[] extractPropertyTokens(string line) {
    char[] sep = {'='};
    var tokens = line.Split(sep, 2);
    if (tokens.Length < 2) throw new ArgumentException("unable to split");
    for (var i = 0; i < tokens.Length; i++) tokens[i] = tokens[i].Trim();
    return tokens;
  }
  private void setProjectProperty(string name, string value) {
    var proj = typeof(Project);
    var prop = proj.GetProperty(capitalize(name));
    if (prop == null) throw new ArgumentException("Unable to find property: " + name);
    prop.SetValue(currentProject, value, null);
  }
  private string capitalize(string s) {
    return s.Substring(0, 1).ToUpper() + s.Substring(1).ToLower();
  }
```

Using reflection makes the code more complex, but it does mean that I don't need to update the parser when I add more properties to the Semantic Model.

Chapter 14

Construction Builder

Incrementally create an immutable object with a builder that stores constructor arguments in fields.

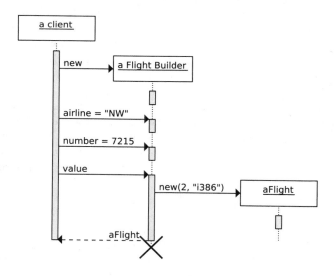

14.1 How It Works

The basic recipe for a Construction Builder is very simple. You need to create an immutable object, which I'll call the product, in a gradual manner. So, take each of the constructor arguments of the product and make a field for each one. Add further fields for any other attributes of the product that you're collecting. Finally, add a method to create and return a new product object assembled from all the data in the Construction Builder.

You may want to add some lifecycle controls to the Construction Builder. Such controls might check if you have enough information already to create the product. You might set a flag once you've returned a product to prevent returning it again, or put the created product in a field. You might raise an error if you try to add new attributes to the Construction Builder once you've created the product.

Multiple Construction Builders can be combined into deeper structures. They can then produce a group of related objects rather than a single object.

14.2 When to Use It

Construction Builder is useful whenever you need to create an object with multiple immutable fields, but you gather the values for these fields gradually. A Construction Builder gives you a coherent place to put all this data before you actually create the product.

The simplest alternatives to Construction Builder is to capture the information in local variables or in loose fields. This works fine for one or two products, but soon gets confusing if you need to create a bunch of objects at once, such as when you're parsing.

Another alternative is to create an actual model object, but after you gather data for an immutable attribute, create a new copy of the model object, with that one attribute changed, and replace the old one. This saves you having to write a Construction Builder, but is generally more awkward to do and follow. In particular, it doesn't work if you have multiple references to the object, or at least it makes it more difficult as you have to replace every reference.

Using Construction Builder is usually the best way to handle this problem, but remember that you only need it when you have immutable fields. If that's not the case, then just create your product objects directly.

Despite the common word "builder," I see this pattern as different from *Expression Builder (343)*. Construction Builder is purely about gradually building up construction arguments; it doesn't attempt to provide a fluent interface. Expression Builders are focused on providing a fluent interface. Certainly it is not unusual to find cases where a single object is both a Construction Builder and an Expression Builder, but that doesn't mean they are the same concept.

14.3 Building Simple Flight Data (C#)

Imagine an application that uses some data about flights. The data is only read by the application, so it makes sense for the domain classes to be read-only.

```
class Flight...
  readonly int number;
  readonly string airline;
  readonly IList<Leg> legs;
  public Flight(string airline, int number, List<Leg> legs) {
    this.number = number;
    this.airline = airline;
    this.legs = legs.AsReadOnly();
  }
  public int Number {get { return number; }}
  public string Airline {get { return airline; }}
  public IList<Leg> Legs {get { return legs; }}

class Leg...
  readonly string start, end;
  public Leg(string start, string end) {
    this.start = start;
    this.end = end;
  }
  public string Start {get { return start; }}
  public string End {get { return end; }}
```

14: Construction
Builder

Although the application may only read the flight data, it's quite possible that it has to gather in such a way that makes it difficult to use constructors to build fully formed objects. In these cases, a simple Construction Builder allows me to gather up the data and build the final object when I have it.

```
class FlightBuilder...
  public int Number { get; set; }
  public string Airline { get; set; }
  public List<LegBuilder> Legs { get; private set; }
  public FlightBuilder() {
    Legs = new List<LegBuilder>();
  }
  public Flight Value {
    get{return new Flight(Airline, Number, Legs.ConvertAll(l => l.Value));}
  }

class LegBuilder...
  public string Start { get; set; }
  public string End { get; set; }

  public Leg Value {
    get { return new Leg(Start, End); }
  }
```

Chapter 15

Macro

Transform input text into a different text before language processing using Templated Generation (539).

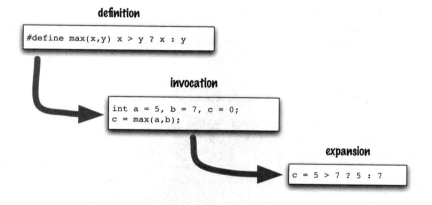

A language has a fixed set of forms and structure that it can process. At times, we see a way to add abstraction to a language by manipulating its input text with a purely textual transformation before that text is parsed by the compiler or interpreter for that language. Since we know the final form we'd like to see, it makes sense to describe the transformation by writing the desired output, with callouts for any parametrizable values.

A Macro allows you to define these transformations, either in a purely textual form or as a syntactic macro that understands the syntax of the underlying language.

183

15.1 How It Works

Macros are one of the oldest techniques for building abstractions in programming languages. In the early days of programming, macros were as prevalent as functions. Since then, they've largely fallen out of favor, mostly for good reasons. But there are still places where they do appear in internal DSLs, particularly in the Lisp community.

I like to separate macros into two main varieties: textual macros and syntactic macros. Textual macros are more familiar and easy to understand—they treat text as text. Syntactic macros are aware of the syntactic structure of the host language, thus making it easier to ensure that they operate on syntactically sensible units of text and produce syntactically valid results. A textual macro processor can operate with any language that's represented as text—which means pretty much any language. A syntactic macro processor is designed to work with only a single language; it is often baked into the tooling for that language, or even into the language specification itself.

To understand how Macros work, I think it's easiest to understand textual macros first, to get a hold of the basic concepts, even if you're more interested in syntactic macros.

15.1.1 Textual Macros

Most modern languages don't support textual macros and most developers avoid them. However, you can use textual macros with any language by using a generic macro processor such as the classic Unix m4 macro processor. Template engines, such as Velocity, are very simple macro processors and can be used for some of the techniques. And although most modern languages shy away from macros, C (and thus C++) has a macro preprocessor built into the basic tooling. C++ gurus mostly tell people to avoid the preprocessor, with good reason, but it's still there.

The simplest form of macro processing is substitution of one string for another. A good example of this being useful is avoiding duplication when specifying colors in CSS documents. Say you have a website, and there's a particular color that you use repeatedly—for table borders, line colors, text highlighting, etc. With basic CSS, you'd have to repeat the color code every time you use it.

```
div.leftbox { border-bottom-color: #FFB595}
p.head { bgcolor: #FFB595 }
```

This duplication makes it harder to update the color, and the use of a raw code makes it harder to understand what's happening. With a macro processor, you can define a special word for your color and use that instead.

```
div.leftbox { border-bottom-color: MEDIUM_SHADE}
p.head { bgcolor: MEDIUM_SHADE }
```

15: Macro

Essentially, the macro processor goes through the CSS file and replaces MEDIUM_SHADE with the color symbol to produce the same text as in the first example above. The CSS file you edit isn't therefore proper CSS; this language doesn't have the ability to define symbolic constants, so you've enhanced the CSS language with a macro processor.

For this example, you could do the substitution using a simple search-and-replace on the input text, essentially using *Textual Polishing (477)*. Although text substitution is staggeringly simple, it is a common use of macros in C programming, specifically for symbolic constants. You can use the same mechanism to introduce common elements to files, like common headers and footers to web pages. Define a marker in your pre-HTML file, run the substitution over it, and get your actual HTML file. A simple trick like this is remarkably handy for small websites that want a common header and footer without duplicating it on every page.

More interesting textual macros are those that allow you to parametrize them. Consider the case where you frequently want to determine the maximum of two numbers, so you repeatedly write the C expression a > b ? a : b. You can write this in the C preprocessor as a macro:

```
#define max(x,y) x > y ? x : y

int a = 5, b = 7, c = 0;
c = max(a,b);
```

The difference between a macro and a function call is that the macro is evaluated at compile time. It does textual search-and-replace for the max expression, substituting the arguments as it goes. The compiler never sees max.

(I should mention here that some environments use the term "macro" for a subroutine. Annoying, but such is life.)

So a macro gives you an alternative to a function call. It has the bonus of avoiding all the overhead of invoking a function—which C programmers often worried about, particularly in the early years. The trouble with macros is that they have a lot of subtle problems, particularly if they use parameters. Consider this macro for squaring a number:

```
#define sqr(x) x * x
```

Seems simple and should work. But try invoking it like this:

```
int a = 5, b = 1, c = 0;
c = sqr(a + b);
```

In this case, the value of c is 11. This is because the macro expansion resulted in the expression a + b * a + b. Since * binds tighter than +, you get a + (b * a) + b rather than (a + b) * (a + b). This is one example where a macro's expansion results in something other than what the programmer was expecting, so I call it a **mistaken expansion**. Such expansions may work most of the time but only break down in particular cases, leading to surprising bugs that are hard to find.

You can avoid that case by using more parenthesis than a Lisper.

```
#define betterSqr(x) ((x) * (x))
```

Syntactic macros avoid much of this because they operate with a knowledge of the host language. However, there are other macro problems that they share. I'll illustrate these first with textual macros.

Let's go back to the max macro and watch me mess this one up.

```
#define max(x,y) x > y ? x : y

int a = 5, b = 1, c = 0;
c = max(++a, ++b);
 printf("%d",c); // => 7
```

This is an example of **multiple evaluation** where we pass in a argument that has a side effect, and the macro body mentions the argument more than once and thus evaluates it more than once. In this case, a and b are both incremented twice. Again, this is a good example of a bug that can be hard to find. It's particularly frustrating because it's hard to predict the various ways macro expansions can go wrong. You have to think differently than you do with function calls, and it's harder to see through consequences, particularly when you start nesting macros.

For some more snakes, consider the following macro. It takes three arguments: a size 5 array of integers, a cap, and a slot for the result. It adds up the numbers in the array and puts either that sum or the cap, whichever is smaller, into the result slot.

```
#define cappedTotal(input, cap, result) \
{int i, total = 0; \
for(i=0; i < 5; i ++) \
  total = total + input[i];\
result = (total > cap) ? cap : total;}
```

We'd call it like this:

```
int arr1[5] = {1,2,3,4,5};
int amount = 0;
cappedTotal (arr1, 10, amount);
```

This works quite nicely (despite the fact it would be better as a function.) Now, look at this slight variation in usage:

```
int total = 0;
cappedTotal (arr1, 10, total);
```

After this code total is 0. The problem is that the name total was expanded into the macro but interpreted by the macro as a variable defined within the macro itself. As a result, the variable passed into the macro is ignored—this error is called **variable capture**.

There is also a reverse of this problem, which doesn't happen in C but does in languages that don't force you to declare variables. To illustrate this, I'll do some textual macros in Ruby—an exercise that's almost too pointless even by the standards of book examples. For our macro processor, we'll use Velocity, which is a fairly well-known tool for generating web pages. Velocity has a macro feature, which I can press into service for this illustration.

We'll use the cappedTotal example again, just as with C. Here is the Velocity macro on the Ruby code:

```
#macro(cappedTotal $input $cap $result)
total = 0
${input}.each do |i|
 total += i
end
$result = total > $cap ? $cap : total
#end
```

15: Macro

It's not very idiomatic Ruby, to put it mildly, but it's conceivable that a new Ruby programmer, fresh from C, might do it this way. Within the macro body, the variables $input, $cap, and $result refer to the arguments when the macro is called. Our hypothetical programmer might use the macro in a Ruby program like this:

```
array = [1,2,3,4,5]
#cappedTotal('array' 10 'amount')
puts "amount is: #{amount}"
```

If you now use Velocity to process the Ruby program before running it and run the resulting file, it all seems to work fine. Here's what it expands to:

```
array = [1,2,3,4,5]
total = 0
array.each do |i|
 total += i
end
amount = total > 10 ? 10 : total
puts "amount is: #{amount}"
```

Now, our programmer went off for a cup of tea, then came back and wrote this code:

```
total = 35
#... lines of code ...
#cappedTotal('array' 10 'amount')
puts "total  is #{total}"
```

He would be surprised. The code works, in that it sets amount correctly. However, he'll sooner or later run into a bug because the variable total is altered behind the scenes when the macro runs. This is because the body of the macro mentions total, so when it's expanded, the expansion changes the value of the variable.

The total variable has been captured by the macro. The consequences of the capture may be different, indeed worse, than the earlier form of variable capture, but both of them stem from the same basic problem.

15.1.2 Syntactic Macros

As a result of all of these issues, macro processing, particularly textual macros, has fallen out of favor in most programming environments. You still run into it in C, but modern languages avoid macros entirely.

There are two notable exceptions—languages that use and encourage syntactic macros: C++ and Lisp. In C++, the syntactic macros are templates which have spawned many fascinating approaches to generating code at compile time. I'm not going to talk about C++ templates any more here. Partly, this is because I'm not very familiar with templates, as my C++ work predates them becoming common. C++ is also not a language noted for internal DSLs; usually, DSLs in the C/C++ world are external. After all, C++ is a complex tool to use even for experienced programmers, which doesn't encourage internal DSL usage. (As Ron Jeffries puts it: It's a long time since I did C++ . . . but not long enough!)

Lisp, however, is another matter. Lispers have been talking about doing internal DSLs in Lisp since the dawn of Lisp, which is a long time since Lisp is one of the oldest programming languages still in active use. This is no surprise, for Lisp is all about symbolic processing—that is, about the manipulation of language.

Macros have penetrated deeper into Lisp's heart than almost any other programming language. Many core features of Lisp are done through macros, so even a beginning Lisp programmer will use them—usually without realizing they are macros. As a result, when people are talking about language features for internal DSLs, Lispers will always talk about the importance of macros. When the inevitable language comparison arguments surface, Lispers can be counted on to belittle any language that doesn't have macros.

(This also puts me in a somewhat awkward pose. Although I've done plenty of dabbling with Lisp, I'd not call myself a serious Lisper and am not active in the Lisp community.)

Syntactic macros do have some powerful abilities, and Lispers do use them. However, much, perhaps most, use of macros in Lisp is to polish the syntax for handling *Closures (397)*. Here's a simple and silly example of a closure for an *Execute-Around Method* [Beck SBPP] in Ruby:

```
aSafe = Safe.new "secret plans"
aSafe.open do
 puts aSafe.contents
end
```

The open method is implemented like this:

```
def open
  self.unlock
  yield
  self.lock
end
```

The key point here is that the content of the closure isn't evaluated until the receiver calls `yield`. This ensures that the receiver can open the safe before running the passed-in code. Compare this approach:

```
puts aSafe.open(aSafe.contents)
```

This doesn't work because the code in the parameter is evaluated before the call to open. Passing the code in a closure enables you to defer the evaluation of that code. **Deferred evaluation** means that the receiving method to a call chooses when, or indeed if, to execute the code that's been passed in.

15: Macro

It makes sense to do the same thing in Lisp. The equivalent call would be:

```
(openf-safe aSafe (read-contents aSafe))
```

We might expect that this can be implemented using a function call like this:

```
(defun openf-safe (safe func)
 (let ((result nil))
  (unlock-safe safe)
  (setq result (funcall func))
  (lock-safe safe)
  result))
```

But this doesn't defer evaluation. In order to defer evaluation, you need to call it like this:

```
(openf-safe aSafe (lambda() (read-contents aSafe)))
```

But this looks way too messy. To get the clean style of call to work, you need a macro.

```
(defmacro openm-safe (safe func)
 `(let (result)
  (unlock-safe ,safe)
  (princ (list result ,safe))
  (setq result ,func)
  (lock-safe ,safe)
  result))
```

This macro avoids the need to wrap functions in lambdas, so we can call this with a clearer syntax.

```
(openm-safe aSafe (read-contents aSafe))
```

A large part (perhaps the majority) of the use of Lisp macros is to provide a clear syntax for the mechanism of delayed evaluation. A language with a cleaner closure syntax doesn't need macros for this.

The macro above will work almost all of the time, but that "almost" indicates problems—for example, if we call it like this:

```
(let (result)
  (setq result (make-safe "secret"))
  (openm-safe result (read-contents result)))
```

This problem is variable capture, causing an error if we use a symbol named result as an argument. Variable capture is a endemic problem for Lisp macros; as a result, Lisp dialects have worked hard to come up with ways to avoid it. Some, like Scheme, have a hygienic macro system, where the system avoids any variable capture by redefining symbols behind the scenes. Common Lisp has a different mechanism: gensyms, essentially an ability to generate symbols for these local variables guaranteeing that they won't collide with anything else. Gensyms are more trouble to use, but they give the programmer the ability to deliberately use variable capture, and there are some situations when deliberate variable capture is useful, although I'll leave that discussion to Paul Graham [Graham].

Apart from variable capture, there is also the potential problem of multiple evaluation, as the parameter safe is used at several points in the expansion definition. To avoid this, I need to bind the parameter to another local variable, which also needs a gensym, which results in this:

```
(defmacro openm-safe2 (safe func)
  (let ((s (gensym))
        (result (gensym)))
    `(let ((,s ,safe))
       (unlock-safe ,s)
       (setq ,result ,func)
       (lock-safe ,s)
       ,result)))
```

Avoiding such issues makes macros a lot harder to write than they might seem at first sight. Despite this, the deferred evaluation with a convenient syntax is used heavily in Lisp, because closures are important for creating new control abstractions and alternative computational models—which is the kind of thing Lispers like doing.

Despite the fact that a large proportion of Lisp macros are written for deferred evaluation, there are other useful things you can do with Lisp macros that are beyond what can be done with syntactically convenient closures alone. In particular, macros provide a mechanism for Lispers to do *Parse Tree Manipulation (455)*.

Lisp syntax seems quirky on first glance, but as you get used to it, you realize that it's a good representation of the parse tree of the program. With each list, the first element is the type of the parse tree node, and the remaining elements are its children. Lisp programs use *Nested Functions (357)* heavily, and the result is a parse tree. By using macros to manipulate the Lisp code before evaluation, Lispers can do Parse Tree Manipulation.

Few programming environments support Parse Tree Manipulation at the moment, so Lisp's support for it is a distinguishing feature of the language. In addition to supporting DSL elements, it also allows for more fundamental manipulations in the language. A good example of this is the standard common Lisp macro setf.

Although Lisp is often used as a functional language—that is, one that doesn't have side effects on data—it does have functions to store data in variables. The basic function for this is setq which can set a variable like this:

```
(setq var 5)
```

15: Macro

Lisp forms lots of different data structures out of nested lists, and it may be that you want to update data in these structures. You can access the first item in a list with car and update it with rplaca. But there are lots of ways to access various bits of data structures, and valuable brain cells are spent on remembering an access function and an update function for each one. So, to help matters, Lisp has setf which, given an access function, will automatically calculate and apply its corresponding update. Thus we can use (car (cdr aList)) to access the second element in the list and (setf (car (cdr aList)) 8) to update it.

```
(setq aList '(1 2 3 4 5 6))
(car aList) ; => 1
(car (cdr aList)) ; => 2
(rplaca aList 7)
aList ; => (7 2 3 4 5 6)
(setf (car (cdr aList)) 8)
aList ;  => (7 8 3 4 5 6)
```

This is an impressive trick, which can seem almost magical. There are limitations on it, which reduce the magic. You can't do this on any expression. You can only do this on expressions that are made up of invertible functions. Lisp keeps a record of inverse functions, such as rplaca being the inverse of car. The macro analyzes its first argument expression and computes the update expression by finding the inverse function. As you define new functions, you can tell Lisp their inverses, and then use setf to do updates.

I'm waving my arms a little here, as setf is more complicated than my brief description implies. But the important fact for this discussion is that, to define setf, you do need macros because setf depends on the ability to parse the input expression. This ability to parse its arguments is the key advantage of Lisp macros.

Macros work well for Parse Tree Manipulation in Lisp because Lisp's syntactic structure is so close to the parse tree. However, macros aren't the only way to do Parse Tree Manipulation. C# is the example of a language that supports Parse Tree Manipulation by providing the ability to get the parse tree for an expression and a library for the program to manipulate it.

15.2 When to Use It

On a first encounter, textual macros are quite appealing. They can be used with any language that uses text, they do all their manipulation at compile time, and they can implement very impressive behaviors that are beyond the abilities of the host language.

But textual macros come with many problems. Subtle bugs like mistaken expansions, variable capture, and multiple evaluation are often intermittent and hard to track down. The fact that macros don't appear in downstream tools means the abstractions they provide leak like a sieve without the wires, and you get no support from debuggers, intelligent IDEs, or anything else that relies on the expanded code. Most people also find it much harder to reason about nested macro expansion than about nested function calls. That could be a lack of practice in dealing with macros, but I suspect it's something more fundamental.

To sum up, I don't recommend using textual macros in anything but the very simplest cases. I think that for *Templated Generation (539)* they work acceptably, providing you avoid trying to be too clever with them—in particular, avoiding nesting the expansions. But otherwise they are simply not worth the trouble.

How much of this reasoning applies to syntactic macros? I'm inclined to say that most of it does. While you are less likely to get mistaken expansions, the other problems still crop up. This makes me very wary of them.

A counterexample to this is the heavy use of syntactic macros in the Lisp community. As an outsider to this world, I feel a certain reluctance to make too much of a judgment. My overall sense is that they do make sense for Lisp, but I'm not convinced that the logic of using them there makes sense for other language environments.

And that, in the end, is the nub of the choice on whether to use syntactic macros. Most language environments don't support them, so there's no choice to worry about. Where you do have them, for example in Lisp and C++, they are often necessary to do useful things, so you have to become at least a little familiar with them. That means that the choice on using syntactic macros is really made for you by your language environment.

The only choice this leaves is whether syntactic macros are a reason to choose a language that has them. For the moment, I see macros as a worse choice than available alternatives, and thus a point deducted from those environments that use them—but with the rider that I haven't worked closely enough with those languages to be completely sure of my judgment.

Chapter 16

Notification

Collects errors and other messages to report back to the caller.

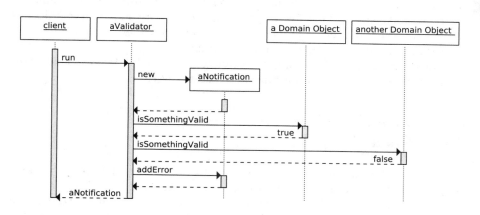

I've carried out some operations that made significant changes to an object model. Now that I'm done, I want to check that the resulting model is valid. I can initiate a validation command; I want to know the answer as a simple Boolean, but if there are errors I want to know more. In particular, I want to know about all the errors rather than have the validation stop at the first error.

A Notification is an object that collects errors. When a validation check fails, it adds an error to the Notification. When the validation command finishes, it returns the Notification. I can then ask the Notification if everything was OK, and if not, delve into the errors.

16.1 How It Works

The basic form of Notification is a collection of errors. During the notified task, I need the ability to add an error to the notification. This can be as simple as adding an error message string, or it can be a more involved error object. When the task is done, the Notification goes back to the caller. The caller invokes a simple Boolean query method to see if all is well. If there are errors, it may interrogate the Notification further to display them.

The Notification usually needs to be available to several methods in the model. It can either be passed in an argument as a *Collecting Parameter* [Beck IP], or it can be stashed in a field if there's an object that corresponds to the task at hand, such as a validator object.

The primary purpose of a Notification is to collect errors, but it's sometimes useful to capture warnings and informational messages too. An error indicates the requested command has failed; a warning occurs for something that doesn't fail but is still a matter of potential concern to the caller. An informational message is just some potentially handy information.

In many ways, a Notification is an object acting like a log file, so many of the features commonly found in logging can be useful here.

16.2 When to Use It

A Notification is useful whenever there is a complicated operation that may trigger multiple errors and you don't want to fail at the first error. If you do want to fail at the first error, then you can simply throw an exception. A Notification allows you to store multiple exceptions to give the caller a fuller picture of what the request led to.

Notifications are particularly useful when a user interface initiates an operation at a lower layer. The lower layer should not try to interact with user interface directly, so a Notification makes an appropriate messenger.

16.3 A Very Simple Notification (C#)

Here's a really simple Notification that I used for a couple of my book examples. All it does is store errors as strings.

```
class Notification...
  List<string> errors = new List<string>();
  public void AddError(String s, params object[] args) {
    errors.Add(String.Format(s, args));
  }
```

Using a format string and parameters makes it a bit easier to use the notification to capture errors, as the client code doesn't need to build the format string.

```
calling code......
  note.AddError("No value for {0}", property);
```

I provide a couple of Boolean methods for the caller to check if there are errors.

```
class Notification...
  public bool IsOK {get{ return 0 == errors.Count;}}
  public bool HasErrors {get { return !IsOK;}}
```

16: Notification

I also provide a method that checks and throws an exception if there are errors. Sometimes this fits the flow of usage better than using the Boolean check methods.

```
class Notification...
  public void AssertOK() {
    if (HasErrors) throw new ValidationException(this);
  }
```

16.4 Parsing Notification (Java)

Here's a different Notification that I use in the example for *Foreign Code (309)*. It is a bit more involved than the C# above and also more specific, as it takes specific kinds of errors.

Since it's part of an ANTLR parse, I put a Notification into the *Embedment Helper (547)* of the generated parser.

```
class AllocationTranslator...
  private Reader input;
  private AllocationLexer lexer;
  private AllocationParser parser;
  private ParsingNotification notification = new ParsingNotification();
  private LeadAllocator result = new LeadAllocator();

  public AllocationTranslator(Reader input) {
    this.input = input;
  }
```

```
public void run() {
  try {
    lexer = new AllocationLexer(new ANTLRReaderStream(input));
    parser = new AllocationParser(new CommonTokenStream(lexer));
    parser.helper = this;
    parser.allocationList();
  } catch (Exception e) {
    throw new RuntimeException("Unexpected exception in parse", e);
  }
  if (notification.hasErrors())
    throw new RuntimeException("Parse failed: \n" + notification);
}
```

16: Notification

This particular Notification handles two specific error cases. The first of these is an exception thrown by the ANTLR system itself. In ANTLR, this is a recognition exception. ANTLR has default behavior for this, but I want to also capture the error in a Notification. I can do this by providing an implementation for an error reporting method in the members section of the grammar file.

```
grammer file 'Allocation.g'......
  @members {
    AllocationTranslator helper;

    public void reportError(RecognitionException e) {
      helper.addError(e);
      super.reportError(e);
    }
  }
class AllocationTranslator...
  void addError(RecognitionException e) {
    notification.error(e);
  }
```

The other case is an error during the parse that the *Embedded Translation (299)* code recognizes. At one point, the grammar is looking for a list of products.

```
grammer file......
  productClause  returns [List<ProductGroup> result]
    : 'handles' p+=ID+ {$result = helper.recognizedProducts($p);}
    ;
class AllocationTranslator...
  List<ProductGroup> recognizedProducts(List<Token> tokens) {
    List<ProductGroup> result = new ArrayList<ProductGroup>();
    for (Token t : tokens) {
      if (!Registry.productRepository().containsId(t.getText())) {
        notification.error(t, "No product for %s", t.getText());
        continue;
      }
      result.add(Registry.productRepository().findById(t.getText()));
    }
    return result;
  }
```

In the first case, I pass ANTLR's recognition exception object to the Notification; in the second case I pass a token and an error message string—again, using the format string convention.

On the inside, the Notification has a list of errors—in this case, instead of a string, I use a more meaningful object.

```
class ParsingNotification...
  private List<ParserMessage> errors = new ArrayList<ParserMessage>();
```

I use a different kind of object for the two different cases. For ANTLR's recognition exception, I use a simple wrapper.

```
class ParsingNotification...
  public void error (RecognitionException e) {
    errors.add(new RecognitionParserMessage(e));
  }

class ParserMessage {}

class RecognitionParserMessage extends ParserMessage {
  RecognitionException exception;

  RecognitionParserMessage(RecognitionException exception) {
    this.exception = exception;
  }
  public String toString() {
    return exception.toString();
  }
}
```

16: Notification

As you can see, the superclass is only a marker to make the generics work. In time, I might add something to it, but for the moment a bare marker suffices.

For the second case, I assemble the incoming data into a different object.

```
class ParsingNotification...
  public void error(Token token, String message, Object... args) {
    errors.add(new TranslationMessage(token, message, args));
  }

class TranslationMessage extends ParserMessage {
  Token token;
  String message;

  TranslationMessage(Token token, String message, Object... messageArgs) {
    this.token = token;
    this.message = String.format(message,  messageArgs);
  }
  public String toString() {
    return String.format("%s (near line %d char %d)",
                   message, token.getLine(), token.getCharPositionInLine());
  }
}
```

By passing the token in, I'm able to provide better diagnostic information.
I provide the usual methods to detect if there are any errors and to print a report of errors if any crop up.

```
class ParsingNotification...
  public boolean isOk() {return errors.isEmpty();}
  public boolean hasErrors() {return !isOk();}

  public String toString() {
    return (isOk()) ? "OK" : "Errors:\n" + report();
  }
  public String report() {
    StringBuffer result = new StringBuffer("Parse errors:\n");
    for (ParserMessage m : errors) result.append(m).append("\n");
    return result.toString();
  }
}
```

16: Notification

I think the most important point here is to build a Notification that makes the calling code as simple and compact as possible. Therefore, I pass all the relevant data to the Notification and let the Notification sort out how to compose error messages from this data.

Part III

External DSL Topics

Chapter 17

Delimiter-Directed Translation

Translate source text by breaking it up into chunks (usually lines) and then parsing each chunk.

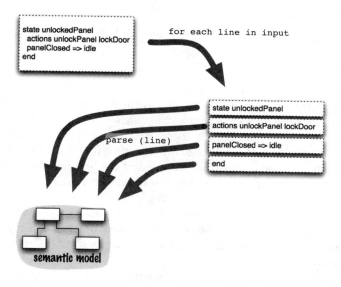

17.1 How It Works

Delimiter-Directed Translation works by taking the input and breaking it down into smaller chunks based on some kind of delimiter character. You can use any delimiter characters you like, but the most common first delimiter is the line ending, so I'll use that for my discussion.

Breaking up the script into lines is usually pretty simple, as most programming environments have library functions that will read an input stream a line at a time. One complication you may run into is if you have long lines and want to break them up physically in your editor. In many environments, the simplest way to do this is to quote the line ending character; in Unix this means using backslash as the last character on a line.

Quoting the line ending looks ugly, however, and is vulnerable to whitespace between the quote and the end of line. As a result, it's often better to use a line continuation character. To do this, you choose some character that, if it's the last non-whitespace character on a line, indicates that the next line is really the same line. When you read in the input, you have to look for the line continuation character and if you see it, patch the next line onto the line you've just read. When you do this, remember you may get more than one continuation line.

How you process the lines depends on the nature of the language you're dealing with. The simplest case is where each line is autonomous and of the same form. Consider a simple list of rules for allocating frequent sleeper points for hotel stays.

```
score 300 for 3 nights at Bree
score 200 for 2 nights at Dol Amroth
score 150 for 2 nights at Orthanc
```

I call the lines here autonomous since none of them affect the other ones. I could safely reorder and remove the lines without changing the interpretation of any line. They're of the same form because each one encodes the same kind of information. Processing the lines is therefore quite simple; I run the same line processing function against each one, this function picks out the information I need (the points to score, the nights stayed, and the hotel name) and translates it into the representation that I want. If I'm using *Embedded Translation (299)*, that means putting it into the *Semantic Model (159)*. If I were using *Tree Construction (281)*, that would mean creating an abstract syntax tree. I rarely see Tree Construction with Delimiter-Directed Translation, so for my discussion here I'm going to assume Embedded Translation (*Embedded Interpretation (305)* is also quite common).

How to pick out the information you want depends on the string processing capabilities you have in your language and on the complexity of the line you have. If possible, the easiest way to decompose the input is to use a string splitter function. Most string libraries have such a function that splits a string into elements separated by a delimiter string. In this case, you can split with a whitespace delimiter and extract, for example, the score as the second element.

Sometimes a string won't split cleanly like this. Often, the best approach is to use a regular expression. You can use groups in the regular expression to extract the bits of the string you need. A regular expression gives you much more expressive power than a string split; it is also a good way to check that the line is syntactically correct. Regular expressions are more complicated, and many people find them awkward to follow. It often helps to break a large regular expression into subexpressions, define each subexpression separately, and combine them (a technique I call a composed regex).

Now, let's consider lines of different forms. This might be a DSL that describes the contents section of a home page for a local newspaper.

```
border grey
headline "Musical Cambridge"
filter by date in this week
show concerts in Cambridge
```

In this case, each line is autonomous but needs to be processed differently. I can handle this with a conditional expression that checks for the various kinds of lines and calls the appropriate processing routine.

```
if      (isBorder())   parseBorder();
else if (isHeadline()) parseHeadline();
else if (isFilter())   parseFilter();
else if (isShow())     parseShow();
else throw new RecognitionException(input);
```

17:
Delimiter-Directed
Translation

The condition checks can use regular expression or other string operations. There's an argument for showing the regular expression in the conditional directly, but I usually prefer using methods.

Apart from purely isomorphic and polymorphic lines, you can get a hybrid where each line has the same broad structure that divides it into clauses, but each clause has different forms. Here's another version of hotel reward points:

```
300 for stay 3 nights at Bree
150 per day for stay 2 nights at Bree
50 for spa treatment at Dol Amroth
60 for stay 1 night at Orthanc or Helm's Deep or Dunharrow
1 per dollar for dinner at Bree
```

Here we have a broad isomorphic structure. There is always a rewards clause, followed by for, followed by an activity clause, followed by at, followed by a location clause. I can respond to this by having a single top-level processing routine that identifies the three clauses and calls a single processing routine for each clause. The clause processing routines then follow the polymorphic pattern of using a conditional of tests and different processing routines.

I can relate this to grammars used in *Syntax-Directed Translation (219)*. Polymorphic lines and clauses are handled in grammars by alternatives, while isomorphic lines are handled by production rules without alternatives. Using methods to break down lines into clauses is just like using subrules.

Handling nonautonomous statements with Delimiter-Directed Translation introduces a further complication, since we now have to keep track of some state information about the parse. An example of this is my introductory state machine where I have separate sections for events, commands, and states. The line unlockPanel PNUL should be handled differently in the events section than in the commands section, even though it has the same syntactic form. It also is an error for a line of this form to show up inside a state definition.

A good way to handle this is to have a family of different parsers for each state of the parse. So the state machine parser would have a top-level line parser, and further line parsers for a command block, event block, reset event block, and state block. When the top-level line parser sees the events keyword, it switches the current line parser over to an event line parser. This, of course, is just an application of the *State* [GoF] design pattern.

A common area that can get awkward with Delimiter-Directed Translation is handling whitespace, particularly around operators. If you have a line of the form property = value, you have to decide whether the whitespace around the = is optional or not. Making it optional may complicate line processing, but making it mandatory (or not allowing it at all) will make the DSL harder to use. Whitespace can get even worse if there is a distinction between one and multiple whitespace characters, or between different whitespace characters such as tabs and spaces.

There is a certain regularity to this kind of processing. There is a recurring programming idea of checking to see if a string matches a certain pattern, then invoking a processing rule for that pattern. Such commonality naturally raises the thought that this would be amenable to a framework. You could have a series of objects, each of which has a regex for the kind of line it processes and some code to do the processing. You then run through all these objects in turn. You can also add some indication of the overall state of the parser. To make it easier to configure this framework, you can add a DSL on top.

Of course I'm not the first person to think of that. Indeed that style of processing is exactly that used by lexer generators such as those inspired by Lex. There is something to be said for using these kinds of tools, but there's also another consideration. Once you've got far enough into this to want to use a framework, then the jump to Syntax-Directed Translation is not much further, and you have a wider range of more powerful tools to work with.

17.2 When to Use It

The great strength of Delimiter-Directed Translation is that it is a technique that is very simple for people to use. Its main alternative, *Syntax-Directed Translation (219)*, requires you to mount a learning curve to understand how to work with grammars. Delimiter-Directed Translation relies purely on techniques that most programmers are familiar with and thus easy to approach.

As is often the case, the downside of this approachability is the difficulty of handling more complex languages. Delimiter-Directed Translation works very well with simple languages, particularly those which don't require much nested context. As complexity increases, Delimiter-Directed Translation can get messy quickly, particularly since it takes thought to keep the design of the parser clean.

As a result, I only tend to favor Delimiter-Directed Translation when you have simple autonomous statements, or maybe just a single nested context. Even then I'd prefer to use Syntax-Directed Translation unless I'm working with a team that I didn't think is prepared to deal with learning that technique.

17.3 Frequent Customer Points (C#)

If you've had the misfortune to be a jet-setting consultant like myself, you'll be familiar with the various incentives that travel companies dole out to try to reward you for traveling too much with opportunities to travel even more. Let's imagine a set of rules for a hotel chain expressed as a DSL like this:

17:
Delimiter-Directed
Translation

```
300 for stay 3 nights at Bree
150 per day for stay 2 nights at Bree
50 for spa treatment at Dol Amroth
60 for stay 1 night at Orthanc or Helm's Deep or Dunharrow
1 per dollar for dinner at Bree
```

17.3.1 Semantic Model

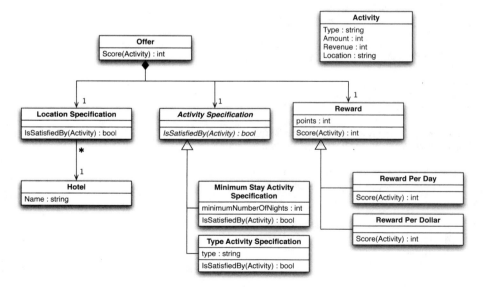

Figure 17.1 *Class diagram of semantic model*

Each line in the script defines a single offer. The main responsibility of an offer is to score the frequent customer points for an activity. The activity is a simple data representation.

```
class Activity...
  public string Type { get;  set; }
  public int Amount { get;  set; }
  public int Revenue { get;  set; }
  public string Location { get; set; }
```

The offer has three components. A location *Specification* [Evans DDD] checks to see if an activity is in the right place to score for this offer; an activity specification checks to see if the activity merits reward points. If both of these specifications are satisfied, then the reward object calculates the score.

The simplest of these three components is the location specification. It just checks the hotel name against a list of stored hotels.

```
class LocationSpecification...
  private readonly IList<Hotel> hotels = new List<Hotel>();

  public LocationSpecification(params String[] names) {
    foreach (string n in names)
      hotels.Add(Repository.HotelNamed(n));
  }

  public bool IsSatisfiedBy(Activity a) {
    Hotel hotel = Repository.HotelNamed(a.Location);
    return hotels.Contains(hotel);
  }
```

I need two kinds of activity specifications here. One checks that activity is a stay of more than the stated amount of nights.

```
abstract class ActivitySpecification {
  public abstract bool isSatisfiedBy(Activity a);
}

class MinimumNightStayActivitySpec : ActivitySpecification {
  private readonly int minimumNumberOfNights;

  public MinimumNightStayActivitySpec(int numberOfNights) {
    this.minimumNumberOfNights = numberOfNights;
  }

  public override bool isSatisfiedBy(Activity a) {
    return a.Type == "stay"
      ? a.Amount >= minimumNumberOfNights
      : false ;
  }
```

The second checks to see if the activity is of the right kind.

```
class TypeActivitySpec : ActivitySpecification {
  private readonly string type;

  public TypeActivitySpec(string type) {
    this.type = type;
  }

  public override bool isSatisfiedBy(Activity a) {
    return a.Type == type;
  }
}
```

The reward classes score the rewards according to the different bases.

```
class Reward {
  protected int points;

  public Reward(int points) { this.points = points; }
  virtual public int Score (Activity activity) {
    return points;
  }
}

class RewardPerDay : Reward {
  public RewardPerDay(int points) : base(points) {}

  public override int Score(Activity activity) {
    if (activity.Type != "stay")
      throw new ArgumentException("can only use per day scores on stays");
    return activity.Amount * points;
  }
}

class RewardPerDollar : Reward {
  public RewardPerDollar(int points) : base(points) {}

  public override int Score(Activity activity) {
    return activity.Revenue * points;
  }
}
```

17.3.2 The Parser

The basic structure of the parser is to read each line of the input and work on that line.

```
class OfferScriptParser...
  readonly TextReader input;
  readonly List<Offer> result = new List<Offer>();
  public OfferScriptParser(TextReader input) {
    this.input = input;
  }
  public List<Offer> Run() {
    string line;
    while ((line = input.ReadLine()) != null) {
      line = appendContinuingLine(line);
      parseLine(line);
    }
    return result;
  }
```

For this example, I want to support "&" as a continuation character. A simple recursive function makes this work.

```
class OfferScriptParser...
  private string appendContinuingLine(string line) {
    if (IsContinuingLine(line)) {
      var first = Regex.Replace(line, @"&\s*$", "");
      var next = input.ReadLine();
      if (null == next) throw new RecognitionException(line);
      return first.Trim() + " " + appendContinuingLine(next);
    }
    else return line.Trim();
  }
  private bool IsContinuingLine(string line) {
    return Regex.IsMatch(line, @"&\s*$");
  }
```

This will turn all continuing lines into one line.

For parsing the line, I begin by stripping out comments and ignoring blank lines. With that done, I begin the proper parsing, for which I delegate to a fresh object.

```
class OfferScriptParser...
  private void parseLine(string line) {
    line = removeComment(line);
    if (IsEmpty(line)) return;
    result.Add(new OfferLineParser().Parse(line.Trim()));
  }
  private bool IsEmpty(string line) {
    return Regex.IsMatch(line, @"^\s*$");
  }
  private string removeComment(string line) {
    return Regex.Replace(line, @"#.*", "");
  }
```

I've used a *Method Object* [Beck IP] to parse each line here, since I think the rest of the parsing behavior is sufficiently complicated that I'd prefer to see it broken out. The method object is stateless, so I could reuse the instance, but I prefer to create a fresh one each time unless there's a good reason not to.

The base parse method breaks the line down into clauses and then calls separate parse methods on each clause. (I could try to do everything in one big regular expression, but I get vertigo thinking of the resulting code.)

```csharp
class OfferLineParser...
  public Offer Parse(string line) {
    var result = new Offer();

    const string rewardRegexp = @"(?<reward>.*)";
    const string activityRegexp = @"(?<activity>.*)";
    const string locationRegexp = @"(?<location>.*)";

    var source = rewardRegexp + keywordToken("for") +
      activityRegexp + keywordToken("at") + locationRegexp;

    var m = new Regex(source).Match(line);
    if (!m.Success) throw new RecognitionException(line);

    result.Reward = parseReward(m.Groups["reward"].Value);
    result.Location = parseLocation(m.Groups["location"].Value);
    result.Activity = parseActivity(m.Groups["activity"].Value);
    return result;
  }

  private String keywordToken(String keyword) {
    return @"\s+" + keyword + @"\s+";
  }
```

17:
Delimiter-Directed
Translation

This is a rather long method by my standards. I thought of trying to break it up, but the core behavior of the method is to divide the regular expression into groups and then map the results of parsing the groups into the output. There's a strong semantic linkage between the definition and the use of these groups, so I felt it was better to have the longer method rather than try to decompose it. Since the crux of this method is the regular expression, I've put the assembly of the regular expression on its own line to draw the eye there.

I could have done all this with a single regular expression instead of the separate regular expressions (rewardRegexp, activityRegexp, locationRegexp). Whenever I run into a complicated regexp like this, I like to break it up into simpler regular expressions that I can compose together—a technique I call a **composed regex** [Fowler-regex]. I find this makes it much easier to understand what's going on.

With everything broken into chunks, I can look at parsing each chunk in turn. I'll start with the location specification, as it's the easiest. Here the main complication is that we can have one location or several locations separated by "or":

```
class OfferLineParser...
  private LocationSpecification parseLocation(string input) {
    if (Regex.IsMatch(input, @"\bor\b"))
      return parseMultipleHotels(input);
    else
      return new LocationSpecification(input);
  }
  private LocationSpecification parseMultipleHotels(string input) {
    String[] hotelNames = Regex.Split(input, @"\s+or\s+");
    return new LocationSpecification(hotelNames);
  }
```

With the activity clause, I have two kinds of activities to deal with. The simplest is the type activity, where I just need to pull out the type of activity.

```
class OfferLineParser...
  private ActivitySpecification parseActivity(string input) {
    if (input.StartsWith("stay"))
      return parseStayActivity(input);
    else return new TypeActivitySpec(input);
  }
```

For hotel stays, I need to pull out the minimum number of nights and choose a different activity specification.

```
class OfferLineParser...
  private ActivitySpecification parseStayActivity(string input) {
    const string stayKeyword = @"^stay\s+";
    const string nightsKeyword = @"\s+nights?$";
    const string amount = @"(?<amount>\d+)";
    const string source = stayKeyword + amount + nightsKeyword;

    var m = Regex.Match(input, source);
    if (!m.Success) throw new RecognitionException(input);
    return new MinimumNightStayActivitySpec(Int32.Parse(m.Groups["amount"].Value));
  }
```

The last clause is the rewards clause. Here I just need to identify the basis of the reward and return the appropriate subclass of the reward class.

```
class OfferLineParser...
  private Reward parseReward(string input) {
    if (Regex.IsMatch(input, @"^\d+$"))
      return new Reward(Int32.Parse(input));
    else if (Regex.IsMatch(input, @"^\d+ per day$"))
      return new RewardPerDay(Int32.Parse(extractDigits(input)));
    else if (Regex.IsMatch(input, @"^\d+ per dollar$"))
      return new RewardPerDollar(Int32.Parse(extractDigits(input)));
    else throw new RecognitionException(input);
  }
  private string extractDigits(string input) {
    return Regex.Match(input, @"^\d+").Value;
  }
```

17.4 Parsing Nonautonomous Statements with Miss Grant's Controller (Java)

I'll use our familiar state machine as an example.

```
events
  doorClosed  D1CL
  drawerOpened D2OP
  lightOn     L1ON
  doorOpened  D1OP
  panelClosed PNCL
end

resetEvents
  doorOpened
end

commands
  unlockPanel PNUL
  lockPanel   PNLK
  lockDoor    D1LK
  unlockDoor  D1UL
end

state idle
  actions unlockDoor lockPanel
  doorClosed => active
end

state active
  drawerOpened => waitingForLight
  lightOn      => waitingForDrawer
end

state waitingForLight
  lightOn => unlockedPanel
end

state waitingForDrawer
  drawerOpened => unlockedPanel
end

state unlockedPanel
  actions unlockPanel lockDoor
  panelClosed => idle
end
```

17:
Delimiter-Directed
Translation

Looking at this language, I see it's divided into several different blocks: command list, event list, reset event list, and each state. Each block has its own syntax for the statements within it, so you can think of the parser being in different states as it reads each block. Each parser state recognizes a different kind of input. As a result, I decided to use the *State* [GoF] pattern, where the main state machine parser uses different line parsers to handle the different kinds of lines it wants to parse. (You can also think of this as *Strategy* [GoF] pattern—the difference is often hard to tell.)

I begin loading the file with a static load method.

```
class StateMachineParser...
  public static StateMachine loadFile(String fileName) {
    try {
      StateMachineParser loader = new StateMachineParser(new FileReader(fileName));
      loader.run();
      return loader.machine;
    } catch (FileNotFoundException e) {
      throw new RuntimeException(e);
    }
  }

  public StateMachineParser(Reader reader) {
    input = new BufferedReader(reader);
  }

  private final BufferedReader input;
```

The run method breaks the input into lines and passes the line to the current line parser, starting with the top level.

```
class StateMachineParser...
  void run() {
    String line;
    setLineParser(new TopLevelLineParser(this));
    try {
      while ((line = input.readLine()) != null)
        lineParser.parse(line);
      input.close();
    } catch (IOException e) {
      throw new RuntimeException(e);
    }
    finishMachine();
  }

  private LineParser lineParser;
  void setLineParser(LineParser lineParser) {
    this.lineParser = lineParser;
  }
```

The line parsers are a simple hierarchy.

```
abstract class LineParser {
  protected final StateMachineParser context;

  protected LineParser(StateMachineParser context) {
    this.context = context;
  }
}

class TopLevelLineParser extends LineParser {
  TopLevelLineParser(StateMachineParser parser) {
    super(parser);
  }
}
```

I make the superclass line parser parse a line by first removing comments and cleaning up whitespace. Once that's done, it passes control to the subclass.

```
class LineParser...
  void parse(String s) {
    line = s;
    line = removeComment(line);
    line = line.trim();
    if (isBlankLine()) return;
    doParse();
  }

  protected String line;

  private boolean isBlankLine() {
    return line.matches("^\\s*$");
  }
  private String removeComment(String line) {
    return line.replaceFirst("#.*", "");
  }

  abstract void doParse();
```

17:
Delimiter-Directed
Translation

When parsing a line, I follow the same basic plan in all the line parsers. The doParse hook method is a conditional statement where each condition looks at the line to see if it matches a pattern for that line. If the pattern matches, I call some code to process that line.

Here's the conditional for the top level:

```
class TopLevelLineParser...
  void doParse() {
    if
      (hasOnlyWord("commands"))    context.setLineParser(new CommandLineParser(context));
    else if
      (hasOnlyWord("events"))      context.setLineParser(new EventLineParser(context));
    else if
      (hasOnlyWord("resetEvents")) context.setLineParser(new ResetEventLineParser(context));
    else if
      (hasKeyword("state"))        processState();
    else failToRecognizeLine();
  }
```

The condition checks use some common condition checks that I place in the superclass.

```
class LineParser...
  protected boolean hasOnlyWord(String word) {
    if (words(0).equals(word)) {
      if (words().length != 1) failToRecognizeLine();
      return true;
    }
    else return false;
  }

  protected boolean hasKeyword(String keyword) {
    return keyword.equals(words(0));
  }

  protected String[] words() {
    return line.split("\\s+");
  }

  protected String words(int index) {
    return words()[index];
  }

  protected void failToRecognizeLine() {
    throw new RecognitionException(line);
  }
```

In most cases, the top level just looks for a block opening command and then switches the line parser to the new one needed for that block. The state case is more involved—I'll come to that later.

I could have used regular expressions in my conditionals instead of calling out methods. So, instead of writing hasOnlyWord("commands") I could say line.matches("commands\\s*"). Regular expressions are a powerful tool. There are reasons I like a method here. First is comprehensibility: I find hasKeyword easier to understand than the regular expression. Like any other code, regular expressions often benefit from being wrapped in well-named methods in order to make them easier to understand. Of course, once I have the hasKeyword method, I could implement it with a regular expression rather than splitting the input line into words and testing the first word. Since many of the tests involved in this parse involve splitting up words, it seems easier to use the word splits when I can.

Using a method also allows me to do more—in this case, check that when I have "commands" I don't have any other text following it on the line. This would have needed an extra regular expression check if I used bare regular expressions in the conditionals.

For the next step, let's look at a line in the command block. There's just two cases here: either a line definition, or the end keyword.

```
class CommandLineParser...
  void doParse() {
    if (hasOnlyWord("end")) returnToTopLevel();
    else if (words().length == 2)
      context.registerCommand(new Command(words(0), words(1)));
    else failToRecognizeLine();
  }

class LineParser...
  protected void returnToTopLevel() {
    context.setLineParser(new TopLevelLineParser(context));
  }

class StateMachineParser...
  void registerCommand(Command c) {
    commands.put(c.getName(), c);
  }
  private Map<String, Command> commands = new HashMap<String, Command>();
  Command getCommand(String word) {
    return commands.get(word);
  }
```

17:
Delimiter-Directed
Translation

As well as controlling the overall parse, I also have the state machine parser acting as a *Symbol Table (165)*.

The code to handle events and reset events is pretty similar, so I'll move right along to look at handling states. The first thing that's different about states is that the code in the top-level line parser is more complicated, so I used a method:

```
class TopLevelLineParser...
  private void processState() {
    State state = context.obtainState(words(1));
    context.primeMachine(state);
    context.setLineParser(new StateLineParser(context, state));
  }

class StateMachineParser...
  State obtainState(String name) {
    if (!states.containsKey(name)) states.put(name, new State(name));
    return states.get(name);
  }
  void primeMachine(State state) {
    if (machine == null) machine = new StateMachine(state);
  }
  private StateMachine machine;
```

The first mentioned state becomes the start state—hence the `primeState` method. The first time I mention a state I put it in the Symbol Table, and therefore use an obtain method (my naming convention for "get one if exists or create if it doesn't").

The line parser for the state block is a touch more complicated as it has more kinds of lines it may match.

```
class StateLineParser...
  void doParse() {
    if (hasOnlyWord("end")) returnToTopLevel();
    else if (isTransition()) processTransition();
    else if (hasKeyword("actions")) processActions();
    else failToRecognizeLine();
  }
```

For actions, I just add them all to the state.

```
class StateLineParser...
  private void processActions() {
    for (String s : wordsStartingWith(1))
      state.addAction(context.getCommand(s));
  }
```

```
class LineParser...
  protected String[] wordsStartingWith(int start) {
    return Arrays.copyOfRange(words(), start, words().length);
  }
```

In this case I could have just used a loop like:

```
for (int i = 1; i < words().length; i++)
  state.addAction(context.getCommand(words(i)));
```

But I think using a loop initializer of 1 instead of the usual 0 is too subtle a change to communicate effectively what I'm doing.

For the transition case I have more involved code in both the condition and the action.

```
class StateLineParser...
  private boolean isTransition() {
    return line.matches(".*=>.*");
  }
  private void processTransition() {
    String[] tokens = line.split("=>");
    Event trigger = context.getEvent(tokens[0].trim());
    State target = context.obtainState(tokens[1].trim());
    state.addTransition(trigger, target);
  }
```

I don't use the splitting into words that I used earlier, since I want drawerOpened=>waitingForLight (without spaces around the operator) to be legal.

Once the input file has been processed, the only thing left is to make sure the reset events are added into the machine. I do this last since the reset events can be indicated before the first state is declared.

```
class StateMachineParser...
  private void finishMachine() {
    machine.addResetEvents(resetEvents.toArray(new Event[resetEvents.size()]));
  }
```

A broad issue here is the division of responsibilities between the state machine parser and the various line parsers. This is also a classic issue with the state pattern: How much behavior should be in the overall context object and how much in different state objects? For this example I've shown a decentralized approach where I try to do as much as possible in the various line parsers. An alternative is to put this behavior in the state machine parser, using the line parsers just to extract the right information from the bunches of text.

I will illustrate this with a comparison of the two ways of doing the command block. Here's the decentralized way I did it above:

```
class CommandLineParser...
  void doParse() {
    if (hasOnlyWord("end")) returnToTopLevel();
    else if (words().length == 2)
      context.registerCommand(new Command(words(0), words(1)));
    else failToRecognizeLine();
  }

class LineParser...
  protected void returnToTopLevel() {
    context.setLineParser(new TopLevelLineParser(context));
  }

class StateMachineParser...
  void registerCommand(Command c) {
    commands.put(c.getName(), c);
  }
  private Map<String, Command> commands = new HashMap<String, Command>();
  Command getCommand(String word) {
    return commands.get(word);
  }
```

17:
Delimiter-Directed
Translation

And here's the centralized way keeping the behavior in the state machine parser:

```
class CommandLineParser...
  void doParse() {
    if (hasOnlyWord("end"))
      context.handleEndCommand();
    else if (words().length == 2)
      context.handleCommand(words(0), words(1));
    else failToRecognizeLine();
  }

class StateMachineParser...
  void handleCommand(String name, String code) {
    Command command = new Command(name, code);
    commands.put(command.getName(), command);
  }
  public void handleEndCommand() {
    lineParser = new TopLevelLineParser(this);
  }
```

The downside of the decentralized route is that, since the state machine parser acts as a Symbol Table, it's constantly being used for data access by the line parsers. Pulling data out of an object repeatedly is usually a bad smell. By using the centralized approach, no other objects need to know about the Symbol Table, so I don't need to expose the state. The downside of the centralized approach, however, is that this puts a lot of logic in the state machine parser, which may make it overcomplicated. This would be more of an issue for a larger language.

Both alternatives have their problems, and I'll confess I don't have a strong preference either way.

Chapter 18

Syntax-Directed Translation

Translate source text by defining a grammar and using that grammar to structure translation.

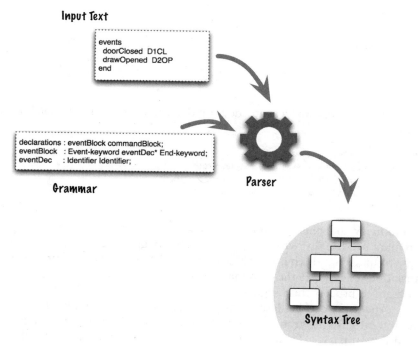

Computer languages naturally tend to follow a hierarchical structure with multiple levels of context. We can define the legal syntax of such a language by writing a grammar that describes how elements of a language get broken down into subelements.

Syntax-Directed Translation uses this grammar to define the creation of a parser that can turn input text into a parse tree that mimics the structure of the grammar rules.

18.1 How It Works

If you've read any book on programming languages, you'll have come across the notion of a grammar. A grammar is a way of defining the legal syntax of a programming language. Consider the part of my opening state machine example that declares events and commands:

```
events
  doorClosed  D1CL
  drawerOpened  D2OP
# ...
end

commands
  unlockPanel  PNUL
  lockPanel    PNLK
# ...
end
```

These declarations have a syntactic form that can be defined using the following grammar:

```
declarations : eventBlock commandBlock;
eventBlock   : Event-keyword eventDec* End-keyword;
eventDec     : Identifier Identifier;
commandBlock : Command-keyword commandDec* End-keyword;
commandDec   : Identifier Identifier;
```

A grammar like this provides a human-readable definition of a language. Grammars are usually written in *BNF (229)*. A grammar makes it easier for people to understand what is legal syntax in a language. With Syntax-Directed Translation we can take the grammar further and use it as the basis for designing a program to process this language.

This processing can be derived from the grammar in a couple of ways. One approach is to use the grammar as a specification and implementation guide for a handwritten parser. *Recursive Descent Parser (245)* and *Parser Combinator (255)* are two approaches to doing this. An alternative is to use the grammar as a DSL and use a *Parser Generator (269)* to automatically build a parser from the grammar file itself. In this case, you don't write any of the core parser code yourself; all of it is generated from the grammar.

However useful, the grammar only handles part of the problem. It can tell you how to turn the input text into a parse-tree data structure. Almost always, you'll need to do more with the input than that. Therefore Parser Generators also provide ways to embed further behavior in the parser, so you can do something like populating a *Semantic Model (159)*. So although the Parser Generator does a lot of work for you, you still have to do a fair bit of programming to create something truly useful. In this way, as in many others, a Parser Generator is an excellent example of a practical use of DSLs. It doesn't solve the whole problem, but does make a significant chunk of it much easier. It's also a DSL with a long history.

18.1.1 The Lexer

Almost always, when you use Syntax-Directed Translation, you'll see a separation between a lexer and the parser. A lexer, also called a **tokenizer** or **scanner**, is the first stage in processing the input text. The lexer splits the characters of the input into tokens, which represent more reasonable chunks of the input.

The tokens are generally defined using regular expressions; here's what such lexing rules might look like for the commands and events example above:

```
event-keyword: 'events';
command-keyword: 'commands';
end-keyword: 'end';
identifier: [a-z A-Z 0-9]*;
```

Here's a very small bit of input:

```
events
  doorClosed  D1CL
  drawOpened  D2OP
end
```

The lexer rules would turn this input into a series of tokens.

```
[Event-keyword: "events"]
[Identifier: "doorClosed"]
[Identifier: "D1CL"]
[Identifier: "drawOpened"]
[Identifier:"D2OP"]
[End-keyword: "end"]
```

Each token is an object with essentially two properties: type and payload. The type is the kind of token we have, for example Event-keyword or Identifier. The payload is the text that was matched as part of the lexer: events or doorClosed. For keywords, the payload is pretty much irrelevant; all that matters is the type. For identifiers, the payload does matter, as that's the data that will be important later on in the parse.

Lexing is separated out for a few reasons. One is that this makes the parser simpler, because it can now be written in terms of tokens rather than raw characters. Another is efficiency: The implementation needed to chunk up characters into tokens is different from that used by the parser. (In automata theory, the lexer is usually a state machine while the parser is usually a push-down stack machine.) This split is therefore the traditional approach—although it is being challenged by some more modern developments. (ANTLR uses a push-down machine for its lexer, while some modern parsers combine lexing and parsing into scannerless parsers.)

The lexer rules are tested in order, with the first match succeeding. Thus you can't use the string events as an identifier because the lexer will always recognize it as a keyword. This is generally considered a Good Thing to reduce confusion, avoiding such things as PL/1's notorious if if = then then then = if;. However, there are cases when you need to get around this by using some form of *Alternative Tokenization (319)*.

If you've been suitably careful in comparing the tokens to the input text, you'll notice something is missing from the token list. Nothing is missing—the "nothing" here being whitespace: spaces, tabs, and newlines. For many languages the lexer will strip out whitespace so that the parser doesn't have to deal with it. This is a big difference to *Delimiter-Directed Translation (201)* where the whitespace usually plays a key structuring role.

If the whitespace is syntactically significant—such as newlines as statement separators, or indentation signifying block structure—then the lexer can't just ignore it. Instead, it must generate some form of token to indicate what's happening—such as a newline token for *Newline Separators (333)*. Often, however, languages that are intended to be processed with Syntax-Directed Translation try to make whitespace ignorable. Indeed, many DSLs can do without any form of statement separator—our state machine language can safely discard all whitespace in the lexer.

Another thing that the lexer often discards is comments. It's always useful to have comments in even the smallest DSL, and the lexer can easily get rid of these. You may not want to discard comments; they may be useful for debugging purposes, particularly in generated code. In this case, you have to think about how you are going to attach them to the *Semantic Model (159)* elements.

I've said that tokens have properties for type and payload. In practice, they may carry more. Often, this information is useful for error diagnostics, such as line number and character position.

When deciding on tokens, there is often a temptation to fine-tune the matching process. In the state controller example, I've said that the event codes are a four-character sequence of capital letters and numbers. So I might consider using a specific type of token for this, something like:

```
code: [A-Z 0-9]{4}
```

The problem with this is that the tokenizer would produce the wrong tokens in cases like this:

```
events
  FAIL FZ17
end
```

In that input, FAIL would be tokenized as a code rather than an identifier, because the lexer only looks at the characters, not the overall context of the expression. This kind of distinction is best left to the parser to deal with, as it has the information to tell the difference between the name and the code. This means that checking for matches of the four-character rule needs to be done later on in the parse. In general, it's best to keep lexing as simple as possible.

Most of the time, I like to think of the lexer as dealing with three different kinds of tokens.

- *Punctuation:* keywords, operators, or other organizing constructs (parentheses, statement separators). With punctuation, the token type is important, but the payload isn't. These are also fixed elements of the language.

- *Domain text:* names of things, literal values. For these, the token type is usually a very generic thing like "number" or "identifier." These are variable; every DSL script will have a different domain text.

- *Ignorables:* stuff that's usually discarded by the tokenizer, such as whitespace and comments.

18:
Syntax-Directed
Translation

Most *Parser Generators (269)* provide generators for the lexer, using the kinds of regular expression rules I've shown above. However, many people prefer to write their own lexers. They are fairly straightforward to write using a *Regex Table Lexer (239)*. With handwritten lexers, you have more flexibility for more complex interactions between the parser and the lexer, which can often be useful.

One particular parser-lexer interaction that can be useful is that of supporting multiple modes in the lexer and allowing the parser to indicate a switch between modes. This allows the parser to alter how tokenizing occurs within certain points of the language, which helps with Alternative Tokenization.

18.1.2 Syntactic Analyzer

Once you have a stream of tokens, the next part of Syntax-Directed Translation is the parser itself. The parser's behavior can be divided into two main sections, which I'll call syntactic analysis and actions. Syntactic analysis takes the stream of tokens and arranges them into a parse tree. This work can be derived entirely from the grammar itself, and in a *Parser Generator (269)*, this code will be automatically generated by the tool. The actions take that syntax tree and do more with it—such as populating a *Semantic Model (159)*.

The actions cannot be generated from a grammar, and are usually executed while the parse tree is being built up. Usually, a Parser Generator grammar file combines the grammar definition with additional code to specify the actions. Often, these actions are in a general-purpose programming language, although some actions can be expressed in additional DSLs.

For the moment, I'll ignore the actions and just look at the syntactic analysis. If we build a parser using only the grammar and thus only doing syntactic analysis, the result of the parse will be either a successful run or a failure. This tells us if the input text matches the grammar or not. You'll often hear this described as whether the parser *recognizes* the input.

So with the text I've used so far, I have this grammar:

```
declarations : eventBlock commandBlock;
eventBlock   : Event-keyword eventDec* End-keyword;
eventDec     : Identifier Identifier;
commandBlock : Command-keyword commandDec* End-keyword;
commandDec   : Identifier Identifier;
```

And this input:

```
events
   doorClosed  D1CL
   drawOpened  D2OP
end
```

I've shown above that the tokenizer splits the input into this token stream:

```
[Event-keyword: "events"]
[Identifier: "doorClosed"]
[Identifier: "D1CL"]
[Identifier: "drawOpened"]
[Identifier:"D2OP"]
[End-keyword: "end"]
```

Syntactic analysis then takes these tokens and the grammar, and arranges them into the tree structure of Figure 18.1.

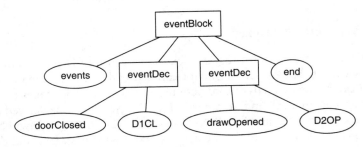

Figure 18.1 *Parse tree for the event input*

As you can see, the syntactic analysis introduces extra nodes (which I've shown as rectangles) in order to form the parse tree. These nodes are defined by the grammar.

It's important to realize that any given language can be matched by many grammars. So for our case here, we could also use the following grammar:

```
eventBlock   : Event-keyword eventList End-keyword;
eventList    : eventDec*
eventDec     : Identifier Identifier;
```

This will match all the inputs that the previous formulation would match; however, it will produce a different parse tree, shown in Figure 18.2.

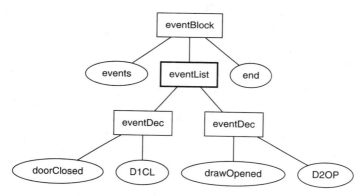

18:
Syntax-Directed
Translation

Figure 18.2 *Alternative parse tree for the event input*

So, in Syntax-Directed Translation a grammar defines how an input text is turned into a parse tree, and we can often choose different grammars depending on how we want to control the parse. Different grammars also appear due to differences in Parser Generator tools.

So far I've talked about the parse tree as if it's something that is explicitly produced by the parser as an output of the parse. However, this is usually not the case. In most cases, you don't ever access the parse tree directly. The parser will build up pieces of the parse tree and execute actions in the middle of the parsing. Once it's done with a bit of the parse tree, it'll discard that bit (historically, this was important to reduce memory consumption). If you are doing *Tree Construction (281)*, then you will produce a full syntax tree. However, in this case you usually don't produce the full parse tree, but a simplification of it called an abstract syntax tree.

You may run into a particular terminological confusion around this point. Academic books in this area often use "parse" as a synonym for syntactic analysis only, calling the overall process something like translation, interpretation, or compilation. I tend to use "parse" much more broadly in this book, reflecting what I see as common usage in the field. Parser Generators tend to refer to the parser as the activity that consumes tokens—so they talk about the lexer and parser as separate tools. Since that's overwhelmingly common, I do that in this section too, although you could argue that, to be consistent with other sections of this book, parsing should include lexing too.

Another terminological muddle is around the terms "parse tree," "syntax tree," and "abstract syntax tree." In my usage, I use **parse tree** to refer to a tree that accurately reflects the parse with the grammar you have with all the tokens present—essentially the raw tree. I use **abstract syntax tree** (AST) to refer to a simplified tree, discarding unnecessary tokens and reorganizing the tree to suit that later processing. I use **syntax tree** as the supertype of AST and parse tree when I need a term for a tree that could be either. These definitions are broadly those you'll find in the literature. As ever, the terminology in software varies rather more than we would like.

18.1.3 Output Production

While the grammar is sufficient to describe syntactic analysis, that's only enough for a parser to recognize some input. Usually, we're not satisfied with recognition; we also want to produce some output. I classify three broad ways to produce output: *Embedded Translation (299)*, *Tree Construction (281)*, and *Embedded Interpretation (305)*. All of these require something other than the grammar to specify how they work, so usually you write additional code to do the output production.

How you weave that code into the parser depends on how you are writing the parser. With *Recursive Descent Parser (245)*, you add actions into the handwritten code; with *Parser Combinator (255)*, you pass action objects into the combinators using the facilities of your language; with *Parser Generator (269)*, you use *Foreign Code (309)* to add code actions into the text of the grammar file.

18.1.4 Semantic Predicates

Syntactic analyzers, whether written by hand or generated, follow a core algorithm that allows them to recognize input based on a grammar. However, there are sometimes cases where the rules for recognition can't quite be expressed in the grammar. This is most notable in a *Parser Generator (269)*.

In order to cope with this, some Parser Generators support semantic predicates. A **semantic predicate** is a hunk of general-purpose code that provides a Boolean response to indicate whether a grammar production should be accepted or not—effectively overriding what's expressed by the rule. This allows the parser to do things beyond what the grammar can express.

A classic example of the need for a semantic predicate is when parsing C++ and coming across T(6). Depending on the context, this could either be a function call or a constructor-style typecast. To tell them apart, you need to know how T has been defined. You can't specify this in a context-free grammar, so a semantic predicate is needed to resolve the ambiguity.

You shouldn't come across the need to use semantic predicates for a DSL, since you should be able to define the language in such a way as to avoid this need. If you do need them, take a look at [parr-LIP] for more information.

18.2 When to Use It

Syntax-Directed Translation is an approach alternative to *Delimiter-Directed Translation (201)*. The principal disadvantage of Syntax-Directed Translation is the need to get used to driving parsing via a grammar, while chopping up via delimiters is usually a more familiar approach. It doesn't take long, however, to get used to grammars, and once you do, they provide a technique that is much easier to use as your DSLs get more complex.

In particular, the grammar file—itself a DSL—provides a clear documentation of the syntactic structure of the DSL it's processing. This makes it easier to evolve the syntax of the DSL over time.

18:
Syntax-Directed
Translation

18.3 Further Reading

Syntax-Directed Translation has been a primary area of academic study for decades. The usual starting-point reference is the famous *Dragon Book* [Dragon]. An alternative route, deviating from the traditional approach to teaching this material, is [parr-LIP].

Chapter 19

BNF

Formally define the syntax of a programming language.

```
grammarDef : rule+;
rule       : id ':' altList ';';
altList    : element+  ( '|' element+ )*;
element    : id ebnfSuffix?
           | '(' altList ')'
           ;
ebnfSuffix : '?' | '*' | '+' ;
id         : 'a'..'z' ('a'..'z'|'A'..'Z'|'_'|'0'..'9')* ;
```

19.1 How It Works

BNF (and EBNF) is a way of writing grammars to define the syntax of a language. BNF (or Backus-Naur Form, to give it its full name) was invented to describe the Algol language in the 60s. Since then, BNF grammars have been widely used both for explanation and to drive *Syntax-Directed Translation (219)*.

You've almost certainly come across BNF when learning about a new language—or rather, you've sort-of come across it. In a wonderful display of irony, BNF, a language for defining syntax, does not itself have a standard syntax. Pretty much any time you run into a BNF grammar, it will have both obvious and subtle differences from any other BNF grammars you've seen before. As a result, it's not really fair to call BNF a language; rather, I think of it as a family of languages. When people talk about patterns, they say that with a pattern, you see it differently every time—BNF is very much like that.

Despite the fact that both syntax and semantics of BNF varies so much, there are common elements. The primary commonality is the notion of describing a language through a sequence of production rules. As an example, consider contacts like this:

229

```
contact mfowler {
  email: fowler@acm.org
}
```

A grammar for this might look something like this:

```
contact      : 'contact' Identifier '{' 'email:' emailAddress '}' ;
emailAddress : localPart '@' domain ;
```

Here the grammar consists of two production rules. Each production rule has a name and a body. The body describes how you can decompose the rule into a sequence of elements. These elements may be other rules or terminals. A terminal is something that isn't another rule, such as the literals contact and }. If you're using a BNF grammar with Syntax-Directed Translation, your terminals will usually be the token types that come out of the lexer. (I haven't decomposed the rules any further. Email addresses, in particular, can get surprisingly complicated [RFC 5322].)

I mentioned earlier that BNF appears in lots of syntactic forms. The one above is that used by the ANTLR *Parser Generator (269)*. Here's the same grammar in a form much closer to the original Algol BNF:

```
<contact>      ::=  contact <Identifier> { email: <emailAddress> }
<emailAddress> ::=  <localPart> @ <domain>
```

In this case, the rules are quoted in angle brackets, the literal text is unquoted, rules are terminated with a newline rather than a semicolon, and "::=" is used as the separator between the rule's name and its body. You'll see all of these elements varied in different BNFs, so don't get hung up on the syntax. In this book, I generally use the BNF syntax used by ANTLR, since I also use ANTLR for any examples that involve Parser Generators. Parser Generators typically use this style, rather than the Algol style.

Now I'll extend the problem by considering contacts that can have either an email address or a telephone number. So, in addition to my original example, we might also get:

```
contact rparsons {
  tel: 312-373-1000
}
```

I can extend my grammar to recognize this by using an alternative.

```
contact : 'contact' Identifier '{' line '}' ;
line    : email | tel ;
email   : 'email:' emailAddress ;
tel     : 'tel:' TelephoneNumber ;
```

The **alternative** here is the | in the line rule. It says that I can decompose the line into either email or tel.

One more thing I'll do is extract the identifier into a username rule.

```
contact  : 'contact' username '{' line '}' ;
username : Identifier;
line     : email | tel ;
email    : 'email:' emailAddress ;
tel      : 'tel:' TelephoneNumber ;
```

The username rule only resolves to a single identifier, but it's worth doing to more clearly show the intent of the grammar—similarly to extracting a simple method in imperative code.

The use of the alternative is pretty limited in this context; it only allows me to have one email or one telephone. As it turns out, alternatives actually unleash an enormous amount of expressive power, but rather than explore that, I'll move on to multiplicity symbols next.

19.1.1 Multiplicity Symbols (Kleene Operators)

A serious contact management application wouldn't give me only one email or telephone as a point of contact. While I won't go too close to what a real contact management application should provide, I will take a step closer. I'll say a contact must have a user name, may have a full name, must have at least one email address, and may have some telephone numbers. Here's a grammar for that:

```
contact  : 'contact' username '{' fullname? email+ tel* '}';
username : Identifier;
fullname : QuotedString;
email    : 'email:' emailAddress ;
tel      : 'tel:' TelephoneNumber ;
```

You'll probably recognize the multiplicity symbols as those used in regular expressions (they are often called **Kleene operators**). Using multiplicity symbols like this makes it much easier to understand grammars.

When you see multiplicity symbols, you'll also often see a grouping construct that allows you to combine several elements to apply a multiplicity rule. So I could write the above grammar like this, inlining the subrules:

```
contact : 'contact' Identifier '{'
  QuotedString?
  ('email:' emailAddress)+
  ('tel:' TelephoneNumber)*
  '}'
  ;
```

I wouldn't suggest doing this, because the subrules capture intent and make the grammar much more readable. But there are occasions where a subrule adds clutter and grouping operators work out better.

This example also shows how longer BNF rules are usually formatted. Most BNFs ignore line endings, so putting each logical piece of the rule on its own line can make a complicated rule clearer. In this case, it's usually easier to put the semicolon on its own line to mark the end. This is the kind of format I've seen most often, and I do prefer this style once the rule becomes too complicated to fit easily on a single line.

Adding multiplicity symbols is usually what makes the difference between EBNF (extended BNF) and basic BNF. However, the terminology here has its usual muddle. When people say "BNF" they may mean basic BNF (i.e., not EBNF) or something more broadly BNFish (including EBNF). In this book, when I refer to a BNF without multiplicity symbols, I'll say "basic BNF"; when I say "BNF" I'm including any BNF-like language, including EBNF-like languages.

The multiplicity symbols I've shown here are the most common ones you're likely to see, certainly with *Parser Generators (269)*. However, there's another form that uses brackets instead:

19: BNF

```
contact  : 'contact' username '{' [fullname] email {email} {tel} '}';
username : Identifier;
fullname : QuotedString;
email    : 'email:' emailAddress ;
tel      : 'tel:' TelephoneNumber ;
```

The brackets replace ? with [..] and * with {..}. There's no replacement for +, so you replace foo+ with foo {foo}. This bracketing style is quite common in grammars intended for human consumption, and it is the style used in the ISO standard for EBNF (ISO/IEC 14977); however, most Parser Generators prefer the regexp form. I'll use the regexp form in my examples.

19.1.2 Some Other Useful Operators

There are a few other operators that I should mention, as I use them in examples in this book and you'll probably run into them elsewhere.

Since I use ANTLR a lot in the this book for my grammars, I use the ~ operator of ANTLR, which I refer to as the up-to operator. The **up-to operator** matches everything up to the element following the ~. So if you want to match all characters up to but not including a close brace, you can use the pattern ~'}'. If you don't have this operator, the equivalent regular expression is something like [^}]*.

Most approaches to *Syntax-Directed Translation (219)* separate lexical analysis from syntactic analysis. You can define lexical analysis in a production-rule style too, but there are usually subtle but important differences as to what kinds of operators and combinations are allowed. Lexical rules are more likely to be close to regular expressions, if only because regular expressions are often used for lexical analysis since they use a finite-state machine rather than a parser's push-down machine (see "Regular, Context-Free, and Context-Sensitive Grammars," p. 96).

An important operator in lexical analysis is the range operator ".." used to identify a range of characters, such as lower-case letters 'a'..'z'. A common rule for identifiers is:

```
Identifier:
  ('a'..'z' | 'A'..'Z')
  ('a'..'z' | 'A'..'Z' | '0'..'9' | '_')*
  ;
```

This allows identifiers that start with a lowercase or uppercase letter, followed by letters, numbers, or underscores. Ranges only make sense in lexical rules, not syntactic rules. They are traditionally also rather ASCII-centric, which makes it difficult to support identifiers in languages other than English.

19.1.3 Parsing Expression Grammars

Most BNF grammars you'll run into are context-free grammars (CFG). However, there's a recent style of grammar called a parsing expression grammar (PEG). The biggest difference between a PEG and a CFG is that PEGs have ordered alternatives. In a CFG, you write:

```
contact : email | tel;
```

which means that a contact can be an email or a telephone number. The order in which you write the two alternatives doesn't affect the interpretation. In most cases, this is fine, but occasionally having unordered alternatives leads to ambiguities.

Consider a case where you want to recognize an appropriate sequence of ten digits as a US telephone number, but want to capture other sequences as just an unstructured telephone number. You could try a grammar like this:

```
tel :  us_number | raw_number ;

raw_number
 : (DIGIT | SEP)+;
us_number
 : (us_area_code | '(' us_area_code ')') SEP? us_local;

us_area_code
    : DIGIT DIGIT DIGIT;

us_local
    : DIGIT DIGIT DIGIT SEP? DIGIT DIGIT DIGIT DIGIT;

DIGIT : '0'..'9';
SEP     : ('-' | ' ' );
```

But this grammar is ambiguous when it gets input like "312–373 1000", because both the us_number and raw_number rules can match it. An **ordered alternative** forces the rules to be tried in order and whichever rule matches first is the one that's used. A common syntax for an ordered alternative is /, so the tel rule would then read:

```
tel: us_number / raw_number ;
```

(I should mention that although ANTLR uses unordered alternatives, they act more like ordered ones. For this kind of ambiguity, ANTLR will report a warning and go with the first alternative that matches.)

symbol	meaning	example
|	alternative	email | tel
*	none or more (Kleene star)	tel*
+	one or more (Kleene plus)	email+
?	optional	fullname?
~	up-to	~'}'
..	range	'0'..'9'
/	ordered alternative	us_tel / raw_tel

19.1.4 Converting EBNF to Basic BNF

The multiplicity symbols make BNF much easier to follow. However, they don't increase the expressive power of BNF. An EBNF grammar using multiplicity symbols can be replaced with an equivalent basic BNF grammar. From time to time, this is important because some *Parser Generators (269)* use basic BNF for their grammar.

I'll use the contact grammar as an example. Here it is again:

```
contact  : 'contact' username '{' fullname? email+ tel* '}';
username : Identifier;
fullname : QuotedString;
email    : 'email:' emailAddress ;
tel      : 'tel:' TelephoneNumber ;
```

The key to the transformation is using alternatives. So, starting with the optional part, I can replace any foo? ; with foo | ; (that is, foo or nothing).

```
contact  : 'contact' username '{' fullname email+ tel* '}';
username : Identifier;
fullname : /* optional */ | QuotedString  ;
email    : 'email:' emailAddress ;
tel      : 'tel:' TelephoneNumber ;
```

You'll notice that I've added a comment to make it clearer what I'm doing. Different tools use different comment syntaxes, of course, but I'll follow the C convention here. I don't like to use comments if I can replace them with something in the language I'm using, but if I can't, I use them without hesitation—as in this case.

If the parent clause is simple, you can fold the alternative into the parent. So a : b? c would transform to a: c | b c. If you have several optional elements, however, you get into a combinatorial explosion, which, like most explosions, isn't something that's fun to be in the middle of.

To transform repetition, again the trick is to use alternatives, in this case with recursion. It's quite common for rules to be recursive—that is, to use the rule itself in its body. With this, you can replace x : y*; with x : y x |;. Using this on the telephone number, we get:

```
contact  : 'contact' username '{' fullname email+ tel '}';
username : Identifier;
fullname : /* optional */ | QuotedString  ;
email    : 'email:' emailAddress ;
tel      : /* multiple */ | 'tel:' TelephoneNumber tel;
```

19: BNF

This is the basic way of handling recursion. To do a recursive algorithm, you need to consider two cases: the terminal case and the next case, where the next case includes the recursive call. In this situation, we have an alternative for each case: the terminal case is nothing, and the next case adds one element.

When you introduce a recursive case like this, you often have the choice of whether to do the recursion on the left or on the right—that is, to replace x : y*; with x : y x | or with x : x y |. Usually your parser will tell you to prefer one over the other due to the algorithm it's using. For example, a top-down parser cannot do left recursion at all, while Yacc can do either but prefers right recursion.

The last multiplicity marker is +. This is similar to * but the terminal case is a single item rather than none, so we can replace x : y+ with x : y | x y (or x: y | y x to avoid left recursion). Doing this to the contact example yields:

```
contact     : 'contact' username '{' fullname email tel '}';
username    : Identifier;
fullname    :  /* optional */ | QuotedString  ;
email       : singleEmail | email singleEmail;
singleEmail : 'email:' emailAddress ;
tel         : /* multiple */ | 'tel:' TelephoneNumber tel;
```

Since the single email expression is used twice in the email rule, I've extracted it into its own rule. Introducing intermediate rules like this is often necessary in transforming to basic BNF; you also have to do this if you have groups.

I now have the contact grammar in basic BNF. It works just fine, but the grammar is much harder to follow. Not only do I lose the multiplicity markers, I also have to introduce extra subrules just to make the recursion work properly. As a result, I always prefer to use EBNF if all else is equal, but I still have this technique for the occasions when basic BNF is necessary.

EBNF	x : y?		x: y*		x: y+
basic BNF	x: /* optional */	y		x: /* multiple */	y x		x: y	y x

19.1.5 Code Actions

BNF provides a way of defining the syntactic structure of a language, and *Parser Generators (269)* typically use BNF to drive the operation of a parser. BNF, however, isn't enough. It provides enough information to generate a parse tree, but not enough to come up with a more useful abstract syntax tree, nor to do further tasks like *Embedded Translation (299)* or *Embedded Interpretation (305)*. So the common approach is to place code actions into the BNF in order for the code to react.

Not all Parser Generators use code actions. Another approach is to provide a separate DSL for something like *Tree Construction (281)*.

The basic idea behind code actions is to place snippets of *Foreign Code (309)* in certain places in the grammar. These snippets are executed when that part of the grammar is recognized by the parser. Consider this grammar:

```
contact : 'contact' username '{' email? tel? '}';
username: ID;
email : 'email:' EmailAddress {log("got email");};
tel : 'tel:' TelephoneNumber;
```

In this case, the message is logged once an email clause is recognized in the parse. A mechanism like this could be used to keep track of when we run into emails. The code in a code action can do anything, so we can also add information to data structures.

Code actions often need to refer to elements that are recognized in the parse. It's nice to log the fact that an email was found, but we might also want to record the email address. To do this, we need to refer to the email address token as we parse it. Different Parser Generators have different ways of doing this. Classic Yacc refers to the tokens by special variables that index the position of the element. So we would refer to the email address token with $2 ($1 would refer to the token email:). Positional references are brittle to changes in the grammar, so a more common approach in modern Parser Generators is to label the elements. Here, this is done ANTLR's way:

```
contact : 'contact' username '{' email? tel? '}';
username: ID;
email : 'email:' e=EmailAddress {log("got email " + $e.text);};
tel : 'tel:' TelephoneNumber;
```

In ANTLR, a reference to $e refers to the element labeled by e= in the grammar. Since this element is a token, I use the text attribute to get the matched text. (I could also get hold of things like the token type, line number, etc.)

In order to resolve these references, Parser Generators run code actions through a templating system, which replaces expressions like $e with the suitable values. ANTLR, in fact, goes further. Attributes like text don't refer to fields or methods directly—ANTLR performs further substitution to get hold of the right information.

Similarly to referring to a token, I can also refer to a rule.

```
contact  : 'contact' username '{' e=email? tel? '}'
  {log("email " + $e.text);}
  ;
username :  ID;
email  : 'email:' EmailAddress ;
tel  : 'tel:' TelephoneNumber;
```

Here the log will record the full text matched by the email rule ("email: fowler@acm.org"). Often, returning some rule object like this isn't too helpful, particularly when we are matching larger rules. As a result, Parser Generators usually give you the ability to define what is returned by a rule when it's matched. In ANTLR, I do this by defining a return type and variable for a rule and then returning it.

```
contact  : 'contact' username '{' e=email? tel? '}'
  {log("email " + $e.result);}
  ;
username :  ID;
email returns [EmailAddress result]
  : 'email:' e=EmailAddress
        {$result = new EmailAddress($e.text);}
  ;
tel  : 'tel:' TelephoneNumber;
```

You can return anything you like from a rule and then refer to that in the parent. (ANTLR allows you to define multiple return values.) This facility, combined with code actions, is extremely important. Often, the rule that gives you the best information about a value isn't the best rule to decide what to do with that data. Passing data up the rule stack allows you to capture information at a low level in a parse, and deal with it at a higher level. Without this, you would have to use a lot of *Context Variables (175)*—which would soon get very messy.

Code actions can be used in all three styles of Embedded Interpretation, Embedded Translation, and Tree Construction. The particular style of code in Tree Construction, however, lends itself to a different approach that uses another DSL ("Using ANTLR's Tree Construction Syntax (Java and ANTLR)," p. 284) to describe how to form the resulting syntax tree.

The position of a code action in a grammar determines when it's executed. So, parent : first {log("hello");} second would cause the log method to be called after the first subrule was recognized but before the second. Most of the time it's easiest to put code actions at the end of a rule, but occasionally you need to put them in the middle. From time to time, the sequence of execution of code actions can be hard to understand, because it depends on the algorithm of the parser. Recursive-descent parsers are usually pretty easy to follow, but bottom-up parsers often cause confusion. You may need to look at the details of your parser system to understand exactly when code actions get executed.

One of the dangers of code actions is that you can end up putting a lot of code in them. If you do this, the grammar becomes hard to see, and you lose most of the documentation advantage it brings. I thus strongly recommend that you use *Embedment Helper (547)* when using code actions.

19.2 When to Use It

You'll need to use BNF whenever you are working with a *Parser Generator (269)*, as these tools use BNF grammars to define how to parse. It's also very useful as an informal thinking tool to help visualize the structure of your DSL, or to communicate the syntactic rules of your language to other humans.

Chapter 20

Regex Table Lexer

by Rebecca Parsons

Implement a lexical analyzer using a list of regular expressions.

pattern	token type
^events	K_EVENT
^end	K_END
^(\\w)+	IDENTIFIER
^(\\s)+	WHITESPACE

Parsers primarily deal with the structure of a language, specifically the way components of the language can be combined. The most basic language components—such as keywords, numbers, and names—can clearly be recognized by the parser. However, we generally separate this stage out into a lexical analyzer. By using a separate pass to recognize these terminal symbols, we simplify the construction of the parser.

Directly implementing a lexical analyzer, also referred to as a lexer, is relatively straightforward. Lexical analyzers stay firmly in the space of regular languages, which means we can use standard regular expression APIs to implement them. For a Regex Table Lexer, we use a list of regular expressions, each associated with the particular terminal symbol. We scan the input, relating individual pieces of the input to the proper regular expressions and generating a stream of tokens naming the individual terminal symbols. It is this token stream that is the input to the parser.

20.1 How It Works

When using *Syntax-Directed Translation (219)*, it's common to separate lexing into a stage of its own. Take a look at that pattern for details on why we separate lexing, some of the conceptual issues around lexing, and how lexing and parsing fit into the broader picture. In this pattern, we'll concentrate on implementing a simple lexer.

The basic algorithm is quite simple. The lexer performs a scan of the input string starting from the beginning, matching tokens as it goes along and consuming those characters. Let's start with a very simple, admittedly ridiculous, example. We have two symbols we want to recognize, the strings Hello and Goodbye. The regular expressions for these symbols are ^Hello and ^Goodbye respectively. The ^ operator is needed to anchor the regular expression match at the start of the string. We'll call our tokens HOWDY and BYEBYE just to be different. Let's see how the basic algorithm works on the input string:

HelloGoodbyeHelloHelloGoodbye

The regular expression for Hello matches the beginning of the string, so we generate the HOWDY token and advance our pointer in the string to the first G. The algorithm would return to the beginning of the list of regular expressions, since ordering matters. Thus, the regular expression for Hello would again be checked against the string starting with G. This check fails, of course. So, we try the next regular expression in the list, the one for Goodbye, and this matches. We add the token BYEBYE to our output token stream, reset the string pointer to be at the second H, and continue. The final output stream for the sentence above is HOWDY, BYEBYE, HOWDY, HOWDY, BYEBYE.

The order of checking the patterns is important so that we can properly handle things like keywords. In the state machine grammar, for example, our keywords also match the rules for identifiers. We order the checks for keywords first, so that the proper token will appear for our keywords. Selection of appropriate tokens is a design decision for the lexical analyzer. In the state machine grammar, we don't attempt to distinguish between codes and names, using a single identifier token for each. This choice is necessary, since the lexer doesn't have the context to know that a four-letter name should match the identifier token, if it isn't in the position where a code is legal. Often, though, the token set includes things like keywords, names, numbers, punctuation, and operators.

We instantiate a particular lexical analyzer by specifying the recognizers, and we use a table or a list to order them. Each recognizer contains the token type, the regular expression to recognize that token, and a Boolean value specifying if this token should be in the output stream. The token type is simply used to identify the token class to the parser. The Boolean allows us to handle things like semantically meaningless whitespace and comments. While these strings are in the input stream and must be handled by the lexer, we don't pass the corresponding tokens on to the parser. The repeated sequential scan of the table enforces the ordering of the matches, and the table of recognizers also makes it simple to introduce additional token types.

The matcher for individual tokens steps through the table of recognizers; if a match occurs, the corresponding input is consumed from the input string and the token is sent to the output stream, assuming the Boolean output flag is set. We populate the tokenValue field of the output token, whether it is needed or not. Generally, token values are only needed for identifiers, numbers, and sometimes operators, but this approach saves us another Boolean flag and simplifies the code. The main scanner method continually invokes the single match method, checking to make sure that some recognition has been successful. Once the input string is consumed and matching has been successful throughout, the token buffer is sent along for processing by the parser.

To help with error diagnostics, you can add information to the token about where that token was in the character stream—for example, a line number and column position.

20: Regex Table
Lexer

20.2 When to Use It

While lexical analysis generators, such as Lex, do exist, there is little need to use them given the prevalence of regular expression APIs. One exception is using ANTLR as the *Parser Generator (269)*, since the lexical analysis and parsing are more tightly integrated in that tool.

The implementation described here is an obvious one for lexical analysis. Its performance clearly depends on the specifics of the regular expression API used. The only time I would suggest not using Regex Table Lexer would be if there is no acceptable regular expression API available.

Given the simple syntax of many DSLs, it is possible for this approach to be used to recognize the full language. As long as the language is regular, this approach applies for the parser as well.

20.3 Lexing Miss Grant's Controller (Java)

The lexical analyzer for the state machine grammar is quite typical. We call out tokens for our keywords, punctuation, and a token type for identifiers. We also have a token type for comments and whitespace, which are just consumed by the lexer. We use the java.util.regex API to specify the patterns and do the matching for us. The input to the lexer is the DSL script to be analyzed, and the output is a token buffer including the token types and their related values. This token buffer becomes the input to the parser.

The implementation is split into the specification of the tokens to recognize and the lexical analysis algorithm itself. This approach makes it easy to add additional token types to the lexer. We use an enumerated type to specify a token's type, with attributes specifying the relevant regular expression and the Boolean value controlling the output of the token. This approach is a clean one in Java, but you could just as easily use a more traditional object. However, the token types do need to be readily available for use in the parser itself.

```java
class ScannerPatterns...
  public enum TokenTypes {
    TT_EVENT("^events", true),
    TT_RESET("^resetEvents", true),
    TT_COMMANDS("^commands", true),
    TT_END("^end", true),
    TT_STATE("^state", true),
    TT_ACTIONS("^actions", true),
    TT_LEFT("^\\{", true),
    TT_RIGHT("^\\}", true),
    TT_TRANSITION("^=>", true),
    TT_IDENTIFIER("^(\\w)+", true),
    TT_WHITESPACE("^(\\s)+", false),
    TT_COMMENT("^\\\\(.)*$", false),
    TT_EOF("^EOF", false);

    private final String regExPattern;
    private final Boolean outputToken;

    TokenTypes(String regexPattern, Boolean output) {
      this.regExPattern = regexPattern;
      this.outputToken = output;
    }
  }
}
```

In the lexical analyzer, we instantiate a table of recognition objects, with the compiled recognizers combined with their token types and the Boolean values.

```java
class ScannerPatterns...
  public static ArrayList<ScanRecognizer> LoadPatterns(){
    Pattern pattern;
    for (TokenTypes t : TokenTypes.values()) {
      pattern = Pattern.compile(t.regExPattern)  ;
      patternMatchers.add(new ScanRecognizer(t, pattern,t.outputToken)) ;
    }
    return(patternMatchers);
  }
```

We define a class for our lexer. The instance variables for the lexer include the recognizers, the input string, and the output token list.

```
class StateMachineTokenizer...
  private String scannerBuffer;
  private ArrayList<Token> tokenList;
  private ArrayList<ScanRecognizer> recognizerPatterns;
```

The main processing loop in the lexer is a do-while loop.

```
class StateMachineTokenizer...
  while (parseInProgress) {
    Iterator<ScanRecognizer> patternIterator = recognizerPatterns.iterator();
    parseInProgress = matchToken(patternIterator);
  }
```

This loop continually invokes the token matcher until the buffer is exhausted or no more matches are possible for the remaining buffer.

The matchToken method steps through the various recognizers in order and attempts to match a single token.

20: Regex Table
Lexer

```
private boolean matchToken(Iterator<ScanRecognizer> patternIterator) {
  boolean tokenMatch;
  ScanRecognizer recognizer;
  Pattern pattern;
  Matcher matcher;
  boolean result;
  tokenMatch = false;
  result = true;

  do {
    recognizer = patternIterator.next();
    pattern = recognizer.tokenPattern;
    matcher = pattern.matcher(scannerBuffer);
    if (matcher.find()) {
      if (recognizer.outputToken) {
        tokenList.add(new Token(recognizer.token, matcher.group()));
      }
      tokenMatch = true;
      scannerBuffer = scannerBuffer.substring(matcher.end());
    }
  } while (patternIterator.hasNext() && (!tokenMatch));

  if ((!tokenMatch) || (matcher.end() == scannerBuffer.length())) {
    result = false;
  }
  return result;
}
```

If a match succeeds, we advance this input buffer to the point just past the match, in this case retrieving the end point using matcher.end(). We check the Boolean for the recognizer that matched and generate the appropriate token if warranted. If no match occurs, we declare failure. The find method in the regex

API scans to the end of the string to find matches. If a scan of the remaining string fails to match, then the overall lexical analysis fails.

The outer loop proceeds as long as the inner loop matches a token, going through the input until the end of the string is reached. The iterator is reset for each pass of the inner loop, ensuring all token patterns are matched in each pass. The result of the parse is a token buffer, where each token has a token type and the actual string value matched in the lexical analyzer.

Chapter 21

Recursive Descent Parser

by Rebecca Parsons

Create a top-down parser using control flow for grammar operators and recursive functions for nonterminal recognizers.

```
boolean eventBlock() {
  boolean parseSuccess = false;
  Token t = tokenBuffer.nextToken();
  if (t.isTokenType(ScannerPatterns.TokenTypes.TT_EVENT)) {
    tokenBuffer.popToken();
    parseSuccess = eventDecList();
  }
  if (parseSuccess) {
    t = tokenBuffer.nextToken();
    if (t.isTokenType(ScannerPatterns.TokenTypes.TT_END)) {
      tokenBuffer.popToken();
    }
    else {
      parseSuccess = false;
    }
  }
  return parseSuccess;
}
```

Many DSLs are quite simple as languages. While the flexibility of external languages is appealing, using a *Parser Generator (269)* to create a parser introduces new tools and languages into a project, complicating the build process.

A Recursive Descent Parser supports the flexibility of an external DSL without requiring a Parser Generator. The Recursive Descent Parser can be implemented in whatever general-purpose language one chooses. It uses control flow operators to implement the various grammar operators. Individual methods or functions implement the parsing rules for the different nonterminal symbols in the grammar.

21.1 How It Works

As in the other implementations, we again separate lexical analysis and parsing. A Recursive Descent Parser receives a token stream from a lexical analyzer, such as a *Regex Table Lexer (239)*.

The basic structure of a Recursive Descent Parser is quite simple. There is a method for each nonterminal symbol in the grammar. This method implements the various production rules associated with the nonterminal. The method returns a Boolean value which represents the result of the match. Failure at any level gets propagated back up the call stack. Each method operates on the token buffer, advancing the pointer through the tokens as it matches some portion of the sentence.

Since there are relatively few grammar operators (sequencing, alternatives, and repetition), these implementation methods take on a small number of patterns. We'll start with processing alternatives, which uses a conditional statement. For the grammar fragment:

```
grammar file...
  C : A | B
```

the corresponding function would simply be:

```
boolean C ()
  if (A())
    then true
    else if (B())
          then true
          else false
```

This implementation clearly checks one alternative and then the other, acting more like an ordered alternatives (p. 233). If you truly need to allow for the ambiguity introduced by unordered alternatives, it might be time for a *Parser Generator (269)*.

After a successful call to A(), the token buffer would now be advanced to begin at the first token past that matched by A. If the call to A() fails, the token buffer remains unchanged.

The sequencing grammar operator is implemented with nested if statements, since we don't continue processing if one of the methods fails. So, the implementation of:

```
grammar file...
  C : A B
```

would simply be:

21: Recursive Descent Parser

```
boolean C ()
  if (A())
    then if (B())
            then true
            else false
    else false
```

The optional operator is a bit different.

```
grammar file...
  C: A?
```

We have to try and recognize the tokens matching nonterminal A, but there's no way to fail here. If we match A, we return true. If we don't match A, we still return true, since A is optional. The implementation is thus:

```
boolean C ()
  A()
  true
```

21: Recursive
Descent Parser

If the match for A fails, the token buffer remains where it was at the entry to C. If the match for A succeeds, the buffer is advanced. The call to C succeeds in either case.

The repetition operator has two major forms: zero or more instances ("*"), and one or more instances ("+"). To implement the one or more instances operator, such as this:

```
grammar file...
  C: A+
```

we would use the following code pattern:

```
boolean C ()
  if (A())
    then while (A())
            {}
          true
    else
          false
```

This code first checks to see if at least one A is present. If that is the case, the function continues to find as many more A's as it can, but it will always return true, because it has matched at least one A—its only requirement. The code for a list that allows zero instances simply removes the outer if statement and always returns true.

The table below summarizes the above using pseudocode fragments to demonstrate the different implementations.

Grammar rule	Implementation
| A \| B | ```
if (A())
  then true
  else if (B())
    then true
    else false
``` |
| A B | ```
if (A())
  then if (B())
    then true
    else false
  else false
``` |
| A? | ```
A();
true
``` |
| A* | ```
while A();
true
``` |
| A+ | ```
if (A())
  then
    while (A());
  else false
``` |

We use the same style of helper functions as in the other sections to keep the actions distinct from the parsing. *Tree Construction (281)* and *Embedded Translation (299)* are both possible in recursive descent.

To make this approach as clean as it is, the methods implementing the production rules must behave in a consistent fashion. The most important rule concerns management of the input token buffer. If the method matches what it is looking for, the current position in the input token string is advanced to the point just past the matched input. In the case of the event keyword, the token position is only moved one spot, for example. If the match fails, the position of the buffer should be the same as it was when the method was called. This is of most importance for sequences. At the beginning of the function, we need to save the incoming buffer position, in case the first part of the sequence matches (like A in the above example) but the match for B fails. Managing the buffer thus allows alternatives to be properly handled.

Another important rule relates to the population of the semantic model or syntax tree. As much as possible, each method should manage its own pieces of the model or create its own elements in the syntax tree. Naturally, any actions should only be taken when the full match has been confirmed. As with the token buffer management for sequences, actions must be deferred until the entire sequence completes.

One complaint about Parser Generators is that they require developers to become familiar with language grammars. While it is quite true that the syntax of
```

the grammar operators does not appear in the recursive descent implementation, a grammar clearly exists in the methods. Changing the methods changes the grammar. The difference is not in the presence or absence of the grammar but in how the grammar is expressed.

21.2 When to Use It

The greatest strength of Recursive Descent Parser is its simplicity. Once you understand the basic algorithm and how to handle various grammar operators, writing a Recursive Descent Parser is a simple programming task. You then have a parser in an ordinary class in your system. Testing approaches work in the same way they always do; in particular, a unit test makes more sense when the unit is a method, just like any other. Finally, since the parser is simply a program, it is easy to reason about its behavior and debug the parser. The Recursive Descent Parser is a direct implementation of a parsing algorithm, making the tracing of flow through the parse much easier to discern.

The most serious shortcoming of Recursive Descent Parser is that there is no explicit representation of the grammar. By encoding the grammar into the recursive descent algorithm, you lose the clear picture of the grammar, which can only live in documentation or comments. Both *Parser Combinator (255)* and *Parser Generator (269)* have an explicit statement of the grammar, making it easier to understand and evolve.

Another problem with Recursive Descent Parser is that you have a top-down algorithm that can't handle left-recursion, which makes it more messy to deal with *Nested Operator Expressions (327)*. Performance will also be usually inferior to a Parser Generator. In practice, these disadvantages aren't such a factor for DSLs.

A Recursive Descent Parser is straightforward to implement as long as the grammar is reasonably simple. One of the factors that can make it easy to deal with is limited look ahead—that is, how many tokens the parser needs to peek forward to determine what to do next. Generally, I wouldn't use Recursive Descent Parser for a grammar that requires more than one symbol of look ahead; such grammars are better suited to Parser Generators.

21: Recursive Descent Parser

21.3 Further Reading

For more information in a less traditional programming language context, [parr-LIP] is a good reference. The *Dragon Book* [Dragon] remains the standard of the programming language community.

21.4 Recursive Descent and Miss Grant's Controller (Java)

We begin with a parser class that includes instance variables for the input buffer, the output of the state machine, and various parsing data. This implementation uses a *Regex Table Lexer (239)* to create the input token buffer from an input string.

```
class StateMachineParser...
  private TokenBuffer tokenBuffer;
  private StateMachine machineResult;
  private ArrayList<Event> machineEvents;
  private ArrayList<Command> machineCommands;
  private ArrayList<Event> resetEvents;
  private Map<String, State> machineStates;
  private State partialState;
```

The constructor for the state machine class accepts the input token buffer and sets up the data structures. There's a very simple method to start the parser, which invokes the function representing our overall state machine.

```
class StateMachineParser...
  public StateMachine startParser() {
    if (stateMachine()) {/* main level production */
      loadResetEvents();
    }
    return machineResult;
  }
```

The method startParser is also responsible for the final construction of the state machine in case of success. The only remaining action not covered by the rest of the methods is to populate the reset event in the state machine.

The grammar rule for our state machine is a simple sequence of the different blocks.

```
grammar file...
  stateMachine: eventBlock optionalResetBlock optionalCommandBlock stateList
```

The top-level function is simply a sequence of the various components of the state machine.

```
class StateMachineParser...
  private boolean stateMachine() {
    boolean parseSuccess = false;
    if (eventBlock()) {
      if (optionalResetBlock()) {
        if (optionalCommandBlock()) {
          if (stateList()) {
            parseSuccess = true;
          }
        }
      }
    }
    return parseSuccess;
  }
```

We'll use event declarations to show how most of the functions work together. The first production constructs the event block, made up of a sequence.

```
grammar file...
  eventBlock: eventKeyword eventDecList endKeyword
```

21: Recursive
Descent Parser

The code for this sequence follows the pattern described above. Notice how the initial buffer position is saved in case the full sequence is not recognized.

```
class StateMachineParser...
  private boolean eventBlock() {
    Token t;
    boolean parseSuccess = false;
    int save = tokenBuffer.getCurrentPosition();
    t = tokenBuffer.nextToken();
    if (t.isTokenType(ScannerPatterns.TokenTypes.TT_EVENT)) {
      tokenBuffer.popToken();
      parseSuccess = eventDecList();
    }
    if (parseSuccess) {
      t = tokenBuffer.nextToken();
      if (t.isTokenType(ScannerPatterns.TokenTypes.TT_END)) {
        tokenBuffer.popToken();
      }
      else {
        parseSuccess=false;
      }
    }
    if (!parseSuccess) {
      tokenBuffer.resetCurrentPosition(save);
    }
    return parseSuccess;
  }
```

The grammar rule for the list of events is straightforward.

```
grammar file...
  eventDecList: eventDec+
```

The eventDecList function follows the pattern exactly. All the actions are performed in the eventDec function.

```
class StateMachineParser...
  private boolean eventDecList() {
    int save = tokenBuffer.getCurrentPosition();
    boolean parseSuccess = false;

    if (eventDec()) {
      parseSuccess = true;
      while (parseSuccess) {
        parseSuccess = eventDec();
      }
      parseSuccess = true;
    }
    else {
      tokenBuffer.resetCurrentPosition(save);
    }
    return parseSuccess;
  }
```

The real work happens when matching the event declaration itself. The grammar is straightforward.

```
grammar file...
  eventDec: identifier identifier
```

The code for this sequence again saves the initial token position. This code also populates the state machine model on a success match.

```
class StateMachineParser...
  private boolean eventDec() {
    Token t;
    boolean parseSuccess = false;
    int save = tokenBuffer.getCurrentPosition();
    t = tokenBuffer.nextToken();
    String elementLeft = "";
    String elementRight = "";

    if (t.isTokenType(ScannerPatterns.TokenTypes.TT_IDENTIFIER)) {
      elementLeft = consumeIdentifier(t);
      t = tokenBuffer.nextToken();
      if (t.isTokenType(ScannerPatterns.TokenTypes.TT_IDENTIFIER)) {
        elementRight = consumeIdentifier(t);
        parseSuccess = true;
      }
    }
```

```
    if (parseSuccess) {
      makeEventDec(elementLeft, elementRight);
    } else {
      tokenBuffer.resetCurrentPosition(save);
    }
    return parseSuccess;
  }
```

Two helper functions invoked here require further explanation. First, consumeIdentifier advances the token buffer and returns the token value of the identifier so it can be used to populate the event declaration.

```
class StateMachineParser...
  private String consumeIdentifier(Token t) {
    String identName = t.tokenValue;
    tokenBuffer.popToken();
    return identName;
  }
```

The helper function makeEventDec uses the event name and code to actually populate the event declaration.

21: Recursive
Descent Parser

```
class StateMachineParser...
  private void makeEventDec(String left, String right) {
    machineEvents.add(new Event(left, right));
  }
```

From the perspective of the actions, the only real difficulty comes in processing states. Since transitions can refer to states that don't yet exist, our helper functions must allow for a reference to a state that has not yet been defined. This property holds true for all the implementations that don't use *Tree Construction (281)*.

One final method is worthy of description. optionalResetBlock implements this grammar rule.

```
grammar file...
  optionalResetBlock: (resetBlock)?
  resetBlock: resetKeyword (resetEvent)* endKeyword
  resetEvent: identifier
```

The implementation we use inlines the different grammar operator patterns, since the rule itself is so simple.

```
class StateMachineParser...
  private boolean optionalResetBlock() {
    int save = tokenBuffer.getCurrentPosition();
    boolean parseSuccess = true;
    Token t = tokenBuffer.nextToken();
```

```
  if (t.isTokenType(ScannerPatterns.TokenTypes.TT_RESET)) {
    tokenBuffer.popToken();
    t = tokenBuffer.nextToken();
    parseSuccess = true;
    while ((!(t.isTokenType(ScannerPatterns.TokenTypes.TT_END))) &
           (parseSuccess)) {
      parseSuccess = resetEvent();
      t = tokenBuffer.nextToken();
    }
    if (parseSuccess) {
      tokenBuffer.popToken();
    } else {
      tokenBuffer.resetCurrentPosition(save);
    }
  }
  return parseSuccess;
}

private boolean resetEvent() {
  Token t;
  boolean parseSuccess = false;

  t = tokenBuffer.nextToken();
  if (t.isTokenType(ScannerPatterns.TokenTypes.TT_IDENTIFIER)) {
    resetEvents.add(findEventFromName(t.tokenValue));
    parseSuccess = true;
    tokenBuffer.popToken();
  }
  return parseSuccess;
}
```

For this method, we return true if the reset keyword is not present, since the whole block is optional. If the keyword is present, we must then have zero or more reset event declarations followed by the end keyword. If these are not present, the match for this block fails and the return value is false.

Chapter 22

Parser Combinator

by Rebecca Parsons

Create a top-down parser by a composition of parser objects.

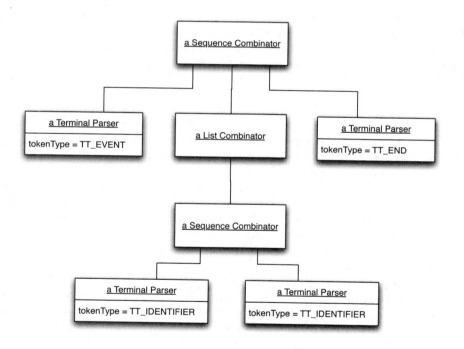

Even though our premise is that *Parser Generators (269)* are not nearly as difficult to work with as they are perceived to be, there are legitimate reasons to avoid them if possible. The most obvious issue is the additional steps in the build process required to first generate the parser and then build it. While Parser Generators are still the right choice for more complex context-free grammars, particularly if the grammar is ambiguous or performance is crucial, directly implementing a parser in a general-purpose language is a viable option.

A Parser Combinator implements a grammar using a structure of parser objects. Recognizers for the symbols in the production rules are combined using *Composites* [GoF], which are referred to as combinators. Effectively, parser combinators represent a *Semantic Model (159)* of a grammar.

22.1 How It Works

As with *Recursive Descent Parser (245)*, we use a lexer, for example a *Regex Table Lexer (239)*, to perform the lexical analysis of the input string. Our Parser Combinator then operates on the resulting token string.

The basic idea behind parser combinators is simple. The term "combinator" comes from functional languages. Combinators are designed to be composed to create more complex operations of the same type as their input. So, parser combinators are combined to make more complex parser combinators. In functional languages, these combinators are first-class functions, but we can do the same with objects in an object-oriented environment. We start with the base cases, which are the recognizers for the terminal symbols in our grammar. We then use the combinators that implement the various grammar operators (such as sequence, list, etc.) to implement the production rules in the grammar. Effectively, for each nonterminal in our grammar, we have a combinator for it, just like in Recursive Descent Parser we have a recursive function for each nonterminal.

Each combinator is responsible for recognizing some portion of the language, determining if there is a match, consuming the relevant tokens from the input buffer for the match, and performing the required actions. These operations are the same as those required by the recursive functions in Recursive Descent Parser. For the recognizer portion of the implementations of various grammar operators below, the same logic that we used in the recursive descent implementation applies. What's really happening here is that we abstract out the fragments of logic associated with processing the grammar operators for top-down parsing and create the combinators to hold that logic. While a Recursive Descent Parser combines those fragments with function calls in inline code, a Parser Combinator combines these by linking together objects in an *Adaptive Model (487)*.

Individual parser combinators accept as input the status of the match so far, the current token buffer, and possibly a set of accumulated action results. Parser combinators return a match status, a possibly altered token buffer, and a set of action results. To make the description easier, assume for the moment that the token buffer and the set of match results are kept as state in the background somewhere. We'll change that later, but this assumption makes the combinator logic easier to follow. Also, we'll concentrate first on describing the recognition logic, and then return to dealing with actions.

Let's first consider a recognizer for a terminal symbol—our base case. The actual recognition of a terminal symbol is easy; we simply compare the token at the current position in the input token buffer to whatever terminal symbol, represented by a token, the recognizer is for. If the token matches, we advance the current position in the token buffer.

Now, let's look at the basics behind the combinators for the various grammar operators. We'll start with the alternative operator.

```
grammar file...
  C : A | B
```

An alternative combinator for C tries one combinator first, say B; if the match status from that combinator is true, the return value for C is the same as that returned by B. We cycle through the alternatives, trying each one. If all alternatives fail, the return value is a failed match status and the input token buffer is unchanged. In pseudocode, this combinator looks like the following:

```
CombinatorResult C ()

if (A())
  then return true
  else
    if (B())
      then true
      else return false
```

As you can see, this logic looks just like the recursive descent algorithm. The sequence operator is a bit more complicated.

```
grammar file...
  C : A B
```

To implement this operator, we need to step through the components in the sequence. If any of these matches fail, we need to reset the token buffer to its input state. For the above grammar rule, the resulting combinator looks like the following:

```
CombinatorResult C ()

  saveTokenBuffer()
  if (A())
    then
      if (B())
        then
          return true
        else
          restoreTokenBuffer
          return false
    else return false
```

22: Parser
Combinator

This implementation and the others below rely on the characteristic behavior of the combinators. If the match succeeds, the tokens relating to that match are consumed in the token buffer. If the match fails, the combinator returns an unaltered token buffer.

The optional operator is straightforward.

```
grammar file...
  C: A?
```

This operator either returns the original tokens or modifies them, based on the match of A. For the above grammar rule, the resulting combinator looks like the following:

```
CombinatorResult C ()

  A()
  return true
```

The list operator for one-or-more lists is our next operator to consider.

```
grammar file...
  C: A+
```

This combinator first checks to make sure that at least one A is present. If it is, then we loop until the match fails and return the new token buffer. If the initial match fails, we return false along with the input tokens.

```
CombinatorResult C ()

  if (A())
    then
      while (A())

      return true
  else
      return false
```

Of course, for an optional list, we would always return true and handle the token buffer appropriately, depending on the match. The code for that would look roughly like the following:

```
CombinatorResult C ()

  while (A())
    return true
```

The combinator implementations shown here are direct implementations of specific rules. The power of parser combinators comes from the fact that we can construct the composite combinators from the component combinators. Thus, the code for specifying the following sequence operation:

```
grammar file...
  C : A B
```

would really look more like this declaration:

```
C = new SequenceCombinator (A,B)
```

where the logic implementing the sequencing is shared across all such rules.

22.1.1 Dealing with the Actions

Now that we know how the recognition works, let's move on to the actions. For the moment, we'll again assume that we've got some state that we manipulate in the actions. The actions can take many forms. In *Tree Construction (281)*, the actions would build up the abstract syntax tree while the parse proceeds. In *Embedded Translation (299)*, the actions will populate our semantic model. The type of the match value will obviously vary based on what the actions are.

We start with our base case again, the terminal symbol combinator. If the match is successful, we populate the match value with the result of the match and invoke the actions on that match value. In the case of an identifier recognizer, for example, we might record it in a *Symbol Table (165)*. For terminal symbols like identifiers and numbers, though, the action often simply records the specific token value for later use.

The sequence operation is more interesting when it comes to actions. Conceptually, once we have recognized all the components of the sequence, we need to call the action on the list of the match values from the individual components. We modify the recognizer to invoke the actions in this way.

22: Parser Combinator

```
CombinatorResult C ()

  saveTokenBuffer()
  saveActions()
  if (A())
    then
      if (B())
        then
          executeActions (aResult, bResult)
          return true
        else
          restoreTokenBuffer()
          restoreActions()
          return false
    else return false
```

We're hiding a great deal in the executeActions method. The match values from the matches for A and B need to be saved so that we can use them in the actions.

Weaving in the actions for the other operators are similar. The alternative operator performs only the actions for the selected alternative. The list operator, like the sequence operator, must operate on all the match values. The optional operator only performs the actions on match, obviously.

The invocations for the actions are relatively straightforward. The challenge is getting the proper action methods associated with the combinator. In languages with closures or other ways of passing functions as parameters, we could simply have the details of the action method passed into the constructor as a function. In languages without closures, such as Java, we need to be a bit more clever. One approach is to extend the operator classes with classes specific to a particular production rule and override the action method to introduce the specific behavior.

As we alluded to above, the actions can be used to construct an abstract syntax tree. In that case, the match values passed to the action function would be the trees constructed for the different components, and the action would combine those parse trees as implied by the grammar rule in question. For example, a list operator will commonly have some node type in the syntax tree representing the list. The list operator action would then create a new subtree with that list node as the root, and make the subtrees from the component matches the children of this root.

22.1.2 Functional Style of Combinators

Now it's time to relax the assumption about manipulating the action results and the token buffer in the background using state. Thought of in the functional style, a combinator is a function that maps an input combinator result value to an output combinator result value. The components of a combinator result value are the current state of the token buffer, the current status of the match, and the current state of the cumulative actions performed so far. Following this style, the sequence operator implementation with actions looks like this:

```
CombinatorResult C (in)
  aResult = A(in)
  if (aResult.matchSuccess)
    then
      bResult = B(aResult)
      if (bResult.matchSuccess)
        then
          cResult.value = executeActions (aResult.value, bResult.value)
          return (true, bResult.tokens, cResult.value)
        else
          return (false, in.tokens, in.value)
    else return (false, in.tokens, in.value)
```

In this version, the saves are unnecessary since the input parameter's value remains valid. This version also makes more explicit how the token buffer is handled and where the action values come from.

22.2 When to Use It

This approach occupies a nice middle ground between *Recursive Descent Parser (245)* and using a *Parser Generator (269)*. A significant benefit of using a Parser Generator is an explicit grammar specification for the language. The grammar in a Recursive Descent Parser is implied in the functions but is difficult to read as a grammar. With the Parser Combinator approach, the combinators can be defined declaratively, as shown in the example above. While it does not use *BNF (229)* syntax, the grammar is clearly specified in terms of the component combinators and the operators. So with Parser Combinator, you get a reasonably explicit grammar without the build complications that tend to come with Parser Generator.

Libraries exist that implement the various grammar operators in different languages. Functional languages are an obvious choice to implement a Parser Combinator, given their support for functions as first-class objects which allows for passing an action function as a parameter to the combinator constructor. However, implementations in other languages are quite possible too.

As with Recursive Descent Parser, Parser Combinator results in a top-down parser, so the same restrictions apply. Many of the advantages of the Recursive Descent Parser also apply, in particular the ease of reasoning about when actions are performed. Even though a Parser Combinator is a very different implementation of a parser, the control algorithm of the parsing can be tracked using the same tools we use for debugging other programs. Indeed, the Parser Combinator approach coupled with an operator library or tested operator implementations allows the language implementer to focus on the actions rather than the parsing.

The biggest downside to a Parser Combinator is that you still have to build it yourself. In addition, you won't get the more sophisticated parsing and error handling features that a mature Parser Generator gives you out of the box.

22: Parser
Combinator

22.3 Parser Combinators and Miss Grant's Controller (Java)

To implement the state machine parser in Java using Parser Combinator, we've got a couple of design choices to make. For this example, we'll use the more functional approach utilizing a combinator result object and *Embedded Translation (299)* to populate the state machine object as we proceed through the parse.

First, let's revisit the full state machine grammar. The productions here are listed in reverse order to match the implementation strategy we're using.

```
grammar file...
   eventDec        : IDENTIFIER IDENTIFIER
   eventDecList    : (eventDec)*
   eventBlock      : EVENTS eventDecList END
   eventList       : (IDENTIFIER)*
   resetBlock      : (RESET eventList END)?
   commandDec      : IDENTIFIER IDENTIFIER
   commandDecList  : (commandDec)*
   commandBlock    : (COMMAND commandDecList END)?
   transition      : IDENTIFIER TRANSITION IDENTIFIER
   transitionList  : (transition) *
   actionDec       : IDENTIFIER
   actionList      : (actionDec)*
   actionBlock     : (ACTIONS LEFT actionList RIGHT)?
   stateDec        : STATE IDENTIFIER actionBlock transitionList END
   stateList       : (stateDec)*
   stateMachine    : eventBlock resetBlock commandBlock stateList
```

To construct a parser combinator for the full state machine, then, we need to construct parser combinators for each of the component terminals and nonterminals in the grammar. The full set of combinators in Java for this grammar is:

```
grammar file...
  //Terminal Symbols
     private Combinator matchEndKeyword
       = new TerminalParser(ScannerPatterns.TokenTypes.TT_END);
     private Combinator matchCommandKeyword
       = new TerminalParser(ScannerPatterns.TokenTypes.TT_COMMANDS);
     private Combinator matchEventsKeyword
       = new TerminalParser(ScannerPatterns.TokenTypes.TT_EVENT);
     private Combinator matchResetKeyword
       = new TerminalParser(ScannerPatterns.TokenTypes.TT_RESET);
     private Combinator matchStateKeyword
       = new TerminalParser(ScannerPatterns.TokenTypes.TT_STATE);
     private Combinator matchActionsKeyword
       = new TerminalParser(ScannerPatterns.TokenTypes.TT_ACTIONS);
     private Combinator matchTransitionOperator
       = new TerminalParser(ScannerPatterns.TokenTypes.TT_TRANSITION);
     private Combinator matchLeftOperator
       = new TerminalParser(ScannerPatterns.TokenTypes.TT_LEFT);
     private Combinator matchRightOperator
       = new TerminalParser(ScannerPatterns.TokenTypes.TT_RIGHT);
     private Combinator matchIdentifier
       = new TerminalParser(ScannerPatterns.TokenTypes.TT_IDENTIFIER);
  //Non-Terminal Production Rules
     private Combinator matchEventDec      = new EventDec(matchIdentifier, matchIdentifier);
     private Combinator matchEventDecList  = new ListCombinator(matchEventDec);
     private Combinator matchEventBlock    = new SequenceCombinator(
       matchEventsKeyword, matchEventDecList, matchEndKeyword
     );
     private Combinator matchEventList     = new ResetEventsList(matchIdentifier);
```

```
private Combinator matchResetBlock    = new OptionalSequenceCombinator (
  matchResetKeyword, matchEventList, matchEndKeyword
);
private Combinator matchCommandDec    = new CommandDec(matchIdentifier, matchIdentifier);
private Combinator matchCommandList   = new ListCombinator(matchCommandDec);
private Combinator matchCommandBlock  = new OptionalSequenceCombinator(
  matchCommandKeyword, matchCommandList, matchEndKeyword
);
private Combinator matchTransition    = new TransitionDec(
  matchIdentifier, matchTransitionOperator, matchIdentifier);
private Combinator matchTransitionList = new ListCombinator(matchTransition) ;
private Combinator matchActionDec     = new ActionDec(
  ScannerPatterns.TokenTypes.TT_IDENTIFIER
) ;
private Combinator matchActionList    = new ListCombinator(matchActionDec);
private Combinator matchActionBlock   = new OptionalSequenceCombinator(
  matchActionsKeyword, matchLeftOperator, matchActionList, matchRightOperator);
private Combinator matchStateName     = new StateName(
  ScannerPatterns.TokenTypes.TT_IDENTIFIER
);
private Combinator matchStateDec      = new StateDec(
  matchStateKeyword, matchStateName, matchActionBlock,
  matchTransitionList, matchEndKeyword
) ;
private Combinator matchStateList     = new ListCombinator(matchStateDec);
private Combinator matchStateMachine  = new StateMachineDec(
  matchEventBlock, matchResetBlock, matchCommandBlock, matchStateList
);
```

22: Parser
Combinator

The terminal symbol combinators don't have a direct analog in the grammar file since we used a lexical analyzer to find them. Past that point, though, the combinator declarations use previously defined combinators and those implementing various grammar operators to create the composite combinator. We'll step through each of these individually.

To describe the parser combinator implementation, we'll start with the simple cases and build up to the final state machine recognizer. We start with a basic Combinator class from which all the other combinators inherit.

```
class Combinator...
  public Combinator() {}
  public abstract CombinatorResult recognizer(CombinatorResult inbound);
  public void action(StateMachineMatchValue... results) { /* hook */}
```

All combinators have two functions. The recognizer maps an incoming CombinatorResult to a result value of the same type.

```
class CombinatorResult...
  private TokenBuffer tokens;
  private Boolean matchStatus;
  private StateMachineMatchValue matchValue;
```

The three components of the result from a combinator are the status of the token buffer, the success or failure of the recognizer, and the object that represents the resulting action value in the token buffer. In our case, we use it simply to hold the token value string from a terminal match.

```
class StateMachineMatchValue...
  private String matchString;
  public StateMachineMatchValue (String value) {
    matchString = value;
  }
  public String getMatchString () {
    return matchString;
  }
```

The second method on a combinator is the method that performs whatever actions relate to the match. The input to the action function is a number of match value objects, one object for each component combinator. For example, a sequence combinator that represents the rule:

22: Parser
Combinator

```
grammar file...
  C : A B
```

would have two match values passed to the action method.

Let's start with the recognizer for the terminal symbols. As an example, we'll use the identifier recognizer. The declaration for this recognizer is:

```
class StateMachineCombinatorParser...
  private Combinator matchIdentifier = new TerminalParser(
    ScannerPatterns.TokenTypes.TT_IDENTIFIER
  );
```

The terminal combinator class has a single instance variable identifying the token symbol to be matched.

```
class TerminalParser...
  public class TerminalParser extends Combinator {
    private ScannerPatterns.TokenTypes tokenMatch;
    public TerminalParser(ScannerPatterns.TokenTypes match) {
      this.tokenMatch = match;
    }
```

The standard terminal recognition function is quite simple as well.

```
class TerminalParser...
  public CombinatorResult recognizer(CombinatorResult inbound) {
    if (!inbound.matchSuccess()) return inbound;
    CombinatorResult result;
    TokenBuffer tokens = inbound.getTokenBuffer();
    Token t = tokens.nextToken();
```

```
if (t.isTokenType(tokenMatch)) {
    TokenBuffer outTokens = new TokenBuffer(tokens.makePoppedTokenList());
    result = new CombinatorResult(outTokens, true, new StateMachineMatchValue(t.tokenValue));
    action(result.getMatchValue());
} else {
    result = new CombinatorResult(tokens, false, new StateMachineMatchValue(""));
}
return result;
}
```

After verifying that the inbound match status is true, we check the current position in the token buffer to see if that value matches the value of our instance variable. If it does, we construct a successful CombinatorResult with the token buffer shifted and the token value from the matched token recorded in the result value. The action method is invoked on this match value, which in this case simply does nothing with it.

Now let's take something a bit more interesting. The event block declaration grammar rule looks like this:

grammar file...
```
eventBlock: eventKeyword eventDecList endKeyword
```

The declaration of the combinator for this rule uses the SequenceCombinator.

class StateMachineCombinatorParser...
```
private Combinator matchEventBlock = new SequenceCombinator(
    matchEventsKeyword, matchEventDecList, matchEndKeyword
);
```

In this case, we again use the null action method, since the real work is actually done elsewhere. The constructor for an instance of SequenceCombinator accepts a list of combinators, one for each of the symbols in the production rule.

class SequenceCombinator...
```
public class SequenceCombinator extends AbstractSequenceCombinator {
    public SequenceCombinator (Combinator ... productions) {
        super(false, productions);
    }
}
```

In this implementation, we've chosen to make separate classes for optional and required sequences, sharing the implementation, rather than introducing an optional operator and adding another level of production rules to the grammar. We extend this base class, AbstractSequenceCombinator, to make both the SequenceCombinator and OptionalSequenceCombinator classes. The common class has an instance variable representing the list of combinators of the sequence and a Boolean value that indicates whether this composite rule is optional or not.

```
class AbstractSequenceCombinator...
  public abstract class AbstractSequenceCombinator extends Combinator {
    private Combinator[] productions;
    private Boolean isOptional;

    public AbstractSequenceCombinator(Boolean optional, Combinator... productions) {
      this.productions = productions;
      this.isOptional = optional;
    }
```

The match function for the shared sequence combinator uses the Boolean value to determine what to do in the case of a a failed match.

```
class AbstractSequenceCombinator...
  public CombinatorResult recognizer(CombinatorResult inbound) {
    if (!inbound.matchSuccess()) return inbound;
    StateMachineMatchValue[] componentResults =
        new StateMachineMatchValue[productions.length];
    CombinatorResult latestResult = inbound;
    int productionIndex = 0;

    while (latestResult.matchSuccess() && productionIndex < productions.length) {
      Combinator p = productions[productionIndex];
      latestResult = p.recognizer(latestResult);
      componentResults[productionIndex] = latestResult.getMatchValue();
      productionIndex++;
    }
    if (latestResult.matchSuccess()) {
      action(componentResults);
    } else if (isOptional) {
      latestResult = new CombinatorResult(inbound.getTokenBuffer(),
          true, new StateMachineMatchValue(""));
    } else {
      latestResult = new CombinatorResult(inbound.getTokenBuffer(),
          false, new StateMachineMatchValue(""));
    }
    return (latestResult);
  }
```

22: Parser
Combinator

We again use the guard clause to return immediately if the inbound match status is false. The match function uses a while loop to step through the different combinators defining the sequence, with the loop halting when the match status is false or when all combinators have been checked. If the overall match succeeds, this means that all combinators in the sequence matched successfully. In this case, we invoke the action method on the array of component match values. If the inbound value was successful, but something in the loop failed, we then need to consult the optional flag. In the case of an optional sequence, this match succeeds with the values and the input tokens returned to their state at the beginning of the match. Naturally, the action method isn't invoked since no match occurred. Otherwise, a failed match is returned from this combinator, with the input values of the tokens and values restored.

An example of an optional sequence is the reset block:

```
class StateMachineCombinatorParser...
  private Combinator matchResetBlock =
    new OptionalSequenceCombinator (matchResetKeyword, matchEventList, matchEndKeyword);
```

for the grammar rule:

```
grammar file...
  optionalResetBlock: (resetBlock)?
  resetBlock: resetKeyword (resetEvent)* endKeyword
  resetEvent: identifier
```

Before moving on to show how we customize actions, let's finish off the grammar operators with the list operator. One production rule using the list operator is the event declaration list, with this grammar rule:

```
grammar file...
  eventDecList: eventDec+
```

and the declaration in the parser appears as:

```
class StateMachineCombinatorParser...
  private Combinator matchEventDecList = new ListCombinator(matchEventDec);
```

The list implementation shown here is for optional lists. We assume for this implementation that the list operator is applied to a single nonterminal. Clearly, this restriction is easy to relax. Given that, however, the constructor accepts only the single combinator, which then also represents the only instance variable in the class.

```
class ListCombinator...
  public class ListCombinator extends Combinator {
    private Combinator production;
    public ListCombinator(Combinator production) {
        this.production = production;
    }
```

The match function is straightforward.

```
class ListCombinator...
  public CombinatorResult recognizer(CombinatorResult inbound) {
    if (!inbound.matchSuccess()) return inbound;
    CombinatorResult latestResult = inbound;
    StateMachineMatchValue returnValues[];
    ArrayList<StateMachineMatchValue> results = new ArrayList<StateMachineMatchValue>();

    while (latestResult.matchSuccess()) {
      latestResult = production.recognizer(latestResult);
      if (latestResult.matchSuccess()) {
        results.add(latestResult.getMatchValue());
      }
    }
```

22: Parser Combinator

```
    if (results.size() > 0) { //matched something
      returnValues = results.toArray(new StateMachineMatchValue[results.size()]);
      action(returnValues);
      latestResult = new CombinatorResult(latestResult.getTokenBuffer(),
          true, new StateMachineMatchValue(""));
    }
    return (latestResult);
  }
```

Since we don't know in advance how many matches will succeed for the list, we use an array list to hold the match values. To make the Java type system happy, we must then transform it into an array of the same type to work with the variable arguments signature of the action method.

As we've mentioned, the actions for all the above combinators, with the exception of the identifier method, are null operations. The actions populating the various components of the state machine are actually associated with other nonterminals. In this implementation, we've used Java inner classes, extending the grammar operator base class, and overriding the action method in it. Let's consider the event declaration production rule:

```
grammar file...
  eventDec: identifier identifier
```

with the declaration in the parser appearing as:

```
class StateMachineCombinatorParser...
  private Combinator matchEventDec = new EventDec(matchIdentifier, matchIdentifier);
```

The class definition is:

```
class StateMachineCombinatorParser...
  private class EventDec extends SequenceCombinator {
    public EventDec(Combinator... productions) {
      super(productions);
    }
    public void action(StateMachineMatchValue... results) {
      assert results.length == 2;
      addMachineEvent(new Event(results[0].getMatchString(), results[1].getMatchString()));
    }
  }
```

This class extends the SequenceCombinator class and overrides the action method. As with all the action methods, the input is simply the list of results from the matches, representing the identifier names for the event declaration. We use the same helper functions as before to load the event into the state machine, extracting the name strings from the relevant match values. The other production follow this same pattern of implementation.

Chapter 23

Parser Generator

Build a parser driven by a grammar file as a DSL.

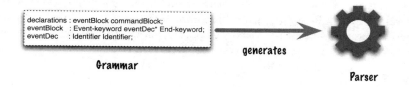

```
declarations : eventBlock commandBlock;
eventBlock   : Event-keyword eventDec* End-keyword;
eventDec     : Identifier Identifier;
```

Grammar

generates

Parser

A grammar file is a natural way of describing the syntactic structure of a DSL. Once you have a grammar, it's tedious work to turn it into a handwritten parser, and tedious work should be done by a computer.

A Parser Generator uses this grammar file to generate a parser. The parser can be updated merely by updating the grammar and regenerating. The generated parser can use efficient techniques that would be hard to build and maintain by hand.

23.1 How It Works

Building your own Parser Generator is no simple task, and anyone who is capable of doing such a thing is unlikely to learn anything from this book. So, here I'll only talk about using a Parser Generator. Fortunately, Parser Generators are common tools, with some useful forms available in most programming platforms, often as open source.

The usual way to work with a Parser Generator is to write a grammar file. This file will use a particular form of *BNF (229)* used by that Parser Generator. Don't expect any standardization here; if you change your Parser Generator, you will have to write a new grammar. For output production, most Parser Generators allow you use *Foreign Code (309)* to embed code actions.

Once you have a grammar, the usual route is to use the Parser Generator to generate a parser. Most Parser Generators use code generation, which may allow you to generate a parser in different host languages. There's no reason, of course, why a Parser Generator shouldn't be able to read a grammar file at runtime and interpret it, perhaps by building a *Parser Combinator (255)*. Parser Generators use code generation due to a mix of tradition and performance considerations—particularly since they are usually aimed at general-purpose languages.

Mostly, you treat the generated code as a black box and don't delve into it. It is, however, occasionally useful to follow what the parser is doing—particularly if you are trying to debug your grammar. In this case, there is an advantage in the Parser Generator using an algorithm that's easier to follow, such as generating a *Recursive Descent Parser (245)*.

I've illustrated many of the patterns in this book using the ANTLR Parser Generator. ANTLR is my usual recommendation for people getting into Parser Generators since it is an easily available, mature tool with good documentation. There's also a nice IDE-style tool (ANTLRWorks) that provides some very handy UI affordances for developing grammars.

23: Parser
Generator

23.1.1 Embedding Actions

Syntactic analysis produces a parse tree; to do something with that tree, we need to embed further code. We place the code in the grammar using *Foreign Code (309)*. Where we place it in the grammar indicates when the code is executed. Embedded code is placed in rule expressions to be executed as a consequence of the recognition of that rule.

Lets take an example of registering events when we see event declarations.

```
eventBlock    : Event-keyword eventDec* End-keyword;
eventDec      : Identifier Identifier {registerEvent($1, $2);}
              ;
```

This would tell us to invoke the registerEvent method just after the parser has recognized the second identifier in an eventDec. In order to pass data from the parse tree into registerEvent, we need some way to refer to the tokens mentioned in the rule. In this case I'm using $1, $2 to indicate the identifiers by position—which is the style of the Yacc Parser Generator.

The actions are usually woven into the generated parser while it is being generated. As a result, the embedded code is usually in the same language as the generated parser.

Different Parser Generator tools have different facilities for embedding code and linking the actions to the rules. While I don't want to go through all the different features that the many tools have, I think it's worth highlighting a couple. I've already talked about linking the embedded code to identifiers. Since the nature of a parser is to create a parse tree, it's often useful to move data around this tree. A common and useful facility is thus to allow a subrule to return data to its parent. To illustrate, consider the following grammar using the ANTLR Parser Generator:

```
eventBlock
 : K_EVENT (e = eventDec {registerEvent($e.result);})* K_END
 ;

eventDec returns [Event result]
 : name = ID code = ID {$result = createEvent($name, $code);}
 ;
```

Here the eventDec rule is set to return a value which the higher-level rule can access and use. (With ANTLR, the actions refer to grammar elements by name, which is usually better than by position.) The ability to return values from rules can make it much easier to write parsers—in particular, it can remove a lot of *Context Variables (175)*. Some Parser Generators, including ANTLR, also have the ability to push data down as arguments to subrules—which allows a lot of flexibility in providing context to subrules.

This fragment also illustrates that the placement of the actions in the grammar defines the moment an action is called. Here, the action in eventBlock is in the middle of the right-hand side, indicating that it should be called after each eventDec subrule is recognized. Placing actions like this is a common feature in Parser Generator.

When using *Syntax-Directed Translation (219)*, a common problem I've seen is to put too much host code in the grammar. When this happens, it's hard to see the structure of the grammar and the host code is difficult to edit—and requires a regeneration to test and debug. The key pattern here is *Embedment Helper (547)*—shift as much code as you can to a helper object. The only code in the grammar should be single method calls.

The actions define what we do with the DSL, and the way you write them therefore depends on the overall DSL parsing approach: *Tree Construction (281)*, *Embedded Interpretation (305)*, or *Embedded Translation (299)*. As Parser Generator isn't really too interesting without one of these, you won't find any examples in this pattern; instead, take a look at those other patterns for examples.

There's another animal that's similar to an action. A **semantic predicate**, like an action, is a block of Foreign Code, but it returns a Boolean that indicates whether the parse for the rule succeeds or fails. Actions don't affect the parsing, but semantic predicates do. You usually use a semantic predicate when you're dealing with areas of a grammar that can't be captured properly in the grammar language itself. They usually appear in more complicated languages, so they tend to crop up more often in general-purpose languages. But if you're having difficulty getting a grammar to work with the grammar DSL itself, then a semantic predicate opens the door to more complicated processing.

23: Parser Generator

23.2 When to Use It

For me, the greatest advantage of using a Parser Generator is that it provides an explicit grammar to define the syntactic structure of the language you're processing. This is, of course, the key advantage of using a DSL. Since Parser Generators are primarily designed to handle complicated languages, they also give you much more features and power than you would get by writing your own parser. While these features may require some effort to learn, you can usually start with a simple set and work your way up from there. Parser Generators may provide good error handling and diagnostics, which, despite my not talking about them, can make a big difference when trying to figure out why your grammar isn't doing what you think it should.

There are some downsides to a Parser Generator. You may be in a language environment where there isn't a Parser Generator—and it's not the kind of thing you should be writing yourself. Even if there is one, you may balk at introducing a new tool to your mix. Since Parser Generators tend to use code generation, they complicate the build process, which can be a significant irritant.

23.3 Hello World (Java and ANTLR)

Whenever you start with a new programming language, it's traditional to write a "Hello World" program. It's a good habit because, when you're not familiar with a new programming environment, there's usually a certain amount of hassle to sort out before you can run even the simplest program.

A Parser Generator like ANTLR is much the same. It's good to get a really simple thing going just to ensure you know what the moving parts are and how they fit together. Since I use ANTLR for several examples in this book, it seems worthwhile to run through pulling it together. The basic steps here are also worth knowing for when you play with a different Parser Generator.

The basic operating model of a Parser Generator is this: You write a grammar file and run the Parser Generator tool on that grammar to produce the source code for a parser. You then compile the parser, together with any other code that the parser works with. Then you can parse some files.

23.3.1 Writing the Basic Grammar

Since we're looking to parse some text, we need some really simple text to parse. Here's such a file:

```
greetings.txt...
  hello Rebecca
  hello Neal
  hello Ola
```

I'm treating this file as a list of greetings, where each greeting is a keyword (hello) followed by a name. Here's a simple grammar to recognize this:

```
Greetings.g...
  grammar Greetings;

@header {
  package helloAntlr;
}

@lexer::header {
  package helloAntlr;
}

script    : greeting* EOF;
greeting  : 'hello' Name;

Name    : ('a'..'z' | 'A'..'Z')+;

WS        : (' ' |'\t' | '\r' | '\n')+ {skip();} ;
COMMENT   : '#'(~'\n')* {skip();} ;
ILLEGAL   : .;
```

23: Parser
Generator

Although simple, the grammar file isn't as simple as I'd like.
The first line declares the name of the grammar.

```
grammar Greetings;
```

Unless I want to put everything in the default (empty) package, I need to ensure that the parser I generate goes into the proper package, in this case helloAntlr. I do this by using the @header attribute in the grammar to weave some Java code into the header of the generated parser. This allows me to weave in the package statement. If I needed to add some imports, I'd do that here too.

```
@header {
  package helloAntlr;
}
```

I do the same with the code for the lexer.

```
@lexer::header {
  package helloAntlr;
}
```

Now come the rules that are the meat of the file. Although ANTLR, like most Parser Generators, uses a separate lexer and parser, you generate both of them from a single file. My first two lines say that a script is multiple greetings followed by the end-of-file, and that a greeting is the keyword token `hello` followed by a Name token.

```
script    : greeting* EOF;
greeting  : 'hello' Name;
```

ANTLR distinguishes tokens by making them start with an uppercase letter. The name is just a string of letters.

```
Name    : ('a'..'z' | 'A'..'Z')+;
```

I usually find it helpful to get rid of whitespace here and declare comments. When things are desperate, comments are a crude but reliable debugging aid.

```
WS        : (' ' |'\t' | '\r' | '\n')+ {skip();} ;
COMMENT   : '#'(~'\n')* {skip();} ;
ILLEGAL   : .;
```

The last token rule (`ILLEGAL`) causes the lexer to report an error if it runs into a token that doesn't fit any of its rules (otherwise such tokens are quietly ignored).

At this point, if you're using the ANTLRWorks IDE, you have enough to run ANTLR's interpreter and verify that it will read the text. The next step is to generate and run a basic parser.

(A small thing, but something that's bitten me a couple of times. If you don't put the EOF at the end of the top rule, ANTLR won't report errors. It effectively stops parsing at the first point of trouble and doesn't think anything went wrong. This is particularly awkward because ANTLRWorks will show an error in its interpreter when this happens—so it's easy to get confused, frustrated, and ready to do violent acts against your monitor.)

23.3.2 Building the Syntactic Analyzer

The next step is to run the ANTLR code generator to generate the ANTLR source files. At this point, it's time to futz with the build system. The standard build system for Java projects is Ant, so I'll use that for my example (although at home I'm more likely to use Rake).

To generate the source files, I run the ANTLR tool, which is contained in the library JAR files.

```
build.xml...
  <property name="dir.src" value="src"/>
  <property name="dir.gen" value="gen"/>
  <property name="dir.lib" value="lib"/>
  <path id="path.antlr">
    <fileset dir="${dir.lib}">
      <include name="antlr*.jar"/>
      <include name="stringtemplate*.jar"/>
    </fileset>
  </path>
```

```
<target name="gen">
  <mkdir dir="${dir.gen}/helloAntlr"/>
  <java classname="org.antlr.Tool" classpathref="path.antlr" fork="true" failonerror="true">
    <arg value="-fo"/>
    <arg value="${dir.gen}/helloAntlr"/>
    <arg value="${dir.src}/helloAntlr/Greetings.g"/>
  </java>
</target>
```

This generates the various ANTLR sources and puts them into the gen directory. I keep the gen directory separate from my core sources. Since they are generated files, I'll tell my source code control system to ignore them.

The code generator produces a number of source files. For our purposes, the key files are the Java sources for the lexer (GreetingsLexer.java) and the parser (GreetingsParser.java).

These are the generated files. The next step is to use them. I like to write my own class to do this. I call this a greetings loader, as ANTLR has already used the word "parser." I set it up with a input reader.

```
class GreetingsLoader...
  private Reader input;
  public GreetingsLoader(Reader input) {
    this.input = input;
  }
```

23: Parser
Generator

I then write a run method which is the one that actually orchestrates the ANTLR-generated files to do their work.

```
class GreetingsLoader...
  public List<String> run() {
    try {
      GreetingsLexer lexer = new GreetingsLexer(new ANTLRReaderStream(input));
      GreetingsParser parser = new GreetingsParser(new CommonTokenStream(lexer));
      parser.script();
      return guests;
    } catch (IOException e) {
      throw new RuntimeException(e);
    } catch (RecognitionException e) {
      throw new RuntimeException(e);
    }
  }
  private List<String> guests = new ArrayList<String>();
```

The basic idea is that I first create a lexer based on the input, followed by a parser that's based on the lexer. I then call a method on the parser that is named the same as the top rule of my grammar. This will then execute the parser on the input text.

I can run this from a simple test.

```
@Test
public void readsValidFile() throws Exception {
  Reader input = new FileReader("src/helloAntlr/greetings.txt");
  GreetingsLoader loader = new GreetingsLoader(input);
  loader.run();
}
```

This runs clean, but it isn't very helpful. All it indicates is that the ANTLR parser didn't blow up when it read the file. That, however, may not even tell you that it read the file without problems. So it's useful to feed the parser some invalid input.

```
invalid.txt...
  hello Rebecca
  XXhello Neal
  hello Ola
```

```
test...
  @Test
  public void errorWhenKeywordIsMangled() throws Exception {
    Reader input = new FileReader("src/helloAntlr/invalid.txt");
    GreetingsLoader loader = new GreetingsLoader(input);
    try {
      loader.run();
      fail();
    } catch (Exception expected) {}
  }
```

With the code as it is so far, that test will fail. ANTLR will print a warning telling you it had trouble, but ANTLR is determined to keep on parsing and recover from errors as much as possible. In general, this is a good thing, but particularly early on it can be frustrating to find ANTLR so tolerant and determined.

So, at this point there are issues. First, all the parser is doing is reading the file—not producing any output. Second, it's hard to tell when it's going wrong. I can fix both these problems by introducing some more code into the grammar file.

23.3.3 Adding Code Actions to the Grammar

With *Syntax-Directed Translation (219)*, there are three strategies I can use to produce some output: *Tree Construction (281)*, *Embedded Interpretation (305)*, and *Embedded Translation (299)*. When starting with something like this, I like to use Embedded Translation. This gives me a simple way to see what's going on.

When I use code actions, I like to use *Embedment Helper (547)*. The simplest way to use Embedment Helper with ANTLR is to take the loader class I already have and add it into the grammar as a loader. If I do this, I can also do something to better notify the user of errors.

The first stage of this process is to modify the the grammar file to inject some more Java code into the generated parser. I use the members attribute to declare the Embedment Helper and override the default error handling function for reporting an error.

```
Greetings.g...
  @members {
    GreetingsLoader helper;
     public void reportError(RecognitionException e) {
       helper.reportError(e);
     }
  }
```

In the loader, I can now provide a simple implementation for error reporting that records errors.

```
class GreetingsLoader...
  private List errors = new ArrayList();
  void reportError(RecognitionException e) {
    errors.add(e);
  }
  public boolean hasErrors() {return !isOk();}
  public boolean isOk() {return errors.isEmpty();}
  private String errorReport() {
    if (isOk()) return "OK";
    StringBuffer result = new StringBuffer("");
    for (Object e : errors) result.append(e.toString()).append("\n");
    return result.toString();
  }
```

Now all I have to do is add a couple of lines to the run method to set up the helper and throw an exception if the parser reports any errors.

```
class GreetingsLoader...
  public void run() {
    try {
      GreetingsLexer lexer = new GreetingsLexer(new ANTLRReaderStream(input));
      GreetingsParser parser = new GreetingsParser(new CommonTokenStream(lexer));
      parser.helper = this;
      parser.script();
      if (hasErrors()) throw new RuntimeException("it all went pear-shaped\n" + errorReport());
    } catch (IOException e) {
      throw new RuntimeException(e);
    } catch (RecognitionException e) {
      throw new RuntimeException(e);
    }
  }
```

With the helper in place, I can also easily add some code actions to report the names of the people I greeted.

```
Greetings.g...
  greeting  : 'hello' n=Name {helper.recordGuest($n);};

class GreetingsLoader...
  void recordGuest(Token t) {guests.add(t.getText());}
  List<String> getGuests() {return guests;}
  private List<String> guests = new ArrayList<String>();

test...
  @Test
  public void greetedCorrectPeople() throws Exception {
    Reader input = new FileReader("src/helloAntlr/greetings.txt");
    GreetingsLoader loader = new GreetingsLoader(input);
    loader.run();
    List<String> expectedPeople = Arrays.asList("Rebecca", "Neal", "Ola");
    assertEquals(expectedPeople, loader.getGuests());
  }
```

This is all very crude, but it's enough to ensure that the Parser Generator is generating something that will parse a file, find errors, and communicate with something that will produce an output. Once this silly example is working, I can add some more useful functionality.

23.3.4 Using Generation Gap

Another way of weaving in the helper and error-handling methods into the parser is to use *Generation Gap (571)*. With this approach, I handwrite a superclass of ANTLR's generated parser. The generated parser can then use the helper's methods as bare method calls.

Doing this requires an option in the grammar file. The whole grammar file then looks like this:

```
Greetings.g...
  grammar Greetings;
  options {superClass = BaseGreetingsParser;}

  @header {
  package subclass;
  }
  @lexer::header {
  package subclass;
  }

  script   : greeting * EOF;
  greeting : 'hello' n=Name {recordGuest($n);};};

  Name    : ('a'..'z' | 'A'..'Z')+;
  WS      : (' ' |'\t' | '\r' | '\n')+ {skip();} ;
  COMMENT : '#'(~'\n')* {skip();} ;
  ILLEGAL : .;
```

I no longer need to override `reportErrors` as I will do that in my handwritten superclass. Here is that superclass:

```java
abstract public class BaseGreetingsParser extends Parser {
  public BaseGreetingsParser(TokenStream input) {
    super(input);
  }

  //---- helper methods
  void recordGuest(Token t) {guests.add(t.getText());}
  List<String> getGuests() { return guests; }
  private List<String> guests = new ArrayList<String>();

  //-------- Error Handling -----------------------------
  private List errors = new ArrayList();

  public void reportError(RecognitionException e) {
    errors.add(e);
  }

  public boolean hasErrors() {return !isOk();}

  public boolean isOk() {return errors.isEmpty();}
```

This class is a subclass of the base ANTLR parser class, so it has introduced itself into the hierarchy above the generated parser. The handwritten class contains the helper and error-reporting code that was in the separate loader class before. However, it's still valuable to have a wrapper class to coordinate the running of the parser.

```java
class GreetingsLoader...
  private Reader input;
  private GreetingsParser parser;

  public GreetingsLoader(Reader input) {
    this.input = input;
  }

  public void run() {
    try {
      GreetingsLexer lexer = new GreetingsLexer(new ANTLRReaderStream(input));
      parser = new GreetingsParser(new CommonTokenStream(lexer));
      parser.script();
      if (parser.hasErrors()) throw new RuntimeException("it all went pear-shaped");
    } catch (IOException e) {
      throw new RuntimeException(e);
    } catch (RecognitionException e) {
      throw new RuntimeException(e);
    }
  }

  public List<String> getGuests() { return parser.getGuests();}
```

Both the inheritance and delegation relationships have their strengths for the *Embedment Helper (547)*. I don't have a strong opinion on the best one to use, and use both of them in this book's examples.

Much more needs to be done for real work, but I think that these simple examples make a good starting point. You'll find more examples of using a Parser Generator, including the gothic security state machine, in the rest of the patterns in this part of the book.

Chapter 24

Tree Construction

The parser creates and returns a syntax tree representation of the source text that is manipulated later by tree-walking code.

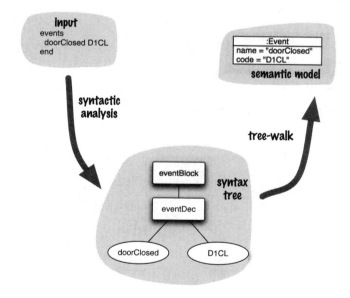

24.1 How It Works

Any parser using *Syntax-Directed Translation (219)* builds up a syntax tree while it's doing the parsing. It builds the tree up on the stack, pruning the branches when it's done with them. With Tree Construction, we create parser actions that

281

build up a syntax tree in memory during the parse. Once the parse is complete, we have a syntax tree for the DSL script. We can then carry out further manipulations based on that syntax tree. If we are using a *Semantic Model (159)*, we run code that walks our syntax tree and populates the Semantic Model.

The syntax tree that we create in memory doesn't need to correspond directly to the actual parse tree that the parser creates as it goes—indeed, it usually doesn't. Instead, we build what's called an **abstract syntax tree**. An abstract syntax tree (AST) is a simplification of the parse tree which provides a better tree representation of the input language.

Let's explore this with a short example. I'll use a declaration of events for my state machine example.

```
events
  doorClosed  D1CL
  drawOpened  D2OP
end
```

24: Tree
Construction

I will parse it with this grammar:

```
declarations : eventBlock commandBlock;
eventBlock   : Event-keyword eventDec* End-keyword;
eventDec     : Identifier Identifier;
commandBlock : Command-keyword commandDec* End-keyword;
commandDec   : Identifier Identifier;
```

to produce the parse tree in Figure 24.1.

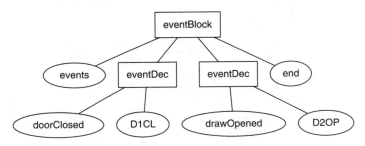

Figure 24.1 *Parse tree for the event input*

If you look at this tree, you should realize that the events and end nodes are unnecessary. The words were needed in the input text in order to mark the boundaries of the event declarations, but once we've parsed them into a tree structure we no longer need them—they are just cluttering up the data structure. Instead, we could represent the input with the syntax tree in Figure 24.2.

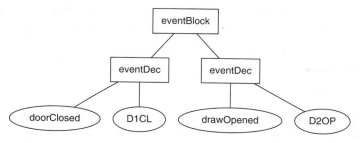

Figure 24.2 *An AST for the event input*

This tree is not a faithful representation of the input, but it's what we need if we're going to process the events. It's an abstraction of the input that's better suited for our purpose. Obviously, different ASTs might be needed for different reasons; if we only wanted to list the event codes, we could drop the name and eventDec nodes as well and just keep the codes—that would be a different AST for a different purpose.

At this point I should clarify my terminological distinctions. I use the term **syntax tree** to describe a hierarchic data structure that's formed by parsing some input. I use "syntax tree" as a general term: parse tree and AST are particular kinds of syntax trees. A parse tree is a syntax tree that corresponds directly to input text, while an AST makes some simplifications of the input based on usage.

In order to build up a syntax tree, you can use code actions in your *BNF (229)*. In particular, the ability of code actions to return values for a node comes in very handy with this approach—each code action assembles the representation of its node in the resulting syntax tree.

Some *Parser Generators (269)* go further, offering a DSL for specifying the syntax tree. In ANTLR, for instance, we could create the AST above using a rule like this:

```
eventDec :   name=ID code=ID -> ^(EVENT_DEC $name $code);
```

The -> operator introduces the tree construction rule. The body of the rule is a list where the first element is the node type (EVENT_DEC) followed by the child nodes, which in this case are the tokens for the name and code.

Using a DSL for Tree Construction can greatly simplify building up an AST. Often, Parser Generators that support this will give you the parse tree if you don't supply any tree construction rules, but you almost never want the parse tree. It's usually preferable to simplify it into an AST using these rules.

An AST built in this way will consist of generic objects that hold the data of for the tree. In the above example, the eventDec is a generic tree node with name and code as children. Both the name and code are generic tokens. If you build up the tree yourself with code actions, you could create real objects here—such as a true event object with the name and code as fields. I prefer to have a generic

24: Tree
Construction

AST and then use second-stage processing to transform that into a Semantic Model. I'd rather have two simple transformations than one complicated one.

24.2 When to Use It

Both Tree Construction and *Embedded Translation (299)* are useful approaches to populating a *Semantic Model (159)* while parsing. Embedded Translation does the transformation in a single step, while Tree Construction uses two steps with the AST as an intermediate model. The argument for using Tree Construction is that it breaks down a single transformation into two, simpler transformations. Whether this is worth the effort of dealing with an intermediate model depends very much on the complexity of the transformation. The more complex the transformation is, the more useful an intermediate model can be.

A particular driver of complexity is the need to make several passes through the DSL script. Things like forward references can be a bit more awkward to use if you are doing all the processing in a single step. With Tree Construction it's easy to walk the tree many times as part of later processing.

Another factor that encourages you to use Tree Construction is if your *Parser Generator (269)* provides tools allowing you to build an AST really easily. Some Parser Generators give you no choice—you have to use Tree Construction. Most give you the option to use Embedded Translation, but if the Parser Generator makes it really easy to build an AST, that makes Tree Construction a more attractive option.

Tree Construction is likely to consume more memory than alternative approaches, as it needs to store the AST. In most cases, however, this won't make any appreciable difference. (Although that certainly used to be a big factor in earlier days.)

You can process the same AST in several different ways to populate different Semantic Models if you need them, and reuse the parser. This may be handy, but if the parsers' tree construction is easy then it may be simpler to use different ASTs for different purposes. It may also be better to transform to a single Semantic Model and then use that as a basis to transform to other representations.

24.3 Using ANTLR's Tree Construction Syntax (Java and ANTLR)

I'll use the state machine DSL from the opening chapter, specifically with Miss Grant's controller. Here's the specific text that I'll be using for the example.

24: Tree
Construction

```
events
  doorClosed   D1CL
  drawerOpened D2OP
  lightOn      L1ON
  doorOpened   D1OP
  panelClosed  PNCL
end

resetEvents
  doorOpened
end

commands
  unlockPanel PNUL
  lockPanel   PNLK
  lockDoor    D1LK
  unlockDoor  D1UL
end

state idle
  actions {unlockDoor lockPanel}
  doorClosed => active
end

state active
  drawerOpened => waitingForLight
  lightOn      => waitingForDrawer
end


state waitingForLight
  lightOn => unlockedPanel
end.

state waitingForDrawer
  drawerOpened => unlockedPanel
end

state unlockedPanel
  actions {unlockPanel lockDoor}
  panelClosed => idle
end
```

24.3.1 Tokenizing

Tokenizing for this is very simple. We have a few keywords (events, end, etc.) and a bunch of identifiers. ANTLR allows us to put the keywords as literal text in the grammar rules, which is generally easier to read. So we only need lexer rules for identifiers.

24: Tree
Construction

```
fragment LETTER : ('a'..'z' | 'A'..'Z' | '_');
fragment DIGIT : ('0'..'9');

ID    : LETTER (LETTER | DIGIT)* ;
```

Strictly, the lexing rules for names and codes are different—names can be any length but codes must be four uppercase letters. So we could define different lexer rules for them. However, in this case it gets tricky. The string ABC1 is a valid code, but also a valid name. If we see ABC1 in the DSL program, we can tell which it is by its context: state ABC1 is different from event unlockDoor ABC1. The parser will also be able to use the context to tell the difference, but the lexer can't. So the best option here is to use the same token for both of them and let the parser sort it out. This means that the parser won't generate an error for five-letter codes—we have to sort that out in our own semantic processing.

We also need lexer rules to strip out the whitespace.

```
WHITE_SPACE  : (' ' |'\t' | '\r' | '\n')+ {skip();} ;
COMMENT  : '#' ~'\n'* '\n' {skip();};
```

24: Tree
Construction

In this case, whitespace includes newlines. I have laid the DSL out in a fashion that suggests that there are meaningful line endings which end statements in the DSL, but as you can now see this isn't true. All whitespace, including the line endings, is removed. This allows me to format the DSL code in any fashion I like. This is a notable contrast to *Delimiter-Directed Translation (201)*. Indeed it's worth remarking that there are no statement separators at all, unlike most general-purpose languages that need something like a newline or a semicolon to end statements. Often, DSLs can get away with no statement separators because the statements are very limited. Things like infix expressions will force you to use statement separators, but for many DSLs you can do without them. As with most things, don't put them in until you actually need them.

For this example, I'm skipping the whitespace which means that it's lost completely to the parser. This is reasonable as the parser doesn't need it—all it needs are the meaningful tokens. However, there is a case where whitespace ends up being handy again—when things go wrong. To give good error reports, you need line numbers and column numbers; to provide these, you need to keep the whitespace. ANTLR allows you to do this by sending whitespace tokens on a different channel, with syntax like WS : ('\r' | '\n' | ' ' | '\t')+ {$channel=HIDDEN}. This sends the whitespace through on a hidden channel so it can be used for error handling but doesn't affect the parsing rules.

24.3.2 Parsing

The lexing rules work the same in ANTLR whether you are using Tree Construction or not—it's the parser that operates differently. In order to use Tree Construction, we need to tell ANTLR to produce an AST.

```
options {
  output=AST;
  ASTLabelType = MfTree;
}
```

Having told ANTLR to produce an AST, I'm also telling it to populate that AST with nodes of a particular type: MfTree. This is a subclass of the generic ANTLR CommonTree class that allows me to add some behavior that I prefer to have on my tree nodes. The naming here is a little confusing. The class represents a node and its children, so you can either think of it as a node or as a (sub)tree. ANTLR's naming calls it a tree, so I've followed that in my code, although I think of it as a node in the tree.

Now we'll move onto the grammar rules. I'll begin with the top-level rule that defines the structure of the whole DSL file.

```
machine : eventList resetEventList? commandList? state*;
```

This rule lists the main clauses in sequence. If I don't give ANTLR any tree construction rules, it will just return a node for each term on the right-hand side in sequence. Usually this isn't what we want, but it does work right here.

Taking the terms in order, the first one gets into events.

```
eventList
  : 'events' event* 'end' -> ^(EVENT_LIST event*);

event  : n=ID c=ID -> ^(EVENT $n $c);
```

There are a few new things to talk about with these two rules. One is that these rules introduce ANTLR's syntax for tree construction, which is the code following "->" in each rule.

The eventList rule uses two string constants—this is us putting the keyword tokens directly into the parser rules without making separate lexer rules for them.

The tree construction rules allow us to say what goes in the AST. In both cases here, we use ^(list...) to create and return a new node in the AST. The first item in the parenthesized list is the token type of the node. In this case we've made a new token type. All items following the token type are the other nodes in the tree. For the event list, we just put all the events as siblings in the list. For the event, we name tokens in the BNF and reference them in the tree construction to show how they are placed.

The EVENT_LIST and EVENT tokens are special tokens that I've created as part of parsing—they weren't tokens produced by the lexer. When I create tokens like this I need to declare them in the grammar file.

```
tokens { EVENT_LIST; EVENT; COMMAND_LIST; COMMAND;
         STATE; TRANSITION_LIST; TRANSITION; ACTION_LIST;
         RESET_EVENT_LIST;
}
```

Figure 24.3 *AST for Miss Grant's event list*

The commands are treated in the same way, and the reset events are a simple list.

```
commandList : 'commands' command* 'end' -> ^(COMMAND_LIST command*);
command : ID ID -> ^(COMMAND ID+);

resetEventList : 'resetEvents' ID* 'end' -> ^(RESET_EVENT_LIST ID*);
```

The states are a bit more involved, but they use the same basic approach.

```
state
  : 'state' ID actionList? transition* 'end'
    -> ^(STATE ID ^(ACTION_LIST actionList?) ^(TRANSITION_LIST transition*) )
  ;
transition : ID '=>' ID -> ^(TRANSITION ID+);
actionList : 'actions' '{' ID* '}' -> ID*;
```

Each time, what I'm doing is collecting together appropriate clumps of the DSL and putting them under a node that describes what that clump represents. The result is an AST that is very similar to the parse tree, but not exactly the same. My aim is to keep my tree construction rules very simple and my syntax tree easy to walk.

24.3.3 Populating the Semantic Model

Once the parser has made a tree, the next step is to walk this tree and populate the *Semantic Model (159)*. The Semantic Model is the same state machine model that I used in the introduction. The interface for building it is pretty simple, so I won't go into it here.

I create a loader class to populate the Semantic Model.

```
class StateMachineLoader...
  private Reader input;
  private MfTree ast;
  private StateMachine machine;

  public StateMachineLoader(Reader input) {
    this.input = input;
  }
```

I use the loader as a command class. Here is its run method that indicates the sequence of steps I use to carry out the translation:

```
class StateMachineLoader...
  public void run() {
    loadAST();
    loadSymbols();
    createMachine();
  }
```

To explain that in English, I first use the ANTLR-generated parser to parse the input stream and create an AST. Then I navigate through the AST to build *Symbol Tables (165)*. Finally, I assemble the objects into a state machine.

The first step is just the incantations to get ANTLR to build the AST.

```
class StateMachineLoader...
  private void loadAST() {
    try {
      StateMachineLexer lexer = new StateMachineLexer(new ANTLRReaderStream(input));
      StateMachineParser parser = new StateMachineParser(new CommonTokenStream(lexer));
      parser.helper = this;
      parser.setTreeAdaptor(new MyNodeAdaptor());
      ast = (MfTree) parser.machine().getTree();
    } catch (IOException e) {
      throw new RuntimeException(e);
    } catch (RecognitionException e) {
      throw new RuntimeException(e);
    }
  }

  class MyNodeAdaptor extends CommonTreeAdaptor {
    public Object create(Token token) {
      return new MfTree(token);
    }
  }
```

MyNodeAdaptor is a second step in telling ANTLR to create the AST with MfTree rather than CommonTree.

The next step is to build the symbol table. This involves navigating the AST to find all the events, commands, and states and load them into maps so we can look them up easily to make the links when we create the state machine.

```
class StateMachineLoader...
  private void loadSymbols() {
    loadEvents();
    loadCommands();
    loadStateNames();
  }
```

Here's the code for the events:

24: Tree
Construction

```
class StateMachineLoader...
  private Map<String, Event> events = new HashMap<String, Event>();

  private void loadEvents() {
    MfTree eventList = ast.getSoleChild(EVENT_LIST);
    for (MfTree eventNode : eventList.getChildren()) {
      String name = eventNode.getText(0);
      String code = eventNode.getText(1);
      events.put(name, new Event(name, code));
    }
  }

class MfTree...
  List<MfTree> getChildren() {
    List<MfTree> result = new ArrayList<MfTree>();
    for (int i = 0; i < getChildCount(); i++)
      result.add((MfTree) getChild(i));
    return result;
  }

  MfTree getSoleChild(int nodeType) {
    List<MfTree> matchingChildren = getChildren(nodeType);
    assert 1 == matchingChildren.size();
    return matchingChildren.get(0);
  }

  List<MfTree> getChildren(int nodeType) {
    List<MfTree> result = new ArrayList<MfTree>();
    for (int i = 0; i < getChildCount(); i++)
      if (getChild(i).getType() == nodeType)
        result.add((MfTree) getChild(i));
    return result;
  }

  String getText(int i) {
    return getChild(i).getText();
  }
```

The node types are defined in the generated code in the parser. When I use them in the loader, I can use a static import to make them easy to refer to.

The commands are loaded in a similar way—I'm sure you can guess what the code for that looks like. I load the states in a similar way, but at this point I only have the name in the state objects.

```
class StateMachineLoader...
  private void loadStateNames() {
    for (MfTree node : ast.getChildren(STATE))
      states.put(stateName(node), new State(stateName(node)));
  }
```

I have to do something like this because the states are used in forward references. In the DSL, I can mention a state in a transition before I declare the state.

This is a case where tree construction works very nicely—there's no problem in taking as many passes through the AST as I need to wire things up.

The final step is to actually create the state machine.

```
class StateMachineLoader...
  private void createMachine() {
    machine = new StateMachine(getStartState());
    for (MfTree node : ast.getChildren(StateMachineParser.STATE)) loadState(node);
    loadResetEvents();
  }
```

The start state is the first declared state.

```
class StateMachineLoader...
  private State getStartState() {
    return states.get(getStartStateName());
  }

  private String getStartStateName() {
    return stateName((MfTree) ast.getFirstChildWithType(STATE));
  }
```

Now we can wire up the transitions and actions for all the states.

```
class StateMachineLoader...
  private void loadState(MfTree stateNode) {
    for (MfTree t : stateNode.getSoleChild(TRANSITION_LIST).getChildren()) {
      getState(stateNode).addTransition(events.get(t.getText(0)), states.get(t.getText(1)));
    }
    for (MfTree t : stateNode.getSoleChild(ACTION_LIST).getChildren())
      getState(stateNode).addAction(commands.get(t.getText()));
  }

  private State getState(MfTree stateNode) {
    return states.get(stateName(stateNode));
  }
```

And finally we add the reset events, which the state machine API expects us to do at the end.

```
class StateMachineLoader...
  private void loadResetEvents() {
    if (!ast.hasChild(RESET_EVENT_LIST)) return;
    MfTree resetEvents = ast.getSoleChild(RESET_EVENT_LIST);
    for (MfTree e : resetEvents.getChildren())
      machine.addResetEvents(events.get(e.getText()));
  }

class MfTree...
  boolean hasChild(int nodeType) {
    List<MfTree> matchingChildren = getChildren(nodeType);
    return matchingChildren.size() != 0;
  }
```

24.4 Tree Construction Using Code Actions (Java and ANTLR)

ANTLR's syntax for Tree Construction is the easiest way to do it, but many *Parser Generators (269)* lack a similar feature. In these cases, you can still do Tree Construction, but you have to form the tree yourself with code actions. With this example, I'll demonstrate how to do this. I'll use ANTLR for this example to save introducing another Parser Generator, but I should stress that I'd never use this technique in ANTLR itself, as the special syntax is much easier to do.

The first thing to decide is how to represent the tree. I use a simple node class.

24: Tree
Construction

```
class Node...
  private Token content;
  private Enum type;
  private List<Node> children = new ArrayList<Node>();

  public Node(Enum type, Token content) {
    this.content = content;
    this.type = type;
  }
  public Node(Enum type) {
    this(type, null);
  }
```

My nodes here are not statically typed—I use the same class for state nodes as for event nodes. An alternative is to have different kinds of nodes for different classes.

I have a small tree constructor class that wraps ANTLR's generated parser to produce the AST.

```
class TreeConstructor...
  private Reader input;

  public TreeConstructor(Reader input) {
    this.input = input;
  }
  public Node run() {
    try {
      StateMachineLexer lexer = new StateMachineLexer(new ANTLRReaderStream(input));
      StateMachineParser parser = new StateMachineParser(new CommonTokenStream(lexer));
      parser.helper = this;
      return parser.machine();
    } catch (IOException e) {
      throw new RuntimeException(e);
    } catch (RecognitionException e) {
      throw new RuntimeException(e);
    }
  }
```

I need an enum to declare my node types. I put this in the tree constructor and statically import it to the other classes that need it.

```
class TreeConstructor...
  public enum NodeType {STATE_MACHINE,
    EVENT_LIST, EVENT, RESET_EVENT_LIST,
    COMMAND_LIST, COMMAND,
    NAME, CODE,
    STATE, TRANSITION, TRIGGER, TARGET,
    ACTION_LIST, ACTION
  }
```

The grammar rules in the parser all follow the same basic format. The rule for events illustrates this nicely and simply.

```
grammar file...
  event returns [Node result]
    : {$result = new Node(EVENT);}
      name=ID {$result.add(NAME, $name);}
      code=ID {$result.add(CODE, $code);}
    ;
```

Each rule declares a node as its return type. The first line of the rule creates that result node. As I recognize each token that's part of the rule, I simply add it as a child.

Higher-level rules repeat the pattern.

```
grammar file...
  eventList returns [Node result]
    : {$result = new Node(EVENT_LIST);}
      'events'
      (e=event {$result.add($e.result);} )* //add event
      'end'
    ;
```

The only difference is that I add the nodes from subrules using $e.result so that ANTLR will pick out the return type of the rule properly.

There's a nonobvious idiom on the line labeled add event. Notice how I have to put the event clause and the code action inside parentheses and have the Kleene star operator apply to the parenthesized group. I do this to ensure that the code action is run once for each event.

I added methods on the node to make it easy to add child nodes with simple code.

```
class Node...
  public void add(Node child) {
    children.add(child);
  }
  public void add(Enum nodeType, Token t) {
    add(new Node(nodeType, t));
  }
```

Normally, I use an *Embedment Helper (547)* with a grammar file. This case is an exception, since the code for building the AST is so simple that calls to a helper wouldn't be any easier to work with.

The top-level machine rule continues this basic structure.

```
grammar file...
  machine returns [Node result]
    : {$result = new Node(STATE_MACHINE);}
      e=eventList {$result.add($e.result);}
      (r=resetEventList {$result.add($r.result);} )?
      (c=commandList {$result.add($c.result);}) ?
      (s=state {$result.add($s.result);} )*
    ;
```

The commands and reset events are loaded the same way as the events.

```
grammar file...
  commandList returns [Node result]
    : {$result = new Node(COMMAND_LIST);}
      'commands'
      (c=command {$result.add($c.result);})*
      'end'
    ;
  command returns [Node result]
    : {$result = new Node(COMMAND);}
      name=ID {$result.add(NAME, $name);}
      code=ID {$result.add(CODE, $code);}
    ;
  resetEventList returns [Node result]
    : {$result = new Node(RESET_EVENT_LIST);}
      'resetEvents'
      (e=ID {$result.add(NAME, $e);} )*
      'end'
    ;
```

Another difference from the grammar with the specific syntax is that I've made special node types for the name and code, which makes the tree-walking code a bit clearer later on.

The final code to show is the parsing of the states.

```
grammar file...
  state returns [Node result]
    : {$result = new Node(STATE);}
      'state' name = ID {$result.add(NAME, $name);}
      (a=actionList {$result.add($a.result);} )?
      (t=transition {$result.add($t.result);} )*
        'end'
    ;
```

```
transition returns [Node result]
  : {$result = new Node(TRANSITION);}
    trigger=ID {$result.add(TRIGGER, $trigger);}
    '=>'
    target=ID {$result.add(TARGET, $target);}
  ;
actionList returns [Node result]
  : {$result = new Node(ACTION_LIST);}
    'actions' '{'
    (action=ID {$result.add(ACTION, $action);}) *
    '}'
  ;
```

The grammar file code is very regular—indeed rather boring. Boring code usually means that you need another abstraction, which is exactly what the special tree construction syntax provides.

The second part of the code is to walk the tree and create the state machine. This is pretty much the same code as the earlier example, the only difference coming from the fact that the nodes I have are slightly different from the previous example.

```
class StateMachineLoader...
  private Node ast;
  private StateMachine machine;

  public StateMachineLoader(Node ast) {
    this.ast = ast;
  }
  public StateMachine run() {
    loadSymbolTables();
    createMachine();
    return machine;
  }
```

I begin with loading up the symbol tables.

```
class StateMachineLoader...
  private void loadSymbolTables() {
    loadStateNames();
    loadCommands();
    loadEvents();
  }
  private void loadEvents() {
    for (Node n : ast.getDescendents(EVENT)) {
      String name = n.getText(NAME);
      String code = n.getText(CODE);
      events.put(name, new Event(name, code));
    }
  }
```

```
class Node...
  public List<Node> getDescendents(Enum requiredType) {
    List<Node> result = new ArrayList<Node>();
    collectDescendents(result, requiredType);
    return result;
  }
  private void collectDescendents(List<Node> result, Enum requiredType) {
    if (this.type == requiredType) result.add(this);
    for (Node n : children) n.collectDescendents(result, requiredType);
  }
```

I've shown the code to loading events, the other classes are similar.

```
class StateMachineLoader...
  private void loadCommands() {
    for (Node n : ast.getDescendents(COMMAND)) {
      String name = n.getText(NAME);
      String code = n.getText(CODE);
      commands.put(name, new Command(name, code));
    }
  }
  private void loadStateNames() {
    for (Node n : ast.getDescendents(STATE)) {
      String name = n.getText(NAME);
      states.put(name, new State(name));
    }
  }
```

I added a method to the node class to get the text for a single child of a type. This feels rather like a dictionary lookup but using the same tree data structure.

```
class Node...
  public String getText(Enum nodeType) {
    return getSoleChild(nodeType).getText();
  }
  public String getText() {
    return content.getText();
  }
  public Node getSoleChild(Enum requiredType) {
    List<Node> children = getChildren(requiredType);
    assert children.size() == 1;
    return children.get(0);
  }
  public List<Node> getChildren(Enum requiredType) {
    List<Node> result = new ArrayList<Node>();
    for (Node n : children)
      if (n.getType() == requiredType) result.add(n);
    return result;
  }
```

With the symbols nicely organized, I can then create the state machine.

```
class StateMachineLoader...
  private void loadState(Node stateNode) {
    loadActions(stateNode);
    loadTransitions(stateNode);
  }
  private void loadActions(Node stateNode) {
    for (Node action : stateNode.getDescendents(ACTION))
      states.get(stateNode.getText(NAME)).addAction(commands.get(action.getText()));
  }
  private void loadTransitions(Node stateNode) {
    for (Node transition : stateNode.getDescendents(TRANSITION)) {
      State source = states.get(stateNode.getText(NAME));
      Event trigger = events.get(transition.getText(TRIGGER));
      State target = states.get(transition.getText(TARGET));
      source.addTransition(trigger, target);
    }
  }
```

The last step is loading the reset events.

```
class StateMachineLoader...
  private void loadResetEvents() {
    if (! ast.hasChild(RESET_EVENT_LIST)) return;
    for (Node n : ast.getSoleDescendent(RESET_EVENT_LIST).getChildren(NAME))
      machine.addResetEvents(events.get(n.getText()));
  }

class Node...
  public boolean hasChild(Enum nodeType) {
    return ! getChildren(nodeType).isEmpty();
  }
```

24: Tree
Construction

Chapter 25

Embedded Translation

Embed output production code into the parser, so that the
output is produced gradually as the parse runs.

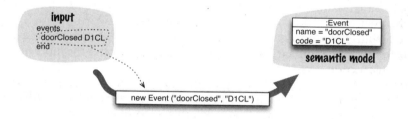

In *Syntax-Directed Translation (219)*, a pure parser merely creates an internal
parse tree, so you need to do more to populate a *Semantic Model (159)*.

Embedded Translation populates the Semantic Model by embedding code into
the parser that populates the Semantic Model at appropriate points in the parse.

25.1 How It Works

Syntactic analyzers are all about recognizing syntactic structures. Using Embedded
Translation, we place code to populate a *Semantic Model (159)* into the parser,
so that we gradually populate the Semantic Model as we carry out the parse.
Most of the time, this implies that the model population code is placed where a
clause of the input language is recognized, although in practice you may place
hunks of population code at various points.

When using Embedded Translation with *Parser Generators (269)*, you usually
see *Foreign Code (309)* incorporating the population code. Most Parser Generators

299

provide a facility to use Foreign Code; the only one I've used that doesn't is intended to work with *Tree Construction (281)*.

One thing that can cause a problem with Embedded Translation is that actions with side effects can often be executed in unexpected places, depending on exactly how rules are recognized by the parsing algorithm. This isn't an issue you get with Tree Construction since Tree Construction only produces a subtree return value. If you find yourself getting into a tangle with Embedded Translation side effects, that's a sign that you should switch to Tree Construction.

25.2 When to Use It

The biggest appeal of Embedded Translation is that it provides a simple way to handle both syntactic analysis and model population in one pass. With *Tree Construction (281)*, you both provide code to build up the AST and write a populator that walks the tree. Particularly for simple cases, which many DSLs are, this two-stage process can be more trouble than it's worth.

The facilities of your *Parser Generator (269)* have an impact on your choice. The better the tree-building features of your Parser Generator the more appealing Tree Construction becomes.

One of the biggest problems with Embedded Translation is that it can encourage complex grammar files, usually due to a poor use of *Foreign Code (309)*. If you are disciplined in using Foreign Code well, this is less likely to be a problem—but a strength of Tree Construction is that it helps to enforce the discipline.

Embedded Translation fits in with a single-pass parse, as all the work is done during syntactic analysis. This means that things like forward references, which are tricky on a single pass, are also tricky with Embedded Translation. To handle them, you often need *Context Variable (175)*, which can further complicate parsing.

The upshot of all this is that the simpler the language and parser, the more appealing is Embedded Translation.

25.3 Miss Grant's Controller (Java and ANTLR)

I'll take the same example I used for *Tree Construction (281)*, with the same tools (Java and ANTLR), but this time handle the parse with Embedded Translation. First of all, this only changes the syntactic analysis—the tokenizing is the same. I won't repeat the tokenizing discussion here; you can pop over to that section ("Tokenizing," p. 285) if you need a refresher.

Another similarity between the two examples is the core BNF grammar. Most of the time, the BNF rules don't vary if you use different parsing patterns; what changes is the supporting code around the BNF. While Tree Construction uses ANTLR's facilities for declaring ASTs, Embedded Translation uses *Foreign Code (309)* to put in Java snippets to populate the *Semantic Model (159)* directly.

Embedded Translation involves putting arbitrary general-purpose code into a grammar file. As in most cases where embedding one language into another is necessary, I like to use an *Embedment Helper (547)*. I've read many grammar files and I find that this pattern helps keep the grammar clear—it isn't buried in the translation code. I do this by declaring a helper in my grammar.

```
@members {
  StateMachineLoader helper;
  //...
```

The top level of the grammar defines the state machine file.

```
machine : eventList resetEventList commandList state*;
```

It shows the same sequence of declarations.

To see some real translation going on, let's look at the handling for the event list:

25: Embedded Translation

```
eventList : 'events' event* 'end';
```

```
event : name=ID code=ID {helper.addEvent($name, $code);};
```

Here we see the typical nature of using Embedded Translation. Much of the grammar file remains plain, but at appropriate points we introduce general-purpose code to perform the translation. Since I'm using an Embedment Helper, all I do is call a single method on that helper.

```
class StateMachineLoader...
  void addEvent(Token name, Token code) {
    events.put(name.getText(), new Event(name.getText(), code.getText()));
  }

  private Map<String, Event> events = new HashMap<String, Event>();
  private Map<String, Command> commands = new HashMap<String, Command>();
  private Map<String, State> states = new HashMap<String, State>();
  private List<Event> resetEvents = new ArrayList<Event>();
```

The call creates a new event object and places it in the symbol table, which is a collection of dictionaries on the loader. The call to the helper passes in the tokens for the name and code. ANTLR uses assignment syntax to mark elements of the grammar so the embedded code can refer to them. The placement of the embedded code indicates when it runs—in this case, the embedded code is run after both child nodes have been recognized.

The commands are done in exactly the same way. The states, however, introduce a couple of interesting issues: hierarchic context and forward references.

I'll start with hierarchic context. The issue here is that the various elements of a state—actions and transitions—occur within the state definition, so when we want to process an action we need to know in which state it is declared.

Earlier on, I drew an analogy to Embedded Translation being rather like processing XML with SAX. This is somewhat true, in that the embedded code just works with one rule at a time. But it's also misleading, because *Parser Generators (269)* can give you much more context during the execution of the code so you don't need to keep it around yourself so much.

In ANTLR, you can pass parameters into rules in order to push down this kind of context.

```
state : 'state' name=ID {helper.addState($name);}
        actionList[$name]?
        transition[$name]*
        'end';

actionList [Token state]
  : 'actions' '{' actions+=ID* '}' {helper.addAction($state, $actions);}
  ;
```

25: Embedded
Translation

Here the state token is passed into the rule for recognizing an action. This way the embedded translation code can pass in both the state token and the command tokens (the "*" indicates they are a list). This provides the right context for the helper.

```
class StateMachineLoader...
  public void addAction(Token state, List actions) {
    for (Token action : (Iterable<Token>) actions)
      getState(state).addAction(getCommand(action));
  }
  private State getState(Token token) {
    return states.get(token.getText());
  }
```

The second issue is that the transition declarations involve forward references to states that haven't been declared yet. In many DSLs, you can arrange things so that no item refers to an identifier that hasn't yet been declared, but the state model can't do this, resulting in forward references. Tree Construction allows us to process the AST in multiple passes, so we can make one pass to pick up the declarations and another pass to populate the states. With multiple passes, forward references aren't a problem since they are resolved on later passes through the AST. With Embedded Translation, we don't have that option.

Our solution here is to use an "obtain" (the term I use for find-or-create) operation on both the references and declarations. Essentially, this means that whenever we mention a state, we implicitly declare it if it doesn't already exist.

```
stateMachine.g...
  transition [Token sourceState]
   : trigger = ID '=>' target = ID {helper.addTransition($sourceState, $trigger, $target);};

class StateMachineLoader...
  public void addTransition(Token state, Token trigger, Token target) {
    getState(state).addTransition(getEvent(trigger), obtainState(target));
  }
  private State obtainState(Token token) {
    String name = token.getText();
    if (!states.containsKey(name))
      states.put(name, new State(name));
    return states.get(name);
  }
```

One of the consequences of this approach is that if we misspell a state in our transition, we will just get a blank state as the transition target. If we're happy with that, we can leave it. It's common, however, to check declarations against usage, in which case we need to keep track of the states created by use and ensure that they are all declared too.

Our language defines the start state as the first state mentioned in the program. This kind of context isn't handled by the Parser Generator particularly well, so we need to resort to what is effectively a context variable.

25: Embedded Translation

```
class StateMachineLoader...
  public void addState(Token n) {
    obtainState(n);
    if (null == machine)
      machine = new StateMachine(getState(n));
  }
```

Handling the reset events is pretty trivial—we just add them to a separate list.

```
stateMachine.g...
  resetEventList : 'resetEvents' resetEvent* 'end' ;
  resetEvent     : name=ID {helper.addResetEvent($name);};

class StateMachineLoader...
  public void addResetEvent(Token name) {
    resetEvents.add(getEvent(name));
  }
```

The single-pass nature of the parser also complicates reset events: They can be defined before we get the first state, and thus before we have a machine to put them on. So I keep them in a field to add them at the end.

```
class StateMachineLoader...
  public void addResetEvent(Token name) {
    resetEvents.add(getEvent(name));
  }
```

The run method of the loader shows the overall sequence of tasks: lexing, running the generated parser, and finishing the model population with the reset events.

```
class StateMachineLoader...
  public StateMachine run() {
    try {
      StateMachineLexer lexer = new StateMachineLexer(new ANTLRReaderStream(input));
      StateMachineParser parser = new StateMachineParser(new CommonTokenStream(lexer));
      parser.helper = this;
      parser.machine();
      machine.addResetEvents(resetEvents.toArray(new Event[0]));
      return machine;
    } catch (IOException e) {
      throw new RuntimeException(e);
    } catch (RecognitionException e) {
      throw new RuntimeException(e);
    }
  }
```

It's not unusual to have code like this following the syntactic analysis—this is also where any semantic analysis would happen.

Chapter 26

Embedded Interpretation

Embed interpreter actions into the grammar, so that executing the parser causes the text to be directly interpreted to produce the response.

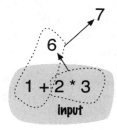

There are many occasions where you may want to run a DSL script and get an immediate result, such as performing a calculation or running a query. Embedded Interpretation interprets the DSL script during parsing, so the result of the parse is the result of the script itself.

26.1 How It Works

Embedded Interpretation works by evaluating DSL expressions as soon as possible, collating results together, and returning the overall result. Embedded Interpretation does not use a *Semantic Model (159)*; instead, the interpretation is done directly on the DSL input. As the parse recognizes each fragment of a DSL script, it interprets as much as it can.

305

26.2 When to Use It

I'm a big proponent of a *Semantic Model (159)*, so I don't usually favor Embedded Interpretation—it is useful when you have relatively small expressions that you just want to evaluate and run. Sometimes, building a Semantic Model just isn't worth the overhead. But I find this is a rare case; even a relatively small DSL is usually simpler to deal with by creating a Semantic Model and interpreting that, rather than trying to do everything in the parser. Furthermore, a Semantic Model provides a stronger foundation if the language grows.

26.3 A Calculator (ANTLR and Java)

A calculator is perhaps the best example case for Embedded Interpretation. It's easy to interpret each expression and compose the results together. It's also a case where the syntax tree for arithmetic is a perfectly good *Semantic Model (159)*, so there's no gain in trying to create the usual Semantic Model that I prefer.

26: Embedded Interpretation

Doing a calculator in ANTLR is a bit awkward, because arithmetic expressions are *Nested Operator Expressions (327)* while ANTLR is a top-down parser. So, the grammar gets a bit more involved.

I begin with a top-level rule. Since arithmetic expressions are recursive, ANTLR needs a top-level rule to know where to start the parse.

```
grammar "Arith.g" ......
  prog returns [double result] : e=expression {$result = $e.result;};
```

I call this top-level rule from a simple Java class that wraps the ANTLR grammar file.

```
class Calculator...
  public static double evaluate(String expression) {
    try {
      Lexer lexer = new ArithLexer(new ANTLRReaderStream(new StringReader(expression)));
      ArithParser parser = new ArithParser(new CommonTokenStream(lexer));
      return parser.prog();
    } catch (IOException e) {
      throw new RuntimeException(e);
    } catch (RecognitionException e) {
      throw new RuntimeException(e);
    }
  }
```

With Nested Operator Expressions, I need to start from the lowest-precedence operators, which in this case are addition and subtraction.

```
grammar "Arith.g" ......
  expression returns [double result]
   : a=mult_exp {$result = $a.result;}
     ( '+' b=mult_exp {$result += $b.result;}
     | '-' b=mult_exp {$result -= $b.result;}
     )*
   ;
```

This shows the basic pattern of the calculator. Each grammar rule recognizes one operator, and the embedded Java code executes the arithmetic based on that input. The rest of the grammar follows this pattern.

```
grammar "Arith.g" ......
  power_exp returns [double result]
   : a=unary_exp {$result = $a.result;}
     ( '**' b=power_exp {$result = Math.pow($result,$b.result);}
     | '//' b=power_exp {$result = Math.pow($result, (1.0 / $b.result));}
     )?
   ;

  unary_exp returns [double result]
   : '-' a= unary_exp {$result = -$a.result;}
   | a=factor_exp {$result = $a.result;}
   ;

  factor_exp returns [double result]
    : n=NUMBER {$result = Double.parseDouble($n.text);}
   | a=par_exp {$result = $a.result;}
   ;

  par_exp returns [double result]
   : '(' a=expression ')' {$result = $a.result;}
   ;
```

26: Embedded
Interpretation

Indeed this calculator is so simple and fits the structure of a syntax tree so well that I don't even need an *Embedment Helper (547)*.

Arithmetic expressions are a common choice for illustrating how to use a parser; many articles and papers use some form of calculator example. But I don't think this is very representative of what you have to deal with when working with a DSL. The big problem with using arithmetic expressions as examples is that they force you to deal with a rare problem (Nested Operator Expression) but avoid the common DSL-related problems that encourage the use of Semantic Model and Embedment Helper.

Chapter 27

Foreign Code

*Embed some foreign code into an external DSL to provide
more elaborate behavior than can be specified in the DSL.*

DSL

```
scott handles floor_wax in MA RI CT when {/^Baker/.test(lead.name)};
```

Javascript

By definition, a DSL is a limited language that only does a few things. Sometimes, however, you need to describe something in the DSL script that is beyond the capabilities of the DSL. One solution may be to extend the DSL to handle this capability, but taking this path may significantly complicate the DSL, removing much of the simplicity that makes it appealing.

Foreign Code embeds a different language—often, a general-purpose language—into certain places in the DSL.

27.1 How It Works

Putting bits of another language into a DSL involves two questions. First, how do we recognize these foreign pieces and weave them into the grammar, and second, how do we execute this code so it can do its job?

Foreign Code only appears in certain parts of a DSL, so the DSL's grammar will mark the spots where it can show up. One wrinkle in handling Foreign Code is that the grammar will not be able to recognize the internal structure of the Foreign Code. As a result, you will usually need to use *Alternative Tokenization (319)* with a Foreign Code and read it into the parser as one long string. You

309

can then either embed that string into the *Semantic Model (159)* in its raw form, or pass it to a separate parser for the Foreign Code in order to weave it more intimately into the Semantic Model. The latter is more involved—it's something you'd only consider if your Foreign Code is another DSL. Often, the Foreign Code is a general-purpose language, in which case the pure string is usually enough.

Once the Foreign Code is in the Semantic Model, we have to decide what to do with it. The biggest issue lies in whether the Foreign Code can be interpreted or needs to be compiled.

Interpreted Foreign Code is usually the easiest, providing you have a mechanism to interoperate the interpreter with the host language. If the host language of the system is also interpreted, it's easy to use the host language itself for Foreign Code. If the host language is compiled, then you'll need to use an interpreted language that can be called from the host language, allowing for some data transfer. Increasingly, we see static language environments gaining the ability to interoperate with interpreted languages. It's usually a bit fiddly, especially when it comes to moving data around. It also might involve introducing another language to the project, which can sometimes be an issue.

The alternative is to embed the host language itself, even if it's a compiled language. The complexity here is that this introduces an extra compilation step into the build process, just like using code generation. Of course if you are actually doing code generation, you have to do this extra compilation step anyway, so adding compiled Foreign Code doesn't make things any more complex. The complexity matters if you're compiling code while interpreting the Semantic Model.

Whenever you use general-purpose Foreign Code, you should seriously consider using an *Embedment Helper (547)*. That way, the only Foreign Code in your DSL script should be the minimum required for the context within the DSL, calling out to the Embedment Helper for any more general processing. One of the big problems with Foreign Code is that a lot of foreign code can overwhelm the DSL, thus losing most of the advantages of readability that the DSL offers. Embedment Helper is an easy technique and is worth it in all but the smallest cases.

Sometimes, the Foreign Code needs to refer to symbols that are defined in the DSL script itself. This only occurs if the DSL script includes variables or other ways to create indirect constructs. While these are omnipresent in general-purpose languages, they are actually not so common in DSLs as DSLs often don't need that kind of expressiveness. As a result, these seem rare in practice, but are nevertheless a familiar case because they crop up in grammars—which are a common case of using Foreign Code. Here's an example of this:

```
allocationRule
  : salesman=ID  pc=productClause lc=locationClause ('when' predicate=ACTION)? SEP
      {helper.recognizedAllocationRule(salesman, pc, lc, predicate);}
  ;
```

Here the Foreign Code is Java. The Java code includes references to salesman, pc, lc, and predicate, all of which are symbols defined in the grammar. When processing the Foreign Code, the *Parser Generator (269)* needs to resolve these references.

27.2 When to Use It

When you're thinking about using Foreign Code, the usual alternative is to extend the DSL to do what you're considering the Foreign Code for. Introducing Foreign Code certainly has its downsides. By using it, you are breaking the abstraction that the DSL gives you. Anyone who reads the DSL now needs to understand the Foreign Code as well as the DSL itself—at least to an extent. Also, using Foreign Code complicates the parsing process and probably complicates the *Semantic Model (159)* as well.

These added complexities have to be weighed against the additional complexity you'd need to add to the DSL to support the capability you need. The more powerful the DSL, the harder it is to understand and use.

So what are the cases that lean to using Foreign Code? One natural case is when you really need a general-purpose language. You certainly don't want to turn your DSL into a general-purpose language, so that pushes you quickly to using Foreign Code.

Another case for Foreign Code is when you only need a capability very rarely in your DSL scripts. A rarely used capability may not be worth extending the DSL for.

Who uses the DSL is a factor in the decision. If the DSL is only used by programmers, then adding Foreign Code is not a problem—they will be able to understand the Foreign Code as much as the DSL. If nonprogrammers will read the DSL, that argues against Foreign Code as they may not be able to understand, and thus engage with, the foreign code. If the Foreign Code is to handle rare cases, however, this may not be a big problem.

27.3 Embedding Dynamic Code (ANTLR, Java, and Javascript)

In order to sell stuff, you need salesmen; if you have many salesmen, you need some way to decide how to allocate the leads to them. A common notion is that of "territories," which are effectively a set of rules for distributing leads to salesmen. These territories can be based on various factors; here's an allocation script that uses US states and products:

27: Foreign Code

```
scott handles floor_wax in WA;
helen handles floor_wax desert_topping in AZ NM;
brian handles desert_topping in WA OR ID MT;
otherwise scott
```

It's a simple DSL where each allocation rule is checked in sequence, and once a deal matches the conditions, the lead is allocated to that salesman.

Now, let's imagine that Scott has got very friendly with an executive at Baker Industries, who operate in southern New England. Since they spend so much time on the golf course together, we want any leads involving floor wax at Baker Industries to go to Scott. To complicate matters, Baker Industries has a number of variations on its name: Baker Industrial Holdings, Baker Floor Toppings, etc. So we decide that we want any lead with a company whose name starts with "Baker" in New England to go to Scott.

To do this, we could extend our DSL, but since it's one of those particular cases that would end up complicating the language, we'll go for some Foreign Code instead. This is what we'd like to say:

```
scott handles floor_wax in MA RI CT when {/^Baker/.test(lead.name)};
```

27: Foreign Code

The foreign code I'm using here is Javascript, which I've picked because it's easily integrated with Java and can be evaluated at runtime, which avoids recompilation when someone changes the allocation rules. The Javascript code isn't exactly super readable—I suspect I'd have to say "trust me" to the sales manager—but it will do the job. I'm also not using *Embedment Helper (547)* here, as the predicate is very small.

27.3.1 Semantic Model

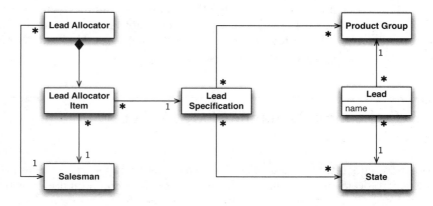

Figure 27.1 *The model for lead allocation*

In this simple model, we have leads, and each lead has a product group and a state.

```
class Lead...
  private String name;
  private State state;
  private ProductGroup product;

  public Lead(String name, State state, ProductGroup product) {
    this.name = name;
    this.state = state;
    this.product = product;
  }

  public State getState() {return state;}
  public ProductGroup getProduct() {return product;}
  public String getName() {return name;}
```

To allocate these leads to salesmen, we have a lead allocator which contains a list of items that link salesmen to lead specifications.

```
class LeadAllocator...
  private List<LeadAllocatorItem> allocationList = new ArrayList<LeadAllocatorItem>();
  private Salesman defaultSalesman;

  public void appendAllocation(Salesman salesman, LeadSpecification spec) {
    allocationList.add(new LeadAllocatorItem(salesman, spec));
  }

  public void setDefaultSalesman(Salesman defaultSalesman) {
    this.defaultSalesman = defaultSalesman;
  }

  private class LeadAllocatorItem {
    Salesman salesman;
    LeadSpecification spec;

    private LeadAllocatorItem(Salesman salesman, LeadSpecification spec) {
      this.salesman = salesman;
      this.spec = spec;
    }
  }
```

27: Foreign Code

A lead specification follows the *Specification* [Evans DDD] pattern, set to match the lead if the lead's attributes are included in the specification's lists.

```
class LeadSpecification...
  private List<State> states = new ArrayList<State>();
  private List<ProductGroup> products = new ArrayList<ProductGroup>();
  private String predicate;

  public void addStates(State... args) {states.addAll(Arrays.asList(args));}
  public void addProducts(ProductGroup... args) {products.addAll(Arrays.asList(args));}
  public void setPredicate(String code) {predicate = code;}

  public boolean isSatisfiedBy(Lead candidate) {
    return statesMatch(candidate)
        && productsMatch(candidate)
        && predicateMatches(candidate)
      ;
  }
  private boolean productsMatch(Lead candidate) {
    return products.isEmpty() || products.contains(candidate.getProduct());
  }
  private boolean statesMatch(Lead candidate) {
    return states.isEmpty() || states.contains(candidate.getState());
  }
  private boolean predicateMatches(Lead candidate) {
    if (null == predicate) return true;
    return evaluatePredicate(candidate);
  }
```

The specification also contains a predicate, which is some embedded Javascript code. The specification evaluates that using Java's Rhino Javascript engine.

```
class LeadSpecification...
  boolean evaluatePredicate(Lead candidate) {
    try {
      ScriptContext newContext = new SimpleScriptContext();
      Bindings engineScope = newContext.getBindings(ScriptContext.ENGINE_SCOPE);
      engineScope.put("lead", candidate);
      return (Boolean) javascriptEngine().eval(predicate, engineScope);
    } catch (ScriptException e) {
      throw new RuntimeException(e);
    }
  }
  private  ScriptEngine javascriptEngine() {
    ScriptEngineManager factory = new ScriptEngineManager();
    ScriptEngine result = factory.getEngineByName("JavaScript");
    assert result != null : "Unable to find javascript engine";
    return result;
  }
```

I add the lead that's being evaluated to the scope of the Javascript evaluation, so that the embedded Javascript code can access the lead's properties.

The lead allocator works by running down the list of items, returning the first salesman with a matching specification.

```
class LeadAllocator...
  public Salesman determineSalesman(Lead lead) {
    for (LeadAllocatorItem i : allocationList)
      if (i.spec.isSatisfiedBy(lead)) return i.salesman;
    return defaultSalesman;
  }
```

27.3.2 Parser

The main driver class for the translation builds a lead allocator as its result.

```
class AllocationTranslator...
  private Reader input;
  private AllocationLexer lexer;
  private AllocationParser parser;
  private ParsingNotification notification = new ParsingNotification();
  private LeadAllocator result = new LeadAllocator();

  public AllocationTranslator(Reader input) {
    this.input = input;
  }

  public void run() {
    try {
      lexer = new AllocationLexer(new ANTLRReaderStream(input));
      parser = new AllocationParser(new CommonTokenStream(lexer));
      parser.helper = this;
      parser.allocationList();
    } catch (Exception e) {
      throw new RuntimeException("Unexpected exception in parse", e);
    }
    if (notification.hasErrors())
      throw new RuntimeException("Parse failed: \n" + notification);
  }
```

The allocation translator also acts as the *Embedment Helper (547)* for the grammar file.

```
grammar...
  @members {
    AllocationTranslator helper;

    public void reportError(RecognitionException e) {
      helper.addError(e);
      super.reportError(e);
    }
  }
```

I'll walk through the grammar file from the top down. I'm using *Embedded Translation (299)*.

Here are the core tokens I'm using:

```
grammar...
  ID  : ('a'..'z' | 'A'..'Z' | '0'..'9' | '_' )+;
  WS  : (' ' |'\t' | '\r' | '\n')+ {skip();} ;
  SEP : ';';
```

This defines the usual whitespace and identifier tokens, together with an explicit semicolon statement separator.

Here's the top-level rule of the grammar:

```
grammar...
  allocationList
    : allocationRule* 'otherwise' ID {helper.recognizedDefault($ID);}
    ;
```

```
class AllocationTranslator...
  void recognizedDefault(Token token) {
  if (!Registry.salesmenRepository().containsId(token.getText())) {
      notification.error(token, "Unknown salesman: %s", token.getText());
      return;
    }
  Salesman salesman = Registry.salesmenRepository().findById(token.getText());
    result.setDefaultSalesman(salesman);
  }
```

I'm assuming the salesmen, products, and states all exist before we interpret the allocation rules, probably in a database. For this example, I'll access this data using *Repositories* [Fowler PoEAA].

At the risk of getting all recursive, you might enjoy the point that this grammar also demonstrates Foreign Code—the code actions in a grammar are an excellent example of Foreign Code. With ANTLR, the Foreign Code gets woven into the generated parser during code generation, which is a different approach from what I'm doing with the Javascript allocation rule. But the same basic Foreign Code pattern is still in play. I'm also using Embedment Helper to keep the amount of Foreign Code down to a minimum.

Now it's time for me to return to the plot and show you the allocation rule.

```
grammar...
  allocationRule
    : salesman=ID  pc=productClause  lc=locationClause ('when' predicate=ACTION)? SEP
        {helper.recognizedAllocationRule(salesman, pc, lc, predicate);}
    ;
```

The rule is pretty straightforward. It calls for a salesman name, product, and location clauses (subrules) as well as an optional predicate token and a separator. The fact that the predicate is a token rather than a subrule is important, because we want to take all the Javascript as a single string and won't parse it further.

I have a single helper call to record the recognition, which I'll go into when we see what the product and location clauses return. I've followed a convention of giving a fully spelled-out name to the labels for a salesman and predicate, because the tokens aren't sufficiently clear. I've used abbreviations for the labels for the subrules because those subrule names are clear, so a full label would be just duplicating the subrule name and thus add noise.

Let's look at the subrules, in particular the product clause.

```
grammar...
  productClause  returns [List<ProductGroup> result]
    : 'handles' p+=ID+ {$result = helper.recognizedProducts($p);}
    ;
```

I've made the clause itself return a list of product groups. As a result, it doesn't populate the *Semantic Model (159)* itself but returns the objects for the parent clause to populate the Semantic Model. I do this because otherwise I need to access the current allocation rule inside the action for the product rule. This would usually require a *Context Variable (175)* which I'd like to avoid. ANTLR has the ability to pass down objects as rule arguments—so I could do that there instead—but I prefer to do all the Semantic Model in the one place.

I still need an action to convert the product tokens to actual product objects. This is just a simple lookup in the repository.

```
class AllocationTranslator...
  List<ProductGroup> recognizedProducts(List<Token> tokens) {
    List<ProductGroup> result = new ArrayList<ProductGroup>();
    for (Token t : tokens) {
      if (!Registry.productRepository().containsId(t.getText())) {
        notification.error(t, "No product for %s", t.getText());
        continue;
      }
      result.add(Registry.productRepository().findById(t.getText()));
    }
    return result;
  }
}
```

27: Foreign Code

The location clause works pretty much the same way, so I'll move on to the meat of this example—grabbing the Javascript. As I indicated above, I do this in the lexer. After all, I don't care about the content of the Javascript, so I'm just going to bung the entire string into the lead specification. There's no point in building or using a Javascript parser, unless I want to check during parsing whether the Javascript is syntactically legal. Since parsing would only detect a syntactic error and not a semantic error, I don't think it's worth the trouble.

I use *Alternative Tokenization (319)* to grab the text. The simplest way is to choose a pair of delimiters that aren't being used for anything else and have a token rule like this:

```
ACTION : '{' .* '}' ;
```

This is a reasonable rule which will work in many situations. However, it does have a potential problem—things go awry if I have any curly brackets inside the

Javascript code itself. I can avoid this by using more unlikely delimiters, for example pairs of characters.

```
ACTION : '{:' .* ':}' ;
```

In ANTLR, however, I can make use of its own ability to handle nested tokens.

```
grammar...
  ACTION : NESTED_ACTION;

  fragment NESTED_ACTION
    : '{' (ACTION_CHAR | NESTED_ACTION)* '}'
    ;
  fragment ACTION_CHAR
    : ~('{'|'}')
    ;
```

It's not quite perfect; I'd be defeated by a Javascript fragment of badThing = "}"; but it should do for most cases.

With the subclause collections, and the Javascript predicate, I can update the Semantic Model.

```
class AllocationTranslator...
  void recognizedAllocationRule(Token salesmanName, List<ProductGroup> products,
                         List<State> states, Token predicate)
  {
    if (!Registry.salesmenRepository().containsId(salesmanName.getText())) {
      notification.error(salesmanName, "Unknown salesman: %s", salesmanName.getText());
      return;
    }
    Salesman salesman = Registry.salesmenRepository().findById(salesmanName.getText());
    LeadSpecification spec = new LeadSpecification();
    spec.addStates((State[]) states.toArray(new State[states.size()]));
    spec.addProducts((ProductGroup[]) products.toArray(new ProductGroup[products.size()]));
    if (null != predicate) spec.setPredicate(predicate.getText());
    result.appendAllocation(salesman, spec);
  }
```

Chapter 28

Alternative Tokenization

Alter the lexing behavior from within the parser.

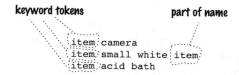

28.1 How It Works

In my simple overview of how *Parser Generators (269)* work, I said that the lexer feeds a stream of tokens to the parser that assembles the stream into a parse tree. The implication is that it's a one-way interaction: The lexer is a source that the parser simply consumes. As it turns out that isn't always the case. There are times when the way the lexer does the tokenizing should change depending on where we are in the parse tree—meaning that the parser has to manipulate the way the lexer does the tokenizing.

For a simple example of this problem, consider listing a bunch of items that might appear in a catalog.

```
item camera;
item small_power_plant;
item acid_bath;
```

Using underscores or camelCase is familiar and normal for geeks like us, but regular human beings are more used to spaces. They would rather read something like:

```
item camera;
item small power plant;
item acid bath;
```

How hard can this be? As it turns out, when you're using a grammar-driven parser, it can be surprisingly tricky, which is why I have a section here to talk about it. (You'll notice that I'm using semicolons to separate the item declarations. You could also use newlines, and indeed may prefer to. I might too, but that introduces another tricky issue, that of handling *Newline Separators (333)*, so I'll use semicolons for now to deal with one tricky issue at a time.)

The simplest grammar allowing us to recognize any amount of words after the item keyword might look like this:

```
catalog : item*;
item : 'item' ID* ';';
```

The trouble is that this breaks down when you have an item that contains the "item" in its name, such as item small white item;.

The problem is that the lexer recognizes item as a keyword, not as a word, and thus hands back a keyword token rather than an ID token. What we really want to do is to treat everything between the item keyword and the semicolon as an ID, effectively altering the tokenization rules for this point in the parse.

Another common example of this kind of situation is *Foreign Code (309)*—which can include all sorts of meaningful tokens in the DSL, but we want to ignore them all and take the foreign code as one big string to embed into the *Semantic Model (159)*.

There are a number of approaches available for this, not all of which are possible with all kinds of Parser Generators.

28.1.1 Quoting

The simplest way to deal with this problem is to quote the text so the lexer can recognize it as something special. For our item names, it means putting them inside some kind of quotation characters, at least when we use the word item. This would read like this:

```
item camera
item small power plant;
item "small white item";
```

This would be parsed with a grammar like:

```
catalog : item*;
item : 'item' item_name ';';

item_name    : (ID | QUOTED_STRING)* ;
QUOTED_STRING : '"' (options{greedy = false;} : .)* '"';
```

Quoting gobbles up all the text between the delimiters, so it is never touched by the other lexer rules. I can then take the quoted text and do whatever I like with it.

Quoting doesn't involve the parser at all, so a quoting scheme has to be used everywhere in the language. You can't have specific rules for quoting particular elements of the language. In many situations, however, this works out just fine.

An awkward aspect of quoting is dealing with delimiters inside the quoted string—something like Active "Marauders" Map where you need quotation marks inside the quoted string. There are ways of dealing with this, which should be familiar to you from regular programming.

The first is to provide an escaping mechanism, such as Unix's beloved backslash or doubling the delimiter. To process item Active "Marauders" Map you would use a rule like this:

```
QUOTED_STRING : STRING_DELIM (STRING_ESCAPE |  ~(STRING_DELIM))* STRING_DELIM;
fragment STRING_ESCAPE:  STRING_DELIM STRING_DELIM;
fragment STRING_DELIM :  '"';
```

The basic trick is to use the delimiters to surround a repeating group where one of the elements of that group is the negation of the delimiter (essentially the same thing as a nongreedy match) and the other alternatives are any escape combinations you need.

You're more likely to see this written in a more compact form.

```
QUOTED_STRING : '"' ('""' |  ~('"'))* '"';
```

28: Alternative
Tokenization

I prefer the long-winded clarity here, but such clarity is particularly rare when it comes to regular expressions.

Escaping works well, but it may be confusing, particularly to nonprogrammers.

Another technique is to pick a more unusual combination of delimiter symbols that are unlikely to appear in the quoted text. A good example of this is the Java CUP *Parser Generator (269)* Most Parser Generators use curly braces to indicate code actions, which is familiar but runs into the problem that curly brackets are a common thing to be found inside C-based languages. So CUP uses "{:" and ":}" as its delimiters—a combination you don't find in most languages, including Java.

Using an unlikely delimiter is obviously only as good as the unlikeliness of its use. In many DSL situations, you can get away with it because there are only a few things you're likely to run into in the quoted text.

A third tactic is to use more than one kind of quoting delimiters, so that if you need to embed a delimiter character, you can do so by switching to an alternative for quoting. As an example, many scripting languages allow you to quote with either single or double quote characters, which has the additional advantage of reducing the confusion caused by some languages using one or the other. (They often have different escaping rules with the different delimiters.) Allowing double or single quotes for the item example is as simple as this:

```
catalog : item*;
item : 'item' item_name ';';

item_name    : (ID | QUOTED_STRING)* ;
QUOTED_STRING : DOUBLE_QUOTED_STRING | SINGLE_QUOTED_STRING ;
fragment DOUBLE_QUOTED_STRING : '"' (options{greedy = false;} : .)* '"';
fragment SINGLE_QUOTED_STRING : '\'' (options{greedy = false;} : .)* '\'';
```

There's a less common option that can occasionally be useful. Some Parser Generators, including ANTLR, use a push-down machine rather than a state machine for lexing. This provides another option for cases where the quoting characters are matching pairs (like "{...}"). This requires a slight variation on my example; imagine that I want to embed some Javascript in the item list to provide an arbitrary condition for when the item should appear in the catalog, for example:

```
item lyncanthropic gerbil {!isFullMoon()};
```

The embedding problem here is that Javascript code can obviously include curlies. However, we can allow curlies, but only if they are matched, by writing the quoting rule like this:

```
catalog : item*;
item : 'item' item_name  CONDITION?';';

CONDITION : NESTED_CONDITION;
fragment NESTED_CONDITION  : '{' (CONDITION_CHAR | NESTED_CONDITION)* '}';
fragment CONDITION_CHAR    : ~('{'|'}') ;
```

This doesn't handle all embedded curlies—it would be defeated by {System.out.print("tokenize this: }}}");}. To conquer that, I'd need to write additional lexer rules to cover any elements that might be embedded in the condition that might include a curly. For this kind of situation, however, a simple solution will usually suffice. The biggest downside to this technique is that you can only do it if the lexer is a push-down machine, which is relatively rare.

28.1.2 Lexical State

Perhaps the most logical way of thinking about this problem, at least for the item name case, is to replace the lexer completely while we are looking at the item name. That is, once we've seen the keyword item, we replace our usual lexer with another lexer until that lexer sees the semicolon, at which point we return to our usual lexer.

Flex, the GNU version of lex, supports a similar behavior under the name of **start conditions** (also referred to as **lexical state**). While this feature uses the same lexer, it allows the grammar to switch the lexer into a different mode. This is almost the same thing as changing the lexer, and certainly enough for this example.

I'll switch to Java CUP for this example code because ANTLR currently doesn't support changing the lexical state (it can't, as the lexer currently tokenizes the entire input stream before the parser starts working on it). Here's a CUP grammar to handle the items:

```
<YYINITIAL> "item"      {return symbol(K_ITEM);}
<YYINITIAL> {Word}      {return symbol(WORD);}

<gettingName> {Word} {return symbol(WORD);}

";"         {return symbol(SEMI);}
{WS}        {/* ignore */}
{Comment}   { /* ignore */}
```

For this example, I'm using two lexical states: YYINITIAL and gettingName. YYINITIAL is the default lexical state that the lexer starts up in. I can use these lexical states to annotate my lexer rules. In this case, you see that the item keyword is only recognized as a keyword token in the YYINITIAL state. Lexer rules without a state (such as ";") apply in all states. (Strictly, I don't need the two state-specific rules for {Word} as they are the same, but I've shown them here to illustrate the syntax.)

I then switch between the lexical states in the grammar. The rules are similar to the ANTLR case, but a little different as CUP uses a different version of BNF. I'll first show a couple of rules that don't get involved in the lexical state switching. First is the top-level catalog rule, which is a basic BNF form of the ANTLR rule.

```
catalog  ::= item | catalog item ;
```

At the other end, there is the rule to assemble the item name.

```
item_name ::=
  WORD:w {: RESULT = w; :}
  | item_name:n WORD:w {: RESULT = n + " " + w; :}
  ;
```

The rule that involves the lexical switching is the rule to recognize an item.

```
item   ::= K_ITEM
  {: parser.helper.startingItemName(); :}
  item_name:n
  {: parser.helper.recognizedItem(n); :}
  SEMI
  ;
```

28: Alternative
Tokenization

```
class ParsingHelper...
  void recognizedItem(String name) {
      items.add(name);
      setLexicalState(Lexer.YYINITIAL);
  }
  public void startingItemName() {
      setLexicalState(Lexer.gettingName);
  }
  private void setLexicalState(int newState) {
      getLexer().yybegin(newState);
  }
```

The basic mechanism is very straightforward. Once the parser recognizes the item keyword, it switches the lexical state to just take the words as they come. Once it finishes with the words, it switches back.

As written, it is pretty easy, but there's a catch. In order to resolve their rules, parsers need to look ahead through the token stream. ANTLR uses arbitrary look ahead, which is partly why it tokenizes the entire input before the parser gets to work. CUP, like Yacc, does one token of look ahead. But this one token is enough to cause a problem with an item declaration like item item the troublesome. The problem is that the first word in the item name is parsed before we change lexical state, so in this case it will be parsed as an item keyword, thus breaking the parser.

It's easy to run into a more serious problem. You'll notice I put the call to reset the lexical state (recognizedItem) before recognizing the statement separator. Had I put it afterwards, it would recognize the item keyword in look ahead before switching back to the initial state.

This is another thing to be careful with when using lexical states. If you use common border tokens (like quotes), you can avoid problems when you only have one token of look ahead. Otherwise, you have to be careful in how the parser look ahead interacts with the lexer's lexical states. As a result, combining parsing and lexical states can easily get pretty messy.

28.1.3 Token Type Mutation

The parser's rules react not to the full contents of the token, but to the token's type. If we can change the type of a token before it reaches the parser, we can change an item keyword into an item word.

This approach is opposite to lexical states. With lexical states, you need the lexer to feed the parser tokens, one at a time; with this approach, you need to be able to look ahead in the token stream. So it's no surprise that this approach is better suited to ANTLR than to Yacc, and I'll therefore switch back.

```
catalog : item*;
item :
  'item' {helper.adjustItemNameTokens();}
  ID*
  SEP
  ;
SEP : ';';
```

There's nothing in the grammar that shows what's going on; all the action occurs in the helper.

```
void adjustItemNameTokens() {
  for (int i = 1; !isEndOfItemName(parser.getTokenStream().LA(i)); i++) {
    assert i < 100 : "This many tokens must mean something's wrong";
    parser.getTokenStream().LT(i).setType(parser.ID);
  }
}
private boolean isEndOfItemName(int arg) {
  return (arg == parser.SEP);
```

The code runs forward along the token stream, turning the token types to ID, until it runs into the separator. (I've declared the token type of the separator here to make it available from the helper.)

This technique doesn't capture exactly what was in the original text, as anything that the lexer skips won't be offered up to the parser. For example, whitespace isn't preserved in this method. If that's an issue, then this technique isn't the right one to use.

28: Alternative Tokenization

To see this used in a bigger context, take a look at the parser for Hibernate's HQL. HQL has to deal with the word "order" appearing either as a keyword (in "order by") or as the name of a column or table. The lexer returns "order" as a keyword by default, but the parser action looks ahead to see if it's followed by "by", and if not changes it to be an identifier.

28.1.4 Ignoring Token Types

If the tokens don't make sense and you want the full text, you can ignore the token types completely and grab every token until you reach a sentinel token (in this case the separator).

```
catalog : item*;
item : 'item' item_name SEP;
item_name : ~SEP* ;
SEP : ';';
```

The basic idea is to write the item name rule so it accepts any token other than the separator. ANTLR makes this easy by using a negation operator, but other

Parser Generators (269) may not have this capability. If you don't, you have to do something like:

```
item  : (ID | 'item')* SEP;
```

You need to list all the keywords in the rule, which is more awkward than just using a negation operator.

The tokens still appear with the correct type, but when you're doing this you don't use the type in this context. A grammar with actions might look something like this:

```
catalog returns [Catalog catalog = new Catalog()]:
  (i=item {$catalog.addItem(i.itemName);})*
  ;
item returns [String itemName] :
  'item' name=item_name SEP
  {$itemName = $name.result;}
  ;
item_name returns [String result = ""] :
  (n=~SEP {$result += $n.text + " ";})*
  {$result = $result.trim();}
  ;
SEP : ';';
```

In this case, the text is taken from every token in the name, ignoring the token type. With *Tree Construction (281)* you'd do something similar, taking all the item name tokens into a single list and then ignoring the token types when processing the tree.

28.2 When to Use It

Alternative Tokenization is relevant when you are using *Syntax-Directed Translation (219)* with tokenization separated from syntactic analysis—which is the common case. You need to consider it when you have a section of special text that shouldn't be tokenized using your usual scheme.

Common cases for Alternative Tokenization include: keywords that shouldn't be recognized as keywords in a particular context, allowing any form of text (typically for prose descriptions), and *Foreign Code (309)*.

Chapter 29

Nested Operator Expression

An operator expression that can recursively contain the same form of expression (for example, arithmetic and Boolean expressions).

$$2 * (4 + 5)$$

Calling Nested Operator Expression a pattern is a bit of a stretch, since it isn't so much a solution as it is a common problem in parsing. This is particularly the case with bottom-up parsers where you need to avoid left recursion.

29.1 How It Works

Nested Operator Expressions have two aspects that can make them a bit tricky—their recursive nature (the rule appears in its own body) and sorting out precedence. Exactly how to deal with these depends in part on the particular *Parser Generator (269)* you are using, but there are some useful general principles that apply. The biggest difference lies in how bottom-up and top-down parsers work with them.

My example problem is a calculator that can handle four common arithmetic operations (+ - * /), parenthesized groups, as well as raising to a power (using "**") and taking a root (using "//"). It also allows a unary minus—referring to a negative number with a minus sign.

This choice of operators means we want several levels of precedence. Unary minus binds tightest, followed by power and root, then multiplication and division, and finally addition and subtraction. I've introduced power and root into the problem as they are right-associative operators while the other binary operators are left-associative.

29.1.1 Using Bottom-Up Parsers

I'll start with bottom-up parsers, because they are the easiest to describe. The basic grammar to handle four-function arithmetic expressions with parentheses looks like this:

```
expr ::=
    NUMBER:n {: RESULT = new Double(n); :}
  | expr:a PLUS expr:b   {: RESULT = a + b; :}
  | expr:a MINUS expr:b  {: RESULT = a - b; :}
  | expr:a TIMES expr:b  {: RESULT = a * b; :}
  | expr:a DIVIDE expr:b {: RESULT = a / b; :}
  | expr:a POWER expr:b  {: RESULT = Math.pow(a,b); :}
  | expr:a ROOT expr:b   {: RESULT = Math.pow(a,(1.0/b)); :}
  | MINUS expr:e         {: RESULT = - e; :}  %prec UMINUS
  | LPAREN expr:e RPAREN {: RESULT = e; :}
  ;
```

This grammar uses the Java CUP *Parser Generator (269)*, which is essentially a version of the classic Yacc system for Java. The grammar captures the structure of expression syntax in a single production rule, with one alternative for each kind of operator we need to work with, together with the base case where there's just a number present.

Unlike ANTLR, my usual choice for examples in this book, you can't put literal tokens into the grammar file, which is why I have token names like PLUS rather than +. A separate lexer translates the operators and numbers into the form that the parser needs.

I'm using *Embedded Interpretation (305)* here to do the calculation, so you see the resulting calculations following each alternative in the code actions. (Code actions are delimited with {: and :} to make it easier to deal with curlies in the code action.) The special variable RESULT is used for the return value; rule elements are labeled with a trailing :label.

The basic grammar rules handle the recursive structure quite directly, but they don't handle precedence: we want 1 + 2 * 3 to be interpreted as 1 + (2 * 3). To do this, I can use a set of precedence declarations.

```
precedence left PLUS, MINUS;
precedence left TIMES, DIVIDE;
precedence right POWER, ROOT;
precedence left UMINUS;
```

Each precedence statement lists some operators at the same precedence level and says how they associate (left or right). The precedence goes from low to high.

The precedence can also be mentioned in the grammar rules, as it is in the unary minus case with %prec UNMINUS. The UMINUS is a token reference that isn't a real token; it's only used to adjust the precedence of that rule. By using this context-dependent precedence, I'm instructing the Parser Generator that this rule doesn't use the default precedence for the "-" operator, but uses the precedence declared for the ghostly UMINUS operator instead.

In programming language terms, the problem that precedence solves is that of ambiguity. Without the precedence rules, a parser with this grammar could parse 1 + 2 * 3 as (1 + 2) * 3 or as 1 + (2 * 3), which makes it ambiguous. The same is true for 1 + 2 + 3 even though we (humans) know it doesn't matter in this case. This is why we have to state the direction of associativity as well, even though it doesn't matter for "+" and "*".

The combination of a simple recursive grammar rule and precedence declarations makes it very easy to handle nested expressions in a bottom-up parser.

29.1.2 Top-Down Parsers

Top-down parsers are more complicated when it comes to Nested Operator Expression. You can't use a simple recursive grammar because it would introduce left recursion. As a result, you have to use a series of different grammar rules, which both solves the left recursion problem and handles precedence at the same time. The resulting grammar, however, is much less clear. Indeed, this lack of clarity is why many people prefer a bottom-up parser.

Let's look at these rules with ANTLR. I'll start with the two top-level rules, which introduce the two operators at the lowest precedence level. For a pure parse, they would look like this:

```
expression : mult_exp ( ('+' | '-') mult_exp )* ;
```

```
mult_exp : power_exp ( ('*' | '/') power_exp )* ;
```

Here you see the pattern for left-associative operators. The body of the rule starts with a reference to the next lowest rule, followed by a repeating group with the operators and right-hand sides. At all times, I mention the next-lowest rule rather than the rule I'm in.

The power and root operators show the pattern for a right-associative operator.

```
power_exp : unary_exp ( ('**' | '//') power_exp )? ;
```

Notice a couple of differences here that make it right-associative. First, the right-hand side rule is a recursive reference to the rule itself, rather than the next lower rule. Second, instead of a repeating group, it's just an optional group. The recursion allows multiple power expressions to be combined together, and the right recursion like this is inherently right-associative.

Unary expressions need to support an optional minus sign.

```
unary_exp
  : '-' unary_exp
  | factor_exp
  ;
```

29: Nested Operator Expression

Notice how I use recursion when the sign is present (to allow multiple minus signs in an expression) but the next lower when it isn't (to avoid left recursion).

Now we get to the lowest level, the atoms of the language (in this case just numbers) and parentheses.

```
factor_exp : NUMBER | par_exp ;

par_exp : '(' expression ')' ;
```

Parenthetic expressions introduce deep recursion as they reference the top-level expression again.

(An ANTLR-specific note: ANTLR can get confused if your grammar only has these rules, as there's no top-level rule that isn't called by other rules (it gives a "no start rule" error message). So you have to add something like prog : expression;.)

As you can see, this is much more complicated than the bottom-up case. You're spending your time massaging the *Parser Generator (269)* rather than expressing intent. The resulting mangled grammars are why many people prefer bottom-up Parser Generators to top-down ones. Advocates of top-down parsing argue that it's only nested expressions that get thus mangled, and that's a worthwhile tradeoff compared to the other problems with bottom-up parsers.

Another consequence of this mangled grammar is that the resulting parse tree is more complicated. You would expect the parse tree for 1 + 2 to look something like:

```
+
  1
  2
```

But instead it looks like:

```
+
  mult_exp
    power_exp
      unary_exp
        factor_exp
          1
  mult_exp
    power_exp
      unary_exp
        factor_exp
          2
```

All the grammar rules for precedence add a lot of clutter nodes to the parse tree. This isn't a huge deal in practice; you need to write code to handle these nodes for the cases when they're useful, but sometimes they are just irritating.

The grammars I've just shown are pure grammars that don't involve any output production. Doing something with the parsing often introduces some additional mangling. To replicate the calculator *Embedded Interpretation (305)*, the top-level rule looks like this:

```
expression returns [double result]
 : a=mult_exp {$result = $a.result;}
   ( '+' b=mult_exp {$result += $b.result;}
   | '-' b=mult_exp {$result -= $b.result;}
   )*
 ;
```

Here, the interplay of code actions and grammar is more involved than I usually like. Since we can have any number of terms at this level (e.g., 1 + 2 + 3 + 4) I need to declare an accumulating variable at the beginning of the expression and accumulate values within the repeating group. Furthermore, since I need to do something different depending on whether it's a plus or minus, I need to widen the alternative—that is, going from ('+'|'-') mult_exp to ('+' mult_exp | '-' mult_exp). This introduces some duplication, but this is often the case once you actually do something with your grammar. *Tree Construction (281)* often reduces this problem, but even so you might want to return a different type of node for plus and minus, which would require widening the alternative.

The examples I've shown above are all using ANTLR, as it's the top-down parser that you're likely to come across. Different top-down parsers have slightly different problems and solutions. Usually they will have documentation on how to deal with left recursion.

29: Nested Operator Expression

29.2 When to Use It

As I indicated earlier, Nested Operator Expression doesn't quite fit my usual description of a pattern, and if I were a better writer I would do something better than include it here as one. As a consequence, this "when to use it" section only serves to flaunt a fixation with consistency which isn't usually something I'm known for.

Chapter 30

Newline Separators

Use newlines as statement separators.

```
first statement
second statement
third statement
```

30.1 How It Works

Using newlines to mark the end of a statement is a common feature of program-ming languages. This fits very well with *Delimiter-Directed Translation (201)* since newlines are used as the main delimiter to break up the input. As a result I have nothing to add here for that context.

With *Syntax-Directed Translation (219)*, however, newline separators are rather more tricky, introducing a number of subtle traps that can trip you up. This section will hopefully point out of few of those traps.

(Of course it's possible to use newlines for a syntactic purpose other than statement separation—but I've yet to come across it.)

The reason that newline separators and Syntax-Directed Translation don't go together too well is that newlines play two roles when you use them as separators. Apart from their syntactic role, they also play a formatting role in providing vertical space. As a result, they can appear in spaces where you wouldn't expect a statement separator to pop up.

Here's what I might think of as the obvious grammar for using line endings as separators:

```
catalog   : statement*;
statement : 'item' ID EOL;

EOL : '\r'? '\n';
ID  : ('a'..'z' | 'A'..'Z' | '0'..'9' | '_' )+;
WS  : (' ' |'\t' )+ {$channel = HIDDEN;} ;
```

333

This grammar captures a simple list of items where each line is the keyword item followed by an identifier of the item. I've got into the habit of using this grammar as my "Hello World" example for parsing, as it's drop-dead simple. This grammar is easy to follow—keyword, identifier, newline—but there are a number of common cases that will trip it up:

- Blank lines in between statements

- Blank lines before the first statement

- Blank lines after the last statement

- Last statement on last line has no end-of-line

The first three above are all blank lines, but they may need different ways of handling them in the grammar, so should all be tested. Making sure you have tests for these cases is probably the most important thing to do. I've got some solutions for these problems below, but the good tests are the key to ensuring that the situations are covered properly.

One way of handling blank lines effectively is to use an end-of-statement rule that matches multiple newlines. The logical place to put this rule is in the lexer, since it's a regular rule (I'm using "regular" here in the language theory sense of the word, meaning I can use a regex to match it). This is somewhat complicated by that last test—where the last line of the file is a statement with a missing end-of-line. To handle that case you need to match the end-of-file character in the lexer, which, depending on your *Parser Generator (269)*, may not be possible. So in ANTLR, to do this I need an end-of-statement rule in the parser grammar.

```
catalog    : verticalSpace statement*;
statement : 'item' ID eos;
verticalSpace : EOL*;
eos : EOL+ | EOF;
```

A missing end-of-line on the last line is often an awkward case. How awkward depends on how the Parser Generator deals with an end-of-file. ANTLR makes it available to the parser as a token, which is why I can match it in the parser rules (and not in the lexer rules). Others make matching an end-of-file very hard or impossible. One option to consider is forcing an end-of-line at the end—either through the lexer (if you can) or perhaps by prelexing. Forcing a final end-of-line can help avoid a few awkward corner cases.

Another approach to dealing with statement terminators—one that avoids the general problem of a missing final terminator—is to think of them as separators instead of terminators. This leads to a rule of this form:

```
catalog : verticalSpace statement (separator statement)* verticalSpace;
statement : 'item' ID;
separator : EOL+;
verticalSpace : EOL*;
```

I've come to prefer this style. Instead of defining an extra verticalSpace rule, I can use separator?.

A third alternative is to think of a statement body as an optional element for each line of the catalog.

```
catalog : line* ;
line : EOL | statement EOF | statement EOL;
statement : 'item' ID;
```

This rule needs to match the end-of-file explicitly in order to handle the missing last end-of-line case. If you can't match the end-of-file, you need something like:

```
catalog : line* statement?;
line : statement? EOL;
statement : 'item' ID;
```

which doesn't read as clearly to me, but also doesn't need the end-of-file matching.

A separate element that can also cause a lot of trouble with newline separators is comments. Comments that match up to the end-of-line are very useful. When you are ignoring newlines, you can easily match comments in such a way that eats the newline (although that can trip you up if there's a final line that's a comment with a missing end-of-line). When you are using newline separators, however, eating a newline can be a real problem since comments often appear at the end of a statement, like this:

```
item laser # explain something
```

If the comment matching eats the newline, then you'll lose the statement terminator too.

It's usually easy to avoid this problem by using an expression like this:

```
COMMENT : '#' ~'\n'* {skip();};
```

which in classical regex terms looks like this:

```
Comment = #[^\n]*
```

A final issue to bear in mind is to provide some form of continuation character for lines that get too long. This is easily handled with a lexer rule like this:

```
CONTINUATION : '&' WS* EOL {skip();};
```

30.2 When to Use It

Deciding to use newline separators is really a pair of decisions: deciding to have statement separators and then deciding to use newlines as the separator character.

The limited structure of a DSL often means that you can live without statement separators. The parser can usually figure out the context of the parse from the

30: Newline
Separators

various keywords you use. As an example, the introductory grammar for Miss Grant's controller doesn't use any statement separators, yet parses quite easily.

Statement separators can make it easier to localize, and thus find, errors. In order for the parser to localize errors it needs some kind of checkpointing marker to tell where it's supposed to be in the parse. Without checkpointing, an error in one line of the script may not be apparent to the parser until several lines later, leading to confusing error messages. Statement separators can often fulfill this role. (Although they are not the only mechanism that can do this; keywords often do this too.)

If you've decided to use statement separators, the choice is between a visible character, such as a semicolon, and a newline. The nice thing about using newlines is that most of the time, you have one statement per line anyway, so using a newline separator doesn't add any syntactic noise to the DSL. This is particularly valuable when working with nonprogrammers, although many programmers (including myself) prefer newline separators as well. The downside with newline separators is that *Syntax-Directed Translation (219)* is made more finicky and you have to use the techniques I've described here. You also need to ensure you have tests to cover the common problem cases. On the whole, however, I still prefer to use newlines rather than a visible statement separator.

Chapter 31

External DSL Miscellany

At the point in time that I'm writing this chapter, I'm very conscious about how long I've spent on this book. As with writing software, there is a point at which you have to cut scope in order to ship your software, and the same is true of book writing—although the bounds of the decision are somewhat different.

This tradeoff is particularly apparent to me in writing about external DSLs. There is a host of topics that are worth further investigation and writing. These are all interesting topics, and probably useful to a reader of this book. But each topic takes time to research and thus delays the book appearing at all, so I felt I needed to leave them unexplored. Despite this, however, I do have some incomplete but hopefully useful thoughts that I felt I could collect here. (Miscellany is, after all, just a fancy sounding name for hodgepodge.)

Remember that my thoughts here are more preliminary than much of the other material in this book. By definition, these are all topics that I haven't done enough work on to merit a proper treatment.

31.1 Syntactic Indentation

In many languages, there is a strong hierarchic structure of elements. This structure is often encoded through some kind of nested block. So we might describe Europe's structure using a syntax like this:

```
Europe {
  Denmark
  France
  Great Britain {
    England
    Scotland
    #...
  }
  #...
}
```

That example shows a common way in which programmers of all stripes indicate the hierarchic structure of their programs. The syntactic information about the structure is contained between delimiters, in this case the curly brackets. However, when you read the structure, you pay more attention to the formatting. The primary form of structure that we read comes from the indentation, not from the delimiters. As a true-blooded Englishman, I might prefer to format the above list like:

```
Europe {
  Denmark
  France
Great Britain {
  England
  Scotland
  }
}
```

Here the indentation is misleading, as it does not match the actual structure shown by the curly brackets. (Although it is informative, as it shows a common British view of the world.)

Since we mostly read structure through indentation, there's an argument that we should use the indentation to actually show the structure. In this case, I can write my European structure like this:

```
Europe
  Denmark
  France
  Great Britain
    England
    Scotland
```

In this way, the indentation defines the structure as well as communicates it to the eye. This approach is most famously used by the Python programming language, it's also used by YAML—a language for describing data structures.

In terms of usability, the great advantage of syntactic indentation is that the definition and the eye are always in sync—you can't mislead yourself by altering the formatting without changing the real structure. (Text editors that do automatic formatting remove much of that advantage, but DSLs are less likely to have that kind of support.)

If you use syntactic indentation, be very careful about the interplay between tabs and spaces. Since tab widths vary depending on how you set the editor, mixing tabs and spaces in a file can cause no end of confusion. My recommendation is to follow the approach of YAML and forbid tabs from any language that uses syntactic indentation. Any inconvenience you'll suffer from not allowing tabs will be much less than the confusion you avoid.

Syntactic indentation is very convenient to use, but presents some real difficulties in parsing. I spent some time looking at Python and YAML parsers and saw plenty of complexity due to the syntactic indentation.

The parsers I looked at handled syntactic indentation in the lexer, since the lexer is the part of a *Syntax-Directed Translation (219)* system that deals with characters. (*Delimiter-Directed Translation (201)* is probably not a good companion for syntactic indentation, since syntactic indentation is all about the kind of counting of the block structure that Delimiter-Directed Translation has problems with.)

A common, and I think effective, tactic is to get the lexer to output special "indent" and "dedent" tokens to the parser when it detects an indentation change. Using these imaginary tokens allows you to write the parser using normal techniques for handling blocks—you just use "indent" and "dedent" instead of { and }. Doing this in a conventional lexer, however, is somewhere between hard and impossible. Detecting indentation changes isn't something that lexers are designed to do, nor are they usually designed to emit imaginary tokens that don't correspond to particular characters in the input text. As a result, you'll probably end up having to write a custom lexer. (Although ANTLR can do this, take a look at Parr's advice for handling Python [parr-antlr].)

Another plausible approach—one that I'd certainly be inclined to try—is to preprocess the input text before it hits the lexer. This preprocessing would only focus on the task of recognizing indentation changes and would insert special textual markers into the text when it finds them. These markers can then be recognized by the lexer in the usual way. You have to pick markers that aren't going to clash with anything in the language. You also have to cope with how this may interfere with diagnostics that tell you the line and column numbers. But this approach will greatly simplify the lexing of syntactic indentation.

> 31: External DSL
> Miscellany

31.2 Modular Grammars

DSLs are the better the more limited they are. Limited expressiveness keeps them easy to understand, use, and process. One of the biggest dangers with a DSL is the desire to add expressiveness—leading to the trap of the language inadvertently becoming general-purpose.

In order to avoid that trap, it's useful to be able to combine independent DSLs. Doing this requires independently parsing the different pieces. If you're using *Syntax-Directed Translation (219)*, this means using separate grammars for different DSLs but being able to weave these grammars into a single overall parser. You want to be able to reference a different grammar from your grammar, so that if that referenced grammar changes you don't need to change your own grammar. Modular grammars would allow you to use reusable grammars in the same way that we currently use reusable libraries.

Modular grammars, however useful for DSL work, are not a well-understood area in the language world. There are some people exploring this topic, but nothing that's really mature as I write this.

Most *Parser Generators (269)* use a separate lexer, which further complicates using modular grammars since a different grammar will usually need a different lexer than the parent grammar. You can work around this by using *Alternative Tokenization (319)*, but that places constraints on how the child grammar can fit in with the parent. There's currently a growing feeling that scannerless parsers—those which don't separate lexical and syntactic analysis—may be more applicable to modular grammars.

For the moment, the simplest way of dealing with separate languages is to treat them as *Foreign Code (309)*, pulling the text of the child language into a buffer and then parsing that buffer separately.

Part IV

Internal DSL Topics

Chapter 32

Expression Builder

An object, or family of objects, that provides a fluent interface
over a normal command-query API.

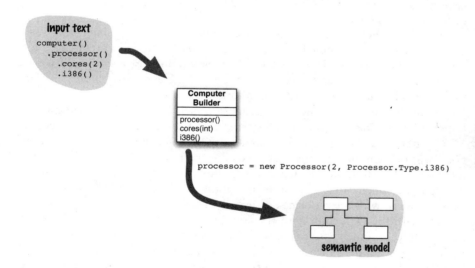

APIs are usually designed to provide a set of self-standing methods on objects. Ideally, these methods can be understood individually. I call this style of API a **command-query API**; it's so normal that we don't have a general name for it. DSLs require a different kind of API, what I call a **fluent interface**, which is designed with the goal of readability of a whole expression. Fluent interfaces lead to methods that make little sense individually, and often violate the rules for good command-query APIs.

An Expression Builder provides a fluent interface as a separate layer on top of a regular API. This way you have both styles of interface and the fluent interface is clearly isolated, making it easier to follow.

32.1 How It Works

An Expression Builder is an object that provides a fluent interface which it then translates into calls on an underlying command-query API. You can think of it as a translation layer that translates the fluent interface into the command-query API. An Expression Builder is often a *Composite* [GoF] using child Expression Builders to build subexpressions within an overall clause.

Exactly how you arrange Expression Builders depends very much of the kind of clause you are dealing with. *Method Chaining (373)* is a sequence of method calls, each returning an Expression Builder; *Nested Function (357)* may use an Expression Builder that is a superclass or a set of global functions. As a result, I can't really give any general rules for what an Expression Builder looks like in this pattern—you need to look at the different kinds of Expression Builders shown in the other internal DSL patterns. What I can do is talk a little about some general guidelines that I think will help you put together a clear layer of Expression Builders.

One of the most notable questions is whether to have a single Expression Builder object for the whole DSL, or whether to use multiple Expression Builders for different parts of the DSL. Multiple Expression Builders usually follow a tree structure that really is a syntax tree for the DSL. The more complex the DSL, the more valuable a tree of Expression Builders is.

One of the most useful tips for getting a clearly separated set of Expression Builders is to ensure you have a well-defined *Semantic Model (159)*. The Semantic Model should have objects with command-query interfaces that can be manipulated without any fluent constructs. You can verify this by being able to write tests for the Semantic Model that don't use any DSLs. It may not be wise to force this rule too much; after all, the whole point of an internal DSL is to make it easier to work with these objects, so usually it will be easier to manipulate them in tests with the DSL than with the command-query interface. But I'd usually include at least some tests that only use the command-query interface.

Expression Builders then can act on top of these model objects. You should be able to test the Expression Builders by comparing the Semantic Model objects they manipulate, using direct calls to the Semantic Model command-query APIs.

32.2 When to Use It

I consider Expression Builder a default pattern—meaning I tend to use it pretty much all the time unless there's a good reason not to.

This, of course, begs the question of when are there occasions when Expression Builder isn't a good idea?

The alternative to using an Expression Builder is to put the fluent methods on the *Semantic Model (159)* itself. The main reason I dislike this is that it intermingles the API for building the Semantic Model with the methods that run the model. Usually, each of these two aspects is quite involved. The Semantic Model execution logic often requires an effort to understand, particularly if it represents an alternative computational model. Fluent interfaces have their own logic to maintain flow. So my argument for an Expression Builder boils down to a separation of concerns. It's easier to understand if we separate building logic from execution logic.

A further reason to separate is that a fluent interface is unusual. Mixing both fluent and command-query methods on the same class intermingles two different ways of representing an API. The fact that fluent APIs are rarer, and thus developers are less familiar with them, exacerbates the situation.

The best argument I see for not using Expression Builder is when the execution logic on the Semantic Model is pretty simple, so that mixing it into the building logic doesn't really add any complexity.

It is, however, pretty frequent to combine the two. This occurs partly because some people aren't aware of Expression Builder, and partly because people don't feel that the additional classes for an Expression Builder are worthwhile. I prefer lots of little classes to a few big classes, so my fundamental design philosophy encourages me to use Expression Builder.

32.3 A Fluent Calendar with and without a Builder (Java)

32: Expression Builder

To explore how an Expression Builder works, I'll explore building up an event calendar with and without a builder. Essentially, I want to add events to a calendar with a DSL like this:

```
cal = new Calendar();
cal.add("DSL tutorial")
  .on(2009, 11, 8)
  .from("09:00")
  .to("16:00")
  .at ("Aarhus Music Hall")
  ;

cal.add("Making use of Patterns")
  .on(2009, 10, 5)
  .from("14:15")
  .to("15:45")
  .at("Aarhus Music Hall")
  ;
```

To do this, I'm creating fluent interfaces for the calendar and event classes.

```
class Calendar...
  private List<Event> events = new ArrayList<Event>();
  public Event add(String name) {
    Event newEvent = new Event(name);
    events.add(newEvent);
    return newEvent;
  }

class Event...
  private String name, location;
  private LocalDate date;
  private LocalTime startTime, endTime;

  public Event(String name) {
    this.name = name;
  }
  public Event on(int year, int month, int day) {
    this.date = new LocalDate(year, month, day);
    return this;
  }
  public Event from (String startTime) {
    this.startTime =parseTime(startTime);
    return this;
  }
  public Event to (String endTime) {
    this.endTime = parseTime(endTime);
    return this;
  }
  private LocalTime parseTime(String time) {
    final DateTimeFormatter fmt = ISODateTimeFormat.hourMinute();
    return new LocalTime(fmt.parseDateTime(time));
  }
  public Event at(String location) {
    this.location = location;
    return this;
  }
```

(The built-in date and time classes in Java are worse than awful, so I'm using JodaTime here, which is very usable.)

This is a nice interface for building up these things, but the style of interface is different to what most people expect for an object. The methods look somewhat odd next to methods like getStartTime() or contains(LocalDateTime). This is particularly so if you want people to be able to change an event outside the DSL context. In this case, you'll need to provide regular command-query mutators, such as setStartTime, as well. (Using a fluent interface outside its context would lead to hard-to-read code.)

The basic idea of an Expression Builder is to move these fluent methods onto a separate builder class that uses regular command-query methods on the domain classes.

```
class CalendarBuilder...
  private Calendar content = new Calendar();

  public CalendarBuilder add(String name) {
    content.addEvent(new Event());
    getCurrentEvent().setName(name);
    return this;
  }
  private Event getCurrentEvent() {
    return content.getEvents().get(content.getEvents().size() - 1);
  }
  public CalendarBuilder on(int year, int month, int day) {
    getCurrentEvent().setDate(new LocalDate(year, month, day));
    return this;
  }
  public CalendarBuilder from(String startTime) {
    getCurrentEvent().setStartTime(parseTime(startTime));
    return this;
  }
  public CalendarBuilder to(String startTime) {
    getCurrentEvent().setEndTime(parseTime(startTime));
    return this;
  }
  private LocalTime parseTime(String startTime) {
    final DateTimeFormatter fmt = ISODateTimeFormat.hourMinute();
    return new LocalTime(fmt.parseDateTime(startTime));
  }
  public CalendarBuilder at (String location) {
    getCurrentEvent().setLocation(location);
    return this;
  }
```

This makes using the DSL a little different.

```
CalendarBuilder builder = new CalendarBuilder();
builder
  .add("DSL tutorial")
    .on (2009, 11, 8)
    .from("09:00")
    .to  ("16:00")
    .at  ("Aarhus Music Hall")
  .add("Making use of Patterns")
    .on (2009, 10, 5)
    .from("14:15")
    .to  ("15:45")
    .at  ("Aarhus Music Hall")
  ;
calendar = builder.getContent();

class CalendarBuilder...
  public Calendar getContent() {
    return content;
  }
```

32: Expression
Builder

32.4 Using Multiple Builders for the Calendar (Java)

Here's an absurdly simple version of using multiple builders with the same Calendar example. To motivate this, let's assume that an event is immutable and all its data has to be created in a constructor. It's a stretch, but it saves me having to make up another example.

With this, I need to capture the data for an event as I build up the fluent expression. I could do this with fields in the calendar builder (e.g., currentEventStartTime) but it seems better to make an event builder to do this (essentially, using a *Construction Builder (179)*).

The DSL script is just the same as with a single object builder.

```
CalendarBuilder builder = new CalendarBuilder();
builder
  .add("DSL tutorial")
    .on  (2009, 11, 8)
    .from("09:00")
    .to  ("16:00")
    .at  ("Aarhus Music Hall")
  .add("Making use of Patterns")
    .on  (2009, 10, 5)
    .from("14:15")
    .to  ("15:45")
    .at  ("Aarhus Music Hall")
    ;
calendar = builder.getContent();
```

32: Expression
Builder

The calendar builder is different in that it stores a list of event builders, and add returns an event builder.

```
class CalendarBuilder...
  private List<EventBuilder> events = new ArrayList<EventBuilder>();

  public EventBuilder add(String name) {
    EventBuilder child = new EventBuilder(this);
    events.add(child);
    child.setName(name);
    return child;
  }
```

The event builder captures the data about an event in its own fields using the fluent interface.

```
class EventBuilder...
  private CalendarBuilder parent;

  private String name, location;
  private LocalDate date;
  private LocalTime startTime, endTime;

  public EventBuilder(CalendarBuilder parent) {
    this.parent = parent;
  }
  public void setName(String arg) {
    name = arg;
  }
  public EventBuilder on(int year, int month, int day) {
    date = new LocalDate(year, month, day);
    return this;
  }
  public EventBuilder from(String startTime) {
    this.startTime = parseTime(startTime);
    return this;
  }
  public EventBuilder to(String endTime) {
    this.endTime = parseTime(endTime);
    return this;
  }
  private LocalTime parseTime(String startTime) {
    final DateTimeFormatter fmt = ISODateTimeFormat.hourMinute();
    return new LocalTime(fmt.parseDateTime(startTime));
  }
  public EventBuilder at (String location) {
    this.location = location;
    return this;
```

32: Expression
Builder

The add method indicates punctuation for the next event. Since the event builder
will receive this call, it needs a method for it, which it delegates to its parent to
build the new event builder.

```
class EventBuilder...
  public EventBuilder add(String name) {
    return parent.add(name);
  }
```

When the builder is asked for its content, it creates the whole structure of
Semantic Model (159) objects.

```
class CalendarBuilder...
  public Calendar getContent() {
    Calendar result = new Calendar();
    for (EventBuilder e : events)
      result.addEvent(e.getContent());
    return result;
  }
```

```
class EventBuilder...
  public Event getContent() {
    return new Event(name, location, date, startTime, endTime);
  }
```

In Java, a variation on this scheme is to make the child builder an inner class of the parent. With this approach, you don't need the parent field. (For examples in this book I've not done this, as I feel this gets a bit too far into Java's idiosyncrasies for a multilanguage book.)

Chapter 33

Function Sequence

A combination of function calls as a sequence of statements.

```
computer();
  processor();
    cores(2);
    speed(2500);
    i386();
  disk();
    size(150);
  disk();
    size(75);
    speed(7200);
    sata();
```

33.1 How It Works

Function Sequence produces a series of calls, unrelated to each other except ordered in a sequence in time; most importantly, there is no data relationship between them. As a result, any relationship between the calls needs to be done through the parsing data, so a heavy use of Function Sequence means you use a lot of *Context Variables (175)*.

To use Function Sequence in a readable way, you usually want bare function calls. The most obvious way to do this is to use global function calls, if your language allows it. This, however, brings two main disadvantages: static parsing data and the fact that the functions are global.

The problem with global functions is that they are visible everywhere. If your language has some kind of namespacing construct, you can (and should) use that to reduce the scope of the function calls to the *Expression Builder (343)*. A particular mechanism to handle this in Java is static import. If your language doesn't support any global function mechanism at all (such as C# and pre-1.5 Java), then

351

you'll need to use explicit class methods to handle the calls. This often adds noise to the DSL.

Global visibility is an obvious disadvantage to global functions, but often the most annoying problem is that they force you to use static data. Static data is often a problem because you can never be entirely sure who is using it—particularly with multithreading. This problem is particularly pernicious with Function Sequence because you need a lot of Context Variables to make it work.

A good solution for both globally visible functions and static parsing data is *Object Scoping (385)*. This allows you to host the functions in a class in the natural object-oriented way and gives you an object to put the parsing data into. As a result, I suggest using Object Scoping if you are using Function Sequence in all but the very simplest cases.

33.2 When to Use It

On the whole, Function Sequence is the least useful of the function call combinations to use for DSLs. Using *Context Variables (175)* to keep track of where you are in a parse is always awkward, leading to code that's hard to understand and easy to get wrong.

Despite this, there are times when you need to use Function Sequence. Often, a DSL involves multiple high-level statements; in this case, a list of statements often makes sense as a Function Sequence as you only need a single result list and Context Variable to keep track of things. So, Function Sequence is a reasonable option at the top level of a language, or at the top level inside a *Nested Closure (403)*. However, below that top level of statements, you want to form expressions using *Nested Function (357)* or *Method Chaining (373)*.

Perhaps the biggest reason to use Function Sequence is that you always have to start your DSL with something, and that something has to be a Function Sequence even if there's only one call in the sequence. This is because all the other function call techniques require some kind of context. Of course, one can argue about whether a sequence with a single element is really a sequence, but that seems the best way to fit it into the conceptual framework I'm using.

A simple Function Sequence is a list of elements, so the obvious alternative is to use a *Literal List (417)*.

33.3 Simple Computer Configuration (Java)

Here is the recurring computer configuration example as a DSL with Function Sequence:

```
computer();
  processor();
    cores(2);
    speed(2500);
    i386();
  disk();
    size(150);
  disk();
    size(75);
    speed(7200);
    sata();
```

Although I've indented the code to suggest the structure of the configuration, that's just arbitrary use of whitespace. The script is really just a sequence of function calls with no deeper relationship between them. The deeper relationship is built up entirely using *Context Variables (175)*.

Function Sequence uses top-level function calls, which I have to resolve in some way. I could use static methods and global state—but I hope that would offend your design taste too much for me to get away with it. So instead I use *Object Scoping (385)*. This does mean that the script has to be kept in a subclass of the computer builder, but that's well worth it to avoid using globals.

The builder contains two types of data: the content of processors and disks that it's building up, and Context Variables to indicate what it's currently working on.

```
class ComputerBuilder...
  private ProcessorBuilder processor;
  private List<DiskBuilder> disks = new ArrayList<DiskBuilder>();

  private ProcessorBuilder currentProcessor;
  private DiskBuilder currentDisk;
```

I'm using *Construction Builders (179)* to capture the data for the (immutable) *Semantic Model (159)* objects.

The call to computer() clears the Context Variables.

```
class ComputerBuilder...
  void computer() {
    currentDisk = null;
    currentProcessor = null;
  }
```

The calls to processor() and disk() create a value for collecting the data and set the Context Variables to track what the builder is currently working on.

```
class ComputerBuilder...
  void processor() {
    currentProcessor = new ProcessorBuilder();
    processor = currentProcessor;
    currentDisk = null;
  }
```

33: Function
Sequence

```
void disk() {
  currentDisk = new DiskBuilder();
  disks.add(currentDisk);
  currentProcessor = null;
}
```

I can then capture the data into the appropriate source.

```
class ComputerBuilder...
  void cores(int arg) {
    currentProcessor.cores = arg;
  }
  void i386() {
    currentProcessor.type = Processor.Type.i386;
  }
  void size(int arg) {
    currentDisk.size = arg;
  }
  void sata() {
    currentDisk.iface = Disk.Interface.SATA;
  }
```

Specifying the speed is a little more complicated, as the call could refer to either processor or disk speed, depending on the context.

```
class ComputerBuilder...
  void speed(int arg) {
    if (currentProcessor != null)
      currentProcessor.speed = arg;
    else if (currentDisk != null)
      currentDisk.speed = arg;
    else throw new IllegalStateException();
  }
```

33: Function
Sequence

When the builder is done building, it can return the Semantic Model.

```
class ComputerBuilder...
  Computer getValue() {
    return new Computer(processor.getValue(), getDiskValues());
  }
  private Disk[] getDiskValues() {
    Disk[] result = new Disk[disks.size()];
    for(int i = 0; i < disks.size(); i++)
      result[i] = disks.get(i).getValue();
    return result;
  }
```

To hook all this with the script, I need to wrap the script into a subclass of the computer builder.

```java
class ComputerBuilder...
  public Computer run() {
    build();
    return getValue();
  }
  abstract protected void build();

public class Script extends ComputerBuilder {
  protected void build() {
    computer();
      processor();
        cores(2);
        speed(2500);
        i386();
      disk();
        size(150);
      disk();
        size(75);
        speed(7200);
        sata();
  }
}
```

33: Function
Sequence

Chapter 34

Nested Function

Compose functions by nesting function calls as arguments
of other calls.

```
computer(
    processor(
        cores(2),
        speed(2500),
        i386
    ),
    disk(
        size(150)
    ),
    disk(
        size(75),
        speed(7200),
        SATA
    )
);
```

34.1 How It Works

By representing a DSL clause as a Nested Function, you're able to reflect the hierarchic nature of the language in a way that's mirrored in the host language, not just in a formatting convention.

A notable property of Nested Function is the way it affects the evaluation order of its arguments. *Function Sequence (351)* and *Method Chaining (373)* both evaluate the functions in a left-to-right sequence. Nested Function evaluates the arguments of a function before the enclosing function itself. I find this most memorable with the "Old MacDonald" example: To sing the chorus, you type o(i(e(i(e())))). This evaluation order has an impact on both how to use Nested Function and when to choose it instead of alternatives.

Evaluating the enclosing function last can be very handy, in that it provides a built-in context to work with the arguments. Consider defining a computer processor configuration:

```
processor(cores(2), speed(2500),i386())
```

The nice thing here is that the argument functions can return fully formed values which the processor function can then assemble into its return value. Since the processor function evaluates last, we don't need to worry about the stopping problem of Method Chaining, nor do we need to have the *Context Variable (175)* that we need for Function Sequence.

With mandatory elements in the grammar, along the lines of parent::= first second, Nested Function works particularly well. A parent function can define exactly the arguments required in the child functions and, with a statically typed language, can also define the return types, which enables IDE autocompletion.

One issue with function arguments is how to label them so as to make them readable. Consider indicating the size and speed of a disk. The natural programming response is disk(150, 7200) but this isn't terribly readable as there's no indication what the numbers mean, unless you have a language with keyword arguments. A way to deal with this is to use a wrapping function that does nothing other than provide a name: disk(size(150), speed(7200)). In the simplest form of this, the wrapping function just returns the argument value, representing pure syntactic sugar. It also means that there's no enforcement of the meaning of these functions—a call to disk(speed(7200), size(150)) could easily result in a very slow disk. You can avoid this by making the nested functions return intermediate data, such as a builder or token—although that is more effort to set up.

Optional arguments can also present problems. If the base language supports default arguments for functions, you can use these for the optional case. If you don't have this, one approach is to define different functions for each combination of the optional arguments. If you only have a couple of cases, this is tedious but reasonable. As the number of optional arguments increases, so does the tediousness (but not the reasonableness). One way out of this problem is to use intermediate data again—tokens can be a particularly effective choice.

If your language supports it, a *Literal Map (419)* is often a good way out of these quandaries. In this case, you get just the right data structure to deal with the issue. The only problem is that C-like languages don't usually support Literal Map.

With multiple arguments in the same call, a varargs parameter is the best choice if the host language supports it. You can also think of this as a nested *Literal List (417)*. Multiple arguments of different kinds end up being like optional arguments, with the same complications.

The worst case of this is a grammar like parent::= (this | that)*. The issue here is that, unless you have keyword arguments, the only way to identify the arguments is through their position and type. This can make picking out which argument is which messy—and downright impossible if this and that have the same types. Once this happens, you are forced into either returning intermediate results, or using a Context Variable. Using a Context Variable is particularly difficult here since the parent function isn't evaluated till the end, forcing you to use the broader context of the language to properly set up the Context Variable.

In order to keep the DSL readable, you usually want Nested Functions to be bare function calls. This implies you either need to make them global functions, or use *Object Scoping (385)*. Since global functions are problematic, I usually try to use Object Scoping if I can. However, global functions can often be much less problematic in Nested Function, because the biggest problem with global functions is when they come with a global parsing state. A global function that just returns a value, such as a static method like DayOfWeek.MONDAY, is often a good choice.

34.2 When to Use It

One of the great strengths—and weaknesses—of Nested Function is the order of evaluation. With Nested Function, the arguments are evaluated before the parent function (unless you use *Closures (397)* for arguments). This is very useful for building up a hierarchy of values because you can have the arguments create fully formed model objects to be assembled by the parent function. This can avoid much of the mucking about with replacements and intermediate data that you get with *Function Sequence (351)* and *Method Chaining (373)*.

Conversely, this evaluation order causes problems in a sequence of commands, leading to the Old MacDonald problem: o(i(e(i(e())))). So, for a sequence that you want to read left to right, Function Sequence or Method Chaining are usually a better bet. For precise control of when to evaluate multiple arguments, use *Nested Closure (403)*.

Nested Function also often struggles with optional arguments and multiple varied arguments. Nested Function very much expects you to say what you want and in the precise order you want, so if you need greater flexibility you'll need to look to Method Chaining or a *Literal Map (419)*. A Literal Map is often a good choice as it allows you to get the arguments sorted out before calling the parent while giving you the flexibility of ordering and optionality of the arguments, particularly with a hash argument.

Another disadvantage of *Nested Function (357)* is the punctuation, which usually relies on matching brackets and putting commas in the right place. At its worst, this can look like a disfigured Lisp, with all the parentheses and added warts. This is less of an issue for DSLs aimed at programmers, who get more used to these warts.

Name clashes are less of a trouble here than with Function Sequence, since the parent function provides the context to interpret the nested function call. As a

34: Nested
Function

result, you can happily use "speed" for processor speed and disk speed and use the same function as long as the types are compatible.

34.3 The Simple Computer Configuration Example (Java)

Here's the common example of stating the configuration of a simple computer:

```
computer(
  processor(
    cores(2),
    speed(2500),
    i386
  ),
  disk(
    size(150)
  ),
  disk(
    size(75),
    speed(7200),
    SATA
  )
);
```

For this case, each clause in the script returns a *Semantic Model (159)* object, so I can use the nested evaluation order to build up the entire expression without using *Context Variables (175)*. I'll start from the bottom, looking at the processor clause.

```
class Builder...
  static Processor processor(int cores, int speed, Processor.Type type) {
    return new Processor(cores, speed, type);
  }
  static int cores(int value) {
    return value;
  }
  static final Processor.Type i386 = Processor.Type.i386;
```

I've defined the builder elements as static methods and constants on a builder class. By using Java's static import feature, I can use bare calls to use them in the script. (Is it only me who finds it confusing that we call them "static imports" but have to declare them with import static?)

The cores and speed methods are pure syntactic sugar—only there to help readability (particularly if you skipped dessert). I toy with calling something that's pure syntactic sugar a "sucratic" function, but maybe that is a step too far for even my neologizing habits. In this case, the sugar also helps with the disk speed—if they needed different return types this could be a problem, but it isn't in this case.

The disk clause has two optional arguments. Since there's only a couple, I'll nap for a while as I write out the combination of functions.

```
class Builder...
  static Disk disk(int size, int speed, Disk.Interface iface) {
    return new Disk(size, speed, iface);
  }
  static Disk disk(int size) {
    return disk(size, Disk.UNKNOWN_SPEED, null);
  }
  static Disk disk(int size, int speed) {
    return disk(size, speed, null);
  }
  static Disk disk(int size, Disk.Interface iface) {
    return disk(size, Disk.UNKNOWN_SPEED, iface);
  }
```

For the top-level computer clause, I use varargs parameter to handle the multiple disks.

```
class Builder...
  static Computer computer(Processor p, Disk... d) {
    return new Computer(p, d);
  }
```

I'm usually a big fan of using *Object Scoping (385)* to avoid littering the code with global functions and Context Variables. However, with static imports and Nested Function, I can use static elements without introducing global trash.

34: Nested Function

34.4 Handling Multiple Different Arguments with Tokens (C#)

One of the trickier areas to use Nested Function is where you have multiple arguments of different kinds. Consider a language for defining properties of an onscreen box:

```
box(
  topBorder(2),
  bottomBorder(2),
  leftMargin(3),
  transparent
);
box(
  leftMargin(2),
  rightMargin(5)
);
```

In this situation, we can have any number of a wide variety of properties to set. There's no strong reason to force an order in declaring the properties, so the usual style of argument identification in C# (position) doesn't work too well. For this example, I'll explore using tokens to identify the arguments to compose them into the structure.

Here's the target model object:

```
class Box {
  public bool IsTransparent = false;
  public int[] Borders = { 1, 1, 1, 1 }; //TRouBLe - top right bottom left
  public int[] Margins = { 0, 0, 0, 0 }; //TRouBLe - top right bottom left
```

The various contained functions all return the token data type, which looks like this:

```
class BoxToken {
  public enum Types { TopBorder, BottomBorder, LeftMargin, RightMargin, Transparent }
  public readonly Types Type;
  public readonly Object Value;
  public BoxToken(Types type, Object value) {
    Type = type;
    Value = value;
  }
}
```

I'm using *Object Scoping (385)* and define the clauses of the DSL as functions on the builder supertype.

```
class Builder...
  protected BoxToken topBorder(int arg) {
    return new BoxToken(BoxToken.Types.TopBorder, arg);
  }
  protected BoxToken transparent {
    get {
      return new BoxToken(BoxToken.Types.Transparent, true);
    }
  }
}
```

I'm only showing a couple of them, but I'm sure you can deduce from these what the rest look like.

The parent function now just runs through the argument results and assembles a box.

```
class Builder...
  protected void box(params BoxToken[] args) {
    Box newBox = new Box();
    foreach (BoxToken t in args) updateAttribute(newBox, t);
    boxes.Add(newBox);
  }

  List<Box> boxes = new List<Box>();
```

```
private void updateAttribute(Box box, BoxToken token) {
  switch (token.Type) {
    case BoxToken.Types.TopBorder:
      box.Borders[0] = (int)token.Value;
      break;
    case BoxToken.Types.BottomBorder:
      box.Borders[2] = (int)token.Value;
      break;
    case BoxToken.Types.LeftMargin:
      box.Margins[3] = (int)token.Value;
      break;
    case BoxToken.Types.RightMargin:
      box.Margins[1] = (int)token.Value;
      break;
    case BoxToken.Types.Transparent:
      box.IsTransparent = (bool)token.Value;
      break;
    default:
      throw new InvalidOperationException("Unreachable");
  }
}
```

34.5 Using Subtype Tokens for IDE Support (Java)

Most languages differentiate between function arguments by their position. So in the above example, we might set the size and speed of a disk with a function like disk(150, 7200). That bare function isn't too readable, so in the above example I wrapped the numbers with simple functions to get disk(size(150), speed(7200)). In the earlier code example, the functions just return their arguments, which aids readability but doesn't prevent someone typing the erroneous disk(speed(7200), size(150)).

34: Nested Function

Using simple tokens, like in the Box example, provides a mechanism for error checking. By returning a token of [size, 150] you can use the token type to check that you have the right argument in the right position, or indeed make the arguments work in any order.

Checking is all very well, but in a statically typed language with a modern IDE, you want to go further. You want autocompletion popups to force you to put size before speed. By using subclasses, you can pull this off.

In the tokens above, the token type was a property of the token. An alternative is to create a different subtype for each token; I can then use the subtype in the parent function definition.

Here's the short script I want to support:

```
disk(
  size(150),
  speed(7200)
);
```

Here's the target model object:

```java
public class Disk {
  private int size, speed;
  public Disk(int size, int speed) {
    this.size = size;
    this.speed = speed;
  }
  public int getSize() {
    return size;
  }
  public int getSpeed() {
    return speed;
  }
}
```

To handle size and speed, I create a general integer token with subclasses for the two kinds of clauses.

```java
public class IntegerToken {
  private final int value;
  public IntegerToken(int value) {
    this.value = value;
  }
  public int getValue() {
    return value;
  }
}
```

```java
public class SpeedToken extends IntegerToken {
  public SpeedToken(int value) {
    super(value);
  }
}
```

```java
public class SizeToken extends IntegerToken {
  public SizeToken(int value) {
    super(value);
  }
}
```

I can then define static functions in a builder, with the right arguments.

```java
class Builder...
  public static Disk disk(SizeToken size, SpeedToken speed){
    return new Disk(size.getValue(), speed.getValue());
  }
  public static SizeToken size (int arg) {
    return new SizeToken(arg);
  }
  public static SpeedToken speed (int arg) {
    return new SpeedToken(arg);
  }
```

With this setup, the IDE will suggest the right functions in the right places, and I'll see comforting red squigglies should I do any reckless typing.

(Another way to approach adding static typing is to use generics, but I'll leave that as an exercise for the reader.)

34.6 Using Object Initializers (C#)

If you're using C#, then the most natural way to handle a pure hierarchy of data is to use object initializers.

```
new Computer() {
  Processor = new Processor() {
    Cores = 2,
    Speed = 2500,
    Type = ProcessorType.i386
  },
  Disks = new List<Disk>() {
    new Disk() {
      Size = 150
    },
    new Disk() {
      Size = 75,
      Speed = 7200,
      Type = DiskType.SATA
    }
  }
};
```

This can work with a simple set of model classes.

```
class Computer {
  public Processor Processor { get; set; }
  public List<Disk> Disks { get; set; }
}

class Processor {
  public int Cores { get; set; }
  public int Speed { get; set; }
  public ProcessorType Type { get; set; }
}
public enum ProcessorType {i386, amd64}

class Disk {
  public int Speed { get; set; }
  public int Size { get; set; }
  public DiskType Type { get; set; }
}
public enum DiskType {SATA, IDE}
```

34: Nested
Function

You can think of object initializers as Nested Functions that can take keyword arguments (like a *Literal Map (419)*) which are restricted to object construction. You can't use them for everything, but they can come in handy for situations like this.

34.7 Recurring Events (C#)

I used to live in the South End of Boston. There was much to like about living in a downtown area of the city, close to restaurants and other ways to pass the time and spend my money. There were irritations, however, and one of them was street cleaning. On the first and third Monday of the month between April and October, they would clean the streets near my apartment and I had to be sure I didn't leave my car there. Often I forgot and I got a ticket.

The rule for my street was that the cleaning occurred on the first and third Monday of the month between April and October. I could write a DSL expression for this.

```
Schedule.First(DayOfWeek.Monday)
  .And(Schedule.Third(DayOfWeek.Monday))
  .From(Month.April)
  .Till(Month.October);
```

This example combines *Method Chaining (373)* with Nested Function. Usually when I use Nested Function, I prefer to combine it with *Object Scoping (385)*, but in this case the functions that I'm nesting just return a value so I don't really feel a strong need to use Object Scoping.

34.7.1 Semantic Model

Recurring events are a recurring event in software systems. You often want to schedule things on particular combinations of dates. The way I think of them these days is that they are a *Specification* [Evans DDD] of dates. We want code that can tell us if a given date is included on a schedule. We do this by defining a general specification interface—which we can make generic, as specifications are useful in all sorts of situations.

```
internal interface Specification<T> {
  bool Includes(T arg);
}
```

When building a specification model for a particular type, I like to identify small building blocks that I can combine together. One small building block is the notion of a particular period in a year, such as between April and October.

```csharp
internal class PeriodInYear : Specification<DateTime>
{
  private readonly int startMonth;
  private readonly int endMonth;

  public PeriodInYear(int startMonth, int endMonth) {
    this.startMonth = startMonth;
    this.endMonth = endMonth;
  }
  public  bool Includes(DateTime arg) {
    return arg.Month >= startMonth && arg.Month <= endMonth;
  }
}
```

Another element is the notion of the first Monday in the month. This class is a little more tricky as I have to walk through sample dates in the month to see which one is the first.

```csharp
internal class DayInMonth : Specification<DateTime> {
  private readonly int index;
  private readonly DayOfWeek dayOfWeek;

  public DayInMonth(int index, DayOfWeek dayOfWeek) {
    this.index = index;
    this.dayOfWeek = dayOfWeek;
    if (index <= 0) throw new NotSupportedException("index must be positive");
  }

  public bool Includes(DateTime arg) {
    int currentMatch = 0;
    foreach (DateTime d in new MonthEnumerator(arg.Month, arg.Year)) {
      if (d > arg) return false;
      if (d.DayOfWeek == dayOfWeek) {
        currentMatch++;
        if (currentMatch == index) return (d == arg);
      }
    }
    return false;
  }
}
```

To walk through the days in a month, this specification makes use of a special enumerator. I set the enumerator with a particular month and year.

```csharp
internal class MonthEnumerator : IEnumerator<DateTime>, IEnumerable<DateTime> {
  private int year;
  private Month month;

  public MonthEnumerator(int month, int year) {
    this.month = new Month(month);
    this.year = year;
    Reset();
  }
```

34: Nested Function

It implements the IEnumerator methods.

```
class MonthEnumerator...
  private DateTime current;
  DateTime IEnumerator<DateTime>.Current { get { return current; } }
  public object Current { get { return current; } }

  public void Reset() {
    current = new DateTime(year, month.Number, 1).AddDays(-1);
  }

  public void Dispose() {}

  public bool MoveNext() {
    current = current.AddDays(1);
    return month.Includes(current);
  }
```

And also implements IEnumerable to allow it to be used in a for-each loop.

```
class MonthEnumerator...
  IEnumerator<DateTime> IEnumerable<DateTime>.GetEnumerator() {
    return this;
  }
  public IEnumerator GetEnumerator() {
    return this;
  }
```

Finally, we have a very simple Month class, which also acts as a specification.

```
class Month...
  private readonly int number;
  public int Number { get { return number; } }
  public Month(int number) {
    this.number = number;
  }
  public bool Includes(DateTime arg) {
    return number == arg.Month;
  }
```

These are useful building blocks, but they can't do much on their own. To really make them sing and dance, I need to be able to combine them into logical expressions, which I do with a couple more specifications.

```
abstract class CompositeSpecification<T> : Specification<T> {
  protected IList<Specification<T>> elements = new List<Specification<T>>();
  public CompositeSpecification(params Specification<T>[] elements) {
    this.elements = elements;
  }
  public abstract bool Includes(T arg);
}
```

```
internal class AndSpecification<T> : CompositeSpecification<T> {
  public AndSpecification(params Specification<T>[] elements)
    : base(elements) {}
  public override bool Includes(T arg) {

    foreach (Specification<T> s in elements)
      if (! s.Includes(arg)) return false;
    return true;
  }
}

internal class OrSpecification<T> : CompositeSpecification<T> {
  public OrSpecification(params Specification<T>[] elements)
    : base(elements) {}
  public override bool Includes(T arg) {
    foreach (Specification<T> s in elements)
      if (s.Includes(arg)) return true;
    return false;
  }
}
```

I trust you can figure out how to implement a NotSpecfication.

One thing I don't like about this model is my usage of the DateTime class. The problem is that DateTime has subsecond precision, but I'm only working at day precision. Using overprecise temporal data types is very common, because usually libraries push us in that direction. However, they can easily result in awkward bugs when you compare two DateTimes that are different below the level of precision you care about. If I were doing this on a real project, I'd make a proper Date class with the correct precision.

34.7.2 The DSL

Here's the DSL text for my old street cleaning schedule:

```
Schedule.First(DayOfWeek.Monday)
  .And(Schedule.Third(DayOfWeek.Monday))
  .From(Month.April)
  .Till(Month.October);
```

Like most realistic DSLs, it uses a combination of internal DSL techniques, namely a mix of *Method Chaining (373)* and Nested Function. I'm not going to worry too much about the Method Chaining here; instead, I'll concentrate on the way Nested Function is used. Since each Nested Function returns a simple value, I don't have a strong need for *Object Scoping (385)* as they won't require any *Context Variables (175)*. As a result, I'll use static methods. As I'm in C#, all the static methods need to be prefixed with their class name. This reads pretty well, although it does add noise compared to an Object Scoping approach.

34: Nested Function

Two of the Nested Functions are calls to return a simple value. `DayOfWeek.Monday` is actually built into the .NET libraries. I added `Month.April` and friends myself.

```
class Month...
  public static readonly Month January = new Month(1);
  public static readonly Month February = new Month(2);
  // I don't need to show more do I?
```

The calls on `Schedule` are a bit different. The initial use of `Schedule.First` is an example of a common feature in these languages—using a bare function to create a starting object to begin the chaining. `Schedule` here is an *Expression Builder (343)*. It's not called "builder" because I think it reads better as just "schedule."

```
class Schedule...
  public static Schedule First(DayOfWeek dayOfWeek) {
    return new Schedule(new DayInMonth(1, dayOfWeek));
  }
```

Like most Expression Builders, the schedule builds up a content, which is a specification.

```
class Schedule...
  private Specification<DateTime> content;
  public Specification<DateTime> Content { get { return content; } }
  public Schedule(Specification<DateTime> content) {
    this.content = content;
  }
```

Notice how the initial call returns a schedule that wraps the first element in the specification. The later call to `Third` is the same (except for the parameter). I would usually argue against writing different methods for something that would be better handled as a parameter, but this is yet another example where you have different rules of good programming when you use an Expression Builder.

It's the Method Chaining that actually builds up the composite structure. Here's the interestingly named `And` method:

```
class Schedule...
  public Schedule And(Schedule arg) {
    content = new OrSpecification<DateTime>(content, arg.content);
    return this;
  }
```

We say "first and third Monday" in our language, but in terms of the specification, it's the first *or* third Monday that matches the Boolean condition. It's an interesting example of where the DSL is opposite to the model in order for both to read naturally.

The period at the end is similarly assembled using Method Chaining calls.

```
class Schedule...
  public Schedule From(Month m) {
    Debug.Assert(null == periodStart);
    periodStart = m;
    return this;
  }
  public Schedule Till(Month m) {
    Debug.Assert(null != periodStart);
    PeriodInYear period = new PeriodInYear(periodStart.Number, m.Number);
    content = new AndSpecification<DateTime>(content, period);
    return this;
  }
  private Month periodStart;
```

Here I use a Context Variable to properly build up the period.

This example uses simple static methods for the Nested Functions. Would it benefit by getting rid of the class names? I think it would read better to say Monday rather than DayOfWeek.Monday. Object Scoping would provide this at the cost of requiring the inheritance relationship. In Java, I could use static imports. The gain isn't huge but would probably be worthwhile.

34: Nested
Function

Chapter 35

Method Chaining

Make modifier methods return the host object, so that multiple modifiers can be invoked in a single expression.

```
computer()
  .processor()
    .cores(2)
    .speed(2500)
    .i386()
  .disk()
    .size(150)
  .disk()
    .size(75)
    .speed(7200)
    .sata()
  .end();
```

35.1 How It Works

Method Chaining rapidly caught on amongst people as an example of what an internal DSL should look like. It caught on a bit too much—people started to assume that Method Chaining was synonymous with fluent interfaces and internal DSLs. My view is that Method Chaining is one of several techniques, but it's still valuable and noticeable.

   Its common form is on an *Expression Builder (343)*. Consider the hard drive in the sketch. Using a regular command-query API, I might set it up like this:

```
//java...
  HardDrive hd = new HardDrive();
  hd.setCapacity(150);
  hd.setExternal(true);
  hd.setSpeed(7200);
```

I create my object, put it in a variable, and then use setters to manipulate its properties. For just three items like this, I'd be more likely to use a constructor, but let's assume there's many more of them. DSLs are often about building up configurations of objects, and doing so in constructors is often tricky. It's also usually difficult to read, since constructors often allow only positional parameters.

Using Method Chaining, I would do something like this:

```
new HardDrive().capacity(150).external().speed(7200);
```

To make the chain work, methods designed to be used in a chain are implemented differently from the common convention for setter methods. In Java, we usually implement a setter method like this:

```
public void setSpeed(int arg) {
  this.speed = arg;
}
```

But a method designed for use in a chain needs to return an object to continue the chain. For this builder, it needs to return itself.

```
private HardDrive speed(int arg) {
  speed = arg;
  return this;
}
```

Returning a value from a modifying method breaks the principle of command-query separation (p. 70). Most of the time I follow that principle, and it's served me well. A fluent interface is one case when we need to break it.

There's a second consequence of using Method Chaining like this—the naming of the method. In many naming conventions, a method like sata() would seem like a query, not a modifier. This naming is very problematic, as it will seriously confuse anyone who is expecting a command-query API. Taken together, Method Chaining violates many common rules of common (command-query) API design.

Not just does Method Chaining change the rules for API design, it also implies a change to formatting conventions. Usually, we try to keep multiple method calls on a single line, but long Method Chaining often does not look good that way, particularly if we want to suggest a hierarchy. As a result, it's often better to format Method Chaining with each call on its own line.

```
new HardDrive()
    .capacity(150)
    .external()
    .speed(7200);
```

Java and C# ignore most newlines, which gives us a lot of flexibility in formatting. There is a general preference to have the periods at the start of the line, as this makes them more noticeable and thus emphasizes the use of chaining. Languages that use newlines as statement separators are less flexible here. Ruby, for example, will work but you need to have the periods at the ends of the lines rather than the beginnings. Putting methods on separate lines also makes debugging easier, as error messages and debugger control usually work on a line-by-line basis. Therefore, it's wise to do less on each line.

35.1.1 Builders or Values

In the example above, I showed Method Chaining on an *Expression Builder (343)*. I prefer keeping Method Chaining, and other fluent APIs, to Expression Builders since that reduces the confusion between the conventions of fluent and command-query APIs.

However, there are cases where it can be useful to use Method Chaining outside of Expression Builders, for example in something like 42.grams.flour. In this case, we are building up an expression through a sequence of *Value Objects* [Fowler PoEAA]. The grams method is defined on integer (using *Literal Extension (481)*) and returns a quantity object, which is the host for the flour method that returns an ingredient. Instead of having a single Expression Builder, we have a sequence of regular objects. Often, when you see this, the objects are Value Objects.

At each step in the expression we see a change to a new type, a phenomenon that my colleague Neal Ford refers to as **type transmogrification**. (I need to mention that term here, as he'll be upset otherwise and won't bring me good tea anymore.)

There are plenty of good developers who are comfortable with using Method Chaining on domain types like this, so I'm cautious about arguing against it. My inclination, however, leads me to prefer using Expression Builders as much as possible, to clearly separate command-query and fluent API styles.

35: Method
Chaining

35.1.2 Finishing Problem

The finishing problem is a common issue with Method Chaining. It boils down to the lack of a clear end-point to a method chain. Imagine a builder for appointments that allows expressions like:

```
//C#...
  var dentist = new AppointmentBuilder()
    .From(1300)
    .To(1400)
    .For("dentist")
    ;
  var dinner = new AppointmentBuilder()
    .From(1900)
    .To(2100)
    .For("dinner")
    .At("Turners")
    ;
```

I would like the returned value to be an `Appointment` object, since that would be the most natural usage. However, the need to continue the method chain means that each method has to return an appointment builder. There's nothing in the chain that tells me when I'm done, so I have to put in some kind of marker method to show the end.

```
Appointment dentist = new AppointmentBuilder()
  .From(1300)
  .To(1400)
  .For("dentist")
  .End
  ;
```

It isn't too bad, but the use of `End` is still a bit of syntactic noise. This is where using *Nested Function (357)* or *Nested Closure (403)* can be a valuable alternative. In C#, you can avoid it by using an implicit conversion operator, although that does mean you'll forgo `var` for an explicit type.

35.1.3 Hierarchic Structure

Tied in with the finishing problem is the problem that Method Chaining doesn't naturally fit a hierarchic structure. Hierarchic structures are common in languages, which is why syntax trees are valuable for thinking about them. Consider the sketch example again:

```
computer()
  .processor()
    .cores(2)
    .speed(2500)
    .i386()
  .disk()
    .size(150)
  .disk()
    .size(75)
    .speed(7200)
    .sata()
  .end();
```

35: Method
Chaining

There's a definite hierarchy to this, but it's suggested by the indentation and not captured in the structure of the code itself. As a result, we have to manage that structure ourselves. This problem also occurs with *Function Sequence (351)*.

A good example of where we have to do this management is checking if we are manipulating the correct disk when we have a method like size. There are a couple of approaches here. One is to use a *Context Variable (175)*, such as `currentDisk`. Each time we see a `disk` method, we can update the Context Variable. We can keep a list of the disks and update the last one in the list each time.

Often, a useful approach is to have a new child builder for the disk. A separate builder allows us to limit the methods available to only those required to provide the information for the disk or a finishing method.

35.1.4 Progressive Interfaces

A valuable variation to the basic Method Chaining approach is to use multiple interfaces to drive a fixed sequence of method-chaining calls. Let's consider building up an email message. We want the programmer to first specify the destination address, any Cc's, the subject, and then the body. We can do this by presenting a sequence of interfaces to the *Expression Builder (343)*. The first interface has only the to method. The to method returns an interface with only the legal next steps: to, cc, and subject. The cc method returns an interface with only cc and subject. The subject method returns an interface with only the body method.

This can work really well in a statically typed language with IDE support. Autocompletion in the IDE can step you through each clause in the DSL by only suggesting the methods that are valid for that point in the chain.

This ability to control which methods are valid in which contexts is similar to that you get by using a child builder. Indeed, you can use a child builder to do the same thing as progressive interfaces, but progressive interfaces are easier if there's no other reason to make a child builder.

Progressive interfaces can be used to enforce mandatory elements in a chain; for this, define an interface that only takes a single mandatory element.

35.2 When to Use It

Method Chaining can add a great deal to the readability of an internal DSL and, as a result, has become almost a synonym for internal DSLs in some minds. Method Chaining is best, however, when it's used in conjunction with other function combinations.

Method Chaining works best when using optional clauses in a language. Method Chaining easily allows a DSL script writer to pick and choose clauses needed for a particular situation. It's difficult to specify in the language that certain clauses must be present. Using progressive interfaces allows some ordering of clauses, but in the end clauses can always be left out. *Nested Function (357)* is the better choice for mandatory clauses.

The finishing problem crops up from time to time. While there are workarounds, usually if you run into this you're better off using a Nested Function or *Nested Closure (403)*. These alternative are also better choices if you are getting into a mess with *Context Variables (175)*.

35.3 The Simple Computer Configuration Example (Java)

Here's the basic computer configuration example done with a healthy dose of
Method Chaining:

```
computer()
  .processor()
    .cores(2)
    .speed(2500)
    .i386()
  .disk()
    .size(150)
  .disk()
    .size(75)
    .speed(7200)
    .sata()
  .end();
```

To start an expression using Method Chaining, you need some method call to
initiate the chain. In this case, I'm using a static method that I can reference in
the DSL script by using a static import.

```
public static ComputerBuilder computer() {
  return new ComputerBuilder();
}
```

I use the computer builder to define the various methods I need for chaining.
It also contains the parse data.

For the processor, I store a *Construction Builder (179)* for the current processor
in a *Context Variable (175)*.

35: Method
Chaining

```
class ComputerBuilder...
  public ComputerBuilder processor() {
    currentProcessor = new ProcessorBuilder();
    return this;
  }
  private ProcessorBuilder currentProcessor;

  public ComputerBuilder cores(int arg) {
    currentProcessor.cores = arg;
    return this;
  }
  public ComputerBuilder i386() {
    currentProcessor.type = Processor.Type.i386;
    return this;
  }
}
```

```
class ProcessorBuilder {
  private static final int DEFAULT_CORES = 1;
  private static final int DEFAULT_SPEED = -1;

  int cores = DEFAULT_CORES;
  int speed = DEFAULT_SPEED;
  Processor.Type type;
  Processor getValue() {
    return new Processor(cores, speed, type);
  }
}
```

As is characteristic for Method Chaining, the builder returns itself with each call in order to continue the chain.

Specifying the disks is a bit more involved, since each disk has its own data. I could define more context variables on the computer builder, just as I did for processor, but in this case I'll use a separate builder to capture the attributes for the disk.

```
class DiskBuilder...
  public DiskBuilder size(int arg) {
    size = arg;
    return this;
  }
  public DiskBuilder speed(int arg) {
    speed = arg;
    return this;
  }
  public DiskBuilder sata() {
    iface = Disk.Interface.SATA;
    return this;
  }
```

The tricky bit here is shuffling between the computer builder and the disk builder and keeping the Context Variables in step. The disk clause introduces a new disk, so the computer builder puts a new disk builder into a context variable and passes the call to it.

```
class ComputerBuilder...
  public DiskBuilder disk() {
    if (currentDisk != null) loadedDisks.add(currentDisk.getValue());
    currentDisk = new DiskBuilder(this);
    return currentDisk;
  }
  private DiskBuilder currentDisk;
  private List<Disk> loadedDisks = new ArrayList<Disk>();
```

```
class DiskBuilder...
  public DiskBuilder(ComputerBuilder parent) {
    this.parent = parent;
  }
  private int size = Disk.UNKNOWN_SIZE;
  private int speed = Disk.UNKNOWN_SPEED;
  private Disk.Interface iface;
  private ComputerBuilder parent;
```

The disk clause also occurs between disks. As a result, I add the current disk to a list of loaded disks before making a new builder. The disk builder will get the disk call if I'm in the middle of making one, so I just forward the call to the computer builder.

```
class DiskBuilder...
  public DiskBuilder disk() {
    return parent.disk();
  }
```

In this example, I have to deal with the finishing problem. I've done the simplest workaround here: an end method. As with the disk clause, the end method can appear as a call to disk builder, so I forward it to the computer builder when that happens.

```
class DiskBuilder...
  public Computer end() {
    return parent.end();
  }
```

In the computer builder, I use the end method to create and return the computer that's been configured.

```
class ComputerBuilder...
  public Computer end() {
    return getValue();
  }

  public Computer getValue() {
    return new Computer(currentProcessor.getValue(), disks());
  }

  private Disk[] disks() {
    List<Disk> result = new ArrayList<Disk>();
    result.addAll(loadedDisks);
    if (currentDisk != null) result.add(currentDisk.getValue());
    return result.toArray(new Disk[result.size()]);
  }

  public ComputerBuilder speed(int arg) {
    currentProcessor.speed = arg;
    return this;
  }
```

35: Method Chaining

This allows me to use the builder in this style:

```
Computer c = ComputerBuilder
  .computer()
    .processor()
    .cores(2)
    .speed(2500)
    .i386()
  .disk()
    .size(150)
  .disk()
    .size(75)
    .speed(7200)
    .sata()
  .end();
```

Otherwise, I need to do something like:

```
ComputerBuilder builder = new ComputerBuilder();
builder
  .processor()
    .cores(2)
    .speed(2500)
    .i386()
  .disk()
    .size(150)
  .disk()
    .size(75)
    .speed(7200)
    .sata();
Computer c = builder.getValue();
```

With this example, I've been inconsistent in my use of the subsidiary builders for the processor and disks. The processor builder is a simple Construction Builder, just used to store the intermediate values. With the disk builder, I've delegated the fluent methods to it. A simple Construction Builder works better for simple cases and full delegation works better for more complicated cases. I've shown both here for pedagogical reasons, although I lean more to full delegation.

The example illustrates quite well many of the issues in using Method Chaining, particularly compared to *Nested Function (357)*. Method Chaining reads very clearly, without much of the syntactic noise that can clutter Nested Function. However, to pull it off, I have to do a lot of fiddling around with Context Variables and cope with the finishing problem.

35: Method
Chaining

35.4 Chaining with Properties (C#)

C# and Java are similar languages, so many of the comments that apply to Java apply to C# too. The biggest difference is that C# has a special property syntax, instead of Java's more fumbly getters and setters. As a result, the regular example would look like this:

```
HardDrive hd = new HardDrive() {
  Size = 150,
  Type = HardDriveType.SATA,
  Speed = 7200
};
```

The chaining case looks almost the same.

```
new HardDriveBuilder()
  .Size(150)
  .SATA
  .Speed(7200);
```

The chaining modifiers for speed and capacity are identical (other than the capitalization convention). There is, however, one interesting variation in handling the external property. By using a property getter for the external property, I can get rid of the unnecessary and annoying parentheses. I implement the property getter like this:

```
private HardDriveBuilder SATA {
  get {
    type = HardDriveType.SATA;
    return this;
  }
}
```

This code should make you feel distinctly uneasy: It's a property getter that's really acting as a setter, returning the object itself rather than the value of the property. This violates all our expectations of how property getters should work. In almost all circumstances, I would call this extremely bad code. It's only acceptable when clearly placed in a fluent context—again, I would confine this abomination to a securely fenced *Expression Builder (343)*.

35.5 Progressive Interfaces (C#)

Autocompletion is one of the joys of modern IDEs. I no longer need to remember what methods are callable on a particular class—I can just hit a key combination and get a menu right there. Since my brain filled up about fifteen years ago, I appreciate having to remember less.

Many DSLs have a definite order in which things can be built up. We can use autocompletion to help signal that if we use progressive interfaces. Suppose we want to build up an email message:

```
message = MessageBuilder.Build()
  .To("fowler@acm.org")
  .Cc("editor@publisher.com")
  .Subject("error in book")
  .Body("Sally Shipton should read Sally Sparrow");
```

We want to ensure that we build up the elements of the message in a particular order: first the destination address, then the Cc's, then the subject, and finally the body. With vanilla Method Chaining, there's nothing to enforce a particular order.

The chocolate sauce in this case is to use multiple interfaces over the *Expression Builder (343)*. I'll start with build.

```
public static IMessageBuilderPostBuild Build() {
  return new MessageBuilder();
}

interface IMessageBuilderPostBuild {
  IMessageBuilderPostTo To(String arg);
}
```

I return an Expression Builder just as I would normally do, but the return type is a special interface that only allows the legal next step in the sequence. The Expression Builder implements that interface, and now I can only make that call next. As an added bonus, my autocompletion menus will now only show me the legal next steps (although it's not perfect, as methods inherited from Object also show up). Thus autocompletion can guide me through the process.

The next step continues the story.

```
public IMessageBuilderPostTo To(String arg) {
  Content.To.Add(new Email(arg));
  return this;
}

interface IMessageBuilderPostTo : IMessageBuilderPostBuild {
  IMessageBuilderPostCc Cc(String arg);
  IMessageBuilderPostSubject Subject(String arg);
}
```

One new thing is that the legal next steps after To include the legal steps after Build. I can show this, without duplicating the body of IMessageBuilderPostBuild, by using inheritance between the interfaces. It's not really that worthwhile in this example, but it's often a useful technique.

The rest of the sequence continues as you'd expect.

35: Method Chaining

```
public IMessageBuilderPostCc Cc(String arg) {
  Content.Cc.Add(new Email(arg));
  return this;
}
public IMessageBuilderPostSubject Subject(String arg) {
  Content.Subject = arg;
  return this;
}
public Message Body(String arg) {
  Content.Body = arg;
  return Content;
}

interface IMessageBuilderPostCc
{
  IMessageBuilderPostCc Cc(String arg);
  IMessageBuilderPostSubject Subject(String arg);
}
interface IMessageBuilderPostSubject {
  Message Body(String arg);
}
```

I have a natural stop method with Body, so I'll have that return the message.

Chapter 36

Object Scoping

Place the DSL script so that bare references will resolve to a single object.

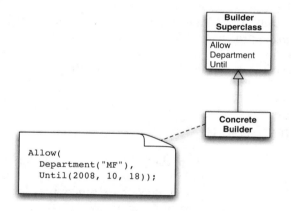

Nested Function (357) and (to an extent) *Function Sequence (351)* may provide a nice DSL syntax, but in their basic forms they come with a serious cost: global functions and (worse) global state.

Object Scoping alleviates these problems by resolving all bare calls to a single object and this avoids cluttering the global namespace with global functions, allowing you to store any parsing data within this host object. The most common way to do this is to write the DSL script inside a subclass of a builder that defines the functions—this allows the parsing data to be captured in that one object.

36.1 How It Works

One of the many useful properties of objects is that each object provides a contained scope for functions and data. Inheritance allows you to use this scope separately from where it's defined. A DSL can use this facility by defining DSL functions on a base class, and then allowing developers to write DSL programs in subclasses. The base class can also define fields to hold any parsing data that's required.

Using a base class like this is an obvious place for an *Expression Builder (343)*. Clients then write DSL programs in a subclass of the Expression Builder. Using inheritance allows them to add other DSL functions in the subclass, or even override base functions in the DSL object if they need to.

Although inheritance is the most common mechanism to use for this kind of work, some languages provide other ways to use Object Scoping. An example of this is Ruby's instance evaluation which provides the facility to take any program code and execute it within the context of a particular object (using the instance_eval method). This allows a DSL writer to write the DSL text without declaring any links to the base class that defines the language.

Another technique that's available in Java is instance initializers. These are not well known nor often used, but can work well for this case.

36.2 When to Use It

Object Scoping solves the niggly problems of globalness within *Nested Function (357)* and *Function Sequence (351)* and as such is always worth considering. Using Object Scoping allows you to have bare function calls in your DSL and have them resolve to instance methods on an object. Not only does this avoid messing with a global namespace, it also allows you to store parsing data in an *Expression Builder (343)*. I find these advantages quite compelling, and thus would always suggest using Object Scoping if you can.

Sometimes, however, you can't. For a start, you need to be using an object-oriented language to do this. I, of course, don't see that as a problem since I prefer using OO languages anyway.

The more common issue is that Object Scoping puts constraints on where your DSL script can go. With the most common inheritance case, it means you must put the DSL script within a method in a subclass of an Expression Builder. This isn't too much of problem for self-contained DSL scripts. Such scripts often sit in their own file and are well-separated from other code. In this case, there is a little syntactic noise to set up the inheritance structure but it's not too obtrusive. (You can avoid even that syntactic noise with techniques like Ruby's instance_eval.)

The real problem is with fragmentary DSLs, where using Object Scoping forces you into an inheritance relationship that may be awkward or even impossible.

Object Scoping is mostly an antidote to global functions, so it's worth remembering that the biggest problems of global functions come with modifying global data. A common case where you don't get this problem is when the global function just creates and returns a new object, such as Date.today(). Static methods, which are effectively global, can very effectively return such objects which can either be regular objects or Expression Builders. If you can arrange your bare functions to be like this, then there is much less need for Object Scoping.

If the DSL framework is set up to allow a user of the DSL to substitute their own subclass of the scoping class for *Object Scoping (385)*, this also makes the DSL more extensible. A user subclass can add more methods to extend the language. Indeed if particular methods are only needed in one script, then that script subclass can define those methods directly.

36.3 Security Codes (C#)

We have a building that houses all sorts of secret projects. As a result, the building is divided into zones, and each zone has security policies that govern what kinds of employees can enter a zone. As an employee approaches a door into the zone, the system checks the employee against the zone's policies and decides whether or not to admit her.

The DSL I'm going to build will support expressing rules like this:

```
class MyZone : ZoneBuilder {
  protected override void doBuild() {
    Allow(
      Department("MF"),
      Until(2008, 10, 18));
    Refuse(Department("Finance"));
    Refuse(Department("Audit"));
    Allow(
      GradeAtLeast(Grade.Director),
      During(1100, 1500),
      Until(2008, 5, 1));
    Refuse(
      Department("k9"),
      GradeAtLeast(Grade.Director));
    Allow(Department("k9"));
  }
}
```

36.3.1 Semantic Model

The *Semantic Model (159)* has a zone class with multiple admission rules. Each admission rule is either an allow rule (specifying conditions to let someone in) or a reject rule (specifying conditions to refuse entry). The admission rule has a body (that we'll explore later) and the method to check if an employee can be admitted.

```
abstract class AdmissionRule {
  protected RuleElement body;
  protected AdmissionRule(RuleElement body) {
    this.body = body;
  }
  public abstract AdmissionRuleResult CanAdmit(Employee e);
}
enum AdmissionRuleResult {ADMIT, REFUSE, NO_OPINION};
```

I handle the two kinds of admission rules through inheritance. Each one provides an implementation of CanAdmit.

```
class AllowRule : AdmissionRule {
  public AllowRule(RuleElement body) : base(body) {}
  public override AdmissionRuleResult CanAdmit(Employee e) {
    if (body.eval(e)) return AdmissionRuleResult.ADMIT;
    else return AdmissionRuleResult.NO_OPINION;
  }

class RefusalRule : AdmissionRule {
  public RefusalRule(RuleElement body) : base(body) {}
  public override AdmissionRuleResult CanAdmit(Employee e) {
    if (body.eval(e)) return AdmissionRuleResult.REFUSE;
    else return AdmissionRuleResult.NO_OPINION;
  }
```

When asked to admit an employee, the zone class runs through the admission rules in order, seeing how they respond.

```
class Zone...
  private IList<AdmissionRule> rules = new List<AdmissionRule>();
  public void AddRule(AdmissionRule arg) {
    rules.Add(arg);
  }
  public bool WillAdmit(Employee e) {
    foreach (AdmissionRule rule in rules) {
      switch(rule.CanAdmit(e)) {
        case AdmissionRuleResult.ADMIT:
          return true;
        case AdmissionRuleResult.NO_OPINION:
          break;
        case AdmissionRuleResult.REFUSE:
          return false;
        default:
          throw new InvalidOperationException();
      }
    }
    return false;
  }
```

If none of the rules give an opinion, the method defaults to refusal (false).

The body of the admission rule is a composite structure of rule elements, essentially a *Specification* [Evans DDD]. The declared type is an interface.

```csharp
internal interface RuleElement {
  bool eval(Employee emp);
}
```

Various implementations all check the attributes of an employee. Here's checking for grades and departments:

```csharp
internal class MinimumGradeExpr : RuleElement {
  private readonly Grade minimum;
  public MinimumGradeExpr(Grade minimum) {
    this.minimum = minimum;
  }
  public bool eval(Employee emp) {
    if (null == emp.Grade) return false;
    return emp.Grade.IsHigherOrEqualTo(minimum);
  }
}

internal class DepartmentExpr : RuleElement {
  private readonly string dept;
  public DepartmentExpr(string dept) {
    this.dept = dept;
  }
  public bool eval(Employee emp) {
    return emp.Department == dept;
  }
}
```

I have a composite element, so I can combine them into logical structures.

```csharp
class AndExpr : RuleElement {
  private readonly List<RuleElement> elements;
  public AndExpr(params RuleElement[] elements) {
    this.elements = new List<RuleElement>(elements);
  }
  public bool eval(Employee emp) {
    return elements.TrueForAll(element => element.eval(emp));
  }
}
```

36: Object
Scoping

So if I want to admit someone who is a senior programmer in the K9 department, I can set up the zone like this:

```csharp
zone.AddRule(new AllowRule(
            new AndExpr(
                new MinimumGradeExpr(Grade.SeniorProgrammer),
                new DepartmentExpr("K9"))));
```

36.3.2 DSL

To use Object Scoping, I create a builder superclass that I can inherit from to form the DSL. Here's the example subclass again that shows the kind of DSL I'm supporting:

```
class MyZone : ZoneBuilder {
  protected override void doBuild() {
    Allow(
      Department("MF"),
      Until(2008, 10, 18));
    Refuse(Department("Finance"));
    Refuse(Department("Audit"));
    Allow(
      GradeAtLeast(Grade.Director),
      During(1100, 1500),
      Until(2008, 5, 1));
    Refuse(
      Department("k9"),
      GradeAtLeast(Grade.Director));
    Allow(Department("k9"));
  }
```

This rule first allows anyone from the MF department in until a cut-off date next year. It then explicitly refuses access to anyone in the finance or audit departments (in separate refusal clauses), finally allowing any director in between fixed hours up to another cut-off date.

Although the underlying model allows arbitrary Boolean expressions, the DSL is simpler. Each admission rule is a conjunction ("and") of its clauses. This is why I need separate refuse statements for the two departments. If I put them in the same clause, it would only refuse people who were in both departments.

Arbitrary Boolean expressions are powerful, but often difficult for people, particularly non-nerds, to follow. So some form of simplified structure can be handy in a DSL.

The DSL is comprised of methods which are defined on the base builder class. This allows me to call them in the subclass without any qualification. The `Allow` method adds a new allow rule to the zone whose body is the conjunction of the method's arguments.

```
class ZoneBuilder...
  private Zone zone;
  public ZoneBuilder Allow(params RuleElement[] rules) {
    var expr = new AndExpr(rules);
    zone.AddRule(new AllowRule(expr));
    return this;
  }
```

I use a vararg method here as a *Literal List (417)*. (If there's only one sub-expression, then the wrapping and expression are unnecessary. I could fix that, but I got a good deal on and expressions, so I haven't bothered.)

Each argument is built up through further functions on the base builder.

```
class ZoneBuilder...
  internal RuleElement GradeAtLeast(Grade grade) {
    return new MinimumGradeExpr(grade);
  }
  internal RuleElement Department(String name) {
    return new DepartmentExpr(name);
  }
```

To add a new element to the system, I define a new expression for the model and a function on the builder.

```
class ZoneBuilder...
  internal RuleElement Until(int year, int month, int day) {
    return new EndDateExpr(year, month, day);
  }

  internal class EndDateExpr : RuleElement {
    private readonly DateTime date;
    public EndDateExpr(int year, int month, int day) {
      date = new DateTime(year, month, day);
    }
    public bool eval(Employee emp) {
      return Clock.Date < date;
    }
  }
```

As well as adding rules for all users of a DSL, I can also extend the DSL for specific DSL programs. Let's imagine it's only my department that wants access restricted to certain hours. I can put that code directly in the subclass.

```
class MyZone...
  private RuleElement During(int begin, int end) {
    return new TimeOfDayExpr(begin, end);
  }

  private class TimeOfDayExpr : RuleElement {
    private readonly int begin, end;
    public TimeOfDayExpr(int begin, int end) {
      this.begin = begin;
      this.end = end;
    }
    public bool eval(Employee emp) {
      return (Clock.Time >= begin) && (Clock.Time <= end);
    }
  }
```

If other script classes want this feature, but I'm unable to modify the library, I can create my own zone builder class that's a subclass of the library zone builder and let my scripts subclass that. I can then put any useful methods into my own abstract zone builder.

36: Object
Scoping

Object Scoping does help in reducing noise in the DSL, but one problem is that it does introduce noise in the code that declares the DSL class. The first two lines (and closing braces) are awkward noise. It could be a little worse; my natural way to use this class would be to pass the zone into the builder in the constructor, but that would force me to add a constructor declaration to the subclass. I avoided that by passing the zone with a separate method.

```
class ZoneBuilder...
  internal void Build(Zone zone) {
    this.zone = zone;
    doBuild();
  }
  protected abstract void doBuild();
```

I call it like this:

```
class DslTest...
  new MyZone().Build(zone);
```

It's a small thing, but saves me a bit of noise in the DSL text. These small things add up.

36.4 Using Instance Evaluation (Ruby)

While Object Scoping is a very valuable pattern, as it provides good names without global artifacts, using subtyping does introduce limitations. For a standalone DSL, the script file needs some head and tail noise to set up the context. For fragmentary DSLs, you need to be in a subclass of the DSL builder to write DSL expressions.

Ruby has a very good mechanism that you can use to get around these problems: instance evaluation. The idea behind instance evaluation is that you can take some text and evaluate it within the context of a particular Ruby object instance. Any bare method calls on the script are resolved to that instance, as if they were inside an instance method of the class itself. This allows you to write a DSL using Object Scoping without needing to bother with any subclassing.

So for the zones example above, I have the following script file:

```
allow {
  department:mf
  ends 2008, 10, 18
}

refuse department :finance

refuse department :audit
```

```
allow {
  gradeAtLeast :director
  during 1100, 1500
  ends 2008, 5, 1
}

refuse {
  department :k9
  gradeAtLeast :director
}
allow department :k9
```

The builder executes this with a simple call.

```
class Builder...
  def load_file aFilename
    self.load(File.readlines(aFilename).join("\n"))
  end
```

The bare function calls can resolve to methods on the builder.

```
class Builder...
  def allow anExpr = nil, &block
    @zone << AllowRule.new(form_expression(anExpr, &block))
  end
```

That's the essence of using instance evaluation to handle Object Scoping. However, while I was putting this example together, there were a couple of other interesting things that I couldn't resist going into. It's crossing the line into language-specific tricks that I usually try to avoid, but it's been a long day, so please indulge me.

In the example code, I tried to follow the structure of the C# example. However, I felt it read better if a multiclause condition used a *Nested Closure (403)* rather than a *Nested Function (357)*. Pulling this off results in a complication. If I have a single clause in an allow or refuse statement, I need to return the value of the clause; if I have a nested block, I need to return an and expression of the values of each clause.

36: Object
Scoping

```
class Builder...
  def form_expression anExpr = nil, &block
    if block_given?
      AndExprBuilder.interpret(&block)
    else
      anExpr
    end
  end
```

For the simple case, I make the method in the builder just return the rule element, so that the rule element is wrapped in the parent allow rule.

```
class Builder...
  def gradeAtLeast gradeSymbol
    return RuleElementBuilder.new.gradeAtLeast gradeSymbol
  end

class RuleElementBuilder
  def gradeAtLeast gradeSymbol
    return MinimumGradeExpr.new gradeSymbol
  end
```

If I have a Nested Closure, I use a child builder for that expression and use instance evaluation on that again, so the expressions in the DSL bind to the child builder rather than the parent.

```
class AndExprBuilder...
  def initialize &block
    @rules = []
    @block = block
  end

  def self.interpret &block
    return self.new(&block).value
  end

  def value
    instance_eval(&@block)
    return AndExpr.new(*@rules)
  end

  def gradeAtLeast gradeSymbol
    @rules << RuleElementBuilder.new.gradeAtLeast(gradeSymbol)
  end
```

This mechanism allows me to handle calls to methods like gradeAtLeast differently in different parts of the DSL. In Ruby, it's nice to use *Function Sequence (351)* inside a Nested Closure as that allows the contents of the group to be separated with newlines rather than commas.

36.5 Using an Instance Initializer (Java)

A way to use Object Scoping in a relatively unobtrusive inline manner is to use an instance initializer. This technique was popularized by JMock; I confess that until I'd seen it used, I completely neglected that language feature. Using it in a DSL script looks like this:

```
ZoneBuilder builder = new ZoneBuilder() {{
  allow(department(MF));
  refuse(department(FINANCE));
  refuse(department(AUDIT));
  allow(
    gradeAtLeast(DIRECTOR),
    department(K9));
}};
zone = builder.getValue();
```

The builder that makes this work looks pretty much the same as the one in C#.

```
class ZoneBuilder...
  private Zone value = new Zone();
  public Zone getValue() {
    return value;
  }
  public ZoneBuilder refuse(RuleElement... rules) {
    value.addRule(new RefusalRule(new AndExpr(rules)));
    return this;
  }
  public ZoneBuilder allow(RuleElement... rules) {
    value.addRule(new AllowRule(new AndExpr(rules)));
    return this;
  }
  public RuleElement gradeAtLeast(Grade g) {
    return new MinimumGradeExpr(g);
  }
  public RuleElement department(Department d) {
    return new DepartmentExpr(d);
  }
```

The trick is the use of double curly brackets in the DSL script. This creates not an instance of the zone builder, but an inner class that's an instance of a *subclass* of the zone builder. This one-off subclass has the code between the double curly braces woven into the constructor. You can always do this sort of thing in Java, although I've not seen it that widely used. Since the code between the double curlies is in a subclass of zone builder, we have the Object Scoping that we need.

36: Object
Scoping

Chapter 37

Closure

A block of code that can be represented as an object (or first-class data structure) and placed seamlessly into the flow of code by allowing it to reference its lexical scope.

```
var threshold = ComputeThreshold();
var heavyTravellers = employeeList.FindAll(e => e.MilesOfCommute > threshold);
```

Also known as: lambda, block, or anonymous function

You have a collection of objects and want to filter them in various ways. Writing a method for each filter leads to duplication in the setup and processing of the filter.

By using a Closure, you can factor the setup and processing of the filter and pass in an arbitrary block of code for each filter condition.

37.1 How It Works

Closures are a language feature that, despite being around for a long time, has only recently begun to make its way onto the radar of many software developers. This is probably because the languages that have and use closures, such as Lisp and Smalltalk, weren't part of the C culture that drove the development of the current mainstream languages.

I use the term Closure in this book, but naturally there is no standard term for this language element. You also see them referred to as lambdas, anonymous functions, and blocks. Each language that uses them usually has its own term for them. For example, lispers use "lambda," smalltalkers and rubyists use "block." Although they are called blocks in Smalltalk and Ruby, it isn't the same as blocks in C-based languages.

Now that I've got the terminological babble out of the way, I can actually say what they are. Here's my starting definition: A Closure is a code fragment that can be treated as an object. To get serious about this, we need an example.

Let's consider the problem of getting a subset of data from a collection. Imagine we have a list of employees and we want all employees who are heavy travelers.

```
int threshold = ComputeThreshold();
var heavyTravellers = new List<Employee>();
foreach (Employee e in employeeList)
  if (e.MilesOfCommute > threshold) heavyTravellers.Add(e);
```

Somewhere else in the code, we need to get a list of employees who are managers.

```
var managerList = new List<Employee>();
foreach (Employee e in employeeList)
  if (e.IsManager) managerList.Add(e);
```

These two code fragments contain a lot of duplication. In both cases, we want a list that is formed by taking the members of the original list, running a Boolean function against each element, and collecting those for which the function returns true. Removing that duplication is a simple thing to envisage, but difficult to write in many languages because the thing that varies between the two code fragments is a chunk of behavior—which is often not easy to parametrize.

The most obvious way to parametrize something like this is to turn it into an object. What I need is a method on a list that will allow me to select from the list based on a separate object that I pass in.

37: Closure

```
class MyList<T> {
  private List<T> contents;
  public MyList(List<T> contents) {
    this.contents = contents;
  }
  public List<T> Select(FilterFunction<T> p) {
    var result = new List<T>();
    foreach (T candidate in contents)
      if (p.Passes(candidate)) result.Add(candidate);
    return result;
  }
}
interface FilterFunction<T> {
  Boolean Passes(T arg);
}
```

I can then use it to select managers like this:

```
var managers = new MyList<Employee>(employeeList).Select(new ManagersPredicate());
```

```
class ManagersPredicate : FilterFunction<Employee> {
  public Boolean Passes(Employee e) {
    return e.IsManager;
  }
}
```

There's a certain programming satisfaction in doing this, but there's so much code in setting up the predicate object that the cure is worse than the disease. This is especially true when we look at the heavy travelers case. Here I need to pass a parameter into the predicate object, which means I need a constructor in my predicate:

```
var threshold = ComputeThreshold();
var heavyTravellers = new MyList<Employee>(employeeList)
                          .Select(new HeavyTravellerPredicate(threshold));

class HeavyTravellerPredicate : FilterFunction<Employee> {
  private int threshold;
  public HeavyTravellerPredicate(int threshold) {
    this.threshold = threshold;
  }
  public Boolean Passes(Employee e) {
    return e.MilesOfCommute > threshold;
  }
}
```

Essentially, a Closure is a more elegant solution to this problem—one that makes it much easier to create a hunk of code and pass it around like an object.

You'll notice I've made my examples in C#. I did this because in the past few years, C# has evolved steadily towards a more convenient use of Closures. C# 2.0 introduced the notion of anonymous delegates, which are a big step in this direction. Here's the heavy traveler example again using anonymous delegates:

```
var threshold = ComputeThreshold();
var heavyTravellers = employeeList.FindAll(
  delegate(Employee e) { return e.MilesOfCommute > threshold; });
```

37: Closure

The first thing to notice here is that there's much less code involved. The duplication between this expression and a similar one for finding managers is vastly reduced. In order to make this work, I've used a library function on the C# list class, similar to the select function I wrote myself for the handwritten predicate. C# 2 introduced a number of changes to the libraries that took advantage of delegates. This is an important point—for Closures to be really useful in a language, the libraries need to be written with Closures in mind.

A third point that this fragment illustrates is how easy it is to use the threshold parameter—I just use it in my Boolean expression. I can put any local variable that's in scope into this expression, which saves all the faffing around with parameters that the predicate object version needed.

This reference to variables in scope is what formally makes this expression a Closure. The delegate is said to close over the lexical scope of where it's defined.

Even if we take the delegate and store it somewhere for later execution, those variables are still visible and usable. Essentially, the system needs to take a copy of the stack frame to allow the Closure to still have access to everything it should see. Both the theory and implementation of this are quite tricky—but the result is very natural to use.

(Some people define "closure" only to mean an instantiated hunk of code that closes over some variables in lexical scope. As is often the case, the use of the word "closure" is very inconsistent.)

C# 3 went a step further. Here's the heavy travelers expression again:

```
var threshold = ComputeThreshold();
var heavyTravellers = employeeList.FindAll(e => e.MilesOfCommute > threshold);
```

You'll notice there's really little change here—the main factor is that the syntax is much more compact. This may be a small difference but it's a vital one. The usefulness of Closures is directly proportional to how terse they are to use. This syntax makes them far more readable.

There is a second difference, which is an important part of making the syntax terser. In the delegate example, I needed to specify the type of the parameter Employee e. I don't need to indicate that type with the lambda because C# 3.0 has a type inference capability, meaning that, since it can figure out the type of the result of the right-hand side of the assignment, you don't have to specify it on the left.

The consequence of all this is that I can create Closures and treat them just like any other object. I can store them in variables and execute them whenever I wish. To illustrate this, I can make a club class that has a field for a selector:

```
class Club...
  Predicate<Employee> selector;
  internal Club(Predicate<Employee> selector) {
    this.selector = selector;
  }
  internal Boolean IsEligable(Employee arg) {
    return selector(arg);
  }
```

and use it like this:

```
public void clubRecognizesMember() {
  var rebecca = new Employee { MilesOfCommute = 5000 };
  var club = createHeavyTravellersClub(1000);
  Assert.IsTrue(club.IsEligable(rebecca));
}

private Club createHeavyTravellersClub(int threshold) {
  return new Club(e => e.MilesOfCommute > threshold);
}
```

This code creates a club in one function, using a parameter to set the threshold. The club contains the Closure, including the link to the now-out-of-scope parameter. I can then use the club to execute the Closure at any future time.

In this case, the selector Closure isn't actually evaluated when it's created. Instead, we create it, store it, and evaluate it later (possibly multiple times). This ability to create a block of code for later execution is what makes Closures so useful for *Adaptive Models (487)*.

Another language featured in this book that uses Closures heavily is Ruby. Ruby was built with Closures from early days, so most Ruby programs and libraries use them extensively. Defining a club class looks like this in Ruby:

```
class Club...
  def initialize &selector
    @selector = selector
  end
  def eligible? anEmployee
    @selector.call anEmployee
  end
```

and we use it like this:

```
def test_club
  rebecca = Employee.new(5000)
  club = create_heavy_travellers_club
  assert club.eligible?(rebecca)
end
def create_heavy_travellers_club
  threshold = 1000
  return Club.new {|e| e.miles_of_commute > threshold}
end
```

In Ruby, we can define a Closure either with curly braces, as above, or with a do...end pair.

```
threshold = 1000
return Club.new do |e|
  e.miles_of_commute > threshold
end
```

The two syntaxes are almost entirely equivalent. In practice, people use the curlies for one-liners and the do...end for multiline blocks.

The sad part about this nice Ruby syntax is that you can only use it to pass a single Closure into a function. If you want to pass multiple Closures, you have to use a less elegant syntax.

37: Closure

37.2 When to Use It

Like many programmers who have used languages with good support for Closures, I find I miss them a great deal when using a language without them. They are a valuable tool to take chunks of logic and arrange them to eliminate duplication and support custom control structures.

Closures play a couple of useful roles in DSLs. Most obviously, they are an essential element for *Nested Closure (403)*. They also can make it easier to define an *Adaptive Model (487)*.

Chapter 38

Nested Closure

Express statement subelements of a function call by putting them into a closure in an argument.

```
computer do
  processor do
    cores 2
    i386
    speed 2.2
  end
  disk do
    size 150
  end
  disk do
    size 75
    speed 7200
    sata
  end
end
```

38.1 How It Works

The basic idea of a Nested Closure is similar to that of *Nested Function (357)*, but the child expressions of the function call are wrapped in a closure. To show the difference, here's a call to create a new processor using Nested Function in Ruby:

```
processor(
  cores 2,
  i386
)
```

Now with a Nested Closure:

```
processor do
  cores 2
  i386
end
```

Instead of passing two Nested Function arguments, I pass a single Nested Closure argument which contains the two Nested Functions. (I'm using Ruby here, as it provides closures in a syntax which is suitable for this discussion.)

Placing the subelements in a Nested Closure has an immediate consequence for my implementation—I have to put in code to evaluate the closure. With a Nested Function, I don't need to do this since the language automatically evaluates the cores and i386 functions before calling the processor function. With a closure argument, the processor function is called first and the closure is only evaluated when I explicitly program it to. So, usually I'll evaluate the closure within the body of the processor function. The processor function can also carry out other tasks before and after the closure evaluation, such as setting up *Context Variables (175)*.

In the example above, the contents of the closure is a *Function Sequence (351)*. One of the problems of a Function Sequence is that the multiple functions communicate using hidden Context Variables. While you still have to do this inside a Nested Closure, the processor function can create the Context Variable before evaluating the closure and tear it down afterwards. This can greatly reduce the problem of Context Variables appearing all over the place.

Another choice for the subelements is to use *Method Chaining (373)*. Here, there is the additional benefit that the parent function can set up the head of the chain and pass it into the closure as an argument.

```
processor do |p|
  p.cores(2).i386
end
```

It's also quite common to pass in a Context Variable as an argument.

```
processor do |p|
  p.cores 2
  p.i386
end
```

In this case, we have a Function Sequence but with the Context Variable explicitly present. This often makes it easier to follow, without adding too much clutter.

Bare functions written inside a Nested Closure are evaluated in the scope where they are defined—so, again, it's usually wise to use *Object Scoping (385)*. Passing in an explicit Context Variable or using Method Chaining allows you to avoid this, as well as to organize the builder code into different builders.

Some languages allow you to manipulate the context that a closure is executed in. This can allow you to use bare functions and still use multiple builders. The example with Ruby's `instance_eval` ("Using Instance Evaluation (Ruby)," p. 412) shows how this can work.

In the examples I've shown above, I've put all the subelements of the parent function into a single closure. It's also possible to use multiple closures. The advantage of this is that it allows you to evaluate each subclosure independently. A good example of where this is handy is where you have a conditional expression, such as this example in Smalltalk:

```
aRoom
  ifDark: [aLight on]
  ifLight: [aLight off]
```

38.2 When to Use It

Nested Closure is a useful technique because it combines the explicitly hierarchic structure of *Nested Function (357)* with the ability to control when the arguments are evaluated. Control of evaluation provides you with a lot of flexibility, helping you to avoid many of the limitations of Nested Function.

The biggest limitation of Nested Closure is the way the host language supports closures. Many languages don't provide closures at all. Those that do often provide the syntax in a way that doesn't jive terribly well with DSLs, such as with an awkward keyword.

It's usually worth thinking of Nested Closure as a enhancement to Nested Function, *Function Sequence (351)*, and *Method Chaining (373)*. The explicit control of evaluation gives you different advantages with each technique. All of these, however, boil down to the fact that you can do specific setup and tear-down operations on either side of the closure invocations. With Function Sequence, this means you can prepare *Context Variables (175)* right before they are used by the closure. With Method Chaining, you can set up the head of the chain before invoking the closure.

38: Nested Closure

38.3 Wrapping a Function Sequence in a Nested Closure (Ruby)

For a first example, I'll start with what I might consider as the most straightforward case: using a Nested Closure in conjunction with a *Function Sequence (351)*. Here is the DSL script:

```
class BasicComputerBuilder < ComputerBuilder
  def doBuild
    computer do
      processor do
        cores 2
        i386
        processorSpeed 2.2
      end
      disk do
        size 150
      end
      disk do
        size 75
        diskSpeed 7200
        sata
      end
    end
  end
end
```

To begin the discussion, let's compare this with a version using Function Sequence alone, which would look like this:

```
class BasicComputerBuilder < ComputerBuilder
  def doBuild
    computer
      processor
        cores 2
        i386
        processorSpeed 2.2
      disk
        size 150
      disk
        size 75
        diskSpeed 7200
        sata
  end
end
```

From the script's point of view, the only change with Nested Closure is to add the do...end closure delimiters. By adding these, I introduce an explicit hierarchic structure to what otherwise is a linear sequence with a formatting convention. The extra syntax doesn't strike me as troubling because it's marking the structure from the reader's point of view and in a way that makes sense to the reader.

Now, let's move on to the implementation. As usual, I'm using *Object Scoping (385)* so I can have bare functions resolve against an *Expression Builder (343)*. (A note for rubyists: I'm using subtyping here for pedagogical reasons, but with

Ruby I'd usually use `instance_eval`.) We can see the basic structure of using Nested Closure by looking at the clause for `computer`.

```
class ComputerBuilder...
  def computer &block
    @result = Computer.new
    block.call
  end
```

I pass in the closure as an argument (Ruby refers to closures as "blocks"), set up some context, and then call the closure. The processor function can then use this context and repeat the process for its children.

```
class ComputerBuilder...
  def processor &block
    @result.processor = Processor.new
    block.call
  end
  def cores arg
    @result.processor.cores = arg
  end
  def i386
    @result.processor.type = :i386
  end
  def processorSpeed arg
    @result.processor.speed = arg
  end
```

I do the same for the disks. The only difference is that this time, I use the more idiomatic `yield` keyword to call the implicitly passed-in block. (This is a mechanism Ruby uses to simplify working with a single block argument.)

```
class ComputerBuilder...
  def disk
    @result.disks << Disk.new
    yield
  end
  def size arg
    @result.disks.last.size = arg
  end
  def sata
    @result.disks.last.interface = :sata
  end
  def diskSpeed arg
    @result.disks.last.speed = arg
  end
```

38: Nested
Closure

38.4 Simple C# Example (C#)

For contrast, here is pretty much the same example using C#:

```
class Script : Builder {
  protected override void doBuild() {
    computer(() => {
      processor(() => {
        cores(2);
        i386();
        processorSpeed(2.2);
      });
      disk(() => {
        size(150);
      });
      disk(() => {
        size(75);
        diskSpeed(7200);
        sata();
      });
    });
  }
}
```

As you can see, the structure is exactly the same as in the Ruby example; the big difference is that there's a lot more punctuation in the script.

The builder also looks remarkably similar.

```
class Builder...
  protected void computer(BuilderElement child) {
    result = new Computer();
    child.Invoke();
  }
  public delegate void BuilderElement();
  private Computer result;
```

The computer function follows the same pattern that we see in the Ruby case: pass the closure argument, do any setup, invoke the closure, then do any teardown. The most notable difference with C# is that we have to define the type of the closure we pass in with a delegate clause. In this case, the closure has no arguments and no return type, but with a more complicated case we might need several different types.

The rest of the code is similarly similar to the Ruby case, so I'll save the ink.

To my eyes, Nested Closure works much less well in C# than it did in Ruby. Ruby's do...end closure delimiters flow more naturally to me than C#'s () => {...}, particularly when you also add the mandatory parentheses into the mix. (You can also use {...} as closure delimiters in Ruby.) The more used you are to C# notation, the less that will bother you. Furthermore, this example doesn't pass arguments into the closure—which adds more punctuation to the Ruby case but actually makes the C# easier to read since the empty parentheses now have something to surround.

38.5 Using Method Chaining (Ruby)

Nested Closure can work in a couple of different styles. Here's an example using *Method Chaining (373)*:

```
ComputerBuilder.build do |c|
  c.
    processor do |p|
      p.cores(2).
        i386.
        speed(2.2)
    end.
    disk do |d|
      d.size 150
    end.
    disk do |d|
      d.size(75).
        speed(7200).
        sata
    end
end
```

The difference here is that each call passes in an object to the closure that's used at the head of a chain. This use of closure arguments may add noise to the DSL script (as does the need to now wrap method arguments in parentheses), but one benefit is that you no longer need *Object Scoping (385)* and thus can easily use the code in a fragmentary style.

Invoking the build method creates an instance of the builder and passes it into the closure as an argument.

```
class ComputerBuilder...
  attr_reader :content
  def initialize
    @content = Computer.new
  end
  def self.build &block
    builder = self.new
    block.call(builder)
    return builder.content
  end
end
```

Another useful part of this approach is that it makes it easy to factor the various builder methods into a group of small, cohesive *Expression Builders (343)*. The processor clause introduces a new builder (using the more compact yield keyword).

38: Nested Closure

```
class ComputerBuilder...
  def processor
    p = ProcessorBuilder.new
    yield p
    @content.processor = p.content
    return self
  end

class ProcessorBuilder
  attr_reader :content
  def initialize
    @content = Processor.new
  end
  def cores arg
    @content.cores = arg
    self
  end
  def i386
    @content.type = :i386
    self
  end
  def speed arg
    @content.speed = arg
    self
  end
end
```

Disks are also handled with a disk builder.

```
class ComputerBuilder...
  def disk
    currentDisk = DiskBuilder.new
    yield currentDisk
    @content.disks << currentDisk.content
    return self
  end
class DiskBuilder
  attr_reader :content
  def initialize
    @content = Disk.new
  end
  def size arg
    @content.size = arg
    self
  end
  def sata
    @content.interface = :sata
    self
  end
  def speed arg
    @content.speed = arg
    self
  end
end
```

Apart from allowing better factoring of the builder methods, it also allows me to use an unqualified speed method for both the processor and the disk without ambiguity.

38.6 Function Sequence with Explicit Closure Arguments (Ruby)

In the previous example, we saw there are several advantages to breaking down the language layer into multiple *Expression Builders (343)*. With this approach, each builder is smaller and more cohesive; we also allow clauses in different parts of the language to use the same name (as in processor and disk speed). The explicit closure arguments also allow us to easily use the DSL in a fragmentary context.

While *Method Chaining (373)* gives us these advantages, the resulting DSL script can look rather awkward. The interplay between Nested Closure and Method Chaining doesn't necessarily fit will. Certainly, most of the Ruby DSLs I've looked at do not use this style.

Instead, they use *Function Sequence (351)* within each closure but pass an explicit closure argument to allow multiple builders. In this style, our computer configuration script looks like this:

```
ComputerBuilder.build do |c|
  c.processor do |p|
    p.cores 2
    p.i386
    p.speed 2.2
  end
  c.disk do |d|
    d.size 150
  end
  c.disk do |d|
    d.size 75
    d.speed 7200
    d.sata
  end
end
```

38: Nested Closure

The big difference in the DSL script is that you have separate statements for each clause in the DSL. On every statement, you have to state the passed-in object as the receiver of the method call. Although this adds more text to the statement, it results in a more regular style of code that rubyists find easier to work with.

The implementation is very similar to the Method Chaining case. Again, I have a computer builder at the top level with a class method that creates an instance and passes it to the supplied closure.

```ruby
class ComputerBuilder...
  attr_reader :content
  def initialize
    @content = Computer.new
  end
  def self.build
    builder = self.new
    yield builder
    return builder.content
  end
end
```

The processor clause introduces a new builder.

```ruby
class ComputerBuilder...
  def processor &block
    p = ProcessorBuilder.new
    yield p
    @content.processor = p.content
  end
```

```ruby
class ProcessorBuilder
  attr_reader :content
  def initialize
    @content = Processor.new
  end
  def cores arg
    @content.cores = arg
  end
  def i386
    @content.type = :i386
  end
  def speed arg
    @content.speed = arg
  end
end
```

I'll leave you the barely existing challenge of figuring out what the disks look like.

38.7 Using Instance Evaluation (Ruby)

Passing in explicit closure arguments yield many advantages, but at the cost of constantly mentioning the name of the argument. Ruby gives us a particularly nifty technique to help deal with this: instance evaluation (using the instance_eval method).

When you call a Ruby block, the block is evaluated in the context of where it's defined. In particular, any bare functions (or fields) are resolved to the object in which it's defined. Using instance_eval, you can change this by telling some other object to execute the block within its context, which means any bare methods will now resolve to the new object. The following code demonstrates the difference:

```
class StaticContext < Test::Unit::TestCase
  def identify
    return "in static context"
  end
  def test_demo
    o = OtherObject.new
    assert_equal "in static context", o.use_call {identify}
    assert_equal "in other object", o.use_instance_eval {identify}
  end
end

class OtherObject
  def identify
    return "in other object"
  end
  def use_call &arg
    arg.call
  end
  def use_instance_eval &arg
    instance_eval &arg
  end
end
```

In effect, using `instance_eval` changes what `self` refers to inside the passed-in block.

We can use this facility to be able to use multiple builders with bare method calls in our DSL script.

```
ComputerBuilder.build do
  processor do
    cores 2
    i386
    speed 2.2
  end
  disk do
    size 150
  end
  disk do
    size 75
    speed 7200
    sata
  end
end
```

The builder takes the block as it did before, but uses `instance_eval` rather than call:

```
class ComputerBuilder...
  def self.build &block
    builder = self.new
    builder.instance_eval &block
    return builder.content
  end
  def initialize
    @content = Computer.new
  end
```

Handling the processor again uses instance_eval:

```
class ComputerBuilder...
  def processor &block
    @content.processor = ProcessorBuilder.new.build(block)
  end
class ProcessorBuilder
  def build block
    @content = Processor.new
    instance_eval(&block)
    return @content
  end
  def cores arg
    @content.cores = arg
  end
  def i386
    @content.type = :i386
  end
  def speed arg
    @content.speed = arg
  end
end
```

As does the disk:

```
class ComputerBuilder...
  def disk &block
    @content.disks << DiskBuilder.new.build(block)
  end
class DiskBuilder
  def build block
    @content = Disk.new
    instance_eval(&block)
    return @content
  end
  def size arg
    @content.size = arg
  end
  def sata
    @content.interface = :sata
  end
  def speed arg
    @content.speed = arg
  end
```

The way I've shown the DSL script use `instance_eval` is typical for a fragmentary context where I'm putting a little bit of DSL into a regular Ruby program. In a self-contained context, I can have the DSL script in its own file, in which case by using `instance_eval` I get rid of any top and tail noise of setting up *Object Scoping (385)*. The whole script file looks like this:

```
computer do
  processor do
    cores 2
    i386
    speed 2.2
  end
  disk do
    size 150
  end
  disk do
    size 75
    speed 7200
    sata
  end
end
```

The builder can then process the whole file by `instance_eval`ing it.

```
class ComputerBuilder...
  def load_file aFileName
    load(File.readlines(aFileName).join("\n"))
  end
  def load aStream
    instance_eval aStream
  end
  def computer
    yield
  end
```

38: Nested
Closure

Using `instance_eval` seems such a good trick that you may wonder if you should ever pass explicit closure arguments. As it turns out, there is a very real choice, one that was crystallized for me by Jim Weirich's experience with his builder library. The builder library is a very nice library to create XML documents using Nested Closures and *Dynamic Reception (427)*. In the first version of the library, Jim used `instance_eval`, but later switched to explicit parameters. The reason is that programmers are used to the call behavior with closures; redefining `self` causes a lot of confusion and makes it very difficult to refer to elements in the static context that you need.

For me, the choice lies in whether you are using the DSL script in a self-contained or fragmentary style. In a fragmentary context, you need to follow the usual conventions with closures, so redefining `self` though `instance_eval` is not a good choice. With self-contained DSL scripts, your code style is different from regular Ruby code; the redefinition then doesn't cause confusion and is worth it to remove the noisy references.

Chapter 39

Literal List

Represent language expression with a literal list.

```
martin.follows("WardCunningham", "bigballofmud", "KentBeck", "neal4d");
```

39.1 How It Works

A Literal List is a language construct for forming a list data structure. Many languages provide a direct syntax for Literal List. The most obvious of these is Lisp's (first second third); Ruby is similar [first, second, third] but not quite as elegant. These structures usually allow lists to be nested; indeed, one way of looking at an entire Lisp program is as a nested list.

Literal Lists are usually used in a function call; the parent function will then take the elements of the list and process them in some way.

Mainstream C-based languages don't provide a useful nested list syntax. There are literal arrays {1, 2, 3} but they often allow only constants or literals inside them, unlike a general syntax which permits any symbol or expression.

One way to get around this problem is to use varargs functions, such as companions(jo, saraJane, leela). In a strongly typed language, these elements will all need to be of the same type to work in a varargs call.

39.2 When to Use It

Literal List may work well when nested inside another element, most often a function call, using a logical grammar such as (parent ::= child*). Often, the items in the list are function calls themselves, so Literal Lists can make *Nested Function (357)* workable. If you look at the examples for Nested Function, you'll see that a Literal List is usually present as a varargs function. (The examples there also

417

talk about some of the issues in this combination, particularly in the presence of strong typing.)

Even if your host language has native syntax for Literal Lists, you're usually better off using a varargs function if that list is used in a function call. That is, I prefer `companions(jo, saraJane, leela)` to `companions([jo, saraJane, leela])`.

It is possible to form just about any DSL using only Literal Lists, essentially mimicking Lisp. This is, obviously, a natural way to write in Lisp, but little more than a fun exercise in other languages where it's more natural to combine lists with other forms of expression.

Chapter 40

Literal Map

Represent an expression as a literal map.

```
computer(processor(:cores => 2, :type => :i386),
         disk(:size => 150),
         disk(:size => 75, :speed => 7200, :interface => :sata))
```

40.1 How It Works

A Literal Map is a language construct, present in many languages, that allows you to form a map data structure (also known as a dictionary, hashmap, hash, or associative array). It's normally used in a function call where the function takes the map and processes it.

The biggest problem with using a Literal Maps in a dynamically typed language is the lack of a way to communicate and enforce the valid names for the keys. In addition to the fact that you'll have to write code to handle unfamiliar keys yourself, there's no mechanism to indicate to the DSL script writer which keys are correct. A static language allows to avoid this problem by defining enums of a particular type to be the keys.

In a dynamically typed language, the keys of a Literal Map are usually a symbol data type (or, failing that, a string). Symbols are the natural choice and are easy to process; some languages offer syntax shortcuts to make it easy to use symbol keys, as they are so common. Ruby, for example, can replace {:cores => 2} with {cores: 2} as of version 1.9.

Just as I treat a varargs function call as a form of *Literal List (417)*, I treat a function call with keyword arguments as a form of Literal Map. Indeed, keyword arguments are even better, as they often allow you to define valid keywords. Sadly, keyword arguments are even rarer than a literal map syntax.

If you have a literal list syntax but not a literal map, you can use literal lists to represent maps—this is what Lisp does with an expression like (processor (cores

2) (type i386)). In other languages, you can achieve that by using a construct similar to processor("cores", 2, "type" "i386"), treating arguments as alternating keys and values.

Some languages, Ruby for example, allow you to omit the delimiters for a literal map when you are only using one of them within a particular context. So, instead of writing processor({:cores => 2, :type => :i386}), you can shorten it to processor(:cores => 2, :type => :i386).

40.2 When to Use It

Literal Map is a great choice when you need a list of different elements where each element should appear no more than once. The common lack of key validation is annoying but, overall, the syntax is usually the best choice for this case. There's a clear communication that each subelement can only appear at most once, and the map data structure is ideal for the called function to process.

If you don't have Literal Maps, you can make do with a *Literal List (417)*, or use *Nested Functions (357)* or *Method Chaining (373)*.

40.3 The Computer Configuration Using Lists and Maps (Ruby)

Following its scripting language tradition, Ruby provides very good literal syntax for lists and maps. Here's how we can use this syntax for the computer configuration example:

```
computer(processor(:cores => 2, :type => :i386),
         disk(:size => 150),
         disk(:size => 75, :speed => 7200, :interface => :sata))
```

I'm not using just Literal Map here; as usual, it's good to mix Literal Map with other techniques. Here I have three functions: computer, processor, and disk. Each of these functions takes a collection as an argument: computer takes a *Literal List (417)*, the others take a Literal Map. I'm using *Object Scoping (385)* with a builder class that implements the functions. Since this is Ruby, I can use instance_eval to evaluate the DSL script in the context of an instance of the builder, which saves me from having to make a subclass.

I'll start with processor.

```
class MixedLiteralBuilder...
  def processor map
    check_keys map, [:cores, :type]
    return Processor.new(map[:cores], map[:type])
  end
```

Making use of a Literal Map is simple; I just pick the necessary items out of the map using the keys. The danger with using a map like this is that it's easy for the caller to introduce an incorrect key by accident, so it's worth a little checking here.

```
class MixedLiteralBuilder...
  def check_keys map, validKeys
    bad_keys = map.keys - validKeys
    raise IncorrectKeyException.new(bad_keys) unless bad_keys.empty?
  end

class IncorrectKeyException < Exception
  def initialize bad_keys
    @bad_keys = bad_keys
  end
  def to_s
    "unrecognized keys: #{@bad_keys.join(', ')}"
  end
end
```

I use the same approach for the disk.

```
class MixedLiteralBuilder...
  def disk map
    check_keys map, [:size, :speed, :interface]
    return Disk.new(map[:size], map[:speed], map[:interface])
  end
```

Since everything is a simple value, I can create the domain object and return it within each *Nested Function (357)*. The computer function can create the computer object, using a vararg for the multiple disks.

40: Literal Map

```
class MixedLiteralBuilder...
  def computer proc, *disks
    @result = Computer.new(proc, *disks)
  end
```

(Using a "*" in the argument list enables variable arguments in Ruby; in the argument list, *disks indicates a vararg. I can then refer to all the disks passed in as an array named disks. If I call another function with *disks, the elements of the disks array are passed in as separate arguments.)

To process the DSL script, I get the builder to evaluate the script using instance_eval.

```
class MixedLiteralBuilder...
  def load aStream
    instance_eval aStream
  end
```

40.4 Evolving to Greenspun Form (Ruby)

As with other elements in an internal DSL, a good DSL uses several different techniques together. So in the previous example, I used *Nested Function (357)* and *Literal List (417)* as well as Literal Map. Sometimes, however, it's interesting to push a single technique as far as it can go just to get a sense of its capabilities. It's quite possible to write even a fairly complex DSL expression using only Literal List and Literal Map. Let's see what that might look like:

```
[:computer,
  [:processor, {:cores => 2, :type => :i386}],
  [:disk, {:size => 150}],
  [:disk, {:size => 75, :speed => 7200, :interface => :sata}]
]
```

In this version, I've replaced all the function calls with Literal Lists, where the first element in the list is the name of the item to be processed and the rest of the list contains the arguments. I can process this array by first evaluating the Ruby code and then passing it to a method that interprets the computer expression.

```
class LiteralOnlyBuilder...
  def load aStream
    @result = handle_computer(eval(aStream))
  end
```

I handle each expression by checking the first element of the array and then processing the other elements.

```
class LiteralOnlyBuilder...
  def handle_computer anArray
    check_head :computer, anArray
    processor = handle_processor(anArray[1])
    disks = anArray[2..-1].map{|e| handle_disk e}
    return Computer.new(processor, *disks)
  end
  def check_head expected, array
    raise "error: expected #{expected}, got #{array.first}" unless
      array.first == expected
  end
```

This essentially follows the form of a *Recursive Descent Parser (245)*. I say that the computer clause has a processor and multiple disks, and I call the methods to process them, returning a newly created computer.

Handling a processor is straightforward—just unpick the arguments out of the provided map.

```
class LiteralOnlyBuilder...
  def handle_processor anArray
    check_head :processor, anArray
    check_arg_keys anArray, [:cores, :type]
    args = anArray[1]
    return Processor.new(args[:cores], args[:type])
  end
  def check_arg_keys array, validKeys
    bad_keys = array[1].keys - validKeys
    raise IncorrectKeyException.new(bad_keys) unless bad_keys.empty?
  end
end
```

Handling the disks works the same way.

```
class LiteralOnlyBuilder...
  def handle_disk anArray
    check_head :disk, anArray
    check_arg_keys anArray, [:size, :speed, :interface]
    args = anArray[1]
    return Disk.new(args[:size], args[:speed], args[:interface])
  end
```

One thing to notice about this approach is that it gives me complete control over the order of evaluation of the elements of the language. I choose here to evaluate the processor and disk expressions before creating the computer object, but I can do things pretty much any way I wish. In many ways, this DSL script is like an external DSL encoded in internal literal collection syntax instead of a string.

This form mixes lists and maps, but it's also possible to do this using only Literal List, which might appropriately be called Greenspun form.

40: Literal Map

```
[:computer,
 [:processor,
  [:cores, 2,],
  [:type, :i386]],
 [:disk,
  [:size, 150]],
 [:disk,
  [:size, 75],
  [:speed, 7200],
  [:interface, :sata]]]
```

(I'll leave it as an exercise for the reader to determine why I call this piece of programming whimsy "Greenspun form.")

All I've really done here is replace each map with a list of two-element sublists, where each sublist is a key and value.

The main loading code is the same, breaking down the symbolic expression (sexp) for the computer into a processor and several disks.

```
class ListOnlyBuilder...
  def load aStream
    @result = handle_computer(eval(aStream))
  end
  def handle_computer sexp
    check_head :computer, sexp
    processor = handle_processor(sexp[1])
    disks = sexp[2..-1].map{|e| handle_disk e}
    return Computer.new(processor, *disks)
  end
```

The difference comes with the subclauses, which need some extra code as an equivalent of looking up things in a map.

```
class ListOnlyBuilder...
  def handle_processor sexp
    check_head :processor, sexp
    check_arg_keys sexp, [:cores, :type]
    return Processor.new(select_arg(:cores, sexp),
                         select_arg(:type, sexp))
  end
  def handle_disk sexp
    check_head :disk, sexp
    check_arg_keys sexp, [:size, :speed, :interface]
    return Disk.new(select_arg(:size, sexp),
                    select_arg(:speed, sexp),
                    select_arg(:interface, sexp))
  end
  def select_arg key, list
    assoc = list.tail.assoc(key)
    return assoc ? assoc[1] : nil
  end
```

Using only lists does result in a more regular DSL script, but using a list of pairs as a map doesn't fit in so well with Ruby's style. Either case isn't as good as the earlier example which mixed function calls with literal collections.

Yet this approach of nested lists does lead us to another place where this style is natural. As many readers will have long ago realized, this is essentially what Lisp looks like. In Lisp, the DSL script might look like this:

```
(computer
  (processor
    (cores 2)
    (type i386))
  (disk
    (size 150))
  (disk
    (size 75)
    (speed 7200)
    (interface sata)))
```

The list structure is a lot clearer in Lisp. Bare words are symbols by default, and since expressions are either atoms or lists, there's no need for commas.

40: Literal Map

Chapter 41

Dynamic Reception

Handle messages without defining them in the receiving class.

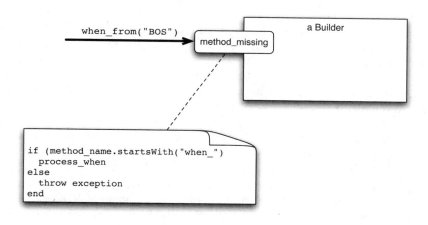

Also known as: Overriding method_missing or doesNotUnderstand

Any object has a limited set of methods defined for it. A client of an object may attempt to invoke a method that isn't defined on the receiver. A statically typed language will spot this at compile time and report a compilation error. As a result, you know you won't get this kind of error at runtime (unless you do some clever fiddling to get around the type system). With a dynamically typed language, you can invoke a nonexistent method at runtime, which usually gives you a runtime error.

Dynamic Reception allows you to adjust this behavior, which means you can respond differently to an unknown message.

41.1 How It Works

Many dynamic languages react to an unknown method invocation by calling a special error-handling method at the top of the object hierarchy. There is no standard name for this method: in Smalltalk it's doesNotUnderstand, and in Ruby it's method_missing. You can introduce your own processing for an unknown method by subclassing these methods in your own class. When you do this, you are essentially dynamically altering the rules for the reception of method calls.

There are many reasons why Dynamic Reception is useful in general programming. One excellent example is supporting automatic delegation to another object. To do this, you define the methods that you wish to handle in the original receiver and use Dynamic Reception to send any unknown messages to a delegate object.

Dynamic Reception can feature in several ways in DSL work. One common use is to convert what might otherwise be method parameters into the name of the method. A good example of this is Rails's Active Record dynamic finders. Say you have a Person class with firstname and lastname properties. With these defined, you can call find_by_firstname("martin") or find_by_firstname_and_lastname("martin", "fowler") without having to define these methods. The code in the Active Record superclass overrides Ruby's method_missing and checks to see if the method call begins with find_by. If so, it then parses the method name to find the property names and uses them to construct a query. You could also do this by passing in multiple arguments, such as find_by("firstname", "martin", "lastname", "fowler"), but putting the property names into the method name is more readable as it mimics what you would actually do if you explicitly defined methods like that.

A method like find_by_name works by taking a single method name and parsing it. Essentially, you are embedding an external DSL in the method name. Another approach is to use a sequence of Dynamic Receptions, like find_by.firstname("martin").and.lastname("fowler") or find_by.firstname.martin.and.lastname. fowler. In this case, the find_by method would return an *Expression Builder (343)* that you can use to build up a query using *Method Chaining (373)* and Dynamic Reception.

41: Dynamic Reception

One of the advantages of doing this is that it can avoid quoting the various parameters, using martin rather than "martin" to reduce noise. If you are using *Object Scoping (385)*, with this mechanism you can use bare symbols for arguments, for example state idle instead of state :idle. You can do this by implementing Dynamic Reception in the superclass so that, once the object has had state invoked, it will override the next unknown method call to capture the name of the state. You can go further by using *Textual Polishing (477)* to remove various bits of noisy punctuation.

41.2 When to Use It

Using Dynamic Reception to move parameters into method names is appealing for a couple of reasons. First, it can mimic what you would genuinely do with a method but with less effort. It's quite reasonable to imagine a person class having a find_by_firstname_and_lastname method; by using Dynamic Reception you are providing this method without having to actually program it. This can be a significant time-saver, particularly if you are using lots of combinations. Certainly, there are other ways you can do it; you can put attribute name into the parameters as in find(:firstname, "martin", :lastname, "fowler"), use a closure like find {|p| p.firstname == "martin" and p.lastname == "fowler"}, or even embed a fragmentary external DSL in a string as in find("firstname == martin lastname == fowler"). Yet many people find that embedding the field names into the method names is the most fluent way to express the call.

Another benefit of replacing parameters by method names is that it can give you better consistency in punctuation. An expression like find.by.firstname. martin.and.lastname.fowler uses dots as the only form of punctuation. This is good, in that people won't get confused as to when they should use a dot and when a pair of parentheses or quotes. For many others, this consistency isn't a virtue; I like separating what is schema from what is data, so I prefer the way find_by.firstname("martin").and.lastname("fowler") puts field names into method calls and the data into parameters.

One of the problems with putting data into method names is that often, programming languages use a different encoding for program text than for their string data; many only allow ASCII, which then wouldn't work for non-ASCII personal names. Similarly, the language grammar rules for method names may exclude valid personal names.

Above all, it's important to remember that Dynamic Reception only pays its way when it allows you to build these structures in general, without any special case handling. This means that it's only worthwhile when you can clearly translate from the dynamic methods to methods that are needed for other purposes. Conditions are good examples of this because they usually call attributes on domain model objects. A find_by_firstname_and_lastname method is effective because I have a Person class that has firstname and lastname attributes. If you need to write special methods to handle particular cases of Dynamic Reception, that usually means you shouldn't be using Dynamic Reception.

Dynamic Reception comes with many problems and limitations. The biggest one, of course, is that you can't do this at all with static languages. But even in a dynamic language, you need to be wary about using it. Once you override the handler for unknown method invocations, any mistake can lead you into a deep debugging trouble. Stack traces often become impenetrable.

There are also limitations on what you can express. You usually can't put in something like find_by.age.greater_than.2 because most dynamic languages won't

41: Dynamic Reception

allow "2" in a method name. You can dodge around that with something like find_by.age.greater_than.n2 but that obstructs much of the fluency that you're doing this for.

Since I'm focusing on Boolean expressions here, I should also point out that this kind of method call composition is not a good way of composing complex Boolean conditions. The approach is fine for something simple like find_by.firstname("martin").and.lastname("fowler"), but once you get to statements like find_by.firstname.like("m*").and.age.greater_than(40).and.not.employer.like("thought*"), you're running down a road that forces you to implement a kludgy parser in an environment not well-suited for it.

The fact that expressions using Dynamic Reception don't work well for complex conditionals isn't a reason to avoid them for simple cases. Active Record uses Dynamic Reception to provide dynamic finders for simple cases, but deliberately does not support more complex expressions, encouraging you to use a different mechanism instead. Some people don't like that, preferring a single mechanism, but I think it's good to realize that different solutions may work best at different complexities, so you should provide more than one.

41.3 Promotion Points Using Parsed Method Names (Ruby)

For this example, let's consider a scheme that assigns points to travel itineraries. Our domain model is an itinerary that consists of items, where each item might be a flight, hotel stay, car hire, etc. We want to allow a flexible way for people to score frequent travel points, such as scoring 300 points for taking a flight out of Boston.

Using Dynamic Reception, I'll show how to support the following cases. First is a simple case of one promotion rule.

41: Dynamic
Reception

```
@builder = PromotionBuilder.new
@builder.score(300).when_from("BOS")
```

In another case, we can have multiple promotion rules matching different kinds of elements. Here we score for flying out of a particular airport and staying an a particular hotel brand within the same itinerary:

```
@builder = PromotionBuilder.new
@builder.score(350).when_from("BOS")
@builder.score(100).when_brand("hyatt")
```

And finally, we have a compound flight rule, where we score for flying out of Boston on a particular airline (which may not be around any more when you read this).

```
@builder = PromotionBuilder.new
@builder.score(140).when_from_and_airline("BOS","NW")
```

41.3.1 Model

The model here has two parts: itineraries and promotions. The itinerary is just a collection of items, which could be anything. For this simple example, I just have flights and hotels.

```ruby
class Itinerary
  def initialize
    @items = []
  end
  def << arg
    @items << arg
  end
  def items
    return @items.dup
  end
end

class Flight
  attr_reader :from, :to, :airline
  def initialize airline, from, to
    @from, @to, @airline = from, to, airline
  end
end

class Hotel
  attr_accessor :nights, :brand
  def initialize  brand, nights
    @nights, @brand = nights, brand
  end
end
```

Promotions are a set of rules, each rule having a score and a list of conditions.

```ruby
class Itinerary...
  def initialize rules
    @rules = rules
  end

class PromotionRule...
  def initialize anInteger
    @score = anInteger
    @conditions = []
  end
  def add_condition aPromotionCondition
    @conditions << aPromotionCondition
  end
```

41: Dynamic Reception

The approach here scores an itinerary against a promotion. It does this by scoring each rule against the itinerary and summing up the results.

```
class Itinerary...
  def score_of anItinerary
    return @rules.inject(0) {|sum, r| sum += r.score_of(anItinerary)}
  end
```

The rule scores an itinerary by checking if all its conditions match the itinerary; if so, it returns its score.

```
class PromotionRule...
  def score_of anItinerary
    return (@conditions.all?{|c| c.match(anItinerary)}) ? @score : 0
  end
```

Each score line in the DSL is a separate rule. So,

```
@builder = PromotionBuilder.new
@builder.score(350).when_from("BOS")
@builder.score(100).when_brand("hyatt")
```

is one promotion with two rules. Either or both of them could match a given itinerary. In contrast,

```
@builder = PromotionBuilder.new
@builder.score(140).when_from_and_airline("BOS","NW")
```

is one rule with two conditions. Both conditions have to match to score the points.

To handle this, I have an equality condition object that I can set with appropriate names and values.

```
class EqualityCondition
  def initialize aSymbol, value
    @attribute, @value = aSymbol, value
  end
  def match anItinerary
    return anItinerary.items.any?{|i| match_item i}
  end
  def match_item anItem
    return false unless anItem.respond_to?(@attribute)
    return @value == anItem.send(@attribute)
  end
end
```

Using equality conditions in the method name like this is very limited. However, the underlying model allows me to have any kind of condition as long as it knows how to match an itinerary. Some of these conditions could be added through the DSL, others through other means, such as a closure.

```
example......
  rule = PromotionRule.newWithBlock(520) do |itinerary|
    flights = itinerary.items.select{|i| i.kind_of? Flight}
    flights.any? {|f| f.from == "LAX"} and
      flights.any? {|f| f.to == "LAX"} and
      flights.all? {|f| %w[NW CO DL].include?(f.airline)}
  end
  promotion = Promotion.new([rule])

class BlockCondition
  def initialize aBlock
    @block = aBlock
  end
  def match anItinerary
    @block.call(anItinerary)
  end
end
```

This kind of flexibility can be quite important. It allows people to use the DSL to handle simple cases simply, but provides an alternative mechanism to handle more complicated cases.

41.3.2 Builder

The basic builder wraps a collection of promotion rules that it builds up, returning a new promotion object as needed.

```
class PromotionBuilder...
  def initialize
    @rules = []
  end
  def content
    return Promotion.new(@rules)
  end
```

The score method creates one of these rules, which it holds in a *Context Variable (175)*. It also creates a particular builder for the condition.

```
class PromotionBuilder...
  def score anInteger
    @rules << PromotionRule.new(anInteger)
    return PromotionConditionBuilder.new(self)
  end
```

The condition builder is the class that uses Dynamic Reception. In Ruby, you do Dynamic Reception by overriding method_missing.

41: Dynamic Reception

```
class PromotionConditionBuilder...
  def initialize parent
    @parent = parent
  end
  def method_missing(method_id, *args)
    if match = /^when_(\w*)/.match(method_id.to_s)
      process_when match.captures.last, *args
    else
      super
    end
  end
end
```

The method_missing hook checks if the caller begins with when_; if not, it forwards to the superclass, which will throw an exception. Assuming we have the right kind of method, it pulls the attribute names out of the method call, checks that they match the arguments, and then creates the appropriate rules.

```
class PromotionConditionBuilder...
  def process_when method_tail, *args
    attribute_names = method_tail.split('_and_')
    check_number_of_attributes(attribute_names, args)
    populate_rules(attribute_names, args)
  end
  def check_number_of_attributes(names, values)
    unless names.size == values.size
      throw "There are %d attribute names but %d arguments" %
        [names.size, values.size]
    end
  end
  def populate_rules names, args
    names.zip(args).each do |name, value|
      @parent.add_condition(EqualityCondition.new(name, value))
    end
  end
end
```

This approach is unsurprisingly similar to Active Record's dynamic finders. If you're curious about those, take a look at Jamis Buck's description (http://weblog.jamisbuck.org/2006/12/1/under-the-hood-activerecord-base-find-part-3).

41.4 Promotion Points Using Chaining (Ruby)

Now I'll take the same example and work it using chaining. I'll use the same model and (mostly) the same example conditions. As the DSL is different, the conditions are formulated differently. Here's the simple single selection of flights out of Boston:

```
@builder.score(300).when.from.equals.BOS
```

In this case, I'm passing all the arguments to the condition as methods rather than parameters (although I'm keeping the score as a parameter, just to be inconsistent). I'm also indicating the operator for the condition as a method.

Here's the case with two separate scores:

```
@builder.score(350).when.from.equals.BOS
@builder.score(100).when.brand.equals.hyatt
```

Finally, here I have a compound condition:

```
@builder.score(170).when.from.equals.BOS.and.nights.at.least._3
```

The compound condition is more involved than the one I used in the previous example. For this one, I'm taking advantage of the ability to use other operators, as well as showing the kind of smudge you need to make in order to pass a numeric parameter as a method name.

41.4.1 Model

The model is almost identical to the one I used in the previous example. The only change is that I've added an extra condition.

```
class AtLeastCondition...
  def initialize aSymbol, value
    @attribute, @value = aSymbol, value
  end
  def match anItinerary
    return anItinerary.items.any?{|i| match_item i}
  end
  def match_item anItem
    return false unless anItem.respond_to?(@attribute)
    return @value <= anItem.send(@attribute)
  end
end
```

41.4.2 Builder

The differences from the previous example lie in the builder. As before, I have a promotion builder object that holds a bunch of rules and produces a promotion when needed.

```
class PromotionBuilder...
  def initialize
    @rules = []
  end
  def content
    return Promotion.new(@rules)
  end
end
```

The score method adds a rule to the rules list.

41: Dynamic
Reception

```
class PromotionBuilder...
  def score anInteger
    @rules << PromotionRule.new(anInteger)
    return self
  end
```

The when method returns a more specific builder to capture the attribute name.

```
class PromotionBuilder...
  def when
    return ConditionAtributeNameBuilder.new(self)
  end
end

class ConditionAtributeNameBuilder < Builder
  def initialize parent
    @parent = PromotionConditionBuilder.new(parent)
    @parent.name = self
  end
end

class Builder
  attr_accessor :content, :parent
  def initialize parentBuilder = nil
    @parent = parentBuilder
  end
end

class PromotionConditionBuilder < Builder
  attr_accessor :name, :operator, :value
```

To build the condition, I create a little parse tree. Each condition in an expression has three parts: name, operator, and condition. So I make a builder for each of the parts, as well as a parent builder to tie the conditions together. As a result, when I create the name builder, I also create the condition builder parent to prepare the tree.

The attribute name builder will look for a suitable name for the attribute we are testing, since this name will vary depending on the model class's attributes. I use Dynamic Reception.

```
class ConditionAtributeNameBuilder...
  def method_missing method_id, *args
    @content = method_id.to_s
    return ConditionOperatorBuilder.new(@parent)
  end
```

This captures the name and returns the operator builder to capture the operator.

The operator builder will only have a fixed set of operators to work off, so it doesn't need to use Dynamic Reception.

```ruby
class ConditionOperatorBuilder < Builder
  attr_reader :condition_class
  def initialize parent
    super
    @parent.operator = self
  end
  def equals
    @content = EqualityCondition
    return next_builder
  end
  def at
    return self
  end
  def least
    @content = AtLeastCondition
    return next_builder
  end
  def next_builder
    return ConditionValueBuilder.new(@parent)
  end
end
```

The basic behavior of the operator builder is similar to the name builder: Capture the operator and return a new builder for the final part (the value). There are a couple of interesting points. Firstly, the content of this builder is the appropriate condition class from the model. Secondly, the at method just returns itself, as it's pure syntactic sugar—only there to make the expression readable.

The final builder is the value builder which captures the value using Dynamic Reception.

```ruby
class ConditionValueBuilder < Builder
  def initialize parent
    super
    @parent.value = self
  end
  def method_missing method_id, *args
    @content = method_id.to_s
    @content = @content.to_i if @content =~ /^_\d+$/
    @parent.end_condition
  end
end
```

41: Dynamic Reception

If the value is a number, I need some jiggery-pokery, hence the use of a leading underscore "_3" to represent "3" in the DSL script. (In Ruby, "_3".to_i will parse the string to an integer, ignoring the underscore and returning 3.)

This method also ends this part of the expression, so it tells its parent to populate the model.

```
class PromotionConditionBuilder...
  def end_condition
    content = @operator.build_content(@name.content, @value.content)
    @parent.add_condition content
    return @parent
  end

class ConditionOperatorBuilder...
  def build_content name, value
    return @content.new(name, value)
  end

class PromotionBuilder...
  def add_condition cond
    current_rule.add_condition cond
  end
  def current_rule
    @rules.last
  end
```

At this point, I've consumed the little parse tree and created the condition object in the model. If I have a compound condition, I repeat the process.

```
class PromotionBuilder...
  def and
    return ConditionAtributeNameBuilder.new(self)
  end
```

Making little parse trees like this isn't a common way to do an internal DSL; it's usually easier to just build the model up as you go. But with a conditional expression like this, it makes sense.

Overall, however, I'm not too keen on building up expressions using this approach. It seems to me that once you start parsing sequences of method calls like this, you might as well just switch to an external DSL where you get more flexibility. The desire to build up parse trees is a smell indicating that the internal DSL is doing too much work.

41.5 Removing Quoting in the Secret Panel Controller (JRuby)

In the introduction, I showed an example of how you could use Ruby as an internal DSL for the secret panel controller. The code looks like this:

```
event :doorClosed, "D1CL"
event :drawerOpened,  "D2OP"
event :lightOn, "L1ON"
event :doorOpened, "D1OP"
event :panelClosed, "PNCL"

command  :unlockPanel, "PNUL"
command  :lockPanel,   "PNLK"
command  :lockDoor,    "D1LK"
command  :unlockDoor,  "D1UL"

resetEvents :doorOpened

state :idle do
  actions :unlockDoor, :lockPanel
  transitions :doorClosed => :active
end

state :active do
  transitions :drawerOpened => :waitingForLight,
              :lightOn => :waitingForDrawer
end

state :waitingForLight do
  transitions :lightOn => :unlockedPanel
end

state :waitingForDrawer do
  transitions :drawerOpened => :unlockedPanel
end

state :unlockedPanel do
  actions :unlockPanel, :lockDoor
  transitions :panelClosed => :idle
end
```

In this example code, I don't use any Dynamic Reception, relying on simple function calls. One of the disadvantages of this script is that there's a lot of quoting, in particular every reference to an identifier needs Ruby's symbol marker (the initial ":" in the names). Compared to an external DSL, this feels like noise. If I use Dynamic Reception, it's possible to get rid of all of the symbol quoting and produce a script like this:

41: Dynamic
Reception

```
events do
  doorClosed    "D1CL"
  drawerOpened  "D2OP"
  lightOn       "L1ON"
  doorOpened    "D1OP"
  panelClosed   "PNCL"
end
```

```
commands do
  unlockPanel "PNUL"
  lockPanel   "PNLK"
  lockDoor    "D1LK"
  unlockDoor  "D1UL"
end

reset_events do
  doorOpened
end

state.idle do
  actions.unlockDoor.lockPanel
  doorClosed.to.active
end

state.active do
  drawerOpened.to.waitingForLight
  lightOn.to.waitingForDrawer
end

state.waitingForLight do
  lightOn.to.unlockedPanel
end

state.waitingForDrawer do
  drawerOpened.to.unlockedPanel
end

state.unlockedPanel do
  panelClosed.to.idle
  actions.unlockPanel.lockDoor
end
```

The starting point for implementing this is a state machine builder class. This class uses *Object Scoping (385)* using instance_eval. The build occurs in two stages, first evaluating the script and then doing some postprocessing.

```
class StateMachineBuilder...
  attr_reader :machine
  def initialize
    @states = {}
    @events = {}
    @commands = {}
    @state_blocks = {}
    @reset_events = []
  end
  def load aString
    instance_eval aString
    build_machine
    return self
  end
```

To evaluate the script, the builder has methods that correspond to the main clauses of the DSL script. I'm using the same *Semantic Model (159)* that I used in the introduction; the JRuby builder populates Java objects.

The first clause to look at is the event declarations, which I make by calling the events method on the state machine builder, passing in a block that contains the individual event declarations.

```
class StateMachineBuilder...
  def events &block
    EventBuilder.new(self).instance_eval(&block)
    self
  end

  def add_event name, code
    @events[name] = Event.new(name.to_s, code)
  end

class EventBuilder < Builder
  def method_missing name, *args
    @parent.add_event(name, args[0])
  end
end

class Builder
  def initialize parent
    @parent = parent
  end
end
```

The events method evaluates the block immediately in the context of a separate builder which uses Dynamic Reception to process every method call as an event declaration. With each event declaration, I create an event from the Semantic Model and put it into a *Symbol Table (165)*.

I use the same basic technique for commands and reset events. By using a different builder, I can keep each one simple and clearly scope what each builder is recognizing.

The state declaration is more interesting. Again, I use a closure to capture the body of the declaration, but there are a couple of differences. The obvious one from the script is that I indicate the name with Dynamic Reception.

41: Dynamic Reception

```
class StateMachineBuilder...
  def state
    return StateNameBuilder.new(self)
  end

  def addState name, block
    @states[name] = State.new(name.to_s)
    @state_blocks[name] = block
    @start_state ||= @states[name]
  end
```

```
class StateNameBuilder < Builder
  def method_missing name, *args, &block
    @parent.addState(name, block)
    return @parent
  end
end
```

The second difference is in the implementation. Instead of evaluating the *Nested Closure (403)* right away, I squirrel it away in a map. By deferring the evaluation till later, I can avoid worrying about the forward references between states. I can wait to deal with the state bodies until I've declared all the states and fully populated the Symbol Table with them.

The last point is that I treat the first-named state as the start state by using an additional variable which I populate only if it's still nil—which means that the first state will be in there.

Populating this data finishes evaluating the script; now, the second stage is the postprocessing.

```
class StateMachineBuilder...
  def build_machine
    @state_blocks.each do |key, value|
      if value
        sb = StateBodyBuilder.new(self, @states[key])
        sb.instance_eval(&value)
      end
    end
    @machine = StateMachine.new(@start_state)
    @machine.addResetEvents(
            @reset_events.
            collect{|e| @events[e]}.
            to_java("gothic.model.Event"))
  end

class StateBodyBuilder < Builder
  def initialize parent, state
    super parent
    @state = state
  end
```

The first step of postprocessing is to evaluate the bodies of the state declarations, again by creating a specific builder and instance_evaling the block with it.

The body can contain two kinds of statements: declaring actions and declaring transitions. The action case is handled by a specific method.

```
class StateBodyBuilder...
  def actions
    return ActionListBuilder.new(self)
  end
  def add_action name
    @state.addAction(@parent.command_at(name))
  end
```

```
class ActionListBuilder < Builder
  def method_missing name, *args
    @parent.add_action name
    return self
  end
end

class StateMachineBuilder...
  def command_at name
    return @commands[name]
  end
```

The actions creates another builder which absorbs all method calls as command names. This allows you to specify multiple actions in a single line with chaining.

While actions use a special method, analogous to a keyword in an external DSL, transitions use Dynamic Reception.

```
class StateBodyBuilder...
  def method_missing name, *args
    return TransitionBuilder.new(self, name)
  end
  def add_transition event, target
    @state.addTransition(@parent.event_at(event), @parent.state_at(target))
  end

class TransitionBuilder < Builder
  def initialize parent, event
    super parent
    @event = event
  end
  def to
    return self
  end
  def method_missing name, *args
    @target = name
    @parent.add_transition @event, @target
    return @parent
  end
end

class StateMachineBuilder...
  def event_at name
    return @events[name]
  end
  def state_at name
    return @states[name]
  end
```

Here I use an unknown method to start a specific builder to capture the target state with a further use of Dynamic Reception. I also allow to as syntactic sugar.

By doing all of this, I can get rid of all the ":" on symbols. The question, of course, is whether it's worth the trouble. To my eye, I like the way the event and command list turn out, but I'm not so keen on the states. I could, of course, use

41: Dynamic
Reception

a hybrid approach with Dynamic Reception for the things I like and symbol references where Dynamic Reception isn't helping. A mixture of techniques is often the best bet.

Getting rid of the symbol ":" is nice, but I still have the quotes around command and event codes. I could use a similar technique to deal with those as well.

Chapter 42

Annotation

Data about program elements, such as classes and methods,
which can be processed during compilation or execution.

```
@ValidRange(lower = 1, upper = 1000, units = Units.LB)
private Quantity weight;
@ValidRange(lower = 1, upper = 120, units = Units.IN)
private Quantity height;
```

We are used to classifying the data in our programs and making rules about how they work. Customers can be grouped by region and have payment rules. Often, it is useful to make these kinds of rules about elements of the program itself. Languages usually provide some built-in mechanisms to do this, such as access controls that allow us to mark classes and methods as public or private.

However, there are often things we would like to mark that go beyond what a language supports, or even should reasonably support. We might want to restrict the values that an integer field might take, mark methods that should be run as part of testing, or indicate that a class can safely be serialized.

An Annotation is a piece of information about a program element. We can take this information and manipulate it during runtime, or indeed during compile time if the environment supports this. Annotations thus provide a mechanism to extend the programming language.

I've used the term Annotation here, as that is the term used in the Java programming language. A similar syntax predated this in .NET, but its term "attribute" is too widely used for other concepts, so I prefer to follow the Java terminology. However, the concept here is more broad than the syntax, and the same benefits can be achieved without this kind of special syntax.

42.1 How It Works

There are two topics in using Annotations: defining them and processing them. Although both depend on facilities that vary from language to language, definition and processing are relatively independent of each other, in that the same processing technique can be used for Annotations defined in different ways.

To fit in with our general model of DSLs, the defining syntax represents how the Annotations work as an internal DSL. In each case, they develop a *Semantic Model (159)* by attaching data to the runtime model of a program that's built into a language. Later processing steps correspond to the running of the Semantic Model; as with any DSL, these can involve model execution and code generation.

42.1.1 Defining an Annotation

The most obvious way to define an Annotation is to use specially designed syntax that some languages have. So, in Java we can mark a test method like this:

```
@test public void softwareAlwaysWorks()
```

or, in C#, like this:

```
[Test] public void SoftwareAlwaysWorks()
```

Both languages allow parameters to their annotations, so you can do something like:

```
class PatientVisit...
  @ValidRange(lower = 1, upper = 1000, units = Units.LB)
  private Quantity weight;
  @ValidRange(lower = 1, upper = 120, units = Units.IN)
  private Quantity height;
```

Using a purpose-designed syntax is the most obvious, and often the easiest, way to put together annotations. However, there are other techniques that you can use.

One of the most natural ways to specify an Annotation is to use class methods. Let's consider a case where we want to add a valid range annotation that indicates a specific legal range for a field. Let's say we want to limit a patient's height between 1 and 120 (inches) and weight between 1 and 1000 (pounds). (Usually we'd use a Quantity here, but we'll use an integer to keep it simple.) We specify these ranges in Ruby like this:

```
valid_range :height, 1..120
valid_range :weight, 1..1000
```

In order to make this work, we define a class method called valid_range. This method takes two arguments, the name of the field and the range to limit that field to. The class method can then do whatever it likes with this data. It can just add the bare data into a structure, mirroring what the built-in syntax does, or it can directly create and store validator objects.

Using class methods like this can be almost as easy as using purpose-designed syntax. The biggest issue is that the class method call needs the name of the program element it's annotating. This leads to some extra verbiage, but also gives the programmer the freedom to separate the annotations from the annotated declarations. That is a big payoff for languages that make this easy—there's little need to provide a special annotation syntax.

Using class methods like this does raise some issues to keep in mind. For the annotations to be stored, they need to be executed. The Ruby example above is executed when the code is loaded. Some languages may need additional mechanics to ensure this is done. The simplest way to store annotation data is with class variables, but many languages share class variables across a class and its subclasses, which wouldn't mess up this example but could lead to problems in other cases.

I've described this technique in object-oriented terms, but you can do basically the same thing with any language that allows you to easily represent its elements. So, you could define a Lisp structure that tagged function names with data. That structure could live anywhere as long as it could be found by later processing.

A common technique used in statically typed languages is a marker interface. This involves defining an interface with no methods and implementing it. The presence of the interface effectively tags the class for later processing. This technique only works on classes, not methods or fields.

Naming conventions provide a simple form of annotation. This was what was done in many xUnit implementations—test methods were tagged by the convention of having their name begin with test. For simple annotations, this can work rather well, but you're limited in that multiple annotations are difficult to support and parameters are practically impossible.

In all these cases, the annotations are processed by the built-in language constructs to build up a *Semantic Model (159)*. In addition to the usual internal DSL limitations—the syntax of the DSL is limited by the syntax of the host language—there is a further limitation for Annotations. With Annotations, the Semantic Model has to be based on the fundamental representation of the program itself. In an object-oriented program, the foundational representation is that of classes, fields, and methods. The Semantic Model of the Annotations is a decoration of that structure—you can't practically build a completely separate and independent Semantic Model.

42: Annotation

42.1.2 Processing Annotations

Annotations are defined in the source code but are available for processing at later stages—typically during compilation, program loading, or during regular runtime operation.

Processing during regular operation is probably the most common case. This involves using the annotations to control some aspect of an object's behavior. A simple example of this is running test methods in xUnit-style testing frameworks. These tools allow tests to be defined as methods in test classes. Not all methods are test methods, so some annotation scheme is used to identify the tests. A test runner program finds these test methods and runs them.

Database mapping can work in a similar way. Here, a database mapping program interrogates the attributes to find how the fields in the program map to persistent storage structures. It then uses this information to map data.

This kind of processing can be done both at program load and when the processing is used. Validation annotations, such as those shown above, can be partially processed during program startup to create validator objects which are attached to classes. These validators can then be used to validate objects during the execution of the program.

These runtime uses of Annotations correspond to the general approach of model execution of DSLs. As with any DSL, there is also the alternative of code generation. If you have a dynamic language, this code generation can be done during runtime—usually during program load. It can take the form of generating new classes, or adding methods to existing classes.

For compiled languages, generating code at runtime is usually more complicated. It can be possible to run the compiler at runtime and link modules dynamically, but this can be awkward to set up. Another option is when the language provides hooks in its compiler to process annotations—as this is currently done in Java.

Of course code can be generated before compilation. So for the validation example, we could generate a validation method either in the host class or as a separate object. This code would then be part of the program as it compiles. Such intimate intermixing of written and generated code can be confusing, however.

Bytecode postprocessing offers another route for compiled programs. In this approach, we let the compiler compile the program, and after compilation we manipulate the bytecode to add generated steps.

Processing can occur in multiple places with multiple definitions of the processing. If we are building a web application and need to define validations on fields, we'd like to run those validations in multiple places. For best responsiveness, we want to run them in the browser using Javascript. But we can never rely on that, as the user can always get around them, so we also need to run the validations on the server. Using Annotation, we can create a runtime check for the server and generate Javascript to validate in the browser without duplicating code. Both checks can be fully derived from a single Annotation.

42.2 When to Use It

The wide-scale use of Annotations is still relatively new in mainstream programming languages. We are still learning when best to use them.

The key feature of Annotations is that they allow you to separate definition from processing. The validation example is a good illustration of this. If we want to ensure the valid range of a field, then an obvious way to do this is as part of the setting method. The problem with this is that it combines the definition of the constraint with when that constraint is enforced—in this case, forcing the validation to occur when changing a value.

There are many cases when it's useful to check constraints at other times, perhaps allowing a user to fill a form but only validating when that form is submitted. To get a validate-on-submit behavior, you might have an overall validate method on an object—but, again, you define the constraints at the same time when they are checked.

Separating the two allows you to check constraints at different times, perhaps even applying different subsets of constraints at different times. It can also make the code clearer by letting the definitions of the constraints stand alone, so a programmer can see the constraint definition not cluttered by the mechanics of running the checks.

So the strength of Annotations lies where it makes sense to separate definition and processing. You might want to do this because you want processing to change independently of definition, or because you want to make definition easier to understand by letting it stand alone.

The downside of using Annotations is that it is more awkward to follow both definition and processing. If you need to understand them together, then Annotations force you to look in two disconnected places. The processing code is also generic, which may make it even harder to follow.

A corollary to this is that the definition of an Annotation should be declarative and not involve any logic flow. Furthermore, it shouldn't imply any ties to when the processing logic occurs, or any ordering of processing Annotations attached to the same or different program elements.

42: Annotation

42.3 Custom Syntax with Runtime Processing (Java)

For our first code example of annotations, I'll use the most obvious case: a language that has a custom syntax for annotations—in this case Java, which added them with version 1.5 (or 5, or whatever number they are using these days).

Here's how to specify a valid range for an integer value:

```
class PatientVisit...
  @ValidRange(lower = 1, upper = 1000, units = Units.LB)
  private Quantity weight;
  @ValidRange(lower = 1, upper = 120, units = Units.IN)
  private Quantity height;
```

To make this work, I need to define an annotation type like this:

```
@Target(ElementType.FIELD)
@Retention(RetentionPolicy.RUNTIME)
public @interface ValidRange {
  int lower() default Integer.MIN_VALUE;
  int upper() default Integer.MAX_VALUE;
  Units units() default Units.MISSING;
}
```

In Java's annotation system, the annotation type itself is effectively an object that has only fields, which must be literals or other annotations.

As a result of this, all the processing of annotations is done elsewhere. I'll trigger validation processing by having objects validate themselves.

(This is a side note to the topic at hand, but I think it's important to point out that having an object validate itself in this way is not always the correct strategy. When you validate something, you always do so for a context, and that context is usually some action involving that object. The validation approach I'm using here implies validation is correct for all contexts where you use this code. Sometimes this is the case, but often it isn't.)

```
class DomainObject...
  boolean isValid() {
    return new ValidationProcessor().isValid(this);
  }
public class PatientVisit extends DomainObject
```

All the domain object method does is delegate to the validation processor.

```
class ValidationProcessor...
  public boolean isValid(Object arg) {
    for (Field f : arg.getClass().getDeclaredFields())
      for (Annotation a : f.getAnnotations())
        if (doesAnnotationValidationFail(arg, f, a)) return false;
    return true;
  }
  public boolean doesAnnotationValidationFail(Object obj, Field f, Annotation a) {
    FieldValidator validator = validatorMap().get(a.annotationType());
    if (null == validator) return false;
    return !validator.isValid(obj, f);
  }
  private Map<Class, FieldValidator> validatorMap() {
    Map<Class, FieldValidator> result = new HashMap<Class, FieldValidator>();
    result.put(ValidRange.class, new ValidRangeFieldValidator());
    return result;
  }
```

The validation processor scans the target object class for annotations, figures out which ones are validations, gets hold of a specific validator object for each annotation, and runs that validator against the object.

Most of this code only needs to be run once, as annotations don't change at runtime. I'll leave it up to you to find a more efficient way of running this setup code, if you promise to only do it if you know it's a performance bottleneck.

The link between annotation and a processing class is made by a dictionary built in validatorMap(). If you have a scheme where annotations can contain code, then the annotation could implement the isValid method itself. I could also include the name of the validator class in the annotation as one of its fields. I didn't do this because I generally prefer, at least in Java, to make annotations independent of the processing mechanism.

I then have the validator object check the range.

```
class ValidRangeFieldValidator...
  public boolean isValid(Object obj, Field field) {
    ValidRange r = field.getAnnotation(ValidRange.class);
    field.setAccessible(true);
    Quantity value;
    try {
      value = (Quantity)field.get(obj);
    } catch (IllegalAccessException e) {
      throw new RuntimeException(e);
    }
    return (r.units() == value.getUnits())
      && (r.lower() <= value.getAmount())
      && (value.getAmount() <= r.upper());
  }
```

42.4 Using a Class Method (Ruby)

Ruby is an example of a language where there's no custom annotation syntax, yet where annotations are widely used. In Ruby, we define annotations with a class method called directly within the body of the class.

```
class PatientVisit < Domain Object...
  valid_range :height, 1..120
  valid_range :weight, 1..1000
```

(For the Ruby examples, I'm using integers rather than quantities to keep the examples simpler. Feel free to spank me if you ever see me doing this with production code.)

Code like this, directly in the body of the class, is run when the class is loaded, so it works well for this kind of initialization:

```
class DomainObject...
  @@validations = {}

  def self.valid_range name, range
    @@validations[self] ||= []
    v = lambda do |obj|
      range.include?(obj.instance_variable_get("@" + name.to_s))
    end
    @@validations[self] << v
  end
end
```

The implementation here is pretty straightforward. I store the validators using a class variable. I need to make this class variable a hash indexed by the actual class, as a class variable's value is shared across all subclasses.

Whenever valid_range is called, it begins by initializing the hash's value to an empty array if necessary. It then creates a closure, taking a single argument, that carries out the validation and adds it to the array.

I'll also give each object a method to validate itself.

```
class DomainObject...
  def valid?
    return @@validations[self.class].all? {|v| v.call(self)}
  end
```

Using a class variable with a hash to store differing values per class is really a way of implementing a class instance variable. I can do this directly in Ruby like this:

```
class DomainObject...
  class << self; attr_accessor :validations; end

  def self.valid_range name, range
    @validations ||= []
    v = lambda do |obj|
      range.include?(obj.instance_variable_get(name))
    end
    @validations << v
  end
end
```

```
class DomainObject...
  def valid?
    return self.class.validations.all? {|v| v.call(self)}
  end
```

42.5 Dynamic Code Generation (Ruby)

One of the nice things about working with a dynamic language is the ability to add to the code at runtime. I can use this to show a further enhancement with processing Annotations. In this case, I want to not just provide an overall method to validate an object, but also provide methods to validate individual fields. Thus, using our patient visit example, I want to have not just a valid? method, but also the field-specific methods valid_height? and valid_weight? on my patient visit class. I want these methods to be automatically generated, so that any field that has a validation annotation will automatically get the field-specific validation method.

The nice thing about this is that I don't need to modify the annotation calls in the patient visit class; they can remain the same as the simpler case.

```
class PatientVisit...
  not_nil :height, :weight
  valid_range :height, 1..120
  valid_range :weight, 1..1000
```

I use the class instance variable approach to storing the validators. The difference is that instead of storing my validators as simple closures, I make field validator classes that take the field name and a closure as arguments.

```
class DomainObject...
  class << self; attr_accessor :validations; end

  def valid?
    return self.class.validations.all? {|v| v.call(self)}
  end

class FieldValidator
  attr_reader :field_name
  def initialize field_name, &code
  @field_name = field_name
  @code = code
  end
  def call target
  @code.call target
  end
end
```

If I use the object validation method, all the validators run the same as before. The extra step is this method:

```
class DomainObject...
  def self.define_field_validation_method field_name
  method_name = "valid_#{field_name}?"
  return if self.respond_to? method_name
  self.class_eval do
   define_method(method_name) do
    return self.class.validations.
     select{|v| v.field_name == field_name}.
     all? {|v| v.call(self)}
   end
  end
  end
end
```

This method tests to see if it has already been defined. If not, we use `define_method` to add a new method to the patient visit class. This method selects those validations that apply to the given field and runs just those. (I have to wrap the call to `define_method` inside `class_eval` because `define_method` is actually a private method. I could avoid this by using `class_eval` with a string.)

Chapter 43

Parse Tree Manipulation

*Capture the parse tree of a code fragment to manipulate it
with DSL processing code.*

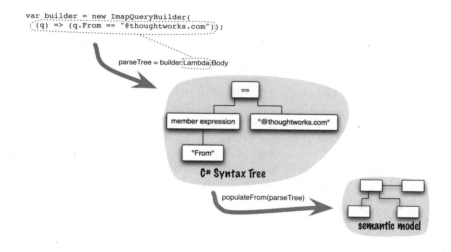

```
var builder = new ImapQueryBuilder(
    (q) => (q.From == "@thoughtworks.com"));
```

parseTree = builder.Lambda.Body

C# Syntax Tree

populateFrom(parseTree)

semantic model

When you write code in a closure, that code is available to be executed at some
future time. Parse Tree Manipulation allows you to not only execute the code
but also examine and modify its parse tree.

43.1 How It Works

In order to use Parse Tree Manipulation, you need a programming environment
that supports taking a code fragment and turning it into a parse tree that you
can work with. This is a relatively rare programming language feature—rare

both in that few languages support it and in that, even when it is supported, it's rarely used. While I have not made any detailed survey of tools that support this, I can use the ones I have to give a rough picture of how one might use this kind of capability. The three examples I'll talk about are C# (from version 3.0), Ruby's ParseTree library, and Lisp.

C# and ParseTree operate in a similar way. You invoke a library call on a fragment of source code, and the library returns a data structure of that code's parse tree. In C#, you can only do this on an expression inside a lambda. This limitation to expressions means you can't take code with multiple statements. ParseTree allows you to take a class, a method, or a string containing Ruby code.

In C#, the returned data structure is a hierarchy of expression objects. These objects are purpose-built for representing parse trees, with an inheritance hierarchy for different kinds of operators. ParseTree returns nested Ruby arrays, with simple built-in types, such as symbols and strings, as leaves.

In both C# and Ruby, you then write a tree walker to walk the parse tree and examine it. In C#, the parse tree is immutable, but you can transform it by copying and modifying it as you copy. Both libraries provide a mechanism for taking a subtree and turning it back into executable code.

The approach Lisp takes is rather different. Lisp source is itself essentially a serialized parse tree of nested lists. Lisp provides syntactic macros that allow you to examine and manipulate any Lisp expression. The programming style is different, as it uses macros, but you can achieve much the same effects.

Although Parse Tree Manipulation allows you write an expression in your host language, you usually can't use any expression you like. There are usually limits on what you can handle in expressions. In these situations, it's important to fail fast should you get an expression that you can't handle. Usually, when you walk over a parse tree, you know that the nodes in that tree will conform to what you expect. With Parse Tree Manipulation, your parse tree can contain any legal construct in the host language, so you have to do some checking yourself as you walk it.

Usually you won't need, or want, to walk the entire parse tree of the expression. Most cases involve walking some parts of the tree, but leaving substantial subtrees for evaluation. That way you don't have to build an entire parser, but only parse the bits you need to populate your *Semantic Model (159)*, and evaluate subtrees as soon as you don't need to do further navigation.

43.2 When to Use It

Parse Tree Manipulation allows you to express logic in your host programming language and then manipulate that expression with more flexibility than you would be able to get otherwise. With that, a driving reason to use Parse Tree Manipulation with a DSL is the desire to use a fuller range of the host language's features to express something, instead of the pidgin of the usual internal DSL constructs.

Being able to make use of the host language isn't the whole point of using Parse Tree Manipulation. After all, one of the advantages of internal DSLs is that you can intermix the full host language with DSLish constructs as much as you like. The key difference is that usually, you can only manipulate the executable results of the host language—you can't dive into host language expressions and manipulate their structure.

Even so, there's not that many examples when you need to use Parse Tree Manipulation for a DSL. (Like most things, Parse Tree Manipulation has many uses outside a DSL context, which I'm not going to touch on here.) One of the best ones to consider is the driving force behind .NET's support for Parse Tree Manipulation—Linq.

Linq allows you to express query conditions—essentially Boolean expressions—using the standard .NET languages. These conditions can then be evaluated on .NET data structures—that much is trivial. The interesting thing is to take a C# condition and turn it into a SQL query—this allows you to write database queries without knowing SQL, or to write queries that will be executed against different data sources. In order to pull this off, you need to take the C# condition, turn it into a parse tree, and then walk the parse tree and generate the equivalent SQL. Essentially, you are doing source-to-source translation from C# to SQL (or some other target). Parse Tree Manipulation is good for these cases, as it allows you to use a familiar syntax for your conditions when your target language is not well known or you want multiple targets.

Another way to use Parse Tree Manipulation is to change the parse tree to carry out a useful manipulation. One example is changing all method calls on a certain object to be redirected to another object. But it's not clear how useful that kind of surgery is in a DSL context (which is the focus of this book).

I also worry a bit that Parse Tree Manipulation is one of those techniques where the intricacies of doing it may be just too appealing for many programmers. It's an appeal that can blindside people into missing other, simpler, ways of achieving the same goal.

43: Parse Tree
Manipulation

43.3 Generating IMAP Queries from C# Conditions (C#)

Some of you may be familiar with the IMAP protocol for interacting with email servers. If you use IMAP, your email stays on the server and is brought down to the client only for reading or caching. As a result, if you want to search your email, that search needs to be done on the server.

To search with IMAP, your email client sends a search request. That search request is, like all IMAP commands, a string. There is a DSL that is used to express the IMAP search conditions. I won't go into all the details here (if you want them, go to [RFC 3501]) but will just show a simple example. Let's say I want to find all emails containing the phrase "entity framework," sent by someone other than at thoughtworks.com, since 23rd of June 2008. Using IMAP, I would encode this query in a search command as SEARCH subject "entity framework" sentsince 23-jun-2008 not from "@thoughtworks.com".

IMAP's search command DSL provides a good domain-specific query language for email. For this exercise, however, we want to express our query in C#, like this:

```
var threshold = new DateTime(2008, 06, 23);
var builder = new ImapQueryBuilder((q) =>
  (q.Subject == "entity framework")
  && (q.Date >= threshold)
  && ("@thoughtworks.com" != q.From));
```

43.3.1 Semantic Model

My first step is to create a *Semantic Model (159)* for the IMAP output. This is a simple IMAP query object that contains elements for each clause in the query. These elements will be anded together to form the complete query.

```
class ImapQuery...
  internal List<ImapQueryElement> elements = new List<ImapQueryElement>();
  public void AddElement(ImapQueryElement element) {
    elements.Add(element);
  }

interface ImapQueryElement {
  string ToImap();
}
```

I'm declaring an interface here for the query elements. This interface has two implementations: one to handle the basic query clauses (from "@thoughtworks.com") and the other to handle negations (not).

```
class BasicElement : ImapQueryElement {
  private readonly string name;
  private readonly object value;
  public BasicElement(string name, object value) {
    this.name = name.ToLower();
    this.value = value;
    validate().AssertOK();
  }

class NegationElement : ImapQueryElement {
  private readonly BasicElement child;
  public NegationElement(BasicElement child) {
    this.child = child;
  }
```

Although this query is a conjunction, IMAP can express general Boolean expressions. Doing so is more awkward, but then most email queries can be handled very nicely as a conjunction. This is where IMAP makes the common case easy, but allows you to be more expressive in the relatively rare situations that need it. For my purposes of illustrating this pattern, a simple conjunction will do fine.

Each basic query element has a keyword and value, mirroring the way IMAP forms its search language. In this situation, I'm adding some error checking into each element, throwing an exception should any of them be in error.

```
class BasicElement...
  private Notification validate() {
    var result = new Notification();
    if (null == Name)
      result.AddError("Name is null");
    if (null == Value)
      result.AddError("Value is null");
    if (!stringCriteria.Contains(Name) && !dateCriteria.Contains(Name))
      result.AddError("Unknown criteria: {0}", Name);
    if (stringCriteria.Contains(Name) && !(Value is string))
      result.AddError("{0} needs a string argument, got {1}", Name, Value.GetType());
    if (dateCriteria.Contains(Name) && !(Value is DateTime))
      result.AddError("{0} needs a DateTime argument, got {1}", Name, Value.GetType());
    return result;
  }
  private readonly static string[] stringCriteria = { "subject", "to", "from", "cc" };
  private readonly static string[] dateCriteria =
    { "since", "before", "on", "sentbefore", "sentsince", "senton"};

class Notification...
  public void AssertOK() {
    if (HasErrors) throw new ValidationException(this);
  }
```

With this command-query interface, I can construct the model for my query like this:

```
var expected = new ImapQuery();
expected.AddElement(new BasicElement("subject", "entity framework"));
expected.AddElement(new BasicElement("since", new DateTime(2008, 6, 23)));
expected.AddElement(new NegationElement(
  new BasicElement("from", "@thoughtworks.com")));
```

With a Semantic Model in place, I can now generate the code for the IMAP search command. This is very simple code generation—just pushing out the result for each IMAP element.

```
class ImapQuery...
  public string ToImap() {
    var result = "";
    foreach (var e in elements) result += e.ToImap();
    return result.Trim();
  }
```

43: Parse Tree Manipulation

```
class BasicElement...
  public string ToImap() {
    return String.Format("{0} {1} ", name, imapValue);
  }
  private string imapValue {
    get {
      if (value is string) return "\"" + value + "\"";
      if (value is DateTime) return imapDate((DateTime)value);
      return "";
    }
  }
  private string imapDate(DateTime d) {
    return d.ToString("dd-MMM-yyyy");
  }

class NegationElement...
  public string ToImap() {
    return String.Format("not {0}", child.ToImap());
  }
```

43.3.2 Building from C#

This *Semantic Model (159)* allows me to represent and generate search commands for IMAP queries (or at least for the subset of IMAP queries I'm using here). Now, let's look at the builder to create them from C#.

The builder takes an appropriate lambda in its constructor.

```
class ImapQueryBuilder...
  private readonly Expression<Func<ImapQueryCriteria, bool>> lambda;
  public ImapQueryBuilder(Expression<Func<ImapQueryCriteria, bool>> func) {
    lambda = func;
  }
```

In order to write the expression in the closure, we need some object that can act as the receiver for the keywords of the query (subject, sent, from). This object won't ever do anything at runtime; it's only there to provide the methods to help me compose the query. As a result, the return values of its methods are irrelevant as they'll never actually be called.

```
class ImapQueryBuilder...
  internal class ImapQueryCriteria {
    public string Subject {get { return ""; }}
    public string To {get { return ""; }}
    public DateTime Sent {get { return DateTime.Now; }}
    public string From {get { return ""; }}
```

To build the query, I use a lazily evaluated property.

```
class ImapQueryBuilder...
  public ImapQuery Content {
    get {
      if (null == content) {
        content = new ImapQuery();
        populateFrom(lambda.Body);
      }
      return content;
    }
  }
  private ImapQuery content;
```

The heart of the work is done by populateFrom—a recursive tree walk.

```
class ImapQueryBuilder...
  private void populateFrom(Expression e) {
    var node = e as BinaryExpression;
    if (null == node)
      throw new BuilderException("Wrong node class", node);
    if (e.NodeType == ExpressionType.AndAlso) {
      populateFrom(node.Left);
      populateFrom(node.Right);
    }
    else
      content.AddElement(new ElementBuilder(node).Content);
  }
```

At this point, I confront the fact that, despite my desire to allow clients to construct IMAP queries in C#, they can't use *any* C#. My Semantic Model can only handle a subset of possible C# expressions. The expression must consist of one or more element expressions connected by the && operator. Each of these element nodes must be a particular binary operator for which one side must be a keyword—a call to an IMAP query criteria object. There are then rules about what operators go with which keywords. String-oriented keywords (from, subject, to) can only take == and !=. Date-oriented keywords (sent, date) can take any equality or comparison operators.

As a result, I know that the only elements I'll have to navigate through are binary expressions, so populateFrom throws an exception if it sees anything else. If the operator in the expression is && I can just recurse to the children. The interesting case is the element node—and there's enough logic there that I've put it into a separate class.

```
class ElementBuilder...
  private BinaryExpression node;
  public ElementBuilder(BinaryExpression node) {
    this.node = node;
    assertValidNode();
  }
```

These element nodes have two children: One is a keyword node (e.g., q.To) and one is some arbitrary C# that will return the value that will be compared in the query. I'm allowing the keyword and value to appear in any order, since that commutativity is expected in the host language.

To be a keyword, the child must have a method call on an instance of my criteria object. I'll need to be able to extract that keyword from the child node, so I write a method that takes a child node and returns the keyword if it's a keyword expression, or null if it's not.

```
class ElementBuilder...
  private string keywordOfChild(Expression node) {
    var call = node as MemberExpression;
    if (null == call) return null;
    if (call.Member.DeclaringType != typeof(ImapQueryBuilder.ImapQueryCriteria))
      return null;
    return call.Member.Name.ToLower();
  }
```

This utility method is very useful. Its first use is to allow me to check that I actually have a valid element node to work on. For this, I need to ensure that one of the children is indeed a keyword node.

```
class ElementBuilder...
  private void assertValidNode() {
    if (null == keywordOfChild(node.Left) && null == keywordOfChild(node.Right))
      throw new BuilderException("expression does not contain keyword", node);
    if (!isLegalOperator)
      throw new BuilderException("Wrong kind of operator", node);
  }
```

Not only do I check that one of the children is a keyword node, I also need to check that I have a legal operator for the kind of keyword I have.

```
class ElementBuilder...
  private bool isLegalOperator {
    get {
      ExpressionType[] dateOperators = {
        ExpressionType.Equal, ExpressionType.GreaterThanOrEqual,
        ExpressionType.LessThanOrEqual, ExpressionType.NotEqual,
        ExpressionType.GreaterThan, ExpressionType.LessThan
      };
      ExpressionType[] stringOperators = {
        ExpressionType.Equal, ExpressionType.NotEqual
      };
      return (isDateKeyword())
              ? dateOperators.Contains(node.NodeType)
              : stringOperators.Contains(node.NodeType);
    }
  }
  private bool isDateKeyword() {
    return dateKeywords.Contains(keywordMethod());
  }
```

```
private static readonly string[] dateKeywords = { "sent", "date" };
private string keywordMethod() {
  return keywordOfChild(node.Left) ?? keywordOfChild(node.Right);
}
```

You might notice here that I'm doing a bit more checking for date keywords. For string keywords, I'm relying on the Semantic Model to tell me if I try to create an element with an illegal keyword. I have to handle the date keywords differently since there is a mismatch between the C# expression and the Semantic Model. If I want to find emails sent since a certain date, the natural way to say this in C# is something like q.Sent >= aDate; however, IMAP does this with sentsince aDate. Essentially, I need the combination of the C# keyword plus the operator to determine the correct IMAP keyword. As a consequence, I have to check the C# date keywords in the builder as they are part of the input DSL but not the Semantic Model.

By checking that I have a valid node in the constructor, I can simplify my later logic to extract the right data from the node.

Now let's look at exactly that. I begin with a content property which separates the simple string case from the more complicated date case.

```
class ElementBuilder...
  public ImapQueryElement Content {
    get {
      return isDateKeyword()? dateKeywordContent() : stringKeywordContent();
    }
  }
```

For the string case, I create a basic query element using whatever the keyword is and the value from the other side of the node. If the operator is !=, I wrap that basic element inside a negation.

```
class ElementBuilder...
  private ImapQueryElement stringKeywordContent() {
    switch (node.NodeType) {
      case ExpressionType.Equal:
        return new BasicElement(keywordMethod(), Value);
      case ExpressionType.NotEqual:
        return new NegationElement(new BasicElement(keywordMethod(), Value));
      default:
        throw new Exception("unreachable");
    }
  }
```

To determine the value, I don't need to parse the value node. Instead I can just toss the expression back to the C# system to get it. This allows me to put any legal C# into the value side of my elements without having to deal with it in my navigation code.

43: Parse Tree
Manipulation

```
class ElementBuilder...
  private object Value {
    get {
      return (null == keywordOfChild(node.Left))
               ? valueOfChild(node.Left)
               : valueOfChild(node.Right);
    }
  }
  private object valueOfChild(Expression node) {
    return Expression.Lambda(node).Compile().DynamicInvoke();
  }
```

Dates are more complicated, but I use the same basic approach. The IMAP keyword I'll need depends on both the keyword method in the node and the value of the operator. In addition, I need to throw in negations when I need to. As the first step, I'll tease out the keyword method.

```
class ElementBuilder...
  private ImapQueryElement dateKeywordContent() {
    if ("sent" == keywordMethod())
      return formDateElement("sent");
    else if ("date" == keywordMethod())
      return formDateElement("");
    else throw new Exception("unreachable");
  }
```

With the right date keyword sorted out, I'll then break things out by the operator type.

```
class ElementBuilder...
  private ImapQueryElement formDateElement(string prefix) {
    switch (node.NodeType) {
    case ExpressionType.Equal:
      return new BasicElement(prefix + "on", Value);
    case ExpressionType.NotEqual:
      return new NegationElement(new BasicElement(prefix + "on", Value));
    case ExpressionType.GreaterThanOrEqual:
      return new BasicElement(prefix + "since", Value);
    case ExpressionType.GreaterThan:
      return new NegationElement(new BasicElement(prefix + "before", Value));
    case ExpressionType.LessThan:
      return new NegationElement(new BasicElement(prefix + "since", Value));
    case ExpressionType.LessThanOrEqual:
      return new BasicElement(prefix + "before", Value);
    default:
      throw new Exception("unreachable");
    }
  }
```

Notice that I'm taking advantage of the similar names of the date-oriented IMAP keywords that I deal with. My first code for this had separate switch statements for each keyword, but I realized that by doing the prefix trick I could remove the duplication. The code's a little cleverer than I like, but I think it's worth that to avoid duplication.

43.3.3 Stepping Back

That sums up the implementation of IMAP search, but I need to mention a couple more things before I leave this example.

The first point is a difference between how I've described the example and how I built it. In describing the example, I found it easier to look at each part of the implementation separately: populating the *Semantic Model (159)* with a command-query interface, generating the IMAP code, walking through the parse tree. I think looking at each aspect separately makes it easier to understand—which is also why the code is separated that way.

However, I didn't actually build it that way. I did the example in two stages; first, I just supported simple conjunctions of basic elements, and then I added the ability to handle negations. I wrote the code for all elements on the first pass and then extended and refactored each section when adding the negations. I always advocate building software like this, feature by feature, but I don't think that's the best way to explain the final result. So don't let the structure of the final result and the way I explain it fool you into thinking that it is how it's built.

The second point I want to share is that although walking a parse tree like this yields that geeky pleasure of using fancy parts of a language, I wouldn't actually build an IMAP DSL this way. An alternative is a dose of simple *Method Chaining (373)*.

```
class Tester...
  var builder = new ChainingBuilder()
    .subject("entity framework")
    .not.from("@thoughtworks.com")
    .since(threshold);
```

Here's all the implementation I need to do this:

```
class ChainingBuilder...
  private readonly ImapQuery content = new ImapQuery();
  private bool currentlyNegating = false;

  public ImapQuery Content {
    get { return content; }
  }
  public ChainingBuilder not {
    get {
      currentlyNegating = true;
      return this; }
  }
```

43: Parse Tree Manipulation

```
private void addElement(string keyword, object value) {
  ImapQueryElement element = new BasicElement(keyword, value);
  if (currentlyNegating) {
    element = new NegationElement((BasicElement) element);
    currentlyNegating = false;
  }
  content.AddElement(element);
}
public ChainingBuilder subject(string s) {
  addElement("subject", s);
  return this;
}
public ChainingBuilder since(DateTime t) {
  addElement("since", t);
  return this;
}
public ChainingBuilder from(string s) {
  addElement("from", s);
  return this;
}
```

It's not utterly trivial—including the negation makes me use a messy *Context Variable (175)*—but it's still small and simple. I'd need to add methods to support more keywords, but they would still be simple.

Of course, one of the main reasons this is so much simpler is that the structure of the internal DSL is more similar to the IMAP query itself. In fact, it's really just the IMAP query expressed as Method Chaining. Its advantage over using IMAP itself boils down to IDE support. Some people might prefer the more C#ish syntax that the Parse Tree Manipulation example gives you, but I must admit I'm happier with the IMAPish version.

Chapter 44

Class Symbol Table

Use a class and its fields to implement a symbol table in order to support type-aware autocompletion in a statically typed language.

```
public class SimpleSwitchStateMachine extends StateMachineBuilder {
    Events switchUp, switchDown;
    States on, off;
    protected void defineStateMachine() {
        on.transition(switchDown).to(off);
        off.transition(switchUp).to(on);
    }
}
```

Modern IDEs provide lots of powerful and compelling features to make programming easier. A particularly useful one is type-aware autocompletion. In my C# and Java IDEs, I can type the name of a variable, type the period, and get a list of all the methods that are defined on that object. Even people like me who enjoy dynamically typed languages have to admit that this is a benefit of statically typed languages. When working in an internal DSL, you don't want to give up this capability for typing the name of a symbol in the DSL. However, the most common ways of expressing DSL symbols are to use strings or a built-in symbol type—so there's no relevant type information.

Class Symbol Table allows you to make symbols statically typed in the host language by defining each symbol as a field in a *Expression Builder (343)*.

44.1 How It Works

The base of making this work is to write your DSL script inside a single *Expression Builder (343)* class. This builder will usually be a subclass of a more general Expression Builder where you can place the behavior needed for all your scripts. The script's Expression Builder will then consist of a method for the script itself and fields for the symbols. So, if you have tasks in your DSL and need to define three of them in your script, you'll have a field declaration like this:

```
Tasks drinkCoffee, makeCoffee, wash;
```

A class named Tasks is, like so many things in DSL processing, an unconventional name. Again, the readability of the DSL is trumping my usual code style rules. By defining fields like this, I can now refer to them in the DSL script as fields; also, the IDE will offer autocompletion for them, and the compiler will check them.

Just defining the fields, however, is not enough. When I refer to a field in the DSL script, it refers to the contents of the field, not the field definition. While I'm writing code, the IDE knows about both; but when I run the program, the link to definition of the field disappears, leaving me with only the field contents. In normal life, this isn't a problem, but to make our Class Symbol Table we need a link to the field definition at runtime.

We can provide this by populating each field with a suitable object before the script is executed. A good way to do this is to use the class instance as the active script—put code in the constructor to populate the fields and the script inside an instance method. The contents of the fields are usually small Expression Builders that link to the underlying *Semantic Model (159)* object and also contain the field name to help with cross-referencing. In terms of a *Symbol Table (165)*, the field name acts as the key and the builder acts as the value; but occasionally, you will need another kind of key access, which is why it's handy for the builders in the field to keep the field name.

The DSL script will usually refer to the field by the field literal itself—which is the whole point. To refer to the wash task, I can just type the wash field name in the DSL script. However, as we're processing the DSL script, we'll need the builders in the fields to refer to each other. This will sometimes involve looking up fields by name, or iterating through all fields of a certain type. Doing this will require more tricky code, usually using reflection. Usually there's not too much of it and, provided it's well encapsulated, it shouldn't make the language too difficult to process.

44.2 When to Use It

The primary consequence of using Class Symbol Table is that it provides full static typing of all the DSL language elements. The big benefit this gives us is that it allows IDEs to use all the sophisticated tools based on static typing—such as type-aware autocompletion. It also provides compile-time type checking on the DSL script, which matters a lot to many people (but rather less to me).

With such a focus on IDE capabilities, I see this technique as much less useful if you don't have an IDE that takes advantage of static types. It also does not bring much benefit in a dynamically typed language.

The downside of this technique is that you have to bend your DSL significantly to fit within the type system. The resulting builder classes look very odd; also, you have to put your DSL scripts in a place where they can take advantage of these facilities, such as all in the same class. These restrictions may make the DSL harder to read and use.

So for me, the fundamental tradeoff is between the restrictions on the DSL script and the benefits of the IDE support. I've got rather dependent on good IDE support in languages where it's available, which would prompt me to use techniques like this to get it.

If you want this kind of static type support, you can often get what you need by using enums as symbols (see *Symbol Table (165)* for an example of this).

44.3 Statically Typed Class Symbol Table (Java)

I used Class Symbol Table for the Java example in the introduction, so that seems like a good example to show how this works.

The DSL script is in a specific class.

```
public class BasicStateMachine extends StateMachineBuilder {

    Events doorClosed, drawerOpened, lightOn, panelClosed;
    Commands unlockPanel, lockPanel, lockDoor, unlockDoor;
    States idle, active, waitingForLight, waitingForDrawer, unlockedPanel;
    ResetEvents doorOpened;

    protected void defineStateMachine() {
        doorClosed. code("D1CL");
        drawerOpened. code("D2OP");
        lightOn.     code("L1ON");
        panelClosed.code("PNCL");

        doorOpened. code("D1OP");

        unlockPanel.code("PNUL");
```

44: Class Symbol Table

```
lockPanel.  code("PNLK");
lockDoor.   code("D1LK");
unlockDoor. code("D1UL");

idle
  .actions(unlockDoor, lockPanel)
  .transition(doorClosed).to(active)
  ;

active
  .transition(drawerOpened).to(waitingForLight)
  .transition(lightOn).  to(waitingForDrawer)
  ;

waitingForLight
  .transition(lightOn).to(unlockedPanel)
  ;

waitingForDrawer
  .transition(drawerOpened).to(unlockedPanel)
  ;

unlockedPanel
  .actions(unlockPanel, lockDoor)
  .transition(panelClosed).to(idle)
  ;
  }
}
```

The DSL script is housed in its own class. The script itself is in one method, and the fields of the class represent the symbol table. I've set things up so the DSL script class is a subclass of a builder—this way I can have the superclass builder control the way the script is run. (Using a subclass like this also allows me to use *Object Scoping (385)*, although I don't need it here.)

```
class StateMachineBuilder...
  public StateMachine build() {
    initializeIdentifiers(Events.class, Commands.class, States.class, ResetEvents.class);
    defineStateMachine();
    return produceStateMachine();
  }
  abstract protected void defineStateMachine();
```

I define the public method to run the script on the superclass; it executes the code to set up the Class Symbol Table fields before running the script. In this case, running the DSL script performs a basic preparation of the information for the state machine, and a second pass actually produces the *Semantic Model (159)* objects. So, running a script has three distinct stages: initializing the identifiers (generic), running the DSL script (specific), and finally producing the model state machine (generic).

I need the first step of initializing the identifiers, since any reference to a field in the DSL script refers to the contents of the field rather than the field itself. In this case, the suitable objects are specific identifier objects that hold the name of the identifier and refer to the underlying model object. Doing this ends up being a bit more messy than I'd like, as I want to write generic code for setting up the identifiers to avoid duplicating setup code. However, any generic code doesn't know about the specific type of the identifier being set up, and so has to determine it dynamically.

Hopefully, this will become a little clearer when we look at an example—in this case, the event builder class (Events). The first thing to discuss is the name of the class. Any style book on object-oriented programming will wisely tell you to avoid plural class names, and I agree with that advice. However, here a plural name reads better in the context of the DSL, so this is another case of general coding rules being broken to make a good DSL script. The DSL naming doesn't alter the fact that it is truly a builder of events, so I'll refer to it as the event builder class in my text (and similarly for its siblings).

The event builder extends a general identifier class.

```
class Identifier...
  private String name;
  protected StateMachineBuilder builder;

  public Identifier(String name, StateMachineBuilder builder) {
    this.name = name;
    this.builder = builder;
  }
  public String getName() {
    return name;
  }

public class Events extends Identifier {
  private Event event;
  public Events(String name, StateMachineBuilder builder) {
    super(name, builder);
  }
  Event getEvent() {
    return event;
  }
```

44: Class Symbol Table

There is a simple division of responsibility here, with the identifier class carrying the responsibilities needed for all identifiers, and the subclasses carrying what's needed for specific types.

Let's look at the first step of running the script—initializing the identifiers. Since many identifier classes need to be initialized, I have some generic code to do that. This way I can provide a list of classes which are identifiers, and the code will initialize all fields of those classes.

```
class StateMachineBuilder...
  private void initializeIdentifiers(Class... identifierClasses) {
    List<Class> identifierList = Arrays.asList(identifierClasses);
    for (Field f : this.getClass().getDeclaredFields()) {
      try {
        if (identifierList.contains(f.getType())) {
          f.setAccessible(true);
          f.set(this, Identifier.create(f.getType(), f.getName(), this));
        }
      } catch (Exception e) {
        throw new RuntimeException(e);
      }
    }
  }
}
```

```
class Identifier...
  static Identifier create(Class type, String name, StateMachineBuilder builder)
      throws NoSuchMethodException, InvocationTargetException,
          IllegalAccessException, InstantiationException
  {
    Constructor ctor = type.getConstructor(String.class, StateMachineBuilder.class);
    return (Identifier) ctor.newInstance(name, builder);
  }
```

Doing it this way is more tricky than I like, but it avoids having to write duplicate initializing methods. Essentially, I look through every field on the DSL script object, and if the type of the field is one of those I've passed in, I initialize it with a special static utility method that finds and calls the right constructor. As a result, once I've called initializeIdentifiers, I have all of these fields populated with objects that will help me construct the state machine.

The next step is to execute the DSL script itself. The DSL script executes by building up suitable intermediate objects to capture all the information about the state machine.

The first step is defining the codes for the events and commands.

```
class Events...
  public void code(String code) {
    event = new Event(getName(), code);
  }
```

Since the code has all the information I need to create a model event object, I can create it on calling code and put it inside the identifier (the command builder looks just the same).

The event and command builders are degenerately simple *Expression Builders (343)*. The state builder is a bit more of a builder, as it needs several steps.

Since a state model object isn't immutable, I can create it in the constructor.

```
class States...
  private State content;
  private List<TransitionBuilder> transitions = new ArrayList<TransitionBuilder>();
  private List<Commands> commands = new ArrayList<Commands>();

  public States(String name, StateMachineBuilder builder) {
    super(name, builder);
    content = new State(name);
  }
```

The first building behavior I'll show is creating the actions. The basic behavior here is simple—I go through the supplied command identifiers and store them in the state builder.

```
class States...
  public States actions(Commands... identifiers) {
    builder.definingState(this);
    commands.addAll(Arrays.asList(identifiers));
    return this;
  }
```

If the DSL script always defines the codes before it defines the states (as I've done here), I could save myself the need to store command builders in the state builder and instead put the model command objects into the model state object. However, this would lead to errors if I define a state before its action codes. Using the builder as an intermediate object allows me to work it either way.

There is a bit of trickiness here. The DSL makes the assumption that the first mentioned state is the start state. As a result, I have to check, whenever I begin defining a state, if this is the first state I define, and if so make it the start state. Since it's only the overall state machine builder that can really tell if a state is the first one to be defined, I want the machine builder to make the decision about whether to set a state as first.

```
class StateMachineBuilder...
  protected void definingState(States identifier) {
    if (null == start) start = identifier.getState();
  }
```

The state builder does need to call the machine builder to tell it that it's being defined, but it shouldn't know what the machine builder is going to do with that information, as that's the secret of the machine builder. So I make what is effectively an event notification call from the state builder (since that is all it knows) and let the machine builder decide what to do on that event. This is a good example of naming being important in communicating what I think the responsibilities and relative knowledge of the objects should be.

The other thing we can do with a state builder is to define a transition. As this requires a couple of steps, it's a dash more complicated. I begin with the transition method, which creates a separate transition builder object.

44: Class Symbol
Table

```
class States...
  public TransitionBuilder transition(Events identifier) {
    builder.definingState(this);
    return new TransitionBuilder(this, identifier);
  }

class TransitionBuilder...
  private Events trigger;
  private States targetState;
  private States source;

  TransitionBuilder(States state, Events trigger) {
    this.trigger = trigger;
    this.source = state;
  }
```

Since I don't need to mention the transition builder's type in the DSL script, I can give it a more meaningful name. Its only builder method is the to clause, which adds itself to the source state builder's list of transition builders.

```
class TransitionBuilder...
  public States to(States targetState) {
    this.targetState = targetState;
    source.addTransition(this);
    return source;
  }
```

These are the elements I need to capture all the specific information in the DSL script. When the script is run, I have a data structure of intermediate data: The builders are captured in the fields of the DSL script object itself. I now need to run through this structure to produce a fully wired up model state machine.

```
class StateMachineBuilder...
  private StateMachine produceStateMachine() {
    assert null != start;
    StateMachine result = new StateMachine(start);
    for (States s : getStateIdentifers())
      s.produce();
    produceResetEvents(result);
    return result;
  }
```

Most of the work here is going through all the state builders, getting them to produce their wired-up model objects. To find all these states, I need to get all the objects out of the fields of the script class, so again I use some reflective trickery to find all fields of the state builder's type.

```
class StateMachineBuilder...
  private List<States> getStateIdentifers() {
    return getIdentifiers(States.class);
  }
  private <T extends Identifier> List<T> getIdentifiers(Class<T> klass) {
    List<T> result = new ArrayList<T>();
    for (Field f : this.getClass().getDeclaredFields()) {
      if (f.getType().equals(klass))
        try {
          f.setAccessible(true);
          result.add(((T) f.get(this)));
        } catch (IllegalAccessException e) {
          throw new RuntimeException(e);
        }
    }
    return result;
  }
```

To produce its model object, the state builder wires up the commands and produces its transitions.

```
class States...
  void produce() {
    for (Commands c : commands)
      content.addAction(c.getCommand());
    for (TransitionBuilder t : transitions)
      t.produce();
  }

class TransitionBuilder...
  void produce() {
    source.getState().addTransition(trigger.getEvent(), getTargetState().getState());
  }
```

The last step is to produce the reset events.

```
class StateMachineBuilder...
  private void produceResetEvents(StateMachine result) {
    result.addResetEvents(getResetEvents());
  }
  private Event[] getResetEvents() {
    List<Event> result = new ArrayList<Event>();
    for (Events identifier : getIdentifiers(ResetEvents.class))
      result.add(identifier.getEvent());
    return result.toArray(new Event[result.size()]);
  }
```

44: Class Symbol Table

Using a class and its fields as a symbol table does involve a bit of tricky code in places, but the benefit is full static typing and IDE support. That's usually a worthwhile tradeoff.

Chapter 45

Textual Polishing

Perform simple textual substitutions before more serious processing.

```
3 hours ago => 3.hours.ago
```

Internal DSLs are often easier to develop, particularly if you're not comfortable with parsing. However, the resulting DSLs contain host language artifacts that can are awkward for nonprogrammers to read.

Textual Polishing uses a series of simple regular expression substitutions to smooth some of these out.

45.1 How It Works

Textual Polishing is a very simple technique. It involves running a series of text substitutions on the DSL script before it gets to the parser. A simple example is if readers find the use of dots for method calls off-putting. A simple substitution of dots for spaces can turn 3 hours ago into 3.hours.ago. More involved patterns can turn 3% into percentage(3). The output of the Textual Polishing is an expression in an internal DSL.

Specifying the polishing is a simple matter of writing a sequence of regular expression substitutions—which most language environments support. The tricky thing, of course, is getting the regular expressions correct so you don't get unwanted substitutions. A space in a quoted string probably should not be turned into a dot, but that makes the regex much harder to write.

I've seen Textual Polishing most often in dynamic languages, where you can evaluate text at runtime. Here, the language reads in the DSL expression, polishes it, then evaluates the resulting internal DSL code. You can, however, also do this with a static language. In this case, you'd run the polishing before compiling the DSL script—which does introduce another step into the build process.

While Textual Polishing is mostly an internal DSL technique, there are a few cases where it can be useful with external DSLs. When certain things are hard to spot with the usual lexer and parser chain, a preprocessing of Textual Polishing before lexing can make things more helpful. Semantic indentation and possibly semantic newlines are examples.

You can think of Textual Polishing as a simple application of textual *Macros (183)*, with all the corresponding problems.

45.2 When to Use It

I confess I'm rather wary of Textual Polishing; my feeling is that if you use a little, it doesn't help much, and if you use it a lot, it gets very complicated, so it may then be better to use an external DSL. Although the basic notion of repeated substitutions is simple, it's very easy to make mistakes in the regular expressions.

Textual Polishing cannot do anything to change the syntactic structure of the input, so you are still tied to the basic syntactic structure of the host language. Indeed, I think it's important to keep the prepolished DSL and the resulting internal DSL expressions recognizably similar. The resulting internal DSL should be as clear as possible for programmers to read—the polishing is only a visual convenience for nonprogrammers.

If you find the noise characters in an internal DSL annoying, an alternative approach to Textual Polishing is to use an editor that supports syntax coloring and set it up to color the noise characters with a very gentle color that fades into the background. That way, a reader's eye is more likely to skip over them. If you set it to the same color as the background, you make these characters disappear completely.

If you find yourself doing a lot of polishing, I strongly suggest that you explore using an external DSL instead. Once you get up the learning curve of writing a parser, you'll get much more flexibility, and it will be easier to maintain the parser than the sequence of polishing steps.

45: Textual
Polishing

45.3 Polished Discount Rules (Ruby)

Consider an application that processes discount rules against orders. A simple discount rule might be to discount the price by 3% if the order's value is greater than $30,000. To capture that phrase in a Ruby internal DSL, I might use an expression like this:

```
rule = DiscountBuilder.percent(3).when.minimum(30000).content
```

Not too bad, but still a bit awkward for nonprogrammers. Some of the awkwardness I remove by using object scoping. If I can put the expressions as lines in a separate file, I can use Ruby's instance_eval (a form of *Object Scoping (385)*) to evaluate each line.

```
processing code...
  input = File.readlines("rules.rb")
  rules = []
  input.each do |line|
    builder = DiscountBuilder.new
    builder.instance_eval(line)
    rules << builder.content if builder.has_rule?
  end
```

Then my rules file can have lines like this:

```
percent(3).when.minimum(30000)
```

With this technique, I also move the call of content (the *Method Chaining (373)* end method) to the processing code, which gets it out of the user-visible part of the DSL. The check builder_has_rule? is needed since it evaluates each line, and if that line is a comment, there won't be a rule defined. Similarly, if the rule is malformed, there'll be errors, but I'll neglect handling that for this example.

This may be good for programmers, but domain experts may prefer a different formulation—something like this:

```
3% if  value at least $30000
```

I can get this formulation into the above DSL by using Textual Polishing. The polishing is a series of textual substitutions.

```
class DiscountRulePolisher...
  def polish aString
    @buffer = aString
    process_percent
    process_value_at_least
    process_if
    replace_spaces
    return @buffer
  end
```

The first transformation is to turn 3% into percent(3).

```
class DiscountRulePolisher...
  def process_percent
    @buffer = @buffer.gsub(/\b(\d+)%\s+/, 'percent(\1) ')
  end
```

This is the basic approach: Make a suitable regex, match it, and replace it with the call that you need in the actual internal DSL.

45: Textual
Polishing

In this example, I'm expecting the various elements to be separated by whitespace, just as I would when tokenizing an external DSL. As a result, it's valuable to ensure that all of the regexes have boundary expressions at both ends. In most cases, this boundary is \b (word boundary), but occasionally I need something else (such as \s+ here since "%" doesn't constitute a word boundary).

The "at least" is handled the same way, albeit with a more complicated regex.

```
class DiscountRulePolisher...
  def process_value_at_least
    @buffer = @buffer.gsub(/\bvalue\s+at\s+least\s+\$?(\d+)\b/, 'minimum(\1)')
  end
```

Our domain expert prefers "if" to "when." In an unpolished internal DSL, this is a problem because it's a Ruby keyword, but polishing can fix that.

```
class DiscountRulePolisher...
  def process_if
    @buffer = @buffer.gsub(/\bif\b/, 'when')
  end
```

An alternative here is to rename the when method to something like my_if or _if. Doing this makes it easier to see the correspondence between the polished text and the resulting DSL.

My last step is to replace the spaces with method call dots, and the result will now be valid Ruby in my internal DSL.

```
class DiscountRulePolisher...
  def replace_spaces
    @buffer = @buffer.strip.gsub(/ +/, ".")
  end
```

This doesn't look too bad, but the code is only enough to process this one particular example. To handle more cases, the code will have to get more complex and much more ugly. So in this case, I'd be keeping a careful eye on it, ready to reach for an external DSL to use instead.

Chapter 46

Literal Extension

Add methods to program literals.

```
42.grams.flour
```

46.1 How It Works

Literals, such as numbers and strings, often make a good starting point for DSL expressions. Traditionally, however, they are built-in types with fixed interfaces, so you can't extend them. More languages now allow you to add methods to third-party classes using techniques like C#'s extension methods and Ruby's open classes. This capability is particularly handy for DSLs, as it allows you to start a method chain with a literal.

As with most method chains, one important decision is whether to use an *Expression Builder (343)*. If you don't use an Expression Builder, you have to ensure that all the intermediate types have the appropriate fluent methods defined on them. Using an Expression Builder avoids this, but you have to ensure you can get from the builder to the underlying object cleanly.

Take the expression 42.grams. What should be the result type of this? I see three main options: a number, a quantity, or an Expression Builder. With a number, you generally choose one unit to be your canonical unit, for example with weight you might use kilograms. In this case, 42.grams would result in 0.042, and 2.oz would yield 0.567.

One thing to watch for here is what my colleague Neal Ford calls **type transmogrification.** 42.grams starts with an integer, but turns into a floating point. This means that all the further methods in the chain have to be defined on multiple numeric types.

With a quantity, 42.grams turns into a quantity object with a magnitude of 42 and a unit of grams. In general, I much prefer quantities to simple numbers for representing dimensioned values; quantities represent my intent better and also

481

allow me to define useful behavior (such as alerting me to problems with 42.grams + 35.cm). Sadly, almost all language platforms lack a built-in quantity class, but at least you can easily define it yourself with any fluent methods you need. Since the magnitude of the quantity is encapsulated, you greatly reduce the type transmogrification problem, because all the following methods are defined on quantity. However, quantity still has the fluent methods which may make the quantity class harder to understand.

The final option is to use an Expression Builder, so 42.grams would yield a recipe builder instance. At this point, you can use one or more Expression Builders and have full control over how the rest of the expression works. The problem here is that you need to ensure the calling code can easily unpack the subject from the builder. This isn't a problem for expressions such as:

```
ingredients {
  42.grams.flour
  2.grams.nutmeg
}
```

but is a problem if you want an expression like 42.grams + 3.oz. I tend to prefer an Expression Builder most of the time, but it really depends on the context of its use.

46.2 When to Use It

Literal Extension has become a popular illustration of how to make APIs more fluent, particularly by advocates of languages which are able to do it. The ability to add methods to third-party classes was not something supported in mainstream OO languages (although Smalltalk always made it possible). It can help a good deal in improving fluency, although there's also the suspicion that some of this enthusiasm is fondness of a new toy.

In some environments, there is a serious concern that adding methods like this to literals will bloat the interface of those literal classes. These Literal Extensions are only needed in some contexts, so if they appeal in more contexts they can make a class's interface much more confusing. If this is the case, then you have to weigh the usefulness of the Literal Extension versus the problems it adds by complicating the literal class's interface. Some language environments allow you to state that Literal Extensions are bound to a namespace, which avoids this problem.

46.3 Recipe Ingredients (C#)

Without stressing my creativity any further, I decided to steal this example from my colleague Neal Ford, who's been using it in several articles and talks. It's simply a C# formulation of the sketch.

```
var ingredient = 42.Grams().Of("Flour");
```

For this case, I'll use domain types rather than an *Expression Builder (343)*. I begin with adding a Grams method to integer.

```
namespace dsl0rcas.literalExtension {
  public static class RecipeExtensions {
    public static Quantity Grams(this int arg) {
      return new Quantity(arg, Unit.G);
    }
```

I usually don't show namespaces in my examples, but in this case it's relevant—it means that the Grams method will only show up if I'm in the right namespace.

I return a quantity, which is simple illustration of the quantity pattern.

```
public struct Quantity {
  private double amount;
  private Unit units;
  public Quantity(double amount, Unit units) {
    this.amount = amount;
    this.units = units;
  }
}

public struct Unit {
  public static readonly Unit G = new Unit("g");
  public String name;
  private Unit(string name) {
    this.name = name;
  }
}
```

Although quantity is a class I'm writing, I don't think the Of method belongs on it—because Of is part of a DSL for a limited purpose, while the quantity class can be used as part of a general library. So I use an extension method again.

```
public static Ingredient Of(this Quantity arg, string substanceName) {
  return new Ingredient(arg, SubstanceRegistry.Obtain(substanceName));
}
```

The DSL code creates ingredient objects.

46: Literal
Extension

```
public struct Ingredient {
  Quantity amount;
  Substance substance;
  public Ingredient(Quantity amount, Substance substance) {
    this.amount = amount;
    this.substance = substance;
  }
```

```
public struct Substance {
  private readonly string name;
  public Substance(string name) {
    this.name = name;
  }
```

I use strings in the DSL to name the ingredients, resolving them to objects with a registry acting like a *Symbol Table (165)*.

```
private static SubstanceRegistry instance = new SubstanceRegistry();
public static void Initialize() { instance = new SubstanceRegistry(); }
private readonly Dictionary<string, Substance>
              values = new Dictionary<string, Substance>();
public static Substance Obtain(string name) {
  if (!instance.values.ContainsKey(name))
    instance.values[name] = new Substance(name);
  return instance.values[name];
}
```

Part V

Alternative Computational Models

Chapter 47

Adaptive Model

*Arrange blocks of code in a data structure to implement an
alternative computational model.*

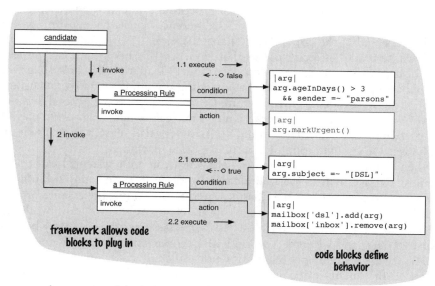

change program behavior by adding rules to data structure

Programming languages are designed with a particular computational model in
mind. For mainstream languages, this model is an imperative model with code
organized in an object-oriented way. This approach is currently favored because
it's worked out to be a suitable compromise between power and understandability. However, this model isn't always the best one for a particular problem. Indeed,
often the desire to use a DSL comes with a desire to use a different computational
model.

Adaptive Model allows you to implement alternative computational models within an imperative language. You do this by defining a model where the links between elements represent the behavioral relationships of the computational model. This model usually needs references to sections of imperative code. You then run the model either by executing code over it (procedural style) or by executing code within the model itself (object-oriented style).

47.1 How It Works

As we write software, we regularly build models of the bits of the world the software is working with. A catalog system captures information about products and prices; a media web site has news stories, advertising, and tags that describe how they should go together. These models may be pure data structures (data models) or compose data with the code that manipulates them (object models). But even in an object model, the flow of processing is dictated by the code. The data it operates on is different, and its differences cause changes in detail of the processing, but the broad flow remains the same.

The state model of secret panels that I opened this book with is a different kind of beast. Depending on which state model I load a particular system with, I get a big change in the overall behavior of the system. Essentially, the instantiation of the state model is the program. Certainly, there is the general *Semantic Model (159)* of a state machine; this is a constant factor and a constraint on what any particular state machine can do. But in a very real sense, the program that executes is the configuration of a particular state machine.

When a model takes the primary behavioral role in a system, I call this an Adaptive Model. As with most boundaries in software, the one around Adaptive Models is fuzzy, but I find the classification useful. To me, the essence of using an Adaptive Model is the sense that you are changing the program by altering the instances and their relationships. This sense dissolves the boundary between code and data, and we enter a world with new possibilities and new problems. Some software communities relish this world—the Lisp community is particularly strong on the duality of code and data—but for many developers it's a world that's both entrancing and scary.

Adaptive Models exist independently from DSLs in that you can have an Adaptive Model in a system without a DSL in sight and get most of the benefits of using one. The DSL's role here is to make it easier to program the Adaptive Model by providing a language in which you can describe your intentions more clearly. The examples I used for the difference between the command-query API and the various DSLs illustrate this point. One of the hardest parts in using an Adaptive Model is to figure out what it's supposed to do—a DSL can be a big help in overcoming that.

My examples in this book use in-memory object models as Adaptive Models, but Adaptive Models can take many forms. An Adaptive Model can be a data structure interpreted by procedural code. A common use of Adaptive Model is to store the model in a database and have it interpreted by other applications. Workflow systems often use this style.

When I see an Adaptive Model stored in a relational database, I often find that it goes with a (usually crude) projectional editor (p. 136), usually using forms and fields to edit the Adaptive Model. While this is serviceable, there are many advantages to using a DSL instead. DSLs are often better at giving the whole picture of a behavior, although visualization techniques can also do that. Perhaps the best argument for a textual DSL is that it allows you to easily put the Adaptive Model under version control. I find it deeply troubling when core system behavior isn't kept under a proper source code control system.

Adaptive Models are often represented by data structures that take well-known graph structures. As a result, you may find textbooks on algorithms and data structures very helpful in working with them.

47.1.1 Incorporating Imperative Code into an Adaptive Model

When I created the initial state machine example, I deliberately made it so that all the behavioral elements could be described through simple data. The actions in the state machine are simply represented by transmitting a command code. It's common, however, for Adaptive Models to interplay much more closely with imperative code. In another state machine, I might want actions to do a wider range of things, or put conditions on my transitions as guards. To do this within the Adaptive Model would mean complicating it with a range of imperative expressions that I already have in my host programming language. Often, a better alternative is to embed regular programming language code into the Adaptive Model data structure.

A good example of this is a rule in a *Production Rule System (513)*. Such a rule has two parts: a Boolean condition and an action. It's often useful to represent these in the host language.

The most natural way to do this is with a closure.

```
rule.Condition = j => j.Start == "BOS";
rule.Action = j => j.Passenger.PostBonusMiles(2000);
```

47: Adaptive Model

Closures work well because they allow you to easily embed arbitrary blocks of code into data structures. A closure is the most direct statement of my intention here. The big drawback of using closures is that many languages don't have them. If that is the case with yours, you need to resort to some workarounds.

Probably the easiest workaround is to use a *Command* [GoF]. To do this, I create little objects that wrap a single method. My rule class then uses one for the condition and one for the action.

```
class RuleWithCommand {
  public RuleCondition Condition { get; set; }
  public RuleAction Action { get; set; }
  public void Run(Journey j) {
    if (Condition.IsSatisfiedBy(j)) Action.Run(j);
  }
}

interface RuleCondition {
  bool IsSatisfiedBy(Journey j)
}

interface RuleAction {
  void Run(Journey j);
}
```

I can then set up a particular rule by making a subclass.

```
var rule = new RuleWithCommand();
rule.Condition = new BostonStart();
rule.Action = new PostTwoThousandBonusMiles();

class BostonStart : RuleCondition {
  public bool IsSatisfiedBy(Journey j) {
    return j.Start == "BOS";
  }
}

class PostTwoThousandBonusMiles : RuleAction {
  public void Run(Journey j) {
    j.Passenger.PostBonusMiles(2000);
  }
}
```

Most of the time I can reduce the amount of subclasses I need by parametrizing the commands.

```
var rule = new RuleWithCommand();
rule.Condition = new JourneyStartCondition("BOS");
rule.Action = new PostBonusMiles(2000);

class JourneyStartCondition : RuleCondition {
  readonly string start;
  public JourneyStartCondition(string start) {
    this.start = start;
  }
  public bool IsSatisfiedBy(Journey j) {
    return j.Start == this.start;
  }
}
```

```
class PostBonusMiles : RuleAction {
  readonly int amount;
  public PostBonusMiles(int amount) {
    this.amount = amount;
  }
  public void Run(Journey j) {
    j.Passenger.PostBonusMiles(amount);
  }
}
```

In a language without closure support, something like this is usually where I would prefer to go.

Another option is to use the name of a method and invoke it using reflection. I don't like this approach, as it circumvents the mechanisms of the underlying environment just a bit too much.

I've described using commands as a workaround, and when you're looking at it from the Adaptive Model viewpoint, that's true. However, if you're populating the Adaptive Model with a DSL, then commands become more attractive. In many situations, the DSL will wrap common cases in parameters anyway, which leads naturally to parametrized commands. To use the full expressiveness of closures in the DSL means using closures either in an internal DSL or *Foreign Code (309)* in an external DSL. The latter, in particular, is something you should use only rarely.

47.1.2 Tools

A DSL is a valuable tool for an Adaptive Model since it allows people to configure the instance of a model using a programming language that makes its behavior more explicit. However, a DSL is not really enough to work with an Adaptive Model when it gets more complicated. Other tools come in handy.

It's often difficult to follow what an Adaptive Model is doing since it uses a computational model that people are less familiar with. As a result, it's particularly important to use some kind of tracing when executing the model. The trace should capture how the model processed its inputs, leaving a clear log of why it did what it did. This greatly helps answering the question, "Why did the program do that?"

A model can also produce alternative visualizations of itself, where you tell the model to produce a descriptive output of a model instance. A graphical description is often very useful. I've seen some very handy visualizations produced using Graphviz, a tool for automatically laying out node-and-arc graph structures. The state diagram picture of the secret panel control system is a good example of this. Various kinds of reports that show what the model looks like from different perspectives can also be useful.

Such visualizations are a simple equivalent of the multiple projections of a language workbench. Unlike those projections, they aren't editable—or rather, the cost to make them editable is usually prohibitive. But such visualizations can

47: Adaptive Model

still be extremely useful. You can build them automatically as part of your build process and use them to check your understanding of how the model is configured.

47.2 When to Use It

An Adaptive Model is the key to using an alternative computational model. Using an Adaptive Model allows you to build a processing engine for an alternative computational model that you can then program for specific behavior. So, once you have an Adaptive Model for a *Production Rule System (513)*, you can execute any set of rules by loading them into the model. I would usually advise that any of the alternative computational models mentioned in this book should be implemented with an Adaptive Model.

Of course this is somewhat of a glib answer—it begs the question of when would you want to use an alternative computational model? That is a qualitative decision on what best seems to fit your problem. I don't have any rigorous approach to making this decision. My best suggestion is to try expressing the behavior according to a different computational model and see if that seems to make it easier to think about. Doing this often means prototyping a DSL to drive the model, since the Adaptive Model alone may not provide enough clarity.

A lot of the time, this involves considering a common computational model. The other patterns in this part of the book give you a starting point; if one of these seems to fit, then it's worth a try. It's less common to find that you want an entirely new computational model, but it isn't unknown. Often such a realization can grow from the way a framework changes over time. A framework can begin by just storing data, but as more behavior worms its way in, you can see a Adaptive Model beginning to form.

Adaptive Models come with a particularly large disadvantage: they can be very hard to understand. I commonly come across cases where programmers complain bitterly about being unable to understand how an Adaptive Model works. It's as if a bit of magic is embedded in the program, and a lot of people find this kind of magic rather scary.

The scariness comes from the fact that an Adaptive Model results in implicit behavior. No longer can you reason about what the program does by reading the code. Instead, you have to look at a particular model configuration to see how the system behaves. Many developers find this enormously frustrating. It's often difficult to write a clear program that expresses your intent, but now you have to decode it from a data model that's hard to navigate. Debugging can be a nightmare. You can make it easier by producing tools to help with this, but then you'll spend time building the tools rather than working on the true purpose of the software.

Usually, there are a couple of people around who understand the Adaptive Model. They are big fans of it, and can be incredibly productive by using it. Everyone else, however, steers well clear.

This phenomenon genuinely puts me in two minds. I'm the kind of person who finds Adaptive Models very powerful. I'm comfortable with finding them and using them—and I feel that a well-chosen Adaptive Model can greatly improve productivity. But I also have to recognize that they can be an alien artifact to most developers—and sometimes, you have to forgo the gains of an Adaptive Model because it's not good to have a magic section in a system that people are fearful of touching. If the few people who understand the Adaptive Model would move on, nobody will be able to maintain that part of the system.

One hope I have is that using DSLs can alleviate this problem. Without a DSL, it's very hard to program an Adaptive Model and understand what it does. A DSL can make much of that implicit behavior explicit by capturing the configuration of the Adaptive Model in a language nature. My sense is that as DSLs become more common, more people will become comfortable with Adaptive Models and thus able to realize the productivity benefits they provide.

47: Adaptive Model

Chapter 48

Decision Table

*Represent a combination of conditional statements
in a tabular form.*

Premium Customer	X	X	Y	Y	N	N
Priority Order	Y	N	Y	N	Y	N
International Order	Y	Y	N	N	N	N
Fee	150	100	70	50	80	60
Alert Rep	Y	Y	Y	N	N	N

conditions

consequences

When you have code that composes several conditional statements, it can often be hard to follow exactly what combinations of conditions lead to what outcomes.

A Decision Table improves understandability by representing the group of conditions as a table, where each column shows the outcome for a particular combination of conditions.

48.1 How It Works

A decision table is divided into two sections: conditions and consequences. Each condition row indicates the state of that condition; for a simple two-value Boolean condition, each cell in the row will be either true or false. There are as many columns in the table as needed to capture each combination of conditions, so for n two-value Booleans you'll have 2^n columns.

Each consequence row represents values of a single output from the table. Each cell represents the value matching the conditions in the same column. So for the case in the sketch, if we have a domestic, regular order from a premium customer, the fee is $50 and we don't alert a representative. A Decision Table only needs a single consequence, but can happily accept more.

As in the case of the sketch, it's quite common to have a three-valued Boolean logic, where the third value is "don't care," indicating that this column is valid for any value of the condition. Using don't-care values can remove a lot of repetition in the table, keeping it more compact.

A valuable property of decision tables is that you can determine whether all the permutations of conditions have been captured as columns, and thus indicate missing permutations to the user. It may well be the case that some combinations cannot happen; this can be captured as an error column, or the semantics of the table can allow for missing columns, treating them as errors.

A table can get more complex if we want to introduce more arbitrary enumerations, numeric ranges, or string matches. We can capture each such case as a Boolean, but then the table needs to know that, if we have conditions like $100 > x > 50$ and $50 >= x$, these conditions cannot be both true at the same time. Alternatively, we can have just a single condition row for the value of x and allow the user to type the ranges in the cells. The latter approach is usually easier to work with. If we have more complex condition values, it will be more awkward to compute all the permutations, and may be better to treat an unmatched case as an error.

As usual, I'd advise building a separate Decision Table *Semantic Model (159)* and parser. With both of these, you'll need to decide how generic to make them. You can build a model and parser for just a single Decision Table case. Such a table would have its condition rows fixed in the table code, together with the number and types of its consequences. You'll usually still want the column values to be configurable, so that it's easy to change the consequence values for each combination of conditions.

A more generic Decision Table would allow you to configure the conditions and consequence types. Each condition would need some way of indicating the code to run to evaluate a condition (a method name or a closure). The type of input and each consequence would be needed for a strongly typed language configured at compile time.

Similar decisions are needed for the parser. The parser could be for a fixed table, even if it configures a generic Semantic Model. To be more flexible, you need something akin to a simple grammar for the table structure so the parser can properly interpret the input data.

Decision Tables are very simple to follow, and indeed edit, and so are particularly suited to capturing information from domain experts. Many domain experts are familiar with spreadsheets, so a good tactic is to allow the domain experts to edit the tables in a spreadsheet and then import the spreadsheet into the system. Depending on the spreadsheet program and your platform, there are lots of ways of doing this. The crudest (but often effective) way is to save the decision table in a simple text form, such as CSV. This usually works because the table is pure values, no formulae are needed. Other approaches include inter-operating with the spreadsheet program—for example, starting up and talking to a running instance of Excel. Spreadsheets like Excel that have their own pro-gramming language can be programmed to receive, edit, and transmit decision table data to a remote program.

48.2 When to Use It

Decision Tables are a very effective way to capture the results of a set of interact-ing conditions. They communicate well both to programmers and domain experts. Their tabular nature allows domain experts to manipulate them using familiar spreadsheet tools. Their biggest disadvantage is that they do take some effort to set things up so they can be edited and displayed easily, but this effort is usually quite small compared to be communicative benefit they provide.

Decision Tables can only handle a certain degree of complexity—no more than what you can capture in a single (if complex) conditional expression. If you need to combine multiple kinds of conditionals, consider a *Production Rule System (513)*.

48.3 Calculating the Fee for an Order (C#)

Here I'll outline a Decision Table that can handle the example I've shown in the sketch.

48.3.1 Model

The *Semantic Model (159)* here is a Decision Table. I've decided to create for this example a generic Decision Table that can handle any number of conditions, each of which supports three-value Booleans. I'm using C# generics to specify the input and output types for the Decision Table. Here's the class declaration and fields:

```
class DecisionTable <Tin, Tout>{
    readonly List<Condition<Tin>> conditions = new List<Condition<Tin>>();
    readonly List<Column<Tout>> columns = new List<Column<Tout>>();
```

The table needs two kinds of configuration: conditions and columns, each of which gets its own class. The conditions are parametrized with the input type, and the columns with the output (consequence) type. I'll begin with the conditions.

```
class DecisionTable...
  public void AddCondition(string description, Condition<Tin>.TestType test) {
    conditions.Add(new Condition<Tin>(description, test));
  }

public class Condition<T> {
  public delegate bool TestType(T input);
  public string description { get; private set; }
  public TestType Test { get; private set; }
  public Condition(string description, TestType test) {
    this.description = description;
    this.Test = test;
  }
}
```

This allows me to configure the conditions for the example table with this code:

```
var decisionTable = new DecisionTable<Order, FeeResult>();
decisionTable.AddCondition("Premium Customer", o => o.Customer.IsPremium);
decisionTable.AddCondition("Priority Order",    o => o.IsPriority);
decisionTable.AddCondition("International Order",   o => o.IsInternational);
```

The input type for the decision table is an order. I won't go into details, since it's just a dummy for this example. The output is a special class that just wraps the output data.

```
class FeeResult {
  public int Fee { get; private set; }
  public bool shouldAlertRepresentative { get; private set; }
  public FeeResult(int fee, bool shouldAlertRepresentative) {
    Fee = fee;
    this.shouldAlertRepresentative = shouldAlertRepresentative;
  }
}
```

The next part of setting up the table is to capture the column values. Again, I use a class for the column.

```
class Column <Tresult> {
  public Tresult Result { get; private set; }
  public readonly ConditionBlock Conditions;
  public Column(ConditionBlock conditions, Tresult result) {
    this.Conditions = conditions;
    this.Result = result;
  }
}
```

The column has two parts. The result is the type that handles the consequences. This type is the same output as the output type of the decision table itself. The condition block is a special class that represents one combination of condition values.

```
readonly List<Bool3> content = new List<Bool3>();
public ConditionBlock(params Bool3[] args) {
  content = new List<Bool3>(args);
}
```

I've made a three-valued Boolean class to represent the values in the conditions. I'll describe how they work later on, but for the moment we can assume that there's just three legal instances of Bool3, corresponding to true, false, and don't care.

I can now configure the columns like this:

```
decisionTable.AddColumn(new ConditionBlock(Bool3.X, Bool3.T, Bool3.T),
  new FeeResult(150, true));
decisionTable.AddColumn(new ConditionBlock(Bool3.X, Bool3.F, Bool3.T),
  new FeeResult(100, true));
decisionTable.AddColumn(new ConditionBlock(Bool3.T, Bool3.T, Bool3.F),
  new FeeResult(70, true));
decisionTable.AddColumn(new ConditionBlock(Bool3.T, Bool3.F, Bool3.F),
  new FeeResult(50, false));
decisionTable.AddColumn(new ConditionBlock(Bool3.F, Bool3.T, Bool3.F),
  new FeeResult(80, false));
decisionTable.AddColumn(new ConditionBlock(Bool3.F, Bool3.F, Bool3.F),
  new FeeResult(60, false));
```

```
class DecisionTable...
  public void AddColumn(ConditionBlock conditionValues, Tout consequences) {
    if (hasConditionBlock(conditionValues)) throw new DuplicateConditionException();
    columns.Add(new Column<Tout>(conditionValues, consequences));
  }
  private bool hasConditionBlock(ConditionBlock block) {
    foreach (var c in columns) if (c.Conditions.Matches(block)) return true;
    return false;
  }
```

This describes how to configure a decision table, but the next question is how it works. At the heart of the table is the three-valued Boolean. I've written this polymorphically, using a different subclass for each value:

```
public abstract class Bool3 {
  public static readonly Bool3 T = new Bool3True();
  public static readonly Bool3 F = new Bool3False();
  public static readonly Bool3 X = new Bool3DontCare();
  abstract public bool Matches(Bool3 other);

  class Bool3True : Bool3 {
    public override bool Matches(Bool3 other) {
      return other is Bool3True;
    }
  }
}
```

```
class Bool3False : Bool3 {
  public override bool Matches(Bool3 other) {
    return other is Bool3False;
  }
}
class Bool3DontCare : Bool3 {
  public override bool Matches(Bool3 other) {
    return true;
  }
}
```

A single Bool3 has a Matches method that compares to another value. Similarly, the condition block compares its list of Bool3s against another condition block.

```
public bool Matches(ConditionBlock other) {
  if (content.Count != other.content.Count)
    throw new ArgumentException("Conditon Blocks must be same size");
  for (int i = 0; i < content.Count(); i++)
    if (!content[i].Matches(other.content[i])) return false;
  return true;
}
```

This method is a "matches" method, not an "equals" method because it's not symmetric. (This means that Bool3.X.Matches(Bool3.T), but not vice versa).

The matching of condition blocks is the core mechanism. Now, once I have a decision table configured, I can run it on a particular order to get a fee result.

```
class DecisionTable...
  public Tout Run(Tin arg) {
    var conditionValues = calculateConditionValues(arg);
    foreach (var c in columns) {
      if (c.Conditions.Matches(conditionValues)) return c.Result;
    }
    throw new MissingConditionPermutationException(conditionValues);
  }
  private ConditionBlock calculateConditionValues(Tin arg) {
    var result = new List<bool>();
    foreach (Condition<Tin> c in conditions) {
      result.Add(c.Test(arg));
    }
    return new ConditionBlock(result);
  }
```

With this, we can see how the decision table model is configured and how it runs. But before we move onto the parser, I think it's worth showing the code that the decision table can use to ensure it has a column to match every permutation of conditions.

The top level of this code is straightforward. I write a function to find any missing permutations by generating every possible permutation for a given number of conditions and checking if it is matched by the columns.

```
class DecisionTable...
  public bool HasCompletePermutations() {
    return missingPermuations().Count == 0;
  }
  public List<ConditionBlock> missingPermuations() {
    var result = new List<ConditionBlock>();
    foreach (var permutation in allPermutations(conditions.Count))
      if (!hasConditionBlock(permutation)) result.Add(permutation);
    return result;
  }
```

This begs the question of how do I generate all the permutations. I found it easier to do this in a two-dimensional matrix and then pull out each column of the matrix as a permutation.

```
class DecisionTable...
  private List<ConditionBlock> allPermutations(int size) {
    bool[,] matrix = matrixOfAllPermutations(size);
    var result = new List<ConditionBlock>();
    for (int col = 0; col < matrix.GetLength(1); col++) {
      var row = new List<bool>();
      for (int r = 0; r < size; r++) row.Add(matrix[r, col]);
      result.Add(new ConditionBlock(row));
    }
    return result;
  }
  private bool[,] matrixOfAllPermutations(int size) {
    var result = new bool[size, (int)Math.Pow(2, size)];
    for (int row = 0; row < size; row++)
      fillRow(result, row);
    return result;
  }
  private void fillRow(bool[,] result, int row) {
    var size = result.GetLongLength(1);
    var runSize = (int)Math.Pow(2, row);
    int column = 0;
    while (column < size) {
      for (int i = 0; i < runSize; i++) {
        result[row, column++] = true;
      }
      for (int i = 0; i < runSize; i++) {
        result[row, column++] = false;
      }
    }
  }
```

The code for generating the permutations is trickier than I'd like, but it seemed easier to write using a matrix data structure. In situations like this, I'm quite happy to use the data structure that makes it easiest to write some code and then transform the result into the data structure I actually want to consume. It reminds me of my engineering days when you would get a problem that's difficult to solve in your usual coordinate system; you'd then transform the problem to a coordinate system that made it easier to solve the problem, solve it, and transform it back again.

48.3.2 The Parser

When working with a tabular form like this, often the best form of editor is a spreadsheet. There are lots of ways to get data from a spreadsheet into a C# program, and I'm not going to try to describe them here. Instead, I'll write the parser to operate on a simple interface for a table.

```
interface ITable {
  string cell(int row, int col);
  int RowCount {get;}
  int ColumnCount {get;}
}
```

I'll parse the table in the spirit of *Delimiter-Directed Translation (201)* but using rows and columns instead of a stream of delimiter-separated tokens.

For the model, I wrote a generic decision table that I could use with any table of three-value Booleans. For the parser, however, I'll write one specifically designed for this table. It is possible to write a general table parser and configure it for this case, but I thought I'd leave that as an exercise for you to do on some cold winter night.

The basic structure of the parser is a command object that takes an ITable as input and returns a decision table as output.

```
class TableParser...
  private readonly DecisionTable<Order, FeeResult>
                    result = new DecisionTable<Order, FeeResult>();
  private readonly ITable input;
  public TableParser(ITable input) {
    this.input = input;
  }
  public DecisionTable<Order, FeeResult> Run() {
    loadConditions();
    loadColumns();
    return result;
  }
```

As is my habit with command objects, I provide the parameters to the command in the constructor and use a run method to do the work.

The first step is to load the conditions.

```
class TableParser...
  private void loadConditions() {
    result.AddCondition("Premium Customer", (o) => o.Customer.IsPremium);
    result.AddCondition("Priority Order", (o) => o.IsPriority);
    result.AddCondition("International Order", (o) => o.IsInternational);
    checkConditionNames();
  }
```

A potential problem here is that the table might reorder the conditions or change them without updating the parser. So I do a simple check on the condition names.

```
class TableParser...
  private void checkConditionNames() {
    for (int i = 0; i < result.ConditionNames.Count; i++)
      checkRowName(i, result.ConditionNames[i]);
  }
  private void checkRowName(int row, string name) {
    if (input.cell(row, 0) != name) throw new ArgumentException("wrong row name");
  }
```

Loading the conditions doesn't really pull any data from the table, other than the check of the condition names. The main purpose of the table is to provide the conditions and consequences for each column, which I load in the next step.

```
class TableParser...
  private void loadColumns() {
    for (int col = 1; col < input.ColumnCount; col++ ) {
      var conditions = new ConditionBlock(
        Bool3.parse(input.cell(0, col)),
        Bool3.parse(input.cell(1, col)),
        Bool3.parse(input.cell(2, col)));
      var consequences = new FeeResult(
        Int32.Parse(input.cell(3, col)),
        parseBoolean(input.cell(4, col))
        );
      result.AddColumn( conditions, consequences);
    }
  }
```

As well as picking out the right cells from the input table, I also need to parse the strings into appropriate values.

```
class Bool3...
  public static Bool3 parse (string s) {
    if (s.ToUpper() == "Y") return T;
    if (s.ToUpper() == "N") return F;
    if (s.ToUpper() == "X") return X;
    throw new ArgumentException(
      String.Format("cannot turn <{0}> into Bool3", s));
  }
```

```
class TableParser...
  private bool parseBoolean(string arg) {
    if (arg.ToUpper() == "Y") return true;
    if (arg.ToUpper() == "N") return false;
    throw new ArgumentException(
      String.Format("unable to parse <{0}> as boolean", arg));
  }
```

Chapter 49

Dependency Network

*A list of tasks linked by dependency relationships. To run
a task, you invoke its dependencies, running those tasks
as prerequisites.*

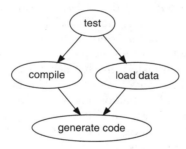

Building a software system is a common predicament for software developers. At various points, there are various things that you may want to do: just compile the program, or run tests. If you want to run tests, you need to make sure your compilation is up-to-date first. In order to compile, you need to ensure you've carried out some code generation.

A Dependency Network organizes functionality into a directed acyclic graph (DAG) of tasks and their dependencies on other tasks. In the case above, we would say that the test task is dependent upon the compilation task, and the compilation task is dependent upon the code generation task. When you request a task, we first find any tasks it depends on and ensure they are executed first, if needed. We can navigate through a dependency network to ensure that all the prerequisite tasks necessary for the requested task are executed. We can also make sure that even if a task crops up more than once through different dependency paths, it's still executed only once.

49.1 How It Works

In the opening example above, I presented a **task-oriented** description where the network is a set of tasks with dependencies between them. An alternative way is a **product-oriented** style where we focus on the products we want to create and the dependencies between them. I'll illustrate the difference by considering the case where we carry out a build by doing some code generation and then compiling. In the task-oriented approach, we would say that we have a code generation task and a compilation task, with the compilation task depending on the code generation task. In the product-oriented style, we would say that we have an executable which is created by a compilation process, and some generated source files that are created by code generation. We then state the dependencies by saying that the code-generated source files are a prerequisite to building the executable. The difference between these two may seem oversubtle at the moment, but hopefully will get clearer as I continue.

The way a dependency network is run is by requesting that we either run a task (process-oriented) or build a product (product-oriented). We typically refer to this requested product or task as the **target**. The system then finds all the prerequisites of the target and continues finding the prerequisites of the prerequisites of the . . . until it has a full list of all the transitive prerequisites that need to be run or built. It invokes each task, using the dependency relationships to ensure that no task is invoked before its prerequisites. An important property of this is that no task is executed more than once, even if traversing the network means you run into the same item several times.

To talk about this, I'll introduce a slightly larger example that will also allow me to get away from the ever-present example of software builds. Let's consider a production facility for magical potions. Each potion has ingredients, which are substances that often need to be made themselves from other substances. So, in order to create a health potion, we need clarified water and octopus essence (I'm ignoring quantities here). To create the octopus essence, we need an octopus and clarified water. To create the clarified water, we need dessicated glass. We can state the links between these products (I'm using a product-oriented approach here) as a series of dependencies:

- `healthPotion => clarifiedWater, octopusEssence`

- `octopusEssence => clarifiedWater, octopus`

- `clarifedWater => dessicatedGlass`

In this case, we want to ensure that the task to produce clarified water is only run once when we request a health potion—even though there are multiple dependencies running into it.

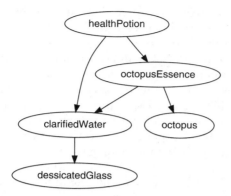

Figure 49.1 *A graph showing the dependency links between substances needed for a health potion*

It's often easy to think of physical things in this way—for example, consider the clarified water product to be something that fits in a metal bucket. The same notion, however, also makes sense for information products. In this case, we could build a production plan that includes information about what's needed to produce each substance. We don't want to make a production plan for clarified water unless we need to—it's a lot of computing resources when you're running your programs on a hamster-powered auto-abacus.

With dependency networks, there are two main errors that can come up. The most serious error is a **missed prerequisite**—something we ought to have built but didn't. This is a serious error which can result in an erroneous answer; it's also nasty because it can be hard to spot—everything looks like it works correctly but the data is all wrong because we didn't get a prerequisite. The other error is an **unnecessary build**, such as calculating the production plan for clarified water twice. In most cases, this only results in a slower execution, as the tasks are often idempotent. It can cause more serious errors if they aren't.

A common feature of a Dependency Network, particularly the product-oriented case, is that each product keeps a track of when it was last updated. This can further help to reduce unnecessary builds. When we request a product to be built, it only actually executes the process if the output product's last-modified date is earlier than any of the prerequisites. For this to work, the prerequisites need to be invoked first so they can rebuild if necessary.

I'm making a distinction here between *invoking* a task and *executing* it. Every transitive prerequisite is invoked, but a prerequisite is only executed if it's necessary. So, if we invoke octopusEssence, it invokes octopus and clarifiedWater (which, in turn, invokes dessicatedGlass). Once all the invocations have finished, octopusEssence compares the last-modified dates of the clarifiedWater and octopus production plans and only executes itself if either of those prerequisites is later than octopusEssence's production plan's last-modified date.

49: Dependency Network

In a task-oriented network, we often don't use last-modified dates. Instead, each task keeps track of whether it's already executed during this target request and only executes on the first invocation.

The fact that it's easier to work with persistent last-modified dates is a strong reason to prefer the product-oriented style to the task-oriented. You can use last-modified information in a task-oriented system, but to do this, each task has to handle this responsibility itself. Using product-orientation with last-modified dates allows the network to decide on execution. This capability doesn't come for free; it only works if the output will always be the same if none of the prerequisites change. Thus everything that could make a change to the output needs to be declared in prerequisites.

The task/product distinction surfaces in build automation systems. The traditional Unix Make command is product-oriented (the products are files), while the Java system, Ant, is task-oriented. One potential issue with product-oriented systems is that there isn't always a natural product. Running tests is a good example of this. In this case, you need to make something like a test report that keeps track of things. Sometimes, the outputs are only there to fit in with the dependency system; a good example of such a pseudo-output is a touch file—an empty file that's only there for its last-modified date.

49.2 When to Use It

A Dependency Network works for problems where you can divide the computation up into tasks with well-defined inputs and outputs. The ability of a Dependency Network to only execute tasks that are needed makes it suitable for resource-intensive tasks, or tasks which take an effort to get going—such as remote operations.

As with any alternative model, Dependency Network is often tricky to debug when things go wrong. It's therefore important to log invocations and executions so you can see what's going on. Coupled with the desire to only execute when needed, this leads me to a recommendation to prefer relatively coarse-grained tasks for the network.

49.3 Analyzing Potions (C#)

It's not often that you see examples of the manufacturing of magical potions in software texts, so I thought it was time to shed a little light on the business challenges of such enterprises. My domain experts tell me that in the very competitive world of potion manufacture, there is regular tweaking of the recipes. This leads to a problem, as there are various analyses they need to make of the potions to maintain quality control, but these analyses are expensive and time consuming. Consequently, you cannot redo the analysis every time you make a potion; instead, you only redo it every time you change the recipe. Furthermore, every substance in the manufacturing chain can cause changes to characteristics downstream, so if I analyze an upstream substance, I need to ensure I have up-to-date analyses on all the downstream substances that use its output.

So, let's take the example of a basic health potion. Its inputs include clarified water, which itself has an input of dessicated glass. If I need to analyze the MacGuffin Profile for a recipe of health potion, I need to see the profile for its input (the clarified water). If I'm still on the same recipe for clarified water that I used last week, then I don't need to redo the clarified water analysis. However, if the recipe for dessicated glass has changed since I last did that analysis, then I will need to redo the work.

This is a Dependency Network. Each substance has its inputs as prerequisites for determining its profile. If any prerequisite of a substance has an out-of-date profile, we need to reanalyze its profile first, and then reanalyze the requested substance's profile.

I'll examine specifying this Dependency Network as an internal DSL in C#. Here is the sample script:

```
class Script : SubstanceCatalogBuilder {
  Substances octopusEssence, clarifiedWater, octopus, dessicatedGlass, healthPotion;
  override protected void doBuild() {
    healthPotion
      .Needs(octopusEssence, clarifiedWater);

    octopusEssence
      .Needs(clarifiedWater, octopus);

    clarifiedWater
      .Needs(dessicatedGlass);
  }
```

The script uses *Object Scoping (385)* and *Class Symbol Table (467)*. I'll talk about parsing it later; first, let's have a look at the *Semantic Model (159)*.

49.3.1 Semantic Model

49: Dependency Network

The data structure of the *Semantic Model (159)* is simple: a graph structure of substances.

```
class Substance...
  public string Name { get; set; }
  private readonly List<Substance> inputs = new List<Substance>();
  private MacGuffinProfile profile;
  private Recipe recipe;

  public void AddInput(Substance s) {
    inputs.Add(s);
  }
```

Each substance has a recipe and a MacGuffin profile. All we really need to know is that they have a date. (If I told you more, killing would only be the start of what I'd have to do to you.)

```
class MacGuffinProfile...
  public DateTime TimeStamp {get;  private set;}
  public MacGuffinProfile(DateTime timeStamp) {
    TimeStamp = timeStamp;
  }

class Recipe...
  public DateTime TimeStamp { get; private set; }
  public Recipe(DateTime timeStamp) {
    TimeStamp = timeStamp;
  }
```

The Dependency Network behavior occurs whenever I ask for the profile. First, the invocation is passed back along with the inputs, so that every transitive input to the substance is invoked. Then, each one checks to see if it is no longer up-to-date and recalculates if necessary.

```
class Substance...
  public MacGuffinProfile Profile {
    get {
      invokeProfileCalculation();
      return profile;
    }
  }
  private void invokeProfileCalculation() {
    foreach (var i in inputs) i.invokeProfileCalculation();
    if (IsOutOfDate)
      profile = profilingService.CalculateProfile(this);
  }
```

By calling invoke on its inputs before doing its own check, I ensure that each input substance is up-to-date before checking itself. If a substance appears more than once in the input chain, it will be invoked many times, but it only calculates its profile once. This is essential, since the profiling service call is expensive, particularly to the kittens.

The check for being up-to-date relies on the timestamps of profiles and recipes.

```
class Substance...
  private bool IsOutOfDate {
    get {
      if (null == profile) return true;
      return
        profile.TimeStamp < recipe.TimeStamp
          || inputs.Any(input => input.wasUpdatedAfter(profile.TimeStamp));
    }
  }
  private bool wasUpdatedAfter(DateTime d) {
    return profile.TimeStamp > d;
  }
```

49.3.2 The Parser

The parser is a straightforward form of *Class Symbol Table (467)*. Here is the script again:

```
class Script : SubstanceCatalogBuilder {
  Substances octopusEssence, clarifiedWater, octopus, dessicatedGlass, healthPotion;
  override protected void doBuild() {
    healthPotion
      .Needs(octopusEssence, clarifiedWater);

    octopusEssence
      .Needs(clarifiedWater, octopus);

    clarifiedWater
      .Needs(dessicatedGlass);
  }
```

The script is contained in a class. The fields in the class are various substances. I use *Object Scoping (385)* to allow the script class to make bare function calls. The parent class carries out the build, returning a list of substances.

```
class SubstanceCatalogBuilder...
  public List<Substance> Build() {
    InitializeSubstanceBuilders();
    doBuild();
    return SubstanceFields.ConvertAll(f => ((Substances) f.GetValue(this)).Value);
  }
  protected abstract void doBuild();
```

The first step in the build is to populate the fields with instances of substance builders. The substance builders have the odd name of Substances so that the DSL reads better.

```
class SubstanceCatalogBuilder...
  private void InitializeSubstanceBuilders() {
    foreach (var f in SubstanceFields)
      f.SetValue(this, new Substances(f.Name, this));
  }
  private List<FieldInfo> SubstanceFields {
    get {
      var fields = GetType().GetFields(BindingFlags.Instance | BindingFlags.NonPublic);
      return Array.FindAll(fields, f => f.FieldType == typeof (Substances)).ToList();
    }
  }
```

Each substance builder holds a substance and the fluent methods to populate it. In this case, the substance's properties are read-write, so I can build up the values as I go along.

Chapter 50

Production Rule System

Organize logic through a set of production rules, each having a condition and an action.

```
if
   candidate is of good stock
   and
   candidate is a productive member of society
then
   candidate is worthy of an interview

if
   candidate's father is a member
then
   candidate is of good stock

if
   candidate is English
   and
   candidate makes ten thousand a year
then
   candidate is a productive member of society
```

There are many situations that are easily thought of as a set of conditional tests. If you are validating some data, you can think of each validation as a condition where you raise an error if the condition is false. Qualifying for some position can often be thought of as a chain of conditions where you qualify if you make it all the way up the chain. Diagnosing a failure can be thought of a series of questions, with each question leading to new questions, and hopefully to the identification of the root fault.

The Production Rule System computational model implements the notion of a set of rules, where each rule has a condition and a consequential action. The system runs the rules on the data it has through a series of cycles, each cycle identifying the rules whose conditions match, then executes the rules' actions. A Production Rule System is usually at the heart of an expert system.

513

50.1 How It Works

The basic structure of the rules in a Production Rule System is pretty simple. You have a set of rules where each rule has a condition and an action. The condition is a Boolean expression. The action can be anything, but may be limited depending on the context of the Production Rule System. For example, if your Production Rule System is only doing validation, then your actions may only be raising errors, so each action may specify which error to raise and what data to provide to the error.

The more complex part of a Production Rule System is deciding how to execute the rules. Doing this for general expert systems can be very involved, which is why a whole community of expert systems and a market of tools have developed. As is often the case, however, the fact that a general Production Rule System is very complicated doesn't mean that you can't build a simple Production Rule System for limited cases.

A Production Rule System usually puts all the control of rule execution into a single component, often called a **rule engine, inference engine,** or **scheduler.** A simple rule engine operates in a series of inference cycles. The cycle begins by running all of the conditions of the available rules. Each rule whose condition returns true is then said to be **activated.** The engine keeps a list of activated rules, called an **agenda.** When the engine has finished checking the rules' conditions, it then looks at the rules on the agenda with the intention of executing these rules' actions. Executing the action of a rule is called **firing** the rule.

The sequence in which the rules are fired may be determined in different ways. The simplest approach is to fire the rules in an arbitrary sequence. In this case, the way in which the rules are written doesn't determine the sequence of firing—which can help keep the computation simple. Another approach is to always fire the rules in the order they are defined in the system. The filter rules of an email system are a good example of this. You define your filters specifically so the first one that matches will process the email, and any rules that might match later won't get fired.

Another sequencing approach is to define rules with a priority, in expert system circles often referred to as **salience.** In this case, the rule engine will pick the rule with the highest priority on the agenda to fire first. Using priorities is often considered a smell; if you find yourself using priorities a lot, you should reconsider whether a Production Rule System is the appropriate computational model for your problem.

Another variation in a rule engine is whether to check the rules for activation after each rule is fired, or whether to fire all the rules on the agenda before rechecking. Depending on how the rules are structured, this may affect the behavior of the system.

When you look at a rule base, you'll often find different groups of rules, with each group being a logical part of the overall problem. In this case, it makes sense to divide the rules up into separate **rule sets** and evaluate them in a particular order. So, given some rules that do basic validation of data and others that determine qualification, you might choose to run the validation rule set first, and only if there are no errors, to run the qualification rule set.

50.1.1 Chaining

The common case of a series of validation rules is the simplest kind of Production Rule System. In this case, you scan all the rules, and those that fire add an error or warning to some form of log or *Notification (193)*. One cycle of activation and firing is enough, because the actions of the rules don't change the state of the data that the Production Rule System is working with.

Often, however, rule actions will change the state of the world. In this case, you need to reevaluate the rule conditions to see if any of them have become true, in which case they get added to the agenda. This interaction between rules is known as **forward chaining**: You start with some facts, use rules to infer more facts, these facts activate more rules, which create more facts, and so on. The engine stops only when there are no more rules on the agenda.

For the simple sequence in the sketch, all of the rules would be checked first. If the second two rules are both activated and fired, then the first rule gets activated and fired.

Another approach is to work the other way around. In this style, you begin with a goal and examine the rule base to see which rules have actions that would make this goal true. You then take these rules and make them subgoals to find further rules that support them. This style is called **backward chaining**; it is less common in simple Production Rule Systems as it's much more involved to get a simple case working. As a result, my discussion here is focused more on forward-chaining or nonchaining engines.

50.1.2 Contradictory Inferences

One of the great advantages of rules is that you can state each rule independently and let the Production Rule System figure out the consequences. But this strength comes with a problem. What if you get chains of inferences that contradict each other? We may have a series of rules for membership in a local military reenactment club that says that to join the freedom-loving American revolutionary army, you have to be over 18, American citizen, have your own imitation musket, etc. Then there's another rule in section 4.7 which says that British citizens may join the club but can only be part of the army of the cruel tyrants. This works well for a few years, till I turn up as dual citizen; now we have one rule that says I can join the revolutionary army and another that says I can't.

The biggest danger here is that we may not notice this can happen at all. If the consequence of these rules is to change the value of the isEligibleForRevolutionaryArmy Boolean, then whichever rule runs last will win. Unless we have a defined sequence or priority values on the rules, this could lead to an incorrect inference, or even different inferences depending on hidden qualities in the rule execution sequence.

There are two broad ways to tackle contradictory rules. One is to design the rule structure to avoid them. This involves ensuring that the way the rules run avoids contradiction, perhaps by the way the rules update the data, or by organizing rule sets, or by playing with priorities. In our example, we could start with all the eligibility conditions set to false, and only allow them to be changed to true. This convention would force whoever wanted to keep out the Brits to write the rule in a different way, surfacing the potential contradiction while writing the rules. You have to be careful because a mistake can sneak in a rule that will potentially subvert the design.

An alternative approach is to record all the inferences in such a way that tolerates contradiction, allowing you to spot a contradiction should you get one. In this case, instead of having a Boolean value for eligibility, you would create a separate fact object whose key is eligibilityForRevolutionaryArmy and the value is a Boolean. Once you're done running the rules, you'd look for all the facts with the key you're interested in. You could then spot if you had facts with the same key but different values. The *Observation* [Fowler AP] pattern is one way to handle this kind of situation.

In general, you need to be careful of circles in your rule structure, where multiple rules are arranged so that one keeps the next one firing endlessly. This can happen with contradictory rules that keep arguing with each other, and with rules that get into a positive feedback loop.

Tools specifically designed for Production Rule Systems have their own techniques for dealing with such problems.

50.1.3 Patterns in Rule Structure

While I have seen a few rule bases, I can't claim to have done any kind of reasonable study of how rule systems tend to be organized. But those few I have seen did reveal a few common patterns in the structure of the rules.

A common, and simple, case is validation. This is simple because all the rules usually have a simple consequence: raising some form of validation error. There's little, if any, chaining. I suspect most people who work seriously with Production Rule Systems wouldn't consider these to be rule systems since they are so simple—and, certainly, it seemed an overkill to me to use a specialized rules tool for something like this. However, this kind of simple structure is a nice one for you to write yourself.

Determining eligibility is somewhat more involved. In this kind of rule base, you are trying to assess whether a candidate is eligible for one or more agreements. It could be a system assessing which, if any, insurance policy someone qualifies for, or determining what discount scheme an order may fall into. In this case, the rules can be structured as a progression of steps where lower-level rules lead to higher-level inferences. You can avoid contradictions by keeping all the inferences positive, perhaps with some separate route for disqualifications.

More involved still is some kind of diagnostic system where you observe some problems and want to determine the root cause. Here, you're much more likely to get contradictions, so having something like *Observation* [Fowler AP] is more important.

50.2 When to Use It

A Production Rule System is a natural choice when you have behavior that feels like it is best expressed as a set of if-then statements. Indeed, just writing control flow like that is often a good starting point for evolving into a Production Rule System.

The big danger with Production Rule System is that they are so seductive. A small example is easy to understand and demos well to nonprogrammers. What isn't clear from simple demos is that it may become very hard to reason about what a Production Rule System is doing as it gets bigger, particularly if you are using chaining. This can make debugging very difficult.

This problem is often exacerbated by a rule engine tool. It's very easy to stretch a tool—to use it in lots of places without realizing how difficult it is to modify until you've already built something too large. Thus there is an argument to building something simple yourself, which you can tune to your particular needs as well as use to learn more about the domain and how a Production Rule System can fit in with it. Once you've learned more, you can evaluate whether it's worth replacing your simple Production Rule System with a tool.

I'm not saying that rule engines are always a bad idea, although I've yet to see one that's worked well. What is important is that you should treat them with caution and understand what you are getting into when you use them.

50.3 Validations for club membership (C#)

Validations are a good simple example of a Production Rule System, as they are common and usually don't involve any chaining. For the example problem, I'll consider the first stage of an application for joining some imaginary Victorian English club. To process these applications, I'll use two separate rule sets. The first will do validation on the basic application data, just to make sure the form is filled out properly. The second rule set will evaluate eligibility for an interview, and I'll describe that in the second example.

Here are a few of the validation rules:

- Nationality must not be null.

- University must not be null.

- Annual income must be positive.

50.3.1 Model

There are two bits of the model I need to describe. The first, and really simple, bit is the data about the person that the rules will work on. This is a simple data class with properties for the various things we're interested in.

```
class Person...
  public string Name { get; set; }
  public  University? University { get; set; }
  public  int? AnnualIncome { get; set; }
  public  Country? Nationality { get; set; }
```

Now I'll move on to the rule processing part. The basic structure of the validation engine is a list of validation rules.

```
class ValidationEngine...
  List <ValidationRule> rules = new List<ValidationRule>();

interface ValidationRule {
  void Check(Notification note, Person p);
}
```

To run the engine, all I do is run each of the rules, collecting the result in a *Notification (193)*.

```
class ValidationEngine...
  public Notification Run(Person p) {
    var result = new Notification();
    foreach (var r in rules) r.Check(result, p);
    return result;
  }
```

The most basic validation rule takes a predicate and a message to record if it fails.

```
class ExpressionValidationRule : ValidationRule {
  readonly Predicate<Person> condition;
  readonly string description;
  public ExpressionValidationRule(Predicate<Person> condition, string description) {
    this.condition = condition;
    this.description = description;
  }
  public void Check(Notification note, Person p) {
    if (! condition(p))
      note.AddError(String.Format("Validation '{0}' failed.", description));
  }
```

I can then set up and run rules using the command-query interface with code like this:

```
engine = new ValidationEngine();
engine.AddRule(p => p.Nationality != null, "Missing Nationality");
var tim = new Person("Tim");
var note = engine.Run(john);
```

50.3.2 Parser

For this example, I'll use a simple internal DSL. I'll make direct use of C#'s lambdas to capture the rules. My DSL script starts like this:

```
class ExampleValidation : ValidationEngineBuilder {
  protected override void build() {
    Validate("Annual Income is present")
      .With(p => p.AnnualIncome != null);
    Validate("positive Annual Income")
      .With(p => p.AnnualIncome >= 0);
```

I'm using *Object Scoping (385)* so I can define validation with a simple call to the Validate method, followed by a bit of method chaining to capture the predicate.

Creating the builder sets up an engine. The validate method sets up a child rule builder to capture the rule information.

```
abstract class ValidationEngineBuilder {
  public ValidationEngine Engine { get; private set; }
  protected ValidationEngineBuilder() {
    Engine = new ValidationEngine();
    build();
  }
  abstract protected void build();
  protected WithParser Validate(string description) {
    return new ValidationRuleBuilder(description, Engine);
  }
}

class ValidationEngine...
  public void AddRule(Predicate<Person> condition, string errorMessage) {
    rules.Add(new ExpressionValidationRule(condition, errorMessage));
  }

interface WithParser {
  void With(Predicate<Person> condition);
}
```

Using a progressive interface here feels a bit of overkill, since there's only one method present on the rule builder. But I think the interface name helps communicate what the parser is looking for.

50.3.3 Evolving the DSL

These validations work well to capture the logic—but, hopefully, once you've written a few expressions to look for null values, you'd begin to think there should be a better way to do these null checks. If such checks are common, you can place the null check logic in the rule, so all we have to do in the script is state which property should not be null.

One way to do this, which works in many languages, is to write the name of the property as a string and use reflection to check the logic. So I would have this line in the DSL script:

```
MustHave("University");
```

To support this, I need to augment the model and parser.

```
class ValidationEngineBuilder...
  protected void MustHave(string property) {
    Engine.AddNotNullRule(property);
  }

class ValidationEngine...
  public void AddNotNullRule(string property) {
    rules.Add(new NotNullValidationRule(property));
  }

class NotNullValidationRule : ValidationRule {
  readonly string property;
  public NotNullValidationRule(string property) {
    this.property = property;
  }
  public void Check(Notification note, Person p) {
    var prop = typeof(Person).GetProperty(property);
    if (null == prop.GetValue(p, null))
      note.AddError("No value for {0}", property);
  }
```

I want to stress here that I didn't need to change the *Semantic Model (159)* to support this. Instead, I could easily put this code in the builder:

```
class ValidationEngineBuilder...
  protected void MustHaveALT(string property) {
    PropertyInfo prop = typeof(Person).GetProperty(property);
    Engine.AddRule(p => prop.GetValue(p, null) != null,
                   String.Format("Should have {0}", property));
  }
```

It's often an easy reflex to put this kind of logic in the builder, but I urge you not to fall for it. If I put the logic in the Semantic Model, it will be able to make a much better use of the information, since it knows what it's doing. For example, this allows the Semantic Model to generate code for this validation should you want to embed Javascript in a form. But even without a need like this, my preference is to put smarts in the Semantic Model as much as possible. It isn't any more work than putting it in the builder, but it keeps the knowledge of the rules where it's most useful.

The string argument is all very well, but it does have disadvantages, particularly in an environment like C# with static typing and good tool support. It would be nicer to capture the property name with a mechanism that has its place within C#, so we can use autocompletion and static checking.

Fortunately, this can be done in C# by using lambda expressions. The DSL script for a not-null check looks like this:

```
MustHave(p => p.Nationality);
```

Again, I implement it in the model, with a simple call from the builder.

```
class ValidationEngineBuilder...
  protected void MustHave<T>(Expression<Func<Person, T>> expression) {
    Engine.AddNotNullRule(expression);
  }

class ValidationEngine...
  public void AddNotNullRule<T>(Expression<Func<Person, T>> e) {
    rules.Add(new NotNullValidationRule<T>(e));
  }

class NotNullValidationRule<T> : ValidationRule {
  readonly Expression<Func<Person, T>> expression;
  public NotNullValidationRule(Expression<Func<Person, T>> expression) {
    this.expression = expression;
  }
  public void Check(Notification note, Person p) {
    var lambda = expression.Compile();
    if (lambda(p) == null) note.AddError("No value for {0}", expression);
  }
}
```

I've used an expression of the lambda here, rather than just the lambda. This is so that I can print out the text of the code in the error message when the validation fails.

50.4 Eligibility Rules: extending the club membership (C#)

The previous example showed validation rules for the input form for our fictional club. This example now looks at eligibility rules, and gets a little more involved as it includes some forward chaining. The top-level rule says that a candidate is considered for interview if he (and for a club like this it must be a "he") is of good stock and a productive member of society.

```
class ExampleRuleBuilder : EligibilityEngineBuilder {
  protected override void build() {
    Rule("interview if good stock and productive")
      .When(a => a.IsOfGoodStock && a.IsProductive)
      .Then(a => a.MarkAsWorthyOfInterview());
```

As with the previous example, I'm using an internal DSL with *Object Scoping (385)* using a superclass, although I'll describe the details of the parsing later. There are various rules for determining good stock and what it means to be a productive member of society. Two ways to be of good stock are to have your father as a member or to be militarily accomplished.

```
Rule("father member means good stock")
  .When(a => a.Candidate.Father.IsMember)
  .Then(a => a.MarkOfGoodStock());
Rule("military accomplishment means good stock")
  .When(a => a.IsMilitarilyAccomplished)
  .Then(a => a.MarkOfGoodStock());
Rule("Needs to be at least a captain")
  .When(a => a.Candidate.Rank >= MilitaryRank.Captain)
  .Then(a => a.MarkAsMilitarilyAccomplished());
Rule("Oxbridge is good stock")
  .When(a => a.Candidate.University == University.Cambridge
          || a.Candidate.University == University.Oxford)
  .Then(a => a.MarkOfGoodStock());
```

These rules illustrate an important property of a Production Rule System—the various rules are open-ended, in that I can easily add new rules that say what it means to be of good stock. I can add these rules without altering the rules that are already in place. The downside is that there's no single spot in the rule base text where I can be sure of finding *all* the conditions. One way to deal with this is to have a tool capable of finding all the rules that have a consequence of calling MarkOfGoodStock.

The other leg of what makes someone eligible for an interview is the issue of being a productive member of society, which is typical English refined double-speak for saying how much you earn.

```
Rule("Productive Englishman")
  .When(a => a.Candidate.Nationality == Country.England
          && a.Candidate.AnnualIncome >= 10000)
  .Then(a => a.MarkAsProductive());
Rule("Productive Scotsman")
  .When(a => a.Candidate.Nationality == Country.Scotland
          && a.Candidate.AnnualIncome >= 20000)
  .Then(a => a.MarkAsProductive());
Rule("Productive American")
  .When(a => a.Candidate.Nationality == Country.UnitedStates
          && a.Candidate.AnnualIncome >= 80000)
  .Then(a => a.MarkAsProductive());
```

```
Rule("Productive Solider")
  .When(a => a.IsMilitarilyAccomplished
    && a.Candidate.AnnualIncome >= 8000)
  .Then(a => a.MarkAsProductive());
```

A club like this naturally prefers Englishmen, but will take others providing they are sufficiently well heeled.

Looking at the patterns in use here, we see that the list of rules is defined using *Function Sequence (351)*. The details for each rule use *Method Chaining (373)* for the When and Then clauses, and *Nested Closure (403)* for capturing the contents of the condition and action for each rule.

50.4.1 The Model

The model for eligibility is similar to the validation one, but a little more complicated in order to handle the different consequences and the forward chaining. The first part is the data structure used to report the results of the logic—this is an application.

```
class Application...
  public Person Candidate { get; private set; }
  public bool IsWorthyOfInterview { get; private set; }
  public void MarkAsWorthyOfInterview() { IsWorthyOfInterview = true; }
  public bool IsOfGoodStock { get; private set; }
  public void MarkOfGoodStock() {IsOfGoodStock = true;}
  public bool IsMilitarilyAccomplished { get; private set; }
  public void MarkAsMilitarilyAccomplished() { IsMilitarilyAccomplished = true; }
  public bool IsProductive { get; private set; }
  public void MarkAsProductive() { IsProductive = true; }
  public Application(Person candidate) {
    this.Candidate = candidate;
    IsOfGoodStock = false;
    IsWorthyOfInterview = false;
    IsMilitarilyAccomplished = false;
    IsProductive = false;
  }
```

Like the Person earlier on, it's mostly a simple data class, but it does have a somewhat unusual structure. All the properties are Booleans that start false and can only be changed to true. This enforces some structure in the rules system to avoid undetected contradictions.

Each eligibility rule takes a pair of closures, one for the condition and another for consequence, with a textual description.

50: Production
Rule System

```
class EligibilityRule...
  public string Description { get; private set; }
  readonly Predicate<Application> condition;
  readonly Action<Application> action;
  public EligibilityRule(string description,
                    Predicate<Application> condition, Action<Application> action)
  {
    this.Description = description;
    this.condition = condition;
    this.action = action;
  }
```

I can load eligibility rules into a rule set.

```
class EligibilityRuleBase {
  private List<EligibilityRule> initialRules = new List<EligibilityRule>();
  public List<EligibilityRule> InitialRules {
    get { return initialRules; }
  }
  public void AddRule(string description, Predicate<Application> condition,
                Action<Application> action)
  {
    initialRules.Add(new EligibilityRule(description, condition, action));
  }
```

Running the engine is a bit more involved due to the forward chaining. The basic cycle is to check the rules, place those that can be activated onto the agenda, fire the rules on the agenda, and then check to see if more rules can be activated.

```
class EligibilityEngine...
  public void Run() {
    activateRules();
    while (agenda.Count > 0) {
      fireRulesOnAgenda();
      activateRules();
    }
  }
```

I use some further data structures to keep track of the running of the rules.

```
class EligibilityEngine...
  public readonly EligibilityRuleBase ruleBase;
  List<EligibilityRule> availableRules = new List<EligibilityRule>();
  List<EligibilityRule> agenda = new List<EligibilityRule>();
  List<EligibilityRule> firedLog = new List<EligibilityRule>();
  readonly Application application;
  public EligibilityEngine(EligibilityRuleBase ruleBase, Application application) {
    this.ruleBase = ruleBase;
    this.application = application;
    availableRules.AddRange(ruleBase.InitialRules);
  }
```

I copy the rules from the rule base into a list of available rules. When a rule is activated, I remove it from that list (so it can't be activated again) and put it on the agenda.

```csharp
class EligibilityEngine...
  private void activateRules() {
    foreach (var r in availableRules)
      if (r.CanActivate(application)) agenda.Add(r);
    foreach (var r in agenda)
      availableRules.Remove(r);
  }
```

```csharp
class EligibilityRule...
  public bool CanActivate(Application a) {
    try {
      return condition(a);
    } catch(NullReferenceException) {
      return false;
    }
  }
```

I trap null references in CanActivate, just treating them as failures to activate. This allows me to write a conditional expression like anApplication.Candidate. Father.IsMember without having to do any null checking when I write the rule—moving that responsibility to the model.

When I fire a rule, I remove it from the agenda and put it on a log of fired rules. Later I can use the log to provide a trace for diagnostic purposes.

```csharp
class EligibilityEngine...
  private void fireRulesOnAgenda() {
    while (agenda.Count > 0) {
      fire(agenda.First());
    }
  }
  private void fire(EligibilityRule r) {
    r.Fire(application);
    firedLog.Add(r);
    agenda.Remove(r);
  }
```

```csharp
class EligibilityRule...
  public void Fire(Application a) {
    action(a);
  }
```

50: Production Rule System

50.4.2 The Parser

As I said earlier, I'm using a similar structure for the eligibility rule builder as I did for the validation rules—with *Object Scoping (385)* using a superclass.

```
abstract class EligibilityEngineBuilder {
  protected EligibilityEngineBuilder() {
    RuleBase = new EligibilityRuleBase();
    build();
  }
  public EligibilityRuleBase RuleBase { get; private set; }
  abstract protected void build();
```

I define a rule as a *Function Sequence (351)* of calls to Rule.

```
class EligibilityEngineBuilder...
  protected WhenParser Rule(string description) {
    return new EligibilityRuleBuilder(RuleBase, description);
  }

class EligibilityRuleBuilder : ThenParser, WhenParser{
  EligibilityRuleBase RuleBase;
  string description;
  Predicate<Application> condition;
  Action<Application> action;
  public EligibilityRuleBuilder(EligibilityRuleBase ruleBase, string description) {
    this.RuleBase = ruleBase;
    this.description = description;
  }
```

I use *Method Chaining (373)* on a child rule builder with progressive interfaces to capture the rest of the rule. The first clause is When.

```
class EligibilityEngineBuilder...
  interface WhenParser {
    ThenParser When(Predicate<Application> condition);
  }

class EligibilityRuleBuilder...
  public ThenParser When(Predicate<Application> condition) {
    this.condition = condition;
    return this;
  }
```

It is followed by Then.

```
class EligibilityEngineBuilder...
  interface ThenParser {
    void Then(Action<Application> action);
  }

class EligibilityRuleBuilder...
  public void Then(Action<Application> action) {
    this.action = action;
    loadRule();
  }
  private void loadRule() {
    RuleBase.AddRule(description, condition, action);
  }
```

Chapter 51

State Machine

Model a system as a set of explicit states with transitions between them.

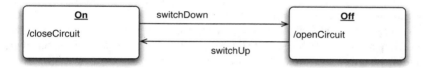

Many systems react to stimuli differently, depending on some internal property. Sometimes it's useful to classify these different internal states and describe both the differences in response and what causes the system to move between these states. A State Machine can be used to describe and perhaps to control this behavior.

51.1 How It Works

State Machines are a common thing to find both in software and in discussions about software—which is why I used a State Machine in the opening example for this book. The degree to which a State Machine is used varies with the situation, as does the form of State Machine in use.

To explore this, I'll use a different example, one that is less clear-cut than the one in the Introduction. Let's consider an order processing system. Once I've created an order, I can freely add or remove items in that order, or cancel it. At some point, I have to provide payment for the order. Once I've paid for it, the order is eligible to be shipped, but before that I can still add or remove items or cancel the order. Once it's shipped, I can't do any of that.

I can describe this order using the state transition diagram of Figure 51.1.

51: State Machine

527

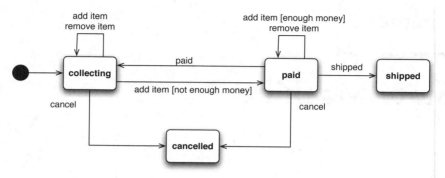

Figure 51.1 *UML state machine diagram for an order*

At this point, I need to address the meaning of "state." In general use, we often refer to the state of an object as the combination of the values of its properties. In this reading, removing an item from an order changes its state. However, the state machine diagram doesn't reflect all these possible states; instead, it only shows a few states. These are the states that are interesting in terms of the model, in that they affect the behavior of the system. I'll refer to this smaller set of states as **machine states**. So, while removing an item changes the state of the order, it doesn't change its machine state.

This state model is a useful way of thinking about the behavior of the order, but this doesn't mean that we want a state machine model in our software. The model can help us understand that we need a check on the cancel method to verify that we are in the appropriate state. But this can simply be a guard clause in the cancel method.

Similarly, tracking what machine state the order is in could be a status field on the order, but it could also be completely derived. You could determine if you are in the paid state by checking if the payment authorization amount is greater than or equal to the overall cost of the order. The diagram may still be a useful way to visualize how the order works, but you don't need the model to be manifest in the software.

State Machines, like other alternative computational models, come in several varieties which share many common elements but with notable differences. I'll start with the common elements. The essence of a State Machine is that it has a notion of multiple states that the machine can be in. We can then define multiple transitions on each state, where each transition is triggered by an event and causes the machine to move to a target state. This target state is often, but not necessarily, a different state. The resulting behavior of the machine is the definition of the states and the events that trigger the movement between states.

Figure 51.1 shows a diagrammatic representation of such a network. The collecting state has four transitions defined on it. These say that if the machine, when in that state, receives a cancel event, it moves to the cancelled state. A paid event leads to the paid state, the add item and remove item events both lead back to the collecting state. The add item and remove item events are separate transitions, even though they go to the same target.

A general question with state machines is how they react to an event that isn't defined on the state that the machine is currently in. Depending on the application, such an event may be an error, or it may be safely ignored.

Figure 51.1 also introduces another notion, that of a guarded transition. When in the paid state, if the machine gets an add item event, it takes a different transition depending on whether there's enough money or not. The Boolean conditions on the transitions should not overlap, otherwise the state machine won't know where to go. Guarded transitions don't have to appear on all State Machines; indeed the introductory example doesn't have them.

Figure 51.1 describes several machine states and the events that cause the machine to move between them, but it is still a passive model as it does not invoke any actions that cause changes to the system. To have an *Adaptive Model (487)* with a State Machine, we need a way to bind actions into the machine. Over the years, several schemes have come up to do this. There are two places you can sensibly bind actions to: the transitions or the states. Binding an action to a transition means that the action is executed whenever the transition is taken. Binding an action to a state most commonly means that the action is invoked when you enter the state. But you can also see actions bound to exits from a state too. Some machines allow internal actions that are invoked when an event is received in that state—like a transition back to itself, but perhaps without triggering any entry actions again.

Different action-binding approaches suit different problems and different personalities. I don't have any strong guidelines to offer, other than to keep it as simple as it can reasonably be to model your behavior. Many implementations of state machine techniques have gone for the maximum expressiveness of the machine—such as the very expressive state machine models used by the UML. But small state machines suitable for DSLs can often work well with much simpler models.

51.2 When to Use It

I have that horrible feeling when I know that almost the only thing I can say is that you should use a State Machine when the behavior you're specifying feels like a State Machine—that is, when you have a sense of movement, triggered by events, from state to state. In many ways, the best way to see if a State Machine is appropriate is to try sketching one on paper and, if it fits well, to try it in action.

There is one danger area where the smidgeon of language theory I gave earlier ("Regular, Context-Free, and Context-Sensitive Grammars," p. 96) can be helpful. Remember that State Machines are limited to parsing regular grammars,

51: State Machine

meaning they can't handle matching arbitrarily nested parentheses. If your behavior has anything like that, you may run into the same problem.

51.3 Secret Panel Controller (Java)

In many places in this book, starting with the Introduction, I've used a simple state machine as an example. For all the cases where I've mentioned it, I've used a single *Semantic Model (159)*, which I describe in the Introduction. The state behavior doesn't do guarded transitions and binds very simple actions to state entry. The actions are simple, in that they don't involve executing an arbitrary code block but only sending a numeric code message. This simplifies the state machine model and the DSLs to control it (which is very important for an example like this).

Part VI

Code Generation

Chapter 52

Transformer Generation

*Generate code by writing a transformer that navigates the
input model and produces output.*

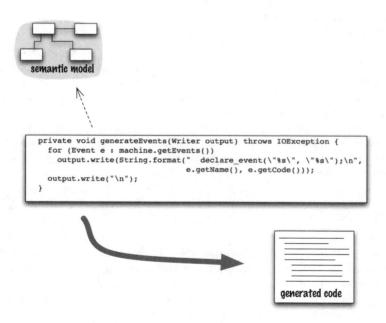

```
private void generateEvents(Writer output) throws IOException {
    for (Event e : machine.getEvents())
        output.write(String.format("  declare_event(\"%s\", \"%s\");\n",
                                   e.getName(), e.getCode()));
    output.write("\n");
}
```

52.1 How It Works

Transformer Generation involves writing a program that takes the *Semantic
Model (159)* as input and produces an output in the form of source code for the

target environment. I like to think of transformers in terms of input-driven and output-driven sections. Output-driven transformation starts from the required output and dives into the input to gather the data it needs as it goes. Input-driven transformation walks the input data structure and produces output.

For an example, consider generating a web page based on a catalog of products. An output-driven approach would start with the structure of the web page, perhaps with a routine like this:

```
renderHeader();
renderBody();
renderFooter();
```

An input driven transformation looks instead at the input data structure and navigates through that, perhaps like this:

```
foreach (prod in products) {
  renderName(prod);

  foreach (photo in prod.photos) {
   renderPhoto(photo);
  }
}
```

Often, transformers use a combination of the two approaches. I seem to regularly run into situations where the outer logic is output-driven, but it calls routines that are more input-driven. The outer logic describes the broad structure of the output document, dividing it into logical sections, while the inner section produces output driven by a particular kind of input data. In any case, I find it useful to think of each routine in the transformation as either input-driven or output-driven and to be conscious of which I'm using.

Many transformations can go directly from Semantic Model to target source, but for more complicated transforms it can be useful to break down the transformation into multiple steps. A two-step transform, for instance, would walk the input model and produce an output model. This output model would be a model, rather than a text, but more oriented towards the generated output. A second step might then walk the output model and produce the output text. Using a multistep transform is useful when the transform is complicated, or if you have multiple output texts to produce from the same input that share some characteristics. With multiple output texts, you can produce, in the first-stage transform, a single output model with the common elements. The difference between the output texts can then be placed in varying second stages.

With a multistage approach, you can also mix techniques, for example using Transformer Generation for the first stage and *Templated Generation (539)* for the second stage.

52.2 When to Use It

A single-stage Transformer Generation is a good choice when the output text has a simple relationship with the input model and most of the output text is generated. In this case, Transformer Generation is very easy to write and doesn't require introducing a templating tool.

Transformer Generation with multiple stages can be very useful when the relationship between input and output is more complex, as each stage can handle a different aspect of the problem.

If you use *Model-Aware Generation (555)*, you can usually populate the model with a simple sequence of calls, which is easy to generate with Transformer Generation.

52.3 Secret Panel Controller (Java generating C)

Using *Model-Aware Generation (555)* often goes with Transformer Generation as the separation between generated code and static code is clear, allowing any sections of generated code to have very little static code. So in this case, I'll generate the code for the secret panel controller from the example in Model-Aware Generation. To save you flipping pages, here is the code I need to generate:

```
void build_machine() {

  declare_event("doorClosed", "D1CL");
  declare_event("drawerOpened", "D2OP");
  declare_event("lightOn", "L1ON");
  declare_event("doorOpened", "D1OP");
  declare_event("panelClosed", "PNCL");

  declare_command("lockDoor", "D1LK");
  declare_command("lockPanel", "PNLK");
  declare_command("unlockPanel", "PNUL");
  declare_command("unlockDoor", "D1UL");

  declare_state("idle");
  declare_state("active");
  declare_state("waitingForDrawer");
  declare_state("unlockedPanel");
  declare_state("waitingForLight");

  /* body for idle state */
  declare_action("idle", "unlockDoor");
  declare_action("idle", "lockPanel");
  declare_transition("idle", "doorClosed", "active");

  /* body for active state */
```

```
declare_transition("active", "lightOn", "waitingForDrawer");
declare_transition("active", "drawerOpened", "waitingForLight");

/* body for waitingForDrawer state */
declare_transition("waitingForDrawer", "drawerOpened", "unlockedPanel");

/* body for unlockedPanel state */
declare_action("unlockedPanel", "unlockPanel");
declare_action("unlockedPanel", "lockDoor");
declare_transition("unlockedPanel", "panelClosed", "idle");

/* body for waitingForLight state */
declare_transition("waitingForLight", "lightOn", "unlockedPanel");

/* reset event transitions */
declare_transition("idle", "doorOpened", "idle");
declare_transition("active", "doorOpened", "idle");
declare_transition("waitingForDrawer", "doorOpened", "idle");
declare_transition("unlockedPanel", "doorOpened", "idle");
declare_transition("waitingForLight", "doorOpened", "idle");
}
```

The output that I need to generate has a very simple structure, evident from the way I construct the outer routine of the generator.

```
class StaticC_Generator...
  public void generate(PrintWriter out) throws IOException {
    this.output = out;
    output.write(header);
    generateEvents();
    generateCommands();
    generateStateDeclarations();
    generateStateBodies();
    generateResetEvents();
    output.write(footer);
  }
  private PrintWriter output;
```

This code is a typical output-driven outer routine of a transformer. I might as well go through each of these steps in the order they come in. The header just writes out the static stuff I need at the top of the file.

```
class StaticC_Generator...
  private static final String header =
    "#include \"sm.h\"\n" +
    "#include \"sm-pop.h\"\n" +
    "\nvoid build_machine() {\n";
```

When I create the generator, I create it with the state machine that it will work on.

```
class StaticC_Generator...
  private StateMachine machine;
  public StaticC_Generator(StateMachine machine) {
    this.machine = machine;
  }
```

The first time I use this is to generate the event declarations.

```
class StaticC_Generator...
  private void generateEvents() throws IOException {
    for (Event e : machine.getEvents())
      output.printf("  declare_event(\"%s\", \"%s\");\n", e.getName(), e.getCode());
    output.println();
  }
```

The commands and state declarations are similarly easy.

```
class StaticC_Generator...
  private void generateCommands() throws IOException {
    for (Command c : machine.getCommands())
      output.printf("  declare_command(\"%s\", \"%s\");\n", c.getName(), c.getCode());
    output.println();
  }

  private void generateStateDeclarations()throws IOException {
    for (State s : machine.getStates())
      output.printf("  declare_state(\"%s\");\n", s.getName());
    output.println();
  }
```

Next, I generate the body (actions and transitions) for each state. In this case, I have to declare all the states before I can declare transitions since I'll get an error if I forward-reference a state.

```
class StaticC_Generator...
  private void generateStateBodies() throws IOException {
    for (State s : machine.getStates()) {
      output.printf("  /* body for %s state */\n", s.getName());
      for (Command c : s.getActions()) {
        output.printf("  declare_action(\"%s\", \"%s\");\n", s.getName(), c.getName());
      }
      for (Transition t : s.getTransitions()) {
        output.printf(
          "  declare_transition(\"%s\", \"%s\", \"%s\");\n",
          t.getSource().getName(),
          t.getTrigger().getName(),
          t.getTarget().getName());
      }
      output.println();
    }
  }
```

52: Transformer Generation

This also demonstrates a flip into an input-driven style. The code that's generated in each case follows the structure of the input model. This is fine, as it doesn't matter in which order I declare actions and transitions. This code also shows generating a comment with dynamic data.

Finally, I generate the reset events.

```
class StaticC_Generator...
  private void generateResetEvents() throws IOException {
    output.println("  /* reset event transitions */");
    for (Event e : machine.getResetEvents())
      for (State s : machine.getStates())
        if (!s.hasTransition(e.getCode())) {
          output.printf(
            "  declare_transition(\"%s\", \"%s\", \"%s\");\n",
            s.getName(),
            e.getName(),
            machine.getStart().getName());
        }
  }
```

Chapter 53

Templated Generation

*Generate output by handwriting an output file and placing
template callouts to generate variable portions.*

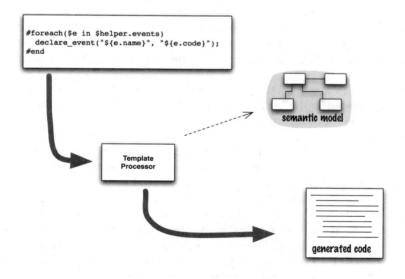

```
#foreach($e in $helper.events)
  declare_event("${e.name}", "${e.code}");
#end
```

Template
Processor

semantic model

generated code

53.1 How It Works

The basic idea behind Templated Generation is to write the output file you desire,
inserting callouts for all the bits that vary. You then use a template processor
with the template file and a context that can fill the callouts to populate the real
output file.

Templated Generation is a very old technique, familiar to anyone who has
used mail-merge facilities in a word processor. Templated Generation is very

539

common in web development, as many websites with dynamic content use Templated Generation. In those forms, the entire document is a template, but Templated Generation also works in smaller contexts too. The old faithful printf function in C is an example of using Templated Generation to print out a single string at a time. In the context of code generation, I usually use Templated Generation for the cases where the whole output document is a template, but printf reminds us that Templated Generation and *Transformer Generation (533)* can be very intermixed. Textual macro processors, another old standby in software development, are another form of Templated Generation.

With Templated Generation, there are three main components: templating engine, template, and context. The **template** is is the source text of the output file, with the dynamic parts represented by callouts. The callouts involve references to the context which will populate the dynamic elements when the generation takes place. The **context** therefore acts as a source for dynamic data—essentially, the data model for the template generation. The context may be a simple data structure or a more complex programmatic context; different templating tools use different forms of context. The **templating engine** is the tool that brings template and context together to produce the output. A controlling program will execute the templating program with a particular context and template to produce an output file, and may run the same template with multiple contexts to produce multiple outputs.

The most general form of template processors allow arbitrary host code expressions to be placed in the callouts. This is a common mechanism used by tools like JSP and ASP. Like any form of *Foreign Code (309)*, it needs to be used with care, otherwise the structure of the host code can overwhelm the template. I strongly recommend that, if you have a template processor that embeds arbitrary host code, you confine yourself to simple function calls within the callouts, preferably using an *Embedment Helper (547)*.

Because it's common for template files to get thoroughly messed up due to too much host code, many template processors don't allow arbitrary host code in the callouts. Such tools provide a specific **templating language** to be used in the callouts instead of host code. This templating language is usually quite restricted to encourage simpler callouts and preserve the clarity of the template structure. The simplest kind of templating language treats the context as a map and provides expressions to look up values in that map and insert them into the output. While this mechanism is sufficient for simple templates, there are common cases where you need more.

A common driver for more complex templating is the need to generate output for items in a collection. This usually requires some kind of iterative construct, such as a loop. Conditional generation is another common need, where different template output is needed depending upon a value in the context. Often, you find duplication of chunks of template source, which suggests the need for some kind of subroutine mechanism inside the template language itself.

I'm not going to delve into the different ways that various templating systems handle these cases, although that is an interesting diversion. My general advice here is to be as minimalist as possible, since the strength of Templated Generation is directly proportional to how easy it is to visualize the output file by looking at the template.

53.2 When to Use It

The great strength of Templated Generation is that you can look at the template file and easily understand what the generated output will look like. This is most useful when there is quite a lot of static content in the output while the dynamic content is occasional and simple.

So the first indication that you may want to use Templated Generation is a lot of static content in the generated file. The greater the proportion of static content, the more likely that it will be easier to use Templated Generation. The second thing to consider is the complexity of the dynamic content you need to generate. The more you use iterations, conditionals, and advanced templating language features, the harder it is to comprehend what the output will look like from the template file. When this happens, you should consider *Transformer Generation (533)* instead.

53.3 Generating the Secret Panel State Machine with Nested Conditionals (Velocity and Java generating C)

Generating code for nested conditionals in a state machine is a good case where the static output is relatively large and the dynamic part is fairly simple—all good indications for Templated Generation. For this example, I'll generate the code that I discussed in the example for *Model Ignorant Generation (567)*. To give you a sense of what we want, here is the entire output file:

```
#include <stdio.h>
#include <stdlib.h>
#include <assert.h>
#include <string.h>
#include "sm.h"
#include "commandProcessor.h"

#define EVENT_doorClosed "D1CL"
#define EVENT_drawerOpened "D2OP"
#define EVENT_lightOn "L1ON"
#define EVENT_doorOpened "D1OP"
#define EVENT_panelClosed "PNCL"
```

```
#define STATE_idle 1
#define STATE_active 0
#define STATE_waitingForDrawer 3
#define STATE_unlockedPanel 2
#define STATE_waitingForLight 4
#define COMMAND_lockDoor "D1LK"
#define COMMAND_lockPanel "PNLK"
#define COMMAND_unlockPanel "PNUL"
#define COMMAND_unlockDoor "D1UL"

static int current_state_id = -99;

void init_controller() {
  current_state_id = STATE_idle;
}
void hard_reset() {
  init_controller();
}
void handle_event_while_idle (char *code) {
  if (0 == strcmp(code, EVENT_doorClosed)) {
    current_state_id = STATE_active;
  }
  if (0 == strcmp(code, EVENT_doorOpened)) {
    current_state_id = STATE_idle;
    send_command(COMMAND_unlockDoor);
    send_command(COMMAND_lockPanel);
  }
}
void handle_event_while_active (char *code) {
  if (0 == strcmp(code, EVENT_lightOn)) {
    current_state_id = STATE_waitingForDrawer;
  }
  if (0 == strcmp(code, EVENT_drawerOpened)) {
    current_state_id = STATE_waitingForLight;
  }
  if (0 == strcmp(code, EVENT_doorOpened)) {
    current_state_id = STATE_idle;
    send_command(COMMAND_unlockDoor);
    send_command(COMMAND_lockPanel);
  }
}
void handle_event_while_waitingForDrawer (char *code) {
  if (0 == strcmp(code, EVENT_drawerOpened)) {
    current_state_id = STATE_unlockedPanel;
    send_command(COMMAND_unlockPanel);
    send_command(COMMAND_lockDoor);
  }
  if (0 == strcmp(code, EVENT_doorOpened)) {
    current_state_id = STATE_idle;
    send_command(COMMAND_unlockDoor);
    send_command(COMMAND_lockPanel);
  }
}
```

```
void handle_event_while_unlockedPanel (char *code) {
  if (0 == strcmp(code, EVENT_panelClosed)) {
    current_state_id = STATE_idle;
    send_command(COMMAND_unlockDoor);
    send_command(COMMAND_lockPanel);
  }
  if (0 == strcmp(code, EVENT_doorOpened)) {
    current_state_id = STATE_idle;
    send_command(COMMAND_unlockDoor);
    send_command(COMMAND_lockPanel);
  }
}
void handle_event_while_waitingForLight (char *code) {
  if (0 == strcmp(code, EVENT_lightOn)) {
    current_state_id = STATE_unlockedPanel;
    send_command(COMMAND_unlockPanel);
    send_command(COMMAND_lockDoor);
  }
  if (0 == strcmp(code, EVENT_doorOpened)) {
    current_state_id = STATE_idle;
    send_command(COMMAND_unlockDoor);
    send_command(COMMAND_lockPanel);
  }
}

void handle_event(char *code) {
  switch(current_state_id) {
  case STATE_idle: {
    handle_event_while_idle (code);
    return;
  }
  case STATE_active: {
    handle_event_while_active (code);
    return;
  }
  case STATE_waitingForDrawer: {
    handle_event_while_waitingForDrawer (code);
    return;
  }
  case STATE_unlockedPanel: {
    handle_event_while_unlockedPanel (code);
    return;
  }
  case STATE_waitingForLight: {
    handle_event_while_waitingForLight (code);
    return;
  }
  default: {
    printf("reached a bad spot");
    exit(2);
  }
  }
}
```

53: Templated
Generation

The engine I'm using here is Apache Velocity, which is a common and easy to understand templating engine available for Java and C#.

I can look at this overall file as segments of dynamic content that need to be generated. Each segment is driven by a collection of elements that I can iterate through to generate the code for that segment.

I'll begin by looking at how I generate the event definitions, such as #define EVENT_doorClosed "D1CL". If you follow how this works, the rest pretty much falls into place.

I'll start with the code in the template.

```
template file...
  #foreach ($e in $helper.events)
  #define $helper.eventEnum($e) "$e.code"
  #end
```

Unfortunately, one of the confusions here is that both the C preprocessor (itself a form of Templated Generation) and Velocity both use "#" to indicate template commands. #foreach is a command for Velocity while #define is a command for the C preprocessor. Velocity will ignore any commands it doesn't recognize, so it will just treat #define as text.

#foreach is a Velocity directive to iterate over a collection. It takes each element from $helper.events in turn and runs its body with $e set to that element. In other words, this is a typical for-each style construct.

$helper.events is a reference to the context of the template. I'm using an *Embedment Helper (547)* and have thus placed just the helper, in this case an instance of SwitchHelper, into the Velocity context. The helper is initialized with a state machine, and the events property provides access to it.

```
class SwitchHelper...
  private StateMachine machine;

  public SwitchHelper(StateMachine machine) {
    this.machine = machine;
  }
  public Collection<Event> getEvents() {
    return machine.getEvents();
  }
}
```

Each event is an object from the *Semantic Model (159)*. As a result, I can use the code property directly. However, creating a constant to reference in the code is a little more work; for this, I put some code in the helper.

```
class SwitchHelper...
  public String eventEnum(Event e) {
    return String.format("EVENT_%s", e.getName());
  }
}
```

Of course there's no absolute need to use a constant here; I could just use the event code itself. I generate the constant because I prefer even my generated code to be readable.

As is usually the case, the commands use exactly the same mechanism as the events, so I'll leave that code to your imagination.

To generate the states, I need to sort out an integer constant.

```
template file...
  #foreach ($s in $helper.states)
  #define $helper.stateEnum($s) $helper.stateId($s)
  #end

class SwitchHelper...
  public Collection<State> getStates() {
    return machine.getStates();
  }
  public String stateEnum(State s) {
    return String.format("STATE_%s", s.getName());
  }
  public int stateId(State s) {
    List<State> orderedStates = new ArrayList<State>(getStates());
    Collections.sort(orderedStates);
    return orderedStates.indexOf(s);
  }
```

Some readers may be uncomfortable with me generating and sorting a list of states every time I need an ID. Rest assured that if this was a performance issue, I'd cache the sorted list, but since it isn't I don't.

With all the declarations generated, I can now generate the conditionals. First, the outer conditional switches on the current state.

```
template file...
  void handle_event(char *code) {
    switch(current_state_id) {
  #foreach ($s in $helper.states)
    case $helper.stateEnum($s): {
      handle_event_while_$s.name (code);
      return;
    }
  #end
    default: {
      printf("reached a bad spot");
      exit(2);
    }
    }
  }
```

The inner conditionals switch on the input event. I've broken these into separate functions.

```
template file...
  #foreach ($s in $helper.states)
  void handle_event_while_$s.name (char *code) {
  #foreach ($t in $helper.getTransitions($s))
    if (0 == strcmp(code, $helper.eventEnum($t.trigger))) {
      current_state_id = $helper.stateEnum($t.target);
  #foreach($a in $t.target.actions)
    send_command($helper.commandEnum($a));
  #end
    }
  #end
  }
  #end
```

To get the transitions for each state, I need both the transitions defined in the Semantic Model and the reset event transitions.

```
class SwitchHelper...
  public Collection<Transition> getTransitions(State s) {
    Collection<Transition> result = new ArrayList<Transition>();
    result.addAll(s.getTransitions());
    result.addAll(getResetTransitions(s));
    return result;
  }

  private Collection<Transition> getResetTransitions(State s) {
    Collection<Transition> result = new ArrayList<Transition>();
    for (Event e : machine.getResetEvents()) {
      if (!s.hasTransition(e.getCode()))
        result.add(new Transition(s, e, machine.getStart()));
    }
    return result;
  }
```

Chapter 54

Embedment Helper

An object that minimizes code in a templating system by providing all needed functions to that templating mechanism.

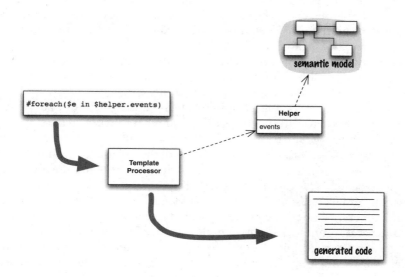

Many systems allow you to extend the capability of a simple representation by embedding general-purpose code into that representation to do things that otherwise would not be possible. Examples include embedding code into web page templates, putting code actions into grammar files, and putting callouts into code generation templates. This mechanism of general-purpose *Foreign Code (309)* adds a lot of power to the representation it's embedded into, without complicating the basic representation itself. However, a common problem when you do this is that the Foreign Code can end up being quite involved and obscure the representation that it's embedded into.

Embedment Helper moves all the complex code to a helper class, leaving only simple method calls in the host representation. This allows the host representation to be dominant and retain its clarity.

54.1 How It Works

The basic idea behind Embedment Helper is similar to a refactoring. Create the Embedment Helper, make the Embedment Helper visible to the host representation, and take all the code from the host representation and move it to the Embedment Helper, leaving just a method call behind.

There's only one potentially tricky technical aspect to this, which is getting an object into the visible scope when processing the host representation. Most systems give you some mechanism to do this—they need to in order to call libraries—but it's sometimes a bit messy.

Once you have the Embedment Helper visible, any code that's more than a simple method call should move into the Embedment Helper, so the only code left in the host representation is simple calls.

This leaves another complication in this technique, which isn't anything particularly technical: How to ensure that it's clear what the code in the Embedment Helper is doing? The key to this, as with any abstraction, is careful naming of the methods, so they clearly state the intention of the called code without revealing its implementation. This is the same basic skill as method and function naming in any context—a central skill of a good programmer.

Embedment Helper is often used with *Templated Generation (539)*, and when you find this combination, a common question is whether the Embedment Helper should generate output. I often hear this as an absolute point: Helpers must never generate output. I don't agree with this absoluteness. Certainly, there is a problem with generating output in the helper—any such output isn't visible from the template. Since the whole point of Templated Generation is that you see the output with holes, such hiding of generated material is, without doubt, a problem.

However, I think that this problem has to be weighed against the complexity of retaining the output in the template and the more complicated constructs of *Foreign Code (309)* you may need if you want to avoid generating output in it. This is a balance that you have to consider in each case, and although I would say it's good to avoid generating from the Embedment Helper, I'm not inclined to agree that it is always better than the alternative.

54.2 When to Use It

I'm very suspicious of patterns that someone claims should always be used, but Embedment Helper is one of those things I would always suggest doing, except in really trivial cases. I've looked at a fair bit of code using *Foreign Code (309)* in my time, and I see a huge difference if Embedment Helper is present. Without it, it's hard to see the host representation, so much so that it rather defeats the purpose of using an alternative representation at all. For instance, a grammar file with lots of Foreign Code in actions makes it very hard to see the basic flow of the grammar.

While preserving the clarity of the host representation is the critical reason for using Embedment Helper, there's another benefit in terms of tooling. This is most evident if you use a sophisticated IDE. In this case, any embedded code can't be edited with the IDE's tooling, but if you move it to a Embedment Helper, you're back in your full editing environment. Even simple text editors benefit a bit by simple things such as code coloring, which usually won't work properly for embedded code.

Still, there is one situation where you don't need an Embedment Helper: where you are using classes that act as a natural home for providing this kind of information. An example of this is if you are doing *Templated Generation (539)* with a *Semantic Model (159)*. In this case, much of the behavior that you would have in an Embedment Helper can reasonably be part of the Semantic Model itself—provided this doesn't make the Semantic Model too complex.

54.3 Secret Panel States (Java and ANTLR)

Perhaps the easiest way to explain how Embedment Helper works is to show what it looks like when you don't use it. For this, I'll take an ANTLR grammar file, pretty much the same one I used in the example for *Embedded Translation (299)*. I won't show the entire grammar file, but here are a few of the rules:

```
machine   : eventList resetEventList commandList state*;
eventList : 'events' event* 'end';

event : name=ID code=ID
        {
          events.put($name.getText(),
                  new Event($name.getText(), $code.getText()));
        };
```

```
state : 'state' name=ID
        {
            obtainState($name);
            if (null == machine)
                machine = new StateMachine(states.get($name.getText()));
        }
      actionList[$name]?
      transition[$name]*
      'end'
      ;

transition [Token sourceState]
   : trigger = ID '=>' target = ID
        {
          states.get($sourceState.getText())
            .addTransition(events.get($trigger.getText()),
                           obtainState($target));
        };
```

Along with the code in the code actions, I also need to set up *Symbol Tables (165)* and any general functions that can avoid duplicated code, such as obtainState. I do this in the members section of the grammar file.

With such inlined code, grammar files can have more lines of Java than of the grammar DSL. For comparison, here's what it looks like with an Embedment Helper:

```
machine : eventList resetEventList commandList state*;

eventList : 'events' event* 'end';

event : name=ID code=ID {helper.addEvent($name, $code);};

state : 'state' name=ID {helper.addState($name);}
        actionList[$name]?
        transition[$name]*
        'end';

transition [Token sourceState]
 : trigger = ID '=>' target = ID {helper.addTransition($sourceState, $trigger, $target);};
```

The difference is moving the code to the helper. To do this, the first step is to put a helper object into the generated parser. ANTLR allows me to do this by declaring a field in the members section.

```
@members {
  StateMachineLoader helper;
//...
```

This will put a field in the generated parser class. I set its visibility to package so that I can manipulate it with another class. I could make it private and provide getters and setters, but I don't think that's worthwhile in this case.

In the overall flow of running this program, I have a loader class that orchestrates the parse. It holds the state machine result, and I create it with a reader.

```
class StateMachineLoader...
  private Reader input;
  private StateMachine machine;

  public StateMachineLoader(Reader input) {
    this.input = input;
  }
```

The run method executes the parse and populates the machine field.

```
class StateMachineLoader...
  public StateMachine run() {
    try {
      StateMachineLexer lexer = new StateMachineLexer(new ANTLRReaderStream(input));
      StateMachineParser parser = new StateMachineParser(new CommonTokenStream(lexer));
      parser.helper = this;
      parser.machine();
      machine.addResetEvents(resetEvents.toArray(new Event[0]));
      return machine;
    } catch (IOException e) {
      throw new RuntimeException(e);
    } catch (RecognitionException e) {
      throw new RuntimeException(e);
    }
  }
```

The ANTLR parse is initiated by the line parser.machine. You'll see that I set the helper in the line before that. In this case, the loader class also acts as the helper. The loader is really quite simple, so it seems better to add the helper behavior to the loader than to make them separate classes.

I then have methods on the helper to handle the various calls. I won't show them all; here's the one for adding an event:

```
class StateMachineLoader...
  void addEvent(Token name, Token code) {
    events.put(name.getText(), new Event(name.getText(), code.getText()));
  }
```

To keep the amount of code in the grammar file to the minimum, I pass in the token and let the helper extract the text payload.

One thing I often fret about when using a *Parser Generator (269)* is whether I should use event-oriented or command-oriented naming for my Embedment Helper. In this case, I've used command-oriented names: addEvent and addState. Event-oriented names would be something like eventRecognized and stateNameRecognized. The argument for event-oriented names is that it doesn't imply any action on the helper, leaving it up to the helper to decide what to do. This is particularly handy if you use different helpers with the same parser that do different things in reaction to the parse. The problem with event-oriented names is that you can't tell what's

54: Embedment Helper

going on by just reading the grammar. In a case where I'm only using the grammar for one activity, I'd rather be able to read the grammar and see from the naming what's happening at each step.

In this example, I used a separate object as a Embedment Helper. Another approach I can use with ANTLR is to use a superclass. The superClass option in ANTLR allows me to set any class as the superclass of the generated parser. I can then use the superclass as the Embedment Helper, putting all the necessary data and functions in there. The benefit of this is that I can say addEvent rather than helper.addEvent.

54.4 Should a Helper Generate HTML? (Java and Velocity)

A common rule I hear is that a Embedment Helper should not generate any of the output. I don't consider this to be a useful rule, but I felt that an example would be a good way to explore the tradeoffs a bit more. The example isn't really connected to DSLs, as it involves creating HTML, but the principles are the same and it saves me having to dream up another contrived example.

Suppose we have a collection of person objects, and we want to print out their names in an unordered list. Each person may have an email address or an URL. If they have an URL, we want a link around the name pointing to the URL; if an email address, we want a mailto link; but there must be no link if there's neither. Using Velocity as my templating engine, here's the code to show that:

```
<ul>
#foreach($person in $book.people)
  #if( $person.getUrl() )
  <li><a href = "$person.url">$person.fullName</a></li>
  #elseif( $person.email )
  <li><a href = "mailto:$person.email">$person.fullName</a></li>
  #else
  <li>$person.fullName</li>
  #end
#end
</ul>
```

The problem with this is that I now have a bunch of logic in my template file. This logic can obscure the template layout itself, which is exactly what a Embedment Helper can help with. Here's an alternative layout using the Embedment Helper to generate the output:

```
template file...
  <ul>
  #foreach($person in $book.people)
    <li>$helper.render($person)</li>
  #end
  </ul>

class PageHelper...
  public String render(Person person) {
    String href = null;
    if (null != person.getEmail()) href = "mailto:" + person.getEmail().toString();
    if (null != person.getUrl())   href = person.getUrl().toString();
    if (null != href)
      return String.format("<a href = \"%s\">%s</a>", href, person.getFullName());
    else
      return person.getFullName();
  }
```

By moving the logic to the helper, I make it easier to follow the template at the cost of some of the HTML not being visible in the template.

But before contemplating the tradeoff fully, I should point out that often in these arguments there is an important middle ground to explore. This is where some of the logic can go into the Embedment Helper without having it generate output.

```
template file...
  <ul>
  #foreach($person in $book.people)
    #if( $helper.hasLink($person) )
    <li><a href = "$helper.getHref($person)">$person.fullName</a></li>
    #else
    <li>$person.fullName</li>
    #end
  #end
  </ul>

class PageHelper...
  public boolean hasLink(Person person) {
    return (null != person.getEmail()) || (null != person.getUrl());
  }
  public String getHref(Person person) {
    if (null != person.getUrl()) return person.getUrl().toString();
    if (null != person.getEmail()) return "mailto:" + person.getEmail().toString();
    throw new IllegalArgumentException("Person has no link");
  }
```

My point here is that putting some output generation in the Embedment Helper is a reasonable choice. The more complicated the logic and the more complicated the overall template, the more I gain by moving output generation to the Embedment Helper where I can factor it better. The biggest objection to this occurs when you have separate people working on the template (such as an HTML designer) and the code. This leads to a coordination cost for some changes. For

54: Embedment Helper

Chapter 55

Model-Aware Generation

Generate code with an explicit simulacrum of the semantic model of the DSL, so that the generated code has generic-specific separation.

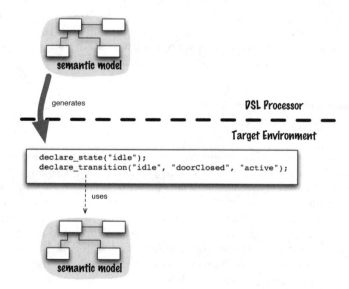

When you generate code, you embed within that code the semantics of the DSL script. By using a Model-Aware Generation, you replicate some form of the *Semantic Model (159)* in the generated code in order to preserve the separation of generic and specific code within the generated code.

55.1 How It Works

The most important aspect of Model-Aware Generation is that it preserves the principle of generic-specific separation. The actual form that the model takes in the generated code is much less important, which is why I like to say that the generated code contains a simulacrum of the *Semantic Model (159)*.

It's a simulacrum model for many reasons. Usually, you are generating code because of limitations in the target environment—these limitation often make it harder to express a Semantic Model than you would like. As a result, lots of compromises will need to be made, which makes the Semantic Model less effective as a statement of the intent of the system. However, it's important to realize that this isn't such a big deal as long as you keep the generic-specific separation.

Since the simulacrum model is a self-standing version of the Semantic Model, you can, and should, build and test the model without using any code generation. Ensure the model has a simple API to populate it. The code generation will then generate configuration code that calls this API. You can then test the simulacrum model using testing scripts that use this same API. This allows you to build, test, and refine the core behavior of the target environment with running the code-generation process. You can do this with a relatively simple test population of the model, which should be easier to understand and debug.

55.2 When to Use It

Using a Model-Aware Generation has many advantages compared to using *Model Ignorant Generation (567)*. The simulacrum model without generation is easier to build and test, because you don't have to rerun and comprehend code generation while working on the simulacrum model. Since the generated code is now made up of API calls on the simulacrum model, that code is much easier to generate, which makes the generator simpler to build and maintain.

The main reason to not use Model-Aware Generation is due to limitations in the target environment. Either it's too hard to express even a simulacrum model, or there are performance problems with having a simulacrum model at runtime.

In many cases, you are using DSLs as a front end to an existing model. If you are generating code to work with the model, then you are using Model-Aware Generation.

55.3 Secret Panel State Machine (C)

For an example of Model-Aware Generation, I'll turn again to the secret panel state machine that I started this book with. I'm now imagining a situation where we've run out of Java-enabled toasters to run our security system, and our new batch are only programmable in C. As a result, we need to generate the C code from the existing Java semantic model.

In this writeup, I won't talk about actually generating the code; for that, take a look at the example in *Transformer Generation (533)*. Here I'll concentrate on what the final code, both generated and handwritten, might look like with a Model-Aware Generation.

There are many ways you can implement a model like this in C. Essentially, I'm doing it as a data structure plus routines that navigate over this data structure in order to produce the behavior we need. Each physical controller only controls a single device, so we can store the data structure as static data. I shall also avoid heap allocations and allocate all the memory I need from the beginning.

I've built the data structure as a set of nested records and arrays. At the top of the structure is a controller.

```
typedef struct {
  stateMachine *machine;
  int currentState;
} Controller;
```

You'll notice that I represent the current state as an integer. As you'll see, I use integer references in the simulacrum model to represent all the various links between different parts of the model.

The state machine has arrays for states, events, and commands.

```
typedef struct {
  State states[NUM_STATES];
  Event events[NUM_EVENTS];
  Command commands[NUM_COMMANDS];
} stateMachine;
```

The sizes of the various arrays are set through macro defines.

```
#define NUM_STATES 50
#define NUM_EVENTS 50
#define NUM_TRANSITIONS 30
#define NUM_COMMANDS 30
#define NUM_ACTIONS 10
#define COMMAND_HISTORY_SIZE 50
#define NAME_LENGTH 30
#define CODE_LENGTH 4
#define EMPTY -1
```

55: Model-Aware Generation

Events and commands have their name and code.

```
typedef struct {
  char name[NAME_LENGTH + 1];
  char code[CODE_LENGTH + 1];
} Event;

typedef struct {
  char name[NAME_LENGTH + 1];
  char code[CODE_LENGTH + 1];
} Command;
```

The state struct holds actions and transitions. Actions are integers corresponding to the commands, while transitions are pairs of integers for the trigger event and target state.

```
typedef struct {
  int event;
  int target;
} Transition;

typedef struct {
  char name[NAME_LENGTH + 1];
  Transition transitions[NUM_TRANSITIONS];
  int actions[NUM_COMMANDS];
} State;
```

Many C programmers would prefer to use pointer arithmetic rather than array indices to navigate through the array structures, but I'd rather avoid inflicting pointer arithmetic on my non-C readers (not to mention myself, as my C was never very good even before it got rusty). There is a broader point here. I believe that generated code should be readable even if it isn't edited, because it will often be used for debugging. To make it readable, you have to understand your target audience, such as who is doing the debugging. To use this example, even if you as a generator writer are comfortable with pointer arithmetic, you should be wary of using it in the generated code if the people reading that code aren't comfortable.

To finish off the data structure, I declare the state machine and the controller as static variables, which means there are only one of them.

```
static stateMachine machine;
static Controller controller;
```

All of these data definitions are done within a single .c file. This way, I can encapsulate the data structure behind a bunch of externally declared functions. The specific code only knows about these functions and is, rightly, ignorant about the data structure itself. In this case, ignorance is truly bliss.

When I initialize the state machine, I put zero bytes into the first character of the string record, effectively making them blank.

```
void init_machine() {
  int i;
  for (i = 0; i < NUM_STATES; i++) {
    machine.states[i].name[0] = '\0';
    int t;
    for (t = 0; t < NUM_TRANSITIONS; t++) {
      machine.states[i].transitions[t].event = EMPTY;
      machine.states[i].transitions[t].target = EMPTY;
    }
    int c;
    for (c = 0; c < NUM_ACTIONS; c++)
      machine.states[i].actions[c] = EMPTY;
  }
  for (i=0; i < NUM_EVENTS; i++) {
    machine.events[i].name[0] = '\0';
    machine.events[i].code[0] = '\0';
  }
  for (i=0; i < NUM_COMMANDS; i++) {
    machine.commands[i].name[0] = '\0';
    machine.commands[i].code[0] = '\0';
  }
}
```

To declare a new event, I look for the first blank event and insert the data there.

```
void declare_event(char *name, char *code) {
  assert_error(is_empty_event_slot(NUM_EVENTS - 1), "event list is full");
  int i;
  for (i = 0; i < NUM_EVENTS; i++) {
    if (is_empty_event_slot(i)) {
      strncpy(machine.events[i].name, name, NAME_LENGTH);
      strncpy(machine.events[i].code, code, CODE_LENGTH);
      break;
    }
  }
}
```

```
int is_empty_event_slot(int index) {
  return ('\0' == machine.events[index].name[0]);
}
```

assert_error is a macro that checks the condition and, if it's false, calls an error function with the message.

```
#define assert_error(test, message) \
do { if (!(test)) sm_error(#message); } while (0)
```

Note that I've wrapped the macro in a do-while block. It looks odd, but prevents awkward interactions if the macro is used inside an if statement.

Commands are declared in the same way, so I'll skip that code.

States are declared through a number of functions. The first one just declares the name of the state.

55: Model-Aware
Generation

```
void declare_state(char *name) {
  assert(is_empty_state_slot(NUM_STATES - 1));
  int i;
  for (i = 0; i < NUM_STATES; i++) {
    if (is_empty_state_slot(i)) {
      strncpy(machine.states[i].name, name, NAME_LENGTH);
      break;
    }
  }
}

int is_empty_state_slot(int index) {
  return ('\0' == machine.states[index].name[0]);
}
```

Declaring the actions and transitions is a bit more complicated, as we have to look up the ID of the action based on the name. Here's the actions:

```
void declare_action(char *stateName, char *commandName) {
  int state = stateID(stateName);
  assert_error(state >= 0, "unrecognized state");
  int command = commandID(commandName);
  assert_error(command >= 0, "unrecognized command");
  assert_error(EMPTY == machine.states[state].actions[NUM_ACTIONS -1],
               "too many actions on state");
  int i;
  for (i = 0; i < NUM_ACTIONS; i++) {
    if (EMPTY == machine.states[state].actions[i]) {
      machine.states[state].actions[i] = command;
      break;
    }
  }
}

int stateID(char *stateName) {
  int i;
  for (i = 0; i < NUM_STATES; i++) {
    if (is_empty_state_slot(i)) return EMPTY;
    if (0 == strcmp(stateName, machine.states[i].name))
      return i;
  }
  return EMPTY;
}

int commandID(char *name) {
  int i;
  for (i = 0; i < NUM_COMMANDS; i++) {
    if (is_empty_command_slot(i)) return EMPTY;
    if (0 == strcmp(name, machine.commands[i].name))
      return i;
  }
  return EMPTY;
}
```

The transitions are similar.

```c
void declare_transition (char *sourceState, char *eventName,
                         char *targetState)
{
  int source = stateID(sourceState);
  assert_error(source >= 0, "unrecognized source state");
  int target = stateID(targetState);
  assert_error(target >= 0, "unrecognized target state");
  int event = eventID_named(eventName);
  assert_error(event >=0, "unrecognized event");
  int i;
  for (i = 0; i < NUM_TRANSITIONS; i++){
    if (EMPTY == machine.states[source].transitions[i].event) {
      machine.states[source].transitions[i].event = event;
      machine.states[source].transitions[i].target = target;
      break;
    }
  }
}

int eventID_named(char *name) {
  int i;
  for (i = 0; i < NUM_EVENTS; i++) {
    if (is_empty_event_slot(i)) break;
    if (0 == strcmp(name, machine.events[i].name))
      return i;
  }
  return EMPTY;
}
```

I can now use these declaration functions to define a complete state machine — in this case, the familiar one for Miss Grant.

```c
void build_machine() {

  declare_event("doorClosed", "D1CL");
  declare_event("drawerOpened", "D2OP");
  declare_event("lightOn", "L1ON");
  declare_event("doorOpened", "D1OP");
  declare_event("panelClosed", "PNCL");

  declare_command("lockDoor", "D1LK");
  declare_command("lockPanel", "PNLK");
  declare_command("unlockPanel", "PNUL");
  declare_command("unlockDoor", "D1UL");

  declare_state("idle");
  declare_state("active");
  declare_state("waitingForDrawer");
  declare_state("unlockedPanel");
  declare_state("waitingForLight");
```

55: Model-Aware
Generation

```
/* body for idle state */
declare_action("idle", "unlockDoor");
declare_action("idle", "lockPanel");
declare_transition("idle", "doorClosed", "active");

/* body for active state */
declare_transition("active", "lightOn", "waitingForDrawer");
declare_transition("active", "drawerOpened", "waitingForLight");

/* body for waitingForDrawer state */
declare_transition("waitingForDrawer", "drawerOpened", "unlockedPanel");

/* body for unlockedPanel state */
declare_action("unlockedPanel", "unlockPanel");
declare_action("unlockedPanel", "lockDoor");
declare_transition("unlockedPanel", "panelClosed", "idle");

/* body for waitingForLight state */
declare_transition("waitingForLight", "lightOn", "unlockedPanel");

/* reset event transitions */
declare_transition("idle", "doorOpened", "idle");
declare_transition("active", "doorOpened", "idle");
declare_transition("waitingForDrawer", "doorOpened", "idle");
declare_transition("unlockedPanel", "doorOpened", "idle");
declare_transition("waitingForLight", "doorOpened", "idle");
}
```

This population code is the code that would be generated by a code generator (see "Secret Panel Controller (Java generating C)," p. 535).

I should now show the code that makes the state machine work. In this case, this is the function that's called to handle an event with a given event code.

```
void handle_event(char *code) {
  int event = eventID_with_code(code);
  if (EMPTY == event) return;  //ignore unknown events
  int t = get_transition_target(controller.currentState, event);
  if (EMPTY == t) return; //no transition in this state so shrug
  controller.currentState = t;

  int i;
  for (i = 0; i < NUM_ACTIONS; i++) {
    int action = machine.states[controller.currentState].actions[i];
    if (EMPTY == action) break;
    send_command(machine.commands[action].code);
  }
}
```

```
int eventID_with_code(char *code) {
  int i;
  for (i = 0; i < NUM_EVENTS; i++) {
    if (is_empty_event_slot(i)) break;
    if (0 == strcmp(code, machine.events[i].code))
      return i;
  }
  return EMPTY;
}

int get_transition_target(int state, int event) {
  int i;
  for (i = 0; i < NUM_TRANSITIONS; i++) {
    if (EMPTY == machine.states[state].transitions[i].event) return EMPTY;
    if (event == machine.states[state].transitions[i].event) {
      return machine.states[state].transitions[i].target;
    }
  }
  return EMPTY;
}
```

So that's the working state machine model. There are a few points to note about it. First, the data structure is somewhat primitive, as it involves walking through an array to look up the various codes and names. In defining the state machine, this is probably no big deal, but in running the machine we might be better off replacing the linear search with a hash function. Since the state machine is well encapsulated, this is easy to do, so I'll leave it as an exercise for the reader. Changing such implementation details of the model doesn't affect the interface of the configuration functions that define new state machines. This is an important encapsulation.

The model does not include any notion of reset events. The various reset events that are defined through the DSL scripts and the Java semantic model are just turned into extra transitions in the C state machine. This makes running the state machine simpler, and is an example of a typical tradeoff where I prefer simplicity of operation to clearly stating intent. For the true *Semantic Model (159)*, I prefer to keep as much intent as I can, but for a model in a generated target environment I value capturing intent a little less.

I could go further in simplifying the executing state machine by removing all the names for events, commands, and states. These names are only used while configuring the machine and aren't used at all during the execution. So I could use some lookup tables that I discard once the machine is fully defined. Indeed the declaration functions could just use integers, something like declare_action(1,2);. While this isn't anywhere near as readable, you can argue that it matters less as this code is generated anyway. In these situations I'm inclined to keep the names, as I prefer even generated code to be readable, but more importantly it allows the state machine to produce more useful diagnostics when things go wrong. I'd sacrifice this, however, if space was really tight in the target environment.

55: Model-Aware
Generation

55.4 Loading the State Machine Dynamically (C)

Generating code in C in the above example means that to set up a new state machine, we need to recompile. Using a Model-Aware Generation also allows us to build state machines at runtime, by driving the code generation through another file.

In this case, I can express the behavior of a particular state machine through a text file such as this:

```
config_machine.txt...
  event doorClosed D1CL
  event drawerOpened D2OP
  event lightOn L1ON
  event doorOpened D1OP
  event panelClosed PNCL
  command lockDoor D1LK
  command lockPanel PNLK
  command unlockPanel PNUL
  command unlockDoor D1UL
  state idle
  state active
  state waitingForDrawer
  state unlockedPanel
  state waitingForLight
  transition idle doorClosed active
  action idle unlockDoor
  action idle lockPanel
  transition active lightOn waitingForDrawer
  transition active drawerOpened waitingForLight
  transition waitingForDrawer drawerOpened unlockedPanel
  transition unlockedPanel panelClosed idle
  action unlockedPanel unlockPanel
  action unlockedPanel lockDoor
  transition waitingForLight lightOn unlockedPanel
  transition idle doorOpened idle
  transition active doorOpened idle
  transition waitingForDrawer doorOpened idle
  transition unlockedPanel doorOpened idle
  transition waitingForLight doorOpened idle
```

I can generate this file from the Java *Semantic Model (159)*.

```
class StateMachine...
  public String generateConfig() {
    StringBuffer result = new StringBuffer();
    for(Event e : getEvents()) e.generateConfig(result);
    for(Command c : getCommands()) c.generateConfig(result);
    for(State s : getStates()) s.generateNameConfig(result);
    for(State s : getStates()) s.generateDetailConfig(result);
    generateConfigForResetEvents(result);
    return result.toString();
  }

class Event...
  public void generateConfig(StringBuffer result) {
    result.append(String.format("event %s %s\n", getName(), getCode()));
  }

class Command...
  public void generateConfig(StringBuffer result) {
    result.append(String.format("command %s %s\n", getName(), getCode()));
  }

class State...
  public void generateNameConfig(StringBuffer result) {
    result.append(String.format("state %s\n", getName()));
  }
  public void generateDetailConfig(StringBuffer result) {
    for (Transition t : getTransitions()) t.generateConfig(result);
    for (Command c : getActions())
      result.append(String.format("action %s %s\n", getName(), c.getName()));
  }
```

To run the state machine, I can easily interpret config_machine using *Delimiter-Directed Translation (201)* with the simple string-processing functions built into the standard C library.

The overall function to build the machine works by just opening the file and interpreting each line as it goes.

```
void build_machine() {
  FILE * input = fopen("machine.txt", "r");
  char buffer[BUFFER_SIZE];
  while (NULL != fgets(buffer, BUFFER_SIZE, input)) {
    interpret(buffer);
  }
}
```

The standard C function strtok allows me to break a string into tokens separated by whitespace. I can pull the first token and then dispatch to a specific function to interpret that kind of line.

55: Model-Aware
Generation

```
#define DELIMITERS " \t\n"

void interpret(char * line) {
  char * keyword;
  keyword = strtok(line, DELIMITERS);
  if (NULL == keyword) return; // ignores blank lines
  if ('#' == keyword[0]) return; // comment
  if (0 == strcmp("event", keyword)) return interpret_event();
  if (0 == strcmp("command", keyword)) return interpret_command();
  if (0 == strcmp("state", keyword)) return interpret_state();
  if (0 == strcmp("transition", keyword)) return interpret_transition();
  if (0 == strcmp("action", keyword)) return interpret_action();
  sm_error("Unknown keyword");
}
```

Each specific function pulls the necessary tokens and calls the static declare functions that I defined in the previous example. I'll just show events, as all the others look pretty much the same.

```
void interpret_event() {
  char *name = strtok(NULL, DELIMITERS);
  char *code = strtok(NULL, DELIMITERS);
  declare_event(name, code);
}
```

(Repeated calls to strtok with a NULL first argument pull further tokens from the same string as the previous call to strtok.)

I don't consider this textual format a DSL, as I designed it to make it easy to interpret, not for readability by humans. It's useful to have a certain amount of human readability—such as using the names of states, events, and commands—as that helps in debugging. Still, in this case human readability was a distant second to ease of interpretation.

The point of this example is to illustrate that code generation for a static target language does not mean you cannot use runtime interpretation. By using Model-Aware Generation, I can compile just the generic state machine model together with a very simple interpreter. My code generator then just generates the text file to be interpreted. This allows me to use C for my controllers, but without having to recompile to make a change in the state machine. By generating a file that's designed for ease of interpretation in the environment I have available, I can minimize the cost of the interpreter. I could, of course, go a step further and put the full DSL processor in C—but this would raise the processing demands of the C system and require more involved C programming. Depending on the particular situation, that may be a viable option, and we would no longer be in the world of Model-Aware Generation.

Chapter 56

Model Ignorant Generation

Hardcode all logic into the generated code so that there's no explicit representation of the Semantic Model (159).

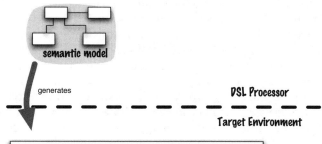

```
void handle_event(char *code) {
  switch(current_state_id) {
  case STATE_idle: {
    if (0 == strcmp(code, EVENT_doorClosed)) {
      current_state_id = STATE_active;
    }
    return;
  }
  case STATE_active: {
...
```

56.1 How It Works

One of the advantages of code generation is that it allows you to produce code that would be too repetitive to write by hand in a controlled way. This opens up implementation options that, usually, you would wisely shy away from because of duplicating code. In particular, this allows you to take behavior usually represented through data structures and encode them in control flow.

567

To use Model Ignorant Generation, I can start by writing an implementation of a particular DSL script in the target environment. I prefer to start with a very simple and minimal script. The implementation code should be clear, but can freely intermingle generic and specific code, and I don't have to worry about repetition in the specific elements, since these will be generated. This means I don't have to think about clever data structures, usually preferring procedural code and simple structures.

56.2 When to Use It

Target environments often involve languages with limited facilities for structuring programs and building a good model. In these situations, it's not possible to use *Model-Aware Generation (555)*, so Model Ignorant Generation is pretty much the only option. The second main reason for using Model Ignorant Generation is when using Model-Aware Generation results in an implementation that demands too much runtime resources. Encoding logic in control flow may reduce memory needs or increase performance; if these are sufficiently critical, then Model Ignorant Generation is a good way to get there.

On the whole, however, I prefer to see Model-Aware Generation if it's possible. It's usually easier to generate code with Model-Aware Generation, which results in a generation program that's simpler to understand and modify. Having said that, using Model Ignorant Generation often makes the generated code easier to follow. This has the converse effect that it can be easier to figure out what to generate, although harder to write the code to generate it.

56.3 Secret Panel State Machine as Nested Conditionals (C)

Again, I'll turn to the secret panel state machine I used in the Introduction. One of the classic state machine implementations uses nested conditionals which allow you to evaluate your next step using conditional expressions based on your current state and the received event. For this example, I'll show what a nested conditional implementation for Miss Grant's controller would look like. To see how I might generate this code, see the example in *Templated Generation (539)*.

There are two conditions that I need to evaluate: the incoming event and the current state. I'll start with the current state.

```
#define STATE_idle 1
#define STATE_active 0
#define STATE_waitingForDrawer 3
#define STATE_unlockedPanel 2
#define STATE_waitingForLight 4

void handle_event(char *code) {
  switch(current_state_id) {
  case STATE_idle: {
    handle_event_while_idle (code);
    return;
  }
  case STATE_active: {
    handle_event_while_active (code);
    return;
  }
  case STATE_waitingForDrawer: {
    handle_event_while_waitingForDrawer (code);
    return;
  }
  case STATE_unlockedPanel: {
    handle_event_while_unlockedPanel (code);
    return;
  }
  case STATE_waitingForLight: {
    handle_event_while_waitingForLight (code);
    return;
  }
  default: {
    printf("in impossible state");
    exit(2);
  }
  }
}
```

Testing the state involves a static variable which holds the current state.

```
#define ERROR_STATE -99
static int current_state_id = ERROR_STATE;
void init_controller() {
  current_state_id = STATE_idle;
}
```

Each subsidiary function now does a further conditional check based on the received event. Here's the case for the active state:

```
#define EVENT_drawerOpened "D2OP"
#define EVENT_lightOn "L1ON"
#define EVENT_doorOpened "D1OP"

#define COMMAND_lockPanel "PNLK"
#define COMMAND_unlockPanel "PNUL"
```

```c
void handle_event_while_active (char *code) {
  if (0 == strcmp(code, EVENT_lightOn)) {
    current_state_id = STATE_waitingForDrawer;
  }
  if (0 == strcmp(code, EVENT_drawerOpened)) {
    current_state_id = STATE_waitingForLight;
  }
  if (0 == strcmp(code, EVENT_doorOpened)) {
    current_state_id = STATE_idle;
    send_command(COMMAND_unlockDoor);
    send_command(COMMAND_lockPanel);
  }
}
```

The other subsidiary functions look very similar, so I won't repeat them.

While this code would be too repetitive to write by hand for different machines, when generated it is quite easy to follow.

Chapter 57

Generation Gap

Separate generated code from non-generated code
by inheritance.

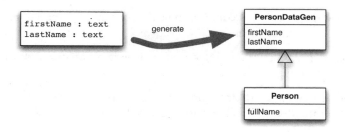

One of the difficulties of code generation is that generated code and handwritten code need to be treated differently. Generated code should never be edited by hand, otherwise you can't safely regenerate it.

Generation Gap is about keeping the generated and handwritten parts separate by putting them in different classes linked by inheritance.

This pattern was first described by the late John Vlissides. In his formulation, the handwritten class was a subclass of the generated class. My description is a little different, based on the use I've seen; I really wish I were able to talk it through with him.

57.1 How It Works

The basic form of Generation Gap involves generating a superclass, which Vlissides refers to as the core class, and hand-coding a subclass. This way you can always override any aspect of the generated code that you like in the subclass.

The handwritten code can easily call any generated features, and the generated code can call hand-coded features by using abstract methods—which the compiler can check are implemented by the subclass—or hook methods which are only overridden when needed.

When you refer to these classes from outside, you always refer to the handwritten concrete class. The generated class is effectively ignored by the rest of the code.

A common variation I've seen is to add a third class, a handwritten class that is a superclass of the generated class. This is done to pull out any logic of the generated class that doesn't depend on the variations triggered by the code generation. Instead of generating the nonvarying code, having it in a superclass allows it to be better tracked by tools, particularly IDEs. In general, my suggestion with code generation is to generate as little code as possible. This is because any generated code is more awkward to edit than handwritten code. Whenever you change generated code, you need to rerun the code generation system. Refactoring capabilities of modern IDEs won't work properly with generated code.

So, potentially you end up with three classes in an inheritance structure:

- **Handwritten base class** contains logic that doesn't vary based on the parameters to code generation.

- **Generated class** contains logic that can be generated automatically from the generation parameters.

- **Handwritten concrete class** contains logic that can't be generated and relies on generated features. This class is the only one that should be mentioned by other code.

You don't always need all three of these classes. If you don't have any unvarying logic, you don't need the handwritten base class. Similarly, if you never need to override the generated code, you can skip the handwritten concrete class. Thus another reasonable variation of Generation Gap is a handwritten superclass and a generated subclass.

Often, you find more complex structures of generated and handwritten classes, related by both inheritance and general calling use. The interplay of code generation and handwriting does lead to a more complicated class structure—this is the price you pay for the convenience of code generation.

A wrinkle that pops up with Generation Gap is the question of what to do when you have handwritten concrete classes some of the time, but not all of the time. In this case, you have to decide what to do for those classes that don't have a handwritten class. You could make the generated class the named class used by calling code, but that causes a lot of confusion over naming and usage. As a result, I prefer to always create a concrete class, leaving it empty if it has nothing to override.

This still leaves a question—should the programmer create these empty classes by hand, or should the code generation system create them? If there's only a few and they change rarely, then it's fine to leave it to a programmer. However, if you have a lot of them and they change frequently, then it's good to tweak the code generation system to check if there's an existing concrete class and generate an empty one if not.

57.2 When to Use It

Generation Gap is a very effective technique that allows you to create one logical class split into separate files to keep your generated code separate. You do need a language with inheritance to pull it off. Using inheritance means that any members that can be overridden need to have sufficiently relaxed access controls to make them visible to subclasses—that is, not private in Java or C#'s schemes.

If your language allows you to put code for one class in multiple files, such as C#'s partial classes or Ruby's open classes, then this is an alternative to Generation Gap. The advantage of partial class files is that it allows you to separate generated and handwritten code without using inheritance—everything is in one class. A downside of C#'s partial classes is that while it's good for adding features to generated classes, it doesn't give you a mechanism to override features. Ruby's open classes do handle this by evaluating the handwritten code after the generated code—which allows you to replace a generated method with a handwritten one.

The common early alternative to Generation Gap was generating code into a marked area of a file between comments that said something like code gen start and code gen end. The trouble with this was that it was confusing, leading to people modifying the generated code and awkward source control diffs. Keeping generated code in separate files is almost always a better idea if you can find a way to do it.

Although Generation Gap is a nice approach, it isn't the only way to keep generated code separate from handwritten code. Often, it works well just to put the two in separate classes with calls between them. Collaborating classes are a simpler mechanism to use and understand, so in general I prefer them. I am only pushed to Generation Gap when the call interaction becomes more complicated—for example, when there is a default behavior in the generated class that I want to override for special cases.

57.3 Generating Classes from a Data Schema (Java and a Little Ruby)

A common topic for code generation is generating the data definitions for classes based on some form of data schema. If you are writing a *Row Data Gateway* [Fowler PoEAA] to access a database, you might generate much of this class from the database schema itself.

57: Generation Gap

I'm feeling too lazy to mess around with SQL or XML schemata today, so I'll pick something simpler. Let's assume I'm reading simple CSV files, so simple that they don't even do any quotes and escaping. For each file, I have a simple schema file to define the filenames and the data type for each field. So I have a schema for people:

```
firstName : text
lastName : text
empID : int
```

and some sample data:

```
martin, fowler, 222
neal, ford, 718
rebecca, parsons, 20
```

From this, I want to generate a Java *DTO* [Fowler PoEAA] with the right type for each field in the schema, getters and setters for each field, as well as the ability to run some validations.

When generating code is in a compiled language like Java, the build process can often get in the way. If I write my code generator in Java itself, I have to compile my code generator separately from compiling the rest of my code. This makes for a messy build process, particularly when working with an IDE. An alternative approach is to use a scripting language for code generation; then I only have to run a script to generate code. This simplifies the build process at the cost of introducing another language. Of course my view is that you should always have a scripting language at hand anyway, since there's always a need to automate tasks with scripts. In this case, I use Ruby, since that's my scripting language of choice. I'll use *Templated Generation (539)* with ERB which is Ruby's built-in templating system.

The *Semantic Model (159)* for the schema is very simple. The schema is a collection of fields with a name and type for each field.

```
class Schema...
  attr_reader :name
  def initialize name
    @name = name
    @fields = []
  end

class Field...
  attr_accessor :name, :type
  def initialize name, type
    @name = name
    @type = type
  end
```

Parsing the schema file is pretty easy—I just read each line, split it into tokens around the colon, and create the field objects. Since this parsing logic is so simple, I don't break the parsing code away from the Semantic Model objects themselves.

```ruby
class Schema...
  def load input
    input.readlines.each {|line| load_line line }
  end

  def load_line line
    return if blank?(line)
    tokens = line.split ':'
    tokens.map! {|t| t.strip}
    @fields << Field.new(tokens[0], tokens[1])
  end

  def blank? line
    return line =~ /^\s*$/
  end
```

Once I've populated the Semantic Model, I can use it to generate the data classes. I'll start with the field definitions and methods that access them. I want to generate code like this:

```java
public class PersonDataGen extends AbstractData {

  private String firstName;
  public String getFirstName () {
    return firstName ;
  }
  public void setFirstName (String arg ) {
    firstName = arg;
  }
  protected void checkFirstName(Notification note) {};

  private String lastName;
  public String getLastName () {
    return lastName ;
  }
  public void setLastName (String arg ) {
    lastName = arg;
  }
  protected void checkLastName(Notification note) {};

  private int empID;
  public int getEmpID () {
    return empID ;
  }
  public void setEmpID (int arg ) {
    empID = arg;
  }
  protected void checkEmpID(Notification note) {};
```

I set up the generated class to be a subclass of the nonvarying hand-coded class. I don't use this class for the basic definition of the fields, but I'll show some usage shortly.

To do this, I make a template.

```
public class <%=name%>DataGen extends AbstractData {
  <% @fields.each do |f| %>
  private <%= f.java_type %> <%= f.name %>;
  public <%=f.java_type%> <%=f.getter_name%> () {
    return <%=f.name%> ;
  }
  public void <%= f.setter_name %> (<%= f.java_type %> arg ) {
    <%= f.name %> = arg;
  }
  protected void <%= f.checker_name %>(Notification note) {};
  <% end %>
```

The template refers to a number of methods on the Semantic Model that assist with the code generation.

```
class Field...
  def java_type
    case @type
      when "text" : "String"
      when "int"  : "int"
      else raise "Unknown field type"
    end
  end

  def method_suffix
    @name[0..0].capitalize + @name[1..-1]
  end

  def getter_name
    "get#{method_suffix}"
  end

  def setter_name
    "set#{method_suffix}"
  end

  def checker_name
    "check#{method_suffix}"
  end
```

Generating fields like this allows me to override the getter and setter methods, or add new methods to the class. In this case, I can return capitalized names and add the ability to form a full name.

```
public class PersonData extends PersonDataGen {
  public String getLastName() {
    return capitalize(super.getLastName());
  }
  public String getFirstName() {
    return capitalize(super.getFirstName());
  }
  private String capitalize(String s) {
    StringBuilder result = new StringBuilder(s);
    result.replace(0,1, result.substring(0,1).toUpperCase());
    return result.toString();
  }
  public String getFullName() {
    return getFirstName() + " " + getLastName();
  }
```

Apart from data access, I also want to have validation. For the moment, I'll do this by adding code to the hand-coded subtype. However, I want to ensure that all the validation methods can easily be run together. This I can do by adding code to the base handwritten class.

```
class AbstractData...
  public Notification validate() {
    Notification note = new Notification();
    checkAllFields(note);
    checkClass(note);
    return note;
  }
  protected abstract void checkAllFields(Notification note);
  protected  void checkClass(Notification note) {}
```

The validate method here calls an abstract method to check all the fields individually and an empty hook method for validation checks that involve multiple fields. The idea is that I can override the hook method in my concrete handwritten class. The generated class will implement the abstract method using the same information used to generate the fields.

```
class PersonDataGen...
  protected void checkAllFields(Notification note) {
    checkFirstName (note);
    checkLastName (note);
    checkEmpID (note);
  }
```

As you may have noticed in the earlier code example, these check methods are themselves just empty hook methods. I can override them to add some validation behavior.

```
class PersonData...
  protected void checkEmpID(Notification note) {
    if (getEmpID() < 1) note.error("Employee ID must be postitive");
  }
```

Bibliography

[Dragon] Aho, Alfred V., Monica S. Lam, Ravi Sethi, and Jeffrey D. Ullman. *Compilers: Principles, Techniques, and Tools*. 2nd Edition. Addison-Wesley. 2006. ISBN 0321486811.

[Anderson] Anderson, Chris. *Essential Windows Presentation Foundation*. Addison-Wesley. ISBN 0321374479.

[Beck IP] Beck, Kent. *Implementation Patterns*. Addison-Wesley. ISBN 0321413091.

[Beck TDD] Beck, Kent. *Test-Driven Development*. Addison-Wesley. ISBN 0321146530.

[Beck SBPP] Beck, Kent. *Smalltalk Best Practice Patterns*. Addison-Wesley. ISBN 013476904X.

[Cross] Cross, Bradford. *The Compositional DSL vs. Computational DSL Smack Down*. http://measuringmeasures.blogspot.com/2009/02/compositional-dsl-vs-computational-dsl.html.

[Evans DDD] Evans, Eric. *Domain-Driven Design*. Addison-Wesley. ISBN 0321125215.

[Fowler-regex] http://martinfowler.com/bliki/ComposedRegex.html.

[Fowler and Sadalage] http://martinfowler.com/articles/evodb.html.

[Fowler PoEAA] Fowler, Martin. *Patterns of Enterprise Application Architecture*. Addison-Wesley. ISBN 0321127420.

[Fowler AP] Fowler, Martin. *Analysis Patterns*. Addison-Wesley. ISBN 0201895420.

[Fowler Refactoring] Fowler, Martin. *Refactoring*. Addison-Wesley. ISBN 0201485672.

[Freeman and Pryce] Freeman, Steve and Nat Pryce. "Evolving an Embedded Domain-Specific Language in Java." In: *Companion to the 21st ACM SIGPLAN Conference on Object-Oriented Programming Systems, Languages, and Applications.*. www.jmock.org/oopsla2006.pdf.

[Fowler rake] http://martinfowler.com/articles/rake.html.

[GoF] Gamma, Erich, Richard Helm, Ralph Johnson, and John Vlissides. *Design Patterns*. Addison-Wesley. ISBN 0201633612.

[Graham] www.paulgraham.com/onlisp.html.

[Herrington] Herrington, Jack. *Code Generation in Action*. Manning. ISBN 1930110979.

[Kabanov et al.] Kabanov, Jevgeni, Michael Hunger, and Rein Raudjärv. *On Designing Safe and Embedded DSLs with Java 5.*

[Hohpe and Woolf] Hohpe, Gregor and Bobby Woolf. *Enterprise Integration Patterns.* Addison-Wesley. ISBN 0321200683.

[Meszaros] Meszaros, Gerard. *xUnit Test Patterns.* Addison-Wesley. ISBN 0131495054.

[Meyer] Meyer, Bertrand. *Object-Oriented Software Construction.* Addison-Wesley. ISBN 0136291554.

[parr-antlr] Parr, Terence. *The Definitive Antlr Reference.* Pragmatic Bookshelf. 2007. ISBN 0978739256.

[parr-LIP] Parr, Terence. *Language Implementation Patterns.* Pragmatic Bookshelf. 2009. ISBN 193435645X.

[RFC 3501] http://tools.ietf.org/html/rfc3501.

[RFC 5322] http://tools.ietf.org/html/rfc5322.

[Yoder and Johnson] www.adaptiveobjectmodel.com/WICSA3/ArchitectureOfAOMsWICSA3.htm.

[Voelter] www.voelter.de/data/pub/ProgramGeneration.pdf.

Index

Bold numbers indicate definitions of terms.

Addison Wesley

REGISTER
THIS PRODUCT

informit.com/register

Register the Addison-Wesley, Exam Cram, Prentice Hall, Que, and Sams products you own to unlock great benefits.

To begin the registration process, simply go to **informit.com/register** to sign in or create an account. You will then be prompted to enter the 10- or 13-digit ISBN that appears on the back cover of your product.

Registering your products can unlock the following benefits:

- Access to supplemental content, including bonus chapters, source code, or project files.
- A coupon to be used on your next purchase.

Registration benefits vary by product. Benefits will be listed on your Account page under Registered Products.

About InformIT — THE TRUSTED TECHNOLOGY LEARNING SOURCE

INFORMIT IS HOME TO THE LEADING TECHNOLOGY PUBLISHING IMPRINTS Addison-Wesley Professional, Cisco Press, Exam Cram, IBM Press, Prentice Hall Professional, Que, and Sams. Here you will gain access to quality and trusted content and resources from the authors, creators, innovators, and leaders of technology. Whether you're looking for a book on a new technology, a helpful article, timely newsletters, or access to the Safari Books Online digital library, InformIT has a solution for you.

informIT.com

THE TRUSTED TECHNOLOGY LEARNING SOURCE

Addison-Wesley | Cisco Press | Exam Cram
IBM Press | Que | Prentice Hall | Sams

SAFARI BOOKS ONLINE

informIT.com
THE TRUSTED TECHNOLOGY LEARNING SOURCE

PEARSON

InformIT is a brand of Pearson and the online presence for the world's leading technology publishers. It's your source for reliable and qualified content and knowledge, providing access to the top brands, authors, and contributors from the tech community.

Addison-Wesley • Cisco Press • EXAM/CRAM • IBM Press. • QUE • PRENTICE HALL • SAMS • Safari Books Online

LearnIT at InformIT

Looking for a book, eBook, or training video on a new technology? Seeking timely and relevant information and tutorials? Looking for expert opinions, advice, and tips? **InformIT has the solution.**

- Learn about new releases and special promotions by subscribing to a wide variety of newsletters. Visit **informit.com/newsletters**.

- Access FREE podcasts from experts at **informit.com/podcasts**.

- Read the latest author articles and sample chapters at **informit.com/articles**.

- Access thousands of books and videos in the Safari Books Online digital library at **safari.informit.com**.

- Get tips from expert blogs at **informit.com/blogs**.

Visit **informit.com/learn** to discover all the ways you can access the hottest technology content.

Are You Part of the IT Crowd?

Connect with Pearson authors and editors via RSS feeds, Facebook, Twitter, YouTube, and more! Visit **informit.com/socialconnect**.

informIT.com
THE TRUSTED TECHNOLOGY LEARNING SOURCE

PEARSON

Addison-Wesley • Cisco Press • EXAM/CRAM • IBM Press. • QUE • PRENTICE HALL • SAMS • Safari Books Online

Try Safari Books Online FREE
Get online access to 5,000+ Books and Videos

FREE TRIAL—GET STARTED TODAY!
www.informit.com/safaritrial

Find trusted answers, fast
Only Safari lets you search across thousands of best-selling books from the top technology publishers, including Addison-Wesley Professional, Cisco Press, O'Reilly, Prentice Hall, Que, and Sams.

Master the latest tools and techniques
In addition to gaining access to an incredible inventory of technical books, Safari's extensive collection of video tutorials lets you learn from the leading video training experts.

WAIT, THERE'S MORE!

Keep your competitive edge
With Rough Cuts, get access to the developing manuscript and be among the first to learn the newest technologies.

Stay current with emerging technologies
Short Cuts and Quick Reference Sheets are short, concise, focused content created to get you up-to-speed quickly on new and cutting-edge technologies.

Your purchase of **Domain-Specific Languages** includes access to a free online edition for 45 days through the Safari Books Online subscription service. Nearly every Addison-Wesley Professional book is available online through Safari Books Online, along with more than 5,000 other technical books and videos from publishers such as Cisco Press, Exam Cram, IBM Press, O'Reilly, Prentice Hall, Que, and Sams.

SAFARI BOOKS ONLINE allows you to search for a specific answer, cut and paste code, download chapters, and stay current with emerging technologies.

Activate your FREE Online Edition at
www.informit.com/safarifree

> **STEP 1:** Enter the coupon code: QKMEHBI.

> **STEP 2:** New Safari users, complete the brief registration form.
> Safari subscribers, just log in.

If you have difficulty registering on Safari or accessing the online edition, please e-mail customer-service@safaribooksonline.com